1 MONTH OF
FREE
READING

at
www.ForgottenBooks.com

By purchasing this book you are eligible for one month membership to ForgottenBooks.com, giving you unlimited access to our entire collection of over 1,000,000 titles via our web site and mobile apps.

To claim your free month visit:

www.forgottenbooks.com/free930284

ISBN 978-0-260-14096-8
PIBN 10930284

REPORTS OF CASES

DECIDED IN THE

COURT OF QUEEN'S BENCH,

BY

H. C. W. WETHEY,

BARRISTER-AT-LAW AND REPORTER TO THE COURT.

CHRISTOPHER ROBINSON, Q.C.,

EDITOR.

VOL. XL.

CONTAINING THE CASES DETERMINED
FROM TRINITY TERM, 40 VICTORIA, TO HILARY TERM, 40 VICTORIA,
WITH A TABLE OF THE NAMES OF CASES ARGUED,
A TABLE OF THE NAMES OF CASES CITED,
AND A DIGEST OF THE PRINCIPAL MATTERS.

TORONTO:
ROWSELL & HUTCHISON.
1877.

ROWSELL AND HUTCHISON, LAW PRINTERS, TORONTO.

JUDGES

OF THE

COURT OF QUEEN'S BENCH

DURING THE PERIOD OF THESE REPORTS.

THE HON. ROBERT ALEXANDER HARRISON, C.J.
"   "   JOSEPH CURRAN MORRISON, J.
"   "   ADAM WILSON, J.

Attorney-General:
THE HON. OLIVER MOWAT.

A TABLE

OF

CASES REPORTED IN THIS VOLUME.

A TABLE

NAMES OF CASES CITED IN THIS VOLUME.

A.

B.

B.

C.

D.

D.

G.

H.

H.

I.

I.

J.

K.

L.

M.

M.

Mc.

O.

P.

P.

R.

R.

R.

S.

S.

W.

W.

REPORTS OF CASES

COURT OF QUEEN'S BENCH.

TRINITY TERM, 40 VICTORIA, 1876.

August 28th to September 9th.

Present :

THE HON. ROBERT ALEXANDER HARRISON, C.J.
"   JOSEPH CURRAN MORRISON, J.
ADAM WILSON, J.

WOOD ET AL. V. CHAMBERS.

Guarantee—Construction.

Defendant's son, living at St. Catharines, applied to the plaintiffs, merchants in Hamilton, to supply him with goods, and on the 12th April they wrote to him that they would execute his order if he could get the endorsation of his father. On the 13th the son wrote to them to send the goods, and that he would get his father's endorsation if required. On the 17th the plaintiffs wrote proposing, in view of future business, and to save the trouble of getting an endorsement with each transaction, that the father should give a continuous guarantee. The son on the 19th wrote that he would get this, and urged them to send the goods at once, which they did on the same day, with a form of guarantee for the father to sign. On the 21st the son wrote to his father, who lived at Woodstock, "I am buying some goods" from the plaintiffs, and enclosing the guarantee for his signature. The father, not liking this form, wrote another, as follows: "Woodstock, 20th April, 1875. Gentlemen—In consideration of your supplying my son with what goods he may from time to time require of you this season, on your usual terms of credit, I do hereby guarantee the payment of the same." The defendant, as the Court inferred from the evidence, was not aware when he signed this that his son had already obtained any goods from the plaintiffs. After the guarantee, in May and June, further goods were purchased by the son.

Held, that the guarantee applied only to the goods purchased after it, not to those previously furnished.

1—VOL. XL U.C.R.

ACTION on a guaranty. Pleas. 1. That defendant did not guarantee or promise, &c., as alleged. 2. That the plaintiffs, without the consent of the defendant, gave time to the defendant beyond the time, &c.

The case was tried at the last Spring Assizes at Hamilton, before Wilson, J.

At the trial the guaranty proved was as follows:

WOODSTOCK, 26 April, 1875.

Messrs. Wood & Leggat:

GENTLEMEN: In consideration of your supplying my son, S. W. Chambers, of St. Catharines, hardware merchant, with what goods he may from time to time require of you this season, on your usual terms of credit, I do hereby guarantee the payment of the same.

Yours truly,
W. CHAMBERS.

It appeared that in the early part of April, 1875, defendant's son, who resided at St. Catharines, was desirous of getting some goods from the plaintiffs, who were merchants in Hamilton, and on the 12th April they wrote to the son that having made enquiries respecting his financial position, and finding them not as satisfactory as they would like, they would execute his order in hand if he could get the endorsation of his father, the defendant. On the 13th April, the son wrote, "Send on the goods as soon as possible, and I will give you my note with my father's endorsation, if required. Write me at once whether you will fill the order at an early date or not, as I am in want of the goods." In reply, the plaintiffs wrote, 17th April: "We have your favour stating that your father will guarantee your purchase: order will be filled at once. In view of future business we propose to you to give us your father's continuous guarantee letter to obviate the trouble of having endorsation for each transaction. Should this meet your views, please let us know, and we shall send you form of letter." On the 19th, the son, in reply, wrote: "I am perfectly willing to give you a letter of guarantee from my father, if it is absolutely required. Please send form, and I will get my father to sign and forward it to you. Please send on the goods ordered as soon as possible, as I am entirely out of a great many of the articles." On the same day, 19th April, the plaintiffs wrote to the son, " We enclose invoice of goods ordered sent off on 17th inst., which we trust will arrive duly, and open to your satisfaction. We also enclose letter of guarantee for your father's signature, which please have executed, attested, and returned." On the 21st April, the son wrote to the defendant, his father, who resided in Woodstock : " I am buying some goods from Messrs. Wood & Leggat, of Hamilton, and they want me to get a guarantee letter from you, so that I can buy the goods at low prices. As I never did any business with their house before, and they are not personally acquainted with me, they do not care to supply me on my own account. The goods I am getting there is only a small lot until I can get the others from Montreal on the opening of navigation. I enclose the letter of guarantee, which please sign, and return to me as soon as possible."

On the 27th of April the son wrote to the plaintiff enclosing the guarantee in question. " I now beg to hand you a letter of guarantee from my father, which I trust will prove perfectly satisfactory." On the same day he wrote to his father : " The letter of guarantee to Messrs. Wood & Leggat of Hamilton is perfectly satisfactory, and I would just repeat what I said before, that they are a firm I do not usually buy from, and do not intend to do so, only that I was out of some goods, and had to buy in Hamilton to keep me going till opening of navigation."

It appeared that the son before the 13th of April had ordered certain goods to the amount of $1006 64 without communicating with the defendant, and the plaintiff Leggat stated at the trial that he sent these goods in pursuance of the son's letter of the 13th of April, without defendant's endorsation or guarantee, merely on the son's promise to get his father's endorsation if necessary, and the goods were sent to the son on the 17th of April, having no security for the $1006 64, at the time the goods were sent, and the

plaintiffs received the letter of guarantee on the 28th of
April. After that date, on the 13th, 14th, 17th, 29th of
May and 5th of June further goods were purchased by
the son.

It appeared also, that on the 2nd of June, 1875, the
plaintiff wrote to the defendant: "Your letter of guarantee,
dated the 27th of April, guarantees your son's account
for the season. Please to say whether this means until the
end of the present year 1875. On the 4th of June defendant wrote in reply. " In answer to your query : the letter
you refer to means for the amount of goods purchased by
my son about that time, and extends for the period of credit
you gave him and has nothing to do with subsequent transactions." This letter was forwarded to the plaintiffs enclosed in a letter of the son, dated the 5th of June, enquir-
ing whether the plaintiffs were going to ship him some
goods he had ordered lately. On the 9th of June the
plaintiffs wrote the son in reply, with that letter before
them, that they considered the letter of guarantee to cease
from that date, and that they were unwilling to continue
the account without the father's guarantee continued as
agreed upon when the account was opened. We may
remark in reference to your father's letter, wherein he states
that he only guaranteed your first purchase, that the letter
of guarantee contemplated more, as it reads what goods
he may from time to time require of you this season.".
And on the 16th of July the plaintiffs enclosed a statement
of their account and notes for the son's signature, and
"your father's endorsation, which please have completed and
returned to us as early as practicable, as your father has
intimated his guarantee has ceased." The son refused to
give endorsed notes, as they held his father's guarantee.

It appeared that after the defendant's letter of the 4th
of June the plaintiffs supplied no more goods. Evidence
was given shewing the usual terms of credit, but as nothing
turns upon it in the judgment it is not necessary to set it
out.

The defendant in his evidence said that when he gave

the guarantee all the information he had of dealings with the plaintiffs was that contained in the letter of his son. of the 21st of April, and that he did not know that his son had bought any goods : that his son enclosed a guarantee for him to sign in that letter, but he did not like it, and sent the one in question : that he made no enquiry when he signed it.

The son testified that the defendant was not aware before he gave the guarantee that he had bought goods from the plaintiffs other than by his letter of the 21st of April, and he explained the meaning of the words "I am buying goods," &c., in that letter viz., that he was going to Hamilton that same day to buy goods : that on his way he met the traveller for a hardware Montreal house, and he induced him to give him an order for goods and so he did not go to Hamilton, and this happened after he had mailed the letter to the defendant, and that he then sent the guarantee to the defendant for signature, as he did not think he could get goods from the plaintiffs until he had the guarantee or shewed them he had sent for it. And he also swore that when he enclosed the guarantee in his letter of the 27th he did not intend it to cover the goods he had bought before.

The learned Judge, after considering the case in its various bearings, the case being tried without a jury, excluded the purchase made before the guarantee, and found a verdict for the plaintiffs for the after-purchased goods, and reserved leave to the plaintiffs to move to increase the verdict by the amount of $1037.

In Easter term May 15, 1876, *MacKelcan*, Q. C., moved accordingly.

In the same term, May 17, 1876, *Osler* for the defendant, moved a cross-rule to enter a verdict for the defendant, on the ground that the second plea of the defendant was proved.

Both rules were argued this term, August 29, 1876. *Osler*, for defendant, shewed cause to the plaintiff's rule, and supported his own. The goods supplied by plaintiffs to defendant's son were supplied before any guarantee was given by the father. Parol evidence cannot be admitted to vary the terms of that guarantee, and to shew that it was given as to goods supplied in the past : *Simmons* v. *Keating*, 2 Stark. 426 ; *Chitty* on Contracts, 8th ed., 471 ; *Broom* v. *Batchelor*, 1 H. & N. 255 ; *Oldershaw* v. *King*, 2 H. & N. 399, 517 ; *McCarthy* v. *Vine*, 22 C. P. 458, 462 ; *Chalmers* v. *Victors*, 16 W. R. 1046, S. C. 18 L. T. N. S. 481 ; *Browne* on Frauds, 2nd ed., sec. 191. As to the defendant's rule, the account furnished to Chambers, and the fact that the notes were taken two or three months after, shews that the term of credit was extended. Taking Chambers's evidence and the account, it is impossible to avoid the inference that the term of credit was six months. He cited *De Colyar* on Guarantees, p. 307, 307, 320.

MacKelcan, Q. C., contra. The guarantee applies to all goods of the season, whether before or after the date of the guarantee : *Edwards* v. *Jevons*. 8 C. B, 436, 444 ; *Hoad* v. *Grace*, 7 H. & N. 494 ; *Johnston* v. *Nicholls*, 1 C. B. 251 ; *White* v. *Woodward*, 5 C. B. 810 ; *Steele* v. *Hoe*, 14 Q. B. 431 ; *Bainbridge* v. *Wade*, 16 Q. B. 89 ; *Colbourn* v. *Dawson*, 10 C. B. 765 ; *Shaw* v. *Campbell*, 10 U. C. R. 117 ; *Wood* v. *Priestner*, L. R. 2 Ex. 66 ; *Heffield* v. *Meadows*, L. R. 4 C. P. 595 ; *Laurie* v. *Scholefield*, L. R. 4 C. P. 622 ; *Coles* v. *Pack*, L. R. 5 C. P. 65 ; *Leathley* v. *Spyer*, L. R. 5 C. P. 565 : *Nottingham, Hide, Skin & Fat Market Co., limited* v. *Bottrill*, L. R. 8 C. P. 694. The date of the guarantee should be read so as to apply to the real date : *Mercer* v. *Peterson*, L. P. 2 Ex. 304, 309.

September 26, 1876. MORRISON, J.—The principal question raised by the plaintiffs' rule is, whether the defendant is liable for the goods sold or sent to the debtor his son before he gave the guarantee in question. After the best consideration I can give to the case, although not free from some doubt, I am of opinion that he is not.

Now what are the facts ? The son applies to the plain-

tiffs to furnish him with certain goods. They write to him
they will do so upon his giving his note for the amount,
endorsed by his father. He writes, send me the goods as
soon as possible, and I will give you my note with my
father's endorsation if required; and requests them to write
if they will do so or not. The plaintiffs reply that as he states
his father will do so his order will be filled at once, and in
their letter they suggest, or rather propose, that in view of
future transactions that the son give to them his father's
continuous guarantee letter to obviate the trouble of having endorsations for each transaction, and if that should
meet his (the son's) view to let them know, and they would
send him a form of letter. Two days after the son replies
that he was willing to do so if absolutely required. The
goods then purchased, those now in question, are sent to
the son, and in their letter to the son enclosing the invoice
of the goods which were sent off two days previous, they
enclose a letter of guarantee for the defendant's signature,
and two days after the son writes to the defendant, who
resides at Woodstock, enclosing the guarantee, and asking
him to return it as soon as possible. In that letter the son
says: I am buying some goods (not that he had bought
from the plaintiffs) and they want a guarantee letter from
you so that I can buy the goods at low prices; that as they
were not personally acquainted with him (the son,) they did
not care to supply him on his own account: that the goods was
only a small lot until he got the others from Montreal. The
defendant upon this does not sign the letter of guarantee
sent by the plaintiffs as he did not like it—what it was
does not appear—but he writes one of his own and forwards it to the son, which is as follows: (Here the learned
Judge read the guarantee set out ante p. 2.)

There is no evidence that previous to signing the guarantee the defendant was aware that his son had then purchased over $1000 worth of goods; on the contrary, the
defendant swore that he had not such knowledge, and the
son testifies to the like effect.

Now can we say that the language of this guarantee is

capable of being construed to extend to and cover goods
previously sold to the debtor, or that it contemplates any
other than goods to be supplied after the giving of the
guarantee ?

As said by Tindal, C. J., in *Alnutt* v. *Ashenden*, 5 M. &
G. 392, 397, "Applying to this guarantee that rule of construction which has been so often laid down, that we must
give to words used their natural meaning," there is nothing
ambiguous in its terms or any language tending to shew that
it referred to a past transaction or existing debt ; the consideration on its face is not, as appears in many of the cases,
defectively stated or ambiguous, and there is no evidence of
any other consideration but the one mentioned on its face ;
and if, as the plaintiffs contend, it intended to cover the
past transaction, then there was no consideration to support a promise to pay the existing debt of the son.

I do not think it necessary to refer to many of the
numerous cases to be found in the books, as each case depends upon the particular words used in the guarantee—
the defective or ambiguous terms in which it is couched,
and the co-existing surrounding circumstances at the time
it was given.

In *Hoad* v. *Grace*, 7 H. & N. 494, it was held that the
words "for goods supplied" ought to be read for goods to
be supplied. The words were, " As Mr. Davis informs me
you require some person as guarantee for goods supplied to
him by you in his business, I have no objection to act as
such, for payment of your account."

Pollock, C. B., said, 496 : " It seems to me that must
mean for goods to be supplied, because, if the goods were
already supplied, no guarantee would be wanted."

Bramwell, B., said, p. 496 : " It is of little use looking at
former cases because one writing can scarcely be proof of the
meaning of another. However, I read the guarantee thus :
' In consideration of your supplying,' or ' if you will supply goods.' Because if it means ' for goods already supplied
by you and for which he owes you the money, I will be
guarantee,' in the first place, that is not an apt way of

expressing it, and in the next place, it is impossible to suppose that the parties would not have named some period for which the credit was to be given."

No doubt we may look at the co-existing circumstances when the guarantee was given in order to see the intention of the parties, but it seems to me that principle is only applicable when the instrument is defective or ambiguous, or when it would have no operation except the particular construction intended, and which it was capable of receiving. Here the language of the guarantee is, in my opinion, only capable of one construction, viz., that it is applicable only to the future. If the words were capable of two constructions, viz., that it applied to goods previously supplied as well as those to be supplied, then do the facts appearing at the trial justify our coming to the conclusion that the defendant had any knowledge of a previous sale. My brother Wilson from his note at the trial appears to have been of that opinion.

The evidence, in my opinion, shews that at the time the defendant signed the guarantee he was not aware of any goods being then furnished to the son. There is no evidence that such fact was communicated to him. * The son carries on business at St. Catharines. The defendant lives at Woodstock, and the first intimation of any dealing between the plaintiffs and the son was communicated in the son's letter of the 21st of April, when he encloses the guarantee for his signature. The goods in question were then sold to and sent to the son, and the whole tenor of that letter was well calculated to lead the defendant only to think that the son required the guarantee to enable him upon it in future to purchase goods from the plaintiffs at low prices. There is no intimation to the defendant that he had then already received $1,000 worth on the strength of the defendant endorsing his note or giving the guarantee.

The impression made on my mind by the whole evidence is, that the son intentionally concealed from the defendant the fact that he had then purchased a lot of goods from the plaintiffs, and that the probability is, that if he

had asked him to guarantee the amount he had then bought
he would have declined giving any guarantee. That I
take to be the position of the defendant at the time he
signed the guarantee, and that he only intended it to
apply to the future.

On the other hand, the plaintiffs' own testimony shews
that they sent the goods to the son without any security,
but solely depending on the son's promise that he would
give his own note for the amount endorsed by the defendant.

I may here remark that in cases where parol evidence is
given to explain the meaning of such instruments the
guarantee must be so expressed that it will cover the
liability contended for.

In *Leathley* v. *Spyer*, L. R. 5 C. P. 595, at p. 606, Montague
Smith, J., in giving judgment says : " No doubt, the written
guarantee must contain language which is capable of being
applied to the liability which is sought to be enforced; but
extrinsic circumstances may be given in evidence for the
purpose of shewing the meaning of the instrument, and
to what debts it was intended to apply." And after referring to the extrinsic circumstances in that case shewing
that the defendant had knowledge of a certain fact,—"the
inference I draw from that is, that it was given not only
with knowlege of the altered position of things, but with
a view to that partnership. That alone would not be
enough, if the language of the guarantee did not warrant
it."

And the same learned Judge, in *Heffield* v. *Meadows*, L.
R. 4 C. P. 595, at p. 600, said: " We may therefore look at
the surrounding circumstances in order to see for what it
was given, and to what transactions or dealings it was
intended to apply, not to alter the language, but to fill up
the instrument where it is silent, and to apply it to the
subject matter to which the parties intended it to be
applied." I refer also to *Wood* v. *Priestner*, L. R. 2 Ex. 66.

On the whole I am of opinion that the plaintiffs' rule
should be discharged. As to the defendant's rule to enter

a verdict on the second issue, after a perusal of the evidence, I think the defendant failed to establish his plea—
the evidence was contradictory but preponderating in favour
of the plaintiffs—and that his rule should be discharged.

HARRISON, C. J., and WILSON, J., concurred.

Both rules discharged.

———

THOMAS RUPERT AND JOSEPHINE RUPERT v. JAMES
JOHNSTON, JAMES MOORE, AND ANTOINETTE SMITH
PRINYER.

Donatio mortis causâ—Gift inter vivos—Delivery.

B., who died in 1874, had made a will in which there was a devise to theplaintiff, his illegitimate daughter; but this having given offence to his
family he destroyed it and made another, and at the same time signed
a promissory note, payable to the plaintiff, for $2,000. He placed this
note in a pocket book, where it remained till after his death, but shortly
before his death he shewed it to a witness, and said it was to be paid
after his death, and then handed it with the pocket book to the witness,
but afterwards took them back. He told this witness that he would
talk more about it to her another time, and asked her to tell P.,
his legitimate daughter and his executrix, that he had shewn the witness the note, which the witness did, and told the testator that she had
done so. It was proved also that he said he had made provision for
the plaintiff.
Held, that the plaintiff could not recover, for the note could not be
claimed by her either as a *donatio mortis causa* or as a gift *inter
vivos,* there having been no delivery of it by the testator.
Quære, whether such a note may, by manual delivery, be the subject of
a gift.

DECLARATION.

First count : for conversion by the defendants of two
promissory notes made by one John Burley, payable to
Josephine Rupert, the wife of Thomas Rupert, for the sum
of $4,000 each.

Second count, in assumpsit : that John Burley made the
promissory notes in the first count mentioned, payable to
Josephine Burley, now the wife of Thomas Rupert, and

then delivered them to the defendants, to be by them kept for the said Josephine, and to be delivered to her upon and after the death of the said John Burley, and the defendants received the notes upon that understanding. It then averred that John Burley departed this life on 7th February, 1874, of which the defendants had notice, and the plaintiffs, since his death, requested delivery of the notes, but defendants neglected and refused to deliver the same.

The defendant Antoinette Smith Prinyer pleaded :—

To the first count : 1. Not guilty. 2. Notes not the property of the plaintiffs, or either of them. 3. John Burley did not make the notes, or either of them.

And as to the second count : 1. Not guilty. 2. Notes not made by Burley. 3. Notes not delivered to the defendant Antoinette Smith Prinyer, as alleged.

The remaining defendants pleaded :—

To the first count : 1. Not guilty. 2. Notes not the property of the plaintiffs or either of them.

And to the second count : 1. Did not detain the notes as alleged. 2. Burley did not make the notes. 3. No value for the making of the notes by Burley. 4. Notes not the property of the plaintiffs. 5. Notes never delivered to the defendants.

Issue.

The cause was tried before Burton, J., and a jury, at the last Spring Assizes, for the county of Hastings.

John Burley died in February, 1874. The plaintiff Josephine Rupert was an illegitimate daughter of his. The defendant Antoinette Smith Prinyer was a legitimate daughter. He died in the house of the latter. Shortly before his death, he made a will, in which there was a devise to Josephine Rupert. This gave great offence to some members of the family. In consequence, he destroyed that will, and executed another will, from which the name of the plaintiff was omitted. Contemporaneously with the latter will, he signed a document in the following form :

$2,000.   For value received, I promise to pay Mrs. Josephine Rupert, wife of Thomas Rupert, the sum of two thousand dollars, to be paid as follows :—two hundred dollars the year after my death, and the sum of two hun-dred dollars annually thereafter, until the said sum of two thousand dollars be paid.

(Signed)   JOHN BURLEY.

Cressy, 19th March, 1873.

The instrument was stamped as a promissory note.

After writing it, he placed it and some other papers in his pocket book, where it remained up to and after the time of his death. Shortly before his death, he had some conversation with *Elizabeth Hill*, a witness called at the trial on behalf of the plaintiffs. He told her he had a good deal of trouble about his former will. He then asked the witness to bring his coat and give him his pocket book. The coat was at the time hanging behind a door within his sight.. She did as requested. He then took out of the pocket book two papers which he said were notes. One of them was the note in question. He shewed her his signature to them, and said they were to be paid to the parties after his death, that he had provided for them, &c. He promised to talk to the witness about them more by and bye. He handed his coat, will, and the notes to the witness, but afterwards took them back. He said he wanted Mr. Hill,. the husband of the witness, to read over the will, and see that it was all right. He said he would afterwards tell her what he wanted done with the notes. He requested her to tell the defendant Mrs. Prinyer that he had shewn the notes to the witness, that they were in the pocket book, and he wished them taken care of. The witness at once mentioned the fact to Mrs. Prinyer, and told her the father wished the notes taken care of. When witness next saw Burley, he asked if the witness had mentioned the matter to his daughter, the defendant. She answered in the affirmative. He then said the witnesses to his will knew that the notes were with the will, and what he in-tended them for, and the provision he proposed for his daughter. He said the daughter, (meaning Mrs. Rupert), got into trouble. He told the witness he had something more to say to her before he died, but he was speechless.

the next time she saw him, and never afterwards said anything more to her about the notes or anything else.

The notes were intended for two persons. One of them
was for the plaintiff. In the course of conversation with
the witness, he said they were to be paid by his estate.
The witness kept the will till after his death, and then
gave it to her husband.

Lucy Miller and the defendant Antoinette Smith Prinyer,
was each appointed an executrix of his last will.

Lucy Miller was next called as a witness for the plaintiffs. She testified to a conversation which the defendant
had with her about two notes found in the pocket book of
the deceased.

The defendant *Antoinette Smith Prinyer* was next called
as a witness for the plaintiffs. She, under subpœna, produced the note. She admitted that she found it in the
pocket book of the deceased. She proved the handwriting
to be that of the deceased. She admitted a demand made
upon her for the note by the male plaintiff on behalf of his
wife. She also swore that her father said to her a few
days before he died, " I want you to take my pocket book,
and keep it," and " give it to no one." He at the time
pointed to his coat. Afterwards the defendant found the
pocket book in the coat, opened it, and found the notes.
She did not recollect any conversation with Mrs. Hill about
the notes.

James Johnston, who was also one of the executors to
the will, swore that the last witness denied to him any
knowledge of the notes.

Other witnesses gave similar testimony bearing on the
conduct of the defendant.

One witness, *Carter,* swore that the deceased, just after
the last will was signed, told him that he had made provision for Josephine, " for she was as much his daughter
as any of the other children."

Thomas Rupert, the plaintiff, also swore that the deceased
in his lifetime told him he intended to make provision for
Mrs. Rupert.

The estate was proved to be worth $40,000 or $50,000, with liabilities of about $8,000.

On objection being made by counsel for the defendants, to the recovery of the plaintiffs, the learned Judge non-suited the plaintiffs, reserving leave to enter a verdict for the plaintiffs, if the Court should be of opinion that there was evidence to go to the jury to sustain either count of the declaration.

During Easter Term, May 17, 1876, *L. Wallbridge*, Q.C., obtained a rule calling on defendants to shew cause why the nonsuit should not be set aside, and a verdict entered for the plaintiffs against Antoinette Smith Prinyer, for the sum of $2,000, pursuant to leave reserved at the trial, on the ground that the delivery of the agreement produced and proved at the trial was a *donatio mortis causâ*, or was a *donatio inter vivos;* and why the names of the defendants Johnston and Moore should not be struck out of the record, on the plaintiffs paying their costs to them.

During this term, September 5, 1876, *Britton*, Q.C., shewed cause for the defendant, Antoinette Smith Prinyer. There was neither a good *donatio mortis causâ : Bunn* v. *Markham*, 7 Taunt. 224; *Tate* v. *Hilbert*, 2 Ves. Jr. 111; *Tiffany* v. *Clarke*, 6 Grant 474; *Blain* v. *Terryberry*, 9 Grant 286; *Veal* v. *Veal*, 6 Jur. N. S. 527; *Story's* Eq. Jur. sec. 607 c.; *Mills* v. *Mills*, 8 P. Wms. 35, 38; *Shower* v. *Pilck*, 4 Ex. 478; nor a good gift *inter vivos: Regina* v. *Carter*, 13 C. P. 611; *Irons* v. *Smallpiece*, 2 B. & Al. 551; *Viet* v. *Viet*, 34 U. C. R. 104; and if the plaintiffs are entitled to recover, the damages should only be nominal: *Doyle* v. *Eccles*, 17 C. P. 644.

Delamere, for the remaining defendants, had no objection, if the Court saw fit, to the making of the rule absolute to strike their names out of the writ on payment of costs: *Hawkins* v. *Platt*, 2 Esp. 663.

Wallbridge, Q. C., contra. There was a good *donatio mortis causâ: Bunn* v. *Markham*, 7 Taunt. 224; *Watson's* Compendium of Equity 129; *Taylor's* Eq. Jur. 199, 200; and the damages should be the face value of the security: *Bromage* v. *Lloyd*, 1 Ex. 32.

September 26, 1876. HARRISON, C. J.—This is a case in which the Court would naturally struggle to carry out the intention of the deceased, but may, owing to existing rules of law, struggle in vain.

The instrument signed by the deceased on 19th March, 1873, although not payable to bearer or order, is a good promissory note, and if it had been delivered by the maker before his death to the payee, would have enabled the latter to sue upon it as a promissory note.

But as there was no such delivery it is sought to make the instrument available to the payee either as a gift *inter vivos*, or as a *donatio mortis causâ*.

The first question is, whether such an instrument can be said to be the subject of such a gift.

There is no doubt that there may be a good donation of any thing which has a physical existence, and admits of a corporal delivery, as, for example, of jewels, gems, a bag of money, a trunk of goods : *Story's* Eq. Jur., 10th ed., sec. 607 *a.*

Besides it is now established that when a man delivers to another such an instrument as a policy of insurance, debenture, bond, bill of exchange, or promissory note, the delivery of the instrument confers on the donee all the rights to the chose in action arising out of the instrument : *Duffield* v. *Hicks*, 1 Dow & Clark 1, overruling *Duffield* v. *Elwes*, 1 Sim. & Stu. 239 ; *Veal* v. *Veal*, 27 Beav. 303 ; *Rankin* v. *Weguelin*, 27 Beav. 309 ; *Witt* v. *Amis*, 1 B. & S. 109, S. C., 33 Beav. 619.

The delivery of a cheque or promissory note made by the donor himself stands, however, on a somewhat different footing. The cheque is no more than an order to obtain a certain sum of money. The promissory note is no more than a promise to pay a certain sum of money. While there are authorities that go far to sustain the delivery of the cheque, we find none to sustain the delivery of the promissory note as being the subject of a gift. See *Boutts* v. *Ellis*, 4 DeG. M. & G. 249 ; *Hewitt* v. *Kaye*, L. R. 6 Eq. 198 ; *Bromley* v. *Brunton*, L. R. 6 Eq. 275 ; *Beak* v. *Beak*, 26 L. T. N. S. 281.

But conceding (as there was no argument on the point at the bar), that such a note may, by manual delivery, be the subject of a gift, we shall proceed to enquire whether the gift was so made as to render it effectual to the female plaintiff either as a gift *inter vivos*, or as a *donatio mortis causâ*.

In *Irons* v. *Smallpiece*, 2 B. & Al. 551; it was held that the verbal gift of a chattel, without actual delivery, does not pass the property to the donee. This decision was approved of in *Shower* v. *Pilck*, 4 Ex. 478; *Power* v. *Cook*, L. R. 4 Ir. C. L. R. 247; 258, and followed in *Case* v. *Dennison*, 11 Am. 222. The better rule now appears to be that a gift of a chattel *inter vivos* may be good without actual delivery, but is revocable until the donee has made some statement or done some act testifying his acquiescence in the gift. *The London and Brighton R. W. Co.* v. *Fairclough*, 2 M. & G. 691 note; *Lunn* v. *Thornton*, 1 C. B. 379; *Ward* v. *Audland*, 16 M. & W. 862, 871; *Winter* v. *Winter*, 4 L. T. N. S. 639; *Regina* v. *Bertles*, 13 C. P. 607; *Viet* v. *Viet*, 34 U. C. R. 104. See also *Bourne* v. *Fosbrooke*, 18 C. B. N. S. 515; *Douglas* v. *Douglas*, 22 L. T. N. S. 127; *Gray* v. *Barton*, 14 Am. 181; *Minor* v. *Rogers*, 16 Am. 69.

There was nothing here shewn which can be construed as amounting either to a delivery by the deceased or acquiescence by the plaintiff in the life time of the deceased. On the contrary, it clearly appears that the gift was not to take effect till after the death of the donor.

Next, can the instrument be held effective as a gift *mortis causâ*.

This, according to *Story*, is a sort of amphibious gift, something between a legacy and a *donatio inter vivos*. *Story's* Eq. Jur. 10th ed., sec. 606.

It differs from a legacy in these respects:

1. It need not be proved—nay, it cannot be proved as a testamentary act.

2. It requires no assent or other act on the part of the executor to perfect the title of the donee.

3—VOL. XL U. C. R.

It differs from a gift *inter vivos* in several respects, in which it resembles a legacy.

1. It is ambulatory, incomplete, and revocable during the donor's life time.

2. It is liable to the debts of the donor upon a deficiency of assets. *Story*, Eq. Jur., 10th ed., sec. 606 *a*.

It is properly a gift of personal property by a party who is in peril of death, upon condition that it shall presently belong to the donee in case the donor shall die, but not otherwise. *Ib*. sec. 606. See further *Cosnahan* v. *Grice*, 15 Moore P. C. 215.

To make the gift effective, there must be a delivery of it to the donee or his agent, subject to be defeated by subsequent personal revocation, or by his recovery or escape from the impending death or peril: *Story*, Eq. Jur. sec. 606.

And there must not only be delivery to the donee, but such a delivery as to indicate on the part of the donor a present determination to part with all dominion over the gift. *Hawkins* v. *Blewett*, 2 Esp. 663; *Bunn* v. *Markham*, 7 Taunt. 224; *Reddel* v. *Dobree*, 10 Sim. 244; *Powell* v. *Hellicar*, 26 Beav. 261, S. C., 5 Jur. N. S. 232. See also *Thompson* v. *Heffernan*, 4 Dru. & W. 285; *Tiffany* v. *Clarke*, 6 Grant 474; *Blain* v. *Terryberry*, 9 Grant 286.

In the case now before us for decision, there was no delivery. The deceased spoke of his intention to give. But he placed the notes in his pocket book, where they were before he spoke to Mrs. Hill about them, and where they remained till after his death. He intended to tell her "what he intended done with the notes," but was never able to do so. His desire, however, was plainly that some other than his executrix should have a knowledge of the existence of the notes. His exhibition of them to Mrs. Hill was in pursuance of that desire. His request that she should tell the executrix what she had seen, indicates the same desire. His subsequent enquiry as to whether she had done as requested, manifested not only his desire, but his anxiety on the point. He said "he intended the notes for his daughter." Unfortunately for that daughter, who

was as much the object of his love in his dying hours as
daughters born under more favourable circumstances, the
facts of the case denote no more than an intention.   It does
not appear that the father ever divested himself for one
moment of the notes.   It is impossible to hold that there
was a delivery of them, either to the donee or to any
agent for her.   And as a *donatio mortis causâ* cannot
exist without a delivery, the gift fails as a *donatio mortis
causâ : Gough* v. *Findon et al.,* 7 Ex. 48.

The plaintiff was, we infer, an object of the testator's
bounty in his first will.   That will, for some reason, gave
offence to the legitimate members of his family.   He, however, was resolved, if possible, to benefit the plaintiff,
although compelled to omit her name from his last will.
He endeavoured to accomplish the strong desire of his dying
hours by making the promissory note in question.   All that
can in law be said of the transaction is, that it is an in-
formal legacy, an attempted testamentary gift, a nuncu-
pative will: *Gough* v. *Findon,* 7 Ex. 48; *Mitchell* v. *Smith,*
4 De. G. J. & S. 422 ; *Dunne* v. *Boyd,* L. R. 8 Ir. Eq. 609.

Such a testamentary request or bequest, unfortunately
for the plaintiff, is of such imperfect obligation, that it is
not binding in a Court of law : Consol. Stat. U. C. ch.
16 sec. 83.

Nor do we see any clear ground on which the assistance
of a Court of equity can be invoked.

In *Milroy* v. *Lord,* 4 DeG. F. & J. 264, 274, Lord
Justice Turner said : " I take the law of this Court to be
well settled, that, in order to render a voluntary settlement
valid and effectual, the settlor must have done everything
which, according to the nature of the property comprised
in the settlement, was necessary to be done in order to
transfer the property, and render the settlement binding
upon him.   He may of course do this by actually transferring the property to the persons for whom he intends to
provide, and the provision will then be effectual, and it will
be equally effectual if he transfers the property to a
trustee for the purpose of the settlement, or declares that

he himself holds it in trust for those purposes; and if the property be personal, the trust may, as I apprehend, be declared either in writing or by parol; but, in order to render the settlement binding,-one or other of those modes must, as I understand the law of this Court, be resorted to, for there is no equity in this Court to *perfect an imperfect gift.*"

In *Warriner* v. *Rogers*, L. R. 16 Eq. 340, 349; this language is quoted with approbation by Bacon, V. C., who says: "Nothing can be more clear and distinct than the exposition of the law contained in the sentences I have read, and to my judgment nothing more satisfactory, if I were at liberty, (which I am not), to pronounce an opinion upon it."

In *Moore* v. *Moore*, L. R. 18 Eq. 474, 482; Hall, V. C., in referring to the foregoing cases, says: "I do think it very important to keep a clear and definite distinction between cases of imperfect gift and cases of declaration of trust, and that we should not extend beyond what the authorities have already established declarations of trust, so as to supplement and supply what, according to the decisions of highest authority, would otherwise be imperfect gifts." See further *Tiffany* v. *Clarke*, 6 Grant 474.

Without deciding or pretending to decide as to the equitable rights (if any), of the plaintiff, we fear all that remains for her is, to appeal from our decision to the heart and conscience of her sister, and to support that appeal as best she can by the dying request of their common father.

MORRISON, J., was not present at the argument and took no part in the judgment.

WILSON, J., concurred.

Rule discharged.

GEARING V. NORDHEIMER.

Building agreement—Omission to sign specifications—Right to sue on quantum meruit.

The plaintiff agreed in writing, on the 19th February, to build a house for the defendant according to the plans and specifications of one R., with alterations made by I., for $25,000. Afterwards some alterations were agreed upon, and on the 30th April a contract was executed by plaintiff and defendant by which the plaintiff was to build the house for $26,596, and this contract recited that the plaintiff had agreed to do all the work required according to certain plans and specifications prepared by R., with certain suggestions and amendments made by I., and signed by the plaintiff, subject to the various stipulations and conditions mentioned in the contract. The plans were signed by the plaintiff, but not the specifications; but he finished the building according to the specifications prepared, and from time to time obtained certificates for payment from the architect for the work executed as under the contract, in accordance with its provisions, by which the money was to be paid on such certificates, no extra work was to be paid for without a written order, and in the event of any dispute the architect was to be the sole and final judge.

Held, that the plaintiff's omission to sign the specifications could not entitle him to set aside the contract as not complete, and to claim for the work done as upon a *quantum meruit,* without the architect's certificates.

DECLARATION : on the common counts.

Pleas : never-indebted, payment, and set-off.

The trial took place before Burton, J., at the last Toronto Winter Assizes, without a jury.

The plaintiff's counsel, in opening his case to the Court, stated the contention on the part of the plaintiff to be, that there was no perfected sealed contract under which the work in question, viz., the building of a dwelling house for the plaintiff, was done, and that the plaintiff was entitled to recover for such work under the common counts : that the defendant contended there was a perfect and binding contract under which the work was completed; and that if the plaintiff established his contention as a matter of law, the amount claimed was to be determined by an arbitrator.

It appeared that the plaintiff proposed to build a dwelling house for the defendant, according to plans and specifications made by one Reck, a New York archi-

tect, and on the 19th of February, 1872, the plaintiff and
defendant both executed an instrument, by which the
plaintiff proposed to build the house according to the plans
and specifications of Mr. Reck; with the alterations made
therein by Mr. Irving, and as agreed on between the plaintiff and defendant previously on the 15th February, such
alterations to be specified in detail by Mr. Irving, for
$25,000, payable according to Mr. Irving's certificate, &c.

The agreement contained various and usual stipulations
and conditions, which it is unnecessary to refer to at length,
and at the end: " I hereby agree, when the specifications
are received, to execute a formal contract, with all the usual
stipulations and provisions inserted by architects in
contracts of a similar nature." On the 30th of April,
1872, after various interviews between the parties and
architects, alterations and additions were agreed on which
increased the contract price by $1,596.06 ; and on that day
a more formal contract was signed. That contract recited
that whereas the party of the first part, the defendant, was
about to erect a dwelling house (stating where) according
to certain plans and specifications prepared by Henry
Reck, architect, of New York, with certain suggestions and
amendments, and conditions, made by William Irving,
architect, of the city of Toronto ; and whereas the plaintiff
had contracted and agreed to do the whole of the works
required in the erection of the said dwelling house, com-
prising, &c. (setting out all the works), and other works
connected therewith, according to certain plans and specifications prepared by Henry Reck, architect, of New York,
with certain suggestions, amendments, and additions made
by William Irving, architect, of the city of Toronto, and
signed by the said party of the second part (the plaintiff)
upon the terms and conditions thereinafter mentioned, &c.,
and for the price of $26,596.06, to be paid to him by the
defendant as thereinafter provided.

Then followed the usual covenants. Among them : And
it is understood and agreed between the parties that the
plans and specifications aforesaid shall be taken to explain

each other : that the amended plans shall take precedence
of the original tracings where alterations have been made;
but both the original and amended plans are to be taken
to elucidate the design of the said dwelling house ; and it
is also distinctly understood that the alterations noted in
reading of the specifications shall be and is considered a
part of the contract. Also, that no work done, or material
furnished in and about or connected with the works, over
and above what is mentioned in the said plans and specifications, shall, in any case, be paid for by the plaintiff
unless the same be specially ordered and directed in writing, as necessary and proper, by the defendant, or the
architect, &c., whether the same are extra or additional to
the said plans and specifications, or whether the same shall
have been contemplated at the time of the execution of the
agreement. The defendant covenanted thereby to pay the
plaintiff the sum of $26,596.06, as stated therein, and upon
the certificate, &c., of the architect.

It was also agreed by and between the parties that in
case the defendant, or the said architect, should desire to
have any part of the work done in a different manner, or
to have extra work done, or to omit something that is now
specified, he or they may do so in writing, and the work
shall be done in such different manner, and such extra
work shall be done, and such thing shall be diminished or
omitted accordingly ; and the architect shall be the sole
judge as to the additional price to be allowed to the plaintiff therefor, or of the sum it is proper to deduct from the
amount aforesaid on account thereof, as the case may be ;
and his decision shall be final and conclusive. And that in
all cases of dispute or difference the decision of such architect shall be final, binding, and conclusive on the parties
thereto. He shall be the sole judge in all disputes which
may happen or arise between them in relation to the said
works, or this agreement, or extra work, and the price to
be paid for the extra work, if any or more, which may be
performed or allowed in the said building, or about the
same, and his decision in all or any of such cases shall be

binding on all parties thereto, provided that such decision shall be given in writing, within one month after the completion of the building and works.

At the time the agreement was executed by the parties, the plans were signed by the plaintiff, but he omitted to sign the specifications. The specifications, according to the architect's testimony, were ready at the time, and in the hurry of the business were neglected to have been signed, and it was a mere oversight. The defendant was of opinion that they were not ready, or rather did not include the alterations agreed on at the time.

The fact, however, appeared that there were specifications, and that the plaintiff had them in March, and knew what they were before he executed the contract, and the evidence went to shew that they were ready at the time of the signing of the contract, and that the works proceeded under them until the work was finished in accordance with them. There was no evidence that the plaintiff objected to those under which he worked. He also, from time to time, received certificates from the architect, certifying that he was entitled to certain amounts under the contract, until the completion of the building.

The plaintiff, on these facts, contended that the contract was not a perfect one, and that he was entitled to sue on the common counts.

The learned Judge was of opinion, from authorities cited at the trial, he ought to find a verdict for the plaintiff, which he did, giving nominal damages, and ordering that the case be referred to an arbitrator.

During Hilary term, February 12, 1876, *Hector Cameron*, Q.C., obtained a rule to set aside the verdict, and to enter a nonsuit or verdict for defendant, on the ground that the verdict was against law and evidence, and that the plaintiff was not entitled to recover on the common counts, there being a valid and binding sealed contract relating to the alleged causes of action sued for, and the work being done under such contract; and because the plaintiff was estopped from denying the existence of such completed contract, and the signature by him of the specifications therein mentioned, the work having been in fact done under such contract and specifications.

During this term, August 28, 1876, *C. Robinson*, Q. C., *Lash* with him shewed cause. There was not a complete contract, and the plaintiff was entitled on a *quantum meruit: Gooch* v. *Snarr*, 34 U. C. R. 616; *Sellin* v. *Price*, L. R. 2 Ex. 189; *Crawford* v. *Brown*, 17 U. C. R. 126, and the cases collected in R. & J. Dig. 587; *Roscoe's* Nisi Prius, 181; *Addison* on Contracts, 7th ed., 19.

Hector Cameron, Q. C., contra. The word "signed," in the contract, only applied to suggestions of Irving, and did not require the specifications to be signed. The plaintiff did sign the provisional contract in which he agreed to sign specifications, and he could now be compelled to sign these specifications, but if there is no other contract the provisional contract governs. Gearing went on with the work after signing the provisional contract, and never asked for specifiations, and took certificates which referred to the contract. His own account is "to amount as per contract $26,596." Irving and he went through the account together. Then Gearing produced the working specifications. *Boileau* v. *Rutlin*, 2 Ex. 665, and *Taylor* on Evidence, 6th ed., pp. 766, 1353, 1496, shew that a bill in Chancery is admissible to prove its existence. Although the signing of the specifications was omitted, yet as the parties worked on them, and paid on them, they would bind: *Pattinson* v. *Luckley*, L. R. 10 Ex. 330. *Gooch* v. *Snarr*, 34 U. C. R. 616 and *Weeks* v. *Maillardet*, 14 East 568, are distinguishable; both are decisions on pleading. *Sellin* v. *Price*, L. R. 2 Ex. 189, is also distinguishable, as it turned on the peculiar provisions of the English Bankruptcy Law. He also referred to *Dyer* v. *Green*, 1 Ex. 71.

September 26, 1876. MORRISON, J.—I am of opinion that the defendant is entitled to our judgment.

The principal facts appearing in the case are: that on the 19th of February, 1872, the plaintiff proposed and agreed to build the dwelling house in question for the defendant, according to the plans and specifications of Mr. Reck, with alterations made by Mr. Irving, for $25,000; and agreeing to execute a more formal agreement, with the usual stipulations, &c. Afterwards some alterations were agreed upon; and finally, on the 30th of April, a contract was executed by the plaintiff and defendant for the building of the house for $26,596.06, the contract reciting that the plaintiff had agreed to do all the work required, &c., according to certain plans and specifications prepared by Mr. Reck, with certain suggestions, amendments, &c., made by William Irving, architect, and signed by the plaintiff, subject to the various stipulations and conditions mentioned in the contract.

At the time of the execution of the contract the plans were signed by the plaintiff, but he omitted to sign the specifications, which, according to the evidence, were prepared for that purpose. The plaintiff proceeded with the work under the contract, and he finished the building according to the specifications so prepared; and he, from time to time as the work progressed, obtained, as the contract provided, certificates for payments for the work executed under the contract, plans, and specifications, until the completion of the building.

Such are the main facts. The plaintiff now contends that because he did not sign, or omitted to sign, the specifications which he worked under, and which were otherwise specifically referred to and indicated in his contract, that he is at liberty to say that the contract he executed was not a perfected contract; and that he is entitled to say to the defendant, "I am not bound by it, nor by the architect's certificates, &c., and you must pay me according to the value of the work done and material provided," &c.

It certainly seems to me to be a monstrous proposition that a builder who enters into and executes such a contract, and who inadvertently or intentionally omits to identify

the specifications by writing his name on them, the specifications being otherwise clearly and specifically referred to
and identified in the contract, should, after having worked
by them and completed his contract, receiving the contract
price from time to time under it, nevertheless, when
the building is finished in pursuance of the contract,
plans, and specifications, then for the first time turns
round and says, "The contract is not a perfected one, and I
am entitled to disregard it." I have been unable to find
any authority exactly in point, for the reason no doubt
that so unreasonable a proposition as the plaintiff contends
for has been seldom put forward.

In *Dyer* v. *Green*, 1 Ex. 71, the plaintiff in an interpleader suit tendered in evidence a bill of sale, which
assigned certain goods, furniture, plate, &c., "which are
particularly enumerated and described in a certain schedule
hereunto annexed." The schedule was not annexed to the
deed, and it was also inadmissible for want of a stamp.
The bill of sale was objected to as incomplete, and the
learned Judge, at the trial, thought, as the bill of sale referred to the schedule, the latter was an instrument explanatory of the mode in which the deed operated, and ruled
against the plaintiff; and a verdict being found for the defendant, a rule was obtained, and the Court, without hearing the plaintiff, ordered a new trial.

Pollock, C. B., who tried the cause, said, p. 73 : "If *Duck*
v. *Braddyll*, McClel. 217, 13 Pri. 455, had been cited at the
trial, I should have received the deed without the inventory.
* * The question here is, does the deed operate without
the inventory ; if it does, the inventory is merely referred
to as a memorandum for the more certain knowledge of the
articles."

Alderson, B., in giving the judgment of the Court, said,
p. 73 : "The deed must be considered as enumerating all the
articles ; it in fact does so by describing them as articles
in a particular house." And after referring to *Weeks* v.
Maillardet, 14 East 569, (to which we were referred in this
case,) said, "Here the deed is sensible without the schedule."

So here the deed cannot be said to be inoperative by reason of the plaintiff omitting to identify the specifications by his signature. It certainly is quite clear and sensible without such signature, as the contract refers to and indicates the particular plans and specifications.

I find, however, a late case, *Pattinson* v. *Luckley*, L. R. 10 Ex. 330, and to which we were referred by Mr. Cameron, which has a strong bearing on the case before us, and in my judgment, in principle, is decisive on this point. That was a case like this of a building contract, and the action on a *quantum meruit*. The defendant in answer set up the contract in which appeared an *erasure* in a material point, and the jury found that it was made by the architect after the plaintiff had signed the contract. The plaintiff contended that the document was void. The Court held that notwithstanding the erasure the conditions were either still the governing document, or at least must be looked at to see what were the real terms of the contract, and that the plaintiff could not recover. The plaintiff got a verdict, and a rule was obtained to set it aside and to enter a non-suit, &c.

Bramwell, B., in giving judgment said p. 333, " The rule must be absolute. It is remarkable that there is no authority on the point, but on principle I think our judgment should be for the defendant. We must assume that the verdict was correct, that the document was altered after execution without the consent of the plaintiff, and upon the authorities I think we must hold that the defendant was as responsible for the alteration as if he had made it himself, since it was made by the person who was holding the document for the defendant and for his benefit. The question is not what the defendant could do against the plaintiff—not what the defendant's rights are. It may be, that if the plaintiff had done none of the work, and the defendant had sought to enforce the contract after having spoiled the document, on the authority of *Powell* v. *Divett*, 15 East 29 he would have been unable to enforce the contract ; or that, if the plaintiff had done the work badly the defendant could not have enforced the contract by an action for bad building. I give no opinion on that question; if it were necessary to decide it, I should desire further time for consideration. But the question we must decide is, on what terms he is entitled to be paid. I am strongly inclined to think that he is entitled to be paid on the terms actually agreed on. If he fails to shew any bargain, he is not entitled to be paid at all. In the case of goods sold and delivered, it is easy to shew a contract from the retention of the goods; but that is not so where work is done on real property; and the plaintiff, therefore, in shewing what the bargain was, must shew all the terms. It is no use to answer, as Mr. Herschell did, that he has made out a *primâ facie* case by telling half the truth. We must have the whole truth. I doubt, therefore, if the document has been so spoiled as not to be still the intrinsically governing document—because, if not, there are innumerable difficulties Suppose the claim on the *quantum meruit* were to the plaintiff's detriment, instead of being to his advantage would he be deprived of his right to sue on the contract? Surely not. Then, has he an option to sue on a *quantum meruit* or on the document at his pleasure? No doubt there are cases where a man may so conduct himself as to give an option, but they do not apply here. The question is, what was the contract? Not what is it the plaintiff's pleasure to say the contract was. * * But if I am wrong, and the instrument is not intrinsically binding, still I think it may be looked at to see the terms of the contract. Upon this point the case of *Earl of Falmouth* v. *Roberts*, 9 M. & W. 471, is material, and the observations of Parke, B., are of great value in shewing what our conclusion ought to be; that even if we hold that the instrument ceased to have any intrinsic operation, still we must look at it to see the terms of the bargain. The plaintiff, therefore, must make out his case in accordance with those terms. But it is admitted that he has been paid for all works for which the architect has certified, and that if he is bound by the terms of the conditions which make the architect's certificate a condition precedent to the right to payment, the verdict is wrong. I think that he is bound by those conditions, and that the rule must therefore be absolute to enter the verdict for the defendant."

And Cleasby, B., said, p. 335, "The contract remains: the disability is on the person who altered it: it would be ridiculous to suppose that his act has destroyed the rights of others. * * This is not a contract to pay a sum of money or do one thing, but an agreement operating over twelve months or more. It is to be acted on from time to time, and as it has been acted on, it is impossible to say one can undo what has been done, and that payments can be recovered back, and that the agreement ceased to be operative while it was being acted on and treated as binding by both parties. That is a satisfactory ground on which to rest our decision."

And Pollock, B., said, p. 336, "We are asked to infer another contract, shutting out what we know occurred, and what was the essence of the contract. By our decision we are carrying out substantially the real contract."

I refer also to the case of *Ranger* v. *Great Western R. W. Co.*, 5 H. L. 72. There the plaintiff contracted under seal to do certain works. In the contract there was a stipulation that if the company thought proper to make any additions to the original works, they could do so by written instructions, signed by their engineer. A verbal arrangement was entered into for the execution of certain extensions, allowing for a variance in the prices, but stipulating with the exception of that variance that all the provisions of the contract should be considered as applicable to the extension work, one of the provisions being the necessity of the engineer's certificate. The work was done by the contractor under that arrangement. It was held he could not afterwards reject the terms of the contract, and sue as upon a *quantum meruit.*

The Lord Chancellor Lord Cranworth, in giving judgment, at p. 101, said, after referring to the contract, "The terms so arranged were the terms according to which the works were in fact done, and though the terms stipulated for by the contract, viz:, that the authority for any additional work should be in writing, signed by the engineer, were not, (so far as appears), adhered to, yet it certainly is not open to the appellant * *   to reject its terms and to claim remuneration on a *quantum meruit,* as if no such express agreement had been come to. It might have been open to argument on the part of the respondents, that they are not bound to pay for works done under the terms of a parol contract made with their agent, and not authorized by them ; but they have not raised such a point, and certainly the appellant can have no right beyond that which the parol agreement confers on him."

On the common sense principles enunciated in these cases, assuming that the plaintiff's omission to sign the specifications rendered the contract inoperative or voidable, our judgment in this case should be for the defendant. We see clearly the terms of the contract under which the dwelling house was built and finished. It would be ridiculous, as said by Cleasby, B., to suppose the plaintiff's omission to write his name in the specifications destroyed the rights of others after the contract was acted on and fulfilled and treated as binding. The case of *Gooch* v. *Snarr,* 34 U. C. R. 616, in this Court cited by the plaintiff, is quite distinguishable. I may here remark, as I thought during the argument, that if the plaintiff's signature to the specification is so essential in determining the rights of the parties I see no reason why he should not sign them now or be compelled to do so. He would only be carrying out what he agreed to do by his agreement of 19th of February, and what he recited he had done in the contract under judgment.

The rule, in my opinion, should be absolute to enter a nonsuit.

HARRISON, C. J., and WILSON, J., concurred.

Rule absolute.

MEMORANDA.

During this term the following gentlemen were called to the Bar :—

PHILIP MCKENZIE, THOMAS HUNTER PURDON, JOHN TOBIAS LENNOX, HEBER ARCHIBALD, WILLIAM BURTON DOHERTY, FRANCIS RYE, ALEXANDER JOHN B. MACDONALD, EMMANUEL THOMAS ESSORY.

IN THE

QUEEN'S BENCH, AND COURT OF APPEAL.

HARRIS V. SMITH ET AL.

Easement—Right of way—Severance of tenements—When the right will pass
—"Appurtenances"—Pleading.

Declaration for breaking and entering the plaintiff's close, being a yard in the rear of a certain shop and premises, and throwing down a brick wall there.

Plea : that before the alleged trespass one J. D. was seized in fee of the said shop and premises, and of the said close : that the occupiers of the shop enjoyed as of right and without interruption a certain way on foot and with cattle from a public lane over said close to said shop and premises, and therefrom over said close to the lane : that after-wards J. D., by deed, dated 12th July, 1849, demised the shop and premises, *with all the appurtenances*, to L. & W. as trustees for a term of years, which it was agreed by the deed should be renewed, and which was afterwards renewed ; and that the defendants became and are assignees of the term, and took possession of the shop and premises under the assignment : that after the demise to L. and W., the executors of J. D. demised to S. the said close, subject to said way, and the same afterwards became vested for a term in the plaintiff : that afterwards the defendants during their term, and in their own right, entered the close to use said way, and in using the same broke down part of said wall, which obstructed said way. On demurrer to this plea :

Held, by HARRISON, C. J., that the plea might be read as alleging a defined way, necessary and convenient for the enjoyment of defendants' property before the lease from J. D., constructed across the plaintiff's close, for the use and enjoyment of defendants' shop, and visible to all persons when the plaintiff acquired title : that so reading the plea, the way might be said to be an "appurtenance" to defendants' premises, which passed from J. D. by the deed under which defendants claimed ; and that the plea therefore was good.

On appeal this judgment was reversed, on the ground that the plea could not be read as alleging an apparent and continuous easement necessary for the proper enjoyment of defendants' premises, without which it would not pass under the deed.

Per BURTON, J.—Upon a severance of tenements, easements used as of necessity, or in their nature continuous, will pass by implication of law; easements not continuous or apparent, but used from time to time only, will not.

Per PATTERSON, J.—A right of way is not such a continuous easement as

5—VOL. XL U. C. R.

to pass by implication of law with a grant of the land; only a way of
necessity will so pass.   A way used by the owner of two tenements
over one for access to the other, is not in law appurtenant to the
dominant tenement, so as to pass with a grant of it under the word
"appurtenances," unless the deed shews an intention to extend the
meaning of that word, and to embrace the way, or the grant is of all
ways "used and enjoyed," or words are used shewing an intention to
include existing ways, in which case a defined existing way will pass.

DEMURRER.   Declaration: that the defendants broke and
entered a close of the plaintiff, being a yard in the rear of
a certain shop and premises, known as No. 14 King street
east, in the city of Toronto, and a certain brick wall of
the plaintiff then standing upon the close, broke down and
destroyed, &c.

Ninth plea, on equitable grounds: that long before the
alleged trespasses one Joseph Dennis was seized in fee of
the said shop and premises, known as No. 14 King street
east, in the said City of Toronto, and also of the said close;
and the occupiers of the said shop and premises enjoyed as
of right and without interruption "a certain way" on foot,
and with cattle, from a certain public lane, over the said
close, to the said shop and premises, and from said shop
and premises over said close to the said lane, at all times
of the year, for the more convenient occupation of the said
shop and premises; and afterwards the said Joseph Dennis,
by deed dearing date the 12th July, 1849, duly demised
the said shop and premises, " with all the appurtenances," to
one James Leary and one James Witherow, as trustees for
certain persons, for the term of twenty-one years; and by
said deed, it was agreed that at the expiration of the said
term the said Dennis, if living, or his executors if he were
deceased, would renew the said lease in favour of the said
cestuis que trust for a further term of twenty-one years,
with all rights and appurtenances thereto belonging; and
before the expiration of the said first mentioned term the
said Joseph Dennis died, having first, by his last will and
testament, duly executed in manner and form required to
pass real estate in the Province of Ontario, devised all the
land aforesaid, subject to said demise and agreement to

certain executors, who took upon themselves the execution of the said will; and upon the expiration of the said first mentioned term the said executors, in execution of the aforesaid agreement, by deed demised the said shop and premises, with the said appurtenances, to the said *cestuis que trust* for a further term of twenty-one years; and the said *cestuis que trust* by deed duly assigned the same to the defendants, and thereunder the defendants entered into the said shop and premises, with the appurtenances, so demised as aforesaid; and at the time of the alleged trespasses the defendants were possessed thereof under said demises and assignments; and also before the alleged trespasses, and after the first herein recited demise, the executors of said Dennis by deed duly demised to one W. C. Spiller the said close, subject to the said way, and to said rights of renewal; and by a certain *mesne* assignment the said close, subject to said way as aforesaid, became vested for a certain term in the plaintiff, and at the time of the alleged trespasses the plaintiff was possessed thereof under said demise and the said assignments; and afterwards, during their said term, and in their own right, defendants broke and entered the said close of the plaintiff for the purpose of using the said way, and in using the same, and because the said brick wall had been placed and was then wrongfully in the said way, obstructing the same, the defendants necessarily broke down said wall for using said wall, doing no unnecessary damage in that behalf, which are the alleged trespasses.

Demurrer to the plea, because: 1. It does not allege that the way was necessary for the beneficial and useful occupation of the shop and premises.

2. It is not shewn how the right of way was appurtenant, so as to pass as one of the appurtenances.

3. It is not alleged that there was any grant of the right of way.

4. It is shewn that Joseph Dennis was owner in fee of both the shop and the close, and it is not alleged that there was any severance, without which no grant by implication could arise, and no express grant is alleged.

5. For all that appears by the plea, Joseph Dennis prior to the alleged devise may have been in actual occupation of both the shops and the close, in which case no right of way could pass unless expressly granted.

6. The plea does not allege a prescriptive right of any grant of the way.

March 14, 1876.   The demurrer was argued before Harrison, C. J., sitting alone, by *Ritchie*, for the plaintiff, and *Allan Cassels*, for the defendant.

The arguments and cases cited were similar to those in the reasons for and against the appeal; post p. 48.

HARRISON, C. J.—The law of easements is perhaps as intricate a subject as any in the law of England. It has grown together atom by atom, as cases have arisen from the earliest time to the present day; theories have been advanced in the older decisions and have been modified or wholly rejected in later times, and it is only in quite recent years that some of the most important doctrines of the law have been established by the Courts: *Goddard* on Easements, iv.

The general rule is, that upon the conveyance of part of an estate a grant of all such rights and easements over the residue retained by the vendor as are necessary to the due enjoyment of the part conveyed will, if there be nothing in the conveyance to the contrary, be presumed: 1 *Dart* V. & P., 5th ed., 537.

The most apt illustration of this rule is, a way of necessity: *Pinnington* v. *Galland*, 9 Ex. 1; *Gayford* v. *Moffatt*, L. R. 4 Ch. 133; *Davies* v. *Sear*, L. R. 7 Eq. 427.

But apparently the rule, on the principle of implied grant, has been extended to *quasi* easements not of absolute necessity, and yet in some sense essential to the enjoyment of the property conveyed.

The leading case in favour of this extension of the rule is *Pyer* v. *Carter*, 1 H. & N. 916.

No case has been more vehemently attacked, or more

warmly defended by Judges of great eminence, than *Pyer* v. *Carter.*

The argument on the part of the defendant here is, that *Pyer* v. *Carter* is good law, and that the principles of it are applicable in support of the plea, to the sufficiency of which the plaintiff has demurred.

In *Pyer* v. *Carter*, 1 H. & N. 916, it was held that where the owner of two or more adjacent houses sells and conveys one of them to a purchaser, the purchaser is entitled to the benefit and subject to the burthen of all existing drains communicating with the other house, without any express reservation or grant for that purpose.

Lord Campbell, in *Ewart* v. *Cochrane*, 7 Jur. N. S. 925, (House of Lords) fully approved of *Pyer* v. *Carter*, and of the principles on which it was decided.

On the other hand, Martin, B., in *Dodd* v. *Birchall*, 8 Jur. N. S. 1180, 1182, 1 H. & C. 113, is reported to have said : "I think the case of *Pyer* v. *Carter* went to the extreme verge of the law."

Sir J. Romilly, M. R., in *Suffield* v. *Brown*, 9 Jur. N. S. 999, approved of *Pyer* v. *Carter* to the fullest extent, and held it to apply to "a regulation to allow bowsprits to overhang a wharf as they had previously done."

But Lord Westbury, in 10 Jur. N. S. 111, 4 DeG. J & S. 185, reversed the decision of the Master of the Rolls, and in every respect disapproved of *Pyer* v. *Carter*, saying he could not look upon the case as "rightly decided," and wholly refused "to accept it as *any* authority."

Lord Chelmsford, in *Crossley* v. *Lightowler*, L. R. 2 Ch. 478, approved of Lord Westbury's view of the law as expressed in *Suffield* v. *Brown*.

But Lord Justice Mellish, on the contrary, in *Watts* v. *Kelson*, L. R. 6 Ch. 166, 171, speaks of *Pyer* v. *Carter* "as good sense and good law," saying that "most of the common law Judges have not approved of Lord Westbury's observations on it."

The principles of *Pyer* v. *Carter*, as applicable to a mill race, conduit for smoke, or other visible permanent and

continuous *quasi* easement, have been in this Province
approved in *Young* v. *Wilson*, 21 Grant 144, 611, and
Culverwell v. *Lockington*, 24 C. P. 611.

In this restricted form, the principles of *Pyer* v. *Carter*
have been followed in the United States in *Lampman* v.
Milks, 21 N. Y. 505; *Bitterworth* v. *Crawford*, 46 N. Y.
349, 7 Am. 352.   See further *Powell* v. *Sims*, 13 Am.
629. And some of the United States cases decide that the
principles of *Pyer* v. *Carter* are applicable to roads and
alleys of a *permanent* and *obvious* character: *United
States* v. *Appleton*, 1 Sumner 492, 500; *Seibert* v. *Levan*,
8 Barr 383; *Huttemeier* v. *Albro*, 18 N. Y. 48, 2 Bosw.
546; *Smyles* v. *Hastings*, 22 N. Y. 217, 220.

The principles of *Pyer* v. *Carter* have not, either in
England or the United States, been held to extend to
rights of way which are invisible and not in any manner
permanently established.

In *Watts* v. *Kelson*, L. R. 6 Ch. 166. 172, Lord Justice
Mellish said: " Where a man walks over his own land in a
particular direction he is not using anything, he is merely
going where he pleases on his own property; but when there
is a *structure* erected for a purpose connected with a certain part of his property, the case is quite different.   I am
not satisfied that if a man *construct* a paved road over
one of his fields to his house, solely with a view to the
convenient occupation of the house, a right to use *that
road* would not pass if he sold the house separately from
the field."

To pass rights which are not properly servitudes, but are
used in like manner as servitudes, there must on the face
of the grant be an intention shewn to pass such rights.

In *Goddard*, 71, it is said: " All easements *properly* so
called, to which a land owner has a right in the soil of a
third person, will pass to a grantee of the land under the
general words of conveyance, ' together with all easements
and appurtenances,' and even if the word ' easements' is
omitted, the word ' appurtenances' is sufficient to carry
these rights."   In support of these propositions he refers to

Whalley v. *Tompson*, 1 B. & P. 371 : *Morris* v. *Edgington*,
3 Taunt. 24 ; *Skull* v. *Glenister,* 7 L. T. N. S. 826; *Beaudely*
v. *Brook*, Cro. Jac. 184; *Pinnington* v. *Galland*, 9 Ex. 1 ;
Barlow v. *Rhodes*, 1 C. & M. 439. But he continues :
" These *quasi* easements which have never existed or which
have ceased to exist, as easements properly so called, by
reason of unity of ownership will not generally pass under
a conveyance of the *quasi* dominant tenement 'with the
appurtenances.'" He refers to the language of Eyre, C. J.,
in *Whalley* v. *Tompson*, 1 B. & P. 371, 375 : *Morris* v. *Edgington*, 3 Taunt. 24, and *Plant* v. *James*, 5 B. & Ad. 791,
4 A. & E. 749 in support of the last proposition.

In *Morris* v. *Edgington*, 3 Taunt. 24, Mansfield, C. J., intimated that in a conveyance where the words used were,
" and all other ways and easements to the said demised
premises belonging and appertaining," it might be shewn
in evidence that there was some way appurtenant in
alieno solo to satisfy the words of the grant.

In *Barlow* v. *Rhodes et al.*, 1 C. & M. 439, it was held
that the words "with all ways thereto belonging, or in anywise appertaining" in a conveyance, will not pass a way
strictly not appurtenant, unless the parties appear to have
intended to use the words in a sense larger than their
ordinary legal sense.

In *Plant* v. *James*, 5 B. & Ad. 791, 794, Lord Denman
said: " Nothing is more clear than that under the word
'appurtenances,' according to its legal sense, an easement
which has become extinct, or which does not exist in point
of law by reason of unity of ownership, does not pass. *
* * If the grantor wishes to *revive* or *create* such a
right, he must do it by express words, or introduce the
terms, 'therewith used and enjoyed,' in which case easements existing in point of fact, though not existing in
point of law, would be transferred to the grantee." See
further *Wardle* v. *Brocklehurst*, 1 E. & E. 1058.

So in the same case in error, 4 A. & E. 749, 761, Tindal, C.
J., says : " We all agree that, where there is a unity of seizin
of the land, and of the way over the land, in one and the

same person, the right of way is either extinguished or suspended, according to the duration of the respective estates in the land and the way; and that, after such extinguishment, or during such suspension of the right, the way cannot pass as 'appurtenant' under the ordinary legal sense of that word."

In *Pheysey et ux.* v. *Vicary*, 16 M. & W. 484, Parke, B., says, p. 496 : " The only thing that would pass by the word 'appurtenances,' as used in this will. would be a way of necessity. That, however, would not be itself a continuous or permanent easement, but one to be exercised from time to time while the necessity continued to occur. There seems to be slight if any ground for holding this to be such."

In *Worthington* v. *Gimson*, 2 E. & E. 618, 626, Crompton, J., cites with approval, *Gale* on Easements, 3rd ed., 76, where it is said, " Other easements, such as ordinary rights of way, will not pass upon a severance of the tenements, unless the owner 'uses language to show that he intended to create an easement *de novo*.'

In *Pearson* v. *Spencer*, 1 B. & S. 571, 583, Blackburn, J., says : " We do not think that on a severance of two tenements any right to use ways which, during the unity of possession, have been used and enjoyed in fact passes to the owner of the dissevered tenement, unless there be something in the conveyance to shew an intention to create the right to use the ways *de novo*.   *   *   *   *   But when, as in the present case, property devised or granted is landlocked, and there is no other way of getting at it without being a trespasser, so that it cannot be enjoyed without a way of some sort over the lands of the testator or grantor, it is clear that a way of necessity is created *de novo*."

The decision in *Pearson* v. *Spencer* was, on the ground of a way of necessity, affirmed in 3 B. & S. 761.

In *Worthington* v. *Gimson*, 6 Jur. N. S. 1053, it was held that a right of way did not pass under the words " together with all and every their rights, members, easements, and appurtenances," Hill, J., saying that the word "appurtenances" was used in the deed only in its strict legal sense.

In *Baird* v. *Fortune*, 7 Jur. N. S. 926, it was held that the word "appurtenances" alone was not sufficient to convey the right to pass over the grantor's soil the sea shore or part of it to take sea ware.

In *Polden* v. *Bastard*, L. R. 1 Q. B. 156, S. C., 4 B. & S. 258, it was held that the right to use a pump situate on adjoining premises belonging to the grantor, did not pass under a devise of the house as "now in the occupation of T. A."

In *Thomson* v. *Waterlow*, L. R. 6 Eq. 36, it was held by Lord Romilly that a right of way of some kind, not particularly described, did not pass under the words "together with all ways, easements, and appurtenances thereto appertaining, and with the same now or heretofore occupied or enjoyed."

In *Langley et al.* v. *Hammond*, L. R. 3 Ex. 161, the decision of Lord Romilly was approved, and it was held that an ordinary right of way did not pass under the words "ways therewith now used, occupied, and enjoyed."

In *Watts* v. *Kelson*, L. R. 6 Ch. 166, 169, Lord Romilly held that the right to use an artificial water-course did not, in the absence of words of express grant, pass, but his decision was reversed by the Lords Justices, who held that as the easement was one apparent, continuous, and permanent, it passed according to the principles of *Pyer* v. *Carter*, 1 H. & N. 916.

In *Culverwell* v. *Lockington*, 24 C. P. 611, where the words of the demise were, "all that house and premises, situate," &c., the right to use a stovepipe running into and through a portion of the adjoining premises, was held to pass.

In *The United States* v. *Appleton*, 1 Sumner 492, 500, Mr. Justice Story said: "The general rule of law is, that when a house or store is conveyed by the owner thereof, everything then belonging to, and in use, for the house or store, as an incident or appurtenance, passes to the grantee."

In that case the contest was as to the use of side doors and windows and a passage as used at the time of the grant.

Reliance was placed on the language of the grant "with

all ways," &c.   But the learned Judge said, at p. 502:
"This is wholly unnecessary; for whatever are properly
incidents and appurtenances of the grant, all pass without
the word "appurtenances,' by operation of law."   See further
Huttemeier v. *Albro*, 18 N. Y. 48, 2 Bosw. 546, and
Kent v. *Waite*, 10 Pick. 138.

The general rule now is, that the surrounding circumstances may be looked at for the purpose of determining
the subject matter of contract, grant, or devise.   See
McCarthy v. *Vine*, 22 C. P. 458 ; *Wyld* v. *London & Liverpool & Globe Ins. Co.*, 33 U. C. R. 284 ; *Castle* v. *Fox*, L. R.
11 Eq. 542 ; *Mead* v. *Parker*, 15 Am. 110.

Lord Wensleydale in *Baird* v. *Fortune*, 7 Jur. N. S.
926, 928' said : "No parol evidence can be used to add or
detract from the description in the deed, or to alter it in
any respect; but such evidence is always admissible to
shew the condition of every part of the property, and all
other circumstances necessary to place the Court   *   *
in the position of the parties to it, so as to enable it to
judge of the meaning of the instrument."

Mr. Justice Story says in the *United States* v. *Appleton*,
1 Sumner 492, 501 : "It has been very correctly stated at
the Bar, that in the construction of grants the Court ought
to take into consideration the circumstances attendant
upon the transaction, the particular situation of the parties,
*   *   *   the state of the thing granted, for the purpose
of ascertaining the intention of the parties."

Mr. Justice Seldon in *Lampman* v. *Milks*, 21 N. Y. 505,
507, said : "The parties are presumed to contract in reference to the condition of the property at the time of the
sale."

I feel much difficulty in attempting to decide this case
without knowing something more of "the way" than is
mentioned in the plea, and without having before me the
deeds under which the plaintiff claims and the deeds under
which the defendant claims, "subject to the said way."

The question is one of intention to be gathered from the
deeds and the surrounding circumstances.

If the alleged right of way was no more than a right of the owner to go hither and thither over his own land, I should without hesitation hold on the authorities that the right to use such a way was not conveyed by the owner of the fee to the defendant under the word "appurtenance." But if before the making of the leases under which the plaintiff and defendants claim there was a constructed or clearly defined way which the owner used for the enjoyment of the shop, and that this is the way to which he has subjected the land held by the defendants, I should think, looking at the deeds under which the parties claim, so far as set forth in the plea, that such a way might, under the recent authorities, and without straining them, be held to be "an appurtenance" to the defendants' property, and a *quasi* servitude on the property of the plaintiff : in other words, that the word "appurtenance" instead of being read in its strict legal meaning, may, in the light afforded by the deeds and the surrounding circumstances, be read in a broad sense, so as to effectuate the intention of the parties.

The latter holding is, I think, more in accordance with the decision of the Lords Justices, in *Watts* v. *Kelson*, L. R. 6 Ch. 166, overruling the decision of the Master of the Rolls, as to the artificial water-course. than would be a contrary holding.

Besides I find that the decision of Lord Romilly in *Thomson* v. *Waterlow*, L. R. 6 Eq. 36, and the remarks of approval of it made in *Langley* v. *Hammond*, L. R. 3 Ex. 161, have not been very cordially followed in the recent case of *Kay* v. *Oxley*, L. R. 10 Q. B. 360.

The facts in the last mentioned case were that defendant was the owner in fee of a dwelling-house, together with a cottage and stable belonging to it called "Roseville," and was also the owner in fee of an adjoining farmstead and farm, having a private road which led from a high road to the farm buildings, and passed close to one side of the stable to Roseville. By deed dated 1st May, 1870, defendant demised Roseville to one Hudson for ten years.

Hudson entered on the premises, and built over the stable a hay loft with two openings towards the private farm road, having first obtained permission from the defendant to do so, and also permission from the defendant and then tenant of the farm to use the farm road for the purpose of bringing hay, straw, &c., to the loft, that being the only access to the openings in the loft. Hudson and the sub-tenants occupying Roseville continued during the term to use the road, and so continued till May, 1870. The plain-tiff then purchased Roseville from the defendant. The deed conveyed Roseville to the plaintiff, " together with all ways, rights of way, easements, and appurtenances to the said dwelling-house, cottage, and hereditaments, or any of them appertaining, or with the same or any of them now or heretofore demised, occupied, or enjoyed, or reputed as part or parcel of them, or any of them, or appurtenant thereto." The defendant obstructed the road. It was admitted by counsel for the defendant that the way was not one of necessity, but he argued that the words used in the deed were sufficient to pass the right to the way as appurtenant, although the way was on the lessor's own land.

Blackburn, J., said, in delivering judgment, at p. 365 : " Mr. Herschell says that, where a man is occupier of two ad-joining pieces of land, and uses both for the convenience of himself as the actual occupier of both, anything that he may do on the one is *primâ facie* not appurtenant to the other, and would not pass as appurtenant ; and that when he passes across the close to the other, he exercises the right of going from one to the other merely for his convenience as occupier of the two, and that he does not *primâ facie* enjoy or occupy the way as appurtenant to the other, and that the way would not pass as a right enjoyed, or as appurtenant ; but though that may *primâ facie* appear to be the case, yet if there be facts of owner-ship, and user of a road by a man across land for the enjoyment and exclusive convenience of himself as occu-pier of the adjoining lands, notwithstanding the cases cited, I do not think, in point of law, we can say that the *fact* of the road having been so enjoyed only during the time he had unity of possession or unity of seizin *prevents it being enjoyed as appurtenant.*"

He then proceeds to' review the cases—*Thomson* v. *Waterlow*, L. R. 6 Eq. 36, 40, and *Langley* v. *Hammond*, L. R. 3 Ex. 161—which are supposed to decide the contrary, and on examination of the evidence held that the way was appurtenant, so as to pass by the deed.

Mr. Justice Lush also agreed, saying among other things, p. 369 : " The only question is, whether the words of this conveyance manifest an intention that the mode of access which had been used by the tenant of Roseville to the hay loft for the purpose of conveying fodder there, should pass to the plaintiff under that conveyance as a right of way." And in speaking of *Thomson* v. *Waterlow*, L. R. 6 Eq. 36, said, p. 370 : " That case is obscurely stated, but I collect from the terms of the judgment that there had been *no specific defined portion* of the soil appropriated by the owner as *a road-way* to the severed property as *appurtenant to it*, but that he had been used to ride across one field in *any* direction he thought proper in order to get to another field."

The result was, that there was judgment for the plaintiff.

If the way here was a certain defined way necessary and convenient for the comfortable enjoyment of the defendant's property before and at the time of the lease from 'Dennis, I think on the principles enunciated in *Pyer* v. *Carter*, 1 H. & N. 916, the right so to use would be an implied part of the grant of the property to which in ordinary language it might be said to be " appurtenant," and to which the remaining property might be said to be " subject."

Although *Pyer* v. *Carter* was at the time of its decision, and for some time afterwards thought to be a great advance on previous decisions it has, as I have already mentioned, really received the approval of the House of Lords in *Ewart* v. *Cochrane*, 7 Jur. N. S. 925.

Lord Campbell in that case, which was the case of a

drain, said: "But the ground upon which I proceed is this —that this is a servitude which the grant implies. I cannot entertain the slightest doubt upon that; I mean on the grant accompanied by the *enjoyment* which *existed* at the time when the grant was made. I consider the law of Scotland, as well as the law of England, to be, that when two properties are possessed by the same owner, and there has been a severance made of part from the other, *anything* which was used, and which was necessary for the comfortable enjoyment of that part of the property which is granted, shall be considered to follow from the grant if there be *the usual words* in the conveyance. I do not know whether the usual words are *essentially* necessary, but where there are the usual words, I cannot doubt that that is the law." Lords Chelmsford and Kingsdown agreed.

In *Pearson* v. *Spencer*, 3 B. & S. 761, 762, Martin, B., speaking of *Pyer* v. *Carter*, said: "I thought that a strange decision, but it has recently been confirmed by the House of Lords."

Wilde, B., in *Pearson* v. *Spencer*, said, at p. 762: " The question may depend on the nature of the way. A path through a man's field may not be used once in six months, but a gravelled path up to his house may be used forty times in a day. On the other hand a drain may only be used occasionally."

A gravelled road or path would be just as visible and perhaps more visible than a drain, and just as necessary and perhaps more necessary for the enjoyment of the particular property than the drain, and so may, in a popular sense, rightly be said to be as "appurtenant" as the drain.

When I say necessary I do not mean so essential that the property will be of no value without the *quasi* easement, but I mean, in the language of Lord Campbell in *Ewart* v. *Cochrane*, that it was necessary for the convenient and comfortable enjoyment of the property, as it existed before the time of the grant.

It may be said that *Ewart* v. *Cochrane* being the case of

a Scotch appeal is not conclusive authority on a question of English law, and that the statement of Lord Campbell as to the identity of Scotch and English laws on the subject is extra-judicial. But what he said is really no more than what was in principle decided in *Pyer* v. *Carter*, 1 H. & N. 916. Instead of restricting *Pyer* v. *Carter* to the case of a drain I think I must accept the principle of the decision, which is as applicable to a paved or certain way as it is to a drain—in the words of Lord Campbell, to *anything* which was used and is necessary for the comfortable enjoyment of that part of the property which is granted. See also *Holker* v. *Poritt*, L. R. 8 Ex. 107, S. C. 10 Ex. 59.

The rule now is, where a pleading demurred to may be read either in a sense in which it is bad or in a sense in which it is good, to read it in the latter sense: *Stanton* v. *Austin*, L. R. 7 C. P. 651. See also *Young* v. *Austen*, L. R. 4 C. P. 553; *Corkling* v. *Massey*, L. R. 8 C. P. 395; *Tench* v. *Swinyard*, 29 U. C. R. 319; *McCulloch* v. *White*, 33 U. C. R. 331, 338; *Redway* v. *McAndrew*, L. R. 9 Q. B. 74.

I think I may read this plea as alleging a way constructed across the defendants' close for the use and enjoyment of the plaintiff's shop—a way visible to all persons at the time the plaintiff acquired title—and the way to which, according to the pleadings, this deed is made subject, and so reading the plea, I think such a way may be said to be "an appurtenance" to the defendants' premises, and to have passed from Dennis to the defendants by the deed under which defendants claim, and to be the way to which, by deed from the owner, the plaintiff's premises are said to be "subject."

Although not free from doubt, I think there must be judgment for the defendants on the demurrer to the ninth plea.

Judgment accordingly.

From the foregoing judgment, the plaintiff appealed to the Court of Appeal.

September 18, 1876. The appeal was argued by *Ritchie*
for the plaintiff, and *Beaty*, Q. C., for the defendants (*a*).

The following reasons, for and against the appeal, sufficiently shew the arguments of counsel and the cases cited.

Reasons for appeal :—

That said ninth plea does not allege any grant of said
way, nor shew any facts from which said grant could be
implied, and said plea, whilst admitting the trespass complained of, does not allege any sufficient justification or
excuse.

That it is not alleged that the said way at the time of the
demise of the shop and premises to defendants was necessary for the convenient and comfortable enjoyment of said
shop and premises, and unless it were so it could not pass
by implied grant.

That it is not alleged that the said way was in existence
at the time of the severance of the plaintiff's close and
defendants' shop and premises, nor that it was an apparent
and continuous easement.

That it is shewn by said plea that Joseph Dennis, prior
to the grant to either plaintiff or defendants, was owner of
both plaintiff's close and defendants' shop and premises, and
said way being therefore a quasi easement could not pass
under the word "appurtenances"; and if defendants intend
to rely on a grant by implication because the way was
visible and apparent, they should set out the facts shewing
that the way was of such a nature as to pass by implication on the grant of the shop and premises.

That for all that appears by said plea, another way may
have been granted to defendants by said Dennis, in lieu of
the way in question. The way in question might not be
at all necessary to secure to defendants the full enjoyment
of their shop and premises.

Under the plea as at present framed, defendants would
be entitled to succeed on proving that a way had existed

(*a*) *Present.*—DRAPER, C. J. of Appeal; BURTON, J. A., PATTERSON
J. A., MOSS, J. A.

during the unity of ownership, and on producing their deed with the word "appurtenances" used therein, without proving that the way was visible or apparent, or that it was at all necessary for the convenient or comfortable enjoyment of defendants' shop and premises, or even that it continued in existence until the time of demise to defendants.

Suffield v. *Brown*, 10 Jur. N. S. 999; *Dodd* v. *Birchall*, 8 Jur. N. S. 1180; *Crossley et al.* v. *Lightowler*, L. R. 2 Ch. 478; *Whalley* v. *Tompson*, 1 B. & P. 371; *Barlow* v. *Rhodes*, 1 C. & M. 439; *Langley* v. *Hammond*, L. R. 3 Ex. 161; *Pearson* v. *Spencer*, 1 B. & S. 571, affirmed 3 B. & S. 761; *Polden* v. *Bastard*, 4 B. & S. 258, affirmed 7 B. & S. 130; *Goddard* on Easements, 71 *et seq.*; *Pheysey* v. *Vicary*, 16 M. & W. 484; *Baird* v. *Fortune*, 7 Jur. N. S. 926; *Thomson* v. *Waterlow*, L. R. 6 Eq. 36; *Gale* on Easements, 5th ed., 614, 617.

Reasons against appeal.

1. The respondents rely on the grounds contained in the judgment of the learned Chief Justice appealed from and the cases cited therein.

2. That it is alleged in the same plea that the right of way was actually enjoyed, and was necessary for the more convenient occupation of the defendants' premises, and was therefore appurtenant: *Morris* v. *Edgington*, 3 Taunt. 24; *Pyer* v. *Carter*, 1 H. & N. 916, 922; *Ewart* v. *Cochrane*, 7 Jur. N. S. 925, 4 Macq. 117; *Kay* v. *Oxley*, L. R. 10 Q. B. 360; *Watts* v. *Kelson*, L. R. 6 Ch. 166, 175; *Kooystra* v. *Lucas*, 5 B. & Al. 830; *Young* v. *Wilson*, 21 Grant 144, 611; *Pearson* v. *Spencer*, 1. B. & S. 571; S. C. 3 B. & S. 761.

3. That the right of way was conveyed by a demise of the shop and premises of the defendants, "with all the appurtenances:" *Skull* v. *Glenister*, 7 L. T. N. S. 826; *Gale* on Easements, 6th ed., 88; *Marquis of Cholmondeley* v. *Clinton*, 2 B. & Al. 637, and other cases cited in the judgment.

4. That it is alleged the plaintiff held his premises under a demise of his close subject to said way, and that he was possessed of said close under the said demise, subject to said way as aforesaid, and is estopped from denying defendants' right, and the plea therefore is sufficient: *Taylor* on Evidence, 6th ed., vol. i., sec. 105; *Taylor* v. *Needham*, 2 Taunt. 278.

September 28, 1876. DRAPER, C. J. OF APPEAL.—The defendants do not support their plea by setting up a claim to this way either by prescription ·or by grant from J. D., nor do they assert that they are entitled to the way as one of necessity. They state that long before the trespass was committed J. D. was seized of the whole premises, *i. e.*, of the shop and of the close over which they claim a way; and that previous occupiers of the shop, &c., as of right enjoyed a certain way. Three things are designated, a shop and premises, a close, and a way; the first and second are stated to belong in fee to J. D. There were occupiers of the shop, &c., who must have held in some way under J. D., and they enjoyed a way across the close. Of their tenure, when and how it began or ceased, nothing appears. But J. D., in 1849, by deed, duly demised the shop and premises to two trustees, between whom and "the occupiers" no privity appears. It is to be assumed from the statement in the plea that J. D., the tenant in fee, was in legal possession of the shop and premises as well as of the close, when he made the demise of July, 1849; and if that be so, as a matter of law and fact the unity of possession would extinguish any existing right of way, and it is not pleaded that J. D. made any grant of it to these trustees or to any one else under whom the defendant claims, unless it would pass by the words appurtenances.

Upon this point *James* v. *Plant*, 4 A & E. 749, is a clear authority, where it was laid down that where there is a unity of seizin of the land, and of the way over the land in one and the same person, the right of way is either extinguished or suspended according to the duration of the respective estates in the land, and that after such extinguishment or during such suspension of the right the way cannot pass as an appurtenant under the ordinary legal sense of that word ; but that in such a case, in order to pass a way existing in point of use, but extinguished or suspended in point of law, the grantor must either use words of express grant or must describe the way in question as one used and enjoyed with the land conveyed ; and the decision in that case (the circumstances which led the Court to construe the word " *appurtenances*" as comprehending a right of way, not existing in the case before us), is directly adverse to the plea demurred to, and the word " *appurtenances*" must receive its strictly legal construction, which does not include a right of way. I refer also to the judgment of Blackburn, J., in *Kay* v. *Oxley*, L. R. 10 Q. B. 360, 365, as sustaining this conclusion, and to *Worthington* v. *Gimson*, 2 E. & E. 618.

Then the plea does not state, nor lead to the conclusion, that the way is one of necessity. I do not by this term mean that he has no other mode of getting to his shop and premises, but that it was necessary for the reasonable and commodious enjoyment of the premises. Whatever the surrounding circumstances may be, the plea discloses nothing but the dry fact that at some time (it must have been before July, 1849,) the occupiers of the shop as of right enjoyed without interruption access across the defendant's close to a public lane : that the owner of the whole property demised the shop and premises to two trustees in trust, but with no word or expression stronger than appurtenances under which it could be contended that a right of way would pass, but he covenanted for a renewal of the term. During the term he died, having devised all the land aforesaid, subject to the demise and agreement, to certain executors, who, on the expiration of the term, by deed demised the shop and premises, with the said appurtenances, to the " *cestui que trust*" for a further term of twenty-one years, and the " *cestui que trust*" by deed duly assigned the same

to the defendants, and thereunder the defendants entered
into the said shop and premises with the appurtenances,
and at the time of the alleged trespasses were possessed
thereof under said demises and assignment. The plea then
states that the executors of J. D. by deed duly demised to
one S. the said close, subject to the way and the said rights
of renewal; and that it became vested in the plaintiff,
who became possessed thereof, and justifies the entry and
breaking down of the wall for the purpose of using the
way.

The ambiguity which is involved in the statement that
certain occupiers of the shops and premises enjoyed as of
right the way claimed by the defendants, while J. D. was
seized in fee thereof, and of the close over which the way
is, not shewing how or whence the right was derived, justly
brings the plea within the old rule, " the plea of every man
shall be construed strongly against him that pleadeth it,
for everie man is presumed to make the best of his owne
case, *Ambiguum placitum interpretari debet contra
proferentem*": *Co.* Lit. 303 *b.* It may well be that these
" occupiers " were tenants at will of J. D., licensed and permitted by him to cross this close while such tenants. The
observations already made on the absence of any allegation
of a transferrible character derived from J. D., are fully
sustained. There is no suggestion of any other right of
way in the plea, and we cannot look out of it for other
facts.

I am of opinion that the judgment of the Court of
Queen's Bench must be reversed, and judgment be entered
for the plaintiff on this demurrer.

The appeal should be allowed with costs.

BURTON, J.—I am of opinion that judgment should be
given for the plaintiff upon this demurrer.

As I read the plea, the shop and the close in rear, over
which the alleged way is claimed, were previously to the
lease from Dennis to Leary and Withrow owned by Dennis.
No easement therefore at that time existed. All his deal-

ings with the land were in the exercise of his ordinary right of ownership. It is not averred, and is probably not material, that any way existed previous to the unity of the title in Dennis, but that it originated with him, he going and allowing his tenants to go where he pleased on his own property.

Such a way, notwithstanding its existence in point of user, cannot pass under the word appurtenances used in this conveyance.

In *Plant* v. *James*, 5 B. & Ad. 791, S. C. in Error, 4 A & E. 749, which was referred in the argument, a way over a certain estate had always existed for the convenient use and enjoyment of a mansion, and had always been occupied and enjoyed with it while they were separate properties, but the right was for a time suspended by unity of possession.

A portion of the lands on which the mansion stood was subsequently conveyed, *together with all ways, easements, and appurtenances thereto belonging, or therewith usually held, used, occupied, or enjoyed, or accepted, reputed, deemed, known, or taken as parcel or member thereof:* the *habendum* referring to the premises thereby granted, with their and every of their appurtenances.

The Court held that the word appurtenances in the *habendum* might be construed with reference to the preceding words of grant, and that, looked at in that light, the word was not confined to what was in legal strictness an appurtenant, such as an easement, which had never been interrupted by unity of possession, or extinguished by unity of seizin, but would let in and comprehend a right of way, which as appeared by the pleadings had been used and enjoyed with part of the lands, and which fell within the operative part of the deed.

In *Worthington* v. *Gimson*, 2 E. & E. 618, 623, it was held that without the words italicised above, no way would have been held to pass under the word "appurtenances."

The Master of the Rolls seemed to think, in *Thompson* v. *Waterlow*, L. R. 6 Eq. 36, that the Judges who decided

James v. *Plant* intended to lay down that even the words there used would not constitute the grant of a right of way, where the user had sprung solely from the convenience of the person who held both tenements, and which convenience ceased to exist when the severance between the closes took place, and that the decision in that case proceeded on the ground that a right of way had existed before the unity of possession, which being revived passed under the words used in that conveyance. If that was the ground of his judgment, I do not think it will be found to be sustained by more recent decisions, and there would seem to be no good reason why a well defined road or way, made by a man over a portion of his property, solely with the view to the convenient occupation of his house, should not pass with the conveyance of the house, if apt general words were used in the conveyance. Lord Justice Mellish, in *Watts* v. *Kelson*, L. R. 6, Ch. 166, 174, seems to be of opinion that it would; and the case of *Kay* v. *Oxley*, L. R. 10 Q. B. 360, seems to decide expressly that such a way would pass, not under the word appurtenances, but under apt words. "It cannot make any difference in law," says Mr. Justice Blackburn, p 367, "whether the right of way was only *de facto* used and enjoyed, or whether it was originally created before the unity of possession, and then ceased to exist as a matter of right, so that in the one case it would be created as a right *de novo*, in the other merely revived. But it makes a great difference, as matter of evidence on the question, whether the way was used and enjoyed as appurtenant."

The Court treated the general words there used as evincing an intention to pass the particular right of way then in question as specifically as if the conveyance had said "including all the ways and easements to the hay loft as the same have been heretofore enjoyed by Gunn."

No such words are to be found in the conveyance as set forth in the pleadings, and the plea must fail unless, as was contended, this can be regarded as an apparent and continuous easement necessary for the proper enjoyment of the premises, and the plea can be read as setting up such an easement.

The distinction to be found in the earlier cases, between easements such as a right of way or easements used from time to time, and easements of necessity or continuous, does not appear to have been weakened by any of the recent decisions; and it would seem to be clear law that upon a severance of tenements, easements used as of necessity or in their nature continuous will pass by implication of law, without any words of grant. Easements which are not continuous or apparent, but are used from time to time only, do not pass unless the deed by appropriate language discloses an intention on the part of the grantor that they should pass.

If there be any facts in reference to this particular right of way which justifies its removal from the one class to the other, then according to the ordinary rules of pleading those facts should have been set forth or it should at least have been averred that it was a way of necessity, or an apparent and continuous easement, so that the opposite party might have the opportunity of taking issue upon them, and contesting them before a jury.

With reference to the contention that the plaintiff is estopped from denying the defendants' right, as the deed to him was made subject to the right of way, the answer was given upon the argument, viz., that that averment means only that it was subject to the rights of those who were entitled to use it, and this plea shews no right in the defendants. I think the plea bad for other reasons, but on those which I have stated the judgment should be given against it on this demurrer.

PATTERSON, J.—This is an appeal from a decision in the Queen's Bench by the learned Chief Justice, sitting alone for the Court, on a demurrer to a plea.

The action is trespass *quare clausum fregit*, and the plea is a plea of justification under an alleged right of way.

The plea alleges that one Dennis was seized of the shop

and premises known as No. 14 King street east in, Toronto,
and also of the close in question : that the occupiers of the
shop and premises enjoyed as of right and without interruption a certain way on foot and with cattle from a public lane, over the close, to the shop and premises, and from
the shop and premises over the close to the lane for the
more convenient occupation of the shop and premises.   So
far the allegation in effect is, that Dennis had a right of
way from his own shop over his own close.   The plea then
proceeds to allege that "afterwards" Dennis, by a deed
dated 12th July, 1849, demised the shop and premises
"with all the appurtenances" to persons who were trustees,
for a term of 21 years, with a covenant that Dennis or his
executors would renew *the lease* for a further term of 21
years, "with all rights and appurtenances *thereto* belonging" : that during the term Dennis died, and his executors,
who were also his devisees, demised the shop and premises
"with the said appurtenances," at the expiration of the
original term of the *cestuis que trustent* of the original lessees,
for a further term of 21 years ; and those lessees assigned to
the defendants ; and the defendants " entered into the shop
and premises with the appurtenances so demised as aforesaid," and at the time of the alleged trespass were possessed
thereof under the said demises and assignment : that
before the trespass and after the first demise, the executors of Dennis by deed demised to Spillen "the said close,
subject to said way and to said rights of renewal," and by a
certain mesne assignment the said close, "subject to said
way as aforesaid," became vested in the plaintiff ; and then
alleges the interruption of the way by the plaintiff, and the
entry of the defendants to remove the obstruction.

The learned Chief Justice arrived at the conclusion that
the plea might be supported upon grounds which, after
examining a number of decisions, he very clearly states
in the following passages, which I extract from his judgment : ".If the way here was a certain defined way, necessary and convenient for the comfortable enjoyment of the
defendants' property before and at the time of the lease from

Dennis, I think, on the principles enunciated in *Pyer* v. *Carter*, 1 H. &. N. 916, the right so to use would be an implied part of the grant of the property to which in ordinary language it might be said to be 'appurtenant,' and to which the remaining property might be said to be 'subject.' * * When I say necessary, I do not mean so essential that the property will be of no value without the supposed easement, but I mean (in the language of Lord Campbell in *Ewart* v. *Cochrane*) that it was necessary for the convenient and comfortable enjoyment of the property as it existed at the time of the grant. * * I think I may read this plea as alleging a way constructed across the plaintiff's close for the use and enjoyment of the defendants' shop—a way visible to all persons at the time the plaintiff's acquired title—and the way to which, according to the pleadings, his deed is made subject; and, so reading the plea, I think such a way may be said to be an 'appurtenance' to the defendants' premises, and to have passed from Dennis to the defendants by the deed under which defendants claim, and to be the way to which, by deed from the owner, the plaintiff's premises are to be 'subject.' "

I am unable to assent to these conclusions either as to the reading of the plea, or as to the effect of the conveyance.

I cannot read the averment that Dennis was seized of both tenements and used the way over one for the convenient enjoyment of the other, and *afterwards* demised the dominant tenement, as an allegation that he was seized or was so using the way *at the time* of the demise. The utmost liberality of construction in favour of the validity of a pleading must stop short of an intendment contrary to the express averment. Even if we should read the plea as alleging that at the making of the first lease the way in question existed, there is no allegation that it continued to be used during the first term of twenty-one years, or was in use when the term was created under which the defendant claims; and I cannot read the plea as alleging that a defined part of the servient tenement was set

apart, or was by any process of construction or fencing,
laid out or dedicated as a private road to the dominant
tenement. These three particulars, or at all events the
second and third, seem to me essential to give to defendants
a starting point for their argument. Possibly they may not
wish the second to be understood as implied in the plea.
They may intend to rely on the first and third, viz., on the
facts that there was a way in use when the first lease was
made, and that it was a defined way; treating it as immaterial whether or not the user continued up to or existed
at the date of the current lease. However this may be,
it is clear that *some* averments which are material to
the defendants' contention are wanting and cannot by any
reasonable intendment be supplied. The plaintiff cannot
by traversing any allegation contained in the plea put in
issue certain facts which, even in the defendants' view, are
essential to the defence. This alone would suffice for the
decision of this demurrer, without any reference to other
obvious faults of the plea. But as the structure of the
plea may be cured by amendment, it is proper to examine
the principles of law on which the rights of the parties
must depend.

The case of *Pyer* v. *Carter*, 1 H. & N. 916, decided that
when the owner of two tenements which occupy the position of *quasi* dominant and *quasi* servient tenement, grants
the servient tenement retaining the other, he reserves by
implication such easements in the servient tenement as are
apparent, and continuous, and necessary for the enjoyment
of the dominant tenement in its then condition.

I quite agree with the learned Chief Justice that this
doctrine is now settled law under the decisions both of the
English Courts and of the Courts in this Province, although
it was questioned by Lord Westbury in *Suffield* v. *Brown*,
10 Jur. N. S. 111, upon grounds of great weight and cogency,
and also in *Crossley* v. *Lightowler*, L. R. 2 Ch. 478, by Lord
Chelmsford, who, however, seems previously to have acted
upon it in *Ewart* v. *Cochrane* in the House of Lords, 7 Jur.
N. S. 925. The effect of the rule in *Pyer* v. *Carter*, 1 H.

N. 916,is to extend to a conveyance of the servient tenement the effect which accompanied a conveyance of the dominant tenement when that was the one first conveyed.

Lord Westbury commenting on a passage in *Gale* on Easements, thus states the rule as applicable to the case of the dominant tenement being first conveyed: "If nothing more be intended by this passage than to state that on the grant by the owner of an entire heritage of part of that heritage, as it is then used and enjoyed, there will pass to the grantee all those continuous and apparent easements, which had been, and are at the time of the grant, used by the owner of the entirety for the benefit of the parcel granted, there can be little doubt of its correctness."

Erle, C. J., in his judgment, in *Polden* v. *Bastard*, L. R. 1 Q. B. 156, in which case the grantee of a tenement claimed an easement as passing by implication with his conveyance, uses these words, p. 161 : "There is a distinction between easements, such as a right of way, or easements used from time to time, and easements of necessity, or continuous easements. The cases recognize this distinction, and it is clear law that upon a severance of tenements, easements used as of necessity, or in their nature continuous, will pass by implication of law without any words of grant; but with regard to easements which are used from time to time only, they do not pass, unless the owner, by appropriate language, shews an intention that they should pass."

This passage is cited by Mellish, L. J., in giving the judgment of the Court of Appeal in Chancery in *Watts* v. *Kelson*, L. R. 6 Ch. 166 at p. 173, as laying down the correct rule ; and the decision in *Watts* v. *Kelson* was founded upon the rule so stated, although it was also held that there were words in the conveyance there in question which would have been sufficient to carry the easement claimed without resorting to the implied grant.

The practical result of the decisions is, that the servient tenement remains burdened with the apparent and continuous easement, whether conveyed before the dominant tenement or not till after it, while the principle on which

this liability rests is not the same in the two cases. When
the owner of the entirety conveys the dominant tenement,
the right to easements, existing in point of user, passes
under the rule that no man shall derogate from his own
grant: *Pomfret* v. *Ricroft* 1 *Wms.* Saund. 569. But when
he sells the servient tenement, retaining the other, he cannot invoke that rule to enable him to claim any reservation
of rights by implication. On the contrary, the principle
of that rule gave great force to the objections of Lord
Westbury to the decision in *Pyer* v. *Carter.* The ground
of decision, as expressed in the judgment in *Pyer* v. *Carter*
1 H. & N. 916, as in *Nicholas* v. *Chamberlain*, Cro. Jac.
121, which it follows, is that the easement is necessary and
quasi appendant to the dominant tenement; and that if,
under the circumstances in that case, the reservation of
right was not implied, the inconveniences and nuisances
in towns would be very great.

Martin, B., illustrates the rule in his remarks in *Dodd* v.
Burchell, 1 H. & C. 113, while he shews that it should
not be extended. He says: "*Pyer* v. *Carter* went to the
utmost extent of the law; but, if considered, that decision
cannot be complained of, for if a man has two fields drained
by an artificial ditch cut through both, and he grants to
another person one of the fields, neither he nor the grantee
can stop up the drain, for there would be the same right
of drainage as before, since the land was sold with the
drain in it. I agree with the law as laid down in that
case, and I think it may be supported without extending
the doctrine to a right of way."

In the case before us, the dominant tenement was the
first conveyed, and the rights of the defendants depend,
therefore, not upon the doctrine enunciated in *Pyer* v.
Carter, 1 H. & N. 916, but upon the rule which has never
been questioned, that the grant of premises carries with it
by implication of law certain easements existing in point
of user, though not strictly easements in point of law. If
the right of way claimed by the defendants is an easement
to which the rule applies, it must be held to pass under a

lease of the tenement, without being either expressly granted or covered by any general words. If it is not an easement of this character it can only pass by force of the terms of the lease.

The law, as I gather it from an examination of the cases cited and others, may be shortly stated in the following propositions :—

A right of way is not an easement of such a continuous character as to pass by implication of law with a grant of the land, the only way which will so pass being a way of necessity.

A way used by the owner of two tenements over one tenement for access to the other is not in law appurtenant to the *quasi* dominant tenement, and therefore will not pass with a grant of that tenement under the general word "appurtenances."

But if the intention appears from the deed to extend the meaning of the word appurtenances beyond its technical signification, and to embrace in it the right of way ; or if the grant is of all ways " used and enjoyed " with the lands granted ; or if other words are used which are appropriate to indicate an intention to include existing ways in the conveyance, then a defined way actually existing and in use (or having existed, if the words are *heretofore used*," &c.) will pass.

Instead of citing authorities for each of these propositions separately, I shall refer to some cases in their chronological order.

In *Barlow* v. *Rhodes*, 1 C. & M. 439, a gateway had been used for each of two tenements. The owner of both the tenements and the gateway conveyed one tenement to the defendant, " together with all ways, roads, rights of road, paths, and passages to the said hereby demised premises, or any part thereof belonging or in anywise appertaining " ; and afterwards conveyed the other tenement and the gateway to the plaintiff. The defendant justified under a claim for right of way through the gateway.

Lord Lyndhurst, C. B., said, p. 447 : " As I am not

satisfied that the parties used these words in any other
sense, I conceive myself bound to give them their ordinary
legal meaning; and 1 am, therefore, of opinion, that the
defendant did not make out his justification."

Bayley, B., said, p. 448: "If you convey the close, with
all ways thereto belonging and appertaining, the easement
will not pass, except in a case of a way of necessity, when
such right of way would pass without any words of grant
of ways."

In *James* v. *Plant*, 4 A. & E. 749, in error from the
King's Bench, Tindal, C. J., said, p. 761: "We agree also in
the principle laid down by the Court of King's Bench, that
in case of an unity of seizin, in order to pass a way existing
in point of user, but extinguished or suspended in point of
law, the grantor must either employ words of express grant,
or must describe the way as one 'used and enjoyed with the
land' which forms the subject matter of the conveyance.
But, agreeing thus far with the Court below, we feel ourselves compelled to differ from it in the application of these
principles to the present case. For we think the intention
of the grantors to pass the way in question to the owner of
the Park Hall estate appears from the deed itself, and that
there are words contained in that deed sufficient to carry
such intention of the parties into effect.   *   *   It appears
therefore judicially to the Court that the way in question
is a way that has always existed for the convenient use
and enjoyment of Park Hall, and has always been held
and occupied and enjoyed therewith; that is, not only
before the unity of seizin of the land and way over it, but
since and during such unity of seizin, and notwithstanding
the effect of it, and indeed up to the very time of the
execution of the deed. This being so, the reasonable inference must be, that in the deed making partition between
the two sisters, it was the intention of the contracting
parties that each sister should take the whole of the estate
allotted to her as her share, in the same plight and condition, as to all its conveniences and means of enjoyment,
as it was held and occupied at the time such partition was

made. * * But, independently of this general inference of intention resulting from the object of the parties being that of effecting a partition, we think the intention of the parties, that the way should pass, is to be inferred more particularly from the frame and texture of the deed itself.'

In *Pheysey* v. *Vicary*, 16 M. & W. 484, there had been unity of ownership of both sets of premises till the death of A. Vicary the younger. The way claimed was over a hard carriage drive from a street in front of both houses. The parties took under a will, and the plaintiff claimed that he had a right of way over that part of the drive which was on the defendants' land. There was another way of access to the plaintiff's premises which abutted at the rear on a highway.

Parke, B., said, at p. 491 : " The way can only pass by one of two modes, viz., either under the word 'appurtenances' in the will or as of necessity," and again, p. 496, " The only thing that would pass by the wor . 'appurtenances' as used in this will, would be a way of necessity. That, however, would not be itself a continuous or permanent easement, but one to be exercised from time to time while the necessity continued to occur.

In *Pinnington* v. *Gallard*, 9 Ex. 1, Martin, B., gave the judgment of the Court, holding that a way of necessity passed under the words "belonging or appertaining," and indeed probably without them.

Worthington v. Gimson, 2 E. & E. 618 was a case of partition. The general words were " with their and every of their rights, members, easements, and appurtenances."

Wightman, J., after referring to *James* v. *Plant* and the words contained in the deed in that case, said, p. 625 : " If we could discover from the deed in the present case any words indicating an intention to pass other than legal incidents to the property as ' appurtenant' thereto, we might put a construction on it in favour of the intention. But there are no such words to be found in the deed."

Compton, J., said, p. 627 : " It would be a dangerous innovation if the jury were to be allowed to be asked to say from the nature of a road whether the parties intended the right of using it to pass."

Hill, J., said p. 627: "I found my judgment upon this, that there is nothing in the deed to indicate that the parties intended to use the word 'appurtenances' in any other than the strict legal sense of the word; and that the right of way claimed by the plaintiff is not within that sense."

The way in question was a defined way which had been used for forty years.

Wardle v. *Brocklehurst*, 1 E. & E. 1065, was a suit about a water course. Williams, J., giving the judgment of the Exchequer Chamber, said: "There has been a variety of decisions upon a species of rights analogous to that now in question, viz., rights of way. A question has often arisen in such cases, where unity of ownership in land and in a right of way over the land has taken place, as to what subsequent grant by the owner is sufficient to convey the continued enjoyment of the easement, as well as the land itself. It seems from these decisions that, inasmuch as the unity of ownership extinguishes the easement, the right of way cannot pass as simply appurtenant to the land to which it was formerly attached, though it continues to exist in point of user. But though it does not exist as a right it will pass by a conveyance of the land, if proper words be used to pass it, as if all ways 'used and enjoyed' with the land, are conveyed."

Pearson v. *Spencer*, 1 B. & S. 571, arose upon a will by which the testator devised a close to each of his two sons. It was conceded that a way of necessity passed—and the point decided merely was, that that way was by a defined way which the testator had used, and up to the point at which the close in question had been entered from that way, notwithstanding that the devisee could have had access to his close after passing over a part only of the way.

Dodd v. *Burchell*, 1 H. & C. 113, is a case very much in point, on the assumption that in the present case the way claimed is a defined way. The dominant tenement was a house fronting on a street, with a garden behind the house.

A passage from the street skirted the side of the house and the garden wall, and led to a cottage built in rear of the garden. A door opened from the back part of the house into the passage, and another from the passage into the garden; and the occupiers of the house had access to the garden by means of the passage, but they had also other means of access. The owner of both tenements conveyed to the defendant, in 1851, the cottage premises, by a description which included that part of the passage which passed the doors into the garden and house; and two years afterwards he conveyed the house and garden to the plaintiff. It is stated that the plaintiff's conveyance made no mention of any right of way, but I do not see the force of that circumstance. The way continued to be used by the plaintiff till 1861, when the defendant stopped it. It was contended on the principle on which *Pyer* v. *Carter*, 1 H. & N. 916, was decided, that, on the conveyance to the defendant, there was an implied reservation of the way, and that it passed to the plaintiff by the conveyance to him; but that contention was not successful.

Pollock, C. B., said, p. 120: "There is a wide difference between that which is substantial, as a conduit or watercourse, and that which is of an incorporeal nature, as a right of way."

Martin, B., used the words which I have already quoted.

Channel, B., said, p. 121: "It seems to me that the defendant is out of Court, unless this is a way of necessity, and upon the facts I am of opinion that it is not."

In *Polden* v. *Bastard*, 4 B. & S. 258, and in Appeal, L. R. 1 Q. B. 156, the decision was, that a devise of a cottage did not carry with it the right to use a pump in another part of the testator's property, although the occupants of the cottage had used it for some time before the will.

Crompton, J., said, in 4 B. & S. 264: "If this had been an old easement attached to the cottage it would pass by the words 'appertaining or belonging,' but to create a new easement which did not exist before the will must have devised the cottage 'with the pump therewith enjoyed.'"

Erle, C. J., L. R. 1 Q. B. 161, used the words I have already quoted, and added : "The right to go to the well to take water is not a continuous easement, nor is it an easement of necessity."

Gayford v. *Moffatt*, L. R. 4 Ch. 133, decides nothing of direct bearing on the present case. The way in question there was held by Cairns, L. C., to be a way of necessity, and he further held that though the building which was complained of contracted the courtyard over which the way existed, yet as much room was left as the plaintiff was entitled to.

In *Thomson* v. *Waterlow*, L. R. 6 Eq. 36, Lord Romilly, M. R., held that no right of way passed under the general words "heretofore occupied or enjoyed," &c., in the deed before him. The owner, in that case, of closes A. and B. made or used a way for his own convenience across B. to A., and afterwards sold A. There was other access to A.

In *Langley* v. *Hammond*, L. R. 3 Ex. 161, a tenant had surrendered to his lessor a part of his farm yard, "together with all ways, &c., used," &c. The lessor claimed a way over the remaining part of the farm yard where there was no defined road, but where the track along which it was usual to drive from the highway to the farm buildings ran alongside of the surrendered piece of land. It was held that no right of way passed, and *Thomson* v. *Waterlow* was followed, Kelly, C. B., putting his decision on the ground that a right of way would only pass under the general words when it had existed before the unity of seizin.

Bramwell, B., however, held a different view on that point. He said, p. 170 : "I am not prepared to say, and I do not understand the Master of the Rolls to have decided, that a right of way could not pass under words such as those here used, even though there had always previously been unity of ownership and of possession. And should the case arise, I should like for time to consider before I assented to the doctrine supposed to have been laid down. Suppose a house to stand 100 yards from a highway, and to be approached by a road running along the side of a field, used for no other purpose, but only fenced off from the field, which I assume to be the property of the owner of the house, I should wish for time to consider before deciding that on the conveyance of the house, the right to use that road, not being a way of necessity, would not pass under such words as these. The ground on which I think this rule ought to be discharged is, that there is here really no defined road. It is said that it is hard and gravelled, but in truth as soon as you turn out of West street, you do not come into what is a road and nothing else, kept for no other purpose, but into a rick-yard, where the occupier could, and no doubt did, go in any particular direction he desired. But this is not a way of such a definite kind as will pass under general words; it is no more a way (if I may use the illustration) than the short cut a man may take across his room from the piano to the fireplace is a way. In one sense, no doubt, it is a way which he may use, but he only uses it, equally with ways in other directions, by virtue of his rights of possession, not because there is any road made there, but because it is the shortest cut to the place he wishes to get to."

In *Watts* v. *Kelson*, L. R. 6 Ch. 166, the dominant tenement was sold first. There was an express grant of a right of way, and the Master of the Rolls decided that the particular way claimed passed under that grant. There was also an easement claimed in respect of water conducted in an artificial channel or pipe across the servient tenement. The Master of the Rolls decided this did not pass, and the Lords Justices reversed that decision. The cases of *Thompson* v. *Waterlow* and *Langley* v. *Hammond* were cited as authority that only an easement which had existed before the unity of ownership would pass under the general words in a deed.

James, L. J., said, at p. 171 : *"Thomson* v. *Waterlow* comes to little more than this : You have a way from the high road to your house, a way from the house to your garden, from your garden to your orchard, and from your

orchard into your field, to which there is another approach.
Nobody could say that a person who bought the field from
you would have a right to use the way through your house,
garden, and orchard."

And Mellish, L. J., said, at p. 172 : "When a man walks
over his own land in a particular direction he is not using
anything, he is merely going where he pleases on his own
property ; but when there is a structure erected for a purpose connected with a certain part of his property, the case
is quite different. I am not satisfied that if a man construct a paved road over one of his fields to his house, solely
with a view to the convenient occupation of the house, a
right to use that road would not pass if he sold the house
separately from the field." And in giving judgment he says,
at p. 173 : "We are clearly of opinion that the easement in
the present case was in its nature continuous.   There was
an actual construction on the servient tenement extending
to the dominant tenement, by which water was continu-
ously brought through the servient tenement to the dominant tenement for the use of the occupier of the dominant
tenement.   According to the rule, as laid down by Chief
Justice Erle, the right to such an easement as the one in
question would pass by implication of law without any
words of grant, and we think that this is the correct rule ;
but if words of grant are necessary, we also think that
the general words in the case are amply sufficient to pass
the easement.   It was a watercourse with the premises at
the time of the conveyance used and enjoyed.   We may
also observe that in *Langley* v. *Hammond*, L. R. 3 Ex. 161,
Baron Bramwell expressed an opinion, in which we concur,
that even in the case of a right of way, if there was a
formed road made over the alleged servient tenement, to
and for the apparent use of the dominant tenement, a right
of way over such road might pass by a conveyance of
the dominant tenement with the ordinary general words."
The Lord Justice further expressed the opinion that the
watercourse was proved to be necessary for the enjoyment of the dominant tenement, but that even if not neces-

sary the general words in the deed were sufficient to pass
the easement.

Kay v. *Oxley*, L. R. 10 Q. B. 360, the latest case I have
to refer to, is probably a more direct authority upon the
questions before us than any of the others. The plaintiff
bought from the defendant premises, including a stable
which for the preceding ten years had been occupied by a
tenant of the plaintiff, who had built a hay loft opening
on a private road belonging to the defendant, and had used
that road for bringing hay, &c., to the loft. The conveyance to the plaintiff was with all ways, &c., "and appurtenances to the said dwelling-house, cottage, and hereditaments, or any of them appertaining, or with the same or
any of them now or heretofore demised, occupied, or
enjoyed, or reputed as part or parcel of them, or any of
them, or appurtenant thereto."

Blackburn, J., said, p. 365 : "It is not disputed that if the
the conveyance had stopped at the word ' appertaining,' the
plaintiff's case might not have been sustainable; but it goes
on to add the words, : 'or with the same or any of them now
or heretofore demised, occupied, or enjoyed, or reputed as
part or parcel of them, or any of them, or appertaining thereto.
We have now to look at the facts in order to see whether
the particular right of way in question was in fact occupied
or enjoyed, or reputed as appurtenant to Roseville.   * *
If there be acts of ownership and user of a road by a man
across land for the enjoyment and exclusive convenience of
himself as occupier of the adjoining lands, notwithstanding
the cases cited,' (viz., *Thomson* v. *Waterlow*, L. R. 6 Eq. 36,
and *Langley* v. *Hammond.*)   I do not think, in point of
law, we can say that the fact of the road having been so
enjoyed and occupied only during the time he had unity
of possession or unity of seisin prevents its being enjoyed
as appurtenant."

Lush, J., said p. 169 : "The only question is, whether the
words of this conveyance manifest an intention that the
mode of access which had been used by the tenant of Roseville to the hay loft for the purpose of conveying fodder

there, should pass to the plaintiff under that conveyance as a
right of way. * *   The conveyance of the house and
stable, together with the other premises, has these words,
'together—[The learned Judge read the clause.]   The
latter words were clearly intended to pass, if there were
any such thing enjoyed, something not strictly appurtenant to the premises, which could not have been claimed as
a matter of right without these larger words."

These cases fully sustain the propositions I have advanced,
and the effect upon the defendants' position is, that as no
right of way would pass by implication except a way of
necessity, which is not claimed, and as no right of way
would pass under the general words of a conveyance except
a defined way actually used at or before the date of the
conveyance as *quasi* appurtenant to the premises, such an
actual and defined way must be alleged and proved : and
further that, being driven to rely on the general words in
the conveyance, there must be general words appropriate
to describe such a way, and that the word "appurtenances"
is not an appropriate word, and will not by itself pass any
way which is not technically appurtenant.

The appeal must be allowed, and the judgment reversed,
with costs.

Moss, J., concurred.

Appeal allowed.

SITTINGS IN VACATION

·AFTER TRINITY TERM, 1876.

SHARP v. CORPORATION OF THE COUNTY OF PEEL.

High Schools.

A County Council is not authorized under 37 Vic. ch. 27, O., sec. 47, to raise money by by-law for a High School not in existence, but in contemplation only.

September I9, 1876. *Osler* obtained a rule *nisi* to quash by-law 107 of the county council, passed on 30th June, 1876, or, among other things, to quash that part of it which relates to raising the sum of $8,000 for the purpose of assisting high schools, so far as relates to the sum of "$2,000 to be paid over to the board of high school trustees of the *future* high school which *may be formed in the north-western portion of the county*," on the ground that it is not competent for the county council to raise money for a high school not in existence, and the limits of which were not established at the June session of the said council for the year 1876.

It was stated by Mr. Osler that no objection was made to any other portion of the by-law than that which related to the $2,000.

The affidavit of the first deputy reeve of the township of Toronto stated, and it was not denied, " That there exist only two high schools within the county of Peel, namely, one in the town of Brampton, and the other· in the village of Streetsville, respectively, and no other high school has been established or formed within the said county of Peel: that no high school has been formed or established in the north-western portion of the said county of Peel, nor were any steps or proceedings had or taken to form or establish such high school prior to or since the passage of the said by-law."

October 3, 1876. *James Fleming* shewed cause, and cited 37 Vic. ch. 27, sec. 47, sub-secs. 1, 2, as authorizing the by-law.

F. Osler supported the rule, and contended there was no authority for the by-law.

October 13, 1876. GALT, J.—By 37 Vic. ch. 27, sec. 39, " Any county council may (under the restrictions prescribed in the next succeeding section), form a village or town, and the whole or part of one or more adjoining townships within its jurisdiction, into a new or additional high school district in the county." Section 40 enacts, " No additional high school shall be established by a county council in any county except at or before its June session in any year, and unless the high school fund shall be sufficient to allow of an apportionment at the rate of not less than $400 per annum to be made to such additional high school without diminishing the fund which was available for high schools during the next preceding year (*a*). Within this restriction it shall be lawful for the Lieutenant-Governor, on the report and recommendation of the chief superintendent of education, to authorize the establishment of an additional high school in any county at the end of the civil year."

It was conceded on the argument that under the General Municipal Act county councils cannot make such an appropriation as that now complained of, but it was contended that they might do so under sec. 47, sub-secs. 1 and 2 of 37 Vic. ch. 27., O. Those sub-sections are, 1. The council of every county may pass by-laws " For making provision by local assessment, in addition to that required to be made by this Act, for procuring sites for high schools, for erecting, building, repairing, furnishing, warming, and keeping in order high school houses, and their appendages grounds, and enclosures."

2. " For obtaining within the county, or in any city or town separated from the county, as the wants of the people may most require, the real property requisite for

erecting high school houses thereon, and for other high school purposes, and for preserving, improving, and repairing such high school houses, and for disposing of such property when no longer required."

It is very plain that the above provisions have reference only to high schools existing in any high school district already established, and not to raising money for high school purposes in a district which has no existence. Consequently this rule must be made absolute, with costs, to quash so much of the said by-law 107 as relates to raising the sum of $2,000 to be paid to the trustees of the future high school which may be formed in the north-western part of the county.

Rule absolute.

WILLIAM SILVERTHORNE v. NATHANIEL E. LOWE.

Covenant for title—Pleading.

A declaration on a covenant against encumbrances by defendant, or his wife, or any one claiming under them, alleged as a breach that at the time of making said covenant a large sum was in arrear for taxes duly imposed, without shewing that they accrued while defendants owned the land or were caused by his acts. *Held*, bad.

DEMURRER.

This was an action for breach of covenant against encumbrances. The declaration set out the deed from the defendant and his wife to the plaintiff, containing covenants against the acts of the defendant, and of the said wife, or of any person claiming under them. It then alleged as a breach that at the time of the execution and delivery of the said deed, and the making of the said covenants, and in breach thereof, a large sum of money was in arrear for taxes duly imposed, and that the land was duly sold for the payment of the said taxes, whereby the plaintiff was put to costs and expenses, &c., &c.

10—VOL. XL U.C.R.

Plea : setting out the deed in full, whereby it appeared that the sale to the plaintiff was made under a power of sale contained in a mortgage from one Matilda Swayze to the said defendant and Eliza Jane Lowe. It then contained the following covenants : And the said parties of the first part, in pursuance of the Act of short forms of conveyances, covenant with the said parties of the second part that they have the right to convey the said lands to the said party of the second part, notwithstanding any act of the said parties of the first part, and that the said party of the second part shall have quiet possession of the said lands, free from all encumbrances, and that the parties of the first part have done no act to encumber the said lands. It then concluded, " and the defendant Nathaniel E. Lowe, further says that the said defendants, or either of them, never were in possession of the said lands, or the owners."

Demurrer, on the ground that the plea does not shew any legal or equitable defence to the declaration.

Notice was given of exceptions to the declaration, among which were the following : " It is not shewn that the said taxes accrued during the time the defendant owned the said lands, and it is not shewn that the arrearages of taxes were caused by the acts of the defendant."

October 3, 1876. The demurrer and exceptions were argued by *Kerr*, Q. C., for plaintiff, and *McMichael*, Q. C., for defendant.

October 17, 1876. GALT, J.—Nothing was said on the argument in support of the plea ; but it was contended by Dr. McMichael that the declaration was defective, in not averring that the arrears of taxes were occasioned by the default of the defendant, and that as they might have accrued without his knowledge, and before he had any title to or possession of the lands, he was not liable under the limited covenants contained in the deed, unless it was alleged and proved that he was himself in default.

The case of *Harry* v. *Anderson*, 13 C. P. 476, appears to me to be decisive of that now before me. It was also an action for breach of covenant, and the breach alleged was, that at the time of executing the conveyance there were arrears of taxes which the plaintiff was obliged to pay.

Wilson, J., in giving judgment says, at p. 482 : " This is not an action for breach of covenant for quiet enjoyment, but it is of the like consideration whether the charge or encumbrance complained of was made by the defendant or by any one claiming under him; and it is impossible to say that it was ; for the defendant was expressly covenanting for his *own* acts, and against his *own* acts, and not for or against the acts of others. And yet the plaintiff desires to charge the defendant, construing the pleading according to the usual and proper rule, most strongly against the pleader, not for his own acts or for the consequence of them, but for the acts of others, and for the consequence of such acts."

I agree with the opinion expressed by the learned Judge. To hold otherwise would be to decide that there is no distinction between limited and absolute covenants.

Judgment for defendant on exceptions to the declaration.

REGINA V. NICHOL ET AL,

Summary conviction—Notice of appeal—33 Vic. ch. 27, D.

It is not essential that the notice of appeal under 33 Vic. ch. 27, D., from a summary conviction, should be signed by the party appealing. A notice, therefore "that we, the undersigned D. N. and C. N." of, &c., following the form given by the Act in other respects, but not signed, was held sufficient.

June 16, 1876. *J. B. Read* obtained from Gwynne, J., sitting alone, a rule *nisi* calling on the chairman and justices of the county of Simcoe, in general sessions assembled, and Colcough Gowán, hereinafter named, to shew cause why a writ of mandamus should not be granted, commanding the said justices to enter continuances and hear and determine on the merits an appeal of David Nichol and Charles Nichol, appellants, and Colcough Gowan, respondent, from the conviction on the 18th of December, 1875, of the said Nichols by Thomas Macham, a justice of the peace of said county, whereby said Nichols were convicted of obstructing a water-course on a highway in Nottawasaga, and were fined $5 and costs.

The affidavits of the Nichols set out the proceedings up to conviction, the entry into recognizances for the purpose of appealing, and the due service of the notice of appeal and the entry of the appeal at the sessions.   After proof of service of the notice, it was objected by Mr. *Lount*, Q. C., on behalf of the respondent, that the notice of appeal was insufficient, because : 1. The notice did not set out the matter of appeal or ground thereof.   2. That it was not signed by the appellants, or any one on their behalf.

The sessions sustained both the objections, and refused to hear the appeal.

The notice of appeal was as follows :—

"To COKELY GOWAN, Esq., of the township of Nottawasaga, in the county of Simcoe, farmer.

Take notice that we, the undersigned David Nichol and Charles Nichol, of the township of Nottawasaga aforesaid, farmers, do intend to enter and prosecute an appeal at the next general sessions of the peace to be holden at Barrie, in

and for the county of Simcoe, against a certain conviction
or order bearing date on or about the 18th of December,
1875, instant, and made by Thomas Macham, Esquire, one
of her Majesty's justices of the peace for the said county
of Simcoe, whereby the said David Nichol and Charles
Nichol were convicted of having obstructed a water course
on the Queen's highway in Nottawasaga, aforesaid, and
were ordered to pay as a fine therefor the sum of $5 and
costs, which were made up at the sum of $9.10, making in
all the sum of $16.10, which sum was to be paid forthwith.
Dated the 21st day of December, A. D. 1875."

The notice of appeal was not in fact signed.

August 29, 1876. *Lount*, Q. C., shewed cause, and
McCarthy, Q. C., supported the rule.

August 31, 1876. GWYNNE, J.—The question in this
case, is whether, inasmuch as the form of notice of appeal
from a summary conviction given in 33 Vic. ch. 27, D., commences with the words, " Take notice that I, *the undersigned*," and has the letters A. B. at the foot to represent a
signature, it is a peremptory necessity that the notice
should be signed by the party appealing to make the
appeal good and to entitle the appellant to have it heard,
the body of the statute not saying anything as to signature.

By Consol. Stat. C. ch. 103, sec. 88, it was enacted that,
the several forms in the schedule to that Act contained, or
forms to the like effect, should be deemed good, valid, and
sufficient in law.

The form of notice of appeal given in the schedule to
that Act corresponded with the form given in 33 Vic. ch.
27, in the particular now in question.

By the 96th section of 32–33 Vic. ch. 31, D., it is
enacted that the several " forms in the schedule to this Act
contained, varied to suit the case, or forms to the like effect,
shall be deemed good, valid, and sufficient."

The form of notice of appeal in the schedule of that Act
given also corresponded with the form in 33 Vic. ch. 27, D.,
in the particular now in question.

By 33 Vic. ch. 27, sec. 4, D., it is enacted that the form in that Act given shall be *substituted* for the form of notice given in the schedule to 32–33 Vic. ch. 31, D.

The form given by 33 Vic. ch. 27, D., differs from the form given by the previous statutes, by omitting all reference to the grounds of appeal and all statement of such grounds.

The effect, then, of 33 Vic. ch. 27, D., is, as it appears to me, to place the form there given in the schedule to 32–33 Vic. ch. 31, D., so as to necessitate the 96th section of the former, since the passing of the latter, being read thus, "The several forms in the schedule to this Act contained (inserting in the schedule the form of notice of appeal given by 33 Vic. ch. 27, D.) varied to suit the case, or forms to the like effect, shall be deemed good, valid, and sufficient in law;" not that the notice *shall* be in the very form given, but that such form, or any form to the like effect, shall be deemed good and sufficient.

Now, the notice given in this case before me is in the precise form given in 33 Vic. ch. 27, D., except that the signatures of the appellants at the foot of the notice appears to have been inadvertently omitted; and the sole question, therefore, is, does the omission avoid the notice; and I am of opinion that it does not. Suppose the notice had commenced, "Take notice that we, the undersigned, (omitting in the body of the notice the names of the appellants) intend to enter and prosecute an appeal * * against a certain conviction * * made by * * one of her Majesty's justices * * whereby we, the undersigned (omitting names in the body), were convicted of having," &c.; and that such notice was signed by the parties who had been convicted by the conviction referred to in the notice, and who were appealing. Such a notice would, I think, be to the like effect as the form given in the statute.

Well, this notice before me commences: "Take notice that we, the undersigned David Nichol and Charles Nichol, intend to prosecute an appeal against a conviction bearing date * * made by * * whereby the said (already named) David Nichol and Charles Nichol were convicted of having * *"

By this notice it clearly appears that the persons giving the notice were the persons convicted, and that the notice may be read as if it commenced, " Take notice that we, David Nichol and Charles Nichol," leaving out the words " the undersigned ;" or it may be read as, " We, the undersigned, namely, David Nichol and Charles Nichol," &c., in either of which cases I think the form would be to the *like effect* as the form given in the schedule, that is, as if the names of the appellants were, for the third time, named in the notice by being inserted again at the foot, after having been twice named in the body.

The notice complies with the requisites prescribed by the 2nd section of 33 Vic. ch. 27, D., namely, that the persons aggrieved, who must be the persons convicted, shall give a notice *in writing* of such appeal.

We must, I think, read these notices, not with a critical eye, but liberally *ut res magis valeat,* and so as to uphold, not to defeat, the right of appeal given to parties summarily convicted. I think this notice, therefore, sufficient, and that the mandamus must go.

Rule absolute.

McBrian et al. v. The Water Commissioners for the City of Ottawa.

Water commissioners for Ottawa—35 Vic. c. 80, sec. 41—Construction of.

The 35 Vic. ch. 80, sec. 41, incorporating the defendants, as amended
by 36 Vic. ch. 104, sec. 17, O., provides that "all work under the said
commissioners shall be performed by contract, excepting the laying of the
water pipes, and such other works as in the opinion of the engineer of
the said commissioners can be more profitably performed by day work."
Held, that the words "by contract" did not necessarily mean by contract under seal, so as to relieve the defendants from liability for work
done upon an executed parol contract.

SPECIAL case stated by an arbitrator.

Declaration on the common counts, for work and
labour, &c., in making excavations, works, buildings, &c.,
necessary for defendants.

Pleas: 1. Never indebted.   2. Payment; and two other
pleas, on which nothing turns in this report.

At the trial before Patterson, J., at the Fall Assizes of
1875, at Ottawa, the action was referred to arbitration.

The arbitrator has stated a case for the opinion of this
Court, from which it appeared: that the defendants were
incorporated by 35 Vic. ch. 80, O., and that on the 14th
of September, 1874, the plaintiff tendered in writing, at the
foot of the specifications prepared for the works above
referred to, for the construction of said works. On the 16th
of September the defendants accepted by resolution the
tender, "provided they (plaintiffs) executed contract with
their sureties within the space of two days." This contract
(called the first contract) was finally executed on the 16th
of October by the plaintiffs under seal. The defendants did
not execute it.

Subsequently the plaintiffs tendered for the completion
of a contract left uncompleted by one Kavanagh. A written contract (called the second contract) was drawn up as
to this work, but never executed by the defendants or
plaintiffs, or their sureties. The plaintiffs entered upon
the works under each contract, but after some time the
defendants took the works out of their hands.

The arbitrator found, subject to the opinion of the Court on this case, that the value of work done under both contracts, and extra work beyond either, was $2,483.44.

September 12, 1876. The special case was argued by *Osler*, for the plaintiff, and *Richards*, Q.C., contra. ·

The arguments sufficiently appear from the judgment.

September 15, 1876. GWYNNE, J.—The only question really arising upon this special case is, whether or not the effect of the 41st section of the Ontario Act, 35 Vic. ch. 80, as amended by the 17th section of the Ontario Act, 36 Vic. ch. 104, is to bar the plaintiffs from all right to recover. Irrespective of those sections it is admitted that the plaintiffs' right to recover, under the circumstances found by the arbitrator, is undoubted.

The above section of the Act for the construction of water works for the city of Ottawa, as amended, reads:—
" All work under the said commissioners shall be performed by contract, excepting the laying of the water pipes and such other works as, in the opinion of the engineer of the said commissioners (such opinion to be expressed in writing) can be more profitably performed by day work."

What is meant by the words " by contract " in this sentence is not very clear. Every work which is done by one in virtue of an employment by another to do it, is done by contract, express or implied. Even when a person is employed to do day work at an agreed-upon price—or even without a price being agreed upon, the work done by such person is done by *contract*, namely, a contract of hiring by the day at an agreed price, if any be agreed on, or on a *quantum meruit* if no wages be named.

Judging from the contrast drawn in the amending Act between work done " *by contract* " and " *by day work*," I should think that what was meant was a fixed price should be agreed upon for all work, except work coming within the exception. If that be the meaning, then that provision was complied with in respect of the works within what

are called in the special case the first and second contracts.
In the first the price was fixed in the specifications, with
reference to which the plaintiffs made their tender, and in
the second the price was determined by Kavanagh's contract, the plaintiffs undertaking in their tender to do the
work within that contract at three per cent. less than the
price agreed upon between the defendants and Kavanagh.

But what the defendants contend is, that the words "by
contract" in this section must be read "by contract *under
seal.*" The contention of the defendants being, that,
although the defendants, without entering into any sealed
contract, should have succeeded in getting any person to
complete all their works for them to their perfect satisfaction, and should accept the work when completed, and
enjoy the benefit of it, they are by this section relieved
from all obligation to pay a farthing for work so executed.

The Legislature has not thought fit to add the words
"*under seal*" after the words "*by contract*," and I shall not
do so in order to give the construction contended for by the
defendants.

Indeed, if these words were inserted in the clause, the
setting up the defence now urged would, as it appears to
me, in view of the facts found by the arbitrator, be such a
fraud upon the plaintiffs, that in the exercise of our equitable jurisdiction the Court would be justified in restraining
the defendants from setting up any such defence. The
defendants, in my judgment, are equally liable to be sued
in *assumpsit* upon an executed contract, as they would
have been if the 41st section, as amended, had formed no
part of the Act.

But, indeed, there is nothing in the matters found by the
arbitrator to shew that the work executed by the plaintiffs,
both that within what are called the first and second contracts, as well as the extra work, is not all within the
exception to the 41st section, namely, work connected with
"the laying of the water pipes."

However, I do not desire to rest my judgment upon this
narrow basis, although it seems sufficient to support it.

What I proceed upon is, that the defendants, although they have executed no contract under seal, did authorize, by themselves and their engineer, the plaintiffs to execute the work coming within what are called the first and second contracts, and that through their engineer they procured the plaintiffs to do the extra work, the nature of which does not appear; but whatever it was, the defendants have accepted, taken, and enjoyed, and still do enjoy the benefit of the whole of the work done by the plaintiffs, and therefore the plaintiffs are entitled to retain the award, and to have judgment for the whole amount of $2,483.44 awarded by the arbitrator, without any deduction; and the rule will be accordingly.

Judgment for plaintiffs.

ROSS v. McLAY.

Registrar—Notice of action.

Held, that a Registrar was not entitled to notice of an action against him for neglecting and refusing to furnish a statement in detail of fees charged by him, as required by 38 Vic. ch. 17, sec. 7 O., and claiming a mandamus ; such neglect and refusal being an act of omission.

DEMURRER. Declaration : that the defendant was and is registrar of the county of Bruce, and the plaintiff paid him as such registrar certain fees of office, and requested him to furnish to the plaintiff a statement in detail of such fees, and it was the duty of the defendant, on being so requested, to furnish to the plaintiff such statement, and the plaintiff was and is personally interested in being furnished with such statement, and sustains and may sustain damage by the non-performance of his said duty, and the performance of the said duty by the defendant has been demanded by the plaintiff of the defendant : that the

defendant has refused and neglected to perform the same,
and all conditions have been fulfilled, and all things happened, and all times elapsed, necessary to entitle the plaintiff
to the performance of the said duty by the defendant, and
to claim a writ of *mandamus* in that behalf ; and the plaintiff claims a writ of *mandamus* commanding the defendant
to furnish to the plaintiff the said statement in detail of
the said fees.

2. That the defendant was and is registrar of the county
of Bruce, and as such registrar furnished certain abstracts
of title, and made certain searches in the registry books, in
the registry office of the said county, for the plaintiff, and
the defendant wrongfully demanded and exacted from the
plaintiff an excessive amount of fees for the said abstracts
and searches.

3. Common counts—for money payable by the defendant
to the plaintiff for money received by the defendant for the
use of the plaintiff, and for money paid by the plaintiff for
the defendant at his request.   .

Pleas :—8. As to said first and second counts of said
declaration, that no notice in writing was delivered to the
defendant or left at his usual place of abode by the plaintiff,
his attorney or agent of the commencing of this action, one
month before the same was commenced, pursuant to the
the statute in that behalf.

9 As to the common counts that defendant is not
indebted to the plaintiff in any moneys, other than for
fees for abstracts, searches, exhibiting instruments, &c.,
which he may have erroneously exacted and taken from
the plaintiff as registrar of the county of Bruce, and in his
capacity and office as such registrar. And the defendant says
that no notice in writing was delivered to the defendant,
or left at his usual place of abode, by the plaintiff, his
attorney or agent, of the commencing of this action one
month before the same was commenced, pursuant to the.
statutes in that behalf.

Demurrer to the eighth and ninth pleas, on the ground :
that the defendant is not entitled to notice of an action to

recover excessive or extortionate charges of fees, or for money had and received by him as fees of office, over and above the amount limited by law.

October 3, 1876. The demurrer was argued by *Delamere*, for the plaintiff. He relied on *Harrison* v. *Brega*, 20 U. C. R. 324.

Robinson, Q. C., contra, cited *Wilson* v. *Mayor*, *&c.*, *of Halifax*, L. R. 3 Ex. 114, 119; *Poulsom* v. *Thirst*, L. R. 2 C. P. 449.

October 10, 1876. GALT, J.—The first count charges that the defendant, being registrar of the county of Bruce, neglected and refused to furnish the plaintiff with a statement in detail of certain fees and charges made by him as registrar.

The second count is for overcharges on certain abstracts and searches.

The third count is in *indebitatus* assumpsit, for money received by the defendant from the plaintiff.

The eighth plea to the first and second counts is, that the defendant received no notice in writing before action brought, &c.

The ninth plea sets forth that the moneys claimed on the third count were moneys paid to the defendant as registrar, and that no notice of action was given.

As to the plea to the second and third counts, I have already decided in another suit *(a)* between these parties that the defendant is entitled to a month's notice of action, and therefore the demurrer to the plea to the second and third counts will be over-ruled, and judgment entered in favour of the defendant.

As to the plea of want of notice to the first count. It is to be observed that the claim made in that count is for a *mandamus* to compel the defendant to furnish a statement of his fees, &c. This it is his duty to do under sec. 7 of 38,

_____

(a) See the next case.

Vic.; ch. 17, and I can see no reason why the defendant can
claim a month's notice of action. His neglect and refusal
was an act of omission, and under the authority of *Harrison v. Brega*, 20 U. C. R. 324, a registrar is not in such a
case, entitled to a month's notice of action. Judgment
will therefore be in favour of the plaintiff on the demurrer
to the plea to the first count.

There will be no costs.

MICHAELMAS TERM, 40 VICTORIA, 1876.

November 20th to December 9th.

Present :

THE HON. ROBERT ALEXANDER HARRISON, C.J.
    "   JOSEPH CURRAN MORRISON, J.
    "   ADAM WILSON, J.

ROSS v. McLAY.

Registrar—Notice of Action.

A registrar is entitled to notice of an action brought against him to recover back fees charged by him in excess of those allowed by the statute 31 Vic. ch. 20, O.

DEMURRER. Declaration. First count: for that the defendant was and is registrar of the county of Bruce, and as such registrar furnished certain abstracts of title and made certain searches in the registry books, in the registry office-of the said county, for the plaintiff, and the defendant wrongfully demanded and exacted from the plaintiff an excessive amount of fees for the said abstracts and searches.

Second count: for that the defendant is indebted to the plaintiff for money payable by the defendant to the plaintiff for money received by the defendant for the use of the plaintiff, and for money paid by the plaintiff for the defendant, at his request. And the plaintiff claims $500.

Third plea, to the first count: that no notice in writing was delivered to the defendant or left at his usual place of abode by the plaintiff, his attorney or agent, of the commencing of this action, one month before the same was commenced, pursuant to the statutes in that behalf.

Fourth plea, to second count: that the defendant is not

indebted to the plaintiff in any moneys other than for fees for abstracts and searches which may erroneously have been exacted and taken by him as registrar of the county of Bruce, and in his capacity and office of such registrar, from the plaintiff; and the defendant says that no notice in writing was delivered to the defendant or left at his usual place of abode by the plaintiff, his attorney or agent, of the commencing of this action one month before the same was commenced, pursuant to the statutes in that behalf.

Demurrer to the second and fourth pleas, on the grounds: that the defendant is not entitled to notice of action to recover extortionate or excessive charges of fees, or for money had and received by him as fees of office over and above the amount limited by law.

June 2, 1876. *Kerr*, Q. C., for the plaintiff. The first count is for malfeasance. The action is brought under 31 Vic. ch. 20, sec. 18, O. The registrar is not a public officer, as far as the collection of fees is concerned, under Consol. Stat. U. C. ch. 126, secs. 1, 10, 20. *Harrison* v. *Brega*, 20 U. C. R. 324, is distinguishable. As to the second count, see *Leete* v. *Hart*, L. R. 3 C. P. 322; *Cook* v. *Leonard*, 6 B. & C. 351; *Cann* v. *Clipperton*, 10 A. & E. 582; *Downing* v. *Capel*, L. R. 2 C. P. 461; *Morgan* v. *Palmer*, 2 B. & C. 729. As to notice in actions for malfeasance, see *Grant q. t.* v. *McFadden*, 11 C. P. 122; *McWhirter* v. *Corbett*, 4 C. P. 203; *Dale* v. *Cool*, 6 C. P. 544; *Garton* v. *Great Western R. W. Co.*, E. B. & E. 837; *Irving* v. *Wilson*, 4 T. R. 485; *Copland* v. *Powell*, 8 Moore 400, S. C. 1 Bing. 369; *Wallace* v. *Smith*, 5 East 115.

Robinson, Q. C., contra. The cases shew that the form of action makes no difference, the substance only is to be regarded, and this is clearly a suit brought for acts done under the statute. The defendant claimed to be entitled to the fees charged by virtue of the Act, under which alone he could have any claim. *Harrison* v. *Brega*, 20 U. C. R. 324, decided that the Registrar was a public officer within Consol. Stat. U. C. ch. 126; and under 35 Vic. ch. 27 O., a certain proportion of the fees received by him go to the public. He cited *Waterhouse* v. *Keen*, 4 B. & C. 200; *Kent* v. *Great Western R. W. Co.*, 3 C. B. 714; *Selmes* v. *Judge*, L. R. 6 Q. B. 724; *Greenway* v. *Hurd*, 4 T. R. 553; *Roscoe* N. P. 485; *Cummins* v. *Moore*, 37 U. C. R. 130. *Garton* v. *Great Western R. W. Co.*, E B. & E. 837, was decided upon a point of pleading, and is not inconsistent with the previous cases.

June 28, 1876. GALT, J. [After setting out the pleadings.] The case of *Harrison* v. *Brega*, 20 U. C. R. 324, decides that a registrar is a public officer, and as such entitled to the protection given to justices of the peace and other officers as to notice of action and the time within which such action should be brought.

The question raised by these demurrers is, whether in an action like the present, and more particularly as respects the second count, being the ordinary one for money had and received, the defendant can claim that protection. It is important to remark that the writ is sued out against the defendant as an individual, without any reference to his position or character; but in the first count he is expressly sued for misconduct as registrar. The second count makes no allusion to him as registrar; but the plea to that count states expressly that the money therein sought to be recovered was received and taken by him as registrar.

The case of *Waterhouse et al.* v. *Keen*, 4 B. & C. 200, seems to me to be decisive in favour of the defendant. That was an action on the money counts for money had and received, for charging and receiving more toll than the defendant was empowered to collect. To this the general issue by statute was pleaded. By the 10 Geo. III., one of the Acts passed for repairing the line of road of which the defendant was lessee, it was provided that no action should be brought against any one for any thing done under the Act without a certain notice of action being given, and within a limited time. A verdict was entered for the plaintiffs, subject to the opinion of the Court.

The counsel for plaintiffs, on the argument of the case, contended, as was done by Mr. Kerr, that "It was unnecessary to give twenty-one days' notice, &c., for the clause in the statute, requiring those things to be done, applies only to actions of tort. It enacts that the defendant is to be at liberty to plead the general issue, not guilty, and that no action is to be commenced after sufficient satisfaction or tender thereof hath been made to the party aggrieved. It therefore, clearly contemplates actions of tort only."

Bayley, J., in giving judgment, says p. 209: "As to the other question, which is one of more general importance, I am of opinion, that under the protecting clause of 10 Geo. III. the defendant was entitled to twenty-one days notice, * * It is true that many of the expressions in that clause seem to point to actions of tort, but it is material to consider the substance rather than the mere form of the action. In many cases the subject matter of the action is substantially tort, but the plaintiff may waive that tort, and bring assumpsit. If an action be brought in consequence of a thing substantially done in pursuance of the Act of Parliament, it is a case within the Act. * * If the Act of Parliament does not apply to this case, parties may be at liberty to maintain actions for all sums levied under a misconstruction of the Act within a period of six years. And thus the object of the Legislature, which was, that the action should be brought promptly, would be defeated. But it is said that in this case there was not anything done by the defendant in pursuance of the Act; but that expression, as used in this Act of Parliament, means that the thing done should be done by the defendant acting *colore officii;* if he did so act, he is within the protection of the Act of Parliament." See Consol. Stat. ch. 126, sec. 9.

Now, in the present case it is perfectly clear that what the defendant did he did *colore officii*. It is so stated in the first count; and it appears to me that a claim for fees, although it may be erroneous, which can be made only under the provisions of the Act, must be considered as done in pursuance of the Act. If, then, the protection of the statute is only to be invoked when the fees charged are those which the Act allows, there could be no action, and therefore the defendant would need no protection.

Holroyd, J., in his judgment in the same case, says, p. 213: "The first part of the clause requires that no action shall be brought against any person or persons, &c., until twenty-one days' notice thereof shall be given to the clerk of the trustees, or after sufficient satisfaction or tender thereof has been made to the party or parties aggrieved. That shows that the protection of the Act is not confined to actions where the party is justified in what he has done under the Act. The question therefore is, was this action brought against the defendant for an act done in pursuance of the Act of Parliament, according to the legal meaning of those terms. The action in form is, for money had and received to the plaintiffs' use, but in substance it is brought to recover money alleged by the plaintiff to have been unlawfully taken by the defendant as toll, under colour of the authority of the Act. The demanding and taking the toll was an act done in pursuance of the Act. This is a case therefore within the words of the Act."

I should have considered myself justified in relying solely on the authority of this case but for the stress laid by the learned counsel on the part of the plaintiff on *Garton* v. *Great Western R. W. Co.*, E. B. & E. 837, which, he contended, over-ruled the case of *Kent* v. *Great Western R. W. Co.*, 3 C. B. 714, relied on by Mr. Robinson.

It becomes necessary to consider those two cases, and to shew in what respects they differ from the present. I mean as respects the second count; for, as regards the first, the case of *Waterhouse et al.* v. *Keen*, 4 B. & C. 200, is conclusive.

The case of *Kent* v. *Great Western R. W. Co.*, 3 C. B. 714, was an application made to the Court to review the taxation of a bill of costs allowed by the Master for charges preliminary to bringing the action. These charges, which amounted to a considerable sum, had been incurred in preparing and serving a notice of action; the contention on

the part of the defendants being, that a notice of action
was unnecessary, and therefore these costs should not be
allowed. By the charter of defendants it was enacted that
no action should be brought for anything done or omitted
to be done in pursuance of the Act, or in the execution of
the powers or authorities given by the Act, unless twenty
days' previous notice should be given. The company
having, contrary to the provisions of the Act, made excessive charges for the carriage of goods, and claimed and
received the amount of said charges from the plaintiff:—
Held, in an action for money had and received, brought to
recover back the sum so extorted, the company were
entitled to notice of action.

Coltman, J., says, p. 725, "Here, however, the defendants were professing to act solely and entirely under the
authority of their Acts of Parliament. They were, therefore, clearly entitled to a notice of action."

Maule, J., says, "I am of the same opinion. I think
the subject matter of charge in this action was a thing
done, or omitted to be done, in pursuance of the Act.
The plaintiff and the defendants are, in reality, trying in
an action of assumpsit (which makes no difference) whether
under the Act the defendants were entitled to charge certain prices. It is scarcely possible to conceive a case more
distinctly within the purview of the Act. The company
were doing what they considered to be in pursuance of the
Act; and therefore the case is clearly one in which a notice
of action was necessary."

This case was brought under the consideration of the
Court of Exchequer Chamber in the case of *Garton* v. *The
Great Western R.W. Co.*, E. B. & E. 837, 846. By the incorporating Act, it was enacted as above stated in the case of
Kent v. *The Great Western R. W. Co.*, 3 C. B. 714. To a
declaration against the company for money had and received, and on an account stated, the company pleaded that
the action was brought after the statute, and no notice had
been given pursuant to the statute. After verdict and
judgment for the defendants, it was held in the Exchequer

Chamber, that the plea was bad, and judgment was reversed *for the want of an allegation shewing that the
action fell within the class described in the section.*

This is the difference between that case and the present.

Willes, J., says, p. 849, " I also am of opinion that the
plea is bad for want of an averment that the action is
brought 'against any person for anything done or omitted
to be done in pursuance of this Act, or in the execution of
the powers or authorities, or of any of the orders made,
given, or directed by or under this Act.'" The other Judges
concurred.

The plea demurred to in this case asserts as positively as
it can do "that he is not indebted to the plaintiff in any
moneys other than for fees for abstracts and searches,
which may erroneously have been exacted and taken by
him as registrar of the county of Bruce, and in his capacity
and office as such registrar."

If, then, the defendant is not entitled to a notice of action
in this case, I cannot conceive an instance in which the
statute would afford him any protection. The defendant
fills a most important situation, and doubtless has been in
the habit of charging the same rate of fees to all persons.
If, then, he has been mistaken as to the amount of fees
which he could legally claim, he would, without any notice
or opportunity being afforded him of making restitution,
be liable to an action by every person from whom he had
erroneously exacted a larger fee than he was entitled to,
unless he is protected by the statute.

Judgment for defendant.

From this decision the plaintiff brought the case on for
rehearing before the full Court.

Before the demurrer was reheard, the case had been carried
down to trial and a verdict entered for the plaintiff.

May 22, 1876, *C. Robinson,* Q. C., obtained a rule *nisi*
to set aside the verdict and enter a verdict for the defen-

dant, on the ground that no overcharge was proved and the plaintiff shewed no right to recover.

November 27, 1877.   The demurrer and rule *nisi*, were argued by *J, K. Kerr*, Q. C., for the plaintiff, and *Robinson*, Q. C., for defendant.

The argument, as to the demurrer, was similar to that before Galt, J.

December, 29, 1876.   MORRISON, J.—The question of the necessity of a notice of action to a public officer has been fully considered in the case of *McDougall* v. *Peterson*, in which judgment has just been delivered by the learned Chief Justice (*a*).   It is not necessary to say anything in this case, as the principles upon which *McDougall* v. *Peterson* has been decided apply to and govern the case. The judgment of Mr. Justice Galt on the demurrer is affirmed, and judgment must be entered for the defendant.

That being so, the defendant will also be entitled to have his rule made absolute to set aside the verdict and to enter a nonsuit.

Rule accordingly.

(*a*) See the next case.

McDougall et al. v. Peterson.

County attorney—Notice of action.

The defendant, being County crown attorney and clerk of the peace, received certain promissory notes belonging to the plaintiffs with the depositions from a magistrate on the committal of certain persons for obtaining such notes by false pretences. At the trial before the County Judge the prisoners were acquitted, the learned Judge saying that the prosecutors' remedy, if any, was in Chancery. The defendant refused to give the notes up to the plaintiffs on demand, saying that he would return them to the committing magistrate, and the plaintiffs thereupon brought trover and detinue.

The learned Judge, who tried the case without a jury, having found that defendant acted *bonâ fide* in such refusal: *Held*, that he was entitled to notice of action under C. S. U. C. ch. 126 : that he was an officer fulfilling a public duty within that statute; and that the refusal, though erroneous, was an act done by him in the supposed discharge of such duty.

THE first count of the declaration was trover for a number of promissory notes made by different persons, and payable to the Ontario Copper Lightning Rod Company or bearer, in the aggregate amounting to $1,214.77.

The second count was detinue for the same notes.

Pleas: 1. Not guilty by statute, Consol. Stat. U. C. ch. 126, secs. 1, 6, 10, 11, 16, 20.

2. Traverse of the plaintiffs' property, in the notes.

3. On equitable grounds alleging, among other things, that the defendant is County Crown attorney for the county of Wellington, and clerk of the County Judge's Criminal Court for that county : that the notes in question came into defendant's possession as such clerk on a criminal trial before the Judge of the County Court, and that no Judge's order was ever made for their delivery to the plaintiffs.

The plaintiffs took issue on the pleas, and replied specifically to the equitable plea, among other things, that after the criminal trial the notes were demanded openly of the defendant in open Court, and in the presence of the Judge, and the defendant refused to deliver them on the ground that he thought they had been improperly obtained, and

that a suit in Chancery was about to be entered in reference to them.

Issue was taken on the replication.

The cause was tried at the last assizes for the county of
Wellington, before Galt, J., without a jury.

Plaintiffs proved that the notes, which were payable to
the Ontario Copper Lightning Rod Company or bearer,
were the property of the plaintiffs, purchased by them from
the company. They also proved a demand of the notes.
and refusal to give them up before suit.

It appeared on the part of the defence that the defendant is Crown attorney for the county of Wellington, and
clerk of the County Judge's Criminal Court: that the notes
in question were forwarded to him with depositions and
other papers, by the committing magistrate at Fergus, on a
committal of some persons for having obtained some of the
notes by false pretences: that they were received by him
as exhibits and depositions as in any other criminal case:
that they remained in his possession till the trial: that at
the trial they were produced and referred to as evidence :
that the prisoners were acquitted, the Judge saying the
remedy, if any, of the prosecutors was in Chancery: that
after the acquittal of the prisoners an application was
made to the Judge, on behalf of the prosecution, for an
order for the delivery up of the notes to the makers: that
the Judge declined to make the order: that a demand for
an order for the delivery of the notes to the plaintiffs was
then made: that the Judge also declined to make this
order, saying something of the propriety of defendant
returning the notes to the committing magistrate, and
thereupon a demand on behalf of the plaintiffs was made
on defendant for the notes: that defendant was perplexed,
and said proceedings would be taken in equity, and this
was said in consequence of some observations which had
fallen from the Judge about the remedy in equity, and
when the notes were next demanded of defendant he said
he would return them to the committing magistrate from
whom he received them: that he was served with the writ

of summons in this cause within an hour or two afterwards, and was afterwards served with a bill in equity, and notified not to give up several of the notes; and that he had no personal interest in the matter, and was never served with any notice of action.

It was during the trial agreed that several of the notes should be given up to the plaintiffs' attorney to be kept by him until the termination of the Chancery proceedings respecting them, and the remaining notes delivered to the plaintiffs. This was accordingly done.

The learned Judge found as a fact that the defendant acted *bonâ fide,* as crown attorney and clerk of the Criminal Judge's Criminal Court, in refusing to give up the notes.

It was objected on this finding that plaintiffs should be nonsuited, because no notice of action had been given to the defendant.

The learned Judge, without expressing any opinion as to the right of the defendant to notice of action, found a verdict for the plaintiffs for one shilling damages, reserving leave to the defendant to move to enter a verdict for the defendant, if the Court should be of opinion that the objection as to want of notice of action was a good one.

During this term, November 22, 1876, *Guthrie,* Q. C., moved accordingly.

November 30, 1876. *S. Richards,* Q. C., shewed cause. The defendant was not entitled to notice of action: *McArthur* v. *Corbett,* 4 C. P. 203; *Archibald* v. *Haldan,* 30 U. C. R. 30. What defendant did was not an act done, within the meaning of the statute: *Harrison* v. *Brega,* 20 U. C. R. 324; *Harrold* v. *The Corporation of the County of Simcoe,* 16 C. P. 43. The action is in the nature of an action of replevin, in which no notice is necessary: *Folger* v. *Minton,* 10 U. C. R. 423; *Applegarth* v. *Graham,* 7 C. P. 171; *Lewis* v. *Teale,* 32 U. C. R. 108; *Manson* v. *Gurnett,* 2 P. R. 389; *Kennedy* v. *Hall,* 7 C. P. 218; and the Judge had no power to make any order as to the notes: Consol. Stat. C., ch. 99, secs. 88, 89; 32–33 Vic. ch. 21, secs. 113,

13—VOL XL. U.C.R.

114, D.; *Regina* v. *London*, E. B. & E. 509; *Regina* v. *Lord Mayor, &c., of London*, L. R. 4 Q. B. 371; *Regina* v. *Goldsmith*, 12 Cox C. C. 594; *Regina* v. *Smith, Ib.* 597. The action is not one in which there could be a tender of amends: *Golightly* v. *Reynolds*, Lofft 88; *Scattergood* v. *Sylvester*, 15 Q. B. 506; *Horwood* v. *Smith*, 2 T. R. 750; *Peer* v. *Humphrey*, 2 A. & E. 495.

Guthrie, Q.C., contra. The defendant was a public officer under the statute, and was, in the embarrassing situation in which he was unexpectedly placed, entitled to some time for consideration and reflection more than was given to him, and his refusal to give the notes was an act done by him in the performance of his duty: *Davis* v. *Williams*, 13 C. P. 365; *Dews* v. *Riley*, 11 C. B. 434; *Spry* v. *Mumby*, 11 C. P. 285; *Helliwell* v. *Taylor*, 16 U. C. R. 279; *Harrison* v. *Brega*, 20 U. C. R. 324; *Moran* v. *Palmer*, 13 C. P. 528; *Mathers* v. *Lynch*, 28 U. C. R. 354. The reasons for deciding that notice is not necessary in an action of replevin, are inapplicable here: *Fletcher* v. *Wilkins*, 6 East 283; *Harper* v. *Carr*, 7 T. R. 270.

McDonald, on the same side, cited *Carswell* v. *Huffman*, 1 U. C. R. 381.

December 29, 1876. HARRISON, C. J.—The statute gives the protection to justices of the peace, and "to any other officer or person fulfilling any public duty, for anything by him done in the performance of such duty": Consol. Stat. U. C. ch. 126, secs. 1, 20.

The effect of such a statute is to protect persons acting illegally, but in the supposed pursuance and with a *bonâ fide* intention of discharging public duty.

If the officer, in the supposed discharge of duty, had done nothing illegal he would not need the protection of any statute. See *Theobold* v. *Crichmore*, 1 B. & Al. 227; *Wells* v. *Ody*, 2 C. M. & R. 128; *Smith* v. *Hopper*, 9 Q. B. 1005; *Hardwick* v. *Moss et al.*, 7 H. & N. 136; *Selmes* v. *Judge*, L. R. 6 Q. B. 724.

The first question is, whether a clerk of the peace, fulfilling the duty of clerk of the County Judge's Criminal

Court, can be said to be an officer fulfilling a public duty within the meaning of the statute?

The clerk of the peace, by himself or his sufficient deputy, must be in constant attendance on the Court of Quarter Sessions. He gives notice of its being holden or adjourned, issues its processes, records its proceedings, and does all the ministerial acts necessary to give effect to its decisions: *Dick.* Sess. 52, 53. See also Consol. Stat. U. C. ch. 106.

Every clerk of the peace is *ex officio* county attorney for the county of which he is clerk of the peace: Consol. Stat. U. C. ch. 17, sec. 9, and *vice versâ:* 27–28 Vic. ch. 33.

The County Judge, sitting out of Sessions for summary criminal trials, for all the purposes thereof, and proceedings connected therewith, or relating thereto, is constituted a Court of Record: 32–33 Vic. ch. 35, secs. 3, 4, 5., D.

It is the duty of the county attorney or clerk of the peace to draw up the record of proceedings, subpœna witnesses, attend the trial, and perform other duties detailed in secs. 3 and 4 of 32–33 Vic. ch. 35.

The sentence of the Judge is to have the same force and effect as if passed at any Court of General Sessions of the peace: *Ib.*, sec. 3, sub-sec. 3.

The following officers have been held in this province entitled to the protection of such an Act as the Consol. Stat. U. C. ch. 126:

A special constable: *Sage* v. *Duffy*, 11 U. C. R. 30. A pathmaster, *Helliwell* v. *Taylor*, 16 U. C. R. 279. A pound-keeper, *Wardell* v. *Chisholm*, 9 C. P. 125 ; *Davis* v. *Williams*, 13 C. P. 365 ; *Denison* v. *Cunningham*, 35 U. C. R. 383. A registrar, *Harrison* v. *Brega*, 20 U. C. R. 324. A school trustee, *Spry* v. *Mumby et al.*, 11 C. P. 285. A collector of school taxes; *Ib.* The mayor of a town, *Moran* v. *Palmer*, 13 C. P. 528.

In England it has been held that the clerk of a County Court is an officer entitled to the protection of a similar Act: *Dews* v. *Riley*, 11 C. B. 434.

We feel no difficulty in holding that a clerk of the peace, whose office is of great antiquity and of much public

importance, must be classed with the officers named as
entitled in a proper case to the protection of the statute.

But the next contention is, that defendant is not in this
action sued for anything "done" by him while in the
supposed performance of a public duty.

Unless he did something this action cannot be maintained
against him. He is charged with having detained or converted to his own use a number of promissory notes
belonging to the plaintiffs. The detention or conversion is
made to depend on a refusal by defendant as clerk of the
peace to give up notes to the plaintiff which had come
rightfully into his possession as clerk of the peace.

The cases cited by Mr. Richards, to which may be added
Nickling v. *Hamps*, 21 L. T. N. S. 754, and *Lindsay* v.
Candy, L. R. 1 Q. B. D. 348, L. R., 2 Q. B. D. 96, shew that
the learned County Judge did right in refusing to make any
such order as asked of him, and that the plaintiffs were not
to be deprived of their property or dominion by reason of
anything which took place in Court.

This being so, we may assume that the refusal by
defendant was, under the circumstances, a wrongful one,
but if it be held to have been an act *done* by him in the
supposed performance of his official duty he would be
entitled to the protection of the Act: Consol. Stat. U. C.
ch. 124.

In many cases a distinction is attempted to be drawn as
regards public officers between mere nonfeasance and malfeasance. The line is a difficult one to draw, and the con-
quence is, that the cases are not consistent.

In *Davis* v. *Curling*, 8 Q. B. 286, where the action was
against defendant for neglect to remove gravel off a highway, the Court held that defendant was charged with doing
something wrong, that is, keeping the gravel in an improper
place and so held that he was entitled to notice of action.

In *Newton* v. *Ellis*, 5 E. & B. 115, the defendant, who
was sued for neglecting to light at night a hole which he
was lawfully excavating on a public highway, was also
held entitled to notice of action.

The latter case has been followed with approval in *Poulsom* v. *Hirst*, L. R. 2 C. P. 449; *Wilson* v. *Mayor of Halifax*, L. R. 3 Ex. 114; *Joliffe* v. *Wallesley Local Board*, L. R. 9 C. P. 62; *Cairns* v. *Water Commissioners of the City of Ottawa*, 25 C. P. 551.

But this Court as then constituted in *Harrison* v. *Brega,* 20 U. C. R. 324, where the action was against a registrar to recover damages for the negligent omission of a particular registry in an abstract of title furnished by him, held that the registrar was not entitled to notice of action.

In delivering judgment, Sir J. B. Robinson distinguished *Davis* v. *Carling*, and similar cases, and held that they are not cases of mere neglect or nonfeasance, and that the statute does not extend to cases of mere neglect or nonfeasance.

In *Moran* v. *Palmer*, 13 C. P. 528, *Harrison* v. *Brega*, 20 U. C. R. 324, was approved.   Richards, C. J., in delivering judgment said : "We think the distinction suggested by the late Chief Justice of Upper Canada, in *Harrison* v. *Brega*, is the true one as regards notice of action in matters of nonfeasance.   When what is complained of is a negligent omission to do what the defendant was called upon to do in the discharge of the duty of his office, then no notice of action would be required; but where the party neglects to do an act and in that way carrying out the law according to his erroneous idea of his duty, then he is entitled to notice of action."

The latter words embrace the present case.   The defendant refused when demanded to give up the notes.   His act of refusal after demand is the ground of action against him either for the detention or alleged conversion of the notes. In so refusing the defendant was carrying out the law according to his erroneous idea of his duty.

In *Moran* v. *Palmer* the defendant, who was mayor of the town of Guelph, was sued for refusing to endorse an order on a tavern inspector's certificate for a license to sell spirits, with a view to the issue of a license to the plaintiff, and it was held that this was an act done by the defendant in the supposed discharge of his duty.

So here the refusal of the defendant as clerk of the peace to deliver the notes to the plaintiff when demanded, must be equally held an act done by him in the supposed fulfilment of his public duty.

The rule must be absolute.

MORRISON, J., and WILSON, J., concurred.

Rule absolute (a).

RE RICHARD LAKE AND W. B. BLAKELEY, INSPECTOR OF LICENSES FOR THE COUNTY OF PRINCE EDWARD.

Temperance Act of 1864—Delivery of by-law to collector.

The issuers of licenses appointed under 37 Vic. ch. 32, O., supersede the collector of inland revenue under the Temperance Act of 1864; and under that Act and the 39 Vic. ch. 26, O., it was held unnecessary to deliver a copy of a by-law passed on the 29th June, 1875, under the Temperance Act, to the collector of inland revenue.

Semble, that if it had been, the person to whom it was delivered in this case was, under the facts stated, sufficiently shewn to be such collector.

It was objected that the applicant for a mandamus to the inspector of licenses to inspect and report on his premises, so as to enable him to apply for a license, did not shew that he was a natural born or naturalized subject, as required by the by-law; but *Held,* that such objection could not have prevailed, for he was shewn to have been duly licensed up to 1st May, 1876, and no exception had been made to him.

IN Easter Term, May 26, 1876, *Ferguson,* Q. C., obtained a rule calling on Mr. Blakeley, as inspector of licenses for the County of Prince Edward, to shew cause on the fourth day of the next term why a writ of *mandamus* should not issue, commanding him forthwith to inspect the house and premises of Richard Lake, an hotel-keeper in the town of Picton, in the said county, according to law, and in accordance with his duty as such inspector, and to make his report as such inspector, in writing to the Board of License Commissioners for the county, in regard to the said house and premises, the accommodations therein, and the said

---

(a) See *Bullock* v. *Dunlop,* L. R. 2 Ex. D. 43.

Richard Lake, in accordance with his duties in that behalf, so as to enable the said Richard Lake to apply for a license to sell spirituous, fermented, and other manufactured liquors by retail in his said house and premises, the same being those heretofore occupied by the said Richard Lake as an hotel, on grounds disclosed in the affidavits and papers filed.

By-law No. 57, passed on the 22nd of February, 1875, by the town of Picton, appointing an inspector of licenses for taverns and shops in the town, and defining his duties, was filed.

On the 29th of June, 1875, the county passed a by-law —applicable as well to the town of Picton as to the rest of the county—prohibiting the sale of intoxicating liquors and the issuing of licenses therefor in the county.

In Michaelmas Term, November 19, 1875, the applicant obtained a rule in the Court of Common Pleas calling on the county to shew cause why the last mentioned by-law should not be quashed for various reasons assigned, which rule was afterwards, in Hilary Term, 10th of March, 1876, discharged with costs: *Re Lake and the Corporation of the County of Prince Edward*, 26 C. P. 173. The applicant said he has appealed from that decision: that his license expired on the 1st of May, 1876, since which time he had been obliged to cease selling liquors, for want of a license : that he had conformed to all existing laws in order to put himself in a position to obtain a license to sell intoxicating liquors, but he had failed to get a license since the 1st of May, 1876 : that he notified William B. Blakeley, the license inspector, and the license commissioners of the county, about the middle of April, 1876, to have the applicant's premises inspected according to law, and in the latter part of that month he tendered the inspector the requisite sum of money in order to obtain a tavern license, for which he applied, and he also tendered him a bond, as required by law, the sureties to which he approved ; and that the applicant endeavoured to fulfil every other formality necessary, and he believed that he had complied with all Acts of Parliament in force necessary to be complied with in order to obtain and to entitle him to a tavern license : that the inspector refused to inspect the applicant's premises, because he said the by-law of 29th of June, 1875, passed under the Temperance Act of 1864, was in force.

That his house and premises had cost the applicant over $13,000, and they contained all the necessary requirements for a hotel or tavern, and had been used for that purpose for more than fifteen years ; and unless he could obtain a license he would be materially injured and his property will be very much reduced in value.

That he was informed and believed the by-law passed under the Temperance Act was not communicated by delivery of a copy of it, certified by the clerk of the county, to the collector of inland revenue, within whose official district the country is situate, according to section 6 of the Temperance Act of 1864 : that the only delivery of the by-law was a delivery of a copy of it by the clerk of the municipality of the county to one John S. Clute, of the town of Picton, stated to be acting for the collector of inland revenue at the town of Picton, on the 20th September, 1875, upon which copy was a certificate of the clerk of the by-law having been approved by the electors of the county, as he was informed and believed : that he was informed and believed John S. Clute was not at the date of the delivery of the by-law acting for the said collector of inland revenue at Picton, but that he had been suspended before the said illegal delivery of the copy of the by-law to him : that the county of Prince Edward contains a population of about 20,000, and is about forty miles long and in some places is about twenty miles wide, and the town of Picton contains a population of about 3,000, and covers several hundred of acres of land, and no licenses have been issued to any person in the town or county.

The affidavit of William L. Hamilton, of Belleville, stated that he was deputy collector of inland revenue at the town of Belleville, and had been for several years past : that there had been no collector of inland revenue at Belleville for about one year, but one Mr. Stratton acted as such till

December, 1875, and one G. C. Holton now acts as such : that the county of Prince Edward was within the official district of which the deponent is deputy-collector: that no copy of a by-law of the county of Prince Edward had been delivered to him, nor had any such copy been delivered to the said acting collectors, or to either of them, as he believed, and if any such copy had been delivered to either of them he would have known it: that John S. Clute, of Picton, had charge at one time of some ware-houses in said town, and was allowed to take out spirits and receive pay for the same, but he did not otherwise act for the collector of inland revenue and prior to the 13th of September, 1875, he was relieved from that duty, and the department of inland revenue at Ottawa, on the 16th of September last confirmed the action of the acting collec-tor in relieving him, and since that date he had not acted, nor been authorized to act by or on behalf of the acting collector of inland revenue.

The affidavit of Robert Boyle, town clerk of the town of Picton, was filed against the rule. It stated :

That a true copy of the by-law passed on the 29th of June, 1875, was, on the 15th of September, 1875, delivered by the deponent, certified by him as town clerk, to one John S. Clute, of the town of Picton, who was then acting for the collector of inland revenue, in the county of Prince Edward ; and on the same day the deponent delivered a copy of the said by-law certified as aforesaid to one Herman Spafford, of Picton, who was then issuer of licenses for the said county : that at the time of the delivery of the copy of by-law to John S. Clute, he informed the deponent that he was at that time acting for the collector of inland revenue in the county of Prince Edward.

In this term, November 25, 1876, *Beaty*, Q.C., shewed cause. The Temperance Act of 1864, section 6, requires that every by-law passed under it "shall be communicated by delivery of a copy thereof, certified by the clerk or secretary-trea-

surer, to the collector of inland revenue, within whose
official district the municipality affected thereby is situate,"
and section 8 provides that "As regards the prohibition of
issue of licenses, every such by-law shall come into force
from the day of the communication thereof to the collector
of inland revenue." The inspectors of licenses have no
duties to perform under the 37 Vic. ch. 32 sec. 9, O., and the
39 Vic. ch. 26 sec. 27, O., in municipalities in which the Temperance Act of 1864, is in force. The only question then is
whether the Temperance Act of 1864 is in force in the town
of Picton, where the applicant's tavern-stand and property
are situated. It is said it is not in force because it was not
communicated to the collector of inland revenue, but to a
person who was not at the time acting for the collector,
but was then suspended from his duties, and such suspension was on the 16th of September confirmed by the head
department at Ottawa, and since then he has not acted nor
has he been authorized to act for the collector : and it is
also stated of him that he had charge at one time of some
warehouses in Picton, and was allowed to take out spirits
and receive pay for the same, but he did not otherwise act
for the collector of inland revenue. But what is said of
Clute by the town clerk is, that he was then acting for the
collector of inland revenue, and that Clute said when he
was so served with the copy of the by-law that he was then
acting for the collector of inland revenue. If the temperance by-law be not in force, then the applicant has not
shewn that he is entitled to be licensed under the by-law
before then in force in the town of Picton, passed on the
2nd of February, 1875, because that limits the persons to
whom licenses are to be granted to " natural born or naturalized subjects of Her Majesty, and who are of sober life
and conversation," while John Henderson speaks of the
applicant only "as a respectable man and well worthy of
having a tavern license." The duties which were to be
performed by the collector of inland revenue under the Act
of 1864, sections 6, 8, 9, 10, sub-section 2, are now, by
the 37 Vic. ch. 32 secs. 5, 6, 7, 8, transferred to and to be

performed by the issuer of licenses, and it is not shewn that he had not a copy of the by-law delivered to him. But the statute does not require he shall be served with a copy of the by-law, and so the by-law the moment it passed came into operation at once.

Ferguson, Q. C., *Diamond* with him, supported the rule. The Court of Common Pleas did not decide, when the application to quash the by-law was before it, that the by-law was in operation, but only that it was validly passed. The applicant is not here impeaching that decision. What he says here is that, admitting the by-law to have been rightly passed, it has not yet been called into legal and actual operation, because some formalities subsequent to its passing have not been observed, which the statute says shall be taken before it shall exclude any one from claiming to have a tavern license. By the Temperance Act of 1864, secs. 6, 8, 9, a copy of the by-law must be duly delivered to the collector of inland revenue by the clerk of the municipality, before it has any operation whatever upon tavern licenses. And the applicant says this has not been done, and that the applicant has been prejudiced by the collector of inland revenue refusing to grant him his license when he is fully qualified in all respects to have it.

Mr. Hamilton in his affidavit shews he has been deputy-collector of inland revenue at Belleville for several years past : that there has been no collector there for about a year before May, 1876, but that Mr. Stratton acted as collector till December, 1875, and that Mr. Holton has acted as such from that time, and that Mr. Clute was never more than in charge of some warehouses at Picton, to deliver out spirits from them and receive payment for the same, but that he did nothing more than that; and that he was suspended from such duties before the 13th of September, and his suspension was confirmed on the 16th of the same month at headquarters : so that he was never properly a person representing the collector of inland revenue, and if he was, that service upon him during his suspension, which suspension has never been removed, was a valid service. It will not be presumed that the applicant is an alien. All that is wanted here is that the inspector of licenses should inspect the applicant's premises and report according to the statutes, so as to entitle him, if he be found to be duly qualified, to apply for his tavern license.

January 2, 1877.   WILSON, J.—The duty of the collector of inland revenue under the Temperance Act of 1864, when the copy of the by-law has been delivered to him, so far as it is material in this case to consider it, is to issue no license within the limits of the municipality to which the by-law extends, and to issue any license when one has to be issued.

By the 37 Vic. ch. 32 sec. 6, O., the Lieutenant-Governor appoints the issuers of licenses, who supersede therefore the collector of inland revenue under the former Act.

It is not provided that they should have a copy of the by-laws of the different municipalities which relate to the sale or prohibit the sale of spirituous liquors, served upon them, although by the later Act, 39 Vic. ch. 26 sec. 8, O. these inspectors are to be appointed by the Lieutenant-Governor in council "for each city, county, union of counties, electoral riding or division," as he may think fit, and such inspector shall also be the issuer of licenses.

The inspector of licenses is to report, under the 37 Vic. ch. 32 sec. 13, O., and also under the 39 Vic. ch. 26 sec. 9, O., and the report is to enable the board of license commissioners under the last named Act, to exercise their own discretion on such application.

By the 27th section of the same Act, sub-section 3, the board of license commissioners and the inspector appointed under it, are to exercise the powers and duties for the enforcement of the provisions of the Temperance Act of 1864, within the limits of any municipality in which any by-law under the Temperance Act is in force.

These new enactments shew that it was not necessary to deliver a copy of the by-law of the 29th June, 1875, to the collector of inland revenue.

If it had been necessary to do so it is very probable I

should have thought the copy of it was well delivered by giving it to Mr. Clute, who was the only inland revenue officer, so far as has been shewn to us, who was within the limits of the county of Prince Edward, and who had the special charge of several warehouses in which spirits were stored, with power to deliver out the same and receive payment of the duties thereon.

As to the objection that the applicant had not shewn he was a naturalized or natural born subject of Her Majesty, according to the terms of the by-law of February, 1875, I could have given no effect to it, because the applicant shews he was a duly licensed hotel-keeper up to the 1st of May, 1876, and because no exception of any kind was made to the applicant for a license, but the single one that the Temperance Act of 1864 was in force, and the officer had not the power to act.

If it be of any value, it appears the town clerk did, on the 15th of September, 1875, deliver a copy of the by-law to the issuer of licenses for the county, which, although unnecessary, was as near a compliance with the statute as could be made in such a case, when the collector of inland revenue had nothing more to do with the matter.

The grounds of the motion fail, and the rule must be discharged, with costs.

HARRISON, C. J., and MORRISON, J., concurred.

Rule discharged.

HALDAN. V. BEATTY.

Will and probate set aside—Rights of executor.

The plaintiff, as executor of one W., having paid money to defendant, as a legatee under the will, and the will with the probate having been afterwards set aside by a decree of the Court of Chancery, the plaintiff was held entitled to recover back the money.

THIS action was brought by order of the Court of Chancery in two suits of *Wilson* v. *Wilson* and *Duffy* v. *Shea,* bearing date the 29th of April, 1875, and of the report of the Master of the said Court, made in pursuance thereof, and bearing date the 30th of June, 1875.

The plaintiff declared for money payable to him as administrator by the defendant, and for money received by the defendant to the use of the plaintiff as administrator, and for interest and for money due on an account stated.

Pleas: never indebted, and payment. Issue.

The cause was tried at the Fall Assizes, 1876, at Toronto before Galt, J., without a jury.

The defendant was called by the plaintiff, and admitted that she had received all the sums of money which she had stated in her examination in this cause. She said: "I received these moneys from Charles Beatty, as executor to Thomas Wilson's will, as portion of a legacy left me by my son, Thomas Wilson. I have not paid back that money. I have used it."

A number of exhibits were then filed; and after hearing counsel, the learned Judge entered a verdict for the defendant.

It appeared that probate had been granted to Charles Beatty and two other executors in 1873, but that the will had been set aside and vacated by a decree of the Court of Chancery, dated the 5th of April, 1875, and that this was an action to recover the moneys which had been paid to the defendant as a legatee under the will.

The plaintiff had leave to move to enter a verdict for him for $1,015.67, with interest from the dates of the different payments, if the Court should think fit.

In Michaelmas term, Nov. 22, 1876, *Donovan* obtained a rule calling on the defendant to shew cause why the verdict

should not be set aside and a verdict entered for the plaintiff for $1,015.67, with interest thereon from the respective
dates of payment, upon the grounds that the said verdict
is contrary to law and evidence, and should been entered
for the plaintiff; and because the defendant admitted at the
trial that the amount in question had been received and
retained by her, and is still due by her to the plaintiff as
administrator of the estate of the late Thomas Wilson; and
on the further ground that no debt or claim was or is due
from the estate of the late Thomas Wilson to the defendant
to justify the payment to the defendant, or the retention
by her of the amount in question in this action.

November 29, 1876. *O'Donohoe* shewed cause. The
decree of the Vice-Chancellor "that the paper writing,
dated the 5th of July, 1873, purporting to be the last
will and testament of Thomas Wilson, does not constitute, and is not the will of the said testator, and the
same, together with the probate thereof, ought to be
delivered up to be cancelled, and doth order and decree
the same accordingly," was made without jurisdiction, as
the application should have been made to the Court of
Probate. The probate cannot be revoked but by the
Court of Probate; and if it should be revoked, the payments made under it still remain valid, and cannot be
recalled or disputed. It is an absolute protection for and to
everything which has been done under it before revocation.
He referred to *Meluish* v. *Milton,* L. R. 3 Ch. D. 27;
Allen v. *McPherson,* 1 H. L. 191; *Barlow* v. *Browne,* 16
M. & W. 126; *Skyring* v. *Greenwood,* 4 B. & C. 281; *Lub-
bock* v. *Tribe,* 3 M. & W. 607; *Spencer* v. *Parry,* 3 A. & E.
331; *Simms* v. *Denison,* 28 U. C. R. 323; *Baron* v. *Husband,* 4 B. & Ad. 611.

Donovan supported the rule. The payments made to
the defendant cannot be supported. They were pretended
to be made under a will, but that paper which was called
a will is no will. It is a piece of useless paper. And the
Court of Chancery has so declared it. The money paid to

the defendant under it must be money had and received by her to the use of the person who is legally entitled, now that the pretended will is out of the way. And that person is the plaintiff, who is the administrator of Thomas Wilson, to whose estate the money in question belongs. It is of no consequence whether the probate has been revoked or not—but as a fact the decree shews it has been revoked—because these payments were not made by virtue of the probate, but under the authority of the supposed will. The Court of Chancery has the power to avoid and vacate both the will and the probate : *Tichborne* v. *Tichborne*, L. R. 2 P & D 41 ; *Perrin* v. *Perrin*, 19 Grant 259. *Williams* on Executors, 7th ed., 272.

January 2, 1877. WILSON, J.—By the Consol. Stat. U. C. ch. 16, the revocation of probate and letters of administration, and all matters arising out of or connected with the same, are to be exercised in the Surrogate Court, and the Court has full power, jurisdiction, and authority to revoke the same : sections 8' 9.

Any cause or proceeding in the Surrogate Courts in which any contention arises as to the grant of probate or administration, or in which any disputed question may be raised as to law or facts relating to matters and causes testamentary, shall be removable by any party to such cause or proceeding into the Court of Chancery, by order of a Judge of the same Court, to be obtained on a summary application supported by affidavit, of which reasonable notice shall be given to the other parties concerned : section 28.

- "Matters and causes testamentary," shall comprehend all matters relating to the grant and revocation of probate of wills or letters of administration : section 86.

And any cause or proceeding so removed, the Court of Chancery shall have full power to determine, and it may cause any question of fact arising therein to be tried by a jury, and may otherwise deal with the same as with any cause or claim originally entered in the said Court and the final order and decree made by the said Court in any cause or proceeding so removed shall, for the guidance of the Surrogate Court, be transmitted by the Surrogate clerk to the registrar of the Surrogate Court, from which suit or proceeding was removed: section 30.

On the removal of such cause or proceeding the Judge making the order of removal may impose such terms as to payment or security for costs or otherwise as he may see fit, but no cause or proceeding shall be so removed unless it be of such a nature and of such importance as to render it proper that the same should be withdrawn from the jurisdiction of the Surrogate Court and disposed of by the Court of Chancery, nor unless the personal estate of the deceased exceeds $2,000 in value : Section 29.

By Consol. Stat. U. C. ch. 12 sec. 28, the Court of Chancery has jurisdiction to try the validity of last wills and testaments, whether the same respect real or personal estate, and to pronounce such wills and testaments to be void for fraud and undue influence, or otherwise, in the same manner and to the same extent as the Court has jurisdiction to try the validity of deeds and other instruments.

It is useless to refer to any other law when our own statute law is so full and precise on the subject.

Firstly, the Court of Chancery has power to try the validity of wills and testaments, and to pronounce them void in the same manner and to the same extent as the Court has jurisdiction to try the validity of deeds and other instruments.

And, secondly, in any cause or proceeding relating to matters and causes testamentary, on their removal into that Court, it has full power to determine and deal with the same as in or with any cause or claim originally entered in that Court.

And I think we must assume the cause was of that nature that it could be removed into that Court, and that it was duly removed there, and that everything was transacted in due form.

The Court had then, plainly, the power to revoke the
will, and if necessary the probate also, if it required a
special revocation. A probate without a will could have
no validity. And it seems proper the Court, which has
the power to revoke the will, should have the power to
revoke the probate dependent upon it.

What we have to enquire into then is, the effect which
the revocation of the will has in this case.

While the probate is in force payments made under
it to the executor are protected at common law, as we
had occasion to decide upon settled authority, in the case
of *Irwin* v *Bank of Montreal*, 38 U. C. R. 375, and
the Consol. Stat. U. C. ch. 16, sec. 59, affirms the same
doctrine. That section declares that in case any probate or
administration be revoked, all payments *bond fide* made to
any executor, or administrator, under such probate or
administration before the revocation, shall be a legal discharge to the person making the same. And the executor
or administrator who has acted under any such revoked
probate or administration, may retain and reimburse himself
in respect of any payments made by him, *which the person
to whom probate or administration may be afterwards
granted might have lawfully made.* This certainly does
not protect the defendant. She claimed to be entitled to
a legacy under the will. That will has been vacated. There
is no authority then for her to retain the money she got.
She should, as events have turned out, never have got it.
It belongs to the estate of the deceased. The provision of
the statute just referred to is taken from the Imperial
Wills Act.

This action is not brought against the executor, or person who acted as executor, who paid the defendant the
money in question, but against the defendant who actually
got it. If it had been brought against the executor he
would, I presume, have been obliged to make good the
amount, because the failure of the will is in derogation of
his rights, as executor, — he never properly filled that
character : *Williams* on Executors, 7th ed., 556 *et seq.*

The defendant then contends that she is entitled to retain the money because she received it in good faith, and has spent it. That would be a good answer if the plaintiff, or the person he represents, had been in any degree culpable, in which case it would be against good conscience that one who by the carelessness or misconduct of another had received money as his own from that other, and who had spent it, believing it was his own, should afterwards, although guilty of no fault, be called upon by the one who was in default to refund money which had been honestly received and honestly spent, to redeem the carelessness or misconduct of the one who had paid it, and who had led the receiver to believe he had the right to spend it.

It may be this decision is premature, while the contestation as to the validity of the will is still under consideration. If the will shall be authoritatively held to be valid the payment will be good. If it stand as it does at present by decree of the Court annulled, the money must be repaid.

The rule will be absolute to enter a verdict for plaintiff for $1,015.67, with interest.

HARRISON, C. J., and MORRISON, J., concurred.

Rule absolute.

GREER ET UX. V. JOHNSTON.

Bond—8 & 9 Wm. III. c. 11.—Assessment of damages—Execution for penalty.

The plaintiffs sued on a bond in $1,000 penalty, conditioned to convey land, alleging non-performance. A verdict was rendered at the trial for $1,000, and 20 cents for detention, no damages being assessed on the breach; and execution was afterwards issued endorsed to levy the $1,000 and costs taxed. *Held*, the bond being within the statute of 8 & 9 Wm. III. ch. 11, and the plaintiff having paid the 20 cents and costs, that execution must be stayed, for that the penalty could not be levied.

In Easter Term, June 5, 1874, *Harrison*, Q.C., obtained a rule *nisi* in this cause, calling on the plaintiff to shew cause, 1, why the writ of execution issued in the cause should not be set aside or amended, so as to prevent the levy upon the defendant's goods, &c., of the sum of $1,000, the alleged debt; 2, why the levy endorsed on the writ should not be reduced by the sum of $1,000; 3, why all further proceedings should not.be stayed, and a stay of execution entered of record, and the defendant's goods, &c., discharged from the said writ, &c.; or why such other rule or order should not be made as to the Court might seem meet, on the ground that the bond sued on in this action was one within the meaning of the 8 & 9 Wm. III., ch. 11, sec. 8, and execution ought not to have issued for the penalty of the said bond, and the defendant having paid the damages and costs ought not to be subject to a levy of the penalty; and on grounds disclosed in affidavits filed.

It appeared from the papers filed, that this action was brought on a bond, set out in the declaration, in the penal sum of $1,000, subject to a condition that if the defendant should convey and assure to the plaintiff certain lands mentioned in a deed recited in the bond, 2½ acres more or less, as soon as the land could be surveyed, &c., by a good and sufficient deed, &c., then the bond should be void. Breach: non-performance by the defendant. And the plaintiff claimed the debt of $1,000, and $1,000 for the detention thereof.

The defendant pleaded several pleas, upon which issue was taken. The pleadings are fully reported in 32 U. C. R. 77.

The case came down for trial before Gwynne, J., and a jury, and a verdict was rendered in favour of the plaintiff for $1,000 debt, and 20 cents damages for detention.

Upon this finding judgment was entered, and upon the roll was entered the *postea*, viz., finding all the issues in favour of the plaintiffs; and following it, was entered as follows: "And they, the jury, assess the damages of the plaintiff, on occasion of the detention of the within debt, over and above his costs of suit, at 20 cents."

Then followed the entry of judgment. "Therefore it is considered that the plaintiffs do recover against the defendant the said debt of $1,000, and the moneys by the jurors aforesaid, in form aforesaid assessed, and also $277.86 for their costs of suit by the Court here adjudged to the plaintiffs, which said debt, damages, and costs, in the whole amount to $1,278.06."

Upon this judgment a *fi. fa.* issued, following the judgment, and which writ was endorsed to levy the sum of $1,000, being the debt, and $38.06, being the balance of the damages and costs taxed, and $5 for the writ.

It appeared also, from the affidavits filed, that all the costs and the one shilling damages were paid by the defendant to the plaintiff's attorney and sheriff.

During this term, November 25, 1876. *M. C. Cameron*, Q. C., shewed cause, and contended that the judgment was properly entered, and it was on the defendant to shew that he was entitled to the equitable relief he sought.

Osler supported the rule, and referred to this case when before the Court, in 32 U. C. R. 77; *Gainsford* v. *Griffiths*, 1 *Wms.* Saund. 67, 78; *Roberts* v. *Mariett*, 2 *Wms.* Saund. 541; 2 *Chitty's* Arch. Prac., 12th ed., 1008, 1010, 1012; *Darby* v. *Wilkins*, 2 Str. 957,

December 29, 1876, MORRISON, J.—When this case was previously before the Court, *vide* 32 U. C. R. 77, it was then decided that the bond was within the statute of William. On occasion the Court intimated that it would not determine what course the plaintiff ought to take to relieve herself from the difficulty she was in, arising from the way in which she had taken a verdict. No step appears to have been taken by the plaintiff to relieve herself from the difficulty. It is quite clear from the authorities that the plaintiff ought to have assessed her damages on the breach assigned in the declaration, and that under the statute of William she is not entitled to endorse her execution for the amount of the penalty, but only for such damages as may be assessed upon the breaches assigned. The provisions of the statute must be complied with. The penalty in the bond only determines by the consent of the parties the limit to which such damages may be assessed: *Gainsford* v. *Griffith*, 1 *Wms.* Saund, 67.

Now, in this case, the error of the plaintiff was in not assessing damages on the breach assigned in the declaration, only taking a verdict for the amount of the penalty or debt, and one shilling for the detention.

The entry of the judgment, and the execution issued thereon, may be so far good; but the plaintiff was not authorized to endorse her *fi. fa.* to levy the amount of the penalty. That she cannot do, it being a bond within the statute of William; and as the plaintiff did not assess damages under the statute, as said by Sir John Robinson, C. J., in *Brock District Council* v. *Bowen et al.*, 7 U. C. R. at page 476: "No doubt this is a bond within the statute 8 & 9 Wm. III. ch. 11, and that the plaintiffs therefore cannot have final judgment and execution to recover the penalty, but must prove breaches and have damages assessed before the issue on *non est factum* can be of any use to them. The Court would interfere on motion to restrain execution for the penalty."

That is the only course we can follow here; and as it appears that the defendant paid all the costs of the action and judgment, &c., I think the rule should be made absolute for staying all further proceedings under the *fi. fa.,*

and that the defendant's goods, &c., be discharged from
such writ.

HARRISON, C. J., and WILSON, J., concurred.

Rule absolute.

G. HOWDEN V. ANN DONNELLY AND ALEXANDER DONNELLY.

Trespass to land after notice—Right to costs—Suggestion—C. L. P. Act,
sec. 325.

The plaintiff, in an action for trespass to land, in which the pleas were
    only not guilty and leave and license, recovered one shilling damages,
    and the Judge refused to certify for costs. The plaintiff then applied
    for leave to enter a suggestion on the record that the trespasses were
    committed after notice, and for an order, on such entry, that the
    master should tax full costs.
Held, that sec. 325 of the C. L. P. Act not being repealed by the 31 Vic.
    ch. 24, O., the plaintiff was entitled under it to enter the suggestion;
    but that the proviso to that section—not to be found in the correspond-
    ing Imperial enactment, 3 & 4 Vic. ch. 24, sec. 3—would prevent him
    from recovering more than Division Court costs, without a certificate.

TRESPASS.

The declaration alleged that the defendants broke and
entered certain land of the plaintiff, being park lot No. 7
in lot 14, in the 11th concession of the township of Monaghan, in the county of Peterborough, and depastured the
same with cattle.

Pleas, not guilty; and leave and license.

The issues were tried before Patterson, J., at the last
Assizes for Peterborough, without a jury.

The plaintiff and defendant Ann Donnelly were owners
of adjoining lots,—the plaintiff owning park lot 7, and the
defendant Ann Donnelly, park lot 8 in lot 14, in the 11th
concession of Monaghan. There is an allowance for road in
front of each lot, and lying between each lot and the river
Otonabee. Each spring the rise of the water in the river
removed a portion of the fence between the two lots. Last

spring, after the removal of the fence, as defendant had not
rails enough to replace the fence along the line between the
two lots she got permission from the plaintiff so to place
the fence as to reach the river in a shorter course than
along the line, but encroaching upon the lot of the plaintiff.
On the 14th of August following the plaintiff caused a letter to be addressed to the defendant Ann Donnelly, request-
ing her to remove the fence, and informing her that unless it
was at once removed he would bring an action of ejectment
against her.   Defendant, after receiving the letter, asked
for a little time so as to have the line run accurately
between the two lots, and the fence placed on the line ; but
the plaintiff made no reply.   The plaintiff caused the writ
to be issued in the present action on the 24th of August
last. The defendant afterwards removed the fence, and, as
the plaintiff had not sustained any actual damage, the
learned Judge entered a verdict for the plaintiff for one
shilling damages, and refused to certify for costs.

During this term, November 23, 1876, *J. K. Kerr*, Q. C.,
obtained a rule calling on the defendants to shew cause why
the plaintiff should not have leave to enter a suggestion
upon the record, that the trespasses in respect of which the
plaintiff recovered a verdict in this cause were committed
by the defendants upon the plaintiff's premises in respect
to which notice not to trespass had been previously served
upon the defendants on behalf of the plaintiff; and why,
upon such suggestion being entered, the Master should not
be ordered to tax to the plaintiff full costs of suit.

December 6, 1876. *Hector Cameron*, Q. C., shewed
cause.   The plaintiff was not entitled to a verdict, as the
declaration is for a single trespass, and that was met by the
plea of leave and license : *Marrs* v. *Davidson*, 26 U. C R.
641, 651.   The Consol. Stat. U. C. ch. 22, sec. 325, which
leaves untouched the right of a plaintiff to costs for a trespass after written notice, is virtually repealed by 31 Vic.
ch. 24, O.; and the case is not within that section if still in
force.: *Wise* v. *Hewson*, 1 P. R. 232 ; *Har.* C. L. P. A., 2nd
ed., 431.

. *J. K. Kerr*, Q. C., contra. No new assignment was necessary : *Weaver* v. *Hendricks*, 37 U. C. R. 1· Sec. 325 of
the C. L. P. Act is still in force : *Orok* v. *Garvin*, 5 P. R.
169. It is the same as sec. 3 of 3 & 4 Vic. ch. 24, Imp.,
and the construction of the latter has been settled in favour
of the application here made : *Bowyer* v. *Cook*, 4 C. B. 236,
4 D. & L. 816.

December 29, 1876. HARRISON, C. J.—If we had a discretion to refuse to any extent to make absolute this rule,
we should exercise the discretion and refuse to do so ; but
on the authorities cited we are of opinion that we have no
such discretion.

It may be that Mr. Cameron is right in urging that without a new assignment, as the declaration complains of only
one trepass and not several trespasses, the particular trespass is answered by the plea of leave and license, and the
defendants entitled to a verdict. See *Barnes* v. *Hunt*, 11
East 451; *Hayward* v. *Grant*, 1 C. & P. 448 ; *Kavanagh*
v. *Gudge*, 7 M. & G. 316, 322 ; *Bracegirdle* v. *Peacock*, 8
Q. B. 174 ; *Adams* v. *Andrews*, 15 Q. B. 284, 292 ; *Marrs*
v. *Davidson*, 26 U. C. R. 641, 651. But without deciding
whether he is right or wrong, the objection is one to the
verdict and not cause to the rule, after the time for moving
against the verdict has been allowed to pass without a
motion against it.

All that we have now before us is an action for trespass
to land, and a recovery of one shilling damages, after
written notice not to trespass.

The plaintiff insists that in such a case he has a right
to enter a suggestion that the trespass was after notice, and
if that suggestion be true or found true, that he is entitled
to costs without a certificate.

If we are at liberty to refer to the evidence and consider
the propriety of the verdict at all, we find it decided that
the continuance of a fence or other obstruction on the land
of another, after a written notice to remove it, is a new
trespass : *Holmes* v. *Wilson*, 10 A. & E. 503 ; and is clearly.

so for the purposes of such a suggestion as now asked :
Bowyer v. *Cook*, 4 C. B. 236, 246.

A plaintiff, unless deprived of costs by some disentitling
statute, is, where he recovers any damages, no matter how
small, also entitled to costs.

If there were no statutes in force but the statute of
Gloucester, a plaintiff in an action of this kind would be
entitled to costs, whether he gave or did not give a notice
in writing not to trespass.

The C. L. P. Act, sec. 324, provided that if the plaintiff in trespass or case recovered less damages than $8, the
plaintiff should not be entitled in respect of such verdict
to any costs whatever, unless the Judge immediately afterwards certified that the action was really brought to try a
right, besides the right to recover damages, &c.

Then sec. 325 of the same Act provided that "Nothing
in the last section contained shall deprive the plaintiff of
costs in any action brought for a trespass over any land,
waste, close, wood, plantation, or enclosure, or for entering
into any dwelling, out-building or premises in respect to
which notice not to trespass had been previously served
by or on behalf of the owner or occupant of the land tres-
passed over, or upon, or left at the last reputed or known
place of abode of the defendant in such action ; [but nothing
in this or in the last preceding section shall entitle any
plaintiff to recover costs as of an action brought in a superior Court, in any case where by law his action might
properly have been brought in an inferior Court."]

The 31 Vic. ch. 24, O., repealed sec. 324 of the C. L. P.
Act, and provided a substituted section for it, but left sec.
325 untouched.

The substituted section for sec. 324 provides that, "If
the plaintiff, in any action of trespass or trespass on the
case, recovers by the verdict of a jury less damages than
eight dollars, such plaintiff shall not be entitled to recover
in respect of such verdict any costs whatever, whether the
verdict be given on an issue tried, or judgment has passed
by default, unless the Judge or presiding officer, before

whom such verdict is obtained, immediately afterwards, or at any future time to which he may postpone the consideration of the matter, certifies on the back of the record in the form hereinafter prescribed, to entitle the plaintiff to full costs; and in case such certificate be not granted, then the defendant in such action shall be entitled to set off his costs against such verdict and recover judgment and issue execution against the plaintiff for the balance of such costs as between attorney and client, unless the said Judge or presiding officer shall certify as hereinafter provided, upon the record, in manner aforesaid, that the defendant is not entitled to recover his costs in the cause against the plaintiff."

What we have now to consider is, the effect of the omission of the Legislature, intentional or unintentional, to repeal sec. 325, and the interpretation to be placed on the latter section.

The effect of its non-repeal is, without doubt to leave it, as it were, a proviso to the new enactment, which is a substitute for the repealed enactment.

Its interpretation must be the same as that of sec. 3 of the Imp. Stat. 3 & 4 Vic. ch. 24, from which, with the exception of the words at the end in brackets, it has been taken.

It was at first considered doubtful whether, on the construction of sec. 3 of 3 & 4 Vic. ch. 24, the plaintiff should be entitled, whenever a notice in writing not to trespass had been given, to costs without any certificate, although the amount of costs should be less than 40s., or whether it meant that it was imperative on the Judge to certify where a written notice had been given.

While Lord Wensleydale was of the latter opinion: *Sherwin* v. *Swindall*, 12 M. & W. 783; see also *Daw* v. *Hole,* 15 L. J. Q. B. 32; it is now decided that the former is the true construction: *Bowyer* v. *Cook*, 4 D. & L. 816.

The latter case is singularly applicable here.

The plaintiff sued defendant in trespass for placing stumps and stakes on the plaintiff's land. The defendant paid into Court 40s., which the plaintiff took out in satisfaction of that trespass. The plaintiff afterwards gave the defendant notice that unless he removed the stumps and stakes a further action would be brought against him. Held, that the leaving of the stumps and stakes on the land was a new trespass, and that the plaintiff was entitled to costs in an action for their continuance after notice, though he recovered less than 40s., and the Judge refused to certify.

But, in dealing with this application, we must not overlook the words of section 325, which I have placed in brackets, and which are not to be found in the Imp. Stat. 3 & 4 Vic. ch. 24.

These are, "Nothing in this or in the last preceding section contained shall *entitle* any plaintiff to recover costs as of an action brought in the superior Court in any case where by law his action might properly have been brought in an inferior Court."

The effect of these words upon the whole clause is to deprive the plaintiff of full costs, unless he has a certificate for full costs, where the action might properly have been brought in an inferior Court.

There was nothing to prevent the plaintiff, where the only pleas are not guilty and leave and license, from suing in a Division Court.

If the facts be as proposed to be suggested by the plaintiff, he is, in our opinion, entitled to costs, but these as to amount must be Division Court costs and nothing more.

The plaintiff may, if he see fit, after this intimation of opinion, enter a suggestion upon the record to the effect that the trespass, in respect of which the plaintiff has recovered his verdict in this cause, was committed by the defendant upon the plaintiff's premises in respect to which notice not to trespass had been previously served upon the defendant on behalf of the plaintiff.

To this extent we are obliged to make absolute the plaintiff's rule. The remainder of the rule must be discharged.

We cannot, as asked in the remainder of the rule, order

.the Master on the entry of such a suggestion to tax full costs, for at least two reasons:—

1. The suggestion is as to a matter of fact, and may be traversed by defendant, and if traversed may be tried in the ordinary manner : *Watson* v.*Quilter*, 11 M. & W. 760.

2. Even if the plaintiff should ultimately succeed, the only direction we could give the Master, if called upon to give him any, would be to tax only Division Court costs to the plaintiff.

As the rule is in part absolute, and in part discharged, there will be no costs to either party of the present application.

MORRISON, J., and WILSON, J., concurred.

Rule accordingly.

KERR ET AL. V. WILLIAM SLADE STRIPP, ROSAMOND STRIPP, AND T. H. STRIPP.

Married woman—Liability of—35 Vic. c. 16, O.

A married woman in August, 1874, gave a promissory note with her husband, to the plaintiffs, for money due by him, which they accepted on the representation, which was true, that she had separate estate, the only consideration being their forbearance of the husband's debt. *Held*, that she was liable, under 35 Vic. ch. 16, O.

THIS was an action brought by the plaintiffs as payees against the defendants as makers of two promissory notes; the one for $850, dated September 20, 1875, payable at six months, with interest at eight per cent. from date ; the other for $550 of the same date, also payable at six months, with interest at eight per cent. from date.

The defendants William Slade Stripp and T. H. Stripp allowed judgment to go by default.

The defendant Rosamond Stripp pleaded to the first count—1. *Non fecit.* 2. Notes not duly stamped.

And to the second count—1. *Non fecit.* 2. Plaintiffs not the holders. And to the whole declaration, coverture.

The plaintiffs joined issue on all the pleas, and specially replied to the plea of coverture :

1. That the defendant Rosamond Stripp was married after the passing of the Married Woman's Property Act of 1872 ; and after the passing of the Act and while the said Act was in force, one William Slade Stripp, for certain money, then the separate property of the defendant Rosamond Stripp, paid by her to the said William Slade Stripp, conveyed to the defendant Rosamond Stripp certain lands particularly described : that the said real estate was, not affected by the trust of any settlement ; whereby and by force of the statute the said real estate, and the rents. and issues, and profits thereof, were at the time of the making of the contract, and still are held and enjoyed by the said defendant for her separate use, &c. [And that the said notes in the declaration mentioned are the separate contracts of the defendant, and were made by her respecting her said separate real estate, and while the same, and the rents, issues, and profits thereof were held and enjoyed by the defendant.]

2. A similar replication as to other lands described, which were alleged to have been acquired by the defendant by deed, for a valuable consideration, executed by one Nancy Lee.

The words in brackets in the replication were added at the trial.

The plaintiffs took issue on the replications.

The plaintiffs, in order to expedite the proceedings in the cause, elected to try the issues at the Sitting of the County Court of the County of Wentworth, held on 30th June, 1876, before Sinclair, Co. J.

It was agreed between the parties that the evidence taken in a case of *Glasco* v. *Stripp* should be considered as taken in this case, the facts as to the giving and acceptance of the notes being the same, and counsel for the defendant Rosamond Stripp, admitting that the defendant R. S. at the time of the making of the notes held as separate estate the lands mentioned in the replications.

It was also agreed that the learned Judge should enter a a verdict for defendant, Rosamond Stripp, with leave to the plaintiffs to move to enter a verdict for plaintiffs for $1,482.64.

The date of the marriage was admitted to be August, 1874.

It was in *Glasco* v. *Stripp* proved that defendant Rosamond Stripp made the notes : that at the time of the making she had separate property, consisting of real and personal estate, more than sufficient to meet the amount of the notes: that her husband, the co-defendant W. S. S., before and at the time the notes were made was indebted to the plaintiffs : that the plaintiffs apparently were pressing the husband for payment : that the plaintiffs, on the representation and faith of the defendant Rosamond Stripp's separate estate accepted the note ; and that the consideration for the making of the notes, so far as the defendant R. S. was concerned, was the forbearance of the husband's debt, and that there was apparently no other consideration.

During Trinity term last, August 29, 1876, *E. Martin*, Q. C., obtained a rule calling on the defendant R. S. to shew cause why the verdict should not be set aside, and a verdict entered for the plaintiffs, pursuant to leave reserved at the trial.

During this term, November 28, 1876. *McMahon*, Q.C., shewed cause. There was no separate contract or separate debt on the part of the wife for which she could under the Act be held responsible, for it was her debt jointly with her husband, and so not her separate debt, and not being for the benefit of her separate estate, is not within the statute : *Darling* v. *Rice*, 1 Appeal R. 43 ; *McCready* v. *Higgins*, 24 C. P. 337.; *Story's* Eq. Jur., 10th ed., sec. 1401 ; *Willard* v. *Eastham*, 15 Gray 328 ; *Field* v. *McArthur*, 25 C. P. 167. And that being so the plaintiffs failed as to all the defendants: *Chandler* v. *Parkes*, 3 Esp. 76 ; *Jeffray* v. *Frebain*, 5 Esp. 47 ; *Boyle* v. *Webster*, 17 Q. B. 950.

E. Martin, Q. C., supported the rule. The notes were accepted by the plaintiffs from the defendant R. S. on the faith of her separate estate. In order to bind the estate of the married woman it is not necessary to shew that she received any pecuniary benefit: *Lewin* on Trusts, 6th ed., 626 ; *McHenry* v. *Davies*, L. R. 10 Eq. 88; *Wagner* v. *Jefferson*, 37 U. C. R. 551; *Commercial Bank* v. *Merritt*, 21 U. C. R. 358; *Darling* v. *Rice*, 1 Appeal R. 43 ; *London Chartered Bank of Australia* v. *Lempriere*, L. R. 4 P. C. 572 ; *Johnson* v. *Gallagher*, 3 DeG. F. & J. 494; *Boustead* v. *Whitmore*, 22 Grant 222 ; *Adams* v. *Loomis*, 22 Grant 99.

December 29, 1876, HARRISON, C. J.—This case must be decided upon the interpretation to be applied to 35 Vic. ch. 16, O.

The most recent and the most authoritative exposition of the meaning of that statute is to be found in *Darling et al.* v. *Rice*, 1 Appeal R. 43, on an appeal from the decision of the Judge of the County Court of the county of Wentworth. The plaintiffs declared upon a promissory note dated 14th May, 1875, for $250, made by the defendant, a married woman, payable three months after date to the order of P. S. Rice, and by him endorsed to the plaintiffs. The third plea was to the effect that at the time of the making of the note the defendant was the wife of Thomas Rice. The replication was, that the note was, and is, the separate engagement and contract of the defendant. Issue was joined on this replication. A nonsuit was moved on the ground that there was no evidence that the note was given or made in respect of the wife's separate estate. The learned Judge on this objection reserved leave to enter a nonsuit, and subsequently made a rule *nisi* absolute to enter a nonsuit.

The appeal was from this decision. The contention was, that by the words at the end of section 9 of 35 Vic. ch. 17, to the effect that any married woman " may be sued or proceeded against separately from her husband in respect of any of her separate debts, engagements, contracts, or torts, as if she were unmarried," the plaintiff was entitled to judgment without any proof of separate estate.

But the Court of Appeal were of a different opinion, and dismissed the appeal with costs.

Draper, C. J., in delivering his judgment said, p. 46: "The effect of the concluding portion of the 9th section I take to be, that a married woman may be sued separately from her husband, as if she were unmarried, for her separate debts, contracts, and engagements, in a suit at law, as if she were sole, whereas before she was only liable in equity, and in respect to a tort could only have been sued jointly with her husband. It is the procedure which is altered,—the principle on which her liability rests is unaffected."

In a subsequent part of the same judgment the learned Chief Justice said : "I think that to maintain any such suit as the present against a married woman, she must first of all make a contract or engagement, or incur a debt ; next, that the liability to enforce which she is sued or proceeded against must either have arisen in respect of some employment or business in which she was engaged in her own behalf ; or, thirdly, that she was possessed of separate estate."

This is in effect the conclusion reached by the majority of the Court in *Wagner* v. *Jefferson*, 37 U. C. R. 551.,

The head note of that case as reported is not quite accurate. The words "in reference to her separate estate" should be added at the end of it in order to express the conclusions at which I arrived, and in which Mr. Justice Morrison agreed. Mr. Justice Wilson arrived at the same result as we did, but on the ground that the debt sued for was not shewn to be "the separate debt" of the defendant,

There is no pretence that the promissory note sued for here was given in respect of any employment or business of the defendant, and the right, if any, of the plaintiffs to recover must rest on the ground that it is a contract made by the defendant R. S. in reference to her separate estate which, before the Act, could be enforced in a Court of equity.

The arguments against the recovery are,

1. That the debt being the joint debt of the husband, wife, and another, cannot be deemed the separate debt of the wife.

2. That the debt, not being for the benefit of the wife or of her separate estate, is not within the operation of the statute.

These were the only grounds on which the claim of the plaintiffs was resisted before us.

There is nothing in the Act which expressly declares that the wife can only be sued, whether possessed of separate property or not, in respect of her separate engagements. This is an inference which some draw from the reading of the concluding words of section nine. But these words are not "separate debts, separate engagements, separate contracts," &c., but "the separate debts, engagements, contracts," &c. It is not at all clear that the word "separate" controls the words "engagements" and "contracts," as well as the word "debts." If not, there is nothing to exclude an engagement with another as surety or otherwise. What the correct reading may be, it is not here necessary to determine if the words be read as affecting procedure only, and not liability or responsibility.

Following, as we are bound to follow, the decision of *Darling* v. *Rice*, 1 Appeal R. 43, we must hold that the words affect procedure only. This being so, we must follow, as we have already followed, *Merrick* v. *Sherwood*, 22 C. P. 467, and other cases decided by the Court of Common Pleas, holding that where a bill will lie in equity to charge the separate estate of a married woman, her husband there being a necessary party, an action will lie in a Court of law, in respect of her contract, without joining her husband. If the Court of Common Pleas erred in so holding, we must leave it to the Court of Appeal to reverse the error.

Then would the fact that the wife received no direct benefit from the making of the note sued on be a good answer to a bill in equity by the plaintiff seeking to charge her separate estate ? The question thus raised was adverted to by Chief Justice Draper, in *Darling et al.* v. *Rice*, 1 Appeal 43, but in no manner decided.

It is now the settled law of England that a married woman, possessed of a separate estate, has as much power as regards that estate to contract as a *feme sole*, and that she may bind her separate estate for general engagements in no manner in words referring to the separate estate. See *Vaughan* v. *Vanderstegen*, 2 Drew. 165, 182 ; *Mathewman's Case*, L. R. 3 Eq. 781 ; *Butler* v. *Cumpston*, L. R. 7 Eq. 16.

In *Johnson* v. *Gallagher*, 3 DeG. F. & J. 494, a leading case on the subject, it was said by Lord Justice Turner that the separate estates of married women are bound by their debts, obligations, and engagements contracted with reference to and upon the faith or credit of those estates, and that whether they were so contracted is to be judged of by all the circumstances of the case; and although this expression of opinion did not receive the entire approval of Lord Romilly in *Shattock* v. *Shattock*, L. R. 2 Eq. 182, 190, Lord Justice James, in *The London Chartered Bank of Australia* v. *Lempriere*, L. R. 4 P. C. 572, approved of the language of Lord Justice Turner, and dissented from the qualification of it attempted by Lord Romilly.

Now, if a married woman having separate estate has as much power to contract in reference to it as a *feme sole*, what is there to prevent her becoming surety for her husband or for any other person to the extent of her separate estate ?

In *Lewin* on Trusts, 6th ed., p. 626, it is said : " If a *feme covert* execute a bond, even to her husband, or join in a bond with another, even with her husband * * her separate estate, if anticipation be not restrained, is liable." The cases referred to in support of the proposition as to jorning with her husband are *Stanford* v. *Marshall*, 2 Atk. 68 ; *Hulme* v. *Tenant*, 1 Brown C. C. 20, White & Tudor L. C. 679 ; *Heatley* v. *Thomas*, 15 Ves. 596.

In *Stanford* v. *Marshall*, two married women joined their husbands in bonds for money, and it was ordered that the rents and profits of their separate estates should be paid over to creditors in liquidation of the debts.

In *Hulme* v. *Tenant*, the husband borrowed of the plaintiff £50, for which he gave as security a bond executed by
himself and his wife. The following year, having occasion
for a further sum, the husband applied to the plaintiff for
£130, which was advanced, and a new bond for £180 given
by the husband and wife for the amount, and a reference
was ordered to take an account of the rents and profits,
and that the plaintiffs' bond should be paid thereout.

In *Heatley* v. *Thomas*, the married woman executed a
bond to the plaintiff as security for a person who afterwards
became bankrupt, and after her death a bill was filed against
her executors and those of her husband, praying that her
separate estate should be made liable for the payment of
the principal and interest due on the bond to the plaintiff,
and the Court held that it was a valid charge on the estate.

The decisions in England appear to be uniform.

Reference was made in the argument to *Willard* v.
Eastham, 15 Gray 328, a United States decision, as having a
contrary bearing. To this decision may be added *Burns*
v. *Lynde*, 6 Allen 305, 313; *Rogers* v. *Ward*, 8 Allen 387;
Athol Machine Co. v. *Fuller*, 107 Mass. 437; *Heburn* v.
Warner, 112 Mass. 271, S. C., 17 Am. 86; *Goodall* v. *Mc-
Adam et ux.*, 14 How. Pr. 385; *North American Coal Co.*
v. *Dyett*, 7 Paige 9, S. C., in Appeal, 20 Wend. 570, and
the leading case of *Yale* v. *Dederer*, 18 N. Y. 265, 276.

If the decisions in England, on any point raised for
decision before us, are uniform, we should not feel disposed
to weaken their effect because of the contrary decisions of
a foreign country, even if uniform in that country. But
while the decisions in England are uniform in one direction,
the decisions of the United States Courts cannot, on the
point in controversy here, be said to be uniform in the
opposite direction.

In *Yale* v. *Dederer*, 18 N. Y. 265, 278, 281, 282, the
leading case against the English decisions, it was conceded
by Mr. Justice Harris, that in England the decisions have
gone the length of holding that where a married woman
unites with her husband in giving a note to pay his debt,

it shall, without any other evidence of her intention, be charged upon her separate estate; but in New York State he said the decisions had never yet gone so far on the point as the English decisions. It is to be observed that the decision of the Court was not unanimous; Justices Denio and Roosevelt dissented, and Mr. Justice Strong took no part in the judgment.

The case afterwards came before the Court of Appeal in 22 N. Y. 450, where the Court affirmed it, on the ground that, in order to charge separate estate, the intention to do so must be declared in the very contract which is the foundation of the charge. See further *Heburn* v. *Warner*, 17 Am. 86.

This ruling, although in accordance with the decisions of Massachusetts, is plainly contrary to the English decisions: *Mathewman's Case*, L. R. 3 Eq. 781; *Butler* v. *Cumpston*, L. R. 7 Eq. 16.

In the *Corn Exchange Ins. Co.* v. *Babcock,* 1 Am. 601, where all the principal English and American cases will be found reviewed, it was held that where a married woman, possessed of separate estate, endorsed notes as surety for her husband, which endorsement in terms purported to charge her estate. it did charge the separate estate, although the separate estate was not benefited by the endorsement of the notes.

In delivering judgment the Court said, at p. 604: "When a married woman assumes to act in reference to her separate estate, the question is not whether her action is really for her own benefit. The right to act and bind her estate carries with it the right to act unwisely, and to her own injury, if she so wills."

In *Deering* v. *Boyle*, 12 Am. 480, the most recent United States decision bearing on the point which we have seen, the New York State decisions were criticized with some severity, and the English decisions preferred, the Court holding that where a married woman gave a promissory note in payment of her husband's debts, without in terms making it a charge upon her separate estate, that a recovery could be had against her on the note, and her separate estate applied in payment.

It would therefore appear that the weight of authority, English as well as foreign, entirely preponderates in favour of holding the defendant in this case liable.

And this is the conclusion at which I have arrived. This conclusion is not at all opposed to the decision of the Court of Common Pleas, in *McCready at al.* v. *Higgins,* 24 C. P. 233. All the Court decided in that case was, that the real estate of a woman married before 1859, and not settled by any marriage settlement or deed, is not her separate estate.

It may be said that the effect of our Act of 1859, Consol. Stat. U. C. ch. 73 was, as it were, to create a marriage settlement for women married without a settlement, so as to protect their weakness against their husband's power, and their property against the husband's control. This is perfectly true. But the Legislature by the Act of 1872, 35 Vic. ch. 16 O., having given to married women power to contract under certain conditions stated in the Act, the power to contract within these conditions is just as absolute as the power of any man. Men are not relieved from their contracts of suretyship because of no direct benefit to themselves. Women having separate estate have, in this respect, as much power to contract as men in reference to the separate estate. While the Legislature has seen fit to confer the power, it is not for the Courts to limit the responsibilities arising from its exercise. The old-fashioned notion that women need legislative protection even against their husbands is fast fading in the light of so-called advanced modern legislation. It is not for the Courts to question the wisdom of this legislation. It is rather for the Courts to interpret the laws, leaving to the Legislature the right to move, forwards or backwards as the exigencies of society appear to them to demand.

We think the rule must be made absolute to enter a ver–

dict for the plaintiffs for $1,482.64, pursuant to leave reserved.

MORRISON, J., and WILSON, J., concurred.

Rule absolute (a).

ANNIE M. HUTCHINSON ET AL. V. BEATTY.

Free grant territory—Sale of timber by locatee—31 Vic. c. 8, 37 Vic. c. 23, O.

Land within the free grant territory was located on the 12th of August, 1870. On the 2nd of April, 1872, the locatee sold to the defendant all the pine and other timber thereon, stipulating that ten years should be allowed for taking it off, and the defendant paid the purchase money in full. The patents for the lands issued in 1876, and the defendant afterwards cut timber, for which the patentees brought trespass.
Held, that under 31 Vic. ch. 8, and the order in council of 4th October, 1871, confirmed by 37 Vic. ch. 23, O., the locatee had a right to make the sale : that no limitation as to the time within which the timber should be removed could be implied from these statutes; and that the plaintiff therefore could not recover.

THE declaration contained counts in trespass *quare clasum fregit,* trespass to goods, and trover for conversion of goods.

There were the usual traverses.

A special plea, unnecessary to be mentioned, was added at the trial.

The issues were tried at the last assizes for the county of Simcoe, before Hagarty, C. J. C. P., without a jury.

The plaintiffs put in the letters patent for the land in question, to Ellen, Albert, Hubert, Alexander, and Eva Hutchinson, heirs and heiresses of Richard Hutchinson, deceased, and proved the cutting of standing timber by the defendant after the issue of the letters patent. These patents were dated 13th January and 15th March, 1876. The land was granted to the patentees subject to the rights of Annie M. Hutchinson, widow of Richard Hutchinson,

---

(a) See *Kerr* v. *Stripp,* 24 Grant 298.

deceased, under section 11 of the Free Grant and Homestead Act of 1868.

The lands were situate in the township of Ferguson,
within the free grant territory of Ontario, and were located
on the 12th of August, 1870, by Richard Hutchinson.

The defendant put in and proved an agreement under
seal, dated 2nd April, 1872, whereby Richard Hutchinson
sold to the defendant "all the pine, oak, birch, spruce,
hemlock, tamarac, and other merchantable timber growing
or being on the lands," described in the letters patent, for
the sum of $300—$150 cash, and the remainder on time.

The agreement stipulated that "ten years should be
allowed from the date hereof for taking off said timber."

A copy of the order of the Lieutenant-Governor in
council, dated 4th October, 1871, which is recited and confirmed in statute 37 Vic. ch. 23, O., was also put in and
proved.   It was as follows :—

The committee of council have had under consideration the report of
the Honourable the Commissioner of Crown Lands in connection with
timber on unlicensed lands in townships open for sale and location under
" The Free Grants and Homestead Act of 1868," in the Districts of Mus-
koka and Parry Sound, and dated the 26th September, 1871.   The Commissioner under the circumstances set forth in his said report, recommends
that he be authorized to have lists prepared of all lands remaining unsold
and unlocated on the 1st October, instant, in the said townships, and to
offer the same for sale as timber limits or berths, not to exceed 20 square
miles in area, on such a day and place as he may deem advisable.

The rate to be made under the following conditions : 1. Each limit at
its estimated area to the party bidding the highest amount of bonus.   The
bonus and first season's ground rent at the rate of $2 per square mile, to be
paid immediately after the limit is adjudged in each case, by depositing
the amount to the credit of the Crown Lands department in the Bank of
Montreal, and delivering to the officer conducting the sale, the usual bank
draft and certificate of deposit ; 2. License to issue to the successful com-
petitor within one month from the day of sale ; 3. All white and red
pine timber or saw logs cut upon the said limits, to be subject to the following special rate of timber dues :—

White and red pine timber per cubic foot................ $0 02½
White and red pine saw logs per standard of 200 feet
    board measure, Scribner's rule 0 30

All other timber, logs, &c., per tariff fixed by the Crown timber
regulations ; 4. So much of the Crown timber regulations as may in any
manner conflict with this order, to be and are hereby suspended for the
purposes of this sale ; but such regulations to apply in all other respects to
the licenses to be issued, and to be in full force, except when inconsistent
herewith.

The commissioner also recommends that he be authorized to give public notice that the department of Crown Lands will recognize the right of
all purchasers or locatees of free grant lands, who shall have so purchased

or located any lot in the said townships, on or before the 30th September, 1871, and who shall, on that day, have been in the actual occupation of and resident on the lots located, to sell or dispose of all pine trees standing or being on the lots located or purchased and occupied by them, subject to the payment of the above duties, which the department will collect on all timber and saw logs found to have been cut upon any sold or located lot. The committee recommend that the said recommendation be carried out.

NOTE—The rate on saw logs purchased from settlers entitled to sell, reduced to 15cts. per standard by O. C., 22nd November, 1871.

The whole of the purchase money was paid before any of the timber was cut. The only contest at the trial was, as to the cutting of the pine timber.

The learned Chief Justice found the value of the pine timber cut, after the issue of the patent, to be $150.

It was contended that the locatee, under the order in council as confirmed by the statute, had the right to sell the standing timber to the defendant, and that it thereupon became and was the timber of the defendant, notwithstanding the subsequent issue of the letters patent.

The learned Chief Justice found against the defendant, and rendered a verdict for the plaintiff for $150.

During this term, November 21, 1876, *Rose,* for defendant, obtained a rule *nisi* calling on the plaintiffs to shew cause why the verdict should not be set aside, and a verdict entered for the defendant, on the ground that the verdict was against law and evidence.

During the same term, November 29, 1876, *McCarthy,* Q. C., shewed cause. By the express language of the Act of Parliament " trees remaining on the land at the time the patent issues shall pass to the patentee ": 31 Vic. ch. 8, sec. 10, O. No alienation could be effectual without the wife being a party to it: *Ib.,* sec. 13 ; and there was no estoppel in such a case: *Morse* v. *Faulkner,* 1 Anstr. p. 11 ; *Doe d. Irvine* v. *Webster,* 2 U. C. R. 24 ; *Boulter* v. *Hamilton,* 15 C. P. 125 , *Rawle* on Covenants, 4th ed., 399, 436, 443 ; *Jones* v. *Kearney,* 1 Dr. & W. 134, 159 ; *Davis* v. *Tollemache,* 2 Jur. N. S. 564 ; 2 *Dart* V. & P., 5th ed., 810.

Rose, contra. The sale was good notwithstanding the issue of the letters patent, and this, at all events, on prin-

18—VOL. XL U.C.R.

ciples of estoppel : *Boulter* v. *Hamilton*, 15 C. P. 125, 130 ; *Burns* v. *Burns*, 21 Grant 7 ; *Brown* v. *Cockburn*, 37 U. C. R. 592.

December 29, 1873, HARRISON, C. J.—This case may be decided independently of any question of estoppel.

The purchase of the standing timber by the plaintiff was after the passing of the order in council of 4th October, 1871, and before the passing of the statute 37 Vic. ch. 23, O.

The purchase was made of a person who before 30th September, 1871, and who was on that day in the actual occupation of the land on which the timber was growing in the free grant territory.

Such a person had, by the terms of the order in council, power to sell or dispose of all pine trees standing or being on the lots located, and by the statute, " a valid and sufficient authority," to sell or dispose of any pine trees standing or being upon the lands located, subject to the payment of the duties imposed by the order : Section 1.

This person did *before* the issue of the letters patent exercise the power conferred on him and sold the standing timber for a valuable consideration, receiving at the time one-half of the purchase money.

The effect in an ordinary case of vendor and vendee would be, to vest the property in the thing sold in the vendee.

If this were not held to be the effect in the present case, the children and widow of the deceased vendor would be enabled to commit a fraud on the purchaser.

There is nothing in the Free Grant Act of 1868, or in the amending Act of 1873, which provides within what time standing timber sold shall be removed, or that in default of removal within a given time the property in the timber shall be forfeited.

Is is argued that some such limitation must be implied from the concluding part of section 10 of the Act of 1868, which declares that " all trees remaining on the land at the time the patent issues shall pass to the patentee," taken in connection with section 13 of the same Act, which declares that " No alienation, (otherwise than by devise,) and no mortgage or pledge of such land, or of any right or interest therein, by the locatee *after* the issue of the patent, and within twenty years from the date of such location, and during the lifetime of the wife of such locatee, shall be valid or of any effect, unless the same be by deed in which she shall be one of the grantors with her husband," &c.

We must read the Acts of 1868 and 1873 together, and if possible give to each such a construction as not to neutralize the other, and to neither, in the absence of positive language, such a construction as would justify the perpetration of fraud or injustice of any kind.

The defendant is not claiming under any alienation made after the issue of the patent, so that the requirements of section 13 of the Act of 1868 are out of the question.

Then what is the effect of the words, " All trees remaining on the land at the time the patent issues shall pass to the patentee," as used in section 10 of that Act.

These words were used by the Legislature before the passing of the order in council authorizing the locatee to sell pine timber, and before the Act confirming the order in council.

These words ought not therefore to be read as restraining any sale subsequently authorized.

Their obvious purpose as used in the Act of 1868 was, to declare that, whereas before the issue of the letters patent pine timber had been reserved by the Crown, there should, after the patent issued, be no further reservation of the kind ; in other words, that then there being no further need of the reservation, the timber should pass with the land to the patentee.

It never could have been designed by the Legislature that after an authorized sale of the timber by the locatee, who afterwards becomes patentee, the timber should pass to the patentee or his representatives notwithstanding the sale.

The main object of the Act of 1868 was to secure the

bonâ fide settlement of the lands in the free grant territory.

When the Act was passed, the Legislature were apprehensive that persons would locate free grant lands for the mere purpose of stripping them of the pine timber, if any, on them, and afterwards, having stripped the lands of such timber, would abandon them without settlement.

In order, if possible, to avoid this consequence, there was a general reservation of all the pine trees growing or being on the land.

The only exceptions in the Act of 1868 were, when the timber was cut and used for the necessary purpose of building, fencing, and fuel on the land located, and the cutting of trees necessary to be removed in the actual clearing of the land for the purpose of cultivation: Sec. 10.

But, notwithstanding, persons made purchases of timber from the locatees, which was, until the issue of the letters patent, the property of the Crown.

For the purpose of protecting such purchasers, and of enabling all who had located before 30th September, 1871, to sell growing timber, the order in council was passed.

Upon the faith of this order in council various persons purchased from the locatees, for valuable consideration, growing timber coming within the terms of the order.

The right of the Crown to pass such an order was doubted by the Court of Chancery in *Hughson* v. *Cook,* 20 Grant, 238.

The Legislature thereupon enacted the 37 Vic. ch. 23, O. the object of which was to remove all doubt as to the legality of the order in council.

It is plain that it was the intention of the Legislature, when passing the Act of 1873, as far as possible to protect those who, on the faith of the order in council, had paid money for standing timber growing on free grant territory.

The defendant is one of that class, and must, therefore, if possible, be protected.

The effect of the last Act is, to qualify the provisions of the first statute to the extent to which it is necessary to give full effect to the last Act. *Leges posteriores priores contrarias abrogant.*

We think, for the honour of the Crown and of the Legislature, we must read the latter part of section 10 of the Act of 1868 as follows:—" All trees remaining on the land at the time the patent issues (*and not previously lawfully sold or disposed of by the locatee*), shall pass to the patentee."

This is not legislation on our part; it is simply using words to express more clearly what the Legislature has, we think, already in effect expressed. See *O'Connor* v. *The Township of Otonabee et al.*, 35 U. C. R. 73.

It is impossible for us, in the absence of express legislation on the point, to decide that standing timber sold on free grant lands shall be removed in one, two, three, or any other given number of years. The Legislature, and the Legislature alone, has, we apprehend, the power to do so.

The Legislature so far has authorized the sale by the locatee, but made no provision as to time for the removal of the timber.

The rule should be made absolute to enter a verdict for the defendant.

MORRISON, J., and WILSON, J., concurred.

Rule absolute.

WATSON v. CHARLTON.

Order to hold to bail—Sufficiency of affidavits—Rule nisi.

In order to support an order to hold defendant to bail, the plaintiff need not disclose in his affidavit the names of the persons on whose information he founds his belief that defendant is about to leave the province, where he files also other affidavit, stating facts which would justify such belief; in that case, it is the same as if the plaintiff had stated that these deponents had informed him of the facts stated in their affidavits.

A rule *nisi* to set aside the order for such alleged insufficiency in the plaintiff's affidavit must point out the objection specifically.

G. H. Watson, obtained, during this term, November 21, 1876, a rule *nisi* calling on the plaintiff to shew cause why an order of the Judge of the County Court of the county of Peterborough, to hold the plaintiff to bail, and the writ of *capias* issued thereon, should not be rescinded and set aside, and the bond to the sheriff ordered to be delivered up to be cancelled, &c., on the ground that there was no sufficient evidence, or statement on oath, of the intention of the defendant to leave the Province adduced to the Judge of the County Court, to warrant the order; and why the plaintiff should not pay the costs of the application.

The rule was drawn up on reading the copies of the affidavits of the plaintiff and two others, produced to the learned County Court Judge, of his order for the arrrest, and the writ of *capias*.

The affidavit of the plaintiff set out that he had recovered a verdict against the defendant on the 9th day of October last, for $500, for seduction of his daughter : that the defendant was making away with his personal property, and had mortgaged his real estate to the value thereof, and was about to remove to the United States, as he was informed and believed : that it was currently rumoured in the village of Lakefield, where the defendant resided, that he was about to quit the Province for the United States : that he had reason to believe, and did verily believe, that unless the defendant was forthwith apprehended he was about to leave, with the intent to defraud him, the plaintiff, of the amount of his verdict; and that he was apprehensive that unless an order for a writ of *capias*, &c., was made, the defendant would forthwith leave the Province with the intent to defraud him of the amount of the verdict, &c.

The plaintiff's attorney made an affidavit, sworn on the 26th October, in which he stated that some days before he searched the registry office, and found that the defendant had given a mortgage, dated the 3rd of October, on his lands in Lakefield, to one Steele for $500; and on the 17th October, after the verdict referred to, he gave another mortgage to Sherin for $251.

One William Watson made an affidavit, in which he stated that he had reason to believe, and did verily believe, that the defendant was immediately about to quit this Province to go to reside in the United States, with intent to defraud his creditors of the amount of their just claims against him : and that the grounds for his belief were, that since the trial of the cause the defendant had been making away with his personal property and disposing of the same to various persons in and near the village of Lakefield : that the defendant did leave the said village about a week before then for the United States, as he was informed and believed, and that he had returned to the village to remove his family and dispose of the remaining portion of his property with the intent to defraud his creditors, and that he had reason to believe, and did believe, that unless the defendant was forthwith apprehended he would quit this Province and go to the United States with the intent to defraud his creditors.

Upon these affidavits the Judge of the County Court made the order for the arrest of the defendant.

In reply to these affidavits, the defendant filed no affidavit.

During the same term, November 29, 1876, *H. Cameron,* Q. C., shewed cause.

There was sufficient material before the Judge below :

Damer v. *Busby*, 5 P. R. 356. The application here is too large; it should not seek to set aside the *capias*. The statute does not require the names of the informants to be stated. He cited *Brown* v. *Riddell*, 13 C. P. 457; *Jones* v. *Gress*, 25 U. C. R. 574; *Molloy* v. *Shaw*, 5 P. R. 250; *Bowers* v. *Flower*, 3 P. R. 62; *Allman* v. *Kensel*, 3 P. R. 110.

Watson, contra, relied on the grounds taken in the rule, and cited *Gibbons* v. *Spalding*, 11 M. & W. 173; *Graham* v. *Sandrinelli*, 16 M. & W. 191.

December 29, 1876. MORRISON, J.—The principal objection pressed by the defendant's counsel is, that the plaintiff's affidavit does not disclose the name or names of the person or persons from whom he received the information upon which he founded his belief that the defendant was about to quit the Province; and we were referred to *Gibbons* v. *Spalding*, 11 M. & W. 173, and the judgment of Parke, B., in that case, and also to the case of *Graham et. al* v. *Sandrinelli*, 16 M. & W. 191.

In those cases it does not appear that there were any other affidavits filed but those of the plaintiffs, and if that were so here I should think the defendant's contention was right; but in the case before us two other affidavits were filed, one by the plaintiff's attorney, shewing that the defendant a short time before the plaintiff obtained his verdict, and again immediately after, had mortgaged his property. Another person swears that he had reason to believe, and verily believed, that the defendant was immediately about to quit the Province with intent to defraud his creditors, and he states the grounds for such belief.

As said by Richards, C. J., in *Brown* v. *Riddell*, 13 C. P. 457, 460: "If the deponents in those affidavits had informed him (the plaintiff) of the facts there stated, and the plaintiff had stated that he got such information from them, the persons from whom he got the information being mentioned, the evil complained of here would not exist."

The Judge here had these affidavits, with the affidavit of the plaintiff, before him at the time he granted the order, and as said by the learned Chief Justice in the case quoted, it seems to me he was justified in giving as much force to them as if the plaintiff had stated that he had been informed by those deponents of the circumstances stated in their affidavits.

On the whole, I think that the Judge had such facts and circumstances before him as satisfied him there was reasonable and probable cause for believing that the defendant was about to leave the Province.

The defendant files no affidavit contradicting or explaining the facts stated in the plaintiff's affidavit, but rests on his strict rights; and in that respect it was objected that the rule *nisi* did not point to or shew the ground now taken as to the insufficiency of the plaintiff's affidavit.

The only ground stated in the rule is, that there was no sufficient evidence or statement on oath of the intention of the defendant to leave the Province, adduced to the Judge, to warrant the order. I think there was quite sufficient, and the plaintiff has good reason to complain that the rule did not point out the ground now taken, viz., that the plaintiff's affidavit did not disclose the information upon which he grounded his belief; and upon this objection alone I think the plaintiff was entitled to have the rule discharged.

The rule will be discharged, and with costs.

HARRISON, C. J., and WILSON, J., concurred.

Rule discharged.

FISKEN AND GORDON V. MEEHAN.

Promissory note—Accommodation maker and indorser—Relation of suretyship—Consideration.

Action on a note for $1500, dated 25th July, 1872, made ·by defendant payable to the order of S., and alleged to have been endorsed by S. to the plaintiffs.

It appeared that one M., on the 17th January, 1872, had given his bond to the assignee in insolvency of, S., conditioned if S. should fail to pay forty-three cents in the $ by the 10th July, to pay to the assignee $500, or so much as should be required to make up the deficiency. S. got the defendant to make this note for his accommodation, and got F. to endorse it afterwards, in order to give it to M. as security against his bond, which he did. M. having been sued on this bond, compelled F. to pay him the amount of the note, and F. and his partner then sued defendant as maker.

The learned Chief Justice of the Common Pleas, who tried the case without a jury, found that defendant, when he signed the note, understood from S. that F., one of the plaintiffs, would endorse as co-surety, and that defendant would be liable only for half the amount; but that F. knew nothing of this, but endorsed in the ordinary way, considering that defendant would be liable to him for the whole. ·

Held, WILSON, J., dissenting, that the relationship of co-sureties between · F. and defendant was not established, so as to prevent the plaintiffs from recovering from defendant more than half the amount of the note.

Per WILSON, J.—F. and defendant each knew that the other was a surety for S., and that being so, there was the relation of suretyship between them for the common debtor.

Ianson v. *Paxton,* 23 C. P. 439, and its effect as a judgment of our Court of Appeal, commented upon.

Held, also, that M. held the note on a good consideration as between himself and the other parties thereto.

ACTION on a promissory note dated 25th July, 1872, made by defendant, payable to the order of James B. Sorley, for $500, at three months, and endorsed by Sorley to plaintiffs.

Pleas : 1. That defendant did not make the note.

2· That plaintiffs were not the lawful holders.

3. That defendant made the note for the accommodation of the plaintiffs, and there never was any value or consideration for the making or payment of the note by the defendant.

4. That defendant made the note for the accommodation of Sorley, and there never was any value or consideration for the making or payment of the note by the defendant,

and the same was endorsed to the plaintiffs, who always held the same without any value or consideration.

5. That the defendant was induced to make the note by the fraud of Sorley, and the same was endorsed to the plaintiff John Fisken who is, and at the time of the endorsement was, a co-partner in business with the other plaintiff, Thomas Gordon, and who always held the note without any value or consideration; and the said Fisken endorsed the note to one James Metcalf, and the said note was overdue when the same was endorsed to the plaintiffs.

6. Defence on equitable grounds, as to the moiety of the amount of the note: that prior to the making of the note it was agreed between the defendant Sorley and the said Fisken that the defendant and Fisken should become co-sureties with Sorley to the said James Metcalf to the amount mentioned in the note, and there was no consideration to the defendant for the making of the note but the note was given and endorsed solely for the purpose of carrying out the said agreement, and the plaintiffs received the note without consideration except as aforesaid.

Issue.

The cause was tried at the last Spring Assizes, at Toronto, before Hagarty, C. J., without a jury.

For the plaintiffs, *James Sorley* was called : He proved the making of the note by the defendant and his own endorsement of it. He added : I got Fisken to endorse it afterwards to give it to Metcalf as security. I got the note for my accommodation. I endorsed it to Fisken, and gave it to Metcalf, who became security for an obligation of mine which he had ultimately to pay. He was sued and judgment was given against him. He did become surety about the time the note was drawn, and was compelled to pay the debt. After Metcalf had agreed to become surety for me, he declined to become such surety. I asked why. He shewed me two anonymous letters, which made him say he would not do it. I told him I thought I could get Meehan to make a note and Fisken to endorse it as sureties to him. He then agreed to become surety. I was insolvent.

Hoskins purchased the estate. He gave a letter of indemnity to Metcalf and others, stating that if he could
get from the assets such sum as he thought sufficient for
payment of his risk and trouble, he would not claim
anything over that. I think the letter was given before
Meehan's note. I told Meehan that Metcalf had agreed to
take the note in security, adding that I should probably
be able to get Fisken to endorse it, which would make
it good security for Metcalf. I had seen Fisken before
that, and he said if Metcalf would not take Meehan alone,
he, Fisken, would endorse. I did not tell Meehan that
Fisken would be responsible for half the note, nor that if
all came to all Meehan would be liable for half the note,
and Fisken for the other half. I never said anything to
Meehan of a joint liability with Fisken. I never dreamt
of such a thing. Meehan did not say he would be liable
for only half the note. It was not a stipulation of Meehan's
that Fisken should be on the note. After Fisken endorsed
he gave me the note, and I took it to Metcalf. I and
Meehan and Fisken knew it would be given to Metcalf.

John Fisken said : There was no agreement between me
and Meehan to be co-sureties. I simply endorsed the note,
knowing he was liable before me. I knew his circumstances, and that he was good. I don't think I would have
signed as co-surety.

For the defence. *Terence Meehan*, defendant, said: Sorley
asked me if I would not back a note, saying Fisken would
be on it. He said if I had to pay it would be the half,
Fisken would have to pay the other half, but he would see
I was only to have to pay the half. It was on thsse terms
I signed the note.

Cross-examination: I do not know the difference between
backing a note and signing it. Sorly had been surety for
me, and had got me money, signing for me, and I had done
so for him.

Two witnesses, *Midgley* and *Howe*, said they would not
believe Sorley on his oath.

Mr. *Fenton*, assignee of Sorley, said he would rather not
be pressed to state what his opinion of Sorley's character

for veracity was. He produced a bond given him by
Metcalf in January, 1872, for $500, which he said Metcalf
paid in full, and which was all the security he held from
Metcalf.

In reply, *Sorley* was called and said : The bonds given to
Mr. Hoskins for the estate were to be paid in six months.
The note was dated to correspond. This note, dated July,
was given in January. I know the note was not made in
July. It was signed at Meehan's house in winter.

For the defence, *Meehan* was re-called : This note was
brought to me in July—a hot day.

Mrs. *Meehan* said : I remember Sorley coming to my
house during the hot weather. Did not know what he
came for. After he went, my husband told me he had
signed a note for Sorley. I made a memorandum at the
time. This is the book, 1872, July 25th, "Sorley's note will
be due 26th October, 1872."

For the plaintiff, Mr. *Fisken*, re-called, said : I produce
our diary, " Thursday, 25th July, Meehan's note to J. B.
Sorley, endorsed by J. F., due this day, $500." This is in
the book-keeper's writing.

The learned Chief Justice, after referring in very strong
terms to the irregular manner in which the case had been
conducted, found as follows :—

" 1. That Meehan, when he signed the note, understood
from Sorley that Fisken would endorse as co-surety, and
that he, the defendant, would only be liable for half the
amount.

2. That Fisken knew nothing of this, but endorsed the
note in the ordinary way, considering the maker would be
liable to him for the whole.

3. That this note on the evidence seems to have been
given, not as Sorley says, in January, but some months
later, and after Metcalf had executed the bond. I cannot
therefore find it proved that Metcalf got this note as a
consideration for giving this bond.

4. I find that Fisken took up the note in good faith,
believing, and having good reason to believe, that Metcalf

was a *bonâ fide* holder for value, and paid the amount of his bond as bondsman for Sorley.

5. I find the $100 transaction is quite separate from this, and that the defendant is not entitled to credit for it.

Plaintiffs' claim being, the amount of their
    cheque to Metcalf $529 61
Interest 6 87

For this I find the verdict for plaintiffs...$536 48

At the end of the evidence the plaintiff asked to be recalled to prove that there had been a renewal. I refused this after the extraordinary evidence I had heard.

It was not pretended the defendant had ever signed but one note. I think the plaintiff paid it to Metcalf, thinking in good faith he was legally bound to do so."

In Easter term last, May 18, 1876, *Black* obtained a rule calling on the plaintiffs to shew cause why the verdict obtained should not be set aside and a nonsuit entered, or a verdict be entered for the defendant, on the ground that the verdict was contrary to law and evidence and the weight of evidence, in this, that the evidence shews that the promissory note in the pleadings mentioned was made by the defendant for the accommodation of one James B. Sorley, without value or consideration : that the note was afterwards endorsed to one James Metcalf without value or consideration, and that the same was overdue when it was endorsed to the plaintiffs ; or why the amount of the verdict should not be reduced, on the ground that the plaintiffs were co-sureties with the defendant on the said note to Metcalf.

In Trinity term last, September 7, 1876, *Ferguson*, Q. C., shewed cause. The plaintiffs have not shewn on the declaration any title to the note from Metcalf. Application was made at the trial to add such a count, and leave was given to do it if it were necessary. The same leave is asked now. The case of *Stein* v. *Yglesias*, 5 Tyr. 172, 1 Gale 98, shews how the title in such a case should be stated. Metcalf had

given a bond for Sorley, who was insolvent, to Mr. Hoskins,
who bought Sorley's estate, binding himself to pay $500 if
Sorley's estate did not pay 43 cents on the dollar ; four
others besides Metcalf gave bonds for Sorley of the like
nature.   After that bond was given Sorley got the note in
question made by the defendant and endorsed by himself
and Fisken, which he gave to Metcalf in security for the
bond which Metcalf had so given.   The note was given in
pursuance of the giving of the bond—in pursuance of a
precedent request by Metcalf when he gave the bond.
Metcalf got the note before it was due.   He had to pay the
bond, and he compelled Fisken to pay him the amount of
the note.   *Mathers* v. *Lynch*, 28 U. C. R. 354, 365 ; *Doty* v.
Wilson, 14 Johnson, 378; *Osborne* v. *Rogers*, 1 *Wms*. Saund.
356, 357, note *b*, shew there was a good consideration
for the making and endorsation of the note.   Meehan was
a surety for Sorley on the note, but he has no right to
claim contribution with the plaintiffs or with Fisken,
because the defendant and the plaintiffs or Fisken never
so agreed.   Fisken endorsed in the ordinary manner, looking to the parties before him as liable to him.   He never
shared his liability with Meehan.   He is entitled to recover
the full amount of the note.

   Hodgins, Q. C., supported the rule, *Black* with him.
Metcalf gave the bond as surety for Sorley months before
he got the note in question from Sorley for his indemnity,
and so the giving and endorsation of the note were without
consideration or value from Metcalf, and it is not said that
any other person ever gave value or consideration for it :
Crofts v. *Beale*, 11 C. B. 172; *Batson* v. *King*, 4 H. & N.
739 ; *Byles* on Bills, 12th ed., 256; 257.   The defendant
is not therefore liable on the note at all.   If he be liable
for anything it is only for one half of the amount of the
note, because he was a co-surety for Sorley with Fisken.
Sorley told the defendant that Fisken would endorse the
note.   And he also told Fisken that defendant would make
the note, and so Fisken and the defendant knew that each
of them was only a surety with the other of them for

Sorley, and each also that the other was becoming a party
to the note as an accommodation party for Sorley. It was
not necessary that the two should have agreed among
themselves what their respective liabilites were to be in
such a case, or that they were to stand towards each other
as co-sureties. They knew, too, that the note was not to be
discounted, but was to lie with Metcalf for his indemnity:
Ianson v. *Paxton*, in Appeal, 23 C. P. 439, 466; *Reynolds*
v. *Wheeler*, 7 Jur. N. S. 1290; *Craythorne* v. *Swinburne*,
14 Ves. 160; *Dering* v. *Earl of Winchelsea*, 1 Cox 318.
The case of *Mills* v. *The Guardians of the Poor of the
Alderbury Union*, 3 Ex. 590, shews. Fisken could sue
Metcalf for a return of the money paid by him under
the circumstances, as he was not liable to pay it. A
note for past consideration is not a valid note in the
hands of the original party, or in the hands of any one
who did not give value for it: *Lyon* v. *Holt*, 5 M. & W.
250; *Roscorla* v. *Thomas*, 3 Q. B. 234. It was said at
the trial that this was a renewal note, when the incon-
sistency of its date with the prior date of the bond was
shewn; but there was no evidence of it, and it is improbable that it was so, for it was never used in discount. They
referred to *Charles* v. *Marsden*, 1 Taunt. 224; *Sturtevant* v.
Ford, 4 M. & G. 101; *Parr* v. *Jewell*, 16 C. B. 684, as shewing what effect a note given for accommodation has when
not used till past due. The plaintiffs must not be
considered as strangers to the transaction, and as deriving
title from Metcalf. They are in the same position as
Fisken.

January 2, 1877. WILSON, J.—It is settled that if a person
take a promissory note from two joint makers, one of
whom he knows to be a surety for the other at the time he
takes the notes, he is bound in his dealings with the
principal debtor to regard the other as a surety, and if he
give time to the principal without the consent of the other
he will discharge the surety. And the payee of such a
note is bound to regard the actual rights of the respective

parties as principal and surety, although the payee did not agree to treat the one as a surety or otherwise than as the maker of the note. If he do not, an equitable plea setting up such facts will be a good defence : *Pooley* v. *Harradine*, 7 E. & B. 431 ; *Greenough* v. *McClelland*, 2 E. &. E. 424, in Ex. Ch. 429.

It would be a good legal plea if at the time the payee took such a note he agreed with the surety to treat him as a surety, and not only as an ordinary maker of the note: *Manley* v. *Boycot*, 2 E. & B. 46.

If the payee is bound to treat two joint makers as principal and surety if they are so in fact, and he merely knew it, without any agreement on his part so to treat them, the like rule must apply as regards all other or subsequent parties to the note. The third endorser must treat the first and second endorsers as sureties for the maker, if that be their actual position, and if he knew of that relation at the time he took the note or endorsation. So in like manner it must follow that if the second endorser knew at the time of the endorsation to him that the first endorser was only a surety for the maker, he must claim payment from the first endorser only as a surety for the maker, the common debtor, and not as an endorser in strict law—that is, he can claim contribution only, and not full payment.

That being so, I must say that *Ianson* v. *Paxton*, in Appeal, 23 C. P. 439, is directly opposed to the English authorities both at law and in equity, and they are the authorities which ultimately govern our highest Court of Appeal, the Privy Council.

The doubts of two of the Judges who concurred in the reversal of the judgment of the Court below, and the differences of opinion expressed by the other Judges, deprive it of much of its value as a final adjudication.

If I were to find a decision of the Privy Council Division expressly against the decision on a like point of our Court of Appeal, which am I to follow ? I presume that of the highest Appellate Court.

In this case I think, that Fisken and Meehan each knew the other was a surety for Sorley. That being so, there is the relation of suretyship between them for the common debtor. And it is of no consequence that Fisken endorsed in the ordinary way, thinking that Meehan would be liable in full to him, and that he did not agree to join in any suretyship. And so far is this rule carried, that a plea which averred that the payee of a note made by two joint makers had knowledge at the time he took the note of one being surety for the other, and that the note was delivered to the payee on the terms that the one maker should be liable only as surety, was held to be sufficiently proved, although the jury negatived that the payee agreed to treat one maker as a surety or otherwise than as a maker, and negatived also that the surety ever stipulated for such a limited liability : *Greenough* v. *McLelland,* 2 E. & E. 424, 429.

It is also decided that if the creditor did not know at the time he took the instrument that there was the relation of principal and surety between two persons liable to him, but becomes aware of it only after his cause of action has accrued, he must nevertheless deal with them after that as principal and surety : *Liquidators of Overend, Gurney & Co.* v. *Liquidators of Oriental Financial Corporation,* L. R. 7 H. L. 348, 360.

The only remaining question is, whether Metcalf, who certainly knew that Fisken and Meehan were only sureties for Sorley, held the note on a good consideration, so that he was entitled to enforce payment from Fisken and Meehan at law.

His obligation of suretyship for Sorley to the assignee of Sorley's insolvent estate had been incurred on the 17th of January, 1872, before the making or endorsation of the note. The note was given, therefore, not in consideration of Metcalf contracting a liability for and on behalf of Sorley, but was given to Metcalf merely because he had contracted such a liability in time past.

The bond he gave was for $500, conditioned that if Sorley

failed to pay the 43 cents on the dollar by the 10th of July, or should deficiencies arise from any cause after that, in the event of Sorley failing to pay when and so often as occasion might require, to the extent of 43 cents on the dollar, then Metcalf would pay to the assignee of the estate the sum of $500, or so much thereof as should be required to enable the assignee to pay that sum.

The note was not made till the 25th of July, or fifteen days after the bond had become due, and before Metcalf was relieved from his liability as such surety to the assignee for Sorley.

Here I may observe that the great confusion there was at the trial about the time the note was given—whether in January when the bond was given, and dated in July at or about the time the bond was to be paid, or whether it was made just at the time it bears date, and whether Metcalf refused to sign the bond till he got the note, or got it at the time of its date in July—may be cleared up, I think, in this way.

Metcalf signed the bond in January without regard to the notes, and Sorley said Metcalf at first agreed to do so, but afterwards would not do it till he got the note.

Now, what Sorley said Metcalf agreed to do I think he did do without asking any security from Sorley.

When the bond became due on the 10th of July, Metcalf probably wanted security then, and the note was given, which is dated the 25th of July.

That the note was made in July I have no doubt from the evidence, and from the finding also of the learned Chief Justice.

If the bond were due which Metcalf gave, and he had not been indemnified by Sorley, as he was not in my opinion, could he not, as an unpaid and unindemnified surety, call upon Sorly to indemnify him?

I suggested that to counsel during the argument, but it was not answered.

The case of *Wooldridge* v. *Norris*, L. R. 6 Eq. 410, shews that a surety, whose engagement is overdue, may file a bill in the nature of a *quia timet* for payment of the debt, and for his indemnity, although he has paid no part of the debt himself : *Antrobus* v. *Davidson*, 3 Meriv. 569, 578.

Now, if Metcalf could have filed a bill against Sorley for indemnity, he had the right to demand it, and to accept it when given by Sorley without suit.

The case of *Crofts* v. *Beale*, 11 C. B. 172, shews that a note made payable on demand, with interest, given by the maker to the payee, for a pre-existing debt due to the payee by a third person, is not a sufficient consideration to sustain the note, because, being payable *on demand*, there is no forbearance given to the principal debtor : *Balfour* v. *The Official Manager of the Sea Fire Life Ass. Co.*, 3 C. B. N. S. 300.

But here the note given is not payable for three months. That was evidence of a consideration to forbear proceeding against Sorley for that time to enforce indemnity.

In any way of putting the case—that is, whether we are to regard the debt assumed by Metcalf for Sorley as due before the note was given, and that the note was given by way of indemnity, Metcalf then having the right to claim indemnity from Sorley ; or are to regard the note as given for an extension of time or forbearance by Metcalf to claim indemnity, because it was given at the further day of three months—there was a good consideration for the making and endorsation of the note to Metcalf, for which he could maintain an action upon the note against the respective parties to it. That being so, the plaintiff is entitled to maintain an action against Meehan, but in my opinion only for contribution to the extent of one half of the amount which was paid to Metcalf.

If the debt were not due on Metcalf's bond when he got the note, he could not have filed a bill for indemnity against Sorley : *Padwick* v. *Stanley*, 9 Hare 627.

But even if it were not due when the note was given, yet if the note gave a longer day of payment than the day when the bond fell due, that would, in my opinion, still be a case of a good consideration between Metcalf and Sorley.

The right of the surety to have the benefit of all securities given to the creditor arises from the obligation of the principal debtor to indemnify the surety : *Yonge* v. *Reynell*, 9 Hare 809, 818.

From the conclusion I have come to, the rule should be absolute to reduce the verdict to one-half the amount.

HARRISON, C. J.—While agreeing in much of what my learned brother Wilson has said, I am unable to agree with him in the conclusion that the relationship of co-sureties. between plaintiff and defendant is established, so as to prevent plaintiff recovering from defendant the whole amount of the note.

Although the learned Chief Justice of the Common Pleas found that the defendant when he signed the note understood from Sorley, the payee, that the plaintiff Fisken would endorse as a co-surety, the learned Chief Justice also found that the plaintiff Fisken knew nothing of this ; but endorsed the note in the ordinary way, considering the maker would be liable to him for the whole.

In cases such as the present it is, as said by Blake, V. C., in *Ianson* v. *Paxton*, 23 C. P. 439, 469, "material to consider whether the sureties became properly co-sureties, meaning thereby persons with a common interest, and a common burden, and equally bound ; or whether, although called co-sureties they are not simply sureties, only called co-sureties because they have undertaken for a common principal a liability which, according to agreement, may as between them press on the one more heavily than on the other."

Where there is no agreement to the contrary between the parties to a promissory note, their position on the note indicates—not the relation of co-suretyship but of successive liability ; a series of contracts on the part of each with the holder of the note for the time being.

The contract of the maker is to pay the note at maturity. The contract of the first endorser is to pay if the maker do not. The contract of the second endorser, to pay if

the maker and first endorser make default. And so on,
ad infinitum.

"There are," as said by the learned Chief Justice of the
Common Pleas in *Ianson* v. *Paxton*, 22 C. P. 505, 509, "very
few persons in this country who endorse notes with one or
more names prior to their own thereon, who would doubt
for a moment their right to look to such names as responsible before their own for the full amount of the note.".

The intention of the parties, in other words the agreement of the parties, at the time they become co-sureties,
is not to be wholly disregarded.

The distinction between co-suretyship and successive
liability by way of accommodation for the maker of a note
was as long since as 1830 pointed out by Chief Justice
Marshall in the Supreme Court of the United States in
McDonald v. *McGruder*, 3 Peters 470, 473; and has since,
been fully recognized by our Court of Appeal in *Ianson* y.
Paxton, 23 C. P. 505. My brother Wilson was one of the
minority in the Court. The majority embraced not only.
the present Chief Justice of Canada, but all the then
Judges of the Court of Chancery, one of whom is now
also a Judge of the Supreme Court of Canada.

The case is not to be likened to several bonds executed
by several sureties for a common principal to a common
obligee, and nothing more at the time said or done between
the parties, but rather to the execution of several bonds,
with an express agreement between the parties that as
between themselves each shall be liable to the other in the
full amount of the guaranteed liability in the order of their
priority.

It seems to me that under any circumstances we are in
this Court concluded by the decision on the point by the
Court of Appeal. No doubt the Privy Council is the
Court of ultimate appeal for the colonies. But I know of
no decision of the Privy Council actually at variance with
Ianson v. *Paxton*. And even if I differed from the decision
of the Court of Appeal, it would, I conceive, be my duty
in this Court to follow that decision till reversed by that
Court, or overruled by some higher authority.

It is not for a subordinate Court to disregard the decisions of a Court of Appeal; but, on the contrary, it is the duty of the subordinate Court to give full effect to such decisions, whatever its views may be as to their intrinsic wisdom. See *Costello* v. *The Syracuse, Binghampton, and New York R. W. Co.*, 65 Barb. 92, 100.

But when the Appellate Court departs from its own decisions, and leaves it uncertain what its views are upon a question of law, it is the duty of the subordinate Court to give effect to the latest expression of the views of the Appellate Court, leaving to that Court to determine which is the sounder, the earlier or the later decisions: *Ib.*

The only decision in the Court of Appeal bearing on the point raised here is *Ianson* v. *Paxton*, and it is, notwithstanding the dissent of my brother Wilson, who sat as a member of the Court as then constituted, against the conclusion at which my brother Wilson has now arrived.

Besides, if I may be allowed to criticize it, the decision appears to me not only in itself to be a reasonable decision, but in actual harmony with cases which, though at first sight in conflict, are really not so when closely examined.

I must, however, forbear to examine these cases, or in any manner to sit in review on the decision of the Court of Appeal. I must leave that duty to Judges sitting in another place, having larger powers and more extended jurisdiction than I possess in this Court.

In my opinion the rule *nisi* should be discharged.

MORRISON, J., concurred in the conclusion arrived at by Harrison, C. J.

Rule discharged.

In re Devlin and the Hamilton and Lake Erie Railway Co.

R. W. Co.—Train passing along a street—Houses injuriously affected—Right to compensation.

A railway company was permitted by the corporation to run their track along Cherry street in the city of Hamilton, which was only thirty feet wide. The plaintiff, owning a brick cottage and frame house on the street, complained that the trains passing caused the houses to vibrate, and the plaster to fall off the walls, and alleged loss of tenants thereby; but the evidence as to any structural injury caused by the railway was contradictory, and the Court held that it was not sufficiently made out.

Held, affirming the judgment of Hagarty, C. J., C. P., that the plaintiff was not entitled to compensation under the Railway Act.

February 26, 1875. *J. B. Read* obtained from Wilson, J., sitting alone, a rule *nisi* for a mandamus to compel the railway company to serve upon the applicant a notice as to certain property described, of their readiness to pay some sum certain as compensation for the injury likely to arise to the said premises from the exercise of the powers of the railway, and if necessary to name arbitrators, &c., to assess the amount of such compensation.

The facts seemed to be, that the road was brought into Hamilton by consent of the municipality along Cherry street, a narrow street only thirty feet wide. The plaintiff had a brick cottage and a double frame house on the street, and complained of the great injury done to her by the railroad and the user of it: that the passing trains caused the houses to vibrate, and the plaster to fall off the walls.

The affidavits filed on each side were contradictory as to the extent or existence of structural or other injury.

March 30, 1875, before Hagarty, C. J. C. P., *C. Robinson,* Q.C., and *Walker,* for the railway company, shewed cause to the rule, and *J. B. Read,* supported the rule. The arguments were the same as on the rehearing, post p. 164.

May 25, 1876. HAGARTY, C. J. C. P.—I have no doubt whatever but that the running of this road along this narrow street is a most serious injury to any resident along either side of it, or to any owner of houses desiring to rent them.

The affidavits as to any structural injury to the houses, such as injuring the plaster, do not satisfy me that such peculiar injury is established; and I am not prepared to hold the case made out on that ground.

Apart from structural injury, I am afraid the applicant has no redress, so long as no negligence was proved in the working of the railway.

The corporation has been pleased to allow the company to lay their track along this public highway. The highway can still, however, be used for the passage of vehicles

The track cannot be said to create any claim on plaintiff's part. It is there by leave of the municipality. The statute, 33 Vic. ch. 36, sec. 3, O.; empowers the company to construct their line *from any point in the city of Hamilton.*

Having obtained authority to use one of the highways in the city, then the user of the railway, unless with negligence, can apparently give no cause of action.

The law is very fully stated in two or three cases in the House of Lords.

In *The Hammersmith R. W. Co.* v. *Brand,* L. R. 4 H. L. 171, a majority of the Lords held that compensation could not be claimed for damages arising from vibration occasioned (without negligence) by the passing of trains after the railway is brought into use, even though the value of the property had been actually depreciated thereby.

It does not appear that there was any structural injury proved to the houses.

In *Ricket* v. *Metropolitan R. W. Co.,* L. R. 2 H. L. 175, the subject is also discussed.

The latest case I have read is *The Metropolitan Board of Works* v. *McCarthy,* L. R. 7 H. L. 243.

The Lord Chancellor Cairns, and Lords Chelmsford, Hatherley, Penzance, and O'Hagan, deliver judgments as to the state of the general law.

Lord Cairns says, p. 252: " I propose entirely to accept the test which has been applied both in this House and elsewhere, as to the proper meaning of those words as giving a right to compensation, namely, that the proper test is to consider whether the act done in carrying out the works in question is an act which would have given a right of action if the works had not been authorized by Act of Parliament." He adds, at p. 253, that he accepts the test suggested by counsel, "Where by the construction of works there is a physical interference with any right, public or private, which the owners or occupiers of property are by law entitled to make use of, in connection with such property, and which right gives an additional market value to such property, apart from the uses to which any particular owner or occupier might put it, there is a title to compensation, if, by reason of such interference, the property, as a property, is lessened in value."

Applying this test we might ask, would the applicant have any redress by action against persons driving heavy vehicles along the street at a rapid rate, so as to cause her houses to vibrate?

I need not say whether an indictment might lie for nuisance, but I hardly see how any one of the residents along the street can sue for damages. The injury is to the common hurt of all.

The turning of heavy traffic down a hitherto quiet street cannot I think give any cause of action.

Every dweller in large cities knows well that houses vibrate unpleasantly as heavy traffic rolls by. The passing of a railway train is only differing in degree from that of heavy loaded vans.

I am hardly prepared to hold that if a corporation permits steam carriages to pass along a public street an action will lie.

It is not necessary here to discuss how far the permission of the municipality can bar an indictment for an obstruction to public right.

Sec. 12 of the Railway Clauses Act Consol. Stat. C. ch. 66, says that the railway shall not be carried along an existing highway, unless leave has been obtained from the proper municipal authorites therefor.

I find the general law is so very fully discussed in these three cases in the House of Lords that it seems useless to do more than refer to them.

Assuming that no actual structural injury is shewn to be done to plaintiff's houses, her injury seems to be in no way peculiar to herself, but is shared with the rest of the general public.

A quiet street is invaded by new and very noisy traffic, personal comfort is much interfered with, and the use of the houses for occupation or renting purposes much affected.

I am afraid that for all this, however burdensome to the applicant, there is no redress by statutory compensation.

The user of the railway by locomotive engines drawing trains is clearly permitted by the Legislature. So long as no negligence is shewn such user can give no right of action. It is the user of the road that causes all the damage to the plaintiff.

As to the alleged structural injury I have already said I do not think it clearly shewn. The houses have been built some years and plaster has no doubt fallen off, but my mind is not convinced that this is caused by the user of the railway, and if at all, then not beyond what any building of that character would suffer on a street used for heavy traffic.

The frame or lath and plaster houses so common in this country would suffer at least as much as the plaintiff's in any paved street on which omnibuses were constantly passing and repassing. Every person building in a street in a city must run some risk of being annoyed or injured by the increase of heavy traffic.

I am not prepared to hold that a sufficient case is here made out.

It may be well perhaps for the applicant to bring the case before the full Court, and to have some more authoritative decision than that of a single Judge on a question of such undoubted public importance.

If the evidence had been clear and positive as to actual

injury to the fabric of the houses, I should have been inclined to let the mandamus go.

Here, at the best, it merely amounts to an assertion of belief that bits of old plaster had fallen off the walls from the vibration caused by passing trains.

The case of *Day* v. *Grand Trunk R. W. Co.*, 5 C. P. 420, 423, may be quoted. I do not pretend to reconcile all the authorities on this much discussed subject.

The applicant's difficulty seems to be this. She has, I think, no redress for the construction of the railroad along this street with the leave of the municipality, although I feel strongly that she is really seriously injured thereby ; and that for the user of the road without negligence no action lies.

I refuse the application, but make no order as to costs.

————

From the foregoing judgment the applicant appealed, and brought the matter on for re-hearing before the full Court.

November, 27, 1876. *McMichael*, Q.C., for the applicant. The evidence shews that vibration is not the only injury the plaintiff complains of, but that cars were left standing on the street so as to affect the easy approach to the houses to so great an extent as to render it difficult to find tenants for them. The affidavits are contradictory, but on the whole they shew structural injury and loss of tenants.

C. Robinson, Q.C., *Walker* with him, contra. *The Hammersmith R. W Co.* v. *Brand*, L. R. 4 H. L. 171, governs this case. Railways would have to stop outside every city if compensation were granted in such a case as this. There was no evidence of structural injury caused by defendants. They referred to *Day* v. *The Grand Trunk R. W. Co.*, 5 C. P. 420; *Day* v. *Town Council of Guelph*, 15 U. C. R. 126; *The Metropolitan Board of Works* v. *McCarthy*, L. R. 7 H. L. 243; *Ogilvy* v. *Caledonia R. W. Co.*, 2 Macq. H. L.

229; *City of Glasgow Union R. W. v. Hunter*, L. R. 2 Sc. App. 78; *Re Widder & Buffalo v. Lake Huron R. W. Co.*, 20 U. C. R. 638.

HARRISON, C.J.—It is not necessary to reserve our decision. We have read over the affidavits and the judgment of the learned Chief Justice. We think that judgment correct, and we think this case is concluded by the *Hammersmith R. W. Co. v. Brand*, L. R. 4 H. L. 171.

MORRISON, J.—I am of the same opinion.

WILSON, J.—Was not present at the argument, and took no part in the judgment.

Judgment affirmed, with costs.

CHAFFEY V. SCHOOLEY.

Vessel—Unseaworthiness—General average.

The defendant's schooner was engaged to carry a cargo of timber from Spanish River to Chippewa. She left Spanish River with the timber on the 15th October, and anchored on that day at Bayfield Sound, leaking badly, where she remained till the 10th of November, and was then towed by a tug to Sarnia. There she got a steam pump, and with it on board was towed to the Welland canal, where she arrived on the 25th November, and being frozen up the cargo had to be unloaded. The defendant refused to give up the lumber unless, in addition to the freight, the plaintiff would pay his share for general average of (1) the expenses incurred for charges of the tug, $1200; (2) use of hawser, $50; (3) use of steam pump, $315; (4) telegrams, protest, adjustment, $25; (5) extra help discharging, $120.

Held, that if the vessel had been seaworthy the first, second and fifth items would not have been chargeable; and that the third might be; but

Held, also, that the evidence, set out below, shewed the vessel to have been unseaworthy at the commencement of and during the whole voyage, and that the expense was occasioned thereby; and that the defendant therefore had no claim.

REPLEVIN for 204,090 feet of pine timber, carried by the defendant's schooner Wacousta.

The issues are not material, as the whole case was reserved for the Court upon the facts.

The cause was tried before Harrison, C. J., at the last Welland Assizes.

The vessel started on the trip from the plaintiff's ship-yard, at Chippewa, on the 11th of September, 1875, for Spanish River. She took a load of coal at Cleveland for Sarnia on her way, and unloaded it there, and left there on the last day of September or 1st of October, for Spanish River, where she arrived about the 7th or 8th of October: She loaded at Spanish River, and sailed from there on the 15th of October for her destination, and bore for and anchored nine hours after starting at Bayfield Sound, about twenty-two miles from Spanish River, on the same day, and remained there from that day till the 10th or 11th of November.

A tug came to her on the 6th of November, but it left for a steam pump. She did not get one, and she towed the schooner without one, as she was, to Sarnia, which she reached on the 21st of November.

The vessel got a steam pump there, and kept it on board, being towed all the way from the time she first got the tug till she arrived in the locks of the Welland canal, where she arrived on the 25th of November.

She did not lock through for two or three days; then the frost came, and she could not get through, and the lumber had to be unloaded there.

The defendant refused to give the plaintiff the lumber unless he would agree to pay the extra expenses, in addition to the freight. The plaintiff refused to do it, and replevied the lumber.

The evidence further shewed, as follows :—

Edwin Hughes, the master, said he had been on the vessel for three years. She was supposed to be twenty years old. She leaked after leaving Chippewa, before she got into Cleveland, on her way to Spanish River: even when light she would "occasionally break out." She leaked very badly at Cleveland, while at the wharf, and before she took on the cargo of coal; all hands were pumping. He was refused his bill of lading at Cleveland, because it was said the vessel was not seaworthy, and the insurance agent forbid him from leaving till the vessel was caulked. He insured the coal himself, and he agreed to take a tow from Cleveland to Sarnia; but when three miles out he broke away from the tow, and, as he said, "paddled his own canoe." He had to keep pumps working after unloading at Sarnia; pumped her out night and morning. It was blowing fresh with a beam sea when they left Spanish River. The vessel laboured; she made water. There was no sea to cause a good vessel to make water. When he found the vessel making water he bore for Bayfield Sound. There was a snow storm. Made Cape Roberts. Had then run sixteen or seventeen miles from Spanish River. It lulled a while, but the weather again got worse; then made straight for Bayfield Sound. The snow storm was heavy. Went in by the chart. The vessel shot ahead and went on to a mud bank. She listed over: he knew from the way she listed there was a good deal of water in her. She afterwards got off, and he came to anchor. All hands—seven men—went to the pumps, but the water gained on them at the rate of five or six inches an hour: came to the conclusion they could not save her. By three o'clock in the morning the men were driven from the forecastle, and he said, "we were driven from the cabin." She was at anchor. No wind could hurt her. There she filled and settled. She remained there water-logged till the 10th or 11th of November. The tug came on the 6th of November. The foreman of the mill at Spanish River offered to take us with the tug to Spanish River. I declined, for I would lose the freight. She was towed without a steam pump to Sarnia. The deck was then three or four feet under water. The crew were "roosting." Came near losing her once or twice the first evening after leaving Bayfield, and we were nearly lost. All left her and went to the tug. Anchored at that time for two or three days. When she got to Sarnia she drew eighteen feet: could not have got through the flats below that without the steam pump. She got on the flats there. Had hard work to keep her up with the cargo before that one. We had to nail pieces of boards under the counter. The seams there were pretty bad. We used canvass under the boards. We had to caulk in Lake Erie or swim: had men outside of her in the lake to stop some of the worst of the leaks. They could not stop them. She needed caulking before she left on her former voyage. Defendant said she would not hold oakum. I said, if she was not fit to hold oakum, she was not fit to hold lumber. He admitted that he had had differences with the owners.

On *re-examination*, he said: I swore on the 25th of November the vessel was seaworthy. I meant that with good luck and good management she might be seaworthy. I supposed when we left Spanish River she was seaworthy. Although I sailed her for three years, "I was mightily scared of her."

There was evidence given by five witnesses of the seaworthy condition of the vessel for the carriage of lumber.

The parties agreed to leave the case to the Court upon the facts. The verdict was, therefore, formally entered for the plaintiff, and damages assessed at $5.

In this term, November 20, 1876, *James A. Miller* obtained a rule calling on the plaintiff to shew cause why the verdict should not be set aside and a verdict entered for the defendant, on the ground that the evidence shewed the defendant was entitled to a lien upon the cargo for average or the cargo's contributory portion thereof, which the plaintiff, as owner of the cargo, refused to pay or to give an average bond for, and the plaintiff was not entitled to the possession thereof until he had either paid such portion or given the bond as required.

November 29, 1876. *Delamere* shewed cause. The only supposed danger was to the vessel, not to the cargo. The cargo, by the leakage, was injured so far as it could be injured. The vessel at Bayfield Sound was in a place of safety, and the master should have allowed her to be taken back to Spanish River to be repaired. The vessel was unseaworthy. He referred to *Lowndes* on Average, 2nd ed., pp. 126, 127, 128 ; *Walthew* v. *Mavrojani*, L. R. 5 Ex. 116 ; *Gurney* v. *Mackay*, 37 U. C. R. 324 ; *Kemp* v. *Halliday*, L. R. 1 Q. B. 520 ; *Hingston* v. *Wendt*, L. R. 1 Q. B. D. 367 ; *Kopitoff* v. *Wilson*, L. R. 1 Q. B. D. 377 ; *Schloss* v. *Heriot*, 14 C. B. N. S. 59.

James A. Miller supported the rule. If the vessel was not seaworthy the defendant is not entitled to the charges he makes, if they were occasioned by such unseaworthiness. The vessel was shewn to have been seaworthy for the carriage of lumber. The master's evidence to the contrary should not be believed after his oath that she was seaworthy, and when he proved himself that he had had differences with the owners. The vessel and cargo were both in great danger, and the services of the tug and of the steam pump were expenses for which the owners of the cargo should bear their share.

January 2, 1877. WILSON, J.—If the vessel were seaworthy at the commencement of the voyage, and by perils of the sea got afterwards damaged, so that it was necessary to hire a steam pump to save the ship and cargo, the expense of such pump would be a proper item for general average.

In *Birkley* v. *Presgrave*, 1 East 220, the expenses of men hired to pump the ship were in like manner allowed.

It was necessary, also, to have the pump to enable the vessel to pass over the flats below Sarnia.

It was not made a question whether the use of the steam pump for the whole of the voyage was the most economical manner of dealing with the vessel in her water-logged condition, or whether it would have been better to have put into port and made a survey of the vessel, and repaired her if it could be done for a reasonable outlay, to fit her to reach her destination.

Taking the vessel into port for such a purpose, making the survey, and doing everything proper preliminary to the repairs, would have been items of general average.

The repairs would, of course, have been at the expense of the owner.

Probably the $315 charged for the pump, to be divided as general average, may not be an immoderate charge, and may, perhaps, not throw more, or not much more, upon the shipper than his share of items allowable as average would amount to, and in that view it may not be worth considering.

The large item of the bill is $1,250, for the use of the tug for twenty-four days, from Bayfield Sound to the place of destination, and for the use of the hawser.

Is that an item of general average ?

The lumber was carried in the original bottom, although it was damaged, The tug was employed, not to take the vessel to a place of safety, for she was safe in Bayfield Sound, nor to a port to be surveyed and repaired, if the repairs could reasonably be made ; but to enable her to earn her freight.

In *Wilson* v. *The Bank of Victoria*, L. R. 2 Q. B. 203, it was decided that a sailing ship, with an auxiliary steam power, could not, when her sailing gear was so injured by perils of the sea as to be useless, charge for the coal she consumed by the use of her auxiliary steam power as an item of general average, on the ground that such an outlay was a substitution beneficial to all parties, in place of making a greater expenditure, which the master had a right to incur by repairing the ship, which would entail the unloading, storing, and reloading of the cargo, and a long detention : that there was no legal principle on which expense incurred by one course could be apportioned according to what might have been the facts if a different course had been adopted. The Court intimated also that the master was bound to use the auxiliary steam power with which his vessel was supplied for the general good, without claim of any kind upon the shippers, because it was a ship fitted up with such a power.

But it was not said what would have been the case if an engine had been put on board a sailing vessel, or if a tug had been employed to carry her to her destination.

In *Lowndes* on Average, 2nd ed., pp. 153, 154, the subject is discussed. It is there said: "Suppose a ship is at a port of refuge, at which she can be completely repaired, she is not seaworthy to *sail* from that port unless repaired: but she can be safely towed from that port to her place of destination by a steamer. If this course is adopted, who is to pay for the steamer ?"

The writer comes to the conclusion that a custom is requisite—which is in the course of formation—to make these "substituted expenses" the subject of division between the owner and the shipper.

It was the duty of the master to carry the lumber to its place of delivery, and he did take it there in the same bottom in which it was shipped. Whether he carried it by the sails of the schooner, or by an engine he put in her, or by a tug he attached to her, is of no consequence to the shipper, so long as he gets his goods conveyed. In strictness, therefore, as the goods were not in danger in Bayfield Sound, and as the tug was not required to take the ship and goods to a port of safety, but to complete the voyage, so that the freight might be earned, the owner is not entitled, as the law now stands, to charge any part of the expenses of the tug against the shipper as substituted expenses, in lieu of the charges he would have been subjected to if the master had gone into port to repair, and had unloaded and reloaded the cargo.

It would seem to be reasonable that such substituted charges should be allowed in lieu of the others which the master could fairly impose upon the shipper, and that they should not be wholly cast upon the owner, who is really acting for the general good.

In *Benson* v. *Chapman*, 8 C. B. 950, H. L., it was held that an action would not lie against the underwriters for the freight, where it had been completely covered by a bottomry bond which the master gave on the ship, freight and cargo, to meet repairs done in a foreign port ; because the ship, when repaired, finished her voyage and actually earned the freight, and the freight was paid under the bottomry bond, not to the owner, of course, but to the obligee of the bond.

The expense of beating off a privateer, in repairing the ship, sails, &c., sustained in the action, falls on the owner, because it is his duty to defend the ship and goods: *Taylor* v. *Curtis*, 6 Taunt. 608.

So damage done to a ship by putting to sea to avoid a lee shore falls on the owner: *Power* v. *Whitmore*, 4 M. & Sel. 141.

The items claimed are, a portion of the tug charges for twenty-four days......................	$1,200 00
Use of hawser..	50 00
Use of steam pump	315 00
Telegrams—protest—adjustment	25 00
Extra help discharging	120 00
Total..	$1,710 00
Claimed from plaintiff	$897 75
Charged against owner	812 25

The first and second items are not chargeable against the shipper. The third may be, as before mentioned. The fourth is so small it is scarcely worth speaking of. It is probable the cost of adjustment is divisible. The fifth and last item is not allowable. The owner is bound to deliver the goods to the shipper.

The cases and references I rely on are *Moss* v. *Smith*, 9 C. B. 94; *Hallett* v. *Wigram*, 9 C. B. 580; *Rosetto* v. *Gurney*, 11 C. B. 176; *De Cuadra* v. *Swann*, 16 C. B. N. S. 772; *Farnworth* v. *Hyde*, L. R. 2 C. P. 204; *Notara* v. *Henderson*, L. R. 7 Q. B. 225, and *Gurney* v. *Mackay*, 37 U. C. R. 324, where the authorities on the subject of average are very fully collected.

I have stated what, in my opinion, the defendant is entitled to recover, if he can recover at all.

As the defendant declined to give up the lumber on tender of the freight, unless the plaintiff would pay the whole $897.75 or give an average bond, the defendant waived tender of the part the plaintiff should have paid, or he dispensed with a tender: *Scarfe* v. *Morgan*, 4 M. & W. 270; *Kerford* v. *Mondel*, 28 L. J. Ex. 303.

If the defendant should recover these sums, he would, nevertheless, not be entitled to succeed in this action on the merits, as his detainer of the goods upon such a claim was not justified.

But I am of opinion, upon the evidence, that he cannot recover for any of the items, because his vessel was unseaworthy at the beginning of and throughout the whole voyage, and the loss and expense were occasioned solely by the unseaworthy condition of the vessel.

The master's evidence is corroborated by the undeniable facts of the case.

The master, it is true, in making his protest after the voyage was over, swore the vessel was seaworthy, and unquestionably that detracts from the reliability of his other statements to the contrary, and makes it imperative that his hostile testimony should be well confirmed; and I think it is, by the evidence of John Cowan, who says he was caulking the vessel on the day she sailed on this voyage, and she was taken away in an unfinished state; and on many of the other facts of the case. The trouble about insurance at Cleveland on his way up; the leakage of the vessel there; his getting the cargo of coal only on the promise to be very careful of the vessel between Cleveland and Sarnia; his starting with a tug from Cleveland to take the vessel to Sarnia, and cutting loose from her when he got out of Cleveland; the caulking and leakage on the way from Sarnia to Spanish River; the patching all the way along, and her very disabled state when she got on the mud in Bayfield Sound, having then a good deal of water in her; the absence of a sufficient cause to account for a good vessel making so much water, and making it so fast that the pumps had to be discontinued; the vessel remained in that state from the 15th of October till the 25th of November, when she got to her destination.

It was a late and dangerous season of the year in these waters, and the vessel should have been fitted to meet these difficulties and to perform her work.

The cases of *Schloss* v. *Heriot*, 14 C. B. N. S. 59, and.

Kopitoff v. *Wilson*, L. R. 1 Q. B. D. 377, shew that unseaworthiness of the ship, which unseaworthiness is the cause of the extra expense being incurred, is a defence to any claim made by the owner of the ship for such expense.

In *Anderson* v. *Morice*, L. R. 10 C. P. 58, a vessel in smooth water, while at anchor, sank without any assignable cause. There was evidence given that she had been carefully examined and found to be all right. The whole facts went to a jury, and they found she was seaworthy, although they could not, from the many conjectures as to the cause of the loss, account for the sinking of the ship. Here the evidence is not of that character. The general evidence of the master, who was not contradicted by any one on board, corresponds with what the actual condition of the vessel was.

If the vessel had been seaworthy, the plaintiff would have been liable for his share of the $340; but I am of opinion the vessel was not seaworthy. The rule should be discharged with costs.

HARRISON, C. J., and WILSON, J., concurred.

Rule discharged.

ABRAHAMS v. THE AGRICULTURAL MUTUAL ASSURANCE ASSOCIATION.

Fire policy—Non-occupation of premises.

A fire policy, granted to the plaintiff on a dwelling house in a town, contained the following condition: "Unoccupied dwelling houses, with the exceptions undermentioned, are not insured by this association, nor shall it be answerable for any loss by fire which may happen to, in, or from any dwelling-house while left without an occupant or person actually residing therein. The temporary absence of a member or his family, however, none of the household effects being removed, is not to be construed into non-occupancy. And this condition is not contrued to apply to the temporary non-occupation of small dwellings for the accommodation of hired help on a farm, the main dwelling on the same continuing to be occupied. But the main dwelling house must not be unoccupied for longer than forty-eight hours at any one time."

The plaintiff lived several miles from the house, which was leased to a monthly tenant, who had removed his goods within forty-eight hours before the fire, and no one had resided in the house for ten days before. The fire took place on the 10th September, and the tenant's month was up on the 24th. He was in arrear for rent, for which his goods had been distrained, but the plaintiff, who had a person ready to take possession, did not suppose that the tenant would leave until his month was up.

Held, that the exception as to forty-eight hours applied only to dwellings on a farm: that the condition, which required an actual residence of the occupant, was broken; and that the plaintiff could not recover.

Held, also, that a demand of the claim papers and proof of loss, without reference to this condition, could not be construed as a waiver of it: *Canada Landed Credit Co.* v. *The Canada Agricultural Ins. Co.,* 17 Grant 418, dissented from on this point.

No such waiver having been set up at the trial, which took place without a jury, *quære,* as to the propriety of allowing it to be urged in term.

THIS was an action on a fire policy of insurance to recover the amount of a loss.

Besides the ordinary traverses, the defendants pleaded that the policy of insurance was granted by the defendants and accepted by the plaintiff, subject to the conditions endorsed on the policy, one of which was as follows :—

"Unoccupied dwelling houses, with the exceptions undermentioned, are not insured by this association, nor shall it be answerable for any loss by fire which may happen to, in, or from any dwelling house while left without an occupant or person actually residing therein. The temporary absence of a member or his family, however, none of the household effects being removed, is not construed into non-occupancy. And this condition is not construed to apply to the temporary non-occupation of small dwellings for the accommodation of hired help on a farm, the main dwelling on the same continuing to be occupied. But the main dwelling house must not be unoccupied for longer than forty-eight hours at any one time."

The plea concluded with an averment that, at the time of the alleged fire, by which the dwelling house of the plaintiff was burnt, the dwelling house was left without an occupant or person actually residing there.

Issue.

The cause was first tried at the last Spring Assizes for 1874, at Simcoe, before Patterson, J., without a jury.

He found a verdict for the defendants.

This verdict was afterwards, in Trinity term last, set aside, and a new trial ordered at the instance of the plaintiff, on payment of costs.

The second trial was before Hagarty, C. J. C.P., at the last Fall Assizes for the same county, without a jury.

The learned Chief Justice found that the fire took place on Friday, 10th September, 1875, between the hours of nine and ten o'clock at night, and the tenant did not reside (sleep or eat) on the premises for six or eight days before the fire, nor did any other person. The great contest in the cause at the trial was, as to the time of the removal of the tenant's goods. They were removed either on the Wednesday or Thursday before the fire. They were advertised to be sold for rent on Thursday, 9th September. The tenant swore the goods were removed the day before the day fixed for the sale,—that is, Wednesday. Another witness swore to the same effect. Still another witness swore they were not removed till the Thursday afternoon. The defendants, under any circumstances, insisted that for forty-eight hours before the fire the building was wholly unoccupied. This depended on whether the occupation by goods was sufficient, and if so, whether the removal of the goods was on the Wednesday or the Thursday. If the defence should turn on this, the learned Chief Justice found that the defendants had not shewn a removal of the goods forty-eight hours before the fire.

There was no imputation of fraud on the part of the plaintiff.

The plaintiff was guilty of no personal default. He lived several miles from the house, and was not aware before the fire that the tenant had ceased personally to occupy. The tenant held the premises by the month. He was in arrears for rent, and his goods distrained. His month did not expire till 24th September. The landlord did not suppose he would quit the premises before that day, and had a person ready to take possession as soon as the tenant left.

The house was situate in the town of Simcoe and was used as a dwelling house.

The learned Chief Justice did not attempt to construe the condition, but left that to the Court, finding a verdict for the plaintiff for $530.

. During this term, November 23, 1876, *J. H. Ferguson*, obtained a rule calling on the plaintiff to shew cause why the verdict for the plaintiff should not be set aside, and a nonsuit or new trial ordered, on the following grounds:

1. That the evidence shews the premises insured to have been unoccupied at the time of the fire, within the meaning of the condition.

2. That there was no occupation of the premises insured for more than forty-eight hours before the fire.

3. That the verdict was against law and evidence.

During the same term, December 6, 1876, *D. B. Read*, Q.C., shewed cause. A personal occupancy was not intended by the condition; an occupation by goods was, under the circumstances, sufficient; the finding of the learned Chief Justice that there was no non-occupancy for forty-eight hours before the fire was sustained by the evidence, and the company having called for proofs, without insisting on the condition as avoiding the policy, should not now be allowed to raise the defence. He cited *The Canada Landed Credit Co.* v. *The Canada Agricultural Ins. Co.*, 17 Grant 418 : *Shearman* v. *The Niagara Fire Ins. Co.*, 46 N. Y., (1 Sickles)

526 ; *Gillyat* v. *Pawtucket Ins. Co.*, 8 Rh. I. 282 ; *Mc-Annally* v. *Somerset Mutual Ins, Co.*, 2 Pittsburgh 189 ; *Clarke* on Insurance, 176, 178.

McMillan contra. The object of the condition is, to have personal occupation as a preventive against fire, and possession by goods only does not answer this object. Although the plaintiff was not aware of the non-occupancy his agent was, and whether he was or not, there could be no recovery against the plain words of the condition, which the defendants had not in any manner waived : *The Ottawa and Rideau Forwarding Co.* v. *The London, Liverpool, and Globe Ins. Co.*, 28 U. C. R. 518; *Gould* v. *British America Ins. Co.*, 27 U. C. R. 473 ; *Kuntz* v. *Niagara District Fire Ins. Co.*, 16 C. P. 573, 582 ; *Hobson* v. *The Western District Fire Ins. Co.*, 6 U. C. R. 536.

January 2, 1877. HARRISON, C. J.—No question of waiver was raised at the trial before the learned Chief Justice.

Where a cause has been tried without a jury, it is in the power of the Court on motion against the verdict to pronounce the verdict which, in their judgment, the Judge who tried the cause ought to have pronounced : 33 Vic. ch. 7, sec. 6, O.

But it is not fair either to the party in whose favour the verdict is rendered, to the Judge who renders it, or to the Court in which the motion is made against the verdict, in the latter Court for the first time to start a question of fact which was never presented to the Judge for his decision, and on which, for all that appears, if raised at the trial other evidence might have been adduced.

The presumption, where there is a jury, is, that parties who omit to have particular questions of fact submitted for the consideration of the jury do so in the belief that the finding of the jury would, on the questions if submitted, be adverse to them, and so are not allowed afterwards to take any advantage of the omission.

The practice as to the trial of cases without a jury is not

in this respect nearly so strict as where there is a jury, but in principle there is no difference between the two cases.

Whether the tribunal for the trial of the question of fact be Judge or jury, and there is an application for a new trial on the ground that the verdict is against evidence, there is an appeal from the decision as to the questions of fact, and the general rule is, to restrict persons appealing to grounds raised in the Court below.

Mr. Justice Patterson, in *Lawrie* v. *Rathbun*, 38 U. C. R. 255, 282, drew attention to the loose practice at present prevailing in non-jury trials. He said: " It cannot be supposed to have been the intention of the Legislature, in giving power to the Court, by 33 Vic. ch. 7, sec. 6, to pronounce the verdict which, in their judgment, the Judge who tried the case ought to have pronounced, in cases where a verdict is objected to on the ground of insufficiency of the evidence or the erroneous view taken of it by the Judge, that the Court should decide, upon the evidence questions not debated before or decided by the Judge. The question under the statute is, whether the view taken by the Judge was correct or erroneous. The Judge in this case does not appear to have been asked to form any view of the evidence on this question."

But rather than do injustice the Court there and the Courts every day decide questions of fact on the evidence not raised before the Judge at the trial.

It would be well, however, for the attention of the profession to be directed to the looseness of the prevailing practice in non-jury trials, in the hope that there will be more strictness in the future, for strictness in this respect, will be found conducive to the proper administration of justice.

Without concluding the plaintiff by his omission to ask for a ruling or a finding on the question of waiver we shall, as we are desirous if possible to sustain the recovery, proceed to consider it.

It does not appear from the report of the evidence given at the trial that there was any evidence—as a demand by the company of proof papers or anything else—which can be construed as a waiver of the condition now pleaded.

If there was evidence of the kind, the plaintiff ought in some manner, if possible by the pleadings, to have raised the issue of waiver for trial.

But assuming that there was the issue, that there was evidence of the demand of the proof papers, and no reference to the condition pleaded, and assuming that the issue on such evidence was found against the plaintiff, we cannot on the authorities interfere with that finding.

It is true that Vice-Chancellor Mowat, in the case referred to by Mr. Read, of *The Canada Landed Credit Co.* v. *The Canada Agricultural Ins. Co.*, 17 Grant 418, 423, said : "On the contrary, though they were informed of both facts at the same time that they were notified of the fire, instead of electing to hold the policy at an end, they called for, and obtained from the parties concerned, the proofs of loss on the footing of the policy being still in full force. After this election to treat the policy as subsisting, the insurance company was not at liberty to elect to treat it as forfeited." But the defence of non-occupation in that case was, according to the report, open to another answer which was so conclusive as to render unnecessary this expression of opinion. Besides, as pointed out by Hagarty, C. J., in *Stickney* v. *The Niagara District Fire Ins. Co.*, 23 C. P. 372, 382 : "In the report of the case none of the numerous cases in our Common Law Courts are noticed." Hence the learned Chief Justice said : "I do not feel at liberty to lay down any such rule, and must leave it to the Court of Error to declare if it be the law."

No such rule has ever prevailed in Courts of Common Law in this Province. In many cases which I remember, and could name if necessary, there was not only the defence of insufficient proof of loss, but a condition making void the policy, and correspondence about the former without any reference to the latter, and no question of waiver ever raised or attempted to be raised.

If such a rule as suggested by the learned Vice-Chancellor is to prevail, it must to be enacted by the Legislature or established by the Court of Appeal.

The Legislature has already in section 1 of 38 Vic. ch. 65, O., to some extent recognized and provided for such a rule. That section declares that, "Where, by reason of neces-sity, accident, or mistake, the conditions of any contract of fire insurance on property in this Province *as to the proof to be given to the insurance company* after the occurrence of a fire have not been strictly complied with; or where, *after a statement or proof of loss* has been given in good faith by or on behalf of the insured in pursuance of any proviso or condition of such contract, the company, through its agent or otherwise, objects to the loss upon *other* grounds than for imperfect compliance with such conditions, or does not within a reasonable time after receiving such statement or proof, notify the assured in writing *that such statement or proof is objected to,* and what are the particulars in which the same is alleged to be defective, and so from time to time: * * no objection to the sufficiency of such statement or proof, * * shall in any of such cases be allowed," &c.

It has been held that this section does not prevent an insurance company in any of the cases supposed objecting that a policy is void for non-compliance with a condition requring notice of a double insurance, for such an objection is not "to the statement or proof of loss": *Fair* v. *The Niagara District Mutual Ins. Co.,* 26 C. P. 398. See fur-ther *Jones* v. *The Mechanics' Ins. Co.,* 13 Am. 405.

For a similar reason it must be held inapplicable where the objection is not to the statement or proof of loss, but that the property destroyed was at the time of the fire left " without an occupant or person actually residing therein" contrary to the terms of the condition on the policy.

The plaintiff cannot avoid the contest raised by the plea here, and so it becomes our duty to construe the condition set out in the plea, and to determine whether or not it is shewn that the plaintiff is prevented by that condition from recovering in this action.

The question is not as to change of occupation, but what kind of occupation the condition makes necessary, and whether on the evidence that kind of occupation, or rather the want of it, can be said to have existed at the time of the fire.

In this view, the cases cited of *Hobson* v. *The Western District Mutual Fire Ins. Co.*, 6 U. C. R. 536; *Kuntz* v. *The Niagara District Fire Ins. Co.*, 16 C. P. 573; *Gould* v. *The British America Fire Ins. Co.*, 27 U. C. R. 473, 480; and *Ottawa and Rideau Forwarding Co.* v. *London, Liverpool, and Globe Ins. Co.*, 28 U. C. R. 518, have no direct bearing on the question now before the Court.

Mere non-occupation of premises insured at the time of a fire, unless there be a condition to that effect, does not avoid a policy of insurance: *Hawkes* v. *The Dodge County Mutual Ins. Co.*, 11 Wis. 196; *Soye* v. *The Merchants' Ins. Co.*, 6 La. An. 761.

It cannot be affirmed that under all circumstances a vacant house is more exposed to danger of fire than an occupied house. Much would depend on the situation of the house, the neighbourhood, &c. A house may be so situated that to leave it vacant for any length of time would expose it to be fired by some malicious or wantonly wicked person. On the other hand, it may be so situated that its want of occupancy may be to reduce the danger. See *Wustum* v. *City Fire Ins. Co.*, 15 Wis. 138.

The question, whether an unoccupied building is a more hazardous risk than one occupied, has been held not to relate to matters of science or skill, so as to render admissible the testimony of witnesses on the point: *Cannell* v. *The Phoenix Ins. Co.*, 59 Me. 582.

But it is competent to insurance companies to shut out all question as to risk, by providing that non-occupation for a particular time, whether increasing the risk or not, shall absolutely avoid the policy in the event of a fire occuring during such non-occupation; and where such appears to be the clear meaning of the condition, the Court would have no discretion to refuse to give effect to it: *Keith* v. *Quincy Mutual Ins. Co.*, 10 Allen 228.

If the condition be that the policy shall be void, when the condition or circumstances of the property insured shall, "by the act of the insured, his agent or tenant, be in anywise so changed as materially to increase the risk,' the question whether the vacancy of the house for weeks or months had that effect, and whether it was attributable to the conduct of the plaintiff, his agent or tenant, is for the jury under a proper direction from the Bench: *Gamwell* v. *The Merchants' and Farmers' Ins. Co.*, 12 Cush. 167; *Gillyatt* v. *Pawtuckett Mutual Fire Ins. Co.*, 8 Rh. I. 282; *Harrison* v. *City Fire Ins. Co.*, 9 Allen 231; *Luce* v. *Dorchester Mutual Fire Ins. Co.*, 110 Mass. 361; *North American Fire Ins. Co.* v. *Zaenger*, 63 Ill. 464.

In the State of Maine the Legislature has found it necessary to make provision that no advantage shall be taken by insurance companies of such conditions as the one now before us, unless it be made to appear not only that the condition was broken but that the breach increased the risk : *Cannell* v. *The Phœnix Ins. Co.*, 59 Me. 582. In this Province there is no such legislation.

In the absence of such legislation we must determine the meaning of the condition now before us—whether there was increase of risk or not.

The occupation of a dwelling house in general means living in it: *Paine* v. *The Agricultural Ins. Co.*, 5 N. Y. S. C. 619.

Where the word "unoccupied" only is used in a condition of a fire policy, a mere temporary absence of the person insured is not a want of occupation : *Canada Landed Credit Co.* v. *Canada Agricultural Ins. Co.*, 17 Grant 418. See *Shearman* v. *The Niagara Fire Ins. Co.*, 46 N Y. 526.

In *The Canada Landed Credit Co.* v. *The Canada Agricultural Ins. Co.* 17 Grant 418, the condition was, that "If, after insurance being effected, any building or buildings so insured become vacant or unoccupied, notice of the same shall be given to the company, that the directors may decide whether it would be prudent to retain the risk," &c.

Mowat, V. C., in delivering judgment said, p. 423: "I think that the proper construction of the condition is, that it does not relate to an absence from personal occupation for a day or so; that where the non-occupation is longer, the policy remains valid until the assured has had a reasonable time for giving notice to the company; and that if a fire takes place before such reasonable time has expired, the insurance company is bound. I am not prepared to say that three days' time in the present case was an unreasonable time for this purpose."

So in *O'Brien* v. *The Commercial Fire Ins. Co.*, 6 J. & Sp. N. Y. 517; *Sansum's* Insurance Digest, p. 827, where the condition was, that the policy should be void "if the premises shall become vacant or unoccupied," it was held that an absence from ten days to two weeks, the furniture of the insured being in the house, did not make void the policy.

But in *American Ins. Co.* v. *Padfield*, 8 Chicago Legal News, 138; *Sansum*, p. 826, under a like condition, where it appeared that there was at the time of the fire nothing but a table, a crib, and a straw mattress in the house, nor had there been anything else for two months, the premises were held to be vacant and unoccupied at the time of the fire so as to make void the policy.

Where the insurance was upon a machine shop, it was in *Keith* v. *Quincy Mutual Fire Ins. Co.*, 10 Allen 228, held that it was not sufficient to constitute occupancy that the tools remained in the shop, and the plaintiff went through it almost every day to see if things were right.

Where the building was insured, as a brewery and not occupied as a residence when insured, it was held not to be vacant because there was no one residing in the brewery at the time of its destruction by fire: *Commercial Ins. Co.* v. *Spankneble*, 52 Ill. 53.

In *Ashworth* v. *Builders' Mutual Fire Ins. Co.*, 112 Mass. 422, 17 Am. 117, it was held that a dwelling-house and barn were unoccupied where the house was only used by the insured and his servants for the purpose of taking their meals there when engaged in carrying on a contiguous farm, and the barn only used for the purpose of storing hay and farming tools.

Colt, J., in delivering judgment, said, 17 Am. 199: "Occupancy as applied to such buildings implies an actual use of the house as a dwelling place, and such use of the barn as is ordinarily incident to a barn belonging to an occupied house, or at least something more than the use of it for mere storage."

With the aid of the foregoing decisions we must now proceed to interpret the condition relied upon to defeat the claim of the plaintiff.

While in some respects resembling the conditions in all the cases cited, it differs from them all as to its general construction.

The condition, which is a compound one, may be divided as follows :—

1. Unoccupied dwelling houses, *with the exceptions under-mentioned*, are not insured by this association.

2. The association will not be answerable for any loss by fire which may happen to, in, or from any dwelling house while left without an occupant or person actually residing therein.

3. The temporary absence of a member or his family, however, none of the household effects being removed, is not to be construed into non-occupancy.

4. The condition is not intended to apply to the temporary non-occupancy of small dwellings for the accommodation of hired help on a farm, the main dwelling on the same continuing to be occupied; but the main dwelling house must not be unoccupied for longer than forty-eight hours at any one time.

In the reading of this condition, so far as the present case is concerned, which was an insurance on a dwelling house in a town, and not on a farm, we must put aside the portions of the condition which we have numbered 1 and 4.

We put aside the portion No. 1, because there is no complaint that the dwelling house when insured was unoccupied; and we put aside portion No. 4, because it contains the exceptions to No. 1, and applies *only* to insurances on small dwellings for hired help on a farm, where the main dwelling is occupied, or not unoccupied for longer than forty-eight hours at any one time.

All that we have left as applicable to the insurance now before us are the portions Nos. 2 and 3. The former contains the rule, the latter the exception to that rule.

The rule is, that the association is not to be answerable for any loss by fire which may happen while the dwelling house is "left without an occupant or person actually residing therein."

The exception is, the temporary absence of the insured, none of the household effects being removed.

It cannot be said that at the time of the fire in this case none of the household effects of the insured or his tenant were removed. On the contrary, it is beyond dispute that at the time of the fire all had been removed. The contest at the trial was, whether the removal was within forty-eight hours of the fire. As the latter exception, in our opinion, applies only to dwellings on a farm, it cannot avail here.

It follows that the present case falls within the rule (No. 2), and not the exception (No. 3), or any exception to the condition.

Then what is the rule? That the company is not to be answerable for any loss by fire which may happen to any dwelling house *while left without an occupant or person actually residing therein.* The word "or" we suppose is intended for the word "and," so as to require not merely an occupation by furniture, tools, &c., but an actual residence of the occupant, subject, however, to the exception that a temporary absence (none of the household effects being removed) is not to be held non-occupation. See *Keith* v. *Dancy Mutual Fire Ins. Co.,* 10 Allen 228.

This is reading the condition most favourably to the plaintiff, and as being satisfied with an occupation by a tenant, although the condition speaks of an occupation by "a member," meaning the member of the association insured.

Now can it be said that at the time of the fire there was any such occupation ? It is quite impossible to do so ? It is hard that the plaintiff, who is in no manner personally to blame for the non-occupation, and who had in fact no personal knowledge of it, should suffer because of it. But so the contract reads. And if the defendants insist upon it, as they do most strenuously, we cannot do otherwise than read the contract as framed.

The insurers have a right to stipulate for the care and supervision which is involved in occupancy. They have made such a stipulation a part of this contract. The plaintiff accepted the contract with that stipulation in it. It makes no exception for a change of tenants. And it is not made, as to its operation, to depend on increased risk.

The rule must be made absolute.

MORRISON, J., and WILSON, J., concurred.

Rule absolute for nonsuit.

Shannon v. The Gore District Mutual Fire Insurance Company.

Insurance—Double Insurance—Same agent for both companies—Estoppel.

The plaintiff and one Morris, who was local agent at Barrie for defendants and for the Hastings Mutual Insurance Company as well, went together to one M., who filled up two applications for insurance, which were signed by the plaintiff, one for insurance with defendants on his grist mill, and the other for insurance with the Hastings Company on fixed and movable machinery in the mill. The agent, thinking the former insurance was on the building only, and the latter on the machinery only, did not inform defendants of the other insurance, and the application to defendants stated that there was no other insurance on the property.

Held, that there was a further insurance on part of the property insured by defendants; but

Held, also, WILSON, J., dissenting, that the defendants, under the circumstances, could not set it up to defeat the plaintiff's claim, defendants' agent having prepared the application with a full knowledge of the facts.

ACTION on a policy by deed dated 4th May, 1874, for $3,000, for one year from 22nd April, 1874, on a grist mill in Innisfil.

The defendants pleaded a sixth plea, stating further insurances on the property by the plaintiff, which did not subsist with the consent of the directors signified by endorsement on the policy signed by the secretary or other officer of the defendants authorized to do so, or otherwise acknowledged by the defendants in writing, whereby and by force of the statute, the policy was void.

The plaintiff took issue upon the plea, and also replied, that it was further provided by the statute that where notification in writing shall have been received by the company from the insured of his having insured an additional sum on the same property in some other company, the additional insurance should be deemed to be assented to unless the company so notified shall, within two weeks after the receipt of such notice, signify to the party in writing their dissent; and the plaintiff says that shortly after he had effected the further insurances mentioned in the plea, and before the loss occurred, he notified or caused the defendants to be notified in writing of such further insurances, and they did not within two weeks after the receipt of such notices signify to the plaintiff their dissent thereto, and the said loss did not occur within the said two weeks.

And on equitable grounds the plaintiff also replied to so much of the sixth plea as alleges that during the continuance of the policy there subsisted upon the premises, by the act of the plaintiff, a policy of insurance in the Hastings Mutual Insurance Company, that the insurance in the Hastings Mutual Insurance Company was effected by or through the defendants' said local agent in the second and third replications mentioned, by whom the application for insurance on which the defendants issued the said policy was received, and by whom an interim contract of insurance with the plaintiff was duly effected. And the plaintiff says that both said applications for insurance were received by the said agent, and interim receipts therefor were issued by him at the same time, and he was fully aware of the said insurance in the Hastings Mutual Insurance Company, and the defendants by means thereof had full knowledge or notice of the said insurance in the said Hastings Mutual Insurance Company. And the plaintiff further says that the application for insurance by the defendants was filled up at the request or by and on behalf of the said agent, who omitted by error or in mistake to insert or have inserted therein the existence of the said insurance in the said Hastings Mutual Insurance Company, and the plaintiff always believed that the fact of the said insurance in the said Hastings Mutual Insurance Company was known to the defendants, in consequence of which he took no steps, as he otherwise would have done, to have the assent of the defendants' secretary in writing obtained thereto, and he continued to believe so until after the happening of the said loss.

The defendants took issue on both replications, and they demurred to the equitable replication, on the grounds that it does not displace the facts stated in the plea about the insurance in the Hastings Insurance Company, nor is it

.any answer thereto that the said local agent had knowledge
·of the said insurance, nor is the knowledge of the said local
:agent sufficient, within the meaning of the said policy or
the conditions thereof, to bind the company.

Joinder.

The cause was tried at Barrie, before Patterson, J., at
the last Spring assizes, with a jury.

The case rested entirely on the double insurance.

Charles Morris, for the defendants, said: I am local agent
here (Barrie) for the defendants. Was so in April, 1874.
The application for insurance was taken by me. The
policy issued on it. It was written by John Morrow and
signed by plaintiff. I saw him sign it. The written part
-of the diagram is Morrow's writing. At same time of this
application, there was an application by plaintiff for insurance in the Hastings Company, for which also I was agent.

Cross-examination—When I sent forward this application, I knew of the application in the Hastings. I did not
know I should have stated it. I did not intend to put it
down at all. I thought that correct. I did not inform
the company of the Hastings insurance. I did not write a
letter with the application. I thought the Hasting insurance was on machinery, and not on the building as this
was. If I had noticed it, and thought it was necessary to
state the Hastings insurance, I would have spoken to the
plaintiff about it. I had a book of instructions from the
defendants' company. It is used up. It was about the
same as that of the Hastings company.

Re-examination—I did not know that the Gore insurance was mentioned in the Hastings application.

The same witness was afterwards recalled by the plaintiff. He said: The Gore application was read over by Mr.
Morrow. I have no recollection of noticing what was read
about other insurances. I may have paid attention and
may not. I understood this to be an insurance on the
building, and that in the Hastings to be on the machinery.
If I had thought both applications were on the same property, and had noticed the statement in this one that there

was no other insurance on the same property, I would have had it corrected.

Mr. *Morrow* said he wrote the application at the request of Mr. Morris, as he, Morris, thought he, Morrow, was a better penman than he was. When he drew the Gore application there was then no other insurance on the property. (The Gore application having been written before the other one.)

The plaintiff said: When the application was read over to me I do not know that I noticed that it contained the statement that there was no other insurance on the property. I thought there was no necessity to notify the Gore company of the insurance in the Hastings. Mr. Morris said he would make the application all right with the Gore and Hastings, and I supposed he had done so. I knew it was necessary the Gore Company should know of the insurance in the Hastings Company. I thought they had been informed of it by the agent, Mr. Morris. There was no conversation between me and Mr. Morris about that; only the Gore application was read. He said they were both the same. He did not say anything about the Hastings insurance. I did not know how the question about the insurance was answered.

The learned Judge found on the issues, on the equitable replication, that both the applications were prepared on the same occasion, and that they were written by John Morrow at Morris's, the agent's, request, the plaintiff concurring in that request : that Morrow wrote them on behalf of the plaintiff, and not as the act of Morris, and that the application for the defendants' policy was read over to the plaintiff before he signed it : that Morris, the agent, knew of both those applications, and he received them and gave interim receipts effecting interim insurances in both of them, but did not communicate to the head office, nor to any office of the defendants, the fact of the insurance in the Hastings Company : that the defendants had no knowledge of that insurance, except so far as the knowledge of Morris can be imputed to them ; and that although the plaintiff knew the Hastings insurance ought to have been communicated to the defendants, his attention was not directed to the necessity for the statement of it in the application, or to the omission of it from the application ; and that he relied on Morris giving whatever notice of it was necessary, and he took no steps himself to give such notice.

The defendants' counsel, on the opinion of the learned Judge being expressed on the other issues, withdrew all objections to the plaintiff's right to recover upon such other issues, and rested only upon the defence of the double insurance.

The verdict was then entered for the defendants on the issues arising on the sixth plea, and for the plaintiff on the other issues, and the damages were assessed for the plaintiff contingently at $3.309, and leave was reserved to the plaintiff to move to enter a verdict for him on the issues on the sixth plea, and to recover the damages assessed, if the Court should be of opinion that no double insurance existed—that is, that the policy of the defendants' company covered fixed machinery, and that under the conditions in the statute this policy was not avoided.

In Easter term last, May 16, 1876, *McCarthy*, Q.C., obtained a rule calling on the defendants to shew cause why the verdict entered for them on the issues on the sixth plea should not be set aside, and a verdict entered thereon for the plaintiff, and for the damages assessed at $3.309, pursuant to leave reserved, and why the plaintiff should not have liberty to amend the replication to the sixth plea so as to meet the evidence adduced at the trial.

In Trinity term last, August 29, 1876, *J. H. Cameron*, Q.C., shewed cause, *Durand* with him. Morris, the agent of the defendants for taking applications for insurance, was not their agent to receive notice of further insurances. Besides, what is called a notice was the mere knowledge by him that when he was taking their risk, he, being also the agent of the Hastings Mutual Insurance Company at the

the time, took a risk for the latter company on the same
property for the plaintiff. The defendants are expressly
protected by their 37th and 38th rules, which are the same
as the 37th and 38th sections of the 36 Vic. ch. 44, O. He
referred also to the law as it is stated in *Clarke* on Insurance 152-156, and to *Butler* v. *Waterloo County Mutual
Fire Ins. Co.*, 29 U. C. R. 553 ; *Jacobs* v. *The Equitable Ins.
Co.*, 18 U. C. R. 14; *Merritt* v. *Niagara District Mutual
Fire Ins. Co.*, 18 U. C. R. 529; *Bruce* v. *Gore District
Mutual Ass. Co.*, 20 C. P. 207.

McCarthy, Q. C., supported the rule, *Strathy* with him.
If there was a double insurance the equitable replication
was proved by the evidence. It was a question whether
Morrow, who drew the plaintiff's application at Morris's the
agent's request, did so as agent for the plaintiff, or as agent
of the defendants. Morrow did so at Morris' request, because he was a better pennman than Morris. The act must
be considered just as if Morris, the defendants' agent, had
personally done it. It is denied, however, that there was
a double insurance. The Hastings policy is "on fixed and
movable machinery in mill." The defendants' policy is
" on his frame grist mill with stone basement," and in the
application the "building" is valued at $6,000. If the
instrument is a double insurance then it should be reformed,
because it was taken by mistake both of the plaintiff and
of Morris, the agent of the defendants, upon the whole grist
mill, while it should have been, and was to have been, upon
the "building" only, exclusive of machinery. He referred
to *Weinaugh* v. *Provincial Fire Ins. Co.*, 20 C. P. 405 ;
May on Insurance, 448 ; *Storer* v. *Elliot Fire Ins. Co.*,
45 Me. 175. The notice to Morris by what took place
with him at the time of the two applications was a sufficient notice, and in writing, too, if necessary, that the
plaintiff was making another insurance with the Hastings
Company, and it was his duty then to have notified the
defendants of it: *Hatton* v. *Beacon Ins. Co.*, 16 U. C. R.
316 ; *Penley* v. *Beacon Ass. Co.*, 7 Grant 130 ; *Tucker* v.
Provincial Ins. Co., 7 Grant 122 ; *Henry* v. *The Agricul-*

tural Mutual Ass. Association, 11 Grant 125, 131 ; *Burton* v. *Gore District Mutual Fire Ins. Co.,* 12 Grant 156 ; *Rowe* v. *London & Lancashire Fire Ins. Co.,* 12 Grant 311; *Wyld* v. *London, Liverpool & Globe Ins. Co.,* 33 U. C. R. 284, 21 Grant 458 ; *Shannon* v. *Gore District Mutual Ins. Co.,* 37 U. C. R. 380 ; *Cole* v. *Jessup,* 9 Barb. 395 ; *Union Mutual Ins. Co.* v. *Wilkinson,* 13 Wall. 222 ; *North Eastern Fire and Mutual Ins. Co.* v. *Schetller,* 38 Ill. 166 ; *Van Bories* v. *United Life, Fire and Marine, Ins. Co.,* 8 Bush, Ky. 133 ; *Robertson* v. *Bullions,* 9 Barb. 64, 101 ; *Sexton* v. *Montgomery County Mutual Ins. Co.,* 9 Barb. 191 ; *May* on Insurance, 371 ; *Columbia Ins. Co.* v. *Cooper,* 50 Penn. 331 ; *Dresser* v. *Norwood,* 10 Jur. N. S. 851 ; *Ætna Live Stock Fire and Tornado Ins. Co.* v. *Olmstead,* 4 Am. 483, 485.

January 2, 1877. WILSON, J.—I have not seen any of the papers relating to the Hastings insurance. They are not among the exhibits in this cause. I do not know precisely the wording of that application or policy. Taking the description of the property insured from Mr. McCarthy's statement of it—that it was described as "fixed and movable machinery in mill," while the defendants' policy was on a "frame grist mill with stone basement"—I should say that the "mill" would include the "fixed and movable machinery" of it. Perhaps not all the *movable* machinery, but certainly it would include the upper mill stone, which is movable, and which is a fixture although movable: *Liford's Case,* 11 Co. 46 *b.* 50 *b.*

"Steam saw mill" includes not only the building, but all the machinery in it necessary to make it a steam saw mill : *Bigler* v. *New York Central Ins. Co.,* 20 Barb. 635.

So also as to "Starch Manufactory" : *Peoria Marine and Fire Ins. Co.* v. *Lewis,* 18 Ill. 553.

Storer v. *Elliot Fire Ins. Co.,* 45 Me. 175, shews that merchandize insured "in the chambers" of a building before insured, it might be shewn that the goods in the

chambers were not intended to be included in the first
policy.

That I think could not be done in this case, so far as the
defendants are concerned.

This is a case of contract between the owner of the
inheritance and the insurance company. It is not governed
by the law of landlord and tenant, but in my opinion by
the law between vendor and vendee, or between heir and
executor, or mortgagor and mortgagee ; and the machinery
therefore, and all fixtures in the mill were covered by the
insurance of the mill: *Place* v. *Fagg*, 4 M. & R. 277;
Fisher v. *Dixon*, 12 Cl. & F. 312; *Mather* v. *Fraser*, 2 K.
& J. 536, 2 Jur. N. S. 900; *Walmsley* v. *Milne*, 7 C. B. N.
S. 115, and the numerous cases there referred to.

There was therefore a double insurance in fact upon
part of the same property which was insured by the
defendants.

Then had the defendants notice of it? They had not
notice in fact, nor any other notice than that which Morris
their agent, who received the application, had.

The plaintiff signed an application drawn by Morrow at
Morris's request, but for the plaintiff, and not for the
defendants, in which the plaintiff has stated there was "no
other insurance at present on the property." And he
signed it.

That statement was literally true, because that application was written before the one for the Hastings Company,
and there was at that instant no other insurance on the
premises. The interim receipt was not then given, and
would not be given till after the application was complete,
and the premium paid.

But the applications for the two insurances were being
written by the same person, the one immediately following
the other, and in common parlance at the same time. The
two insurances were all the one transaction. Morris was
the agent of both companies. He and the plaintiff went
to Morrow's to fill up the two applications, and he did so,
and they were then signed by the plaintiff. The applica-

tion for insurance with the defendants was read over to. the plaintiff.

From the evidence both the plaintiff and Morris thought the application for the defendants' company was for insurance only on the building, exclusive of all machinery, and that the other insurance was to be upon the machinery and not upon the building. The plaintiff said: "If I had thought both applications were on the same property, and had noticed the statement in this one that there was no other insurance on the same property, I would have had it corrected." Morris gave evidence to the like effect, adding: "If I had noticed it, and thought it was necessary to state the Hastings insurance, I should have spoken to plaintiff about it;" and he had just before said, "I did not intend to put it down at all."

It is useless therefore to talk of notice of the double insurance when neither party thought or believed there was one. They each did just exactly what they intended to do, and neither of them contemplated informing the defendants about the Hastings insurance, simply because they each thought it was unnecessary and useless, because there was no other further or double insurance, as they thought, being made.

The expression in the application of the value of the *building only* being $6,000 does not shew the *insurance* was to be upon the building only, exclusive of the machinery in it, but that the value given was the value of the building only, "exclusive of the land" on which it stood. The application was for insurance "on a grist mill," and the mill is also described as having two run of stones and a. smut machine, and as occupied by the plaintiff as a grist and flour mill.

I am of opinion that on the issues on the sixth plea the plaintiff has failed to prove a notice to the defendants of the Hastings insurance, which is valid by reason of the defendants' failure to dissent from it in two weeks thereafter; and that the following parts of the equitable replication are not proved, that is to say. 1. That Morris, the agent, omitted by error or mistake to insert in the application the insurance in the Hastings Company; 2. That the plaintiff always believed the fact of the Hastings insurance was known to the defendants; 3. That in consequence thereof he took no steps, as he otherwise would, to have had the proper assent obtained; 4. And that he continued to believe so until after the loss by fire.

It is not necessary to consider the effect of the other part of the replication, that Morris was the agent of the two companies, and received the two applications at the same time, and granted also the two interim receipts, and he was therefore fully aware of the insurance in the Hastings Company, and so the defendants had full knowledge and notice thereof, because the facts, as I have already stated, shew there was no idea or belief entertained by either the plaintiff or Morris that the Hastings insurance was, a further or double insurance, and there was apparently no intention that it should be so; and each of them, as I understand it, believed the other thought so too. The question of notice being given to the defendants never entered their minds, and they never intended notice should be given to or be considered as received by Morris, and be in turn communicated by him to the defendants. It was not an omission, error, or mistake not to state the Hastings insurance in the application, nor was it any omission, error, or mistake that Morris did not receive and act upon the knowledge he had as a notice of the Hastings insurance.

Both parties deliberately withheld all mention of the Hastings insurance from being mentioned in the defendants' application, and both parties knew that Morris was not notified and had no knowledge of a double insurance ; and that he was not to communicate the Hastings insurance to the defendants; and that the defendants would have no other notice or knowledge of the insurance upon the premises than the application to them expressly contained; and therefore that part of the replication fails also.

The plaintiff's case, if he have one, is for a reformation of the policy, because he contracted in fact, it is said, with the defendants' agent for an insurance only upon the frame work or structure of the building, and not upon any part of the machinery which was contained in it; and upon the evidence I am of opinion that fact was proved.

If there had been no delay and no loss sustained, there would, I presume, have been relief given.

But I doubt whether the plaintiff can be relieved from the effect of this bargain when he did insure as he thought what he meant to insure, and the only mistake is, that he did not know the term *grist mill* would include the machinery as well as the building. The defendants accepted his application just as he gave it, and have acted upon it up to the time of the loss on the 21st of July thereafter, and they believed their policy covered the machinery as well as the building. The plaintiff meant to sign that application just as it is expressed. The defendants' agent took it just as it is expressed, and the defendants themselves have relied upon it just as it is expressed.

What is there then to reform? The rectification could only be that by the term *grist mill* the plaintiff meant the building without the machinery; but the defendants did not so understand him, although their agent did, but neither he nor the agent ever told them so, and the plaintiff intentionally and deliberately signed the application to be acted on by the defendants just as it stands, and they have done so. Now he says he did not know the meaning of *grist mill*, and yet he must admit that that was the very term he meant to use, and to communicate to the defendants for them to act upon. That is not a mistake to be rectified. It is a ground for rescission of the contract, because the parties were not of one mind. The defendants never meant to contract in any other form than as they have done.

The cases of *Mackenzie* v. *Coulson,* L. R. 8 Eq. 368, and *Powell* v. *Smith,* L. R. 14 Eq. 85, apply here.

In my opinion this is not a case for rectification of the policy.

How such relief should be given in a case like the present, if it could be done, is not very clear.

The declaration states an insurance on the grist mill. The plaintiff says now that it is a wrong description of the property, and he wants it amended. If that is to be done, there should be some claim or prayer made for it, setting out the necessary facts and circumstances to entitle the plaintiff to it, and if it be ordered the declaration should either be amended according to the order made, or else the order made and entered on the record must stand in the place of an actual amendment: *Smith* v. *Iliffe*, L. R. 20 Eq. 666; *White* v. *White*, L. R. 15 Eq. 247; *Powell* v. *Smith*, L. R. 14 Eq. 85.

The rule, I think, should be discharged.

HARRISON, C. J —I agree that there was a further insurance, but think that owing to the fact of the same person being the agent of both companies, and looking at what took place between that person and the plaintiff at the time the insurances were effected, the defendants ought not to be allowed to set up that the additional insurance was not with their consent in writing, so as to defeat the claim of the plaintiff.

It appears to me that the application was prepared by the agent of the defendants, who, at the time he did so and received the plaintiff's money for the defendants, had a full knowledge of the facts now relied upon for the purpose of defeating the contract which he entered into on behalf of the defendants; and that the defendants and not the plaintiff, should suffer either because of the ignorance of the agent as to what was necessary to constitute a double insurance, or his neglect to communicate to the defendants what took place between himself and the plaintiff in reference to it. See *Wing* v. *Harvey*, 5 DeG. McN. &G. 265; *Patterson* v. *The Royal Ins. Co.*, 14 Grant 169; *Hawke* v. *The Niagara District Fire Ins. Co.*, 23 Grant 139; *Wyld* v. *The London and Liverpool & Globe Ins. Co.*, 21 Grant 458, 23 Grant 442; *In re Non-Tariff Fire Ins. Co.*, L. R. 19 Eq. 485.

If the agent were the underwriter, there can be no doubt that such a defence as now set up would not, under the facts proved, be allowed to prevail against the plaintiff's claim.

I think, on the facts, that the defendants are not in this respect in any better position, as against the plaintiff, than their own agent.

The general rule applicable to insurance and other companies, laid down both in English and United States authorities, is, that the company must be bound by the acts of their agent, and that the knowledge of the agent must be held to be the knowledge of the principal.

It is also a general rule, thoroughly recognized in both countries, that where one of two innocent persons must suffer from the misconduct or default of a third, the one who authorized or enabled the third to do the act must be the sufferer.

It would be contrary to the plainest principles of justice to permit insurance companies to employ incompetent agents, and then allow the companies to take advantage of the acts, omissions, or ignorance of the agents to defeat the policies of insurance, for which the companies received the premium moneys and the agents their commission.

Happily, in England insurance companies do not as often attempt to profit by the misconduct, neglect, or ignorance of their agents, as insurance companies in the United States and in Canada.

A retrospect of the most recent decisions of the United States Courts, manifests a continued struggle on the part of the Courts to prevent insurance companies making victims of those who reposed confidence in them, and paid their money for what was supposed to be, and what ought in equity and good conscience to be held, good contracts of insurance.

The tendency of the United States Courts at one time was, by their decisions to give effect to the strict letter of the contract regardless of the surrounding circumstances, and defeat insurance claims even where there was no imputation of dishonesty, but the startling injustice exposed, if not caused by these decisions, for a time compelled the Courts to pause, and now the tendency is strongly in an opposite direction.

Hence it has been recently held that if the application for insurance is taken by the agent of the company, and he is aware of facts material to the risk which are not set forth in the application, the company will be charged with the knowledge, and in such a case an unintentional concealment or misrepresentation will not avoid the policy : *Marshall* v. *Columbian Mutual Fire Ins. Co.*, 27 N. H. 157; *Campbell* v. *The Merchants and Farmers Mutual Fire Ins. Co.*, 37 N. H. 35 ; *Plumb* v. *Cattaraugus County Mutual Ins. Co.*, 18 N. Y. 392.

Much more is this held to be the law where the applicant makes a statement of facts which the agent thinks immaterial, and either from ignorance or negligence omits or misrepresents in the application : *Masters* v. *The Maddison County Mutual Ins. Co.*, 11 Barb. 624 ; *New York Central Ins. Co.*, v. *National Protection Ins. Co.*, 20 Barb. 468 ; *Columbia Ins. Co.* v. *Cooper*, 50 Penn. 331; *Ætna Live Stock Fire and Tornado Ins. Co.* v. *Olmstead*, 4 Am. 483.

An agent of an insurance company authorized to procure applications for insurance, and furnished by the company with printed blanks therefor containing interrogatories to be answered by the applicant with regard to the condition of the property to be insured, has, as incidental to such power, authority to make all necessary explanations of the meaning and effect of the terms employed by the company in their interrogatories; and to agree with the applicant as to the terms which he shall employ to express the facts stated by him in answer to the interrogatories : *Malleable Iron Works* v. *Phœnix Ins. Co.*, 25 Conn. 465. See also *Coombs* v. *The Hannibal Ins. Co.*, 43 Mo. 148 ; *May* v. *The Buckeye Mutual Ins. Co.*, 3 Am. 76, 82 ; *Ætna Live Stock Fire and Tornado Ins Co.* v. *Olmstead*, 4 Am. 483, 486 ; *Commercial Ins. Co.* v. *Spankneble*, *Ib.* 582 ; *The Dayton Ins. Co.* v. *Kelly*, 15 Am. 612.

Such an agent is deemed to be acting within the scope of his authority where he himself fills up the blank application, and if by his fault or neglect it contains a material mis-statement not authorized in the instructions of the party who signs it, the loss must be that of the company and not of the party so insuring: *Rowley* v. *Empire Ins. Co.*. 36 N. Y. 550 ; *Howard Fire Ins. Co.* v. *Bruner*, 23 Penn: 50, 57 ; *Miller* v. *The Mutual Benefit Life Ins.* Co., 7 Am. 122.

The Legislature of the State of Maine, in order if possible to place the rights of the parties beyond the region of judicial conflict, has by section 2 of ch. 34 of the Public Acts of 1861, enacted that any application for insurance drawn by the agent of the insurance company shall be deemed conclusive upon the company, although it contain representations of material facts which are material and untrue. See *Caston* v. *Monmouth Mutual Fire Ins Co.*, 54 Me. 170.

The decisions of the Supreme Court of the United States have, as a rule, at all times and in all places commanded great respect; and in a recent insurance case an eminent Judge of that Court used language which can leave no doubt as to its meaning, and which, I think, when properly understood, must commend itself to all concerned in the administration of justice.

Miller, J., in delivering the judgment in *Union Mutual Ins. Co.* v. *Wilkinson*, 13 Wall. 222, said at p. 233: "It is in precisely such cases as this that Courts of law in modern times have introduced the doctrine of equitable estoppels, or, as it is sometimes called, estoppels *in pais*. The principle is that where one party has by his representation or his conduct induced the other party to a transaction to give him an advantage which it would be against equity and good conscience for him to assert, he would not, in a Court of justice be permitted to avail himself of that advantage. And although the cases to which this principle is to be applied are not as well defined as could be wished, the general doctrine is well understood and is applied by Courts of law as well as equity where the technical advantage thus obtained is set.

up and relied on to defeat the ends of justice or establish
a dishonest claim. It has been applied to the precise class.
of cases of the one now before us in numerous well-con-
sidered judgments by the Courts of this country. Indeed,
the doctrine is so well understood and so often enforced
that if, in the transaction we are now considering, Ball, the
insurance agent, who made out the application, had been in
fact the underwriter of the policy, no one would doubt its.
applicability to the present case. Yet the proposition
admits of as little doubt that if Ball was the agent of the
insurance company, and not of the plaintiff, in what he did
in filling up the application, the company must be held to
stand just as he would if he were the principal."

In a subsequent part of the same judgment the same
learned Judge says p. 234: " Whose agent was Ball in filling up the application ? This question has been decided
differently by Courts of the highest respectability in cases
precisely analogous to the present. It is not to be denied that.
the application, logically considered, is the work of the assured, and if left to himself or to such assistance as he might.
select, the person so selected would be his agent, and he
alone would be responsible. On the other hand, it is well
known, so well that no Court could be justified in shutting
its eyes to it, that insurance companies organized under
the laws of one State, and having in that State their principal business office, send their agents all over the land
with directions to solicit and procure applications for
policies, furnishing them with printed arguments in favour
of the value and necessity of life insurance, and of the
special advantages of the corporation which the agent
represents. They pay these agents large commissions on
premiums thus obtained, and the policies are delivered at,
their hands to the assured. The agents are stimulated by
letters and instructions to activity in procuring contracts,
and the party who is in this manner induced to take out
a policy rarely sees or knows anything about the company
or its officers by whom it is issued, but looks to and relies.
upon the agent who has persuaded him to effect insurance.

as the full and complete representative of the company, in all that is said or done in making the contract. Has he not a right to so regard him? It is quite true that the reports of judicial decisions are filled with the efforts of these companies, by their counsel, to establish the doctrine that they can do all this and yet limit their responsibility for the acts of their agents to the simple receipt of the premium and delivery of the policy, the argument being that, as to all other acts of the agent, he is the agent of the assured. This proposition is not without some support in some of the earlier decisions on the subject; and at a time when insurance companies waited for parties to come to them to seek assurance or to forward applications on their own motion, the doctrine had a reasonable foundation to rest upon. But to apply such a doctrine in its full force to the system of selling policies through agents, which we have described, would be a snare and a delusion, leading, as it has done in numerous instances, to the grossest frauds of which the insurance companies receive the benefits, and the parties supposing themselves insured are the victims. The tendency of the modern decisions in this country is steadily in the opposite direction."

Many United States decisions will be found referred to in my judgment when the parties were before us on demurrer. In addition I would mention *Van Bories* v. *The United Life, Fire, and Marine Ins. Co.*, 8 Ky. 133, in which there will be found cited a great many United States decisions on the point in controversy. The condition of the policy was as here, that "If there is or shall hereafter be made any further insurance on the property hereby insured without being notified to this company, and its consent thereto written hereon, then and in that case this policy shall be of no binding force on this company." It appeared that the United Life, Fire, and Marine Insurance Company and the Kenton Insurance Company had the same agent in Louisville: that the assured obtained from that agent a policy on goods in the company first named, and on the next day obtained from the same agent a policy on the same goods in the company secondly named: that formal notice of the second insurance was never given to the first named company, nor was its consent thereto written on the policy; but it was held that the knowledge of the agent was the knowledge of the company, and that under the circumstances the company ought not to be allowed to defeat the policy on the ground that there was no written consent to the second insurance.

Here both insurances were not only effected by the same agent, but at the same time, and, as the agent knew, with no intention that there should be in fact a double insurance. In furtherance of justice, I think we should hold the defendants bound by what then took place, so as to prevent them after a loss avoiding the policy on the ground that they were not notified in writing of the second insurance.

In my opinion, the plaintiff should, under section 50 of the Administration of Justice Act of 1873, be allowed to strike out all unnecessary allegations from his replication and to make such amendments as are necessary on the facts, according to the views above expressed, for the purpose of avoiding the plea, and that thereupon a verdict should be entered for the plaintiff for $3,309, pursuant to leave reserved at the trial. See *Howeren* v. *Bradburn*, 22 Grant 96.

MORRISON, J.—I concur in the result arrived at by the learned Chief Justice. This is one of those cases in which, in whatever way it may be viewed, we find difficulty in arriving at a clear satisfactory conclusion. The justice of the case is entirely with the plaintiff. I can only view the case as if the agent had effected the insurance in the head office of the defendants, with their sanction and concurrence.

Rule absolute (a.)

(a) See *Billington* v. *The Provincial Ins. Co.*, 24 Grant 299.

MALCOLM SINCLAIR v. THE CANADIAN MUTUAL FIRE
INSURANCE COMPANY.

Mutual Ins. Co.—False statement as to title—Concealment of encumbrance—
36 Vic. ch. 44, sec. 36, O.

The plaintiff, in his application for insurance with defendants, a mutual
insurance company, answered "Yes" to the question, "Does the property to be insured belong exclusively to you?" and to the question,
"If encumbered, state to what amount," he made no answer. The
defendants' agent, who took the application, said the plaintiff told him
there was a mortgage for $100 on the building, which he was about to
have discharged, and that he, the agent, therefore thought it unnecessary to insert it in the application, and gave no notice of it to the
company. The plaintiff said the agent filled up the application, which
he signed without reading it, and that he told the agent of the mortgage, but did not say that he was going to remove it.

Held, that there was no false statement as to title ; and that there was no
concealment as to the encumbrance, for the omission to mention it was
sufficiently explained ; and that the defendants, after the issue of the
policy on the application, and after the fire, could not take advantage
of the omission as avoiding the policy under 36 Vic. ch. 44, sec. 36, O.

Quære, whether the "false statement" or "concealment" mentioned
in that section must not be fraudulent, in order to avoid the policy.

ACTION on a fire policy of insurance.

The policy was dated 1st June, 1875, and was for $300
on a shop and dwelling house occupied by the insured,
$200 on the ordinary contents of the dwelling house, and
$500 on the stock contained in the shop, for three years
from date, subject to and in reference to the terms and
conditions on the policy, and which constituted the basis
of insurance.

The declaration, after setting out the policy and averring
performance of conditions precedent, averred interest in the
insured, and a total loss by fire of the shop and dwelling
house, together with the contents of each, within the time
limited by the policy.

The defendants pleaded several pleas, but the only pleas
necessary to be mentioned are the sixth and seventh.

The sixth plea was to the effect, that in and by the policy
and the statute in that behalf it is provided that the
application of the insured should be taken and considered
as a part and portion of the policy, and that any fraudulent

misrepresentation contained in the application, or any false statement respecting the title or ownership of the applicant, or his circumstances, or the concealment of any incumbrances on the insured property, or on the land on which it might be situated, or if the assured should not be the sole and unconditional owner of the property insured, unless the true title should be expressed therein, then, and in either of such cases, the policy should be void; with an averment that the plaintiff, in and by the application, stated that the property he insured belonged exclusively to him, and concealed from the defendants the fact that the land and building were mortgaged, as the fact was; and that the plaintiff did not express or state the true ownership of the property insured.

The seventh plea was to the effect, that in and by the policy and the statute in that behalf, it is, among other things, provided that concealment by the assured, at the time of effecting the insurance, of any incumbrance on the insured property or the land on which it might be situated, should render the policy void; and alleged that at the time of the application the buildings insured by the policy, and the land on which the same were situated, were encumbered and subject to a mortgage thereon, and that the plaintiff upon the application for insurance did not state the incumbrance thereon, or any incumbrance, but, on the contrary, the plaintiff concealed the incumbrance from the defendants, by which, and by force of the statute in such case made and provided, the policy became void and of no effect.

The plaintiff took issue on the pleas, and required the issues to be tried by a jury, but the learned Judge at the trial made an order dispensing with the jury.

The cause was tried at the last Fall Assizes, for the county of Wellington, before Galt, J., without a jury.

The policy was put in and admitted.

The plaintiff proved a total loss of the insured property by fire, and that the values exceeded those mentioned in the policy. There was no dispute as to the value of household furniture and wearing apparel, but defendants disputed the value of the stock.

The application for the insurance, signed by the plaintiff, was put in and admitted. It was dated 1st June, 1875.

The questions and answers in the application, relied upon by the defendants as making void the policy, were the following :—" 12. Does the property to be insured belong exclusively to you ? Yes. If incumbered, state to what amount ? ——"

The application concluded as follows:—"I hereby declare that the foregoing is a just, full, and true exposition of all the facts and circumstances in regard to the condition, situation, value, and risk of the property to be insured, as far the same are known to me; And I hereby agree and consent that the same, and the diagram of the premises herewith, shall be held to form the basis of the liability of the said company."

It was proved by John Crosson, the agent of the defendants for soliciting risks, that the application was taken by him in the plaintiff's shop; that plaintiff told him there was a mortgage for $100 on the building, which he was about to have discharged, and he, the agent, therefore thought it unnecessary to insert it in the application; and that he omitted to notify the company as to what had taken place about the mortgage.

The plaintiff proved that the agent himself filled up the application: that he, the plaintiff, signed it without reading it; that he told him of the $100 mortgage, but denied that he said he was going to remove it.

Counsel for the defendants moved for a nonsuit, on the ground that the existence of the mortgage was not communicated to the defendants, and on the ground that the plaintiff had not in the application disclosed his true title to the property.

The learned Judge thought the objections fatal to the plaintiff's recovery.

Counsel for the plaintiff applied to reply equitably to the plea, or to amend the declaration by shewing the facts; but the learned Judge, thinking he ought not to allow such an amendment at the trial, nonsuited the plaintiff, but reserved leave to plaintiff to move in term, and if the Court should be opinion that upon such amendment being allowed and sustained, the plaintiff was entitled to recover, in order to save another trial, the learned Judge assessed the damages at $800—the defendants not consenting to the assessment of damages.

During this term, November 23, 1876, *S. Richards,* Q. C., obtained a rule calling on the defendants to shew cause why the nonsuit should not be set aside, and a verdict entered for the plaintiff for $800, or such other sum as the Court might direct, or a new trial had, on the ground that the existence of the mortgage on the building did not invalidate the policy, and it was not under the evidence a breach of the conditions: that even if a breach of the condition 'as to the insurance of the building, it would not invalidate the policy as to the other subjects of insurance: that there was no fraudulent misrepresentation or false statement, or any concealment as to title or as to the mortgage, or any untrue statement as to the title: that defendants, by their agent, were notified of and were aware of the existence of the mortgage, and considered it unnecessary to insert any statement thereof in the application for insurance ; and that on the facts the plaintiff was entitled to recover; and why the plaintiff should not be allowed to amend the pleadings by equitable replication or otherwise, to admit the facts entitling plaintiff to recover, or displace the sixth and seventh pleas.

Duff, during the same term, December 6, 1876, shewed cause. There was a false statement as to title, or concealment, sufficient under section 36 of 36 Vic. ch. 44, O., to make void the policy: *Stickney* v. *The Niagara District Mutual Ins. Co.,* 23 C. P. 372: *Walroth* v. *St. Lawrence County Mutual Ins. Co.,* 10 U. C. R. 525; and what took place between the plaintiff and the agent did not displace the defence: *Martin* v. *The Home Ins. Co.,* 20 C. P. 447, 451; *Shannon* v. *The*

Hastings Mutual Fire Ins. Co., 25 C. P. 470 ; *Shannon* v. *The Gore District Mutual Fire Ins. Co.*, 37 U. C. R. 380 ; *Samo* v. *The Gore District Mutual Fire Ins. Co.*, 26 C. P. 405 ; *Bleakley* v. *The Niagara District Mutual Fire Ins. Co.*, 16 Grant 198.

S. Richards, Q. C., contra. There was no false statement as to ownership : *Hopkins* v. *The Provincial Ins. Co.*, 18 C. P. 74 ; *White* v. *The Agricultural Mutual Ass. Co.*, 22 C. P. 98 ; and the omission to mention the mortgage in the application was not a concealment of it, but an omission which the company by accepting the risk have waived, and should not now be allowed to take advantage of : *Liberty Hall Association* v. *Housatonic Mutual Fire Ins. Co.*, 7 Gray 261, 265 ; *Rowley* v. *The Empire Ins. Co.*, 36 N. Y. 550 ; S. C., 42 N. Y. 557 ; *Union Mutual Ins. Co.* v. *Wilkinson,* 13 Wall. 222 ; *Wilson* v. *Conway Fire Ins. Co.*, 4 Rh. I. 141 ; *Malleable Iron Co.* v. *Phœnix Ins. Co.*, 25 Conn. 465 ; *Laidlaw* v. *London and Liverpool Ins. Co.*, 13 Grant 377 ; *Wyld* v. *The Liverpool & London & Globe Ins. Co.*, 23 Grant 442 ; *Shannon* v. *Gore District Mutual Ins. Co.*, 37 U. C. R. 380.

December 29, 1876. HARRISON, C. J.—The statute makes void a policy of insurance where there is any fraudulent misrepresentation contained in the application therefor, or any false statement respecting the title or ownership of the applicant, or his circumstances, or the concealment of any encumbrance on the insured property, or on the land on which it may be situated : 36 Vic. ch. 44, sec. 36, O.

The contention of the company is, that there was a false statement respecting the title, as well as the concealment of an encumbrance in the application, and that either must avoid the policy.

The defence, if any, of the company, arises under the answer to the twelfth question contained in the application.

That question and answer are as follow :—"12. Does the property to be insured belong exclusively to you ? Yes. If encumbered, state to what amount ? ——" (no answer.)

The fact that the question is not only as to the exclusive ownership, but as to encumbrance, if any, we think shews that there may be an exclusive ownership, within the meaning of the question, although there be an encumbrance on the title.

The question is in effect, " Do you exclusively own the property, or do you own it jointly with others, and if owned by you exclusively, and not jointly by you and others, is it encumbered and to what amount"?

The word "owner," or the still more general words "property belong," have no definite meaning in law, but are applicable to various interests which persons may have in property proposed to be insured : *Laidlaw* v. *The Liverpool and London Ins. Co.*, 13 Grant 377 ; *Hopkins* v. *The Provincial Ins. Co.*, 18 C. P. 74; *White* v. *The Agricultural Mutual Ins. Co.*. 22 C. P. 98.

Men may properly be said to own and to be exclusive owners of the property on which they live, or which they rent to others, although such property be encumbered for some amount, much less than the real value of the property.

To the question, therefore, put to the owner of a mortgaged property, " Does the property exclusively belong to you ? " there is nothing false in the plaintiff answering " Yes," and especially when followed by the enquiry as to the amount of the encumbrance.

The cases of *Walroth* v. *The St. Lawrence County Mutual Ins. Co.*, 10 U. C. R. 525; *Stickney* v. *The Niagara District Mutual Ins. Co.*, 23 C. P. 372 ; *Sherboneau* v. *The Beaver Mutual Fire Ins. Co.*, 30 U. C. R. 472; S. C., 33 U. C. R. 1, cited on the part of the defendants, are not in conflict with this position.

They are so plainly distinguishable from the case now before us, that it is not necessary to take up time in distinguishing them in detail.

We are of opinion that the sixth plea, which alleges a false statement as to title, is not proved.

The seventh plea raises the question whether there was any concealment of the encumbrance for $100.

The omission to write the answer is not necessarily a concealment. It is open to explanation.

When the explanation is, that the amount of the encumbrance was at the time mentioned by the applicant to the agent of the company who prepared the application, but that the latter either thought there was no encumbrance, that the amount was too small to be noticed, or that he was satisfied it would be soon removed, and for any of these reasons, or some other reason, he deemed it unnecessary to answer the question or report the matter to the company, there cannot be truly said to be any concealment on the part of the applicant.

The United States decisions abundantly establish that in any such case as last supposed the company will not be allowed to avoid the policy, even where the answer was no, and the answer was false in fact. See *Masters* v. *Maddison Mutual Ins. Co.*, 11 Barb. 624 : *New York Central Ins. Co.* v. *National Protection Ins. Co.*, 20 Barb. 468 ; *Columbia Ins. Co.* v. *Cooper*, 50 Penn. 331 ; *Ætna Live Stock Fire and Tornado Ins. Co.* v. *Olmstead*, 4 Am. 483.

But where what is complained of is not a false answer, but an omission to give any answer, we apprehend it is too late for the company, after the issue of the policy and after a loss, to seek to take advantage of that omission. The time for objecting to the omission was when the application was submitted for approval.

The company might either then ask for information as to the omission or pass it regardless of the omission. If they adopt the latter course it is not open to them afterwards to take advantage of it to the prejudice of the insured.

In the case of the *Liberty Hall Association* v. *Housahannic Mutual Fire Ins. Co.*, 7 Gray 261, 265, cited by Mr. Richards, the question was, "How are the buildings occupied? How many tenants?" No answer. And it was attempted to defeat the policy by shewing that the premises were at the time used for a hazardous business; but Bigelow, J., in delivering the judgment of the Supreme Court of

Massachussets, said: "The defendants having issued the policy without requiring any answer to the eleventh interrogatory contained in the application concerning the occupation of the building insured, it was fair to infer that they waived the information on that point; and having done so, they cannot now avoid the policy by proof that the premises were used for a hazardous purpose or business."

If it were necessary to determine whether the "false statement" or "concealment" mentioned in sec. 36 must as well as the "misrepresentation," be fraudulent in order to avoid the policy, the cases of *Laidlaw* v. *The Liverpool and London &c., Ins. Co.*, 13 Grant 377, and *Hopkins* v. *The Provincial Ins. Co.*, 18 C. P. 74, would go far to sustain the affirmative of the proposition, but as we are of opinion that there was no false statement, and no concealment, it is unnecessary at present to decide the question.

The rule must be absolute to enter a verdict for the plaintiff for $800.

MORRISON, J., and WILSON, J., concurred.

Rule absolute.

REGINA v. SELOTIS PORTIS AND SAMUEL GILBERT.

Forgery—Evidence.

On an indictment for feloniously offering, &c.,a forged note commonly called
a Provincial note, issued under the authority of 29-30 Vic. ch. 10,
D., for the payment of $5, it appeared that the prisoners had passed
off a note purporting to be a Provincial note under the statute, knowing that the figure 5 had been pasted over the figure 1, and the word
five over the word one. No evidence was given that the note so
altered was a note issued by the Government of Canada, but it was
shewn further, that when the attention of the prisoners was called to
the alteration they said "give it back if it is not good," and that on its
being placed on the counter one of them took it up and refused to
return it, or substitute good money for it. *Held,* that looking at the
particular character of the forgery—*i. e.,* an alteration—and the conduct of the prisoners, the onus was on them to dispute the validity of
the writing, if a defence ; and a conviction was sustained.

Case reserved by Burton, J., at the Fall Assizes at
London.

The two prisoners were tried and convicted before me
at the Autumn Assizes for Middlesex, 1876, on an indictment which charged them with feloniously offering,
uttering, disposing of, and putting off a certain forged
note, commonly called a Provincial note, issued under the
authority of an Act passed by the Legislature of the late
Province of Canada, for the payment of five dollars, with
intent thereby to defraud, well knowing the same to be
forged, contrary to the form of the statute, &c.

The evidence shewed that the prisoners had, with the
knowledge that the figure 5 had been pasted over the figure
1, and the word "five" over the word "one" upon a note
purporting to be a note issued by the government of the
late Province of Canada under the authority of the statute
in that behalf, passed off and uttered the same as a five
dollar note of that denomination ; but no evidence was
given that the note so altered was a note issued by the
Government of Canada, beyond the production of the note
itself.

No objection was taken until the jury returned from
their room into the jury box, and were prepared to deliver
their verdict, when it was objected by the counsel for the
prisoners that no proof had been given of the note being
a Provincial note.

The evidence shewed further, that when the attention

of the prisoners was called to the paper with the impression of the five pasted over the one they both said, "give it back if it is not good and we will give you good money for it;" but upon its being placed on the counter Gilbert took it up and refused to return it or substitute good money for it.

I reserved the point as to whether the conviction can be sustained on the facts I have stated for the consideration of the Court. The note will be produced.

The jury found the prisoners guilty, and I therefore sentenced them to two years imprisonment in the Provincial penitentiary; but I respited the execution of the sentence until after the disposal of the question.

The prisoners are still confined in the London gaol.

December 6, 1876. The case was argued by *Glass*, Q.C., for the prisoners. It should have been proved at the trial that the note in question was a Provincial note, and this was not done. It was not shewn that the prisoners had forged or altered anything that had a legal existence. He cited *Paley* on Convictions, 5th ed., 120; 29–30 Vic. ch. 10, sec. 1; *Rex* v. *Aslett*, 2 Leach 954; *Tasch.* Crim. L., vol. ii., 114, 115.

J. K. Kerr, Q. C., contra. The prisoners were rightly convicted, and the note was sufficiently proved to sustaain the indictment of forgery. He referred to *Arch.* Cr. Pl. 18th ed., 55; *Tasch.* Cr. L. vol.i., 88; *Regina* v. *Elsworth*, 2 East P. C. 86; *Russell* on Crimes, 4th ed., vol. ii., 751; *Clarke* Cr. L. 356; *Regina* v. *Brown*, 3 Allen N. B. 13, 15; *Roscoe* Crim. Ev., 8th ed., 544; *Regina* v. *Ritson*, L. R. 1 C. C. 200, 204.

December 29, 1876. HARRISON, C. J.—The Governor in Council was, by the 29–30 Vic. ch. 10 sec. 1, passed by the Legislature of the late Province of Canada, authorized to. issue Provincial notes payable on demand, of such denominational values, and in such form, and signed by such persons, and in such manner, by lithograph printing or otherwise, as he should from time to time direct, to an amount not exceeding $5,000,000, except as in the Act provided.

It was by section 19 of the same Act declared that. the provisions of Consol. Stat. C. ch. 94, intituled "An Act respecting forgery," relating to the forging and uttering of bank notes, &c., shall be applicable to the Provincial notes to be issued under the Act.

It is now declared by section 10 of 32–33 Vic. ch. 19, D., that "Whosoever forges or alters, or offers, utters, disposes of, or puts off, knowing the same to be forged or altered any   *   *   Dominion or Provincial note   *   * issued under the authority of any Act of the Legislature of any one of the late Provinces of Upper Canada, Lower Canada, or Canada, or of the Parliament of Canada,   *   * with intent to defraud, is guilty of felony."

The indictment charged the prisoners with feloniously offering, uttering, disposing of, and putting off "a certain forged note commonly called a Provincial note issued under the authority of an Act passed by the Legislature of the late Province of Canada," for the payment of $5, with intent thereby to defraud well knowing the same to be forged.

There was evidence of an alteration of what purported to be a Provincial note issued under the Act mentioned, and that the prisoners knowing the note to have been so altered uttered it; but the objection is, that there was no evidence that the writing altered was what it purported to be, viz., a Provincial note, issued under the authority of 29–30 Vic. ch. 10.

The plea of not guilty to such an indictment puts the Crown to proof of all the traversable allegations contained in the indictment.

The allegation that the note altered was a Provincial note is a traversable allegation in this indictment as framed, and the question is, whether as against the prisoners there was any evidence in support of that allegation.

If the prisoners had when uttering the note said it was a Provincial note altered from one to five, this would have been. some evidence against them that the note was, at the time of the uttering a Provincial note altered as alleged.

The conduct of the prisoners here may, we think, be properly taken as an admission by them that the writing was at one time a Provincial note, so as to throw upon them the onus of shewing that it was irregularly or improperly issued.

The case of *Regina* v. *Brown*, 3 Allen N. B. 13 goes far to sustain the conviction.

The prisoner in that case was, as here, convicted on an indictment charging him with feloniously uttering "a certain writing—to wit, a certain bank note," with intent to defraud.

The bank note was described in the indictment as follows:

"	State of Maine	
5 B.	No.	Five
	3364.	5

The President, Directors & Co. of the Casco Bank, will pay five dollars to bearer on demand.

Portland, 1st June, 1853.

John Chute, Cashier.   Eliphalet Greely, Pres't."

The evidence was, that there was a bank at Portland in the State of Maine; which issued notes for five dollars, and that a genuine note of that bank, of which the writing described in the indictment was an imitation, was of the value of five dollars in the State of Maine.

It was insisted by the prisoner's counsel that there should have been evidence that the Casco bank was a corporation in the State of Maine legally authorized to issue notes such as that described in the indictment.

Chief Justice Carter in delivering the judgment of the Supreme Court of New Brunswick said, p. 15: " The writing in question carries on its face the semblance of a bank note issued by a company in the State of Maine, and there is nothing in its frame which shews that it is illegal, even if there were no charter or Act of incorporation authorizing the issue of such notes. The evidence proved that there are genuine instruments, of which this is an imitation,

which are of value in the State of Maine, and if the
illegality of such instruments would afford a defence to
the prisoner, and such illegality could be shewn by the Act
of incorporation or any other evidence, such proof would
lie on him, rather than the negative proof on the Crown."

Assuming that illegality of the note would be a defence
the Court, under the circumstances, held that the onus of
proving illegality lay upon the prisoner.

In *Rex* v. *Aslett*, 2 Leach 954, cited by Mr. Glass,
the presumption of legality was overthrown, for it was in
evidence that the person who signed the exchequer bills, the
subject of embezzlement, was not legally authorized to
do so.

To constitute the crime of forgery it is not necessary
that the writing charged to be forged should be such as
would be effectual if it were a true and genuine writing.

In *Rex* v. *Sterling* 1 Leach 996, which was the case of
the forgery of a will of a living man, the Judges were
unanimously of opinion that an instrument may be the
subject of forgery although in fact it should appear impossible for such an instrument as the instrument forged to
exist, provided the instrument purports on the face of it
to be good and valid as to the purposes for which it was
intended to be made.

This principle has been applied to the forging or uttering
of deeds and other instruments on the face of them purporting to be valid, but which if genuine could be avoided
by extrinsic evidence : *Rex* v. *Lyon*, R. & R. 255 ; *Rex* v.
Froud, Ib. 389, 1 B. & B. 300, and even to the forging
of bills or notes in England although on the face of them
not stamped ; *Rex* v. *Hawkswood*, 2 T. R. 606 *a* ; *Rex* v.
Reculist, 2 Leach 703.

If the writing be on the face of it such as prohibited
and made void by any statute there could, it is apprehended, be no forgery, for as all are presumed to know the
law there could be no fraud : *Rex* v. *Moffatt*, 1 Leach 431.
See further, *Rex* v. *Catapodi*, R. & R. 65.

A forged paper purporting on the face of it to be a bank

note is the subject of forgery although there be no such bank as named : *Rex* v. *McDonald*, 12 U. C. R. 543. See further *Bishop* on Criminal Law, 5th ed., vol. ii., sec. 533 to 546 inclusive.

" Whosoever maliciously and for any purpose of fraud or deceit, forges any document or thing written, printed, or otherwise made capable of being read, or utters any such forged document or thing knowing the same to be forged, is guilty of felony " : 32–33 Vic. ch. 19 sec. 45 D.

Had the indictment contained a count for uttering a forged writing *purporting* to be a note commonly called a Provincial note, issued under the authority of an Act passed by the Legislature of the late Province of Canada, there would have been no doubt as to the correctness of the finding.

We think that looking at the particular character of the forgery—that is to say, an alteration—and the conduct of the prisoners in regard to it, that the onus was on them to dispute the validity of the writing if its invalidity would be a defence.

In so holding we give the prisoners the benefit of every fair presumption of innocence.

If the character of the forgery were an imitation—an entirely false representation of a genuine note, the presumption of innocence would probably cast on the prosecution the obligation, as in cases of counterfeiting, of shewing that the instrument alleged to be forged was really not what it purports to be; but on this point we give no opinion. See 32–33 Vic. ch. 18 sec. 30 D.

The conviction must be affirmed.

MORRISON, J., and WILSON, J., concurred.

Judgment for the Crown.

The Mechanics' Building and Savings Society v. The Gore District Mutual Fire Insurance Co.

Mutual insurance policy—-Assignment to mortgagee—Subsequent insurance by mortgagor—Effect of on rights of mortgagee—Pleading.

A mortgagee, becoming assignee of a policy under the Mutual Insurance Act 36, Vic. ch. 44, O., by an assignment duly ratified by the company, becomes—whether he has given his own note, or the directors have assented to retain the premium note of the mortgagor—a person insured to the extent of his own interest, and is, in the event of loss, entitled to recover in his own name to the extent of his claim. By such assignment he acquires a separate independent interest under the policy, and the policy as against him is not avoided by a contract for further insurance made by the mortgagor without his knowledge, and which he could not prevent, nor by any acts of a similar kind beyond his control.

Held, that although the assignment might by agreement so bind him, the terms of the assignment in this case, hereinafter mentioned, were not sufficiently clear to have that effect.

The declaration alleged that defendants by their policy insured one B. for $3,000 on a manufactory and stock: that afterwards, with defendants' knowledge and consent, he assigned all his interest in the policy to the plaintiffs, as collateral security for a mortgage by B. to them for $3000, on the property insured: that defendants ratified and confirmed said policy to and in favour of the plaintiffs : that the premises were burned; and that by force of the statute the plaintiffs became under the said assignment interested in the said policy as the insured, and entitled to all rights as if they had been the original parties insured.

Defendants pleaded that the assignment was accepted by plaintiffs, and the consent given by defendants, subject to the condition that the plaintiffs should be bound by all the terms and conditions of the policy, as B. was bound by the same, and that the policy should continue voidable as though such assignment had not been executed, and the said policy was not otherwise ratified or confirmed to the plaintiffs : that it was a condition of the policy that any insurance on the premises by the act or with the knowledge of the insured in any other company, without the consent of defendants, should avoid the policy; and that B. effected other insurances, specified, without defendants' consent.

The plaintiffs replied, 2. that the said assignment was not accepted by plaintiff, nor was defendants' consent thereto and the ratification by them to the plaintiffs, as in the declaration and plea mentioned, on the terms or subject to the condition that the plaintiffs should be bound by any terms which would render the policy voidable by any act or omission of B. ; but by virtue of said assignment, consent and ratification, the plaintiffs became entitled to all the rights and subject to all the conditions to which B. had been subject, before the assignment, &c., and not otherwise ; and that the said insurances effected by B. were without the plaintiffs' consent or knowledge; 3. that the alleged insurances effected by B. were not of the same interest as that insured by the plaintiffs under said policy in the declaration mentioned, and said insurances were not effected by plaintiffs or with their knowledge or consent.

Held, that the second replication was bad, as being in effect a demurrer to the plea, and neither traversing nor confessing and avoiding it; and that the plea was bad, and the third replication good.

DEMÚRRER. Declaration: that by a policy of insurance, dated the 28th of January, 1874, duly issued by the
defendants under seal, the defendants did insure one
Julius Peter Billington, therein called J. P. Billington, to
the amount of $3,000, for the term of three years, ending
at noon on the 20th January, 1877, as follows, namely:
$1,000 on his stone and wood, steam power, agricultural
implement manufactory, situate on the west side of Cross
street in the town of Dundas; $1,000 on his tools and
machinery, and $1,000 on his stock, manufactured and
unmanufactured, all contained in the said manufactory,
against loss by fire, not exceeding the sum insured nor the
interest of the said assured in the said property, the said
loss or damage to be estimated according to the true and
actual cash value of the said property at the time the same
should happen, and to be paid within three months after
due proof thereof should be received. And the plaintiffs say
that the said Billington at the time of the making of the
said policy, and from thence until the execution of the
deed of assignment thereof to the plaintiffs, hereinafter mentioned, was interested in the said premises and property so
assured as aforesaid, as the sole unconditional owner thereof to the amount so assured thereon respectively aforesaid;
and after the making of the said policy, and whilst it was
in full force the said Billington, by deed or instrument in
writing under seal, dated the 10th of February, 1874, duly
transferred, assigned, and set over unto the plaintiffs, with
the permission, knowledge, and consent of the defendants,
all his right, title, and interest in the said policy, and all
benefits, &c., to be derived therefrom, as collateral security
to the mortgage for $2,000 and interest, hereinafter referred
to, and the defendants ratified and confirmed the said
policy to and in favour of the plaintiffs; and the plaintiffs,—
by virtue of an indenture dated the 1st February, 1874,
made by and between the said Billington, of the first part,
and the plaintiffs, of the other part, and whereby the said
Billington granted, conveyed, and assured unto the plaintiffs for the purpose of securing to them the payment of

$2,000 and interest, the property on which the said stone
and wood steam power agricultural implement manufactory in the said policy mentioned was (and still is situate),
and the said agricultural implement manufactory, together
with the said tools and machinery therein contained,—were,
and up to the time of the happening of the loss hereinafter
mentioned continued to be interested in the said property
so insured; and afterwards and whilst the said policy and
assignment were in force, the said premises, manufactory,
tools, machinery, and stock, so insured as aforesaid, were
burned and destroyed by fire, whereby the plaintiffs sustained immediate loss and damage by such fire, to the
several amounts so insured thereon respectively, and to the
aggregate amount as aforesaid; and by force of the statute
in that behalf, the plaintiffs became, by virtue of the said
assignment, interested in the said policy as the insured, and
were entitled to all rights and privileges as if they had been
the original parties insured in and by said policy; and all
conditions were fulfilled, and all things happened, and all
times elapsed necessary to entitle the plaintiffs to maintain this action, and nothing happened or was done to prevent them from maintaining the same, yet the defendants
have not paid to the plaintiffs the amount of the said loss
or damage, and the same remains wholly unpaid.

Second plea: that the said assignment and transfer of the
said policy to the plaintiffs in the declaration mentioned,
was accepted by the plaintiffs, and the said consent to the
same was given by the defendants, subject to the condition
that the plaintiffs should be bound by all the terms and
conditions of the said policy as the said J. P. B. was
bound by the same, and that the said policy should continue to be voidable as though such assignment had not
been executed, and the said policy was not ratified or confirmed to the plaintiffs otherwise than by the said consent
to the assignment thereof as collateral security, as in the
declaration and in this plea mentioned: that one of the
terms and conditions of the said policy was, and is, that if
any insurance subsists upon the insured premises by the

act or with the knowledge of the insured in the company of the defendants, and in any other insurance company at the same time, the insurance in the defendants' company shall be void, unless the double insurance subsists with the consent of the directors of the defendants' company, signified by endorsement on the policy signed by the secretary or other officer of the defendants' company duly authorized to do so, or otherwise acknowledged in writing. And the defendants say that the said J. P. B., from the time of the making of the said policy to the time of the damage and loss thereto in the declaration mentioned, continued to be and was interested in the said insured premises, and in the said policy, subject to the said assignment thereof to the plaintiffs as in the declaration mentioned; and that after the making of the said policy, and after the assignment thereof to the plaintiffs as collateral security to the said mortgage, as in the declaration mentioned, and during the continuance thereof, the said J. P. B. effected and procured other insurances to be made on the said premises insured by the policy in the declaration mentioned, that is to say, in the Hastings Mutual Fire Insurance Company, for the sum of $3,000, and in the Canadian Mutual Fire Insurance Company, of $3,000, and in the Provincial Insurance Company for the sum of $6,000, which said double insurances were in force from the time of making thereof until the time of the said damage and loss in the declaration mentioned, and subsisted without the consent of the directors of the defendants, and without notice thereof to the defendants, whereby the said policy in the declaration mentioned became, and was, and is void.

Second replication to the second plea: that the said assignment of the said policy was not accepted by the plaintiffs, nor was the said consent of the defendants thereto, and the ratification and confirmation thereof by them to the plaintiffs, as in the declaration and the said plea mentioned, on the terms or subject to the conditions that the plaintiffs should be bound by any terms or conditions which would render the said policy voidable by any act or omis-

sion by or on the part or behalf of the said J. P. B.; but by
virtue of said assignment and consent, and ratification
thereof by the defendants, the plaintiffs became entitled
to all the rights and privileges thereunder, and were subject
to the conditions to which the said J. P. B. has been subject
prior to the making of the said assignment and the consent
and ratification thereof by the defendants, and not otherwise. And the plaintiffs say that the said alleged insurances
effected by the said J. P. B., in the said plea mentioned,
were not, nor was any or either of them effected by the
act or authority of the plaintiffs, and were without the
knowledge or consent of the plaintiffs. And the plaintiffs
say that as such insured by or with the defendants they
are not affected thereby.

Third replication to the second plea : that the alleged
insurances effected by the said J. P. B. in the said plea
mentioned were not, nor was any or either of them effected
of the same interest as that which was insured by the
plaintiffs by and under the said policy as in the declaration
and said plea alleged, and the plaintiffs had no act in the
effecting of the said insurances or any of them, nor were
they effected by or with the authority of the plaintiffs, nor
with their knowledge or consent.

Demurrer to second and third replications, on the grounds
that the second plea shews that the said J. P. B. is in fact
the insured under the said policy, and the replications do not
deny that the defendants' consent to the assignment of the
said policy to the plaintiffs was accepted by the plaintiffs,
and consented to by the defendants, otherwise than as in
the plea is averred, or that the policy was ratified and confirmed to the plaintiffs otherwise than as in the declaration
and plea mentioned, and the replication does not shew that
the said J. P. B. did not in fact continue to be the
insured under the said policy, or aver any facts which shew
that the plaintiffs are not bound by the acts of the said
J. P. B. in effecting the subsequent insurance.

As to the third replication, that the plea shews that the
said Billington was the insured under the policy declared

upon, and the replication alleges no facts in answer to the plea.

The plaintiffs joined in demurrer, and took the following exceptions to the second plea :—

1. It admits an assignment of the said policy to the plaintiffs, whereby the said loss became payable to the plaintiffs.

2. And a substitution of the plaintiffs for the said J. P. B., as to the conditions of the said policy, is admitted thereby.

September 19, 1876. The demurrer was argued by *McCarthy*, Q. C. and *Osler*, Q. C., for the plaintiffs, and by *Osler* and *Durand*, for the defendants.

The argument was similar to that on the rehearing, *post* p. 229.

September 26, 1876. GALT, J.—This action is brought by the plaintiffs in their own name under the provisions of the Act 35 Vic. ch. 12 O.; but it is plain from the pleadings that, although they claim the whole interest in the policy, their right is restricted to the amount of their mortgage for $2000, and that the original insured was interested in the policy to the full amount, as the receipt by the plaintiffs of the $2000 would discharge his debt, and the plaintiffs never had any right or claim to the balance. It is also admitted by the pleadings that the original insured had been guilty of a breach of the conditions which would render the policy void in his hands. In a case of *Smith* v. *Niagara District Mutual Fire Insurance Co.*, decided by my brother Gwynne, in March last, 38 U. C. R., 570, and which in its circumstances was very similar to the present, he says, "By force of these recent statutes therefore to which I have referred, (meaning the 35 Vic. ch. 12 and 36 Vic. ch. 44, O.) and of this term alleged in the plea to have been expressly contained in the assignment of the policy, to which the defendants assented, it must be held, notwithstanding the decision in *Burton* v. *The Gore District*

29—VOL. XL U.C.R.

Mutual Insurance Co., 12 Grant 156, that the original
legal contract is still the contract in force, which, notwithstanding the assignment, may be avoided by any
act of the person thereby insured that, in the terms
of the contract, it is provided shall avoid the policy,
and that the present plaintiff can only, recover under the
policy in right of Givens. And this I take to be the
law of England as laid down in *Rolt* v. *White*, 9 Jur. N.
S., 343. If it were otherwise the plaintiff in this case might
claim a right to recover even though the insured property
had been destroyed by arson committed by the mortgagor.

In *Chisholm* v. *Provincial Insurance Co.*, 20 C., p. 11,
we held that an assignee of a policy, who sued thereon in
the name of the assignor, could not by an equitable replication, which asserted an interest somewhat similar to what
is asserted here in the declaration, displace a plea that the
premises were destroyed by the arson of the assignor. A
mortgagee has no rights whatever, as it appears to me, to
complain of such a construction being put upon an assignment to him by his mortgagor of a policy effected by the
latter; for a mortgagee has it always in his power to protect
himself by a policy in respect of his own interest directly
effected by himself to the extent of his debt. In such a
policy the mortgagor would have no interest, and upon
payment of the debt insured by the policy to the mortgagee
the insurance company would become entitled to an assignment of the mortgage.   When, instead of taking this mode
of protecting himself, the mortgagee is content to take an
assignment of a legal contract already in existence, it is but
reasonable to hold that he takes the contract subject to all
its incidents, and that he is content to trust in the person
who is the party to the contract doing nothing to avoid it.
It being admitted upon these pleadings that the policy
would be avoided if the action was brought by Givens in
his own right, I must hold that it is equally so when the
action is brought by his assignee."

The present case, so far as respects the third replication,
appears to me to be concluded by the reasoning and judg-

ment of the learned Judge in the above, because it is averred in the plea "that the assignment and transfer of the policy was accepted by the plaintiffs, and the consent of the defendants thereto was given by the defendants, subject to the condition, &c., &c., (as already set forth); and it alleges a forfeiture of the policy by reason of a breach of the condition by the said J. P. B. In reply to this the plaintiffs say that the alleged insurances effected by the said J. P. B. were not effected of the same interest as that which was insured by the plaintiffs under the said policy, &c. It does not deny that the property was the same, and consequently is no answer to the charge that a double insurance existed "upon the insured premises," and it admits that the double insurance was effected by the original insured, who was undoubtedly interested in the policy now sued on.

The demurrer to the second replication remains to be considered. The pleadings disclose this state of facts, namely : one Billington effected an insurance for $3000 on certain property. He subsequently executed a mortgage to the plaintiffs for $2000 on this property, and assigned the policy to them as collateral security, to which assignment. the defendants consented. He afterwards committed a breach of a condition contained in the policy, which rendered it void in his hands. The second replication raises the question as to the terms of the assent to the assignment Had the plaintiffs admitted that those terms as set out by the defendants were binding on them, as was done by the demurrer in *Smith's Case*, it would have been my duty to follow the decision in that case, not only because I consider it is binding on me sitting as a single Judge, but because I fully concur with the reasoning of the learned Judge; but they do not do so, but, on the contrary, aver that by the terms of the assent they are bound not for the acts of Billington, but in the same manner as he was for their own acts. The words of the plea are, "the said consent to the assignment was given by the defendants subject to the condition that the plaintiffs should be bound by all the terms and conditions of the said policy as the said J. P. B. was bound by the same, and that the said policy should continue to be voidable as though such an assignment had not been executed." It then goes on, as already stated, to aver a forfeiture by Billington. To this the plaintiffs replied that the assignment was not accepted by the plain-tiffs, nor was the consent thereto given, &c., on the terms and conditions that the plaintiffs should be bound by any terms or conditions which would render the said policy voidable by any act or omission by and on the part and behalf, &c., &c. The replication is demurred to, on the ground that the said J. P. B. was in fact the insured under the said policy, and the replication does not deny that the defendants' consent to the assignment of the said policy to the plaintiffs was accepted by the plaintiffs and assented to by the defendants otherwise than as in the plea averred.

The difficulty that has arisen in this case has been caused by the form in which the plaintiffs have framed their declaration. They have asserted a right in themselves to claim the whole of the insurance money, when it is mani-fest that the original insured is interested in the policy to a very considerable extent, and also that as respects him the policy is void. In its circumstances this case is very similar to the American case of *Tillou* v. *Kingston Mutual Insurance Co.*, 1 Selden N.Y. 405, and if the consent of the defen-dants to the assignment to the plaintiffs was absolute, with-out any reference to the acts of Billington, the decision would probably be the same, but it is impossible to decide that question on this demurrer. It appears to me that this demurrer should be allowed, with leave to the plaintiffs to amend their declaration by claiming their own interest, and by shewing the terms of their consent, so that an issue may be taken. As the case at present stands, the plaintiffs aver an absolute assignment to them and an unqualified consent. To this the defendants plead that their consent was conditional, and that the plaintiffs were responsible for the acts of Billington, as he was the original insured and continued to be interested. To this the plaintiffs reply admitting that they were to be bound in the same way as Billington had been bound, but they were not to be responsible for his acts. In place of this they should simply have traversed the covenant as set out in the plea.

Judgment for defendants on demurrer.

———

From this decision the plaintiffs appealed, and the case was reheard before the full Court, during this term.

November 27, 1876. *McCarthy*, Q. C., and *Osler*, Q. C., for plaintiffs. After the assignment and ratification of the assignment of the policy to the plaintiffs, no act whatever by Billington, the person originally insured, and the assignor of the policy, could affect or prejudice the plaintiffs' rights as assignees. The effect of the assignment and ratification was not to subject the plaintiffs' interest to be prejudiced or defeated by the acts or conduct of Billington, as the defendants contend, but to confer upon them the ordinary rights of original insurers—or the rights of assignees of the original insurer, subject to the terms and conditions by which the assignor was himself bound. The defendants are attempting to treat the further insurances of Billington after his assignment to the plaintiffs and the defendants' ratification of them, as a double insurance by the plaintiffs, or as one which affected the plaintiffs' rights.

They cited *Burton* v. *Gore District Mutual Fire Insurance Co.*, 14 U. C. R. 342, 12 Grant 156; *Livingstone* v. *Western Assurance Co.*, 14 Grant 461, in Appeal 16 Grant 9; *Westmacott* v. *Hanley*, 22 Grant 382; 35 Vic. ch. 12 sec. 5, O.; 36 Vic. ch. 44 sec. 39, O.; *Fitzgerald* v. *The Gore District Mutual Fire Ins. Co.*, 30 U. C. R. 97; *Tillou* v. *The Kingston Mutual Fire Ins. Co.*, 1 Selden, N. Y. 405; *Phillips* on Insurance, 5th ed., secs. 866–868; *Gale* v. *Lewis*, 9 Q. B. 730.

Osler and *Durand,* contra. The 36 Vic. ch. 44 sec. 39, O. differs from the Consol. Stat. U. C. ch 52 sec. 30. The mortgagee may further insure premises without breach of any of the conditions of the mortgagor's policy. Such an insurance would not be a double insurance. Here the plaintiffs accepted the assignment and confirmation of it, expressly subject to the mortgagor's further or continued acts or dealings with respect to the property.

They referred to *Smith* v. *Niagara District Mutual Insurance Co.,* 38 U. C. R., 570, decided lately by Gwynne, J., in this Court, and to *R. & J.* Dig., p. 1824, for many decisions on this subject. *Chisholm* v. *Provincial Insurance Co.,* 20 C. P. 11; *Kreutz* v. *Niagara District Mutual Fire Insurance Co.,* 16 C. P. 131, 573; *Dickson* v. *Provincial Insurance Co.,* 24 C. P. 157, 170; *Storms* v. *Canada Farmers' Mutual Insurance Co.,* 22 C. P. 75; *Hendrickson* v. *Queen Insurance Co.,* 30 U. C. R. 108, in Appeal 31 U. C. R. 547, 553; *Angell* on Insurance, 2nd ed.; sec. 147.

January 12, 1877. WILSON, J.—The declaration shews an original insurance by Billington with the defendants for $3,000 in all, upon his different properties insured.

That Billington mortgaged the insured property to the plaintiffs for the purpose of securing to them the payment of $2,000 with interest.

That Billington also, by way of collateral security to the mortgage assigned, to the plaintiffs all his interest in the policy, and in all benefits to be derived therefrom, and that the defendants permitted, knew of, and consented to such assignment, and that the fire happened which did the damage complained of while the plaintiffs were mortgagees of the insured property and assignees of the policy.

The defendants say that the assignment of the policy was made to the plaintiffs, and was accepted by them, and the defendants gave their consent to the same, " subject to the conditions that the plaintiffs should be bound by all the terms and conditions of the policy, as the said Billing–

ton was bound by the same, and that the policy should continue to be voidable as though such assignment had not been executed;" and that the policy was assigned, and the assignment of it consented to only "as collateral security." "That one of the terms and conditions of the policy was and is, that if any insurance subsists upon the insured premises by the act or with the knowledge of the insured in the company of the defendants and in any other insurance company at the same time, the insurance in the defendants' company shall be void, unless the double insurance subsists with the consent of the directors of the defendants' company signified, &c.: that Billington, from the time of the making of the policy to the time of the damage and loss was interested in the insured premises and in the policy, subject to the assignment to the plaintiffs; and that after the making of the policy and after the assignment of it to the plaintiffs as collateral security, and during the continuance thereof, the said Billington effected and procured other insurances to be made on the said premises insured, that is to say: * *. * which said double insurances were in force from the time of making thereof until the time of the loss and damage, and subsisted without the consent of the directors of the defendants, and without notice thereof to them—whereby the policy became and was and is void."

The plaintiffs in their second replication say, "that the assignment of the policy was not accepted by them, nor was it consented to and ratified by the defendants on the terms and subject to the conditions that the plaintiffs should be bound by any terms or condition which would render the policy voidable by any act or omission, by or on the part or behalf of Billington; but by virtue of the assignment and ratification the plaintiffs became entitled to all the rights and subject to all the conditions which applied to Billington prior to the assignment and ratification," and that Billington effected the subsequent insurances without the knowledge or consent of the plaintiffs.

The third replication merely alleges that the subsequent

insurances effected by Billington were not "of the same interest as that which was insured by the plaintiffs by and under the said policy as in the declaration mentioned," and that they were effected without the knowledge or consent of the plaintiffs.

The question is, whether a policy for $3,000 to Billington, and assigned by him as collateral security to the mortgage before mentioned—for the payment of $2,000—to the plaintiffs, and the assignment of which was assented to by the defendants, was and is void by reason of Billington effecting subsequent insurances with other insurance companies during the continuance of this policy, *when the plaintiffs did not*, as they have averred in their replication, accept the assignment, and *when the defendants did not* give their assent to it, as is alleged therein, subject to the conditions that the plaintiffs should be bound by any terms or conditions which would render the policy voidable by any act or omission of Billington.

The above allegation is not a direct traverse of the plea. The plea states that the assignment of the policy was made to and was accepted by the plaintiffs, and was consented to by the defendants, subject to the condition that the plaintiffs should be bound by the terms and conditions of the policy as Billington was bound by the same, and that the policy should continue to be voidable, as though such assignment had not been executed.

That the plaintiffs do not directly traverse. They say only that the assignment and consent were not subject to the conditions that they should be bound by any terms or conditions which would render the policy voidable by any act or omission of Billington.

How is it possible for the jury to try a question, such as an issue taken upon these allegations would present to them ?

How can they try whether an assignment and consent made and given upon the terms and conditions stated in the plea, did or did not bind the plaintiffs to such terms and conditions which would make the policy voidable by

Billington's subsequent acts or omissions? That is the purest question of law which a jury cannot try, and which therefore should not have been presented as an allegation of pleading for trial.

A pleading should be so framed that it may be traversed or confessed and avoided, or that an issue in fact or in law may be taken upon it. Here the plaintiffs do not confess, nor avoid, nor do they traverse the plea, nor have they taken an issue either in fact or in law upon it. They have replied matter which a jury cannot try, namely, the effect and operation of the assignment and consent upon the terms and conditions which are set out in the plea. And the plaintiffs have made that still more apparent by the later part of their replication, in which they state " but by virtue of the said assignment and consent the plaintiffs became entitled to all the rights, &c., of the said Billington prior to the said assignment and consent, and not otherwise."

The second replication is in effect, although not in form, a demurrer to the second plea: *Astley* v. *Fisher*, 6 C. B. 572. The replication is bad for the reasons stated, but that leaves the sufficiency of the plea in law upon the exceptions which have been taken to it still to be considered.

The third replication states a fact which a jury can well try, namely, whether the later insurances were effected by Billington of or upon the same interest as that which was insured by the plaintiffs on the policy in the declaration mentioned, and therefore it is free from the vice of the second replication. But the defendants say that it is not a good pleading in law, because the conditions and terms in the plea mentioned are equally applicable and equally avoid the policy sued upon whether Billington made the subsequent insurances upon the plaintiffs' interest under the policy or upon Billington's interest, if such interests can be separated, for that the terms and conditions referred to extend to all insurances made upon the same insured properties. They have therefore rightly demurred to the third replication.

The case then is, firstly, what is the meaning, effect, and operation in point of law of the terms and conditions of the assignment and ratification as they are set out in the second plea; and, secondly, what is their meaning, effect, and operation as modified by the third replication? Do the terms and conditions upon which the assignment and ratification of assignment of the policy were based, as set out in the second plea, avoid the policy as against the plaintiffs by reason of the subsequent insurances which were made upon the same property by Billington? By these terms the plaintiffs were to be bound "by all the terms and conditions of the policy as Billington was bound by the same. And the policy was to continue voidable as though such assignment had not been executed."

By the 36 Vic. ch. 44, sec. 39, O., under which the policy was effected by Billington, in case any property insured by a company under that Act is alienated the policy is void, "but the assignee may have the policy transferred to him, and upon application to the directors such assignee, on giving proper security to their satisfaction for such portion of the deposit or premium note or undertaking as remains unpaid, and with their consent, within thirty days next after such alienation, may have the policy ratified and confirmed to him, and by such ratification and confirmation, said assignee shall be entitled to all the rights and privileges and be subject to all the liabilities and conditions to which the original party insured was entitled and subject: Provided, however, that in cases where the assignee is a mortgagee, the directors may permit the policy to remain in force, and to be transferred to him by way of additional security, without requiring any premium note or undertaking from such assignee, or his becoming in any manner personally liable for premiums or otherwise; but in such cases the premium note or undertaking and liability of the mortgagor in respect thereof shall continue in no wise affected."

Under this enactment the plaintiffs became entitled to all the rights and privileges, and subject to all the liabilities and conditions to which Billington was entitled and subject. The plea does not say the plaintiffs became entitled to the rights and privileges which Billington had, but only that they should be bound by all the terms and conditions of the policy as he was bound by the same. I do not think that prevented the plaintiffs, nor does it prevent them now from claiming all the rights and privileges which he could claim under the policy.

As the matter has been so much disputed it is necessary to examine it somewhat minutely. A fire policy was not assignable at law. It might, like any other security of the like kind, be assigned in equity, and be enforced by the assignee in the name of the assignor against the insurer, if notice were given of such assignment before the policy money was paid over to the insured.

On an assignment made of the policy by a mortgagor to secure the mortgagee, with notice to the insurer, (leaving out of consideration for the present any prohibition against assignment unless the insurer approve of it, and treating the matter independently of our statutes and as if the Mutual Acts and the Act relating to choses in action had not been passed), how then do the parties mortgagor and mortgagee stand with respect to the insurer who has notice of the assignment, and how does he stand with respect to them? Does the mortgagee in equity acquire as against the insurer so notified a claim to indemnity, in effect just as if he had made a separate insurance in his own name? Does the assignment and notice of it separate the rights and interests of the mortgagor and mortgagee to any, and what extent?

I have no doubt that the general conditions of the policy continue to be binding on both mortgagor and mortgagee so far that if the conditions forbid the change of the building insured from a dwelling house to a tavern or factory, or that any business shall be carried on in it to increase the risk, or if it is provided that the policy shall be vacated if a building of a dangerous kind be put up within a certain distance of the insured house, or any thing of that nature, that the mortgagee would be affected by such acts as well as the mortgagor, because it is the acts themselves which defeat the policy, no matter by whom done, whether by the mortgagor, or the tenant, or occupant, and in the case of outside creditors although the act be done by a stranger to both parties. So if the policy provided that fires arising from insurrections or riots should defeat the policy, that condition in like manner, because universal in its application would extend to both mortgagor and mortgagee. These and the like are the general conditions of insurance. They are contained in all policies, and they must be continuing and binding on the assignee as well as upon the person originally insured. It is in that respect like a policy on the life of one effected by another for his own interest, and assigned by the holder of it. Both assignor and assignee are affected by the acts and conduct of the person whose life is insured, although neither the assignor nor assignee can control him. There is no dispute so far. It is too clear, just, and reasonable to contend it should be otherwise. But there is another question. If the policy forbid a further assurance being made on the property on pain of forfeiture, will a further insurance upon it made after assignment by the mortgagor, without the knowledge or consent of the mortgagee, defeat the interest which the mortgagee acquired, whatever interest that may be, by the assignment ?

It is said by one party that the further insurance effected by the mortgagor does defeat the entire policy (1) because that is one of the continuing conditions, as well as the one rendering the premises more hazardous and the like ; (2) because the mortgagee has acquired no further interest in the policy than to prevent its unauthorized surrender or release by the mortgagor, and to have the sole authority, as by an irrevocable letter of attorney, to receive for and on account of the mortgagor the policy money under the assignment ; (3) because the whole insurable interest under that policy and assignment remains still with the mortgagor ; (4) because the money paid to the mortgagee goes in reduction of the mortgagor's debt, and that is just what would in effect happen if the assignment had not been made, for the mortgagor would equally get the benefit of the policy money ; (5) because the assignment does not change the contract, it simply converts one of the parties into a trustee for a third person ; (6) because the fact of its being an assignment shews it cannot be a new contract of indemnity with the insurer; (7) because the object of the clause against further insurance is "to restrain the insured from burdening the premises by lessening his care in preserving them from fire," and that is just as much an object to be maintained after his assignment to a mortgagee as it was before, for in such case he retains while mortgagor the right to insure as fully as he did before he made the mortgage and assignment; and (8) because an assignment of the kind is quite different from an assignment to an absolute purchaser of the entire interest in the property of the insured. I take these objections from *Grosvenor* v. *Atlantic Fire Insurance Co., of Brooklyn,* 17 N. Y. 391 ; *State Mutual Fire Insurance Co.* v. *Roberts,* 31 Penn. 438, and from *Smith* v. *Niagara District Mutual Fire Insurance Co.,* decided by Gwynne, J., 38 U. C. R. 570.

It is said by the other party that the mortgagee acquires a substantial interest in the insured property. (1) That he is interested in its preservation to the extent of his interest, which may be more or less than that of the mortgagor; (2) that he might in respect of that interest insure the premises in his own name; (3) that by taking the assignment and notifying the insurer of it, he does in effect make an insurance to the extent of his interest in his own name and for his own benefit. (4) That a further insurance made by the mortgagor after the assignment and notice, cannot be made upon and in respect of the same interest as that upon which the policy was procured before the making of the mortgage; it would be made by him in effect as trustee to the extent of the mortgage debt, and for himself as to the surplus. (5) That the assignee never bound himself to have the assignment defeated by the future *contracts* of the assignor in derogation of his, the assignee's, vested rights, however much he might be liable to have his rights destroyed by failure of the mortgagor to keep up the premiums, on which the whole insurance was based, or by violation of the general terms—such as by increasing the risk, &c., as before mentioned; but that this condition as to further insurances is in its nature one not governing or applicable to the separate right and interest of the mortgagee; (6) that it would be unreasonable to hold the assignee liable for such an act of the mortgagor, because he could not by any means guard himself against, it while he could protect himself against the failure of the mortgagor to pay the premiums. And (7) as to the other general conditions he would be in no worse condition as to them as assignee than he would be if he were insured in his own name.

It is said by way of illustration, in order to prove that the policy after assignment with notice continues liable to be defeated by any act of the assignor just as it was before the assignment, that if a bond had been made conditional for the payment of so much money if the obligee did not for a certain time begin or carry on some particular business in a certain village, and if the bond were assigned to a mortgagee as collateral security with the consent of the obligor, that the assignee would hold the bond for the money liable, just as the obligee held it, to lose it if the obligee began or carried on business within the specified time in the specified locality. Unquestionably that is so, and would be so both in law and equity, for the due observance of that condition is the basis upon which the money is to be paid by the obligor, and his rights and position are in no way altered by the assignment, and the assignee took it plainly upon the continuance of and subject to the terms of the condition.

It is also said, by way of further illustration of the like argument, that the assignment of a policy to a mortgagor may be "likened to the mortgage of a leasehold estate which was subject to conditions and covenants to be performed by the tenant under a penalty of forfeiture of the estate for nonperformance. In such a case" (it is said), "no one would claim that the landlord by consenting to such mortgage would thereby waive performance of the covenants and conditions contained in the lease. I can therefore perceive no reason why a similar consent of the company in this case should have any different effect, it would often work great injustice": *Buffalo Steam Engine Works* v. *Sun Mutual Insurance Co.*, 17 N. Y. 401, 408.

As to the case of the bond, it may be said that a bond differs materially in some respects from a fire policy of insurance; that they are so far alike that they are each based upon certain continuing permanent conditions, operating at all times and upon all persons, but there are some conditions of the policy divisible in their nature, and which may attach to a particular interest and person in one manner, and to another interest and another person in another manner; that the policy is of a shifting character, varying from time to time according as the interest which it covers is changed, and that it adapts itself from time to time according to such altered circumstances; and that it may be made to answer by an assignment the purposes of a new original policy in favour of the assignee, subject to the general conditions on which it first issued, but not to all of them, and only to such of them as would be embraced in a new policy if one had actually been granted upon the interest in the assignment contained. But it may be likened to a life policy, as before mentioned, in which case the assignee takes it subject to the loss of it by the suicide of the life insured, which is one of the usual conditions of such a policy.

And as to the case of the mortgage of the leasehold interest, it may be said that the mortgagee as assignee of the lease would unquestionably be bound by all such conditions and covenants which run with the land, because he took the place of the lessee; and if the illustration be an apposite one, it would shew that the assignee, as respects his interest, took the place of the assignor, and an independent distinct interest in the property. Perhaps a more appropriate case would be the following one: suppose a lease to be made for twenty years, provided that it should be void if an underlease were made, and the lessee to under-let for five years, and the landlord waived that breach. Could the original lessee, during the continuance of the first underlease by making a second underlease for ten years (the whole of that period being within the twenty years), defeat or enable the original lessor to defeat the first underlease, by reason of the forfeiture arising on the making of the second one? The answer may be that he could not do so.

So far I have been considering the case apart from our statutes and the special terms of the policy contained in the second plea.

The effect of the statute is to entitle the assignee to all the rights and privileges of the original insured, and to subject the assignee to all the terms and conditions to which he was liable.

The assignee now by the late Act may be a mortgagee, whatever doubt there was of it before.

An ordinary assignee, upon giving security for such portions of the deposit or premium note as remains unpaid, may have the policy ratified to him; but as regards a mortgagee it is not necessary he should give security for the unpaid part of the premium note in order to have the policy ratified to him. The directors may, if they please, permit the policy to remain in force, and be transferred to him, without requiring any premium note or undertaking from him, or his becoming personally liable for premiums or otherwise, and in such case the premium note of the mort-gagor in respect thereof shall continue in nowise affected.

I understand the provision as to a mortgagee to mean that he shall be as much an assignee of the policy and entitled to all the rights of the original insured and subject to all his liabilities, on the policy being transferred to him, whether he gives his premium note for the unpaid amount of premium or the directors dispense with it and retain instead thereof the premium note of the original insured.

In either case he is entitled to the rights and subject to the liabilities "to which the original party insured *was* entitled and subject."

If the assignee or mortgagee, on giving his premium note, become a contracting party direct with the company, the mortgagee, in my opinion, becomes equally a direct contracting party with the company when the directors dispense with his premium note, and choose to retain in its stead the one which was given by the mortgagor.

Notwithstanding the statute, the company and the mortgagee might nevertheless agree that the policy, notwithstanding the assignment, should remain as theretofore liable to be avoided by any act or omission of the mortgagor, just as if the assignment had never been made. And the enquiry is, whether that has been done or not? the words being, "and that the policy should continue to be voidable as though such assignment had not been executed." It says the assignee shall be entitled to such rights and subject to such liabilities as the original party insured *was* entitled and subject relating plainly to a past and not to a future, time.

And it does not say the assignment shall be voidable *by any act or omission of Billington*, but generally that it shall be voidable as though the assignment had not been made. Now a full and proper meaning may be given to these words without holding that Billington, after raising money from the mortgagee, and assigning the policy as collateral security therefor, with the consent of the company, shall still be at liberty to defeat it all from no act of the plaintiffs, and from which they could not protect themselves.

It may be read and construed as preserving the rights of the defendants to cancel the policy under the 26th section of the Act, notwithstanding the assignment and ratification, "as though such assignment had not been executed," or as a more emphatic form of declaration that the plaintiffs shall be bound, as assignees, by all the terms and conditions of the policy, as Billington was bound, adding as the emphasis, "and that the policy should continue to be voidable as though such assignment had not been executed."

Or as meaning that if anything had been done or omitted before the assignment by Billington, which avoided the policy, that it should still continue voidable, notwithstanding the assignment and ratification to the plaintiffs.

Or as providing that the assigned policy is to operate just as the original policy would be construed, as liable to be defeated by any alteration made in the premises, or by any increase in the risk, or by any act of that nature done to the prejudice of the defendants without notice to them, and without their approval of such acts, and the payment of an additional premium if it were required. In such a case it is quite right "that the policy should continue to be voidable, as though such assignment had not been executed," because the original policy would have been defeated by any such acts, although they had not been done by the insured or with his knowledge or consent.

A tenant might alter the premises or increase the risks against the will of the insured, or the adjoining proprietor might, by the nature of his building or by the business he carried on in it, increase the risk of the insured on his premises, and such acts he would be powerless to prevent, yet without notice to the insured, and the adoption of such new state of things, the policy would be void or voidable.

It is these and the like acts which would defeat the original policy, which it is intended shall defeat the asssignment, as if the assignment had never been executed.

But it may be said, if any of these acts will defeat the assignment if done by Billington, why should not also his further insurances equally defeat it ? The reason is, that the acts alluded to are acts which would have defeated the policy by whomsover committed, whether by the original insured, or by any other person, while a new or double insurance is an act which can be done by the insured and by no one else, unless there be some peculiar and extraordinary provision expressly covering so unusual a case, and there is no such provision in this case.

The plaintiffs could have insured their own interest without any one's leave. · They would probably have required to specify any other insurances upon the property within their knowledge. If they had so insured, Billington could not by any insurance on his part have damaged their right without a special provision to that effect.

These defendants, with a knowledge of all the facts, elected to insure the plaintiffs by means of an assignment of the original policy to them instead of an original policy in their name.

Their interest became separable from that of Billington They became interested to the extent of $2000 for themselves and to the extent of the remaining $1000, by reason of the absolute assignment, in trust for Billington. If Billington insured any of the property again that would be a double insurance as against him, because as mortgagor and as *cestui que trust* for all in excess of the mortgage he had an interest to the full value of the property, and that second insurance would be a forfeiture because a double insurance of all his rights under the policy.

But I see nothing which enabled him by a further insurance on the same property to constitute it a double assurance by or against the plaintiffs, so as to forfeit their interest without their knowledge or consent.

No one could reinsure their interest but themselves, simply because no one else represented it or had power over it. The clause relied upon, as the plea subsequently shews, relates to a double insurance, and there is no such act chargeable upon the plaintiffs.

The allegation is, that one of the conditions of the policy was, and is, that "if any insurance subsists upon the insured premises by the act or with the knowledge of the insured in the company of the defendants and in any other insurance company at the same time, the insurance in the defendants' company shall be void unless the double insurance subsists with the consent," &c. The question is, who is the *insured* under that condition, the assignor or the assignee of the policy, the plaintiffs or Billington? If it be the plaintiffs there is an end of the pleas, because it is plain the other insurances were not effected by the act or with the knowledge of the plaintiffs.. That the plaintiffs are the insured is, I think, established by the fact that they have the legal title. The provision that the policy should continue to be voidable as if the assignment had never been executed, does not by any process of reasoning prevent the plaintiffs from being the *insured.* It would be in their order and disposition, and not in that of the mortgagor, in case of his insolvency: *Alletson* v. *Chichester*, L. R. 10 C. P. 319. They alone are entitled to the money and to grant acquittances for it. The *double insurance* mentioned has then a true and proper signification—that is, a second insurance by the same person and in the same interest by whom and on which the former insurance was made: 1 *Phill.* on Ins., 5th ed., secs. 359, 366; *Angell* on Ins., 2nd ed., sec. 26; *Goden* v. *London Ass. Co.*, 1 Burr. 489.

Contracts are to be construed in the sense in which the promissor knew the promissee accepted the promise, and when there are two meanings, in that sense which best agrees with the matter of the contract, and which leaves no reasonable doubt of the intent of the parties.

Where the landlord gave authority to a broker to distrain on the goods of the tenant with an indemnity "against all costs the broker might be at on that account," it was held that was an indemnity only in case the landlord had no right to distrain, and not against the acts of the broker's own men: *Draper* v. *Thompson*, 4 C. & P. 84. So an action of covenant lies for rent reserved by indenture and accruing before re-entry for a forfeiture, notwithstanding the lessor under the re-entry was to have the premises again as if the indenture had never been made.

In *Hartshorne* v. *Watson*, 4 Bing. N. C. 178, Tindal, C. J., said, at p. 182: "The proper construction of the condition is, that *from the time of re-entry* the lessor shall have the land as if the indenture had not been made: for the period previous to the re-entry the lessee had it subject to the indenture."

The rule is, that an agreement " ought to receive that. construction which its language will admit, and which will best effectuate the intention of the parties to be collected from the whole of the agreement, and that greater regard is to be had to the clear intent of the parties than to any particular words which they may have used in the expression of their intent" : *Ford* v. *Beech*, 11 Q. B. Ex. Ch. 852, 866. The maxim *verba intentioni debent inservire* applies: *Chitty* on Contracts, 10th ed., 71.

By the 26th section of the Act 36 Vic. ch. 44, O., it is enacted that the company shall be at liberty to cancel any policy by giving to the *insured* notice to the effect that they have cancelled or will cancel the same. Now who is the *insured* under that section ? Is it the assignee and holder of the policy, or the original insured who as mortgagor may or may not have one particle of real interest in it. It may probably be both the assignor and assignee when it is not an absolute assignment, but certainly the assignee of it must be entitled to have notice of it whether the assignor is so or not.

What is the general position of a mortgagee with respect to an insurance effected by his mortgagor ? In *Gardner* v. *Ingram*, 23 L. J. Ch. 478, in a lease there was a covenant by the lessee to insure the demised premises in the joint names of the lessor and lessee, and that the money under the policy should be laid out in reinstating the premises. An insurance was effected. The lessee, the defendant, afterwards mortgaged the demised premises to the plaintiff with a power of sale in case of default. The policy was not assigned by the mortgage, nor was any notice taken of it. The premises were injured by fire. The plaintiff, the mortgagee, rebuilt the premises. The defendant refused to join in the receipt with the lessor to the insurance office. The plaintiff as mortgagee filed this bill to compel him to do so.

The Lord Chancellor affirmed the decision of Knight

Bruce, V. C. He said, "The benefit of the insurance passed
to the mortgagee. When a man insures property under an
absolute covenant to insure and then assigns and charges
the lease to secure a sum of money, he still retains his
interest in the property subject to the charge. Then the
property is burnt and the insurance money becomes payable.
Can the mortgagor claim this money against his own mortgagee when the object of effecting the policy was for the
purpose of reinstating the premises? I am of opinion the
benefit of the policy passed by the mortgage."

In *Lees* v. *Whiteley*, L. R. 2 Eq. 143, the defendants
assigned certain machinery by bill of sale to secure a sum
of money advanced by the plaintiff. The deed contained a
covenant to insure, but no provision was made for the
application of the policy money in case of fire, in liquidation
of the mortgage debt. The machinery was burnt, and it was
held the plaintiff had no claim to the benefit of the policy.

Kindersley, V.C., said, p. 149, there was no policy existing
at the time of the mortgage, "nor is there here a covenant
that the policy money shall be applied in restoring the
premises; but it is merely an assignment by bill of sale of
machinery, with a covenant to insure; and it would be
impossible to hold, as was done in *Garden* v. *Ingram*, 23
L. J. Ch. 478, that the benefit of the policy passed by
the assignment as the policy at the time did not exist.
*   *   * If the plaintiff's contention can be sustained, it must stand on the footing, that by reason
of the covenant to insure there is an implied contract
with the mortgagee that the policy money should be
applied in liquidation of the mortgage debt. *   *   *
Can I imply such a covenant from the language
of the bill of sale? and on examination of the terms of
that instrument I am of opinion that I cannot. Were I to
do so I should be making a new contract between the
parties. It was perfectly competent to the plaintiff to
have stipulated that the policy money should be applied in
liquidation of the mortgage debt or in the restoration of
the premises, but he has not done so; and how can I say

that the parties intend̃ed something which is not stipulated for in this instrument, or make for the plaintiff a better agreement than he thought it necessary to make for himself?

* * In point of fact, the existence of the insurance is obviously to some extent for the benefit of the mortgagee, although there was no obligation on the mortgagor to apply the insurance moneys in any particular way because it is for the interest of the mortgagee that his mortgagors should be in a solvent condition, and that in case their property should be destroyed by fire, he should still have the means of paying the mortgage debt."

If the defendants were a company in course of liquidation, who would prove against them for the policy—the plaintiffs, or Billington? In my opinion it would be the plaintiffs.

As between the mortgagor and mortgagee, if the mortgagee at his own expense, and for his own benefit, insure his debtor's life, he alone is entitled to the benefit of the policy, the mortgagor has nothing whatever to do with it; but if the mortgagor pay the premiums, or they are charged in account to him, the benefit of the policy belongs to him— that is, after payment of the debt, the policy belongs to the mortgagor; or if the debt is not paid in his lifetime the surplus of the policy money after payment of the debt will belong to his estate : *Morland* v. *Isaac*, 20 Beav. 389 ; *Lea* v. *Hinton*, 19 Beav. 324 ; *Drysdale* v. *Piggott*, 2 Jur. N. S. 1078 ; *Gotlieb* v. *Cranch*, 17 Jur. 704.

If it had not been necessary that the assignment of this policy should have been made with the assent of the defendants, it would have been necessary for the plaintiffs to give notice to the defendants of such assignment, to have prevented them from paying the policy money to Billington, or in case of his insolvency to his assignees : *West* v. *Reid*, 2 Hare 249 ; *Gibson* v. *Overbury*, 7 M. & W. 555.

Upon such notice given, their rights to the policy money would be complete. The defendants would have to pay the plaintiffs the loss when it happened, and they would have nothing to do with Billington, his rights being fully vested in, and represented by the plaintiffs, and the accounts between these parties would have to be settled by themselves, and with these accounts the defendants have nothing to do: *Desborough* v. *Harris*, 1 Jur. N. S. 986.

Where the part owner of a vessel transferred by absolute sale, but really by way of mortgage, his interest in the ship, upon which he had a policy before then subsisting ; but had made no assignment of the policy, it was held he had a sufficient interest in the vessel as mortgagor in equity to sue upon the policy: *Hutchinson* v. *Wright*, 4 Jur. N. S. 749.

The mortgagees of a policy of assurance mortgaged to them by a deceased testator to secure a sum of money received after the testator's death under the policy a sum exceeding the amount due to them for the mortgage debt. Held, they being creditors also of the testator for other debts not secured, that they were entitled to retain the balance in their hands in discharge of their unsecured debts: *Spalding* v. *Thompson*, 26 Beav. 637. *Re Haselfoot's Estate, Chauntler's Claim*, L. R. 13 Eq. 327.

This last case shews, as does also the case of *Desborough* v. *Harris*, 1 Jur. N. S. 86, above referred to, that the plaintiffs are entitled to the full amount of the policy money of $3,000 from the defendants, although their mortgage claim is only $2,000, because the defendants have nothing to do with the state of accounts between the plaintiffs and Billington; and that the plaintiffs would be entitled to retain the surplus of this policy money beyond the surplus debt to satisfy any other unsecured claims which they might happen to have against Billington at the time.

The plaintiffs, by the assignment to them with the defendants' consent, became by the statute entitled to all the rights and privileges, and subject to the liabilities and conditions to which "the original party insured" was entitled and subject. The plaintiffs became *the insured* in place of *the original party insured.*

They alone became entitled to sue for the money in case of loss, and to grant a discharge for the same. They represented and had vested in them the entire legal interest in the policy, and in the money secured by it. Their interest became a new one, distinct from that of the original party insured. Whether they gave their premium note or not the defendants could have exacted it if they pleased, or they could dispense with it when the assignees were mortgagees.

They are willing to be dealt with in every way as Billington could have been dealt with for any act or omission of his down to the time of the transfer which he made, and for all his acts, and the acts of any other person, by alteration, &c., which increase the risk, and which would equally defeat a policy granted to the plaintiffs in the first instance ; but they are not willing to be bound by his contracts, made subsequently to the assignment, for further insurance or otherwise, which may defeat, abridge or prejudice their rights under the assignment, nor by his criminal acts, as by arson of the premises, any more than they are bound by the criminal acts of any other person, of the like nature.

In 1 *Phill.* on Ins., 5th ed., sec. 81, it is said that " After a valid assignment and delivery of the policy to the assignee, and notice to the underwriters, the assignor cannot by any act of his intercept or impair the rights of the assignee," and he cites several decisions in favour of that statement, but he gives also several later decisions the other way. The cases of *Buffalo Steam Engine Works* v. *Sun Mutual Insurance Co.,* 17 N. Y. 401 ; *Grosvenor* v. *Atlantic Fire Insurance Co. (of Brooklyn),* 17 N. Y. 391 ; *State Mutual Fire Insurance Co.* v. *Roberts,* 31 Penn. R. 438, (1858) : *Buckley* v. *Garrett,* 47 Penn. R. 204 ; *Illinois Mutual Fire Insurance Co.* v. *Fox,* 53 Ill. R. 151 (1870) ; *Home Mutual Fire Insurance Co.* v. *Hauslein,* 60 Ill. R. 521, are all opposed to the dictum in the text above quoted from *Phil.* on Insurance, vol. i., 5th ed., sec. 81, although the writer does not quote some of the late decisions just mentioned. There is a passage, however, which seems the other way. I take it from U. S. Digest, N. S., 4th vol., at pp. 383, 384 (1873) ; " There is a third class of cases where the assignment may have a twofold operation, and it is not always easy to say which was designed. This occurs where the policy is transferred to a mortgagee of the property insured. Here there are two insurable interests, each of which may be a ground of action, notwithstanding the determination of the other. The mortgagor is entitled to indemnity, as the owner of the equity of redemption ; the mortgagee by virtue of of his lien for the debt ; and as the extinguishment of the mortgage will not affect the right of the mortgagor, so a sale or alienation by the mortgagor will not preclude a recovery by the mortgagee :" *Insurance Co. of Pennsylvania* v. *Trask*, 8 Phil. 32.

The case of *Burton* v. *Gore District Mutual Insurance Co.*, 12 Grant 156, and *Livingstone* v. *Western Assurance Co.*, 14 Grant 461, are expressly in favour of the plaintiffs' contention.

If the clauses in question are to have the effect given to them which the defendants place upon them, I should like to see them more plainly expressed, otherwise the mortgagee's collateral security, liable to be defeated by the contracts or criminal acts of the mortgagor, is not worth the taking, and is certainly not worth all the solemnity with which it is taken and pretended to be guaranteed to him.

I do not rely on the fact of notice to the company of the assignment as of any greater effect at common law, or by the rules of equity, than to prevent the company from thereafter dealing with the mortgagor as the person to receive payment of the money in case of a loss, and as the only person who is interested in the property transferred and affected by the insurance of which notice has been given : *Cook* v. *Black*, 1 Hare 390 ; *Solicitors and General Life Insurance Society* v. *Lamb*, 10 Jur. N. S. 579, 739.

Under the statute the giving of the notice of the assignment is required to prevent the policy from being forfeited. And the assent of the company to the assignment makes that notice fully binding, as it would be in law and in equity if there had been no conditions against assigning without leave, and requiring notice and assent if an assignment be made.

There is a further reason why this assignment should be given effect to as if it were an original policy to the plain-tiffs, and that is to prevent the company from claiming from the plaintiffs an assignment of the mortgage, which they could have done if the plaintiffs had taken out an original policy entirely at their own expense and for their own benefit, so soon as the company had paid the loss to them. They would not be entitled to an assignment of the mortgage if by any arrangement between the mortgagor and mortgagee the insurance was for the benefit of the mortgagor, or if it was procured or maintained at his expense.

Now it avoids all difficulty on the part of the mortgagor to prove that he is the one entitled to the policy money when the policy is in the name of the mortgagee, by pro-viding that the mortgagee may have the policy of the mortgagor assigned to him, the mortgagor still if necessary remaining liable on his premium note. That maintains the true and actual rights of the respective parties.

It gives the mortgagee the benefit of an original policy. It assures to the mortgagor the substantial benefit of the policy, and it prevents the company from claiming to have that money repaid to them by getting in an assignment of the mortgage.

My brother Gwynne, in *Smith* v. *Niagara District Mutual Fire Insurance Co.*, 38 U. C. R. 570, was of opinion the plaintiff in that case would have been in direct privity of contract with the company, and would have been the *insured* under the assignment of the policy, if he had given his premium note to the company.

I do not think the premium note was intended for such a purpose, or can be used to constitute or to perfect the con-tract. The contract is the policy. The premium note is a means to make or a circumstance in the making of the contract.

The mortgagor in this case might have paid in money the amount of the note in place of leaving his note there.

And I do not see why a stranger to the company might not give his note for the premium of the insured, because. the assignee, by section 39, may have the policy assigned to him "on giving *proper security* to their satisfaction for such portion of the deposit, note, or undertaking as remains unpaid." See also sections 47 and 48.

I do not think it necessary to review the different decisions which were cited on the argument, and which I have read with much care, because I have given my reasons at length for the conclusion I have come to, and it is shortly this :— that a mortgagee who becomes the assignee of a fire policy under our Mutual Insurance Act, and which assignment is duly ratified and confirmed to him by the directors of the insurance company, becomes, whether he has given his own premium note or the directors have assented to retain the former premium note of the mortgagor, a person insured with the company to the extent of his own interest, and in the event of loss is entitled to sue for indemnity in his own name, to recompense him for his loss to the extent of his money demand under the policy— that by the assignment and due ratification of it to the mortgagee he acquires a separate and independent interest under the policy, and while he is bound by everything prior to the assignment as the mortgagor was himself bound, and continues bound by the general conditions after the assignment which he would have been bound by if he had taken out a new policy in his own name, he is not bound by a contract for further insurance made by the mortgagor after the assignment of which the mortgagee had no notice or knowledge, and which he could not possibly guard against, nor by a second mortgage made upon nor by a further alienation in any manner of the property, nor by any act of that kind. The assignment could be subjected to such a condition, but the language of the terms upon which the assignment was accepted and ratified do not create such a condition as the defendants have set up.

Full effect can be given to the conditions relied upon consistent with the agreement which the parties have entered into, without straining it to defeat a vested interest by the acts or misconduct of a person for whose acts of the nature referred to the plaintiffs were not plainly made answerable.

The Chief Justice and Mr. Justice Morrison are not answerable for more than the conclusion arrived at.

The judgment will be for the defendants on the demurrer to the second replication, and for the plaintiffs on the demurrer to the third replication and for the insufficiency in law of the second plea.

Judgment accordingly.

BELTZ V. MOLSON'S BANK.

Cheque—Alteration in date—Payment by bank—Negligence.

The plaintiff, a merchant and customer of defendants' bank, having a note payable there on the 28th January, 1873, made a cheque payable to himself or bearer, and left it with defendants to meet the note. The cheque however was not used for that purpose nor returned to the plaintiff, but the note was paid by defendants and charged to the plaintiff's account. The cheque was afterwards, on the 31st January, 1874, presented to the defendants by some one unknown, the year having been changed from 1873 to 1874, and it was paid by defendants without noticing the alteration, and charged to the plaintiff's account. How it got out of defendants' bank was not ascertained.

Held, that the alteration avoided the cheque : that defendants therefore were not warranted in paying it ; and that the plaintiff was entitled to recover back the money.

Quare, whether, if the cheque had not been void, the defendants, on the ground of negligence, would, on the facts more fully stated in the case, have been liable to the plaintiff for paying it.

Per WILSON, J., the cheque must be considered to have been paid when the note for which it was given was handed over by defendants to plaintiff, and on that ground defendants could not have been made liable upon it.

ACTION for money had and received.

Pleas : never indebted, and payment.

The cause was tried at London, at the last Fall Assizes, before Moss, J., without a jury.

This was the second trial. The first trial was by a jury. The verdict was then, on certain answers made to questions left to them, entered for the defendants ; but they found, as an answer to one of these questions, that the cheque in question was delivered to the bank in 1873.

The facts were, that the plaintiff, a merchant doing business in London, and a customer at that time of defendants' bank, had made a promissory note, payable to J. Gillespie or order, for $444.10, at the defendants' bank. The note fell due on the 28th of January, 1873.

The plaintiff said he made a cheque on that day, payable to self or bearer, and took it to the defendants' bank to pay the note when it should be presented by the holder of it at the bank for payment; and he said he asked for the note, and was told the note was not in the bank, but to leave the cheque, and it would be used when the note came in. The plaintiff did so.

The note was in the possession of the Montreal Bank, and a clerk of that bank presented it at the defendants' bank on the 28th of January, 1873. A clerk in the defendants' bank on that same day initialed it to shew it was good, and returned it to the clerk from the Montreal Bank.

The next day, the 29th of January, the note came from the Montreal Bank to the defendants' bank for payment, and the defendants paid it on the 29th, although their bank stamp upon it was the 28th, probably, as Mr. Jeffrey, the manager of the defendants' bank at London said, because it came to the bank early on the morning of the 29th, and before the stamp of the day before had been changed.

The stamps of the two banks upon the note, and the initials of the defendants' ledger-keeper upon it, shewed that the note was used as a voucher for the payment of it by the defendants, and that they did not use the cheque of the plaintiff for that purpose. All these facts were relied upon by the defendants to shew that the plaintiff had not taken his cheque to the defendants' bank to pay the note, as he said and supposed he did, because if he had done so it would have been used as the means and voucher of payment, and not the note itself.

The learned Judge on that point found the plaintiff had taken the cheque to the bank on the 28th of January, 1873.

The plaintiff received the past month's cheques at the beginning of the ensuing month, and he said he did not in February, 1873, receive from the defendants the cheque he had given for the note. His pass-book shewed he was charged with $444.10, the amount of the cheque; but that was also the amount of the note, and he got the note from the bank along with the previous month's cheques. A good deal was said about its being negligence on the part of the plaintiff, who gave a receipt for the January cheques, not to have informed the bank he had not got back his cheque after having signed a receipt to them declaring that he had, and it was contended if he had done so, and the cheque could not have been found, it might never have been paid.

And it was contended that the fact of his having given such a receipt and never stating that it was not correct, was evidence that it was correct—that is, if he left the cheque at the bank that he had got it again, or that if he had not left it at the bank that he could not of course have got it back, and so he had nothing to complain of for not receiving it.

The cheque was afterwards on the 31st of January, 1874, presented to the defendants by some body—who it was was not known—the figure *3*, in the year, 1873, being altered or blotted over so as to make the year 1874; and it was paid by the defendants and charged to the plaintiff.

Upon finding that charge in his pass-book he complained of it, and he now claimed to be entitled to have restored to him that money, which he said the defendants wrongfully took from his account, and delivered over to the unknown person who presented the cheque and got the amount of it.

The learned Judge found a verdict for the plaintiff, and he assessed the damages at $495.38.

In Hilary term, Feb. 11, 1876, *A. F. Campbell* obtained a rule calling on the plaintiff to shew cause why the verdict should not be set aside, and a verdict entered for

the defendants, or why a new trial should not be granted
on the merits.   The case was argued in Easter Term,
June 2, 1876, by *Robinson*, Q.C., and *Rock*, Q.C., for the
plaintiff, and *Magee*, for the defendants, before MORRISON
and WILSON, JJ.   These learned Judges not agreeing in
opinion, a re-argument was directed, which took place in
this term November, 25, 1876.

   Robinson, Q. C., shewed cause, *Roek*, Q. C., with him.
The evidence did shew a case of negligence on the part of
the defendants by their paying a cheque which, on the
face of it, had been so plainly altered in its date from
1873 to 1874.   The clerk in the bank who paid it said,
" If I had noticed the alteration I would have thought
twice about paying it ": *Shearman & Redfield* on Negligence, 3rd ed., sec. 239 ; *Orr* v. *Union Bank of Scotland*,
1 Macq. H. L. Cas. 513 ; *Coles* v. *Bank of England*, 10
A. & E. 437, 449 ; *Bellamy* v. *Marjoribanks*. 7 Ex. 389,
21 L. J. Ex. 70.   Apart from the question of negligence,
however, the case of *Vance* v. *Lowther*, L. R. 1 Ex. D.
176, decided since the last argument, shews that the
alteration of the cheque was in a material part, and so
it was no longer the cheque of the plaintiff.   The defendants therefore had no warrant for paying the money.

   Magee supported the rule.   The finding is not warranted
by the evidence.   The evidence is rather that the cheque
in question was never taken to the bank in January, 1873.
There is no mark upon it, as there would have been if it
had been left there as the plaintiff says, and the plaintiff
must be as much in error about that as he is when he says
he spoke to Mr. Strathy, the manager, then about it, and
Mr. Strathy was not at that time in the bank.   What
writing there is is in favour of the defendants' contention
that the bank never got the cheque at that time.   The
initials and stamping upon the note shewed it was used as
the voucher for payment, and not the cheque, or else the
writing there shews that; if the bank got the cheque, it was
duly returned to the plaintiff.   His own receipt is conclusive upon that point.   And the verbal evidence in every

respect is quite as strong for the bank as it is or can be put for the plaintiff. If the cheque had not been altered the payment of it by the defendapts would not have been negligent or wrongful : *Grant* on Banking, 3rd ed., 70, 72. The alteration of the figure of the year is not evidence of negligence on the part of the bank so as to prevent them from recovering for their payment of it : *Ingham* y. *Primrose*, 7 C. B. N. S..82 ; *Young* v. *Grote*, 4 Bing. 253 ; *Hall* v. *Fuller*, 5 B. & C. 750. The cheque is not void, but is good for the amount on the face of it : *Swan* v. *The North British Australasian Co. (Limited)*, 2 H. & C. 175, 183 ; *Ex parte Swan*, 7 C. B. N. S. 400, 443 ; *The Conflans Stone Quarry Co. (Limited)*, v. *Parker*, L. R. 3 C. P. 1 ; *Bellamy* v. *Marjoribanks*, 7 Ex. 389, 21 L. J. Ex. 70 (*a*).

January 2, 1877. WILSON, J.—This cause was heard before my brother Morrison and myself. It has been twice tried—the first time before a jury, and the second time by a Judge without a jury—and on each occasion the finding has been that the plaintiff did take the cheque of the 28th of January, 1873, to the defendants' bank, and left it with a clerk there with instructions to take up his note due that day, and payable at that bank, where it was presented for payment. We must, therefore, accept that fact to be established as well as it possibly ever can be, and act upon it as a settled fact.

What became of the cheque after that is not known, until on the 31st of January, 1874, it was presented to the defendants and paid by them, the year having apparently been altered from 1873 to 1874.

It is not known positively how the cheque ever got out of the bank after its being first left there, and its payment in the following year. Of course we are assuming it as a fact, as before stated, that the cheque was left there in January, 1873. That it did get out in some way and at some time between these two dates is quite certain.

The defendants say, if they ever got it it was given back to the plaintiff in February with the other January cheques and notes, and for which he gave a receipt.

33—VOL. XL U.C.R.

The plaintiff says he did not get it back because the counterfoil or stump, as he called it, has not been crossed by him as a returned cheque; and "the reason why I did not ask for the cheque was, that it was near the last of the month, and if I asked once for it that was all, and it was then overlooked;" or, as the learned Judge puts it, "he supposed that the cheque would come in at the end of February, and he afterwards overlooked the matter."

The learned Judge, I presume, did find, or was of opinion at any rate, that the plaintiff did not receive the cheque back from the bank, because he has found that from the plaintiff's explanation just given. On this point the learned Judge has said, as to the reason why the plaintiff did not get the cheque back, "I think that is sufficiently explained."

We have then two facts found : 1, that the plaintiff did leave the cheque at the bank on the 28th of January, 1873, for the purpose stated ; and (2) that he did not get it back from the bank till after its payment in January, 1874.

The defendants contend they never got it, and that the plaintiff had it himself from the time he signed it until at some later time it must have been abstracted from his papers.

It must be assumed the defendants did receive the cheque, and in some way by the fraud or wrongful act of some one lost or were deprived of it, and that some one who is unknown got the money upon it ; but whether he was the one who took it or found it, or was a *bonâ fide* holder of it for value, is not known. It is also certain that it was altered in the year of its date before presentation for payment. Upon these facts, the case would seem to turn heavily against the defendants, because if they did not return the cheque to the plaintiff they should have cancelled it, or marked it in some way as having passed through the bank—that is the course of business ; and from not doing so it could again be, as it was, put in circulation.

That is an inference which must follow from the conclusion that the bank did not return the cheque to the plaintiff. I cannot say I should have drawn that conclusion from the evidence, I think I should have formed the contrary opinion.

If the cheque had been presented to the bank in its ·original state without any alteration, the defendants would have been liable upon the additional ground of negligence that they had paid a stale cheque, unless they could have excused themselves by reason of its being at that time early in the year, the 28th of January, and that it was not infrequent to find on such instruments the previous year inserted in place of the new year. The plaintiff's cheque book shews numerous cases of that kind in different years down to periods in January, and one as late as the 4th of February. I will suppose the cheque to have been returned by the defendants to the plaintiff in February, 1873, and that it was taken from or lost by the plaintiff in some way without negligence.

How then would the case stand?

The *bonâ fide* holder for value of a lost or stolen note, bill or check, and without notice, is entitled to recover upon it: *Grant* v. *Vaughan*, 3 Burr. 1516, 1525; *Ingham* v. *Primrose*, 7 C. B. N. S. 82, at p. 85.

The cheque was payable on demand. Being so, it was due at once: *Norton* v. *Ellam*, 2 M. & W. 461; *Bartrum* v. *Caddy*, 9 A. & E. 275.

And if it had once been paid, and afterwards by some means got into circulation without the knowledge of the maker, he could not have been required to pay it even by a *bonâ fide* holder, because the one payment had discharged it.

Here the cheque was altered in its date. The date was a material part of it; it shewed when it was given, and it enabled the bank and others to determine whether they would accept it or not, after the lapse of some reasonable time allowed for that purpose. It was therefore a forgery, for the alteration was made with the intent to deceive: *Regina* v. *Ritson*, L. R. 1 C. C. 200.

A bill, altered by the unauthorized addition of a place of payment avoids it: *Burchfield* v. *Moore*, 3 E. & B. 683.

The alteration of the date of a bill from the 2nd to the 22nd of March avoids it: *Parry* v. *Nicholson*, 13 M. & W. 778.

Inserting the name of a payee on a promissory note avoids it, and, semble, that it is a forgery: *Awde* v. *Dixon,* 6 East 869.

A banker cannot debit his customer with a payment made upon a forged instrument: *Robarts* v. *Tucker*, 16 Q. B. 560, 575, 579 ; *Ex parte Swan*, 7 C. B. N. S. 400, per Willes, J., 448, "As a general rule, no one can found a title upon a forgery."

If the plaintiff were guilty of any neglect in the cheque getting into circulation, it was not that negligence which induced the bank to pay it, but the alteration in the date of it, the act of forgery, and for that the plaintiff is in no way to blame: *Ex parte Swan,* 7 C. B. N. S. 400, 447 ; *Swan* v. *The North British Australian Co. (Limited),* 2 H. & C. 175, 191.

This case may really be rested upon the sole ground that the defendants paid a forged instrument, in which case they are not entitled to claim anything upon it, and then it is wholly unimportant whether defendants ever received the cheque or not.

If the cheque had not been altered, I think the plaintiff still could not have been made liable upon it.

It must be considered to have been a paid cheque when the note for which it was given was handed by the defendants over to the plaintiff. That being so, no subsequent demand can be made upon it by any one against the defendants. It is by the payment overdue in fact: *Bartrum* v. *Caddy*, 9 A. & E. 275.

If it is not to be considered as a paid cheque, it certainly was entirely satisfied and effete, and in such a case the great length of time which had elapsed from its making until its presentation for payment, was clear evidence of its being overdue: *Barough* v. *White*, 4 B. & C. 325 ; *Down* v. *Halling*, 4 B. & C. 330 ; *Rothschild* v. *Corney*, 9 B. & C. 388 ; *Norton* v. *Ellam*, 2 M. & W. 461 ; *Bartrum* v. *Caddy*, 9 A. & E. 275.

And under these circumstances no recovery could be had upon it against the plaintiff.

.I gave a good deal of consideration to this case when it was formerly before us, and I find, by the pretty full note of judgment I then made, that I came substantially to the same conclusion which I now do.

The rule must therefore be discharged.

MORRISON, J.—Since the last argument of this case, *Vance* v. *Lowther*, L. R. 1 Ex. D. 176, cited by Mr. Robinson, appears in the reports, and it seems to me that that is an authority in favour of the plaintiff.

There the cheque was drawn and dated on the 2nd March, 1875. The cheque was entrusted to a clerk of the payee to be placed to his credit in a bank. The clerk absconded, and after altering the date to the 26th March, passed it to the plaintiff for value. Payment of the cheque being refused, the holder brought an action to recover the amount against the drawer of the cheque. At the trial the Judge found as a fact that the plaintiff had not been guilty of negligence in taking the cheque, and held under the circumstances the alteration was not material, and entered a verdict for the plaintiff. On appeal, brought against that decision, the Court held the alteration material, and that the cheque was void, and reversed the decision of the Court below.

In this case the plaintiff's contention is, that the cheque in question was drawn and dated on the 28th of January, 1873, to retire a note made payable at defendants' bank on that day, at which bank the plaintiff kept his bank account, and that the cheque was left with the bank for that purpose, and that he never received it back from the bank. On the part of the defendants it is alleged that it was not so given to or received by the bank, or used for such purpose: that what was done was, that the note in question, payable at the defendants' bank on that day, was paid by the bank and charged to the plaintiff's account. The evidence as to what really did take place is contradictory, and the inferences to be drawn from all the circumstances are not very satisfactory.

We assume it, however, as clear that the cheque was made on the 28th January, 1873 : that whether it was handed to the bank for the purpose of retiring the plaintiff's note, and not returned to him, or not being so used, it was abstracted or stolen from the plaintiff, it was afterwards altered so as to make it a cheque dated 28th January, 1874, by writing over the figure 3 of the year the figure 4. By whom this was done does not appear ; and so altered it was presented to the defendants and paid by them on the 31st January, 1874, to some person unknown, and the question is, whether the defendants having paid this altered cheque are entitled to withhold from the plaintiff the amount, in other words, to debit his account with it.

Upon the authority of the case of *Vance* v. *Lowther*, L. R. 1 Ex. D. 176, the alteration of the cheque was material, and the cheque void, and the plaintiff is entitled to recover on this ground alone. That case in one point of view was not so strong as the one before us. There the alteration might have been effected by the addition of the figure 5 and making the date 25 instead of 2, without arresting the attention of the party holding it. Here the alteration was apparent by altering a 3 into a 4. However, the Court in *Vance* v. *Lowther* did not consider it to be a case in which the question could arise, but they rested their decision upon the ground that the alteration made the cheque void.

I am, therefore, of opinion that the rule should be discharged.

HARRISON, C. J., took no part in the judgment.

Rule discharged.

HALLETT V. WILMOT AND BROWN.

Action against magistrates—Pleading—Damages.

A count alleging that defendants were justices of the peace, &c., and
assuming to act as such justices, but without any jurisdiction or authority in that behalf, caused a distress warrant to be issued against the
plaintiff's goods for $56, which they had adjudged the plaintiff to pay
under and by virtue of a certain conviction made by them without any
jurisdiction, and caused the plaintiff's goods to be sold thereunder,
which conviction was afterwards duly quashed on application of the
plaintiff to this Court, whereby the plaintiff lost the use and value of
his goods, and was put to costs in getting the conviction quashed:
Held, a count in trespass; and *held*, also, that the plaintiff was properly
nonsuited, the cause of action being the seizure of the plaintiff's goods
under warrants, issued upon three convictions of the plaintiff, for alleged
offences under the Act relating to the sale of spirituous liquors, two
only of which had been quashed, and a conviction for assault; and
therefore an act done by defendants in the execution of their duty,
as justices, with respect to matters within their jurisdiction.
Quære, if the plaintiff had been entitled to succeed in trespass, whether
he could have recovered the costs of quashing the convictions as
damages.

FIRST count: that the defendants were justices of the
peace in and for the united counties, &c.; and purporting
and assuming to act as such justices, but without any
jurisdiction or authority in that behalf, caused a distress
warrant to be issued against the goods and chattels of the
plaintiff for $56.50, which the defendants had adjudged the
plaintiff to pay under and by virtue of a certain conviction
before then made by them, without any jurisdiction or
authority in that behalf, had caused the goods and chattels
of the plaintiff, to wit one horse, to be sold thereunder;
and which said conviction was afterwards duly quashed in
due form of law, upon application of the plaintiff to her
Majesty's Court of Queen's Bench, &c., against the same:
whereby the plaintiff lost and was deprived of the use and
value of the horse, and was also put to great costs and
charges in and about the said application against the conviction and procuring of the same to be quashed.

The second and third counts were similar, but referred to
two other convictions.

Fourth and fifth counts: common counts in trespass and
trover.

Plea: not guilty, by statute.

The case was tried before Patterson, J.A., at the last Cobourg Assizes.

From the evidence given at the trial it appeared that the plaintiff had been convicted by the defendants, in the month of December last, on four different offences, three of them for alleged offences under the Act relating to the sale of spirituous liquors, and one for an assault: that on the 8th of January four warrants were issued on such convictions, signed by the defendant Wilmot only, and were delivered to a bailiff, who seized on the 11th of January, and sold on the 17th of January, under these warrants, a horse of the plaintiff: that on the 29th of February three of the convictions, including the one for the assault, were quashed, the remaining one being still in force.

At the close of the plaintiff's case the defendants' counsel submitted that the plaintiff should be nonsuited: that the action was one of trespass: that the seizure was justified: that although the three convictions were quashed, they were matters over which the defendants had jurisdiction; and that under any circumstances the defendant Brown was entitled to a verdict, as he had not signed the warrant of distress. The plaintiff's counsel contended that the defendants had not jurisdiction: that the defendant Brown, under the 5th sec. of ch. 126, Consol. Stat. U. C., was liable; and that the plaintiff was entitled to recover the costs of quashing the conviction.

The learned Judge held that the action entirely failed against Brown: that the convictions were within the jurisdiction of the defendants as magistrates; that all the counts were in effect for trespass in seizing, &c.; and that the warrant under the unquashed conviction justified the seizure; and he nonsuited the plaintiff.

During last term, November 23, 1876, *Hector Cameron*, Q. C., obtained a rule to set aside the nonsuit, on the ground that in law and on the evidence the plaintiff was entitled to recover; and for misdirection of the learned

Judge in ruling that no action would lie against the defendant Brown, who made the convictions, as he had not signed the warrants; nor against Wilmot, as the constable held one warrant on a conviction not quashed, as well as three others on the convictions which were quashed, he having seized under all four warrants: whereas the declaration charges a seizure under convictions which were quashed, and the plaintiff was entitled to recover damages for such seizure, and the costs incurred in quashing the convictions; and for the improper refusal of leave to amend, if an amendment was requisite, to enable the plaintiff to recover the amount improperly collected under the convictions which were quashed, and the costs of quashing the same.

During the same term, December 5, 1876, *J. D. Armour*, Q. C., shewed cause. Three convictions were quashed, and one was not. That one is as ample a protection to the defendants against trespass as the four could have been. There is no count for seizing too much, and a good conviction is shewn to support the sale made. He referred to *Crepps* v. *Durden*, 1 Sm. L. C., 7th. ed., 716; *Dickson* v. *Crabb*, 24 U. C. R. 494; *Moffatt* v. *Barnard*, 24 U. C. R. 498; *Pease* v. *Chaytor*, 32 L. J. M. C. 121; *Bott* v. *Ackroyd*, 28 L. J. M. C. 207; *Cave* v. *Mountain*, 1 M. & G. 257; *Price* v. *Woodhouse*, 1 Ex. 559; *Foxall* v. *Barnett*, 2 E. & B. 928; *Holloway* v. *Turner*, 6 Q. B. 928.

Hector Cameron, Q. C., supported the rule. The first three counts are not in trespass, but are special counts, setting out the facts. Under them the plaintiff was entitled to costs. The convictions were not supported by evidence, nor was there any legal offence charged. He cited *Drew* v. *Lainson*, 11 A. & E. 529; Consol. Stat. U. C. ch. 126 sec. 17; 37 Vic. ch. 32, O., secs. 25, 50.

January 2, 1877. MORRISON, J.—I cannot read the three first counts in the declaration in any other light than as counts in trespass. No particular form of words is necessary; all that is required are, allegations and facts that constitute a trespass. The common short form is that used here in the fourth count, viz: that the defendant seized and took the goods of the plaintiff and disposed of them. In substance and effect I see no distinction between that count and the others. The material allegation in all these counts, and that which constitutes the cause of action, is the seizing or taking of the plaintiff's horse and disposing of it. That is the trespass complained of. The setting out of the circumstances which led to the trespass does not deprive the action of its character. Then, when we look at the facts given in evidence at the trial to support the counts, they clearly shew that the plaintiff is seeking to recover damages for trespass in taking his goods.

The action being, therefore, one of trespass, and as it is clear that the cause of action was for an act done by the defendants in the execution of their duty as justices, and with respect to matters within their jurisdiction, the plaintiff was properly nonsuited: *Dickson* v. *Crabb*, 24 U. C. R. 494; *Moffatt* v. *Barnard*, 24 U. C. R. 498; *Haacke* v. *Adamson*, 14 C. P. 201.

In the latter case my brother Wilson said: "We do not think he should have recovered on the first count (trespass) at all, because the magistrate had jurisdiction of the offence, and by the express provisions of the statute, the remedy in such a case should have been by an action on the case charging malice."

The provisions of the statute, ch. 126, Consol. Stat. U. C., would be rendered nugatory if we were to hold that by the use of some introductory words in a count the form of action could be changed.

Mr. Cameron urged very strongly that the plaintiff was entitled, at all events, to recover the costs of quashing the convictions. Assuming that the plaintiff was entitled to succeed in an action of trespass, I am not prepared to say that the plaintiff would be entitled to recover such costs as damages. I find no case directly in point.

In *Holloway* v. *Turner et al.*, 6 Q. B. 928, which was an

action of trespass for seizing goods' under a judgment
entered upon a warrant of attorney, which was set aside,
the plaintiff had a verdict, including the costs of setting
aside the judgment. A rule was made absolute to reduce
the verdict by that amount; Lord Denman, C. J., saying,
he had no doubt the plaintiff could not sue the defendant
for a trespass *per quod* he was put to expense in removing the cause of the trespass.

And in *Pease* v. *Chaytor*, 32 L. J. M. C. 121—a case where
the defendants were charged in the declaration as acting
without jurisdiction and not *bonâ fide*, &c., and a verdict
being obtained against them, which included the costs of
quashing the order under which the distress warrant was
issued, the order not being made within the time limited
for bringing the action, although the seizure was—
Blackburn, J., in giving judgment, said, at p. 127, after
stating the various dates: "The action was therefore too
late as regards the expense of quashing that order, assuming that these costs might have been recovered as special
damage resulting from the making of the order. It is not
to be inferred that the costs of quashing the order could be
recovered as special damages. All that I can say is, that
even if they could, still, as to them, the action is too late.
But the seizure is in itself a cause of action; and, as far as
regards this cause of action, the defendants are not protected by lapse of time; but the costs of quashing the
order are in no sense part of the damage arising from the
seizure."

In that case the form of declaration was somewhat similar to the counts here; but there were allegations in the
declaration that the justices were not acting *bonâ fide*, &c.,
and also sufficiently shewing that they acted without jurisdiction, and on demurrer it was held good without an
allegation that the warrant was issued maliciously and
without reasonable and probable cause: *Regina* v. *Elring-
ton*, 1 B. & S. 688.

The case was afterwards tried, and a verdict entered for
£70; and a rule was granted to set aside the verdict, and

‑to reduce the amount to 1s.: one ground being that the plaintiff was not entitled to recover the costs of removing and quashing the orders of the defendants. The rule was made absolute for a new- trial, or to reduce the verdict to one shilling.

As we are of opinion that the action is one of trespass, it becomes unnecessary to consider the other points raised during the argument, and the rule will be discharged.

As to the amount in the hands of the magistrate, the proceeds of the sale of the horse, over and above the amount necessary to satisfy the conviction not quashed, the counsel for the defendants says they were and are ready to pay over the amount if the plaintiff will receive it.

HARRISON, C. J., and WILSON, J., concurred.

Rule discharged.

REGINA V. GEORGE STARR.

Larceny—Recent possession—Evidence.

On an indictment for stealing cooper's tools on the 5th of November, 1874, it appeared that the prisoner was not arrested for nearly two years afterwards. During that time—it was not shewn precisely when —he was proved to have sold several of the tools at much less than their value, representing that he was a cooper by trade, and was going to quit it, which was proved to be untrue. It was proved also that he was in the shop from which the tools were stolen the night before they were taken, and frequently; and that when arrested he offered the prosecutor $35 to settle and buy new tools, and offered the constable $100 if he could get clear.

Held, that though the mere fact of the possession by the prisoner, after such a lapse of time, might not alone suffice, yet that all the facts taken together were enough to support a conviction for larceny.

CASE reserved from the County Judge's Criminal Court of Huron, by Isaac F. Toms, Co. J.

The facts were as follow : The indictment was for larceny and receiving. The conviction was for larceny.

There were in fact two questions for determination :—

1. Whether the admissions or offers of the prisoner to settle were admissible.

2. Whether, if admissible, there was on the whole case evidence to go to a jury, if there were one, in support of a charge of larceny.

The things stolen were cooper's tools. They consisted of two adzes, champer knife, a leveller, hand-axe, and other similar articles. They were stolen either on the night of the 5th November or morning of the 6th November, 1874, out of a cooper's shop in Seaforth. The shop was usually locked at night. During the night of 5th November, 1874, it was broken into. A pane of glass had been taken out of the back window, which allowed a person to withdraw the bolt and enter the shop. The prisoner before and at the time of the larceny was at Seaforth. He was in the shop the night before the taking of the tools, and had used one of them. He was frequently in the shop, and the evidence did not point to any other than the prisoner as the thief. The prisoner was not arrested for the stealing till nearly two years afterwards. During that period he was proved from time to time to have sold several of the tools at prices much below their value. He represented that he was a cooper by trade: that he had been working at the cooperage trade for some time and was going to quit it. This statement was proved to be devoid of truth. After his arrest he stated that he had purchased the tools from a party in Brussels: that he purchased them in the presence of a woman now dead; and that the purchase was made in a particular tavern named. His brother proved the purchase of a tool or tools by the prisoner from a man under the influence of drink in a tavern at Brussels; but there was no satisfactory evidence to shew that the purchase was of any of the tools in question. This was in January or February last. The man from whom the tools were purchased, was described by a brother of the tavern-keeper as "a hard-looking case."

The prisoner after his arrest offered the prosecutor $35 to settle, and to purchase a new kit of tools. He told another witness he would give $100 if he could get clear of the tools. He was arrested on the 21st September last. On that day he said to the prosecutor, in the presence of the constable who made the arrest, that he had purchased the tools in a tavern at Brussels. The constable proved the offer to him of $100 by the prisoner, when the latter was being taken to the lock-up. There was no evidence of any inducement offered to the prisoner either by the prosecutor or the constable. But the prosecutor told the constable he was willing to let prisoner go, if the constable would.

December 6, 1876. *J. K. Kerr*, Q. C., appeared for the Crown. He referred to *Arch. Cr. Pl.*, 18th ed., 251; *Roscoe Cr. Ev.*, 8th ed., 50; *Rex* v. *Adams*, 3 C. & P. 600; *Rex* v. *Partridge*, 7 C. & P. 551.

He stated that the prisoner desired to cite *Rex* v. *Crowhurst*, 1 C. & K. 370; *Regina* v. *Wilson*, 7 Cox 310; *Regina* v. *Wilson*, 26 L. T. M. C. 45; *Regina* v. *Taylor*, 8 C. & P. 733.

December 29, 1876. HARRISON, C. J.—There is no ground for excluding the offers made to the prosecutor or the constable. It does not appear that there was any inducement whatever held out by either of them. It would be a waste of time to refer to the authorities on the point: *Archbold's Crim. Pl.*, 18th ed., 389.

But the important question is, whether, assuming this evidence to have been rightly received, there was evidence against the prisoner of larceny.

We regret he was not represented by counsel at the argument before us. But the argument, if any, on his behalf would be,—

1. That there was nothing against him but the fact of possession of the things stolen.

2. That the possession was not a recent one.

3. That he gave a satisfactory account as to his possession.

4. That even if a recent possession, and no satisfactory account given, such possession is not evidence of larceny but of receiving.

Recent possession of stolen property is evidence either that the person in possession stole the property, or that he received it knowing it to have been stolen, according to the other circumstances of the case: *Regina* v. *Densley*, 6 C. & P. 399; *Regina* v. *Smith*, 1 Dears. 494; *Regina* v. *Byrne*, L. R. 4 Ir. C. L. 68; *Regina* v. *McMahon*, 13 Cox. 275.

If no other person be involved in the transaction forming the subject of enquiry, and the whole of the case against the prisoner is, that he was found in possession of the stolen property, the evidence would no doubt point to a case of stealing rather than receiving; but in every case, except indeed where the possession is so recent that it is impossible for any one else to have committed the theft, it becomes a mere question for the jury whether the person found in possession of the stolen property stole it himself or received it from some one else. If there is no other evidence the jury will probably consider, with reason, that the prisoner stole the property, but if there is other evidence which is consistent either with his having stolen the property or with his having received it from some one else, it will be for the jury to say which appears to them the more probable solution: *Regina* v. *Langmead*, 1 Leigh & C. 427, 437, 439, 441.

The rule is, that if stolen property be found recently after its loss in the possession of a person, he must give an account of the manner in which he became possessed of it— otherwise the presumption attaches that he is the thief: Per Bayley, J., in *Rex* v. ———, 2 C. & P. 459.

If the person into whose possession the stolen property is traced gives a reasonable account of how he came by it, as by telling the name of the person from whom he received it, it is incumbent on the prosecutor to shew that that account is false; but if the account given by the prisoner be unreasonable or improbable on the face of it, the onus of proving its truth lies on him. Per Alderson, B., in *Regina* v. *Crowhurst* 1 C. & K. 370.

"Suppose, for instance, a person were to charge me with stealing a watch, and I were to say, I bought it from a particular tradesman whom I name: that is *primâ facie* a reaunable account; and I ought not to be convicted of felony, unless it is shewn that account is a false one": *Ib.*

The decision of Alderson, B., in *Regina* v. *Crowhurst*, 1 C. & K. 370, was followed by Lord Denman in *Regina* v. *Smith*, 2 C. & K. 207.

But it is not to be understood from either of these cases that it is incumbent on the Crown, relying solely on a recent possession of goods, in every case to call as witnesses the persons to whom the prisoner referred, to account for his possession: *Regina* v. *Wilson*, 7 Cox 310.

If in this case there could be said to be recent possession, we could not hold the prisoner's account of how he became possessed of the property satisfactory, and it does not apppear to be much, if any, improved by the testimony of the witnesses called on his behalf to substantiate the account.

The question of what is or is not to be held a recent possession, is to be considered with reference to the nature of the articles stolen: *Rex* v. *Partridge*, 7 C. & P. 551.

Where two ends of woollen cloth in an unfinished state, consisting of about twenty yards each, were lost, and were in the possession of the prisoner two months after being stolen, and still in the same state, it was held that this was a possession sufficiently recent to call on the prisoner to shew how he came by the property: *Ib.*

If the *only* evidence against the prisoner be, that the stolen property was found in his possession three months after the loss of it, the Judge may direct an acquittal: *Rex* v. *Adams*, 3 C. & P. 600. And if it appear that so long a period as sixteen months has elapsed it would not be reasonable to apply the presumption either of stealing or receiving, to the prisoner: *Rex* v. ———— 2 C. & P. 459.

But if there be evidence of *something more* than the mere

fact of the property being in possession of the prisoner for a time which cannot be held to be recent, the case ought not necessarily to be withdrawn from the consideration of the jury: *Rex* v. *Adams*, 3 C. & P. 600.

In this case there was not only the fact of possession (not shewn precisely when as to the different articles), but the fact that the prisoner was in the shop the night before the articles were stolen, the fact that when selling them he represented himself as a cooper going out of business, which was untrue, the fact that the articles were sold by him greatly below their value, and the fact of his offers to the prosecutor and the constable with a view to the prevention of the prosecution.

While any one of these facts, standing by itself, might not be strong enough to raise a reasonable presumption of guilt, the combination of them can, in our opinion, have no other effect.

All the questions submitted for our opinion in the case stated by the learned Judge of Huron, must be answered against the prisoner.

The case is defective in omitting to state whether or not the prisoner has been sentenced. If not sentenced, we order the learned Judge to pass judgment on the prisoner.

MORRISON, J., and WILSON, J., concurred.

Conviction affirmed.

PARKINSON V. HIGGINS ET AL.

Mortgage of vessel—Purchase by mortgagee—Loss of vessel—Right to sue for mortgage money.

Declaration on defendant's covenant by deed to pay money. Plea: that the deed mentioned was a mortgage and re-conveyance of a vessel sold by plaintiff to defendant, to secure the purchase money therefor; and that while the plaintiff was mortgagee the said vessel and all defendant's interest therein was sold, and the plaintiff became the absolute owner of said vessel, whereby the mortgage became merged and satisfied. Replication, on equitable grounds, that the vessel, being a British ship, was seized for wages due to the crew, and sold at Detroit, in the United States, solely through defendant's default: that by the law of the United States the wages formed a lien prior to the mortgage, and the plaintiff, wholly to protect himself, and not to gain any advantage over defendant, became the purchaser: that he offered and was always willing to reconvey and deliver her to defendants on being paid the mortgage money and the sum paid by him at such sale, which defendant refused to pay: that the plaintiff, having possession of the vessel, insured her, and on her loss by the perils of the sea received the insurance money, which the plaintiff is and always has been ready to apply on the purchase money. *Held*, on demurrer, affirming the judgment of GWYNNE, J., a good replication, and that the plaintiff, under the circumstances stated, was not precluded from recovering on the covenant.

DEMURRER. Declaration: that the defendants, by deed bearing date the 23rd April, 1873, covenanted with the plaintiff to pay him $900 on the 1st November, 1874, together with interest at the rate of seven per centum per annum, on the sum of $2,700 from the 23rd April, 1873, but did not pay the same.

Plea 2. On equitable grounds: that before the making of the deed in the declaration mentioned, the plaintiff sold a certain vessel to defendant Elizabeth Jane Higgins, and the said deed was a mortgage and re-conveyance of the vessel to the said defendant, E. J. H., and her husband, to secure the purchase money of the said vessel: that the vessel was afterwards seized and sold at Detroit, under the authority of the Admiralty of the U. S., and the plaintiff became the purchaser, and is now the absolute owner thereof, &c., whereby the said mortgage become satisfied. 3. On equitable grounds: that the deed mentioned being a mortgage as in the last plea mentioned, and while the plaintiff was the mortgagee of the said vessel, and before the commencement of this suit, the said vessel was sold and the plaintiff became, and was, and is, the absolute owner of the said vessel, whereby the said mortgage became merged and satisfied.

Replication, on equitable grounds, to the third plea: that the said vessel was and is a British ship, called the Perry, duly registered under the "Merchant Shipping Act, 1854," at the Port of Montreal, in the Province of Quebec, in the Dominion of Canada, as No. 61,125; and that the said vessel was libelled or charged and seized for wages due to the crew thereof, and for necessaries supplied to the said ship, the said wages and necessaries having accrued due and been supplied after the sale of the said ship by the plaintiff to the defendant Elizabeth Jane Higgins, and the giving of the mortgage in the said plea mentioned, and whilst the said vessel was in the possession of the said defendants, and that the said vessel was condemned and sold at the Port of Detroit, in the second plea mentioned, solely through the default of the defendants, and not in any way with the privity or consent or by the collusion or neglect or default of the plaintiff: that by the laws of the United States of America the said charges constituted and were a prior lien to the said mortgage, which in fact was and is wholly ignored and disregarded by the said United States laws; and the plaintiff, wholly in order to protect himself and not for the purpose of gaining any advantage over the defendants, became the purchaser of the said vessel for a sum which, together with sheriff's fees and other expenses connected therewith, amounted to $2,300 or thereabouts; and that after the said sale and purchase the said plaintiff offered and always was ready and willing to re-convey all his right and estate in the said vessel, and to deliver up the said vessel to the defendants, upon being paid by the defendants the amount due on said mortgage and the said sum paid by him at said sale, but the defendants always wholly refused to pay the said several amounts, and the plaintiff was obliged to retain the said vessel in order to

indemnify and save himself harmless against the loss of
the said money, so as aforesaid paid for the same. And
the plaintiff further says that the plaintiff, having possession of the said vessel, duly insured the same in the Royal
Canadian Insurance Company for the sum of $2,000
and the said vessel was subsequently, without any
default or neglect of the plaintiff, lost by perils of the sea,
and was abandoned by the plaintiff to the said company,
who accepted the same, and who afterwards paid to the
plaintiff the sum of $1,860, being the said sum of $2,000
less the premium on the policy of the said company. And
the plaintiff is ready and willing, and has always been
ready and willing since the said payment, to apply the
said sum of $1,860 on the said sum of $2.300, paid by
the plaintiff for the said vessel as aforesaid.

Demurrer to the replication on the grounds:—1. The
replication admits that the absolute title to the vessel became and was vested in the plaintiff, and while so vested
in the plaintiff that the vessel was disposed of by the
plaintiff, and that he cannot restore the same to the
defendants, and therefore cannot maintain this action.

2. The replication shews and states the plaintiff bought
the said vessel as mortgagee thereof, and to secure the
mortgage made to him, and as such acquired the absolute
title in the vessel, and freed from any claim by the defendants or either of them therein; and he cannot now claim
to have held his estate as purchaser and as mortgagee distinct
and separate thereafter, and such purchase was not adding
a further charge against the defendants on the said mortgage.

3. That the law is, that whenever a mortgagee, whether
by title paramount to his mortgage or otherwise howsoever,
vests the absolute title to real or personal properties in
himself, his estate as mortgagee is merged, and he cannot
afterwards maintain an action upon the mortgage without
being ready to restore the mortgagors to their former and
original position, which the plaintiff's replication shews
cannot be done in this case.

September 5, 1876, the demurrer was argued by *Ferguson*, Q.C., for the plaintiff, and *H. J. Scott*, for the defendant. The argument was similar to that on the rehearing post p. 279.

September 15, 1876. GWYNNE, J.—No question arises upon this demurrer as to the liability of the defendant Elizabeth J. Higgins, who, as appears by the record, is the wife of the other defendant, and entered into the covenant declared upon jointly with her husband, nor, although the precise circumstances attending the alleged seizure, libelling and sale of the vessel in the foreign port are not set forth, does any question arise upon this demurrer as to the sufficiency and validity of such proceedings in view of the particular circumstances of the case, in virtue of which such proceedings were had. The simple question is, whether, under the circumstances appearing in the replication to the third plea, which circumstances, for the purposes of this demurrer, we are to assume to be true, the plaintiff is by the doctrines of equity precluded from suing upon the covenant declared upon.

For the purpose of this argument we must, I think, read the replication as alleging the proceeding in the foreign Court to have been taken *in rem*, the propriety of which, even if enquirable into in this Court, is not disputed upon these pleadings. The simple question then is, when the mortgagor of a British registered ship by his own neglect and default, and while the ship is in his actual possession and control, suffers his ship to be legally seized, libelled, and sold in a foreign port for charges properly charged upon the ship, and for which proceedings *in rem* were duly taken in the foreign Court, and the vessel is duly exposed for sale in such foreign Court to realize such charges, and the mortgagee being apprised thereof, solely for his own protection becomes the purchaser thereof at such sale, and thereupon offers to re-convey her to the mortgagor upon payment of the sums so necessarily advanced by the mortgagee, and the mortgagor refuses or neglects to pay such sum, and thereupon the mortgagee makes use of the vessel and insures her, and is always ready and willing to give her up to the mortgagor upon payment of the charges aforesaid, and the ship is lost by perils of the sea without any default of the mortgagee, whereupon the mortgagee receives the insurance money, and is always thereafter ready and willing to account with the mortgagor for such insurance money as against his, the mortgagee's, claims upon the ship, as mortgagee, and 'for his advances upon the sale in the foreign Court—is the mortgagee under such circumstances precluded from suing upon the mortgagor's covenant to pay the mortgage debt; and I am of opinion that upon no principle of law or equity is the mortgagee under such circumstances so precluded.

Palmer v. *Hendrie*, 27 Beav. 349, has nothing in support of the position that the mortgagee is precluded from suing upon the mortgagor's covenant. The principle of that case is, that it was by the act of the mortgagee, unauthorised by the mortgagor, that it became impossible for the mortgagee to restore the mortgaged property upon payment of the mortgage debt. Neither does *Lockhart* v. *Hardy*, 9 Beav. 349, which was also relied upon by the learned counsel for the defendant, in any respect support his contention. There after foreclosure the mortgagee sold the mortgaged property for a sum which was insufficient to pay the mortgage debt, and under such circumstances it was held he could not sue for the balance upon the mortgagor's covenant. Upon these pleadings before me, I must take it that it was wholly by the mortgagor's default that it became necessary for the mortgagee to intervene for his own protection and that of the mortgagor and that it was wholly by the act of God that the mortgagee is unable to restore the mortgaged property, while he is able and willing to give the mortgagor the benefit of the amount received by way of insurance and so representing the mortgaged property, charging the mortgagor with the necessary advances made by the mortgagee to relieve the vessel from the claims made in the foreign Court, and which, upon assumption that the sale was valid, I think he is entitled to do.

It may be that at a future stage the mortgagee will also have to account to the mortgagor for a reasonable amount for the use of the vessel while in the possession of the mortgagee, but at present the only question is, whether the purchase in the foreign Court, under the circumstances stated in the replication, is a complete bar in equity to the mortgagee suing on the mortgagor's covenant, and I am clearly of opinion that it is not.

The pleading here seems to supply all that seemed necessary to Hagarty, C. J., to make the replication good when this case was before him upon a demurrer to a former replication.

Judgment therefore will be for the plaintiff on the demurrer.

During this term, November 24, 1877, the case was reheard before the full Court. *H. J. Scott*, for the defendant, who appealed, relied on *Palmer* v. *Hendrie*, 27 Beav. 349; *Lockhart* v. *Hardy*, 7 Beav. 349; *Gowland* v. *Garbutt*, 13 Grant 578, and the other cases cited in the judgment on the doctrine in equity as to the right of the mortgagee to sue on the mortgagor's covenant. He contended that the mortgagee by his purchase had put himself in the position of a mortgagee who had foreclosed, and that he could not after he had foreclosed take advantage of any further remedies, and it was out of his power to restore the parties to their original status. He also cited *Paul* v. *Ferguson*, 14 Grant 430.

Ferguson, Q. C., for the plaintiff. The plea is a complete plea of merger. The replication is an answer to that, and shews there was no merger, for merger is a question of intention; and the replication shews there was no intent of the plaintiff to merge his mortgage interest. If not a plea of merger, the declaration states that defendant covenanted to pay the money. The plea does not meet that, it does not say, defendant paid the money or that he did not covenant as alleged. The plaintiff's action cannot be likened to a foreclosure, for that is a voluntary taking

by the mortgagee of the thing mortgaged for the debt
secured, whereas here the plaintiff was forced to buy in
the vessel to save his debt.

December 29, 1876.   HARRISON, C. J.—No question was
raised before us as to the sufficiency of the plea, therefore
we give no opinion as to its sufficiency. It was held by
Hagarty, C. J., to be a sufficient plea: 37 U. C. R. 308.
He also held the replication as then framed to be bad, and
in doing so said, at p. 319, speaking of the plaintiff, " Had
he offered to be redeemed or to convey any interest remaining in him, or made out a case shewing that he purchased
merely to save his rights as mortgagee, or claiming to add
the purchase money to the original mortgage money, I
could understand his right to collect the amount. due on
the covenant at law."

The plaintiff has amended his replication to meet this
suggestion of the learned Chief Justice, and the question is
as to the sufficiency of the replication as now amended.
Mr. Justice Gwynne has held the replication sufficient, and
the appeal is from his decision.

In equity a mortgage, though in form a conveyance of
real estate, is looked upon in substance as a mere security
for payment of money — that is, a pledge of the thing
mortgaged, which the mortgagee undertakes to restore on
payment of the mortgage money.   The right to redeem in
equity on payment of the mortgage money exists till the
equity has been foreclosed.

But there is nothing to prevent the mortgagee opening
the foreclosure, in which event he must be prepared to
restore the property pledged or satisfactorily account for it
as against the mortgagor : in other words, if the mortgagee
has put it out of his power to restore the property mortgaged, equity will not permit him to sue for the mortgage
money.   See *Lockhart* v. *Hardy,* 7 Beav. 349 ; *Palmer* v.
Hendrie, 27 Beav. 349 ; *Gowland* v. *Garbutt,* 13 Grant 578 ;
Burnham v. *Galt,* 16 Grant 417.

. If the mortgagee acquire the property by title paramount, as in the case of land on a sale for taxes, on the

strength of his being mortgagee, and makes his interest a ground of being allowed to purchase, he must submit to be redeemed: *Smart* v. *Cottle*, 10 Grant 59 ; *Schofield* v. *Dickinson,' Ib.* 226 ; *Kelly* v. *Macklem*, 14 Grant 29˙

Where a mortgagor covenanting against incumbrances conveyed part of the mortgaged property to a purchaser, and the mortgagee subsequently released the part so sold from his mortgage, it was held that this release being in accordance with the mortgagor's own obligation as to that part, did not affect the mortgagee's right to recover the mortgage debt: *Crawford* v. *Armour,* 13 Grant 576.

While the replication admits the acquirement of the property by title paramount—see *Castrique* v. *Imrie et al.,* L. R. 4 H. L. 414—it shews that the sale arose through the default of the mortgagor, and that the plaintiff became a purchaser wholly in order to protect himself as a mortgagee, and not for the purpose of gaining any advantage over the mortgagor, and offers to re-convey all the interest he acquired in the vessel or its proceeds on payment of the mortgage money and the purchase money.

If the vessel were still in existence and of more value than the mortgage money, we apprehend that the mortgagee on this statement of facts would have to submit to be redeemed, and if for this purpose the assumed foreclosure were to be taken as opened, there ought to be no difficulty interposed to the assertion of the plaintiff's legal right to recover the purchase money or balance of it still unpaid.

The difficulty, if any, arises because the vessel is not still in existence. The plaintiff as mortgagee having obtained possession of the vessel, insured her for the sum of $2,000, and the vessel was subsequently lost without any default or neglect of the mortgagee. The cause of loss is alleged to be the perils of the sea. The insurance company paid to the mortgagee $1,860, being the amount insured less the premium, and this sum the mortgagee is willing to credit on the mortgage.

The argument before us, on behalf of the mortgagor is, that the vessel was a mere pledge, that a pledgee can only use a pledge at his own peril, and if from any cause in the user the pledge has become lost, the pledgee is not in a position to restore it ; and therefore, whether to blame or not as to the loss, the plaintiff should be restrained from suing for the mortgage money or any part of it : *Jones* on Bailments, 4th ed., 81 ; *Story* on Bailments, 8th ed., sec. 330.

The fallacy of the argument is, that for all purposes it treats the mortgagee of a ship as a mere pledgee of a chattel. It is now held that a mortgagee of a ship has the right of exercising the sound discretion which a prudent owner would exercise to use and employ the ship. See *Langton* v. *Horton*, 5 Beav. 9, 1 *Hare*, 549; *Feltham* v. *Clark*, 1 De. G. & Sm., 307 ; *Gardener* v. *Cazenove*, 1 H. & N. 423; Imp. Stat., 17 & 18 Vic. ch. 104, secs. 70, 71 ; *European & Australian Royal Mail Co.* v. *Royal Mail Steam Packet Co.* 4 K. & J. 676 ; *De Mattos* v. *Gibson*, 1 J. & H. 79, 4 De G. & J. 276 ; *Marriott* v. *The Anchor Reversionary Co.*, 3 De G. F. & J. 177.

The rights and liabilities of mortgagor and mortgagee, although in some respects alike, are not in all respects the same as the rights and liabilities of pledgor and pledgee: *Jones* v. *Smith*, 2 Ves. Jr. 372, 378. See further *Williams* v. *Price*, 1 Sim. & S. 581. A mortgagee of real estate may at the same time take possession of the estate, sue the mortgagor on his covenant, and proceed to foreclose : Per the Master of the Rolls in *Cockell* v. *Bacon*, 16 Beav. 158, 159 ; and in *Palmer* v. *Hendrie*, 27 Beav. 356.

A mortgagee in possession of real estate is not only entitled to use and occupy the property mortgaged, but is not charged with deterioration of the property arising from ordinary decay by time, nor even from the want of repair which has caused a diminution in annual value ; and it has been said that he ought not to be charged with the same degree of care which a man is supposed to take who keeps possession of his own property. But if there be gross or wilful negligence, the mortgagee will be held responsible. He will therefore be liable for the loss occasioned by alterations injurious to the value of the estate, such as the pulling down of cottages and the cutting of timber &c.: *Fisher* on Mortgages, p. 948.

. The fact of the mortgagee allowing the premises to fall into decay does not prevent him from suing for the amount due on the mortgage: *Munsen* v. *Hauss*, 22 Grant 279.

There appears to be no doubt as to the right of a mortgagee in possession to insure not merely his own interest but the interest of the mortgagor as well: *Irving* v. *Richardson*, 2 B. & Ad. 193; *Kerswell* v. *Bishop*, 2 C. & J. 529; *Davies* v. *The Home Insurance Co.*. 3 E. & A. 269.

The mortgagee in this case acquired title paramount to the vessel by reason of the admitted neglect and default of the mortgagor to discharge his proper pecuniary obligations. Having so acquired title the mortgagee had an undoubted right to take possession of the vessel. Having taken possession he, like a prudent man, insured the vessel for an amount of money which is not complained of as being too small. He employed the vessel, as he had a perfect right to do, in the proper business of such a vessel. No complaint is made of anything improper in the use of her. While being so used she was lost by the perils insured against. The plaintiff, who is suing the defendant on his covenant for non-payment of the mortgage money, offers to apply the insurance money less the premium in reduction of the mortgage. All that he claims in this action is the difference between the amount advanced on the mortgage added to the amount advanced to save the vessel when sold in the foreign country, and the amount received from the insurance company. We know of no principle of law, whether administered by Courts of law or equity, which should be held to prevent a recovery under these circum-stances. We are of opinion that Mr. Justice Gywnne was right in holding the replication, as now amended, a good answer to the plea.

MORRISON, J., concurred.

WILSON, J., was not present at the argument, and took no part in the judgment.

Judgment affirmed, with costs.

IN THE MATTER OF PHILO D. BATES.

Conviction—Certiorari—38 Vic. c. 4, O.—By-law.

In the case of a conviction for an offence not being a crime, affirmed on
appeal to the Sessions, the writ of *certiorari* is not taken away by the
38 Vic. ch. 4, O.

Where the conviction purported to be for an offence against a by-law,
but shewed no such offence, it was quashed; and it was held, that it
could not be supported as warranted by the general law.

F. Osler, during Hilary term, February 8, 1876, upon
reading the notice of motion and affidavit of service thereof
upon the Clerk of the Peace for the county of Wentworth,
and upon the Police Magistrate for the city of Hamilton, and
upon John Davis, the informant, obtained a rule calling on
these parties to shew cause why a writ of *certiorari* should
not issue out of this Court, directed to the chairman of the
General Sessions of the Peace for the county of Wentworth, commanding him to return into this Court a certain
record of conviction made by the said Police Magistrate,
on or about the 13th of August, 1875, whereby Philo D.
Bates, the applicant, was, upon the information of the said
John Davis, convicted, "for that he, the said Philo D.
Bates, did on the 7th of August, 1875, unlawfully trespass
with and interfere with the waggon of the said John Davis,
and with his property therein, contrary to the provisions
of a certain by-law of the city of Hamilton," which conviction afterwards, on appeal to the Court of General
Sessions of the Peace, was on the 16th of December, 1875,
affirmed by that Court.

The conviction, a copy of which was annexed to the
applicant's affidavit, stated the offence as follows: "For
that the said defendant, on the 12th of August instant, at
Hamilton, &c., did unlawfully trespass upon and damage
the waggon of one John Davis (the said waggon being
lawfully in the James street market of the said city) contrary to a certain by-law of the municipality of the said
city, passed on the 26th of April, A.D. 1869, and entitled
a by-law," &c.

A certified copy of the by-law was filed.

During this term, November 25, 1876, *M. C. Cameron,* Q. C., shewed cause. The effect of secs. 5, 6 7, of 38 Vic. ch. 4, O., read in connection with 32–33 Vic. ch. 31, secs. 65, 71, D., as amended by 33 Vic. ch. 27, D., is to prevent the issue of a writ of *certiorari* upon an appeal from a summary conviction.

He did not attempt, under the by-law or otherwise, to support the conviction.

F. Osler, contra. The conviction is void, and the *certiorari* has not been taken away in the case of a conviction affirmed by the sessions, where no crime is charged : *Paley* on Convictions, 405, 406, 407 ; *Ke Kaye* 1 D. & R. 436 ; *Rex* v. *Mayor of Liverpool*, 3 D. & R. 275 ; 38 Vic. ch. 11, sec 13, O. ; *Michell* v. *Brown*, 1 E. & E: 267 ; *Regina* v. *Levecque*, 30 U. C. R. 509.

December 29, 1876. HARRISON, C. J.—The only. question argued was, whether in the case of a conviction for an offence not being a crime, there can be a writ of *certiorari* after appeal from the conviction. and conviction affirmed.

The power of the Court to order the issue of a writ of *certiorari* is considered so beneficial to the subject that it is not to be held as taken away by anything short of an express statutory provision : *Re Smith et al.*, 1 Mod. 44, cited by Lord Holt in 1 Ld. Raym. 469, 580 ; *Rex* v. *Moreley*, 2 Burr. 1041 ; *Anon.*, 1 Burr. 245 ; *Rex* v. *Jukes*, 8 T. R. 542, 544.

Mere words giving a right of appeal, although accompanied by a declaration that the decision of the justices in appeal shall be final, are not sufficient for the purpose : 2 *Hawk*. P. C. ch. 27, sec. 23 ; *Rex* v. *Plowright*, 3 Mod. 95 ; *Rex* v. *Justices of Lindsey*, 3 D. & L. 101.

General words of reference to offences created in a former statute, in which the *certiorari* is taken away, are not sufficient without the repetition of the prohibitory. clause as to the *certiorari* or some direct reference to it : *Rex* v. *Terret*, 2 T. R. 735 ; *Re Kaye*, 1 D. & R. 436 ; *Rex* v. *Mayor of Liverpool*, 3 D. & R. 275.

Even where *certiorari* is said to be taken away by statute, a superior Court of law is not absolutely deprived of the power to issue the writ, but its action as to the writ is controlled and limited: *The Colonial Bank of Australasia* v. *Willan*, L. R. 5 P. C. 417.

If it appear either that there is a manifest defect of jurisdiction in the tribunal which made the conviction or order: *Rex* v. *Justices of The West Riding of Yorkshire,* 5 T. R. 629, 633; *Regina* v. *Commissioners, &c., of Chelten-ham*, 1 Q. B. 467 ; *Regina* v. *Rose*, 1 Jur. N. S. 802 ; *Re-gina* v. *Wood*, 5 E. & B. 49; *Regina* v. *Justices of War-wickshire*, 6 E. & B. 837; or manifest fraud in the party procuring it: *Regina* v. *Gillgass*, 12 Q. B. 527. The writ may be issued notwithstanding words purporting to take away the right to issue it: *Colonial Bank of Australasia* v. *Willan*, L. R. 5 P. C. 417. See further *Re Holland*, 37 U. C. R. 214.

Matters on which the defect of jurisdiction depends may be apparent on the face of the proceedings, or may be brought before the Court by affidavit : *The Colonial Bank of Australasia* v. *Willan*, L. R. 5 P. C. 417. See further *Regina* v. *Munro*, 24 U. C. R. 344.

There must of course be certain conditions on which the right of every tribunal of limited jurisdiction to exercise that jurisdiction depends. But those conditions may be founded either on the character and constitution of the tribunal, or upon the nature of the subject-matter of the enquiry, or upon certain proceedings which have been made essential preliminaries to the enquiry, or upon facts or a fact to be adjudicated upon in the course of the en-quiry. It is obvious that conditions of the last, differ ma-terially from those of the three other classes. Objections founded on the personal incompetency of the Judge, or on the nature of the subject-matter, on on the absence of some essential preliminary, must obviously, in most cases, depend upon matters which, whether apparent on the face of the proceedings or brought before the Superior Court by affi-davit, are extrinsic to the adjudication impeached. But an objection that a Judge has erroneously found a fact which, though essential to the validity of his order, he was competent to try, assumes that having general jurisdiction over the subject matter he properly entered upon the enquiry but miscarried in the course of it. The Superior Court cannot quash an adjudication upon such an objection without assuming the functions of a Court of Appeal, and the power to re-try a question which the inferior Judge was competent to decide: Per Sir James W. Colville, in *The Colonial Bank of Australasia* v. *Willan*, L. R. 5 P. C. 417, 442, 443.

If there be jurisdiction substantially, although in some respects exceeded, and the writ of *certiorari* be taken away by statute, the writ will be refused: *Regina* v. *Bristol & Exeter R. W. Co.*, 1 P. &. D. 170, note *d.*, 11 A. & E. 202, note.

Consol. Stat. U. C. ch. 114, as amended by 29-30 Vic. ch. 50, which had so long regulated appeals to the General Sessions, in cases of summary convictions not being for crimes, was repealed by sec. 12, of 38 Vic. ch. 4, O.

The statute which now, in general terms, regulates such appeals when to the General Sessions is 38 Vic. ch. 4, O.

The statute which now regulates appeals from convictions for crime is, 32–33 Vic. ch. 31, sec. 65, as amended by 33 Vic. ch. 27, D.

The latter statute in positive language declares that, " No conviction or order affirmed, or affirmed and amended in appeal, shall be quashed for want of form, or removed by *certiorari* into any of her Majesty's Superior Courts of Record," &c.: Sec. 71.

There is no such enactment as the last mentioned in the statute, 38 Vic. ch. 4, O., but the contention is, that by necessary intendment the latter enactment is a part of the law of the Province.

In support of this contention reference is made to secs. 4, 5, 6 of 38 Vic. ch. 4, O.

Sec. 5: " Where a conviction or order is made by a justice or justices of the peace, or by a police or stipendiary magistrate, under the authority of any statute being in force in Ontario, and in respect to matters within the legislative authority of the Province of Ontario, unless it be otherwise provided by the particular Act under which the conviction or order is made, any party who considers himself aggrieved by the conviction or order may appeal therefrom to the General Sessions of the Peace."

Sec. 6: "In case an appeal lie to the Court of General Sessions of the Peace from a conviction or order, made as aforesaid, under the authority of a statute or law having force in the Province of Ontario, but not enacted by the Legislature of the said Province, the practice and proceedings on the appeal and preliminary thereto, and otherwise in respect thereof, shall be the same as the practice and proceedings under the statute of the Dominion then in force, on an appeal to the General Sessions of the Peace from a conviction before a justice of the peace made under the authority of a statute of Canada."

Sec. 7: "In case an appeal lie to the General Sessions of the Peace from a conviction or order made as aforesaid under the authority of a statute of the Legislature of the Province of the Ontario, the practice and proceedings on the appeal and preliminary thereto, and otherwise in respect thereof, shall be the same as provided in the next preceding section, except that either of the parties to the appeal may call witnesses and adduce evidence in addition to the witnesses called and evidence adduced at the original hearing."

It appears to us that these sections wholly fail to support the contention as to the taking away of the writ of *certiorari*.

They do no more than provide for appeals from convictions to the General Sessions, for the practice and proceedings on such appeals, and for the right of either party on an appeal to adduce evidence in addition to the evidence adduced at the original hearing.

Even if the provisions were in unequivocal language that the decision of the General Sessions should be final, this, on the authorities to which we have referred, would not be sufficient to take away the right to the writ of *certiorari*.

The right to the writ, therefore, as regards appeals to sessions for offences not being crimes, remains in all its integrity.

In the case of appeals to the County Judge, without a jury, the law is different: 38 Vic. ch. 11, secs. 13, 14.

The rule must be absolute for the issue of a writ of *certiorari*, as asked.

MORRISON, J., and WILSON, J., concurred.

Rule absolute.

———

Subsequently, April 24, 1877, a motion was made by *Osler*, before Hagarty, C. J., C. P., to quash the conviction, and cause was shewn to the rule by *Sadleir*. He contended that all words in the conviction referring to the by-law might and should be struck out, and the conviction supported under the general law as to malicious injury to property. *Osler* supported his rule.

April 27, 1877. HAGARTY, C. J.—It appears to me that the judgment of the Queen's Bench has settled all questions as to the right to deal with this conviction after affirmance by the sessions.

I think the rule must be absolute to quash. It purports clearly to be a conviction on a by-law. On reference to that law, there seems to be no pretence of any offence against its provisions being shewn.

I do not think it open to respondent to argue that it can be upheld under any other authority. I refer to *Martin v. Pridgeon*, 1 E. & E. 778, cited by Mr. *Osler*. I cannot say that, except as against the by-law, any offence punishable as in this conviction is shewn.

Rule absolute.

REGINA v. JACKSON.

Indictment for obstructing highway—Previous conviction—Estoppel—Costs—Fine.

Where a defendant had been convicted of nuisance in obstructing a certain highway by a fence, and after removal of such fence by the sheriff under process replaced it upon the same highway, though not in precisely the same line as before:—*Held,* that the former conviction was conclusive against the defendant as to the existence of the alleged highway, and that he could not again raise the question on this indictment for obstructing the same highway.

Where the indictment was removed into this Court *by the prosecutors :* *Held,* that the defendant was not liable to costs; but the Court ordered that one-third of the fine imposed should go to the prosecutors, and suggested that the Government might on application order the remaining two-thirds to be paid to them, the whole fine being less than their costs incurred.

INDICTMENT for obstructing a highway by means of a fence placed by the defendant. It recited a former indictment against the defendant for obstructing a certain street called the town line between the townships of York and Vaughan, &c., by the placing of a fence on it, whereby the highway was obstructed, &c.: that this case was tried and the defendant adjudged guilty, and ordered to remove the obstruction: that the defendant failed to comply, &c.; and that the sheriff under process removed this fence. The present indictment then alleged, that since such removal the defendant rebuilt and put and placed the fence, &c., and suffered it to be and remain upon the said Queen's highway, whereby it was obstructed and encroached upon. The indictment was tried on the civil side of the Toronto Assizes before Gwynne, J.

The defendant was found guilty.

During Hilary term, February 10, 1876, *M. C. Cameron,* Q. C., obtained a rule to set aside the verdict of guilty and for a new trial, the verdict being contrary to law and evidence, and for misdirection, and for the rejection of evidence, &c.

In Easter term, May 31, 1876, the rule was argued by *J. K. Kerr,* Q. C., and *Ferguson,* Q. C., for the Crown, who shewed cause.

M. C. Cameron, Q.C., supported his rule.

September 26, 1876. MORRISON, J.—After considering the evidence and the answers of the jury to the several questions left to them by the learned Judge, we are of opinion that the evidence justified the finding of the jury, and that upon the question of evidence we would not disturb it.

But irrespective of the evidence bearing on the question of the original survey or laying out of the road allowance in question, we are of opinion that the defendant was estopped by the former conviction given in evidence at the trial. The principal question in issue on the trial of the previous indictment was, whether the alleged street or highway designated the town line between the townships of York and Vaughan, the same mentioned in the indictment before us, was a highway, and whether the defendant obstructed it by placing a fence upon it. Upon that indictment the defendant was convicted, and it is alleged in this indictment that after the removal of the obstructing fence by the sheriff under process, the defendant again placed a fence upon the same highway. All this was proved at the trial. Under these circumstances, it was not competent for the defendant upon this trial to dispute or to give evidence to disprove that the highway which was in question in the former indictment was not a public highway, for that question as against this defendant was by the former conviction established, and the evidence at the last trial shews that that was the very same question in dispute, and that after the sheriff removed the fence the defendant again replaced it, not on the identical line where it previously stood, but still upon the highway in question. The former conviction as against this defendant was conclusive as to what was involved in it and found upon the trial of that indictment, viz: whether the defendant had encroached on the highway, say to the extent of 30 feet.

It was however contended on the part of the defendant, that the re-placing of the fence within a short distance of where it previously stood placed the question at large again. We think such a proposition untenable.

So long as the former conviction and judgment stands unreversed, it is conclusive between the same parties of the fact it directly decided. And it seems to us, that in this case all that was necessary for the Crown to do, was to put in evidence the former conviction, and to establish that the nuisance was the same or worse or less objectionable than before. That was done here. If it were otherwise then all that a defendant would have to do to avoid a previous conviction, and to contest the matter again, would be to remove, or, as in this case, after the fence was removed by the judgment of the Court, to replace it in the highway a few inches from the former line, and in that way attempt to shew that the former conviction was erroneous; and so by a trivial change the same issue might be tried year after year. If that were allowable it would be in effect contravening an established principle, that when once a matter in litigation is examined into and decided by the judgment of a competent Court, it shall not be litigated between the same parties. Such being our opinion, it is not necessary for us to consider the points taken in the rule of rejection of evidence and misdirection. Judgment will therefore be for the Crown.

WILSON, J., concurred.

HARRISON, C. J., was not present at the argument, and took no part in the judgment.

————

In this term, December 7, 1876, *Ferguson*, Q.C., appeared for the Crown, and *M. C. Cameron*, Q.C., for the defendant, on a motion for the defendant to appear and receive sentence.

December 29, 1876. MORRISON, J.—This is the case of an indictment for a nuisance in obstructing a highway between the townships of York and Vaughan, by fencing in a portion of the highway in front of the defendant's lot, and which he claimed to be part of his land. The indictment was found at the Sessions, and removed by the Crown into this Court by *certiorari*. The defendant was convicted at the last Toronto Assizes. A rule *nisi* for a new trial being granted after argument was discharged, but the defendant was not sentenced at the Assizes, he having entered into recognizance to appear and receive judgment. Judgment was delivered the term before last, but no rule was issued until this term, to give the defendant an opportunity of removing this obstruction, and he was notified that sentence would be passed last term, and after hearing the parties, the case has stood over until to-day.

It was pressed upon us that the defendant should be ordered to pay the costs of the prosecution. I have looked into the practice in such cases, and I find that in a case like this, when the prosecution has removed the cause into this Court, the defendant is not liable to pay costs—all that we can do is, to adjudge him to pay a fine, and out of that fine the prosecutors, who are the municipality of Vaughan, will be allowed one-third of the fine, upon application to be made for that purpose; and as it is quite clear that one-third of the fine which we will adjudge will not by any means defray the prosecutors' costs, the Government on application may order the remainder of this fine to be paid to the municipality.

It is very much to be deplored that the prosecutors, as well as no doubt the defendant, have each been put to so enormous an expenditure. The amount of the prosecutors' costs, it appears by the affidavit filed, is about $1,500. In cases of this kind where a defendant is *bona fide* asserting a right, as here, the Court generally deals leniently with such a defendant. In this case however we feel it necessary to inflict a heavy fine, as the defendant for so long a period after the intimation of our judgment, and up to the present time, has omitted to remove the obstruction. We shall therefore inflict a fine of $300 to be paid to Her Majesty, and order that the nuisance be abated, and that a *writ de nocumento amovendo* issue, if necessary.

HARRISON, C. J., and WILSON, J., concurred.

Rule accordingly.

REGINA v. COOPER.

Indictment for obstructing highway—Costs—5 & 6 W. & M. c. 11—Fine.

A township municipality prosecuting an indictment for obstructing a highway in the township, which indictment had been removed on defendant's application into this Court, and the defendant convicted thereon:
Held, to be "the party aggrieved" within the 5 & 6 W. & M. ch. 11
sec. 3; and the defendant, having to pay their costs and his own,
amounting to over $400, was fined only $1.

THIS was the case of an indictment for obstructing a
highway in the township of Georgina, tried at the Toronto
Spring Assizes, 1876. The indictment was found at the
Sessions, December, 1875, and removed by *certiorari*, upon
the application of the defendant, into this Court in
January, 1876·

The defendant was convicted and sentence was deferred.

During this term, December 7, 1876, *Badgerow* moved
that the defendant should appear and receive sentence.
An affidavit was filed shewing that the costs of the prosecutors (the municipality of Georgina) amounted to over $400.

Osler, who asked several enlargements for defendants,
stated he did not appear for him, and the case stood over
to enable the Court to see whether they should make an
order as to these costs.

December 29, 1876. MORRISON, J.—The statute 5 & 6,
W. & M. ch. 11, sec. 3, enacts: "If the defendant prosecuting
such writ of *certiorari* be convicted of the offence for which
he was indicted, then the said Court of Queen's Bench shall
give reasonable costs to the prosecutor, if he be the party
aggrieved and injured or be a justice of the peace, &c., or
any other civil officer, who shall prosecute upon the account
of any fact committed or done, that concerned him or them
as officer or officers to prosecute or present, which costs
shall be taxed according to the course of the said Court," &c.

It appears that the municipality of Georgina through its
officers at its expense have prosecuted this indictment, and
the only question is, whether they can be said to be the

party aggrieved within the meaning and spirit of the statute, and I am of opinion they are. The road in question is vested in them; it is their duty to see that all nuisances or obstructions on the highways are removed, and that they be kept in repair and free from all obstructions, and they would certainly fail in their duty if they did not take steps to have obstructions removed. I refer to *Regina* v. *Earl of Waldegrave*, 2 Q.B. 341, and *Rex* v. *Thompkins*, 2 B & Ad. 287. That being the case, we have only to consider what fine we shall impose upon the defendant under the circumstances.

Taking into account the amount of the prosecutors' costs which he will have to pay, as well as his own costs, we adjudge the defendant to pay a fine of one dollar.

HARRISON, C. J., and WILSON, J., concurred.

MEMORANDA.

During this term the following gentlemen were called to the Bar :—

HENRY HATTON GOWAN ARDAGH, JOHN STOCKS FRASER, EDWARD PERRY CLEMENT, WILLIAM HENRY CULVER, DANIEL WEBSTER CLENDENAN, JAMES WILLIAM LIDDELL, JOHN WALLACE NESBITT, ALEXANDER CASIMIR GALT, HARRY SYMONS, ALBERT OGDEN, JACOB LEMON WHITESIDE, FREDERICK WILLIAM CASEY, CHARLES LESLIE FERGUSON, FRANK STAYNER NUGENT, THOMAS EDWARD LAWSON, RICHARD HARCOURT, GEORGE ATWELL COOKE, JAMES COLEBROOKE PATTERSON, JAMES CHESTERFIELD JUDD, ROBERT E. WOOD, MAITLAND McCARTHY, EBENEZER WELBURY SCANE, JAMES WARREN, FRANCES TYRRELL.

HILARY TERM, 40 VICTORIA, 1877.

From February 5th to February 17th.

Present :

THE HON. ROBERT ALEXANDER HARRISON, C. J.
"   "   JOSEPH CURRAN MORRISON, J.
"   "   ADAM WILSON, J.

IN RE HENRY JOSEPH JOHNSON AND THE CORPORATION
OF THE COUNTY OF LAMBTON.

Temperance Act of 1864—Voting for by-law—Poll closed too soon.

Where a by-law under the Temperance Act of 1864 had been carried in a
county by 193 majority, but it appeared that in one township, where the
names of the qualified municipal electors on the assessment roll were
more than 800, the poll was left open only two days, leaving 250 votes
unpolled there, the by-law was set aside.

The names of owners appearing in the sixth column of the roll, under
the heading "Owners and address," should be counted, in order to
ascertain the number of electors, although not appearing in the second
column headed, "Name of occupant or other taxable party," and not
bracketed or numbered in the first column.

September 4, 1876. *C. Robinson,* Q. C., obtained from
Galt, J., sitting for the Court, a rule *nisi* returnable
before the full Court, calling on the Corporation of the
County of Lambton to shew cause why the by-law passed
by the said corporation on 16th June, 1876, prohibiting
the sale of intoxicating liquors and the issuing of licenses
therefor in the said county, under the authority of and for
the enforcement of the Temperance Act of 1864, should
not be quashed with costs, on the grounds :—

1. That the said by-law, although submitted for approval
to the electors of the municipality, was not so submitted
in accordance with the provisions of the said Temperance

Act of 1864, and was not duly approved by the said
municipal electors.

2. That the poll to decide whether or not the said by-
law was approved was not duly taken in the townships of
Bosanquet and Warwick, the votes of the voters of the
said townships residing within the village of Arkona not
having been taken at the polling places appointed and
held in and for the said townships respectively, with the
other votes recorded at such polling places.

3. That the poll was improperly and illegally taken in
and for the village of Arkona, without complying with the
provisions or directions of the said Act, there being no
municipal organization in the said village.

4. That the poll in each of the townships of Warwick,
Bosanquet, and Plympton, was kept open only two days,
there being more than 800 qualified municipal electors
on the assessment rolls of each of the said townships.

5. That in the township of Bosanquet the assessment roll
of the said township for the year 1875 was improperly used
in taking the poll instead of the assessment roll for the year
1876, and thereby a number of persons entitled to vote on
the said by-law were excluded and deprived of their votes.

6. That illegal and improper inducements were held out
and offered at the polling place in the township of Bosanquet,
to induce the electors to vote in favour of the said by-law,
and the election in and for the said township was influenced
and procured by bribery and corrupt practices.

7. That the certificates given at the close of the poll in
and for the municipalities of Forest, Euphemia, Oil Springs,
Brooke, Petrolia, Enniskillen, and Bosanquet, are defective
and irregular, and not in accordance with the requirements
of the said Temperance Act.

8. That the said poll was not taken or held at the time
directed in and by the said Act.

The relator was a resident ratepayer and freeholder of
the town of Sarnia, in the county of Lambton.

The by-law against which he moved was passed by the
council of the county on 16th June, 1876, and afterwards
submitted to the vote of the electors.

It was as follows :—

" A by-law prohibiting the sale of intoxicating liquors and the issuing of licenses therefor, in the county of Lambton, passed the 16th June, 1876."

The council of the municipal corporation of the county of Lambton hereby enacts that the sale of intoxicating liquors, and the issuing of licenses therefor, is, by the present by-law, prohibited within the county of Lambton, under authority and for enforcement of the Temperance Act of 1864.

(Signed)   HUGH SMITH, *Clerk.*

WILLIAM IRELAND, *Warden.*"

[L.S.]

The by-law was published in the Sarnia *Canadian*, a newspaper published in the town of Sarnia, on 28th June, and the 5th, 12th, 19th, and 26th July last.

It was also published in the Sarnia *Observer*, a newspaper also published in the town of Sarnia, on 13th June, and the 7th, 14th, and 21st July last.

The day appointed for the commencement of the polling was the 28th of July last.

The by-law was carried by a majority of 173 votes.

At the time of the voting on the by-law there was no separate assessment roll for the village of Arkona, and no separate municipal organization in the village.

The village had been incorporated on 16th June, 1876, by by-law of the county council.

Prior to the passing of the last mentioned by-law the territory forming the village of Arkona comprised portions of the townships of Bosanquet and Warwick.

On 28th July, the day of the voting on the by-law moved against, a meeting of the electors of Arkona took place in the village.

Seventy-three of the village voters before 16th June, 1876, were electors in the township of Bosanquet, and twenty-two in the township of Warwick.

One G. B. Stephenson was elected chairman of the village meeting, and he appointed one W. H. Stephenson his poll clerk.

The poll in Arkona was as follows :—

For the by-law............................. 17
Against it............... 11
                                            ——
Majority for by-law 6
Total vote................................. 28

Previous to the meeting there was furnished for the purposes thereof, by the clerks of the townships of Bosanquet and Warwick, an abstract of the assessment rolls of these townships, so far as the same related to the village of Arkona.

The Court of Revision for the township of Bosanquet had, on 5th June last, passed the assessment roll for the year 1876, and although there were no appeals to the Judge of the County Court at the time of the voting, the roll had not been confirmed by the County Judge.

On the assessment roll of the township of Bosanquet for the year 1876 there were, according to the relator's affidavits, the names of 856 duly qualified electors, but the roll used was that for 1875, on which there were, according to the relator's affidavits, only the names of 767 electors.

The names of the voters on the roll of 1875, according to the respondents' affidavits, were only 712, of which 45 were included in the list of voters for Arkona.

The names on the roll of Bosanquet for 1876, according to the respondents' affidavits, was only 803, but of that number one elector was under age, the name of an elector was entered twice, two electors before the voting had left the Province, and 73 were assessed for property in Arkona.

The poll in Bosanquet was kept open for two days only, and the same was not closed for the reason that half an hour elapsed without a vote being offered.

The poll in Bosanquet was as follows :—

For the by-law 277
Against it 143
                                        ——
Majority for the by-law................ 134
Total vote 420

The assessment roll used in Plympton was that for
1876. There were on it, according to the relator's affidavits,
833 names of electors. But of these, according to the
affidavits in answer, there were—

Widows	18
Assessed under $100	12
Under age	3
Railway companies	2
Person twice assessed	1
Dead	1
An alien	1
	38
Leaving	795

The roll in Plympton was as follows :—

Against the by-law	321
For it	255
Majority against the by-law.........	66
Total vote	576

The poll in Plympton was kept open only for two days,
and was not closed for the reason that half an hour elapsed
without a vote being offered.

The assessment roll used in Warwick was that for 1876.
There were on it, according to the relator's affidavits, 855
names of electors. The respondents admitted there were
on it, subject to an objection noticed in the judgment, over
800 duly qualified voters.

The poll in Warwick was as follows :—

In favour of the by-law..............	339
Against it	220
Majority for by-law	119
Total vote	559

The affidavits for the relator stated the belief of deponent
that if the poll had been kept open on the third day in
Bosanquet, Plympton, or Warwick, the by-law would have
been defeated by a large majority.

These affidavits also shewed that on the third day a

number of the qualified voters of some of these townships presented themselves at the polling places for the purpose of polling their votes, but found the polling places closed.

There were statements shewing bribery in Bosanquet, to which it is not necessary particularly to advert.

In the county, before and at the time of the polling, there were at least 8,500 electors, of these the votes polled were 5,159, leaving unpolled votes, 3,341.

Bethune, Q. C., shewed cause. [The argument was chiefly as to the third, fourth, and fifth grounds taken in the rule: viz., that the vote in Arkona was irregular: that the poll should have been kept open for a third day in Bosanquet, Plympton, and Warwick, or some or one of these townships, and that the wrong assessment roll was used in Bosanquet.] The affidavits do not support the existence of any such irregularities as supposed; but, assuming them to exist, they were not shewn to have prejudiced the result, and the by-law should be sustained: *Walker* v. *Mitchell*, 4 P. R. 218; *Monk Election Case*, 32 U. C. R. 147; *North Victoria Election Case*, 11 C. L. J. N. S. 163; affirmed, 37 U. C. R. 234. He also referred to 32 Vic. ch. 32, O., sec. 21, sub-sec. 1, sec. 23, sec. 24.

Robinson, Q. C., contra. The result is shewn to have been prejudiced. *Primâ facie* an election is void where the poll is closed too soon: *Regina ex rel. Greeley* v. *Gilbert*, 16 U. C. R. 263; *Regina ex rel. Davis* v. *Wilson*, 3 C. L. J. 265; *Hackney Case*, 2 O'M. & H. 81. If the result might have been different the election cannot stand: *Drogheda Case*, 2 O'M. & H. 202; *Warrington Case*, 1 O'M. & H. 43; *Regina ex rel. Lawrence* v. *Woodruff*, 1 Chamb. R. 119; *Rogers* on Elections, 12th ed., 323. The vote as to Arkona is indefensible: *Regina ex rel. Preston* v. *Preston*, 2 Chamb. R. 178; *Regina ex rel. Alemaing* v. *Zenger*, 1 P. R. 219. He also referred to *Regina ex rel. Lachford* v. *Frizell*, 9 C. L. J. N. S. 27; 32 Vic. ch. 32, secs. 153, 243; *North Victoria Election Case*, 11 C. L. J. N. S. 163, 37 U. C. R. 234.

February 6, 1877.   HARRISON, C. J.—It is made the duty
of any municipal council, when passing a by-law under the
27–28 Vic. ch. 18, to order the same to be submitted for
approval to the municipal electors of the municipality:
Sec. 3.

On the passing of an order for the submission of the by-
law to the electors, the clerk of the municipality must
forthwith cause the by-law to be published for four con-
secutive weeks in some newspaper published weekly, or
oftener, within the municipality, and in the case of a by-
law for a county, post up copies of the by-law in at least
four public places in each municipality of the county.
Sec. 5.

These requirements as to publication have been held to
be imperative : *Coe and the Corporation of Pickering*, 24
U. C. R. 439.   See further *Re Miles and the Corporation
of Richmond*, 28 U. C. R. 333 ; *Re Brophy and the Corporation of Gananoque*, 26 C. P. 290.

Where the by-law is for a county the poll must be taken
in each of the several municipalities of the county : Sub-
sec. 2 of sec. 5.

At such polling the mayor or reeve of the municipality
in which the same is held, &c., shall preside, and the clerk
of the municipality shall attend thereat with the assessment rolls of the municipality then in force, or certified
copies thereof : Sub-sec. 3 of sec. 5.

These requirements, as to the meeting, have also been
held imperative : *Re Hartley and the Corporation of
Emily*, 25 U. C. R. 12.   See further *Re McLean and
the Corporation of Bruce, Ib.* 619.

If at any time after the opening of the poll one half hour
elapses without a vote being offered, the poll may be closed.
Sub-sec. 5 of sec. 5.   Unless for that cause closed earlier
the poll shall, under sub-sec. 6, be kept open :—

1. Till the hour of five o'clock in the afternoon of the day
of the opening thereof, and no longer, if the names of the
qualified municipal electors on the assessment roll of the
municipality are not more than 400 in number.

2. And until the like hour of the next day (Sundays and holidays excluded), if such names are more than 400, and not more than 800.

3. And so on, allowing one additional day for each additional 400 names.

These requirements, as to the days for polling, would appear to be as imperative as the other requirements which have already been noticed, and which have in this Court been held to be imperative.

If one-half or more of all the votes *polled* are against the by-law, the same shall be held to be not approved ; but if more than one half of all the votes *polled* are for the by-law, the same shall be held to be approved : Sub-secs. 10 and 11 of sec. 5.

No by-law, passed under authority of and for enforcement of the Act, shall be set aside by any Court for any defect of procedure, or form whatever : Sec. 37.

It may be that sufficient effect has not been given to this section in the several cases decided in this Court, where by-laws have been set aside for defects of procedure as to publication or to polling, but we must follow the cases where applicable, leaving the Court of Appeal or other higher authority, if necessary, to reverse them. See *Re Brophy and Corporation of Gananoque*, 26 C. P. 290; *Re Day and Corporation of Storrington*, 38 U. C. R. 528; *Re Wycott and Corporation of Ernestown*, *Ib.* 533.

The voting on a by-law is an election, as much as where the question is, which of two or more persons shall be chosen to fill a municipal or parliamentary office.

It is in the election of the municipal electors of a county, city, town, township, or incorporated village to decide whether a by-law prohibiting the sale of intoxicating liquors in the municipality, with a few exceptions in the Act specified, shall or shall not become the law of the municipality.

A bare majority of those who actually vote, whether a majority of the whole of the electors or not, is all that is required to decide the question. See *Re Jenkins and*

Corporation of Elgin, 21 C. P. 325; *Erwin* v. *Township of Townsend, Ib.,* 330. But see also *Re Billings and Corporation of Gloucester,* 10 U. C. R. 273; *McAvoy* v. *Corporation. of Sarnia,* 12 U. C. R. 99, 102.

On the roll of the township of Warwick there were the names of more than 800 electors, provided the names of owners appearing in the sixth column of the roll, under the heading " Owners and address," should be counted, although not appearing in the second column, headed, " Name of occupant or other taxable party," and although not bracketed or numbered in the first column of the roll.

The statute in substance provides that the poll shall be kept open for at least three days if the names of the qualified municipal electors " on the assessment rolls are more than 800." Sec. 5, sub-sec. 6.

These names, although not bracketed or numbered in the first column of the assessment roll, are " on the assessment roll," and appear under the principal heading, " Names and descriptions of persons assessed," and must, we think, be counted. See *Regina ex rel. Lachford* v. *Frizell,* 9 C. L. J. N. S. 27.

The poll in Warwick was kept open only on Friday and Saturday, 28th and 29th July, and not closed for the reason that one half hour elapsed without a vote being offered. It was therefore irregularly closed.

When closed there were about 250 votes unpolled in Warwick, and this alone was more than the majority (173) in favour of the by-law throughout the whole county.

If the poll in Warwick had been opened, as it ought to have been, for a third day, it might have been that the result would have been the defeat of the by-law.

In the *Hackney Case,* 2 O'M. & H. 81, Mr. Justice Grove said, " It seems to me a problem which the human mind has not yet been able to solve, namely, if things had been different at a certain period, what would have been the result of the concatenation of events upon that supposed change of circumstances ?"

In another part of the same judgment (p. 85) the same

learned Judge said, " I cannot say, considering the very large number of electors who have been disabled from voting on the present occasion, that it has been an election which may be fairly taken to represent the voices of the electors of Hackney."

The objections to the election were, that no poll was in fact taken at divers places in the borough, and that at other polling places in the borough did not commence at eight o'clock in the forenoon and continue open up to four o'clock in the afternoon, as required by law.

Notwithstanding a provision in the statute to the effect that "No election shall be declared invalid by reason of a non-compliance with the rules * * if it appears to the tribunal * * that the election was conducted in accordance with the principles laid down in the Act," and that no election should be set aside if it appear to the tribunal that "such non-compliance or mistake did not affect the result of the election," the election was set aside.

The principles of this decision were followed in *The Dudley Election Case*, 2 O'M. & H. 115, and *The Bolton Election Case*, 2 O'M. & H: 138, 142.

They are well expressed by Lord Coleridge in the case of *Woodward* v. *Sarsons*, L. R. 10 C. P. 733, 743, where he says: "An election is to be declared void by the common law applicable to parliamentary elections, if it was so conducted that the tribunal, which is asked to avoid it is satisfied, as a matter of fact, either that there was no real *electing* at all, or that the election was not really conducted under the subsisting election laws. As to the first, the tribunal should be so satisfied, *i. e.,* that there was no real electing by the constituency at all, if it were proved to its satisfaction that the constituency had not in fact had a fair and free opportunity of electing the candidate which the majority might prefer. This would certainly be so, if a majority of the electors were proved to have been prevented from recording their votes effectively according to their own preference, by general corruption or general intimidation, or by being prevented from voting by want of the machinery necessary for so voting, as, by polling stations being demolished, or not opened, or by other of the means of voting according to law not being supplied, or supplied with such errors as to render the voting by means of them void, or by fraudulent counting of votes or false declaration of numbers by a returning officer, or by other such acts or mishaps.   And we think the same result should follow, if by reason of any such or similar mishaps, the tribunal, without being able to say that a majority had been prevented, should be satisfied that there was reasonable ground to believe that a majority of the electors *may have been* prevented from electing the candidate they preferred."

Similar principles have been acknowledged and applied recently in England in the case of parish elections : *Shaw* v. *Thompson*, L. R. 3 Ch. D. 233, 250, 251.

These principles have long been held to govern municipal elections in this Province.   See *Regina ex rel. Lawrence* v. *Woodruff*, 1 Chamb. R. 119 ; *Regina ex rel. Greeley* v. *Gilbert*, 16 U. C. R. 263 ; *Regina ex rel. Davis* v. *Wilson*, 3 U. C. L. J. 165; *Regina ex rel. Walker* v. *Mitchell*, 4 P. R. 218 ; *Regina ex rel. Preston* v. *Touchburn*, before me, March 20th, 1876, in Chambers (*a*).

Whether we follow these principles, or, without regard to them, follow the decisions of this Court under the 27–28 Vic. ch. 18, we must set aside the by-law, and this without in any manner deciding as to the irregularities, if any, complained of in reference to the village of Arkona and the townships of Bosanquet and Plympton.

If there were nothing more shewn than a mere irregularity, we might, in the face of sec. 37 of the Act, hesitate to quash the by-law; but where more than an irregularity appears—where the irregularity is of such character and such magnitude that the result of the election may have been affected—it is our duty to set aside the by-law which

---

(*a*) Now reported, 6 P. R. 344.

depends for its validity on a polling tainted by such an irregularity.

Under the Act, the majority voting have power to bind the minority, however large, intelligent, or respectable the minority. The rights of the minority can only be protected by requiring that the provisions of the statute as to the election have been fairly carried out. If satisfied that these provisions have been substantially observed, or that the non-observance could not have seriously affected the result, it would be our duty to sustain the by-law. But where we clearly see a serious omission to comply with the statute, and where, looking at the number of voters and the number of votes polled, we have reason to believe that but for that omission the result might have been different, it is our duty to set aside the by-law.

There are those who, rightly or wrongly, think it unreasonable that all men should be deprived of the right to purchase and use strong liquors in small quantities because some men cannot use without abusing the privilege. If the majority voting as the Act directs prohibits the use, the minority, regardless of their thoughts or feelings, must submit. But where the voting is not as the Act directs—where if it had been as the Act directs, the Court has reason to believe the result might have been different, the by-law ought not to be sustained.

It is therefore incumbent on those who are interested in the carrying of such a by-law as the one now before us, to take all possible care to see that the provisions of the statute bearing on the election have been reasonably followed. And if in any particular case it is doubtful whether the polling should be for two or three days,—that is, whether there are more or less than the names of 800 electors on the assessment roll of a particular municipality,—it would be only prudent for those supporting the by-law to give the benefit of the doubt to those opposed to it, and allow them the extra day for polling.

Had this course been adopted here, we should not have felt constrained to interfere ; but as it is, we see no other

course open to us on the reading of the statute, as applied
to the evidence before us, than to quash the by-law.

MORRISON, J., and WILSON, J., concurred.

Rule absolute, with costs.

JOHNSTONE V. WHITE.

*Husband and wife—Separate estate—C. S. U. C. ch. 73, 35 Vic. ch. 16—
Ejectment—Outstanding term.*

The plaintiff was married to her present husband in 1859, without any
   marriage settlement, and he, before that year, had reduced into possession the land in question.
Held, that she was not entitled to sue for it without joining her husband
   in ejectment, either under C. S. U. C. ch. 73, or 35 Vic. ch. 16, O.,
   such land not being her separate property, and the husband's interest
   not being divested by the last mentioned Act; and that she would not
   have been entitled even if her husband had not reduced it into possession.
The patent issued in 1836 to C., who apparently had made some agreement for sale to D., who transferred it to the plaintiff. The plaintiff
   in 1846 conveyed the land to her sons, and in 1862 a deed, for a
   nominal consideration, was executed by C. to the plaintiff. The
   learned Judge, who tried the case without a jury, having found that
   this last deed was made to the plaintiff as a trustee to enable the
   title of her sons to be perfected : *Held,* that on this ground also the
   land could not be her separate estate.
The evidence shewed that the plaintiff's son had for some time been in
   possession as a tenant under lease, at a yearly rent. *Semble,* per
   HARRISON, J., that this also would have been a bar to plaintiff's action.

THIS was an action of ejectment brought to recover possession of part of lot 22, in the second or front concession
of the township of Pembroke, particularly described by
metes and bounds.

The writ of summons was issued on 13th June, 1876.

The plaintiff set up two modes of title :—

1. By virtue of a deed from David Clow, the patentee
of the Crown.

2. By length of possession of the plaintiff, prior to the
possession of the defendant.

The defendant, besides denying the plaintiff's title, also set up two modes of title :—

1. By deed from James Stewart Johnstone, and Agnes, his wife.

2. By length of possession.

The cause was tried at the last Fall Assizes at Pembroke, before Gwynne, J.

Lots 21, 22, and 23, in 2nd concession of Pembroke, adjoin each other.

Lots 22 and 23, with other lands, were on 12th November, 1836, granted by the Crown to one David Clow, described in the patent as "of the township of Elizabeth, in the county of Leeds, in the district of Johnstown, yeoman, son of William Clow, the elder, of the same place, an U. E. Loyalist."

One Durrell was the patentee of the adjoining lot 21, in the same township.

Durrell, being on lot 21 as early as 1834, began to clear and cultivate lot 22.

Prior to that there was apparently some agreement for the sale of the lot 22 by Clow to one Dunlop, who afterwards made a sale of it to Durrell, but these agreements or sales were not shewn by any satisfactory evidence.

About six months after Durrell took possession of lot 22, he married the plaintiff. The marriage took place on 11th March, 1835. There were three children of the marriage: James, born 21st April, 1836; William, born 14th June, 1838; and Henry, born on 10th November, 1840. Henry died under age, and without issue.

Durrell occupied lots 21 and 22 up to the time of his death, which took place on 21st October, 1841. After his death, Dunlop executed a formal transfer of lot 22 to the plaintiff.

In the Spring of 1847, the plaintiff married James Stewart Johnstone, who at that time was the owner of the adjoining lot 23.

There was no marriage settlement of any kind.

It did not appear whether or not the plaintiff had any child or children by the second marriage.

Shortly after the marriage, the plaintiff by a deed ante-dated, and bearing date 30th December, 1846, conveyed lot 22 to her sons, William, James, and Henry Durrell. Johnstone was no party to this deed.

From 1835 to 1844, the plaintiff lived on lot 21 with her husband Durrell, who cultivated both lots. After his death, she lived on lot 21 with her sons, cultivating lot 22. Upon her marriage with Johnstone in 1847, she went to live with him on lot 23, he cultivating lots 22 and 23 as one farm, and so lived with him for about seventeen years, when, for some unexplained cause, he left her. He was at the time of the trial living in Manitoba, but the plaintiff has not seen him for about twelve years. He in no manner contributes to her support.

On 28th January, 1862, there was a deed to the plaintiff for a nominal consideration of lot 22, executed by one David Clow, described as "near the village of Lyn, in the township of Elizabethtown," but there was nothing except the name and the place of residence to identify him with the patentee.

The original letters patent were not produced at the trial.

On 30th November, 1865, by deed of that date, the plaintiff and her husband Johnstone conveyed lot 23 to the defendant for a valuable consideration.

At the time, and for a great many years previously, apparently from 1847, there was an old fence so placed as to mark the supposed boundary between lots 22 and 23.

In 1865, the defendant, at considerable expense and without any objection on the part of the plaintiff, renewed the fence.

The contention, on the part of the plaintiff was, that the fence encroached and always did encroach on lot 22.

The land claimed in this action as being part of lot 22, was a small strip lying between the fence and a line recently run by the plaintiff, on the land hitherto occupied by the defendant as being part of lot 23.

William Durrell, the son of the plaintiff, was at the time

of the bringing of the action, and for some years previously, in possession of lot 22, under a lease from the plaintiff, he paying her $100 per annum, supplying her with wood and the use of two cows.

The learned Judge found, among other things, that Johnstone was in possession of the lot till the deed of 1862 was executed by Clow, and that the deed was made to the plaintiff as a trustee to enable' the title of the children to be perfected by estoppel, or else it was a deed to Mrs. Johnstone of land which Johnstone had reduced into possession, and continued in possession of from his marriage in 1847, till he left her in or about 1864.

If the latter, the learned Judge was of opinion that the deed conveyed no separate estate to the plaintiff, to enable her to sue alone in her own name in the lifetime of her husband.

But the learned Judge was rather inclined to think that in equity it should be held that the deed from Clow was executed to enable full effect to be given to the deed dated December, 1846, which was registered in 1851, and so to put the estate altogether out of the plaintiff.

Quacunque via the learned Judge thought the plaintiff ought to fail, and so entered a verdict for the defendant.

During Michaelmas term last, November 23, 1876, *Bethune*, Q. C., obtained a rule calling on the defendant to shew cause why the verdict should not be set aside, and a verdict entered for the plaintiff, pursuant to the Law Reform Amendment Act, on the ground that on the law and evidence the plaintiff was entitled to recover.

During the same term, December 2, 1876, *Beaty*, Q. C., shewed cause. The piece of land claimed is a part of lot 23, and not of lot 22. Even if it were part of lot 22, and that lot belonged to the plaintiff, it was not her separate property so as to entitle her to sue for the recovery of possession of it without joining her husband as a co-plaintiff in the action : *McCready et al.* v. *Higgins*, 24 C. P. 233; *Dingman* v. *Austin*, 33 U. C. R. 190 ; *Mc-*

Guire v. McGuire, 23 C. P. 123; Adams v. Loomis, 22 Grant 99; Wagner v. Jefferson, 37 U. C. R. 551. She had divested herself of the property in favour of her sons, and held the subsequent deed as a trustee for them, and not as her separate estate. There was nothing to shew that the subsequent deed was from the patentee: Doe d. Oliver v. Powell, 1 A. & E. 531; Armstrong v. Stewart, 25 C. P. 198.

Bethune, Q. C., contra. The land in dispute is a part of lot 22, and not of lot 23. Lot 22, at the time of the bringing of the action, was the separate estate of the plaintiff so as to entitle her to sue in her own name: Consol. Stat. U. C., ch. 73, sec. 2; Steels v. Hullman, 33 U. C. R. 471; 35 Vic. ch. 16, secs. 1 & 9, O. If not, an amendment should be allowed by the addition of her husband. The deed which she attempted to make to her children, her husband not being a party thereto, was absolutely void; and it is not now open to the defendant to raise the question of the identity of the patentee, as no such question was raised at the trial.

February 6, 1877. HARRISON, C. J.—This was an action of ejectment brought by the plaintiff for the purpose of determining the boundary line between lots 22 and 23 in the second concession of the township of Pembroke.

Although at one time the right to try a question of boundary in an action of ejectment was a subject of doubt— Lund v. Savage, 12 C. P. 143; Lund v. Nesbitt, Ib. 151. See also Irwin v. Sager, 21 U. C. R. 373, S. C. 22 U. C. R. 22; Sexton v. Paxton, 21 U. C. R. 389,—it has now been decided by the majority of the Court of Error and Appeal that such a question may be tried in such an action: Sexton v. Paxton, 9 U. C. L. J. 207; Hunter v. Baptie et al., 23 U. C. R. 43; Archer v. Kilton, 24 C. P. 195.

The question intended to be tried between the parties was, whether the piece of land described in the writ of ejectment formed a portion of lot 22 or of lot 23 in the 2nd concession of Pembroke.

The learned Judge has not found on that question, but

his finding is based on the assumption that the piece of land in dispute is a portion of lot 22.

We shall, although the action on the facts is not one to be favoured, deal with the case on a similar assumption.

It is not clear on the evidence that the William Clow who in 1862 made a conveyance of lot 22 to the plaintiff, is the William Clow who in 1836 became the patentee of the Crown : See *Armstrong* v. *Stewart,* 25 C. P. 198.

But waiving this, as the point does not appear to have been raised at the trial, and assuming that lot 22 beneficially belonged to the plaintiff from the beginning, and that she had never in any manner divested herself of it, we are of opinion she is not entitled to recover in this action.

She was married to her present husband before 1859, and without a marriage settlement of any kind.

The learned Judge found on the evidence that her husband before 1859 had reduced the land into possession.

The case for the plaintiff rests on the contention that the land sought to be recovered was in some manner her separate estate, so as to entitle her without joining her husband to sue for the recovery of the possession of it.

If the land, on the facts, can properly be held to be her separate estate, the consequence for which the plaintiff contends would appear to flow from the ownership of it. See *McFarlane* v. *Murphy,* 21 Grant 80 ; *Boustead* v. *Whitemore,* 22 Grant 222.

It is, however, the essence of separate estate that it be held exclusively for the benefit of the married woman, and that her husband have no estate or interest in it. See *Wardle* v. *Claxton,* 9 Sim. 524 ; *Royal Canadian Bank* v. *Mitchell,* 14 Grant 412, 420 ; *Field* v. *McArthur,* 27 C. P. 15. See further, *Allan* v. *Walker,* L. R. 5 Ex. 187.

Independently of the Consol. Stat. U. C. ch. 73, and 35 Vic. ch. 16, O., it is beyond controversy that the husband in this case had a freehold interest during the joint lives of himself and his wife, in the land of his wife : *Robertson* v. *Norris,* 11 Q. B. 916 ; *Allan* v. *Levisconte,*

15 U. C. R. 1.   See further, *Doran* v. *Read*, 13 C. P. 393 ;
Weaver v. *Burgess et al.*, 22 C. P. 104.

As the marriage took place before 4th May, 1859, section
1 of Consol. Stat. U. C. ch. 73, is inapplicable.

Then as to the second section. It reads as' follows :—
" Every married woman who, on or before 4th May, 1859,
married without any marriage contract or settlement, shall
and may, from and after 4th May, 1859, notwithstanding
her coverture, have, hold, and enjoy all her real estate not
then, that is on 4th May, 1859, taken possession of by
the husband, by himself or his tenants   *   *   free from
his debts and obligations contracted after the said 4th May,
1859, and from his control or disposition without her consent, in as full and ample a manner as if she were sole and.
unmarried."

The finding of the learned Judge that the husband had
reduced lot 22 into possession before 1859, would render
this section inapplicable. See *McGuire* v. *McGuire*, 23
C. P. 123.

But conceding, for the sake of argument, that this finding was wrong, and that the section is applicable, what
follows ?

It is by section 13 of the same Act declared that any
estate or interest to which a husband may by virtue of his
marriage be entitled in the real property of his wife,.
whether acquired before or after 4th May, 1859, or after
this Act takes effect, shall not during her life be subject to
the debts of the husband. See also section 15.

Section 13 not only recognises the estate of the husband
as tenant by the curtesy, but appears to go further, and to
recognize that by virtue of the marriage the husband.
acquires other estates or interests in the wife's real property, for otherwise the provision that such estate or
interest should not be subject to his debts would be useless, for during the wife's life his estate or interest as
tenant by the curtesy would not be consummate, and could
not be made so subject. See *Emrick et al.* v. *Sullivan*, 25.
U. C. R. 105, 107; *Johnstone* v. *McLellan*, 21 C. P. 304.

The fact that under the Act of 1859 the estate or interest of the husband is for any purpose treated as existing, demonstrates that the estate of the wife in her hands under that Act, whether married before or after 1859, is not her separate estate, so as to enable her solely to sue in respect of it: *Royal Canadian Bank* v. *Mitchell*, 14 Grant 412; *McGuire* v. *McGuire*, 23 C. P. 123; *McCready* v. *Higgins*, 24 C. P. 233; *Wagner* v. *Jefferson*, 37 U. C. R. 557.

If direct authority on the point were necessary, *Scouler et al.* v. *Scouler*, 19 U. C. R. 106, 109, would appear to be such an authority.

In that case, which was after 22 Vic. ch. 34 (of which Consol. Stat. U. C., ch. 73, was a consolidation), it was admitted that Cecilia McOuat, one of the plaintiffs, was a married woman : that her husband was still living, and that he had never reduced her interest in the premises in question into possession. Besides, it was not shewn whether there was any child born of the marriage, nor whether her husband was living in Upper Canada. On an objection that her husband was a necessary party to the ejectment, she was held not entitled to recover.

But it was argued before us, that if the right of the plaintiff to sue alone under Consol. Stat. U. C. ch. 73, does not exist, or is doubtful, the right undoubtedly exists under 35 Vic. ch. 16.

The sections of that Act relied upon are the first and the ninth, but reference may also be made to the eighth:

1. "After the passing of this Act, the real estate of any married woman, which *is* owned by her at the time of her marriage, or acquired in any manner during her coverture, and the rents, issues, and profits thereof respectively, shall without prejudice and subject to the trusts of any settlement affecting the same, be held and enjoyed by her for her separate use, free from any estate or claim of. her husband during her lifetime, or as tenant by the curtesy."

8. "A husband shall not by reason of any marriage which shall take place after this Act shall come into operation, be liable for the debts of his wife contracted before mar-

riage, but the wife shall be liable to be sued therefor, and any property belonging to her for her separate use, shall be liable to satisfy such debts, as if she had con-- tinued unmarried."

9. "A married woman may maintain an action in her own name for the recovery of any   *   *   property, by this or any other Act declared to be her separate property," &c.

Section 8, on the face of it, does not apply to marriages before the passing of the Act.

Section 1, so far as the interest of the husband is con-- cerned, has been held by this Court not to apply to marriages before the passing of the Act: *Dingman* v. *Austin*, 33 U. C. R. 190.

In the latter case, Richards, C. J., said, at p. 193 : "The fair reading of the section seems to me to apply to marriages which take place after the passing of the Act; for it does not say the real estate which was or may be owned by her at the time of her marriage, or acquired in any manner during coverture, shall be held by her, but only *is* owned : that is, speaking of something that is to take place after the passing of the Act."

In *McCready et al.* v. *Higgins*, 24 C. P. 233, the decision of this Court in *Dingman* v. *Austin*, 33 U. C. R. 190, was followed by the Court of Common Pleas.

In *Adams* v. *Loomis*, 22 Grant 99, it was intimated that such portions of the Act as would deprive parties of their vested rights should be so read as not to interfere with such rights, while the portions of the Act that would not have this effect should go into operation as regards women married before as well as after the passing of the Act.

This would seem to be only a natural and reasonable interpretation of the Act, in view of the regard which Courts of Justice and the Legislature are always supposed to entertain for the sanctity of vested rights.

Reading the Act by this rule, it follows that the estate or interest of the husband, in this case existing before the Act of 1859, and preserved if not enlarged by that Act, is--

not divested by the Act of 1872, so that the property in question does not, under the operation of either of the Acts, become her separate property.

This being so, section 9 of the Act, which enables the married woman to sue for her property "by this or any other Act declared to be her separate property," is of no avail to her, and *Scouler et al.* v. *Scouler et al.*, 19 U. C. R. 106, is untouched as an authority against her.

Putting, therefore, the facts on a ground most favourable to the rights of the plaintiff, her action fails.

But we do not wish it to be understood that we have overlooked the point, that as to the land in question she is a trustee for her surviving children, and so, at all events as to their interests, the land cannot be held separate estate : *Wardel* v. *Claxton*, 9 Sim. 524 ; *Field* v. *McArthur*, 27 C. P. 15.

It does not appear that the husband is willing to join his wife in this unjust attempt to disturb his own vendee in the enjoyment of land which the parties intended by the deed of 30th November, 1865, to convey to the defendant, and which has ever since been so held and enjoyed by the defendant. But even if it did appear that the two were willing to join in the attempt, the enterprise is not one which so far commends itself to the approbation of a Court of justice as to make it the duty of this Court in any manner to facilitate it.

On the contrary, the case seems to us to be one in which the Court should rather be astute to find grounds, if possible, to prevent the plaintiff's recovery.

Looking at the case in the latter spirit, we venture to suggest a ground for the defeat of the plaintiff's action which, so far as we know, has been overlooked.

The plaintiff seeks to recover possession of the land in question as part of lot 22. The evidence shews that her son William, her tenant, and not she, is the person entitled to the possession of lot 22. Ejectment will not lie at the suit of a reversioner except to take advantage of a forfeiture. An outstanding term is sufficient to defeat the recovery of possession in an ordinary action of ejectment: *Doe d. Hodsden* v. *Staple,* 2 T. R. 684; *Goodtitle* v. *Jones,* 7 T. R. 43; *Cotterell* v. *Hughes,* 15 C. B. 532; *Doe d. Egremont* v. *Langdon,* 12 Q. B. 711. And even a tenancy from year to year, implied from proof of payment of rent, and not shewn to have been duly determined by a notice to quit or otherwise, is sufficient for that purpose: *Doe d. Warn* v. *Horn,* 3 M. & W. 333; *Doe d. Fellowes* v. *Alford,* 1 D. & L. 470.

But as no such point was raised, either at the trial or on the argument, we do no more than advert to it.

It is only necessary for us in the determination of this case to follow *Scouler et al.* v. *Scouler,* 19 U. C. R. 106, which, although not cited in the argument, is in our opinion, for the reasons already given, in point against the plaintiff's recovery.

The rule nisi must be discharged.

WILSON, J., concurred.

MORRISON, J., was not present at the argument, and took no part in the judgment.

Rule discharged.

STONESS V. LAKE AND WALKER.

Conviction—Insufficiency of information—Waiver of—Variance between-conviction and warrant—C. S. U. C. c. 126 s. 17.

The plaintiff, on an information against him under 37 Vic. ch. 32, O., for selling liquor without a license, was brought before the defendants, magistrates. It was proved that this was his second offence, though the information did not charge it as such. The plaintiff disputed the evidence as to the first conviction, but did not object to the information, and the magistrates convicted and adjudged him to be imprisoned for ten days, which they had power to do only for a second offence. *Held*, that the plaintiff had waived the objection to the information, and that defendants were not liable in trespass.

Held, also, that the variance between the conviction and the warrant for plaintiff's arrest, the former saying nothing as to hard labour and the latter providing for it, could not deprive the defendants of protection under the statute, Consol. Stat. U. C. ch. 126.

Held, also, that in any event defendants could not have been liable for plaintiff's suffering caused by the harsh regulations of the prison during his confinement; and that having been proved to have been guilty of the offence for which he was convicted, he could have recovered only three cents and no costs, under Consol. Stat. U. C. ch. 126, s. 17.

THIS was an action against two justices of the peace.

The declaration contained several counts.

The first alleged that the defendants on 24th January, 1876, at the township of Bedford, unlawfully, vexatiously, vindictively, and maliciously, and without any reasonable or probable cause, caused an assault to be made on the plaintiff, and the plaintiff to be imprisoned in the goal at Kingston, and to be subjected to the rules and regulations of the goal, and to have his hair clipped and shorn off, and his beard, whiskers, and mustaches shorn off for a long time, &c.

The second count alleged that on 6th January, 1876, one Marven Halden laid an information in writing before the defendant Walker as a justice of the peace, to the following effect, " That he hath just cause to suspect and believe, that the defendant did at the township of Loughborough, on 24th or 25th December then last past, sell spirituous or malt liquors, without a license therefor, contrary to the form of the statute in such case made and provided." That the plaintiff was summoned to answer the said offence: that he appeared thereto ; and that the defendants unlawfully, vexatiously, vindictively, and maliciously, and without any reasonable or probable cause, convicted the plaintiff and adjudged him to be imprisoned in the gaol at Kingston, for the space of ten days, and to pay $18.20, for costs, and imprisoned the plaintiff in the said gaol, who was thereupon subjected to the rules and regulations of the gaol, as in the first count alleged.

The third count was trespass for false imprisonment. The remaining counts were for money received by the defendants for the use of the plaintiff, and on an account stated.

The defendants separately pleaded, to the first, second, and thir d counts not guilty, by statutes, Consol. Stat. U. C. ch. 126, secs. 5, 1, 11, and 37 Vic., ch. 32, O. secs. 1-16 ; and, not guilty to the common counts.

Issue

The issues were tried at the last Assizes at Kingston before Wilson J., and a jury.

The information was proved, and was as set out in the second count of the declaration.

The conviction was also proved. It was as follows:—

"Be it remembered that on the 24th January, 1876, Jabez Stoness is convicted before the undersigned, two of Her Majesty's justices of the peace, &c., for that he, the said Jabez Stoness, did at the township of Loughborough, sell spirituous or malt liquor on the 24th or 25th December last past, without a license therefor. And we adjudge the said Jabez Stoness for his said offence to be imprisoned in the common gaol of the said county at Kingston, for the space of ten days, (not saying with hard labour) it being his second offence," &c.

The warrant for the arrest of the plaintiff was also proved. It bore the same date as the conviction, 24th January, 1876. It was signed by both defendants, and authorized an imprisonment *at hard labour* for the space of ten days.

It was also proved that on appeal to the County Judge, an order was, on the 28th January, 1876, made quashing the conviction without costs, and authorizing the discharge of the plaintiff from custody.

On 7th March, 1876, the plaintiff caused notice of action to be served on both of the defendants.

The notice corresponded with the first and second counts of the declaration.

The defendant Lake when served with the notice of action, according to the plaintiff's witness, said the plaintiff had no right of appeal, and that the Judge "would be broke" for quashing the conviction.

The defendant Walker, according to the same witness, said he had gone according to the directions of the Crown attorney, and that he did not care a d.— n about it, as he was worth $20,000, and could fight it.

It was also proved by the plaintiff's witnesses, that defendant Walker before the conviction, said of the plaintiff, that he had taken advantage of him, and as he, plaintiff, had come under his defendant's rod, he should use it. Other similar expressions were proved to have been used by Walker. One was, that there was no evidence against plaintiff, and he was d — d sorry for it.

The action was commenced on 22nd April, 1876. The arrest and imprisonment of the plaintiff under the warrant, and his subsequent release from custody under the order of the County Judge, were proved.

The plaintiff was delivered to the gaoler on 25th January, 1876, and discharged from custody on 28th of the same month. The plaintiff while in gaol was treated like all other prisoners in that gaol sentenced to hard labour. His clothes were removed, he was dressed in prison clothes, his hair was cut close, and he was put to the splitting of wood. No flannel drawers or shirt was allowed as part of the prison clothes, but on the second day, on complaint of the plaintiff, he was allowed to wear his own flannels.

There was evidence that the plaintiff was guilty of the offence of selling spirituous liquor without license on 24th December last, and that this was his second offence as proved before the magistrates, although not so mentioned in the information.

The money sought to be recovered under the common counts, was the amount of money deposited by the plaintiff with one of the defendants, as security for the appeal under 37 Vic. ch. 32, sec. 44, O.

The learned Judge, at the close of the plaintiff's case, thought the defendants had jurisdiction over the offence and over the plaintiff, notwithstanding the omission of the information to charge the offence as a second offence, and that as the defendants had, under 37 Vic. ch. 32, sec. 35, jurisdiction to award hard labour for a second offence, the variance between the warrant and the conviction did not deprive them of jurisdiction, and that there was no evidence of want of reasonable and probable cause; but rather than have the case a second time go down for trial, he decided to leave the case to the jury, reserving if necessary leave to the plaintiff to set aside the nonsuit, and enter a verdict for the plaintiff if the jury should find in his favour.

The defendants proved that on the evidence of the offence being a second offence being given, there was no objection whatever on the part of the plaintiff, who was represented by counsel, to the effect that the information did not so charge it, and the only objection being to the sufficiency of the evidence to prove the second offence.

The defendant Walker, who was called for the defence, denied several of the expressions imputed to him, by witnesses on the part of the plaintiff.

Similar denials were made by the defendant Lake, who was also called as a witness for the defence.

The sheriff was called, and proved the rules of the Frontenac gaol as to prisoners committed with hard labour.

It was contended by the plaintiff, that the real occupant at the time of the sales of the liquor, was one Knight, and not himself.

To this it was answered that the arrangement, if any, with Knight was a colourable one.

The learned Judge asked the jury the following questions:

1. Did Mr. Walker say after the close of the evidence, that there was no evidence to convict Stoness, and that he was d — d sorry for it.

Answer. He did not.

2. Was the plaintiff the occupant of the house and bar-room in question, on the 24th and 25th December last?

Answer. He was.

3. If the magistrates had no jurisdiction, or acted beyond their jurisdiction, what damages (if any) is the plaintiff entitled to?

Answer. $500.

The jury said they found their verdict for defendants, but if the magistrates had no jurisdiction or acted beyond jurisdiction, their verdict was to be $500, for the plaintiff.

The verdict was thereupon entered for defendants, leaving the whole case open to both parties on a motion to the Court.

During Michaelmas Term, December 6, 1876, *Bethune*, Q.C., obtained a rule calling on the defendants to shew cause why the verdict should not be set aside, and a verdict entered for the plaintiff upon all or any of the counts for $500, or for such less sum as the Court should think right, or why the said verdict should not be set aside, and a new trial had between the parties, on the following grounds :—1. On leave reserved at the trial. 2. On the ground of misdirection, that the Judge should have charged the jury that the defendants acted without jurisdiction, or exceeded their jurisdiction, in respect of the matters complained of in each of the first three counts, to wit, in convicting as for a second offence, and in ordering imprisonment and payment of costs, and in committing the plaintiff to imprisonment at hard labour, the information and summons being for a first offence throughout. 3. That the Judge should have charged the jury under the fourth count, that the plaintiff was entitled to recover the sum of $10 deposited by him with the defendants as convicting justices on appeal, the deposit with one being a deposit with both.

Britton, Q. C., shewed cause. The defendants having jurisdiction over the offence and the offender, were protected although acting irregularly under the information, or in the framing of the conviction or warrant : 37 Vic. ch. 32 secs. 35, 44. There is only one offence with different degrees of punishment. Even if there are two offences, and the second should have been stated as a substantive offence, the plaintiff having allowed without objection the defendants to proceed under the information as for the second offence, waived any defect in the information or variance between it and the evidence, and is bound by what took place: 32-33 Vic. ch. 31 secs. 24, 30, D., and under the circumstances, trespass is not maintainable against the defendants : *Pike* v. *Carter*, 3 Bing. 78 ; *Fawcett* v. *Fowlis*, 7 B. & C. 394 ; *Mills* v. *Collett*, 6 Bing. 85; *Connors* v. *Darling*, 23 U. C. R. 541; *Thorpe* v. *Oliver*, 20 U. C. R. 266 ; *Cummins* v. *Moore*, 37 U. C. R. 130 ; *Haacke* v. *Adamson*, 14 C. P. 201 ; *Sprung* v. *Anderson*, 23 C. P. 152 ; *Graham* v. *McArthur*, 25. U. C. R. 479 ; *Haylock* v. *Sparke*, 1 E. & B. 471 ; *Barton* v. *Bicknell*, 13 Q. B. 393. But, assuming want of jurisdiction, the recovery can be for no more than three cents : Consol. Stat. U. C. ch. 126 sec. 17. There can be no recovery in this action against both defendants of the money deposited with one of them under 37 Vic. ch. 32 sec. 44 sub-sec. 2 (*b*), O.,[*Bethune* Q. C., abandoned this,] and under no circumstances can the defendant be held liable for the harshness of the prison regulations : *Cave* v. *Mountain*, 1 M. & G. 257, 264.

Bethune, Q. C., contra. It is not lawful for magistrates under an information for one offence to convict of a different offence : *Martin* v. *Pridgeon*, 1 E. & E. 778 ; *Stephens* v. *Stephens*, 24 C. P. 424 ; *Rex* v. *Pereira*, 2 A. & E. 375 ; *Paley* on Convictions, 195, 196. The statute creates one or more different offences having different kinds of punishment : 37 Vic. ch. 32 sec. 35, O. It is necessary, on the information to shew for which of the offences the charge is laid : *Regina* v. *French*, 34 U. C. R. 403. The magistrates had jurisdiction up to the time of the conviction, but in making such a conviction on such an information, they exceeded their jurisdiction : *Connors* v. *Darling*, 23 U. C.

R. 549. There was no waiver, and could be no waiver, of the insufficiency of the information : Consol. Stat. C. ch. 103. The magistrates therefore acted without jurisdiction; and as there was no information for a second offence, it cannot be said that sec. 17 of the Consol. Stat. U. C. ch. 126, is applicable, so as to restrict the damages to three cents : *Haacke* v. *Adamson*, 14 C. P. 201.

February 7, 1877.   HARRISON, C. J.—The defendants are justices of the peace.

Either they acted with jurisdiction or without jurisdiction.

If with jurisdiction, it is conceded that the plaintiff must fail ; if without, it is contended he must succeed.

It is not at all times easy to discern the line between the two classes of cases.

Indeed, some cases are so near the line, or where the line is supposed to be, that it is difficult to say on which side of the line they really lie.

Wherever there is an arrest, and it can be said there was no jurisdiction, trespass is the proper form of action.

Wherever it can be said that there was jurisdiction the remedy is an action on the case, as for a tort, and it must be expressly alleged and proved that the act was done maliciously and without reasonable or probable cause.

Before it can be said that there is jurisdiction, it must appear not only that the justices have jurisdiction over the offence, but over the person of the offender.   See *Caudle* v. *Seymour*, 1 Q. B. 889 : *Barton* v. *Bricknell*, 13 Q. B. 396 ; *Connors* v. *Darling*, 23 U. C. R. 541 ; *Appleton* v. *Lepper*, 20 C. P. 138 ; *Crawford* v. *Beattie*, 39 U. C. R. 13 .

In order to give jurisdiction over the person of the offender, in the case of a summary conviction, it must either appear that an information has been laid or that the information has been waived : *Rex* v. *Fuller*, 1 Ld. Raym. 509 ; *King* v. *Wheatman*, 1 Doug. 345 ; *Rex* v. *Birnia*, 1 Moo. & Rob. 160 ; *Caudle* v. *Ferguson*, 1 Q. B. 886 ; *Friel* v. *Ferguson*, 15 C. P. 584 ; *Regina* v. *Hurrell*, 3 F. &

F. 271 ; *Turner et al. v. Postmaster-General.* 5 B. & S. 756 ;
Regina v. *Shaw,* 12 L. T. N. S. 470, 473 ; 1 L. & C. 579 ;
Regina v. *Fletcher,* L. R. 1 C. C. 320 ; *Blake* v. *Beech,*
L. R. 1 Ex. D. 320.

Unless some statute require the information to be in
writing or under oath it is not necessary that it should be
either in writing or under oath : *Basten* v. *Carew,* 3 B. &
C. 649 ; *Baxter* v. *Carrer,* 3 B. & C. 649 ; *Regina* v. *Mil-
lard,* 17 Jur. 400, 1 Dears. 166. But see *Brookshaw* v.
Hopkins, Lofft 240.

No objection is to be allowed to any information for any
alleged defect therein, in substance or in form, or for any
variance between such information and the evidence adduced on the part of the informant at the hearing of such
information ; but if any such variance appears to the justice
or justices present and acting at such hearing to be such
that the person summoned and appearing has been thereby
misled or deceived, such justice or justices may, upon such
terms as he or they think fit, adjourn the hearing of the
case to a future day : sec. 5 of Consol. Stat. C. ch. 103 ;
Crawford v. *Beattie,* 39 U. C. R. 13·

Where a defendant appears and cross-examines witnesses
on a charge over which the justice has jurisdiction, whether
there be an information or not for the charge, and whether
required to be in writing or not, he thereby waives the
information : *Turner et al.* v. *The Postmaster General,* 5
B. & S, 756 ; *Regina* v. *Shaw,* 1 L. & C. 579, 12 L. T.
N. S. 470 473 , *Regina* v. *Fletcher,* L. R. 1 C. C. 320. But
where instead of doing so he insists upon the want of an
information or defective information, and does nothing to
waive it, he is entitled to the benefit of the objection :
Blake v. *Beech,* L. R. 1 Ex. D. 320.

The case of *Turner* v. *The Postmaster General,* 5 B. &
S. 756, was a very peculiar one. The appellants were
apprehended and brought before a magistrate, charged with
setting fire to the letters in a pillar box, which by statute
was a felony. On their appearance to answer the charge,
after the examination of some witnesses, there was a remand. At the meeting pursuant to the remand, the

attorney for the prosecution announced his intention of proceeding against them only for the misdemeanor of injuring personal property, and the appellants, without then insisting upon the information for the second offence, cross-examined witnesses adduced in support of it. The Court held that they were rightly convicted of the second offence.

Now, supposing that there were two offences, and not the one offence with different degrees of punishment, and that a second information was necessary, the conduct of the plaintiff, at the hearing before the magistrates, in allowing the magistrates to proceed as if there were such an information, would appear on the authorities to be a waiver of the information, so as to make the conviction a good one.

While it is certainly not competent for a magistrate to take an information for one offence and convict without a further information of a different offence—*Martin* v. *Pridgeon*, 1 E. & E. 778; *Soden* v. *Cray*, 7 L. T. N. S. 324; *Rex* v. *Birckhall*, 10 L. T. N. S. 385—it is competent for the accused by his conduct to waive the necessity for the information, so as to give jurisdiction to convict without the information having been first laid.

The magistrates here supposed that no second information, or amendment of the information before them was necessary, and that all that was necessary was evidence of the offence being a second one. The plaintiff allowed the magistrates without objection to proceed on that supposition, and he himself, by disputing the evidence as to the first conviction, without objecting to the sufficiency of the information, acted as if the supposition were correct.

Where a magistrate has jurisdiction he never can be made liable in an action of trespass for an irregularity in procedure, mistake of law, or erroneous conclusion from facts: *Mills* v. *Collett*, 6 Bing. 85. See further, *Lowther* v. *Earl of Radnor*, 8 East 113; *Pike* v. *Carter*, 3 Bing. 78; *Barton* v. *Bricknell*, 13 Q. B. 396; *Haylock* v. *Spark*, 1 E. & B. 471; *Bott* v. *Ackroyd*, 7 W. R. 720; *Sommerville* v. *Mirehouse*, 1 B. & S. 652; *Sprung* v. *Anderson*, 23 C. P. 152; *McDonald* v. *Stucky*, 31 U. C. R. 577; *Colonial Bank of*

Australasia v. *Willan*, L. R. 5 P. C. 417; *Crawford* v. *Beattie*, 39 U. C. R. 13.

The erroneous view of the sufficiency of an information, where the magistrate under statute has jurisdiction over the offence, and no objection is taken to the information, cannot make the magistrate a trespasser. See *Thorpe* v. *Oliver*, 20 U. C. R. 264, 266.

The statute 37 Vic. ch. 32 sec. 35, O., under which the plaintiff was convicted, declares that any person who shall sell or barter spirituous, fermented or manufactured liquors of any kind, or intoxicating liquors of any kind, without the license therefor required by law, &c., shall for,

1. The *first* offence, on conviction thereof, forfeit and pay a penalty of not less than $20 besides costs, and not more than $50 besides costs.

2. For the *second* offence, on conviction thereof, such person shall be imprisoned in the county gaol of the county in which the offence was committed, to be kept at hard labour for a period not exceeding three calendar months.

3. For the *third*, and any *after* offence, on conviction thereof such person shall be imprisoned in the county gaol of the county in which the offence was committed, to be kept at hard labour for a period of not less than one nor more than three calendar months.

The number of convictions may be ascertained by the production of a certificate under the hand of the convicting justice or by other satisfactory evidence.

The offence described in the section is that of selling or bartering spirituous, fermented or manufactured liquors of any kind, without the license therefor by law required.

It is, of course, possible for the same person at different times to commit this offence, and each committal of the offence after the first is an aggravation of his guilt.

For the first time he is made subject to a pecuniary penalty, limited as to amount.

For the second, he is made subject to imprisonment at hard labour for a period of time without any minimum, and with a maximum of three calendar months.

For the third, and every subsequent time, he is made subject to imprisonment at hard labour with a minimum of one calendar month and a maximum of three calendar months.

The only difference between the second and third and subsequent times of commission is in the minimum of imprisonment—the maximum, three calendar months, being the same.

This kind of legislation is by no means a novelty.

The Legislature have from a very early period of our history endeavoured in certain offences to make the punishment of the hardened offender greater than the punishment of an offender for the first time, and attempted to lay down rules for the governance of such cases.

Take the counterfeiting of coin or the uttering of counterfeit coin for example.

In 1742 the Legislature, by 15 Geo. II. ch. 28, sec. 3, not only provided for the punishment by one year's imprisonment of counterfeiting coin or uttering of counterfeit money, but provided that " if any person having been *once* so convicted shall *afterwards* again utter or tender in payment any false counterfeit money, then such person being thereof convicted shall for such *second* offence be and is hereby adjudged guilty of felony, without benefit of clergy."

In 1799 it was held, as a matter of pleading, that in order to warrant the greater punishment it was necessary to shew in one and the same count of the indictment not only the first, but the second commission of the offence: *Rex* v. *Tandy*, 2 Leach 833.   See further *Rex* v. *Martin*, *Ib*. 923.

The proof of these, being material allegations, is, of course, also necessary : See *Regina* v. *Martin*, L. R. 1 C. C. 214.

By analogy there would appear to be no doubt that in strictness the information under 37 Vic. ch. 32, sec. 35, should shew whether the offender was previously convicted, and if so, whether once or twice, in order to justify the graduated scale of punishment prescribed by the section: *Regina* v. *French*, 34 U. C. R. 403.

If there had been no question of waiver in this case, or no proof of waiver within the meaning of the decisions to which we have referred, we should be obliged to hold that in committing the plaintiff even for ten days to hard labour, there was, on the part of the defendants, either no jurisdiction, or what is much the same, an excess of jurisdiction, so as to render the magistrates liable to be sued in trespass. But because the question of waiver is raised and was proved, we must hold there was jurisdiction, and so that trespass will not lie against defendants.

We must, looking at the conduct of the plaintiff, treat the case as if there were an information shewing a previous conviction of the plaintiff, in which event there was power to imprison for three calendar months at hard labour.

In this view the variance between the conviction and the warrant, the former saying nothing as to hard labour, and the latter providing for hard labour, cannot be such as to deprive the defendants of the protection afforded by the Consol. Stat. U. C. ch. 126, to magistrates acting, although irregularly acting, within their jurisdiction.

It is only when magistrates act irregularly or illegally that they need protection. If it appeared that there was nothing irregular or illegal in their conduct there could be no recovery, and so no necessity for protection of any kind.

One of the protections provided by the Legislature is a calendar month's notice of action.

This is as much required in the case of a magistrate *bonâ fide* acting without jurisdiction, or in excess of jurisdiction, as in the case of a magistrate acting within his jurisdiction : Sec. 10.

The notice of action served by the plaintiff in this case applied only to the first and second counts, and although there was not much question as to the *bona fides* of the defendants, did not cover the third count in trespass.

If we were to hold that there was no jurisdiction or an excess of jurisdiction, we should also have to hold on the evidence that there was no sufficient notice of action.

Therefore, in either aspect of the case, recovery by the plaintiff is impossible.

If it were possible for the plaintiff notwithstanding these objections to maintain his action, there could be no recovery against the defendants for suffering from the harsh regulations of the prison during his imprisonment: *Cave* v. *Mountain*, 1 M. & G. 257, 264 ; *Crawford* v. *Beattie*, 39 U. C. R. 13. And as plaintiff, in the language of the statute, "was actually guilty of the offence of which he was so convicted," he would not be entitled to any sum beyond the sum of three cents as damages for the imprisonment : *Haacke* v. *Adamson*, 14 C. P. 201 ; and could recover no costs whatever of the suit : Sec. 17 Consol. Stat. U. C. ch. 126.

So that, practically there is not much difference between our entering a verdict for the plaintiff for three cents, and allowing the verdict for the defendants' to stand.

The latter, as there was, in our opinion, no misdirection on the part of the learned Judge, is the proper and the only course to be followed.

The policy of the law is as far as possible to prevent persons guilty of crime from taking advantages of the irregularities or blunders of the administrators of the law, when acting in good faith in the discharge of public duty.

MORRISON, J., and WILSON, J., concurred.

Rule discharged (a).

(a) See now 40 Vic. ch. 18, O. Sch. C. p. 153.

BROWN v. THE GREAT WESTERN RAILWAY COMPANY.

R. W. Co.—Two lines crossing—Collision—Use of brakes—Negligence.

The defendants' railway crossed the Grand Trunk Railway on a level. The train on the defendants' line was approaching the crossing, and the air brakes for some reason did not act. It was too late after discovering this to stop the train with the hand brakes, or by reversing the engine, though every effort was made, and a collision occurred with a train on the other line, of which the plaintiff was a conductor, by which he was seriously injured. It was shewn that these brakes were in common use on railways, and that the brakes in question had been twice examined and frequently used on that day, and found all right and effective. The learned Judge, who tried the case without a jury, held that defendants were liable, for that the air brakes should have been applied at a sufficient distance to enable the train to be stopped by other means in case of these brakes giving way.

Per HARRISON, C. J.—The finding was right. Per MORRISON, J.—There was no evidence of negligence, for the defendants were not bound to have any other than the air brakes, and were justified in depending upon them.

WILSON, J., being absent, and the Court thus equally divided, MORRISON, J., withdrew his judgment, so as to avoid the expense of a re-argument, and enable the defendant to appeal.

THIS was an action for negligence.

The declaration alleged that the defendants so negligently and unskilfully drove and managed an engine and train of carriages attached thereto, upon and along a certain railway which the plaintiff was then lawfully crossing in a certain railway carriage, that the said engine and train of carriages were driven and struck against the said railway carriage in which the plaintiff was then lawfully crossing the said railway as aforesaid, whereby the plaintiff was thrown down and wounded, &c.; and the plaintiff claimed $6,000 damages.

Plea, not guilty, by statute, 16 Vic., ch. 99, sec. 10.

Issue.

The case was tried at the last Middlesex Fall Assizes, before Burton, J., without a jury.

The collision took place on 19th June last, where the line of the Grand Trunk R. W. Co. crosses the line of the Great Western R. W. Co., on a level crossing about a mile east of the city of London. There is a man usually in charge of the crossing as signal man. This man is in the employment of the Great Western R. W. Co.

There were also three signals. The first observable to a train passing along the line of the Grand Trunk R. W. Co. is the distant semaphore, which is generally supposed to stand at danger. It is on the line of the Grand Trunk R. W. Co. before reaching the crossing. It is about 150 yards from the junction. If up, the train on the line of the Grand Trunk R. W. Co. comes to a stand at it. If down or let down, the Grand Trunk train proceeds.

On 19th June last a train of the Grand Trunk R. W. Co., of which the plaintiff was a conductor, approached the crossing. The semaphore was up. The plaintiff's train was brought to a stand. Thereupon the semaphore was dropped, and the plaintiff's train proceeded. As his train then approached the crossing the plaintiff observed a train on the line of the Great Western R. W. Co. proceeding at great speed, and this notwithstanding the junction signal which was standing to stop the Great Western train, and to invite the Grand Trunk train. The plaintiff's train was travelling about eight miles an hour. The Great Western train was travelling at between twenty and thirty miles an hour. There was no observable slackening of the speed of the Great Western train.

The Great Western train was about 50 or 60 yards from the crossing when the plaintiff first saw it. Plaintiff saw the signal man throw up his hands to try and stop the Great Western train, but without success. It was then too late to stop the Grand Trunk train. The consequence was, that the Great Western train struck the Grand Trunk train, and the plaintiff received the injuries in respect of which he sued.

On the part of the defence it was shewn that their train, besides having the ordinary brakes and brakesmen, had air brakes. These brakes carry from 80 to 90 pounds pressure of air, which is supplied by a little engine worked with steam from the locomotive. The air is conveyed from a reservoir in rubber pipes to each car, and when in good order works the brakes. The effect when there is nothing wrong is very quick and very powerful. These brakes are

in common use in Canada, the United States, and Great
Britain. They sometimes get out of order, and when out
of order are useless. Those in charge of the defendants'
train relying on the air brakes, which on two occasions on
that day had been examined and found all right, did not
attempt to stop the train till the distance was too short to
stop it otherwise than with the air brakes. The driver of
the train then tried to stop the train, but found that the
air had gone from the brakes. He then whistled on brakes
and reversed his engine, but the distance between the train
and the crossing was too short to admit of the stopping of
the train by these means. The distance from the crossing
then was a little over 200 yards, and the train was going
at the rate of 25 miles an hour.

Air brakes, like everything else in use on a railway, suffer
by wear and tear. They wear out and require renewal, but
they do not often become defective. They are sometimes
used for two or three months without the discovery of any
defect. It is seldom possible to discover the defects, if any,
with the eye. On the day in question, so far as the eye
could discover before the collision, the brakes were free
from defect.

If the ordinary brakes had been used in time the collision
would not have happened. So if the defendants' servants
had not chosen entirely to rely on the air brakes, and allowed
the train to approach so near the crossing that it was too
late for the use of the ordinary brakes, there would have
been no collision. The neglect, if any, of the defendants was
in allowing the train to proceed so near the crossing before
using brakes as to make an accident unavoidable should the
air brakes fail.

It was the duty of the defendants, on sight of the raised
semaphore, in some manner to have brought their train to
a dead stand.

Each train was as nearly as possible on time. The
plaintiff's train was timed to leave London at ten minutes
past one o'clock. The defendants' train was due at London
at fifteen minutes past one o'clock. There would not,

therefore, be many minutes between the two trains, if on
time, at the crossing one mile east of London.

The Grand Trunk train was composed of the engine, five
freight cars, the baggage car, and the passenger car. Plaintiff, after seeing the defendants' train, started for the rear
of his train. He had just got one foot on the platform of
a car when his train was struck and he knocked into the
car. The engine of the defendants' train struck the last
freight car and the baggage car of the plaintiff's train,
threw the freight car on the signalman's shanty and upset
the baggage car on the middle of the Great Western R. W.
Co.'s main line. Plaintiff was in the car which was thrown
from the track, and rolled over with it. It turned upside
down. He was struck on the head and shoulders and
stunned, and his right leg was hurt. He at the time only
felt pain in the leg. He was unable to walk home, and
was taken home in a lumber waggon. A doctor was summoned. Plaintiff had pain in his hip, near the hip joint.
About three week afterwards the plaintiff suffered from
pain in his back, about the base of the spine. Afterwards
his leg became as it were partially paralyzed. It became
numb, and he lost feeling in it. He was unable to turn
his foot from one side to the other, except by taking hold
of it with his hand. He was unable at the trial to use
his leg, except by a kind of dragging of it after him.
Several medical men, as well for himself as the company, examined him. All agreed that he had sustained
some injury of the leg; but some of them thought that
when under examination he exaggerated his injury and
feigned more pain than he actually suffered. This was said
to be the manner of some men when suffering. There was
evidence of spinal injury. There was doubt expressed as
to his ultimate recovery. One of the medical men said
there is always doubt in these cases as to permanent
recovery.

The learned Judge found a verdict for the plaintiff. He
ruled that if the defendants relied upon the air brakes, they
should have applied them a sufficient distance from the

semaphore, so that, in the event of the air brakes giving way, the defendants might resort to other appliances, and by reversing the engine have avoided the collision. He held it was not sufficient for defendants to rely upon the air brakes, if, as in the present case, they were unable to control the train in time to prevent the happening of an accident. He held it was clear that when the brakes gave way the defendants' servants were unable to control the train in time to prevent the accident, and the collision was the consequence. This he held to be negligence for which the defendants were responsible. He also held there was no ground for imputing contributory negligence to the plaintiff.

While the learned Judge was of the clear opinion that the plaintiff was entitled to damages, he had very great difficulty in arriving at the amount. He was of opinion that the plaintiff had sustained a serious injury; but as some of the medical men were clear that to some extent the plaintiff had exaggerated his injuries, it was difficult to say to what extent he had practised deception. But referring to the fact that some witnesses said he might be disabled for some months, and possibly longer, the learned Judge on the whole assessed the damages at $1,000.

During Michaelmas term, November 30. 1875, *Barker*, for the defendants, obtained a rule *nisi* to set aside the verdict, and enter a verdict for the defendants, or to reduce the damages.

Rock, Q. C., shewed cause. If there had been a jury in this case the question of negligence would have been for the jury under a proper direction from the Bench: *Templeman* v. *Hayden*, 12 C. B. 507; *West Chester and Philadelphia R. W. Co.* v. *McElwen*, 67 Penn. 311; *Gayner* v. *Old Colony and Newport R. W. Co.*, 100 Mass. 208. There is no absolute rule of law as to what is negligence: *Philadelphia and Reading R. W. Co.* v. *Spearen*, 47 Penn. 300; *Gee* v. *Metropolitan R. W. Co.*, L. R. 8 Q. B. 161, 175, 177; *Shearman & Redfield* on Negligence, 3rd ed., secs. 11, 84, 87.

43—VOL XL U.C.R.

Here there was a *primâ facie* case of negligence: *Byrne* v. *Boodle,* 2 H. & C. 722 ; *Shearman & Redfield* on Negligence, sec. 280 ; *Ware* v. *Gay et al.,* 11 Pick. 106.   And this *primâ facie* case was not rebutted by the testimony of the defence : *Costello* v. *The Syracuse, Binghampton, and New York R. W. Co.,* 65 Barb, 92.   The amount of damages was, under the circumstances, no more than reasonable.

Barker contra.   There was no *primâ facie* case of negligence against defendants, and if there were the fact that defendants used the best appliances known for the stoppage of trains rebutted the *primâ facie* case : *Readhead* v. *The Midland R. W. Co.,* L. R. 2 Q. B. 414 ; *Wyborn* v. *The Great Northern R. W. Co.,* 1 F. & F. 162, 165 ; *Blyth* v. *The Birmingham Water Works Co.,* 11 Ex. 781 ; *Daniel* v. *The Metropolitan R. W. Co.,* L. R. 5 H. L. 49 ; *Crafter* v. *The Metropolitan R. W. Co.,* L. R. 1 C. P. 304.   The damages were excessive.

February 7, 1877.   HARRISON, C. J.—The question whether a person has been negligent in a particular case, is one of mingled law and fact.

It includes, two questions—

1. Whether a particular act has been performed or omitted.

2. Whether the performance or omission was a breach of legal duty.

The first of these is a pure question of fact, the second a pure question of law.

The extent of the defendants' duty is to be determined by a consideration of the circumstances.   The law imposes duties on men according to the circumstances in which they are called upon to act.   See *Shearman & Redfield* on Negligence, 3rd ed., sec. 11.

Negligence is a relative term, depending on circumstances, and therefore is generally a question for the jury, under a proper direction from the bench : *Philadelphia and Reading R. W. Co.* v. *Spearen,* 47 Penn. 300 ; *Gaynor* v. *Old Colony and Newport R. W. Co.,* 100 Mass. 208.   That which in

ordinary cases where there is a jury, passes between the
Judge and the jury, passes only in the Judge's mind where
he sits in the character of both Judge and jury. Per
Maule, J., in *Templeman* v. *Hayden*, 12 C. B. 507, 511.
But where a Judge, under the Administration of Justice
Act, sits without a jury, finds facts, and gives reasons for
his finding, it is not usually difficult to separate the findings
of the Judge as to matters of fact from his decision as to
matters of law.

The Judge in this case, as a matter of fact, found negligence, because the air brakes were not applied in sufficient
time to make use of the ordinary brakes in the event of
the air brakes failing, and as a matter of law decided that
it was the duty of the defendants so to do.

The latter finding is the one which was chiefly disputed
before us, on the authority of the cases of *Blyth* v. *The
Birmingham Water Works Co.*, 11 Ex. 781; *Readhead* v.
The Midland R. W. Co., L. R. 2 Q. B. 412, L. R. 4
Q. B. 379; *Wyborn* v. *The Great Northern R. W. Co.*, 1 F.
& F. 162; *Daniel* v. *The Directors of the Metropolitan R.
W. Co.*, L. R. 5 H. L. 45; *Crafter* v. *The Metropolitan R.
W. Co.*, L. R. 1 C. P. 300. But each case of alleged negli-
gence must be determined on its own circumstances.

It is the duty of railway companies to use upon their
trains such machinery as is necessary for the stopping of
the train in an emergency : *Smith* v. *The New York and
Harlem R. W. Co.*, 19 N. Y. 127. Hence brakes—*Costello* v.
The Syracuse and Binghampton R. W. Co., 65 Barb. 92;
and brakesmen—*Fleke* v. *The Boston and Albany R. W.
Co.*, 13 Am. 549,—are necessary.

The air brakes, although highly approved and much
used in this country and elsewhere, are, as well known to
railway men, not absolutely safe. If greater safety can be
attained by the use of or ability to use the common brakes
in the event of the air brakes failing, it is not, I think,
unreasonable to ask railway companies crossing each others
lines on the level to be prepared in an emergency to use
the old brakes. In order to do so, the air brakes must be

applied at such a distance from the point of danger as to give the opportunity of using either or both of these descriptions of brakes.   This the defendants omitted to do.

Negligence is the omission to do something which a reasonable man guided upon those considerations which ordinarily regulate the conduct of human affairs would do, or doing something which a prudent and reasonable man would not do : Per Alderson, B., in *Blyth* v. *The Birmingham Water Works Co.*, 11 Ex. 781, 783. · See further, per Brett, J., in *Gee* v. *Metropolitan R. W. Co.*, L. R. 8 Q. B. 175.

The occasional failure of the air brakes is a contingency which, in the conduct and management of a railway train, ought not to be overlooked by those responsible for the running of trains propelled by steam.   It may be said that the ordinary brakes may also be defective.   But the answer is, that by the ability to use both kind of brakes in the event of an emergency the probabilities of danger are diminished.

The chief consideration is the safety of the travelling public.   The effort should be in the management of passenger trains propelled by steam to lessen the danger as much as possible by the use of all available machinery, and the proper management of it.   The safety of the travelling public would not, I think, be satisfied with less care than the learned Judge held to be necessary under the circumstances of this case.   The danger of accident was greatly increased by the fact that two lines of railway, over which several trains pass every day, cross each other at the point, where the accident happened on the level.   Increased danger demands increased precaution.   In such a case it is not, in the interest of the travelling public, too much to ask both the railway companies concerned to use all possible precaution to avoid accident.

There is (as said by Bramwell, B., in *Buck* v. *Williams* 3 H. & N. 318), nothing so certain as that which is unexpected.   In like manner there is nothing so certain as that something extraordinary will happen now and then.

I am not convinced that the learned Judge was wrong in

his finding of the duty. Unless convinced that he was wrong, it is my duty to support his finding. I incline to the opinion, under the circumstances of the case, that he was right.

It was, in my opinion, the duty of the defendants to have applied the air brakes a sufficient distance from the point of danger, so that, in the event of these brakes giving way, resort might be had to the ordinary brakes.

I do not see my way to make the rule absolute on the ground of excessive damages. The finding of a Judge is certainly entitled to as much consideration as the finding of a jury. It is often said that juries lean against corporations. This has never been said of Judges: Per Lord Wensleydale, in *Mayor of Beverley* v. *The Attorney General*, 6 H. L. 332, 333.

The question of the measure of damages in actions for negligence has produced more difficulty than any other branch of the law: Per Wilde, B., in *Gee* v. *The Lancashire R. W. Co.*, 6 H. & N. 211. See also *Rowley* v. *London and North-Western R. W. Co.*, L. R. 8 Ex. 221. Damages in such a case where there is a jury must be left to the common sense of the jury, assisted by the presiding Judge: Per Mellor, J., in *Fair* v. *London and North-Western R.W. Co.*, 21 L. T. N. S. 326. See also per Cockburn, C. J., *Ib.* 327. We cannot presume that Judges are devoid of the common sense so generally credited to juries. When, instead of a jury exercising their common sense, aided by the direction of a Judge, we have a Judge using his own common sense, aided by his knowledge of law, we must at least respect his finding as much as we would the finding of any jury under similar circumstances.

The rule *nisi* should, in my opinion, be discharged.

MORRISON, J.—I regret I cannot concur in the view taken by the learned Chief Justice, for in my judgment the defendants are entitled to have their rule made absolute. I have arrived at this conclusion not without some hesitation, but I cannot satisfy myself, after a careful perusal of the evidence, that as charged in the declaration the plaintiff's injury was caused by the defendants' unskilful and negligent management of their train.

It must be borne in mind that this is not a case of contract, but an action for the defendants having negligently and unskilfully driven an engine, &c., against a railway carriage in which the plaintiff was while crossing a line of rails over which the defendants' train was to pass.

The evidence on the part of the defendants, in my opinion, rebutted the presumption of negligence, and shewed that every reasonable care was used and taken, and that the collision which occurred was not due to any fault or carelessness on the part of the defendants' servants, but that it was owing to an unavoidable accident, and arising from a cause which, from the evidence, could not be reasonably foreseen, and that every effort was promptly made after the discovery of the defect in the working of the air brakes to avoid and prevent the mischief that happened and resulted in the misfortune to the plaintiff.

The air brakes were duly tested and properly examined during the progress of the train at the Suspension Bridge and Hamilton, and were found in good and perfect order, as in fact they were, as they were used and worked that day effectually to stop the train at some twenty-four different points before arriving at the place in question.

In *Stokes* v. *Eastern County R. W. Co.*, 2 F. & F. 691, Chief Justice Cockburn, in addressing the jury, said at page 693 : "You are entitled to expect at the hands of a railway company all that skill, care, and prudence, can do to protect the public against danger and accidents, but you must carry that principle into application as reasonable men. * * * If you are of opinion that the flaw or crack had become *visible* prior to the accident; that upon careful examination—not with the aid of scientific authorities and scientific instruments, but on an *ordinary, reasonably proper and careful* examination, such as we all feel ought to be made before the engines are used, on which the safety of a whole train may depend—this flaw might have been discovered, and that either the examination did *not* take place, or, if it did, and the flaw was discovered, but the man with careless disregard of his own safety and of others whose lives and limbs might be involved, treated all this with supine and reckless indifference, then undoubtedly there is negligence established for which the company are, and ought to be, responsible."

In that case the verdict was for the defendants, and, as said by Mellor, J., in *Readhead* v. *Midland R. W. Co.,* L. R. 2 Q. B. 414, if that was not a proper direction—if questioned, the verdict must have been set aside.

I also refer to an extract of a judgment delivered by Hubbard, J., in *Ingalls* v. *Bills,* 9 Metc. 1, 15, quoted by Mellor, J., in *Readhead's* case, and which that learned Judge considered was supported by the weight of English authority : " That carriers of passengers for hire are bound to use the utmost care and diligence in the providing of safe, sufficient and suitable carriages, &c., in order to prevent those injuries which human care and foresight can guard against; and that if an accident happens from a defect in the coach which might have been discovered and remedied upon the most careful and thorough examination of the coach, such accident must be ascribed to negligence, for which the owner is liable in case of injury to a passenger happening by reason of such accident. On the other hand, where an accident arises from a hidden and internal defect, which a careful examination would not disclose, and which could not be guarded against by the exercise of a sound judgment and the most vigilant oversight, then the proprietor is not liable for the injury, but the misfortune must be borne by the sufferer as one of that class of injuries for which the law can afford no redress in the form of a pecuniary recompense."

I refer generally to the judgment in the case of *Readhead* v. *Midland R. W. Co.,* reported in L. R. 2 Q. B. 412, and in the Exchequer Chamber, L. R. 4 Q. B. 379, as an authority in favour of the defendants, where the subject of due and proper care is discussed at length. As said by Montague

Smith, J., who delivered the judgment of the Exchequer Chamber, " An obligation to use all due and proper care, is founded on reasons obvious to all, but to impose on the carrier the burden of a warranty that every thing he necessarily uses is absolutely free from defects likely to cause peril, when from the nature of things defects must exist which no skill can detect, and the effects of which no care or foresight can avert, would be to compel a man by implication of law, and not by his own will, to promise the performance of an impossible thing, and would be directly opposed to the maxims of law, *lex non cogit ad impossibilia—nemo tenetur ad impossibilia.*"

The case before us furnishes just one of those accidents that could not be avoided, and for which no one is blamable. It seems to me, as suggested by Pollock, C. B., in *Greenland* v. *Chapter*, 5 Ex., at page 248 : " That while a person is expected to anticipate and guard against all reasonable consequences, that he is not, by the law of England, expected to anticipate and guard against that which no reasonable man would expect to occur."

The learned Judge who tried the cause without a jury, seems to have rested his finding of negligence on the part of the defendants on the ground that, as the defendants, in the management of their train, relied on the air brakes, they should have anticipated their giving way as they were approaching the crossing, and have applied them at a sufficient distance from the semaphore, so that, in the event of their giving way, they might have resorted to other appliances, and the reversing of the engine, and in that way avoided the collision ; and that it was not sufficient for them to rely on the air brakes, at the point where they applied them, if they were unable to control their train in time in the event of an accident to them.

I cannot concur in that ruling. I am not prepared to say that they were bound to have any other brakes besides the air brakes, which appear to be an efficient apparatus for arresting the progress of the train, and well adapted for the purpose. They had, however, hand brakes, which

were made use of the moment the engineer discovered that
the air brakes did not work and slow the train.

.It was pressed on us by Mr. Rock that the evidence
shewed that the persons in charge of the train did not
attempt to arrest its progress until within a very short distance of the crossing train. That portion of the evidence
referred to is either a mistake or wrongly reported, for it is
quite inconsistent with the facts, and the rest of the testimony, and is not in accordance with the view taken by the
learned Judge, for the evidence clearly shews that if. the
air brakes had not given way the train would have stopped
at the semaphore, the usual stopping place.

On the whole, I am of opinion that the defendants are
entitled to judgment.

This case was argued before the learned Chief Justice
and myself. As we differ in opinion, the rule must drop, or
the case be re-argued before the full Court. Rather than
put the parties to the expense of a re-argument, I shall
withdraw my judgment, and the defendants can take the
case, if advised, to the Court of Appeal.

WILSON, J., was not present at the argument, and took
no part in the judgment.

STEWART V. COWAN ET AL.

Division Court bailiff—Interpleader issue—Detention of goods after judg-ment for plaintiff—Notice of action—Liability of attorney.

Defendant C., a Division Court bailiff, was employed by the plaintiff to sell certain goods under a chattel mortgage given to the plaintiff by one L. Defendant C. advertised and took possession of them, and afterwards ex-ecutions came into his hands against L., under which the attorney for the execution creditors told him to seize these goods. The plaintiff claimed them, and obtained judgment in his favour upon an inter-pleader issue. Defendant C. refused on demand to give up the goods to the plaintiff until he should consult the attorney, who told him to use his own judgment. The plaintiff having brought trespass and trover.

Held, that C. was liable : that he was not entitled to a demand of perusal and copy of the warrants under which he acted, for the action was not brought by reason of any defect in the process : that the jury were warranted in finding, as they did, that he did not believe that he was discharging his duty as bailiff in refusing to give up the goods after the decision of the interpleader, which finding disentitled him to notice of action : that the execution creditors were also liable ; but that the attorney was not, for he had told C. only to use his own judgment.

DECLARATION : First count : trespass to, and conversion of goods.

Second count : trover.

Pleas : 1. Not guilty.

2. Goods not plaintiff's.

3. That in a suit in the Fifth Division Court of the county of Oxford, between John Moody and Angus Mur-ray, plaintiffs, and John B. Laird, defendant, an execution was issued out of the said Court, and the goods in question in this suit were seized by the defendant Cowan-as bailiff of the said Court ; and thereafter an interpleader order was duly made, whereby it was directed that the said Cowan should retain the said goods until that interpleader should be determined, and it is yet pending and undetermined; which is the conversion complained of.

4. Not guilty, by statute, by Cowan. It was noted in the notes of the trial that this leave to plead was given.

Replications : 1. Issue on the pleas.

2. To third plea : that the plaintiff commenced his said action and declared therein, as aforesaid, not for the tres-

passes and conversion in that plea mentioned, but for that
the defendants on the said 6th day of November, 1875,
upon another and different occasion, and for another and
different purpose than the occasion and purpose in the
third plea mentioned, committed the trespasses and conversion in the declaration mentioned, being other trespasses
and conversion than those in the third plea mentioned.

Issue.

The cause was tried before Gwynne, J., at Woodstock, at
the Fall Assizes, 1876, with a jury.

The evidence for the plaintiff shewed that on the 17th
of April, 1875, John B. Laird gave the plaintiff a chattel
mortgage upon the property in question, filed on 21st of
April, 1875. The debt was $595. It was payable in six
months. When it became due, Laird gave the plaintiff
possession of the goods.

The plaintiff employed Cowan to sell the goods under
the mortgage, and he gave Cowan the key of the place
where the goods were, that he might get them. Cowan
advertised them for sale. After that, Cowan told the
plaintiff that two or three parties had put attachments in
his hands as bailiff of the Division Court, upon judgments
against Laird. The plaintiff asked Cowan why he did not
sell the goods under the mortgage. He said he could not,
for attachments had been placed in his hands. The plain-
tion said he had nothing to do with that. He removed the
goods into a house he had. The plaintiff never got back
any of the goods, nor any of the proceeds of their sale.

There was an interpleader suit, in which the now plaintiff was claimant, and Thompson and McEwan, the execution creditors, and Laird, the debtor, were defendants.
Judgment was given on it in favour of the now plaintiff.

For the defence, *Cowan* said: By the instructions of
Mr. McDonald, the plaintiff's attorney in the Division
Court executions, I seized the goods mentioned in the
mortgage. I then removed to a storehouse of my own.
The present plaintiff claimed the goods. I issued an inter-
pleader summons, which was ultimately decided in favour

of Stewart. I had the goods appraised before I sold a part
of them for rent. They were valued at all they were
worth, from $136 to $150. I have all the rest of the goods
yet, excepting those sold for rent. No demand has been
made upon me for them. McDonald, as the attorney for
the execution creditors, claimed that the mortgage was
not good.

Cross-examination—Stewart brought the chattel mortgage and the key of the house where the goods were,
wanting me to sell the goods for him under the mortgage.
I advertised the goods under the mortgage. After getting
the execution I went to Mr. McDonald, the attorney, for
the execution plaintiff, and asked him what I should do.
He told me to seize under the executions, for that the
mortgage was good for nothing. When judgment was
given in favour of Stewart, Mr. Norris as agent demanded
of me what I was going to do about giving up the goods.
I replied that if Kerr & Co. (the plaintiffs in another
Division Court execution) did not indemnify me I would
give up the goods. [It was shewn he had not Kerr & Co.'s
writ then in his hands, and he said]. I must have been
mistaken as to Kerr & Co.'s writ. I must have said to Mr.
Norris that I would refer to Mr. McDonald, and I took his
advice. I have always been instructed to hold on to the
goods.

It was shewn that the rent he sold for had been paid by
Laird, the tenant.

James F. McDonald said :—I never knew till to-day that
the bailiff had the goods in his possession under the chattel
mortgage. I knew there was such a mortgage : I drew
it. Cowan told me Stewart was claiming the goods he
(Cowan) was about to seize under the executions, and he
wanted to know what to do. I told him if he thought
there were suspicious circumstances he might act at his
pleasure in the matter : that if he seized there would be an
interpleader to test whether the mortgage was good or not.

Henry Constable said : he was one of the valuers of the
goods for Cowan. He valued them at $136. It was a
fair value.

The learned Judge submitted the following questions to the jury; and their answers to the respective questions follow the same:

1. What was the value of the goods in the mortgage mentioned, seized by Cowan in November, 1875 ? A.—$350.

2. Had Cowan, as agent of Stewart, possession of the goods at the time the executions came to his hands on the 6th of November, 1875 ? A.—Yes.

3. Did Cowan, before acting under the executions, consult with Mr. McDonald, the attorney of the execution creditors, as to what he should do ? A.—Yes.

4. Did Mr. McDonald, if consulted, give any and what instructions as to seizing the goods under the executions ? A.—Yes. Seize.

5. Had Cowan any reason to suspect the good faith of the chattel mortgage, or of Stewart's title thereunder ? A.—No.

6. Did Cowan, in acting under the executions, do what he did in the actual belief that he was acting in discharge of his duty as bailiff of the Division Court ? A.—No.

7. Did Mr. Norris, as Stewart's attorney, upon judgment on the interpleader being rendered in favour of Stewart, demand the goods from Cowan ? A.—Yes.

8. If Mr. Norris did so demand them, did Cowan refuse to give them up until he should consult Mr. McDonald ? A.—Yes.

9. Did Cowan in fact subsequently consult Mr. McDonald as to his retaining or giving up the goods? A.—Yes.

10. What instructions, if any, did Mr. McDonald give to Cowan after the determination of the interpleader suit ? A.—To use his own judgment.

Verdict for plaintiff, and damages assessed at $350.

In Michaelmas term, November 23,1876, *Read*, Q.C., for all the defendants but Cowan, and *Osler*, for Cowan, obtained rules calling on the plaintiff to shew cause why the verdict should not be set aside and a new trial granted, because it was.

against law and evidence ; and Cowan was not liable for not giving up the goods to the plaintiff, as there were writs in his hands against them and he was bound to hold them ; and because he was entitled to notice of action, which was not given ; and because no demand in writing was made upon him to give a perusal and a copy of the warrants ; and because McDonald did nothing to entitle the plaintiff to recover the value of the goods against him, or more at most than nominal damages ; and for misdirection, in the learned Judge directing that there was evidence on which to make the defendant McDonald liable.

December 4, 1876, *Ferguson*, Q.C., shewed cause. Cowan, who was a bailiff of the Division Court, was employed by the plaintiff as his agent to take possession of goods for the plaintiff under a chattel mortgage which the plaintiff had got from one John B. Laird. Cowan did so, and while in possession of the goods as the plaintiff's agent, two executions were placed in his hands against the goods of the mortgagor. An interpleader suit was brought, and the plaintiff was adjudged by it to be entitled to the goods as against these executions ; yet the bailiff would not, although the goods were demanded of him, deliver up the goods to the plaintiff, and for that refusal this action is brought. The jury have answered all the questions adversely to the defendants, finding that McDonald directed the seizure and not to deliver up the goods, and that Cowan was not acting in such a manner as bailiff of the Division Court as to entitle him to notice of action under the statute. There was no necessity to demand a perusal and the copy of the warrant, for that is required only when there is a defect in the warrant and the action is brought for that defect: Consol. Stat. U. C. ch. 19, secs. 195, 196 ; *Sayers* v. *Findley et al.*, 12 U. C. R. 155. The following authorities relate to the *bona fides* with which a person acts, in determining whether he is entitled to notice of action or not: *Kine* v. *Evershed*, 10 Q. B. 143 ; *Hughes* v. *Buckland*, 15 M. & W. 346 ; *Horn* v. *Thornborough*, 3 Ex. 846 ; *Norwood* v. *Pitt*, 5 H. & N. 801 ; *Cummins* v. *Moore*, 37 U. C. R. 130.

Osler, for Cowan, supported the rule. There was nothing to justify the finding.

D. B. Read, Q. C., for the other defendants, referred to *Denison* v. *Cunningham,* 35 U. C. R. 383 ; *Anderson* v. *Grace,* 17 U. C. R. 96 ; *McPhatter* v. *Leslie,* 23 U. C. R. 573 ; *Fisken* v. *McMullen,* 12 C. P. 85.

March 10, 1877. WILSON, J.—There was no misdirection complained of at the trial, nor was there any stated in the argument before us. There was no objection either taken at the trial that there had been no written demand upon the bailiff, Cowan, for the perusal of and for a copy of his warrants or the executions he was acting under The objection now taken can be of no effect, if it be still open to the bailiff to take it, because the statute and the authorities referred to shew that such a course is required to be pursued only when the bailiff is sought to be made responsible for some defect in the process under which he acts; and that is not the case here.

The bailiff's case then rests upon his right to a notice of action before being sued. That matter was fully considered by the learned Judge at the trial with his usual care and ability, who was of opinion that—as Cowan had originally got possession of the goods from the plaintiff under his mortgage, and had advertised them for sale under it, and as he still held the goods for the plaintiff after the interpleader was disposed of in the plaintiff's favour, and as agent for the plaintiff, freed from the claims of the executions ; and as he refused, after the decision of the interpleader, to deliver the goods to the plaintiff; and as it appeared he had no pretext for supposing there was anything wrong or suspicious in or with the mortgage, or in or with the plaintiff's title to the goods — it was a question for the jury whether he was acting in the belief that he was discharging his duty as bailiff of the Court by retaining and dealing with the goods as he did adversely to the plaintiff. And, accordingly, he left the evidence upon that point to the jury, who found against the bailiff.

There can be no doubt that there was evidence against
the bailiff sufficient to warrant that finding of the jury if
they believed it; and there can be no doubt of the truth
of it. It was not only proved by the plaintiff's witnesses,
but it was furnished by the bailiff himself.

It would be to pervert the evidence, and to ignore it, if
we were to say that the bailiff, against the opinion of the
learned Judge and of the jury, was acting or believed he
was acting in the discharge of his duty as a bailiff of the
Court in refusing to give to the plaintiff the possession of
his goods after the judgment in his favour establishing his
right to them. He was then, by being relieved from these
execution claims, as he was before the writs were delivered
to him—the private agent of the plaintiff; and it would
be absurd to say that he was at that time still honestly
acting as bailiff of the Court by retaining the goods of his
principal without any just cause or excuse.

As to the execution creditors, they are certainly liable.

Then as to Mr. McDonald, the attorney of the execution
creditors. There appears to be no reason to doubt that
McDonald did before the interpleader direct the bailiff to
seize the goods under the writs; and that his advice was
followed.

This action, however, is not brought for that seizure.
The plaintiff has disclaimed suing for that cause. He has
new-assigned a different seizure, &c., which is the refusal
to deliver the goods upon demand made for them after the
judgment was given in the interpleader suit in the plaintiff's favour.

What then was the evidence against Mr. McDonald as to
conversion, &c., at that time?

The jury found that the bailiff did, after the interpleader cause was over, refuse to deliver up the goods on
demand; and that he consulted with McDonald then
whether he should retain or give up the goods, and Mc-
Donald told him to use his own judgment.

That, in my opinion, did not make McDonald a wrong-
doer towards the plaintiff, and answerable for the bailiff's
conduct.

It is just what one would have said who wanted to have nothing more to do with the matter.

The rule should be made absolute in favour of the defendant McDonald—that a verdict be entered in his favour. It would be useless to send the case down to trial again to effect that object; and the residue of the rules will be discharged.

HARRISON, C. J., and MORRISON, J., concurred.

Rule accordingly.

JAMES A. STEPHENS V. CHARLES STAPLETON.

Division Court bailiff—Notice of action—Sae of business—Evidence of bona fides.

The Consol. Stat. U. C. ch. 126, sec. 10, requiring notice of action, does not apply to the case of a Division Court bailiff acting under an execution, which is specially provided for by ch. 19, sec. 193; and a notice, therefore, to such bailiff, not having endorsed upon it the name and place of abode of the plaintiff, as required by the former, but not by the latter Act, was held sufficient.

Upon the evidence set out in the case, the jury having found that the business carried on by the execution debtor was that of his brother, and carried on by the execution debtor as his agent, a new trial was granted, with costs to abide the event.

THE declaration contained two counts.

The first was trespass *de bonis* as to a large quantity of general groceries, confectionery, fruit, and shop furnishings and fixtures.

The second was trover for the same.

Pleas :—1. Not guilty, by statute: Consol. Stat. U. C., ch. 19, secs. 192 to 198 inclusive; Consol. Stat. U. C., ch. 126, secs. 1, 9, 10, 11, 16, 19, 20.

2. Denial of the plaintiff's property.

Issue.

The issues were tried at the last Assizes for the county of Peterborough, before Patterson, J., and a jury.

One John H. Stephens, a brother of the plaintiff, had been carrying on business in a shop on George street, in the town of Peterborough.

He was not successful in business, and in 1872 his stock-in-trade and other effects were sold by the sheriff under executions to the plaintiff, who was a bookbinder living in Brockville.

The stock-in-trade sold consisted of toys, fancy goods, and fruit.

The brother, notwithstanding, continued as before to carry on the business without any change in the sign over the door, which was "John H. Stephens," but, as it was said, as agent for his brother, he getting nothing but his living out of the business.

It was represented by the wife of John H. Stephens that her husband was to repay the plaintiff out of the proceeds of the business, but this the plaintiff denied.

In 1874 John H. Stephens, without any previous consultation with the plaintiff, and without his permission, but assuming to act as his agent, rented another shop on Simcoe street in the same town, and thenceforward carried on business there in the sale of fruits and confectionery.

None of the stock from the former place of business on George street was removed to Simcoe street.

The stock of the latter place was bought by John H. Stephens. some of the invoices being in his own name, some as agent for his brother, and some in the name of the brother.

There was no sign placed over the Simcoe street shop.

In 1875 it was discovered that John H. Stephens was in difficulties, and the plaintiff sent a person to take stock in both places of business, and afterwards himself took possession.

While the plaintiff was in possession of the Simcoe street business, the bailiff seized the stock at that place.

There was evidence that John H. Stephens had made some returns of the business to the plaintiff: that the plaintiff had put some money in the business, and had once or twice visited Peterborough for the purpose of seeing how the business was getting on, but charging his expenses for so doing to John H. Stephens.

The plaintiff, before action, served a notice of action on the defendant, but the name and place of abode of the plaintiff, although on the face of the notice, was not *endorsed* thereon as required by Consol. Stat. U. C. ch. 126, sec. 10.

Leave was reserved to defendant to move to enter a nonsuit, if the Court should be of opinion that the notice of action was insufficient.

The learned Judge left to the jury for their decision three questions, which, with their answers, are subjoined :

1. Was the transaction of 1872 a real purchase by the plaintiff with his own money, and not merely a pretended purchase made with money furnished by John H. Stephens, or made by way of lending the money to John H. Stephens, or on an understanding that he was to repay it ?   Answer. Real sale.

2. Was the Simcoe street business carried on by the understanding between the plaintiff and his brother as really the plaintiff's business carried on by his brother as his agent, or was it really the business of John H. Stephens ? Answer.   By his brother as agent.

3. If the plaintiff is entitled to recover, what damages should he receive ?   Answer. $390.

The jury afterwards, in answer to a question which the learned Judge asked them, to settle a doubt expressed by defendant's counsel, stated that by the answer to the second question they meant that the business was plaintiff's business.

The learned Judge thereupon entered a verdict for plaintiff for $390.

During Michaelmas term, November 22, 1876, *Armour*, Q. C., obtained a rule calling on the plaintiff to shew cause why the verdict should not be set aside and a new trial had between the parties, on the ground that the verdict was contrary to law and evidence and the weight of evidence, or why a nonsuit should not be entered pursuant to leave reserved at the trial.

J. K. Kerr, Q. C., during this term, February 13, 1877, shewed cause.   He submitted that the question of fraud was on the evidence a proper one for the jury, and that their finding ought not to be disturbed : *Doe d. Roy* v. *Hamilton*, 6 O. S. 410 ; *Williams* v. *McDonald*, 7 U. C. R. 381 ; *Clark* v. *Morrell*, 21 U. C. R. 596. That if the sale to the plaintiff by the sheriff was *bond fide*, it was unnecessary to register the bill of sale : *Kissock* v. *Jarvis*, 6 C. P. 393 : that the notice was sufficient under Consol. Stat. U. C. ch. 19, sec. 194 : that Consol. Stat. U. C. ch. 126 is inapplicable to the case of a Division Court bailiff : *McWhirter* v. *Corbett*, 4 C. P. 208. That if applicable the notice was sufficient under that statute : *Bross* v. *Huber*, 16 U. C. R. 282 ; *Pearson* v. *Ruttan*, 15 C. P. 85 ; *Armstrong* v. *Bowes*, 12 C. P. 539 ; *Dollery* v. *Whaley*, 12 C. P. 105 ; *McPhatter* v. *Leslie*, 23 U. C. R. 573 ; *Anderson* v. *Grace*, 17 U. C. R. 96 ; *Oliphant* v. *Leslie*, 24 U. C. R. 398 ; *Neill* v. *McMillan*, 25 U. C. R. 485 ; *McDonald* v. *Stuckey*, 31 U. C. R. 577 ; *Oram* v. *Cole*, 18 C. B. N. S. 1.

Armour, Q. C., contra. *Bross* v. *Huber*, 18 U. C. R. 282, is inconsistent with *Armstrong* v. *Bowes*, 12 C. P. 539, and *Moran* v. *Palmer*, 13 C. P. 528, and overruled by them. Consol. Stat. U. C. ch. 126, is applicable, and defendant is entitled to all the protection afforded by that statute as well as Consol. Stat. U. C. ch. 19 ; *Anderson* v. *Grace*, 17 U. C. R. 96 ; *Archibold* v. *Haldan*, 30 U. C. R. 30 ; *Dale* v. *Cooley*, 4 C. P. 462 ; *Lough* v. *Coleman*, 29 U. C. R. 367 ; *Pearson* v. *Ruttan*, 15 C. P. 85. The verdict is clearly against evidence and the weight of evidence, and should be set aside.

March 10, 1877. HARRISON, C. J.—The first question is, as to the sufficiency of the notice of action.

It is unnecessary to decide whether the notice is sufficient under Consol. Stat. U. C., ch. 126, sec. 10,—see *Bross* v. *Huber*, 18 U. C. R. 282 ; *Armstrong* v. *Bowes*, 12 C. P. 539; *Moran* v. *Palmer*, 13 C. P. 528—for we are of opinion that that statute is inapplicable to the case of a Division Court bailiff acting under an execution. See *McPhatter* v. *Leslie*, 23 U. C. R. 573.

The reason, good or bad, for deciding, as was done in *McWhirter* v. *Corbett*, 4 C. P. 208, that a sheriff is not under the General Act entitled to notice of action, is applicable to a Division Court bailiff.

We cannot hold the contrary without overruling *McWhirter* v. *Corbett*, 4 C. P. 208; and although this Court, in *Archibald* v. *Haldan*, 30 U. C. R. 30, took occasion to doubt the case, we must leave it to the Court whose decision it is or to some higher Court to overrule it.

So far as Division Court bailiffs are concerned, there is no hardship in holding the Act inapplicable, because as to them the Legislature has made special provision of the most ample character in section 193 of Consol. Stat. U. C. ch. 19.

But one difference between the two Acts is, that while Consol. Stat. U. C., ch. 126, sec. 10, requires an endorsement on the back of the notice " of the name and place of abode of the party intending to sue," the Division Courts' Act only requires "notice in writing of such action, and of the cause thereof": Sec. 193.

The notice in this case is clearly sufficient under the Division Courts' Act. See *Oliphant* v. *Leslie*, 24 U. C. R. 398; *Pearson* v. *Ruttan*, 15 C. P. 85; *Lough* v. *Coleman*, 29 U. C. R. 367; *Moore* v. *Gidley*, 32 U. C. R. 233.

The ground of nonsuit therefore fails.

The remaining question is, whether we should interfere with the verdict on the evidence.

If the stock seized had been that in the George street shop, which had been purchased and paid for by the plaintiff as his own in good faith, according to the finding of the jury, we should, notwithstanding the retention of possession by the former owner and the continuance of his name over the door, have declined to interfere: *Doe d. Roy* v. *Hamilton*, 6 O. S. 410; *Williams* v. *McDonald*, 7 U. C. R. 381.

But there are different considerations applicable to the shop on Simcoe street, which shop was in the first instance opened by the execution debtor entirely on his own responsibility, and apparently carried on for his own profit, and that these considerations ought not to be overlooked by a jury in deciding as to the property in that shop.

If that shop, without any concurrence on the part of the plaintiff, was designed by the execution debtor for his own advantage, and the business therein was carried on really as his own business, the mere addition to his invoices, &c., of the often used and often ill-used word "agent," would not make the property in the shop other than his own. And if his own property at the start, the subsequent adoption, if any, by the plaintiff of what the execution debtor had done, is not as against creditors conclusive to shew change of property.

But as the question is one on the evidence for a jury, and as we think another jury should be asked what they think of the transaction, we for the present forbear to say more about it.

In our opinion the rule must be absolute for a new trial. Costs to abide the event.

MORRISON, J., and WILSON, J., concurred.

Rule absolute.

RE JOHNSON AND MONTREAL AND CITY OF OTTAWA JUNCTION RAILWAY COMPANY.

Award—Motion to set aside—Practice.

A rule *nisi* to set aside an award must be drawn up on reading the award or a copy of it.

The objections taken to the award were, that having been made *ex parte*, and without hearing witnesses, it was void, and it was urged that it might therefore be set aside without producing it; but, *Held* otherwise.

Re Hinton v. *Meade*, 24 L. J. Ex. 140, not followed.

During Easter term last, *Beaty*, Q. C., obtained in Practice Court a rule *nisi* returnable in this Court, calling on the Montreal and City of Ottawa Junction Railway Company to shew cause why the award made by Walter Shanly, Esq., C. S. Gzowski, Esq., and Christopher Robinson, Esq., Q. C., or some of them, should not be set aside, on the following grounds :—

1. That the said award was made by the said arbitrators without any evidence being heard by them from either party, and without any knowledge or understanding of the case of either party or the merits, and without any conscience in the premises.

2. That the arbitrators refused to receive or hear evidence of a witness tendered by the said Johnson, and of witnesses proposed to be examined when the evidence of the said witness (one Hibbard) should be closed.

3. That the arbitrators refused to receive or hear evidence of a witness (one Hibbard) tendered by the said Johnson, except under a condition impossible to be undertaken by counsel for Johnson and on his behalf, and which condition was arbitrary and oppressive, *ultra vires*, and injurious to the interests of Johnson.

4. That the proceedings and the award were irregular, illegal, and not peremptory ; nor *ex parte* under such circumstances as to render the same valid.

5. That if any evidence was heard or received by the arbitrators, it was so received in the absence of Johnson and his counsel, and was *ex parte*.

And on grounds disclosed in affidavits and papers filed.

The affidavits and papers filed disclosed the following facts :

A meeting of the arbitrators was held in the office of Mr. Gzowski, in the city of Toronto, on 25th, 26th, and 27th January, 1876.

The parties appeared by their respective counsel and attorneys, and also several witnesses were summoned on behalf of the plaintiff.

The particulars of plaintiff's claim were handed in and filed.

These were based on the report of the company's engineer on an item estimate, by which it appeared that the value of the work done by the contractors for the construction of the railway, at the time of the suspension of the works, was $345,337, in cash, bonds, and stock of the company, as in the contract mentioned, and that after all credits to which the company were entitled amounting to $77,000, there remained a balance for work done, to the amount of $268,337.

After the particulars were filed a suggestion was thrown out by one of the parties, as to the possibility of an amicable understanding.

The consequence was, an adjournment of the arbitration till the 23rd February last.

On the 23rd February, the arbitrators met pursuant to adjournment, and at the request of the plaintiff there was a further adjournment till 14th March last.

There was no meeting on the 14th March, pursuant to the adjournment.

On the 29th March last, the arbitrators made an appointment for "Tuesday, the fourth day of April next, for proceeding on the reference at the hour of 11 o'clock in the forenoon, at the Romaine Buildings, in the city of Toronto ;" and this on the same day was served on the plaintiff, with a notice to the effect, that in case the plaintiff failed to attend without having previously shewn the arbitrators good and sufficient cause for absenting himself, the arbitrators would, at the request of the defendants, if present, proceed with the reference *ex parte*.

On 4th April last, an enlargement was asked on the part of the plaintiff.

The arbitrators refused the enlargement and requested the plaintiff in good faith to proceed at once with the arbitration.

The arbitrators, at the request of the defendants, proceeded *ex parte*, and on the 4th or 5th April, 1876, made an award.

The parties on the 5th April, were notified in writing of the making of the award, and that it was ready for delivery on payment of fees, amounting to $805.

The plaintiff thereupon served a written notice on the arbitrators, requiring them to file their award in the Court of Queen's Bench, but as the notice was not accompanied by the amount required for fees or any offer to pay the same, the arbitrators refused to part with the award.

No copy of the award was filed on this application, and there was nothing to shew the contents of the award.

During Michaelmas term, December 5, 1876, *Armour*, Q.C., and *Kerr*, Q.C., shewed cause. The rule *nisi* not being drawn up upon reading the award or a copy of it, should be discharged : *Grand River Navigation Co* , v. *McDougall*, 1 U. C. R. 255 ; *Wilkins* v. *Peck*, 4 U. C. R. 263. There was no difficulty in obtaining the award or a copy of it in time for the motion, as the arbitrators' fees if excessive might have been taxed : 29 Vic. ch. 32 ; *McCulloch* v. *White*, 33 U. C. R. 331. The arbitrators, in the exercise of their discretion, had power to refuse a further enlargement or to receive evidence not *bonâ fide* tendered with a view to proceeding with the reference : *Ginder* v. *Curtis*, 14 C. B. N. S. 723 ; *Henry* v. *Parker*, 1 W. R. 25 ; *Larchin* v. *Ellis*, 11 W. R. 281 ; *Tryer* v. *Shaw*, 27 L. J. Ex. 320 ; *Angus* v. *Smythie*, 2 F. & F. 381 ; *Proctor* v. *Jarvis*, 15 U. C. R. 187. There was no *bonâ fide* intention on the part of the plaintiff to proceed with the reference : *Ward* v. *McAlpine*

25 C. P. 121; *Colonial Trusts Co. v. Cameron*, 21 Grant 70; *Hobb* v. *Ferrars*, 8 Dowl. 779; *Russell* on Awards, 4th ed., 191, 192; *Wood* v. *Leak*, 12 Ves. 412; *Gladwin* v. *Chilcote*, 9 Dowl. 550; *Scott* v. *Van Sandau*, 6 Q. B. 237; *Walter* v. *King*, 9 Mod. 63; *Hall* v. *Andelton*, 8 Dowl. 326; *Solomons* v. *Solomons*, 28 L. J. Ex. 129; *Re Henry and the Portsmouth Waterworks R. W. Co.*, 10 W. R. 780; *Ringer* v. *Joyce*, 1 Marshall 404; *Russell* on Awards, 4th ed., 178, 182; *Craven* v. *Craven*, 7 Taunt. 644. And the case is distinguishable from *Hinton* v. *Mead*, 24 L. J. Ex. 140.

M. C. Cameron, Q. C., and *Beaty*, Q. C., contra. The award, whatever it was, was under the circumstances absolutely void: *Re Coombs*, 4 Ex. 839; *Russell* on Awards, 4th ed., 672; *Lund* v. *Hudson*, 1 D. & L. 236; *Crosby* v. *Holmes*, 3 D. & L. 566; *Russell* on Awards, 4th ed., 178, 655; *Redman* on Awards, 99; *Phipps* v. *Ingram*, 3 Dowl. 669; *Pepper* v. *Gorham*, 4 Moore 148; *Harvey* v. *Shelton*, 7 Beav. 456, 464; *Morden* v. *Widderfield*, 6 P. R. 179; *Nickalls* v. *Warren*, 6 Q. B. 615, 618; *Anon.* 2 Chitty R. 44; *Re Hinds*, 2 M. & G. 874; *Thorbun* v. *Barnes*, L. R. 2 C. P. 399; *Johnson* v. *Montreal & Ottawa R. W. Co.*, 6 P. R. 230. At all events there should be relief on payment of costs: *Graham & Waterman* on New Trials, vol iii. 1227, 1274; *Barrett* v. *Wilson*, 1 C. M. & R. 586; *Eads* v. *Williams*, 24 L. J. Ch. 534; *Billings* on Awards, 216; *Wyld* v. *Hope*, 9 M. & W. 161; *Samuel* v. *Cooper*, 2 A. & E. 752; *Blair* v. *Jones*, 6 Ex. 701; *O'Driscoll* v. *McCartney*, 9 Ir. L. R. 570; *Whatley* v. *Moreland*, 2 Cr. M. & R. 374; *Garrett* v. *Salisbury and Dorset Junction R. W. Co.*, L. R. 2 Eq. 358. And under the circumstances it was not necessary to file the award, or a copy of it: *Hinton* v. *Meade*, 24 L. J. Ex. 140.

February 7, 1877. HARRISON, C. J.—It is unnecessary, in the view which we take of this case, to express our opinion on any of the grounds taken for the purpose of setting aside the award.

On the threshold we are met with the difficulty that the award is not before us, and we are not in any manner informed as to its contents.

It is the well settled practice that a rule *nisi* to set aside an award, must be drawn up on reading, "the award or a copy of it," *Barton* v. *Ransom*, 5 Dowl. P. C. 597; *Grand River Navigation Co.* v. *McDougall*, 1 U. C. R. 255; *Wilkins* v. *Peck*, 4 U. C. R. 263; but where the rule is drawn up on reading "the affidavits and papers filed," and it be made to appear that among the affidavits and papers filed there is a verified copy of the award, effect will not be given to the objection: *Haywood* v. *Phillips*, 6 A. & E. 119; *Platt* v. *Hall*, 2 M. & W. 391; *Tracey* v. *Hodgest*, 7 U. C. R. 9.

The practice is the same whether the award be attacked for defects on its face or for objections *dehors* the award: *Sherry* v. *Oke*, 3 Dowl. 349, 1 Har. & W. 119; *Jacobs* v. *Ruttan*, 2 Cham. R. 138.

In *Sherry* v. *Oke* the motion was to set aside the award and enter a verdict for the defendant on the grounds, first, of the joinder of too many defendants, secondly, of a variance in the statement of the contract in the declaration; and on an objection that the rule *nisi* was not drawn up on reading the award or a copy of it, the rule *nisi* was discharged without costs.

In *Jacobs* v. *Ruttan*, 2 Cham. R. 138, a decision in our Practice Court, the motion was to set aside an award on the ground that the arbitrators proceeded with the reference and the arbitration, and made their award *ex parte* without the hearing of evidence on the part of the defendant, and other grounds similar to those taken in the present application, and on an objection that the rule *nisi* was not drawn up on reading the award or a copy of it, the rule *nisi* was discharged, with costs.

Mr. Justice Sullivan, in giving effect to the objection, said that he did not see his way "in overruling the practice of the Court."

The only case inconsistent with the settled practice of

the Court on the point in judgment is, *Re Hinton* v. *Meade*, 24 L. J. Ex. 140, cited by Mr. Beaty on the argument. The case is also reported in 1 Jur. N. S. 46, and 3 Com. Law 325. The best report of it is in the *Jurist.*

An action and all matters in difference were referred to two arbitrators nominated by the plaintiff and the defendant respectively, and a third to be nominated by the two thus appointed. Two of the arbitrators without any reference to the third, made an award. The paper called an award was a nullity : *Wade* v. *Dowling*, 4 E. & B. 44.

The *Jurist* report says " Prentice in Michaelmas term obtained a rule *nisi* to set aside the award ; and on a subsequent day in that term informed the Court that ' the Master refused to draw up the rule unless on reading either the award or a copy of it. Prentice urged that although the precise terms of the award were unknown to the plaintiff, it could not be supposed to be in his favour, and it would be hard to put him to the expense of taking it up.

Parke, B., said, p. 46 : "We think you are right in this application. You do not seek to set aside this award for matter apparent on its face—the objection is, that it is an improper award, and in truth a piece of waste paper. Its contents are consequently immaterial to the present purpose, and the case does not come within the rule of practice which requires that the rule to set aside an award be drawn up on reading the award or a copy."

Hawkins now shewed cause, and objected that the rule ought not to have been drawn up without the award or a copy ; but the Court adhered to its former decision

The reports in the *Law Journal* and the Common Law Reports, although more brief are, in substance the same.

It will be observed that no authorities are cited either on the report of the argument or of the judgment.

We do not find that the case has been approved or applied in any subsequent case.

If it be applicable here and opposed to *Sherry* v. *Oke*, and *Jacobs* v. *Ruttan*, we prefer, under the circumstances, to follow them instead of it.

Where a party seeks to set aside an award, we think he should be in a position to shew at least whether the award is for him or against him, instead of leaving the Court to conjecture its nature or bearing.

The Court will not intend anything for the purpose of setting aside an award.

It is impossible for us in such a case as the present to determine that an award is useless without having an opportunity of knowing something of its contents.

For all that appears the award is in favour of the party who is seeking to set it aside.

If the arbitrators' fees are excessive, and for that reason the award was not obtained from the arbitrators, there was no want of a proper remedy : 29 Vic. ch. 32.

Between the day of the publication of the award and the day of the application for the rule *nisi* to set aside the award, there was ample time to have had the fees taxed and the award delivered on payment of the taxed fees.

If the award be a valid one we ought not, on the materials now before us, to set it aside.   If invalid or useless, our refusal to set it aside will not make it valid.

The rule which requires the award or a copy of it, to be before the Court on an application to set aside the award is so wholesome that we ought not, in the absence of direct and unquestionable authority, to encroach upon it.

If we were to do so in this case we should be groping in the dark for the relief of a party who had it in his power to give us all necessary light and yet withheld it.

The rule *nisi* must be discharged, but, under the circumstances, without costs.

MORRISON, J., concurred.

WILSON, J., was engaged at the Assizes, and was not present when judgment was given.

Rule discharged.

ROONEY ET AL. V. LYON.

Insolvent Act of 1875—Composition and discharge—Withdrawal of claim.

At a meeting of the creditors of an insolvent one L., as receiver in
Chancery of the estate of W., claimed on two notes annexed to his
affidavit, stating that according to his information and belief he held
no security. The amount was then entered among the proved claims.
During the meeting, however, the solicitor for the indorsers on these
notes came in, and shewed that security was held for them, of which
L. was not aware; and L. then stated that owing to this he would
withdraw his proof and notes; and he took no further part in the proceedings. The affidavit had not been marked as received and filed,
and three days afterwards the notes were given up to L. by the
assignee. The claim, nevertheless, had been entered on the list of
debts proved, certified by the official assignee under section 52 of the
Insolvent Act of 1875, and remained there; but in the estimate and
calculations made at the meeting it was not taken into account, being
understood as withdrawn. Afterwards a deed of composition and discharge was procured, the creditors who signed it representing less than
the amount required if this claim were included, but more if it were
excluded.

Held, that the claim should not be considered as proved, having been
erroneously retained and included in the certificate; and that the deed
therefore was valid.

ACTION on two notes, and on the common counts. Pleas,
insolvency and deed of discharge, &c. There were other
pleas, but nothing turned on them.

The cause was tried before Hagarty C. J., C. P., at the
last Toronto Fall Assizes.

It appeared from the evidence at the trial that the
defendant became insolvent, and made an assignment of
his estate to the official assignee: that at the first meeting
of the creditors to prove debts, &c., one Laidlaw made proof
of a claim on behalf of the estate of one White, and his affidavit of proof stated he made the claim as receiver and
manager of the estate of J. & T. White, stating that the
insolvent was indebted to him as such receiver and manager, in the sum of $4,355, being the amount due on two
promissory notes annexed to his affidavit, according to his
information and belief; and that he held no security except
the notes. The affidavit was sworn to on the 28th March,
the day of the meeting.

Mr. Laidlaw was receiver of the White estate under

an order of the Court of Chancery. The amount of the
claim was then entered among the other proved claims.
These notes had indorsers. On the same day, and while
the meeting of creditors was going on, Mr. Wood, solicitor
for the indorsers, came in to the meeting, and stated .
that he represented the indorsers or sureties on the
notes, and he produced a paper shewing that security
was held from the insolvent in real estate for the payment
of the notes, of which security Mr. Laidlaw swore that he
had no previous knowledge, the estate being only in his
hands a short time. Some of the creditors then objected
that the receiver had no right to be at the meeting. He
then retired to another room with Mr. Wood, the solicitor,
and after communication with that gentleman he returned
to the meeting, and stated that owing to the existence of
such security he would not have anything further to do
with the proceedings, and that he would withdraw his
proof and notes, and in fact took no further part. The
affidavit of proof, which was produced at the trial, did
not appear to have been marked as received and filed. On
the 1st April, three days afterwards, the notes were given
up to the receiver by the assignee.

It also appeared from the evidence at the trial that in
the estimate and calculations made at the meeting this
claim was not taken into acccount, and that it was perfectly understood at the meeting that this claim was withdrawn. It appeared from the assignee's testimony that
the claim had been entered on the list of debts proved,
and remained on it notwithstanding what had taken
place at the meeting, and that he had given up the notes.
On the 15th April, 1876, a deed of composition and
discharge was procured by the insolvent. The official
assignee's certificate under the 52nd section of the Insolvent
Act of 1875, certified to the Judge of the County Court
that the total amount of claims proved was $36,239.86 :
that the number of creditors was thirty-five, of which
twenty-one signed the deed, representing $26,360.16—the
$36,239.86 included the Laidlaw claim of $4,335—deduct-

ing that amount would leave $31,884—three-fourths of
which would be $23,913; if included it would be $27,179.
The creditors who signed the deed of composition represented $26,368.16, a sum less than the amount required,
including the alleged proved claim of Laidlaw, and more
than necessary, if excluded.

It was contended on the part of the plaintiffs that Laidlaw's claim was proved; on the part of the defendant the
contrary, and that it ought not to be taken into account.

At the trial the learned Chief Justice entered a verdict
for the plaintiff for the amount claimed, being rather of
opinion that he could not avoid holding that the Laidlaw
claim was one of the proved debts, or that it could be
considered as expunged, and consequently that the
insolvent's discharge was not valid.

In last Michaelmas term, November 23, 1876, *Ferguson*, Q.C.,
obtained a rule *nisi* to enter a verdict for the defendant, on
the ground that the evidence proved the defendant's plea,
and for misdirection of the learned Judge in ruling that in
estimating the three-fourths in value of the debts proved,
the debt of Messrs. J. & J. White—Laidlaw's claim—should
be included, when the said debt was not proved, or if proved
the proof thereof was immediately thereafter, at a meeting
of the creditors, objected to, and was thereafter withdrawn,
and the vouchers shewing such debt taken away, and the
said debt remained in the schedule of the official assignee
by error or mistake only, and such debt should not be
included in estimating such proportion of the creditors,
and without including the same it was manifest from
the evidence that the requisite proportion of the creditors
had executed the deed of composition and discharge.

December 4, 1876, *McMichael*, Q.C., with him *Monkman*,
shewed cause. The certificate of the assignee shews that
the discharge cannot be operative for want of the assent
of the proper proportion of the creditors. Even if Laidlaw did undertake to withdraw his claim, the assignee did
not consider tha the had done so. They cited *Ex parte Parr*,

1 Rose 76 ; *Ex parte Goodman*, 3 Madd. 373 ; *Grugeon* v. *Gerrard*, 4 Y. & C. 119 ; *Deacon* on Bankruptcy 233.

Ferguson, Q.C., supported the rule. The security for the debt in respect of which Laidlaw attempted to prove, was not to J. & J. White, of whose estate he was receiver, but to a third party, Miss McCutcheon, who took the security to secure herself against her endorsement. At all events the claim was wholly withdrawn by Laidlaw, and must be treated as if never made. He referred to *Pike* v. *Dickinson*, L. R. 12 Eq. 64 ; *Ex parte English and American Bank*, L. R. 4 Ch. 49.

February 7, 1877. MORRISON, J.—The only question for our decision is, whether the discharge of the defendant, the insolvent, is valid. The general rule is, that if a party proves a debt on the footing of holding no security, he will not be permitted to withdraw such proof and set up a security.

Ignorance of possessing such a security, it is said, may be a ground for granting relief to parties who have so proved : 1 *Mont. & Ayr.* Bankruptcy, 186.

In *Grugeon* v. *Gerrard*, 4 Y. & C. 119, where one of the partners in a bank proved for the whole amount due on two bills, swearing that the bank held no security except the two bills of exchange, Maule, J., who delivered the judgment of the Court, at p. 131, said : " Great jealousy is properly felt on the part of those who exercise jurisdiction in bankruptcy, against permitting parties who have proved on the footing of holding no security, afterwards to withdraw their proof and set up a security ; but where, as in this case, the proof has obviously been made in ignorance of the existence of the security, it is highly probable that the Court would give relief."

Now, it is quite clear here that Laidlaw, as receiver, when he made the affidavit of proof at the first meeting of the creditors, did so in ignorance of the fact of the existence of mortgage security being held for the payment of these notes. And on being informed during the same

meeting that such was the case, he, Laidlaw, immediately
stated he abandoned his claim, and withdrew his proof, if
made, and took no further part in the proceedings of the
creditors.   The creditors also objected to his claim, and it
appears from the evidence at the trial that it was perfectly
understood at the meeting that the claim was withdrawn,
and in the calculations and estimates then made with a
view to a composition this claim was left out, and in
pursuance of his withdrawing the claim Laidlaw got from
the assignee the two notes and detached them from his
affidavit.   It is also to be noticed that the affidavit or proof
papers are not marked or filed.   The amount of the claim,
however, had been entered in the sheet of proved claims,
and nothing appears as to its withdrawal or being expunged

In cases like the one before us the Court would not be
inclined (except where its interference was invoked as
necessary in the interests of justice) to disturb or unsettle
a deed of composition and an arrangement agreed to
between the insolvent and his creditors after its being completed and carried into effect, and according to the clear
intention of the parties, on account of a mere mistake or
error.   In this case the circumstances shew that the insolvent and the creditors must necessarily have understood
that Laidlaw's claim was withdrawn for the reasons
assigned, and that it was not in any way considered as a
proved claim; and they acted upon that assumption; and
the Judge was also led to believe that the creditors
executing the deed of composition represented three-fourths
in value of the debts proved, which was the fact excluding
the withdrawn claim of Laidlaw; and the Judge must
also have assumed that the amounts certified by the
official assignee were in accordance with the provisions of
the Insolvent Act and entitling the defendant to his discharge.   The certificate on its face if examined would have
been found insufficient, as it included Laidlaw's withdrawn
claim, and if the attention of the Judge or the parties had
been called to it, the error would no doubt have been rectified.   We cannot understand, if the official assignee did not

think that the $26,368.06 represented three-fourths in value of the proved debts, that he would have signed a certificate insufficient, or if he was aware of its insufficiency that he would omit directing the attention of the parties or Judge to the fact. The discharge of the defendant signed by the Judge recites and it is predicated on the fact that the deed of composition and discharge was executed by a majority of the creditors, and who represented at least in value three-fourths of the proved liabilities, shewing clearly that the Laidlaw claim was not considered a proved claim, and inadvertently or by mistake, although withdrawn, it was included in giving the total of the proved liabilities.

On the whole, I am of opinion that the defendant is entitled to our judgment, as the evidence clearly shews that Laidlaw's claim, although withdrawn, was retained or placed in the list of proved claims, and that it was so retained in error and mistake, and ought not to have been included in the amount of proved debts; and that the official assignee in error included it in his certificate; and that the total amount of such liabilities ought to have been $31,884.00, and in fact was, instead of $36,239.86, and such being the case, the discharge was valid.

The rule will therefore be absolute to enter a verdict for the defendant.

MORRISON, J., and WILSON, J., concurred.

Rule absolute.

WILLIAM J. CREIGHTON AND WALTER KENWORTHY v.
    SIMEON HEMAN JANES, HENRY NEWCOMBE, AND
    HEMAN DUNE JANES.

Sale of goods by agent—Power of agent to bind principal.

The defendants, merchants in Toronto, arranged with L. & H. in London,
    England, for a consideration specified, that all goods bought by defen-
    dants in England should be charged to L, & H. by the various sellers,
    with whom L. & H. were to settle.   The plaintiffs' agent K. sold goods
    to defendants on credit, and the plaintiffs' draft on L. & H. having been
    protested, they sued defendants.   The evidence was contradictory as to
    K.'s knowledge of defendants' arrangement with L. & H., and as to
    whose credit the sale was made upon.
The jury were directed that the plaintiff was bound by K.'s arrangement
    for payment, if any, made with defendants; and were asked to say
    whether the goods were sold on the credit of L. & H., looking only to
    them for payment, or to defendants, on their own credit, in the ordinary
    way, and they found for defendants.
Held, that the direction was right; but upon the evidence, more fully
    stated in the case, a new trial was granted on payment of costs.

ACTION for goods sold and delivered.

Pleas : never indebted, and payment.

Issue.

The cause was tried at the last Fall Assizes in the city
of Toronto, before Hagarty, C. J., and a special jury.

The defendants were merchants living in the city of
Toronto, and had been carrying on business in Toronto since
1872.

In 1872 they made an arrangement with Messrs. Lawton
& Head, general agents in London, England, to the effect
that all goods bought by defendants in England would be
by the various houses debited to Lawton & Head, with
whom Lawton & Head were to settle, giving defendants
six months credit from the date of summary of invoices for
each shipment.   Messrs. Lawton & Head were to allow defendants to overdraw on their account to the extent of
£1,000, they paying six per cent. interest on the amount, if
any, of overdraft.   If that limit were exceeded by defendants, then seven per cent. interest was to be charged.   The
commission of Messrs. Lawton & Head was to be three per
cent. on each shipment.   If Messrs. Lawton & Head were

employed as buyers, they were to charge five per cent. If the total purchases in any year exceeded £10,000, the commission was to be reduced to two per cent.

This arrangement was sworn, both by defendant Newcombe and defendant Simeon Heman Janes, to have been communicated to King Huston, the agent of the plaintiffs, before and at the time of the transaction next mentioned; but this was denied by King Huston in his evidence given under a commission.

King Huston, in June, 1875, acting as agent for the plaintiffs, sold in England, to the defendants goods to the value of £199 1s., at six months' credit, plaintiffs to draw for the amount on Messrs. Lawton & Head.

King Huston at the time made a written memorandum which he did not keep, but the contents were sworn by defendant Newcombe to be as follows: "Goods. Charge to Lawton & Head, of London. Invoice to Lawton & Head. One invoice to Lawton & Head. Two for Shipper direct, and one for Burke, Stevens & Co. Draw on Lawton & Head for payment."

King Huston was not only agent for the sale of goods for the plaintiffs, but for several other mercantile firms resident in England, Scotland, Ireland, and France, he receiving from the sellers a commission on his sales.

The plaintiffs, as they swore, having been informed of the sale, but not as to any special terms, decided to carry it out. They were told, as they swore, that Lawton & Head were simply agents for the defendants. They were not at any time told, as they swore, of the special arrangement which appeared to have existed between the defendants and Lawton & Head.

Accordingly the plaintiffs debited the goods to defendants, but before sending them, on the 14th of July, 1875, wrote to Lawton & Head, stating that the longest credit they allowed to any one was six months from the first of the month following the shipment; and as they proposed to ship to defendants that week they would draw on Lawton & Head at six months from the 1st of August, 1875, but

offering, "if any accommodation to Lawton & Head," to
draw at six months from the 15th of August, 1875.

Messrs. Lawton & Head answered, stating their willing-
ness to accept the draft at six months from the 15th of
August, 1875.

It was sworn by the plaintiffs that they knew nothing
of the standing or credit of Messrs. Lawton & Head, and
that they sold the goods solely on the credit of defendants,
although willing as requested to draw on Messrs. Lawton
& Head as the agents of the defendants.

The goods were, on the 15th July, 1875, invoiced by
the plaintiffs to and in the name of the defendants, and
not in the name of Lawton & Head.   One copy of the invoice was sent with the goods to Burke, Stevens & Co., the
forwarders of defendants at Liverpool, and another copy to
defendants themselves in Canada.

The goods and the invoice were in due course received
by S. H. Janes, one of the defendants in Canada.   He observed at the time that the invoice was made out in their
own names as purchasers, and spoke about it to the defendant Newcombe when the latter returned from England.
But Newcombe said it was simply a mistake, and there
would be no difficulty about the matter.   So nothing was
done about it.

On the 16th July, 1875, Lawton & Head drew upon the
defendants at six months for £336 12s., made up as follows :

Plaintiffs' goods	£199	1s.	0d.
Goods of another firm	125	12	7
Charges and commission	11	18	5
	£336	12s.	0d.

Defendants accepted the latter draft, which in October
following was discounted by Lawton & Head with the
Bank of British North America in London.

On the 15th August, 1875, the plaintiffs drew on Lawton
& Head at six months for the amount of their account
against defendants, £199 1s.   The draft was accepted, but
never paid.

Messrs. Lawton & Head in the following December, became bankrupts.

On the 24th December, 1875, plaintiffs wrote defendant Newcombe, who was then in England, informing him of the bankruptcy of Lawton & Head, and that the plaintiffs would look to defendants for payment of the goods in the event of the acceptance of Lawton & Head, then maturing, being dishonoured.

Defendant Newcombe swore that he shewed the latter communication to King Huston, who appeared to be annoyed, tore it up, and said it would be all right.

The plaintiffs, not having received any reply to their letter of the 24th December, 1875, on the 16th February, 1876, wrote a similar letter to defendants, but were again without a reply.

On the 18th February, 1876, Lawton & Head's acceptance matured, and was protested for non-payment.

Plaintiffs thereupon wrote defendants, threatening suit, and on the 1st of April, 1876, began this suit.

There was evidence on the part of the defence shewing that merchants in this country, with a view to having only one creditor in England, and for other reasons, often make such an arrangement with agents in England as represented by the defendants to have been made by them with Messrs. Lawton & Head.

The question of fact which the learned Chief Justice in substance left to the jury was whether the goods were sold by the plaintiffs on the credit of Messrs. Lawton & Head looking only to them for payment, or in the ordinary way to defendants on their credit.

The learned Chief Justice in his charge to the jury told them that the plaintiffs were bound by the undertaking as to payment, if any, made by King Huston at the time of the sale.

The counsel for the defendants objected that the learned Chief Justice should have told the jury that the plaintiffs were not bound by Huston's undertaking as to payment, if any, unless disclosed by him to the plaintiffs.

The learned Chief Justice refused to do so, saying that
he told the jury that as the plaintiffs dealt wholly through
King Huston they were bound by the terms agreed to by
him.

The jury found for the defendants.

During Michaelmas term, November 22, 1876, *Mc-
Michael*, Q.C., obtained a rule calling on the defendants to
shew cause why the verdict should not be set aside and a
new trial had between the parties, on the ground that the
verdict was contrary to law and evidence, and for misdirection of the learned Judge who tried the cause, in ruling that
the plaintiffs were bound by whatever was done by their
agent, and that when the agent reported to the plaintiffs
that he had sold goods to the defendants, and they sold
and delivered such goods, they were nevertheless, without
any notice to them, bound to accept the liability of persons
of whom they had not heard.

During this term, February 12, 1877, *Bethune*, Q. C.,
(*Rose*, with him,) shewed cause. Huston by the terms of
the sale had elected to credit Lawton & Head: *Story* on
Agency, 7th ed., sec. 449; *Hyde* v. *Paige*, 9 Barb. 150; *Butt* v.
Barr, 4 Har. 130; *Patterson* v. *Gandasequi*, 15 East 64,
68 ; *Thompson* v. *Davenport*, 9 B. & C. 86 ; *Hutton* v.
Bulloch, L. R. 8 Q. B. 331 ; *Armstrong* v. *Stokes*, L. R. 7
Q. B. 605. The plaintiffs having adopted the contract are
bound by the terms of it : *Pickering* v. *Busk*, 15 East 38,
43. The question was a proper one for the jury, and their
verdict ought not to be disturbed: *DeBlaquiere* v. *Becker*,
8 C. P. 170.

McMichael, Q. C., (*R. Fleming* with him,) contra. The
question is not one of election, but of express contract.
Huston, who was a mere agent to solicit orders, had no
power to bind the plaintiffs by such a contract of sale as
alleged: *Lockwood* v. *Levick*, 8 C. B. N. S. 603; *Dingle* v.
Hare, 7 C. B. N. S. 145 ; *Hogarth* v. *Wheeler*, L. R. 10 C.
P. 630; *Hutton* v. *Bulloch*, L. R. 9 Q. B. 572; *Hamer* v.

Sharpe, L. R. 19 Eq. 108; *Addison* on Contracts, 7th ed., p. 52; and so the learned Chief Justice was wrong in telling the jury that by the adoption of the contract the plaintiffs adopted the terms of it: *Pollock* on Contracts, 487. Besides, the verdict is against evidence: *Calder* v. *Dobell*, L. R. 6 C. P. 486. The invoice was to the defendants, and they neither repudiated it nor returned the goods.

March 10, 1877. HARRISON, C. J.—This case is not one in which the law as to an undisclosed principal can be applied. It is rather a case of express contract.

The learned Chief Justice told the jury that, as plaintiffs dealt with defendants wholly through Huston, they were bound by the terms of contract agreed to by him.

The objection to the charge taken at the trial was, that the plaintiffs were not bound by what Huston undertook as to whom credit was given, if not disclosed by Huston to the plaintiffs.

This is in effect the objection stated as ground of misdirection in the rule *nisi*.

The contention of the plaintiffs up to a certain point is entitled to prevail, but not to the extent to which they endeavour to push it.

Defendants having accepted the goods, accompanied by an invoice in which the goods were debited to them by the plaintiffs, are *primâ facie* liable to the plaintiffs for payment of the price.

The onus therefore is on the defendants by satisfactory evidence to shew that the contract under which they received the goods was a different contract, and that plaintiffs are bound by it.

Whether the contract was as they represent, is a matter of fact on the evidence: *Calder* v. *Dobell*, L. R. 6 C. P. 486; *Curtis* v. *Williamson*, L. R. 10 Q. B. 57. And whether the plaintiffs are bound by it is the matter of law which arises in the event of the preceding question being answered in the affirmative, and as to which misdirection is charged.

The arrangement alleged to have been made by defendants with Lawton & Head was, according to the testimony for the defence, a common one for merchants in this country to make with general agents in England.

There is nothing to prevent the owner of merchandise selling the same to one person and making the delivery to another.

The learned Chief Justice, in leaving to the jury the question whether the goods were sold by plaintiffs on the credit of Lawton & Head, looking to them only for payment, in effect left to the jury the question whether the contract was for a sale to Lawton & Head, delivery to be made to the defendants.

The finding of the jury adopts the contract for which the defendants contend.

If Huston at the time of the sale were the owner of the goods, and suing defendants in this action for the price, he would certainly be concluded by this finding.

But the question which we must now consider is, whether the plaintiffs in this action are bound by the acts and conduct of Huston in making the sale which, according to the finding, he did for them.

The goods were sold by means of the agency of Huston. It is therefore necessary if possible to understand the character of his agency. It is argued that he was only an agent to solicit orders, and not an agent to sell goods. No such point was, we are informed, made at the trial. Had it been the learned Chief Justice might have been asked to take the opinion of the jury as to the nature of Huston's agency, for it was a question of fact for the jury: *DeBlaquiere* v. *Becker*, 8 C. P. 167.

But as no such question was raised for the consideration of the jury, we cannot now on the evidence assume that the agency was of the restricted kind suggested by counsel. Indeed nothing of the kind is suggested in the evidence. The evidence shews that Huston was an agent to sell goods for the plaintiffs and others doing business in Great Britain and France. If an agent for the sale of goods, we

apprehend that it would be within the bounds of his
authority to sell goods to one person deliverable to another.
His neglect to communicate to his principals the precise
nature of the contract which he made, is something for
which his principals and not his vendees must suffer.
The vendees were justified in assuming that he in all
respects did his duty. The vendees receiving the goods
shortly after the contract, if unaccompanied by the invoice,
would have been justified in assuming that the goods
were delivered in pursuance of the contract. Their disregard of the warning afforded by the invoice was a
circumstance against their present contention, and one
which without doubt was pressed on the consideration of
the jury. They gave an explanation which was satisfactory
to the jury.

Now if we exclude from consideration the invoice and
what was done under it, as " explained away," there is no
evidence of a contract except through the instrumentality
of Huston. It is difficult to understand in that case on
what principle the plaintiffs claim to adopt Huston's agency
without adopting what he did as their agent: See *Armstrong* v. *Stewart*, 25 C. P. 198; or to adopt the contract
which he made without adopting it in its integrity: *Bristow* v. *Whitmore*, 9 H. L. 391.

If a person with or without authority make a contract
of sale on behalf of another, the latter cannot at the same
time "approbate and reprobate it": See per Lord Kingsdown
in *Bristow* v. *Whitmore*, 9 H. L. 417.

The well understood principle of agency in such a case
is, that where a contract has been entered into as agent for
another, the person on whose behalf it has been made cannot take the benefit of the contract without bearing its
burden: Per Lord Cranworth, *Ib.* 404.

This was in effect the ruling of the learned Chief Justice at the trial. No authority has been cited against it.
We sustain it.

The case is an important one to the plaintiffs. It is
equally important to the defendants. And it is important

to the mercantile community.   While the learned Chief
Justice is not dissatisfied with the verdict, he is unable to
say he is satisfied with it.   It may be that the plaintiffs
suffered by not having Huston's evidence *viva voce* before
the jury.   There were several points made by witnesses
for the defence, to which he might, if present, have made
some answer.   It may be that, as contended for by the
plaintiffs, the sale was to the defendants, the reference
being to Lawton & Head, upon whom a draft was to be
drawn for the purchase money, as mere machinery for payment, but not as discharging defendants from payment.
The form of the invoice is in accordance with this view.
We have formed no strong opinion on the evidence either
one way or the other.   But, considering the importance of
the case, if plaintiffs are willing to take a new trial on
payment of costs, we think they should have it; they to
elect and pay the costs on or before the 24th of March
next; failing their election by that day, the rule *nisi* to be
discharged.

MORRISON, J., concurred.

WILSON, J., was not present at the argument, and took
no part in the judgment.

CARROLL V. BURGESS.

Tax sale—Delay in obtaining deed—Registry—29 Vic. ch. 24, sec. 57.

The sheriff, on the 9th October, 1860, sold the land in question for taxes to the plaintiff, gave a certificate of the sale, but for some reason not explained he did not obtain his deed until the 17th September, 1866, and he registered it on the same day, within one year from the passing of 29 Vic. ch. 24. There was no proof of any neglect or misconduct on his part in not procuring the deed sooner.

Held, that the delay in registering did not, under 29 Vic. ch. 24, sec. 57, avoid the deed as against the purchaser of the land who had first registered : that the deed not having been questioned within the time limited by the protecting statutes, was within their operation ; and that the plaintiff, bringing ejectment in 1870, was entitled to recover.

EJECTMENT for a part of lot 3 in the 11th concession of East Zorra, containing five acres.

The plaintiff claimed title under a conveyance thereof for arrears of taxes from Andrew Ross, sheriff of the county of Oxford, bearing date 17th September, 1866.

The defendant, besides denying the title of the plaintiff, claimed title under a conveyance from Alfred H. St. Germain, dated 13th November, 1867.

The case was tried at the last Assizes for the county of Oxford, before Gwynne, J., without a jury.

The lot at one time belonged to Mr. Bettridge. He sold and conveyed the westerly part of it to one Pease, who was living in England. One Goodall was, in 1854, the occupant of the land under Bettridge, and was according to the township roll assessed for statute labour and personal property. The roll also shewed the assessment in respect of the realty. Goodall performed the statute labour for that year, but there was no clear proof that the other taxes for that year were paid.

The south-west quarter of the lot was, in 1854, assessed at £240, and subject according to the roll to the following rates :—

	s.	d.
Lunatic Asylum Tax..............	1	2½
County Rate	8	7
Township Rate	5	8½
Six days' Statute Labour @ 2s.6d.	15	0
Total £1 10 6		

During the year 1854, Henry DeBlaquiere purchased the westerly portion of the lot from Pease, and in the spring of 1855 took possession.

On 2nd February, 1856, Henry DeBlaquiere executed a mortgage on the land to Hugh Barwick, and this mortgage afterwards became the property of the Bank of Montreal, who, on 1st November, 1864, sold and conveyed the land to Henry Curtis, who, on 2nd April, 1867, sold and conveyed to Alfred H. St. Germain, who, on 30th November, 1867, sold and conveyed to Samuel Burgess, the defendant. These deeds were all registered in due course.

Four acres of the lot were on 29th November, 1859, sold for arrears of taxes; but on 17th November, 1860, Henry DeBlaquiere redeemed the portion then sold by paying $28.98.

The proceedings to sell the land for the arrears of taxes which had accrued due in 1854, were not taken till 1860. The land appeared on the roll of the county treasurer as the land of a non-resident. On 11th June, 1860, the warrant was issued for the sale of this and other lands under the hand of James Kintrea, the then treasurer of the county of Oxford, and under the seal of the county. This warrant was on 16th June, 1860, handed to James Carroll, the then sheriff of the county. The south-west quarter of 3, in 11th concession, East Zorra, was described in the warrant as patented and subject to $11.50 for arrears of taxes. The sheriff, on 9th October, 1860, sold the five acres in question to the plaintiff for $15.03, being $11.50 arrears of taxes, and $3.53 expenses. He, on the same day, gave a certificate of the sale to the plaintiff. It was proved that the lot had been advertised for sale in the *Official Gazette*, but there was no proof of advertisement in a local paper.

The plaintiff, for some reason not explained, omitted to take his deed till the 17th of September, 1866. In the meantime Sheriff Carroll had died and Sheriff Ross was appointed his successor. He received the deed from Sheriff Ross, the sheriff of Oxford at that time. It was registered in the county registry office on the day that it was made.

The writ of ejectment was not issued till the 13th of June, 1876.

Several objections were taken to the plaintiff's right to recover, but these were overruled by the learned Judge, who entered a verdict for the plaintiff.

During Michaelmas term last, November 23, 1876. *Ernestus Crombie*, obtained a rule calling on the plaintiff to shew cause why the verdict should not be set aside and a verdict entered for the defendant, or a new trial granted, on the ground that the verdict was contrary to law, evidence, and the weight of evidence, in the following particulars :

1. That the deed to the plaintiff could not be legally given by Sheriff Ross, the Act under which the sale took place only allowing it to be executed by Sheriff Carroll, who made the sale.

2. The lands were not proven to be in arrears for taxes, the township treasurer having made no legal return to that effect.

3. The sale was not advertised in a local paper, nor was a notice thereof posted up in the Court House.

4. The land was illegally sold for statute labour tax.

5. The taxes legally imposed were proved to have been paid.

6. The land was assessed as resident land, and could not be returned as non-resident land.

7. The land being assessed against Goodall for some taxes, which were paid, amounted to a waiver of all further claim for taxes.

8. The Acts confirming sales for taxes do not validate a deed given under the circumstances proved at the trial of this cause.

9. The deed of the plaintiff should have been, but was not, registered to obtain priority against Curtis, under whom defendant claims, and who was a *bona fide* purchaser and held under a registered title, and so the plaintiff's deed is void as against Curtis and his assigns.

10. The land being occupied during the year for which
the taxes were unpaid, taxes could not legally be imposed
on the land as non-resident land, and a sale made for
default of payment of taxes so imposed is illegal.

During this term, February 10, 1877, *D. B. Read*, Q. C.,
shewed cause.   He cited *Cotter* v. *Sutherland*, 18 C. P. 357,
394; Consol. Stat. U. C. ch. 55, secs. 83, 84, 86, 88, 89 ; *Silver-
thorn* v. *Campbell*, 24 Grant 17; 29 Vic. ch. 24 sec. 57 ; *Jones*
v. *Cowden*, 36 U. C. R. 495 ; *Bank of Toronto* v. *Fanning*,
18 Grant 391 ; *Davis* v. *Van Norman*, 30 U. C. R. 437 ;
Greenstreet v. *Paris*, 21 Grant 229 ; 32 Vic. ch. 36 sec. 155,
O.; *Taylor* on Titles, 94, 95.

Osler, contra, abandoned all the objections taken except
the eighth and ninth, and cited *Hamilton* v. *Eggleton*, 22
C. P. 536 ; *Proudfoot* v. *Austin*, 21 Grant 566 ; *Jones* v.
Cowden, 34 U. C. R. 345, 36 U. C. R. 495; Consol. Stat. U.
C. ch. 89 sec. 35, 44 ; 29 Vic. ch. 24 sec. 57.

March 10, 1877. HARRISON, C. J.—It is declared by
section 56 of 29 Vic. ch. 24, that every deed made by a
sheriff or other officer shall be registered within eighteen
months after the sale by such sheriff or other officer ; and
all deeds of lands sold under process issued from any of the
Courts of law or equity in Upper Canada shall be regis-
terd within six months after the sale of such lands, otherwise
the parties respectively claiming under any of such sales
shall not be deemed to have preserved their priority as
against a purchaser in good faith, who may have registered
his deed prior to the registration of such deed from the
sheriff or other officer.

It is by section 57 of the same Act declared that all
deeds of lands sold for taxes or under process of law, before
the passing of this Act, (18th September, 1865), shall be
registered within one year after the passing of this Act,
otherwise the parties claiming respectively under any such
sales shall not be deemed to have preserved their priority
as against a purchaser in good faith who may have acquired
priority of registration.

These sections have been re-enacted in sections 58 and 59 of 31 Vic. ch. 20, O.

Section 56 of 29 Vic. ch. 24, refers to future sales and future deeds.

Section 57 refers to past sales.

The purpose of both sections is in all cases of tax or official sales described to make it obligatory on the purchaser to register his deed, and in default for the time limited subjects him to the loss of priority as against a purchaser in good faith who may have first registered.

It is impossible for a purchaser at a sheriff's sale to register his deed until he has procured it. Nothing in the Act contained in direct language makes it his duty to obtain the deed within any fixed time. The default for which, under certain circumstances, he is to be punished by the loss of his title is the omission to register his deed. And this, where section 57 is applicable, must be done within one year after the passing of the Act (18th September, 1865).

The deed—assuming the Act to apply to the case of a sale before the passing of the Act, and a deed afterwards— was obtained and registered on 17th September, 1866, within one year of the passing of the Act.

Had the plaintiff obtained his deed before the passing of the Act, he might still, in the case of a registered title, have been compelled to register as against a subsequent purchaser for value: Consol. Stat. U. C. ch. 89, secs. 35, 44. See also *Jones* v. *Cowden et al.*, 34 U. C. R. 345, affirmed 36 U. C. R. 486. But as he did not obtain his deed till after the passing of the Act, and as it is not shewn that the omission to procure it sooner was any wilful default of his own, to hold that the mere omission to procure the deed and to register it before the Act of 1865, avoided the deed, as against the subsequent purchaser for value, would be to legislate and not to interpret legislation.

The hardship upon the defendant is just as great as if the deed had been procured in 1861 and not registered till 1866 ; but in that case the plaintiff, if he failed to recover,.

would suffer for an obvious default provided against by the Act, whereas in the present case no such default as pro-vided against is shewn in the evidence.

The plaintiff, who bought before the Act of 1865, who did not procure his deed till after the passing of that Act, and who registered his deed within one year after the passing of the Act, in our opinion did all that the Act requires.

This being so, the plaintiff's case comes under the opera-tion of the protecting statutes. There has been a sale for taxes. There has been a deed given under that sale. There were taxes in arrear at the time of the sale. And the sale was by the proper officer. See 27–28 Vic. ch. 28, sec. 43, and *Bell* v. *McLean*, 18 C. P. 416. The deed has not been questioned within the time limited for the purpose, before any Court of competent jurisdiction. The consequence is that the deed, notwithstanding irregularities, if any, in the assessment or sale, is valid to all intents and purposes, except as against the Crown. See 29–30 Vic. ch. 53, sec. 156; 32 Vic. ch. 36, sec. 155, O.

The only exceptions to the operation of these statutes as yet recognized, are where it is shewn that there were in fact no arrears of taxes at the time of the sale: *Hamilton* v. *Eggleton*, 22 C. P. 536; or a sale by an officer having no authority to sell: *Canada Permanent Building Society* v. *Agnew*, 23 C. P. 200.

The defendant failed at the trial to bring the case under the operation of either of these exceptions.

The plaintiff, on proof that an actual sale did take place by the proper officer, that at the time of sale there were taxes in arrear, and that afterwards a deed was made to him by the proper officer, which deed was registered within the time allowed for the purpose, was in our opinion rightly held entitled to succeed in this action. See *Proudfoot* v. *Austin*, 21 Grant 566.

It is remarkable that the defendant did not shew or attempt to shew some wilful neglect or misconduct, if any, on the part of the plaintiff in reference to the procurement of the deed. None such can, in the absence of evidence, be presumed. The deed was procured and registered on 17th September, 1866. The protecting statute in force at that time was 29–30 Vic. ch. 53, sec. 156. Henry Curtis was then the owner of the land, subject to the sale for taxes. He might within four years thereafter, if the sale was defective, have questioned the deed. Instead of doing so he, on 2nd April, 1867, conveyed to Alfred H. St. Germain, who on 3rd April, 1867, registered his deed. It is to be presumed that St. Germain, before buying, searched the registry office for registries on the land. Whether he did so or not, he is bound by the registries then existing. The plaintiff's deed was one of these. Still St. Germain took no proceedings to question it, and on 30th November, 1867, conveyed the land to the defendant, who, on the 2nd December, 1867, registered his deed. Defendant, if the tax deed was in any manner defective, might himself have taken proceedings to question it. But none of the parties did so. The limitation as to time for doing so was allowed to expire. And nearly ten years after the making and registry of the plaintiff's deed, he brings this action of ejectment on the strength of his deed to recover possession of the land described in it.

We see nothing to prevent his recovery. The argument of hardship is of course no ground for resisting the action in a Court of law. No suggestion is made of any defence on the facts in a Court of equity; and mere hardship is not any better ground of defence in equity than at law: See *Silverthorne* v. *Campbell*, 24 Grant 17.

The rule *nisi* must be discharged.

MORRISON, J., and WILSON, J., concurred.

Rule discharged.

JOHN LAGE, FREDERICK PRIES AND FREDERICK THÉDORF
    v. THE REVEREND WILLIAM MACKENSON, HENRY
    HERMAN, JOHN MINTO, MARTIN STADTLANDER, AND
    HENRY HOFFMAN.

*Religious institutions—36 Vic. ch. 135, O.—Removal and appointment of
    trustees—Ejectment—Proof of title.*

The 36. Vic. ch. 135, secs. 10-12, O., respecting the property of religious
    institutions, authorizes only the appointment of successors to trustees
    dead or legally removed, and does not empower the congregation to
    remove trustees competent and willing to act.
The three plaintiffs in this case claimed title under a conveyance to two
    of them, and to H., one of the defendants, as a trustee of a congrega-
    tion named, alleging that H. had been since removed from the office
    of trustee, and the plaintiff T. appointed in his stead. Defendants
    denied the plaintiffs' title. The conveyance contained no clause for
    the removal of trustees or the appointment of new ones, and the con-
    gregation, under the statute above mentioned, had assumed to appoint
    the plaintiff T. in place of H. *Held*, that the plaintiffs must wholly
    succeed or wholly fail as to the title alleged, and that the appointment
    of T. being invalid, a nonsuit must be entered.

EJECTMENT, to recover possession of a part of lot 29 in
the 4th concession of Brant, containing one acre, particularly described in the writ, which was issued on the 22nd
September, 1876.

The first two defendants who were named in the writ
appeared and defended for the whole of the land described
in the writ. The remaining two defendants were afterwards permitted also to appear and defend as landlords.

The plaintiffs claimed title "under a conveyance from
Ernest Harnock to John Lage, Frederick Pries, two of the
plaintiffs, and the defendant Henry Herman, as trustees of
the Evangelical Lutheran Congregation of Saint Peter in
the township of Brant, the said Henry Herman having
been since removed and discharged from the office of such
trustee, and the said plaintiff Frederick Thedorf having
been appointed in his stead," &c.

The defendant Mackenson, besides denying the title
of the plaintiffs, asserted "title under the defendants
John Minto, Martin Stadtlander, and Henry Hoffman,
who are entitled to the possession of the said lands and

premises as trustees thereof for the congregation of the
Evangelical Lutheran Church, called St. Peter's, in the
township of Brant, in the county of Bruce, as the duly
appointed successors of John Lage, Frederick Pries, and
Henry Herman, who were the original trustees of the said
lands and premises under a deed thereof from Ernest
Harnock," &c. The defendant Mackenson claimed the
possession " as tenant thereof to John Lage, Frederick
Pries, and Henry Herman, up to the 25th September, 1876,
and from that time as tenant thereof to the defendants
John Minto, Martin Stadtlander, and Henry Hoffman."

The defendant Henry Herman, besides denying the title
of the plaintiffs, asserted title in himself to the premises
as a trustee thereof for the congregation of the Evangelical
Lutheran Church, called St. Peter's, in the township of
Brant, under and by virtue of a deed made by Ernest
Harnock," &c.

The cause was tried at the last assizes for the county of
Bruce, before Gwynne, J., without a jury.

The counsel for the plaintiffs asked the counsel for the
defendant Mackenson to say whether he intended to claim
as tenant to the plaintiffs or to deny their title, and the
answer was, that he intended to deny the plaintiffs' title.

The plaintiffs' counsel then, as part of his case, proved
the grant from the Crown of the west half of lot 29 in the
4th concession of Brant to John Wilken, or Wilkin, dated
24th July, 1866 ; a deed of the same land from John Wilken
and Mary, his wife, barring dower, to Ernest Harnock,
dated 27th April, 1867, registered 26th June, 1867; and a
deed from Ernest Harnock and Sophia his wife, barring
dower, of the land described in the writ, to John Lage,
Frederick Pries, two of the plaintiffs, and the defendant
Henry Herman, dated 12th February, 1868, registered
18th February, 1868.

The grantees in the latter deed were described as
" trustees for a congregation of Evangelical Lutherans in
the township of Brant." The consideration expressed was
$20. The habendum was to the grantees, " and their

successors in office, to and for the purpose of a chapel for'
the use of the said Evangelical Lutheran Congregation,
according to the rules, regulations, discipline, practices,
and doctrines of the Evangelical Lutheran Church."

The deed contained no clause for the removal of trustees
or for the appointment of new trustees.

The congregation was formed, and a church, manse, and
other necessary buildings erected on the lot.

The defendant Mackenson, in 1872, withdrew from the
Synod of the German Lutheran Church of Canada.

The congregation gradually increased in numbers till
1876, when there were said to be ninety-five men and as
many women members of the congregation.

The defendant Mackenson, in January, 1876, called a
meeting of the congregation, which was attended by about
fifty of the male members of the congregation. This meeting was for the purpose of adopting and subscribing to
rules which he had prepared for church discipline. The
rules were distasteful to many of the congregation, who
refused to be bound by them.

The pastor declined to serve at the baptism, marriage, or
funeral of any' member of the congregation who refused
to subscribe to the rules.

The consequence was a split in the congregation. Forty-
nine members signed the rules, but the remainder of the
congregation refused to do so.

The plaintiffs were, at a meeting called in June, 1876
under section 10 of 36 Vic. ch. 135, O., chosen trustees by
those who were opposed to the pastor and his rules.

The defendants, excluding Herman and the pastor, were,
at a meeting called on the 25th September, 1876, three
days after the issue of the writ of ejectment under the
same statute, chosen trustees by those who were in favour
of the pastor and his rules.

It was objected, among other things, on the part of the
defence, as a ground of nonsuit, that the congregation had
no authority to appoint new trustees until the trustees
under the deed had been legally removed for breach of
trust, or had died.

The learned Judge held that as the defendants Minto, Stadtlander, and Hoffman, only acquired title, if any, after the commencement of the suit, there should be a verdict against them, and that as the defendant Mackenson had put the plaintiffs to proof of title, and as under any circumstances there was title in two of the plaintiffs under the deed there should be a recovery against him ; but he felt great difficulty as to the defendant Herman, who simply claimed under the original deed of trust. Herman's defence raised the question whether he had been legally removed from the trust, and the plaintiff Thedorf appointed his successor, in connection with his co-trustees Lage and Pries. The learned Judge ruled that the pastor Mackenson had no power to deprive the members of the congregation for refusing to sign rules prepared by himself as their pastor, not only of the offices of the church, but also of the civil right to control the property conveyed to trustees "for the purpose of a chapel for the use of an Evangelical Lutheran congregation, according to the rules, regulations, disciplines, practices, and doctrines of the Evangelical Lutheran Church," and therefore that members of the congregation refusing to sign the rules were competent to appoint, and to be appointed, trustees of the property, so that the three plaintiffs had the right to recover against the defendant Herman as well as the other defendants.

The learned Judge entered a verdict for all the plaintiffs against all the defendants.

During Michaelmas term, December 8, 1876, *Ferguson*, Q.C., obtained a rule calling on the plaintiffs to shew cause why the verdict should not be set aside, and a nonsuit or a verdict for the defendants or the defendant Herman entered, on the grounds :—

1. That the verdict is contrary to law and evidence in this, that the evidence shewed that the land in question was granted and conveyed to the plaintiffs Lage and Pries and the defendant Herman, and does not shew Herman's

title to have been divested or vested in any other, and he being so entitled jointly with two of the plaintiffs, and there being no question of ouster raised, there could not be any recovery as against him.

2. That there was misdirection in holding that the professed appointment of the plaintiffs as trustees of the property in question, in manner shewn by the evidence, in lieu of the plaintiffs Lage and Pries and the defendant Herman, was a good and lawful appointment, and that those who professed to make such appointment had, under the circumstances, disclosed power to do so, when on the contrary he should have ruled that there was not any power or authority to remove the original trustees or any of them.

During this term, February 14, 1877, *C. Robinson*, Q. C., shewed cause. The recovery in ejectment is divisible both as to land and parties. The defendant Mackenson having put the plaintiffs to proof of title, cannot now be allowed to claim title under them or any two of them : See the cases referred to *R. & J.* Dig. 1171. The recovery must be supported against him and the recovery against the trustees who acquired title after the commencement of the suit, must also be supported. The defendant Herman not having limited his defence to a joint tenancy with the plaintiffs, and denied ouster, the recovery should also be sustained as against him : *McCallum* v. *Boswell*, 15 U. C. R. 343; *Lyster* v. *Ramage*, 26 U. C. R. 233; *Leach* v *Leach*, 24 U. C. R. 321; *Yeoman* v. *Steiner*, 5 P. R. 466. The original trust deed containing no provision for the removal of trustees, it was competent for the congregation, under section 10 of 36 Vic. O. to remove the trustees and elect others in their stead; and the plaintiffs having been so elected in place of the trustees named in the deed, must recover against all the defendants, including Herman, who was one of the original trustees named in the deed : *Smallwood* v. *Abbott*, 18 U. C. R. 564, and other cases in *R. & J.* Dig. 663, 4.

Ferguson, Q. C., contra. The plaintiffs in this action must succceed on the strength of their own title, which is not under the original deed, but under that deed coupled with the subsequent appointment of the plaintiffs as trustees for the congregation. The plaintiffs could not be appointed successors to the trustees named in the deed till the latter were removed; and although section 10 of 36 Vic. ch. 135, O. provides for the appointment of successors to trustees removed, it does not provide for the removal of trustees. Sec. 29 of the Ejectment Act is inapplicable, because the plaintiffs do not claim simply under the deed in common with defendant Herman. It was unnecessary, therefore, and would have been irregular for defendant to serve a notice under that section. The title set up by the plaintiffs is not sufficient to overcome his title under the deed. There can therefore be no recovery against him.

March 10, 1877. HARRISON, C. J.—The difficulties as to procedure to some extent obstruct the clear view which one would desire to obtain of the facts and the law applicable thereto in this case.

These difficulties can only be removed by obtaining, if possible, a correct understanding of the operation of the several clauses of the Ejectment Act which bear upon the case.

The question for trial in an action of ejectment is, according to the language of sec. 21 of Consol. Stat. U. C. ch. 27 (the Ejectment Act), "whether the statement in the writ of the title of the claimants is true or false, and if true, then which of the claimants is entitled, and whether to the whole or part," &c.

The section appears to make the action divisible both as to persons and parties: see *McNab* v. *Stewart*, 15 C. P. 189; *McBride* v. *Lee*, 16 C. P. 317; *Wilson* v. *Baird*, 19 C. P. 98, 105; but the recovery, whether by all or some of the plaintiffs, must be in respect of "the title" alleged: See sec. 5.

The language of the section, in speaking of the statement of title as in "the writ," is not quite accurate; for the writ demands possession without any statement of title. The statement of title intended to be set up must appear in the notice thereof "attached to the writ": Sec. 4.

The plaintiff, in the absence of amendment, is at the trial to be confined to proof of the title set up, &c.: Sec. 5 as amended by 36 Vic. ch. 8, sec. 62, O. See further *Pettigrew v. Doyle*, 17 C. P. 34, 459; *Hartshorn v. Early*, 19 C. P. 139; *Armstrong v. Armstrong*, 21 C. P. 4.

The defendant by an appearance, without more, denies the title alleged, and puts the plaintiff to proof of that and no other title: *Canada Co. v. Weir*, 7 C. P. 341; *Shore v. McCabe*, 10 C. P. 26; *Colby v. Wall*, 12 C. P. 95; *Fairman v. White*, 24 U. C. R. 123. But if the plaintiff proves the title alleged, and there be no notice of title on the part of the defendant, the latter is without defence: *Burke v. Battle*, 17 C. P. 478.

Where there is a notice of title on the part of the defendant, and the plaintiff's title be proved, then and not till then the question arises as to the sufficiency of the defendant's title: See *Canada Co. v. Weir*, 7 C. P. 341, 343; *Burke v. Battle*, 17 C. P. 478; *Brandon v. Cawthorne*, 19 U. C. R. 368, and *Cartwright v. McPherson*, 20 U. C. R. 251.

Where the defendant not only by his appearance denies the plaintiff's title, but by his notice of title alleges title under the plaintiff, if defendant, on being asked to elect, disclaims the plaintiff's title and puts plaintiff to proof of title, defendant will not be allowed afterwards to set up a tenancy under the plaintiff: *Doe Maitland v. Dillabough*, 5 U. C. R. 214; *Houghton v. Thompson*, 25 U. C. R. 557; *Wilson v. Baird*, 19 C. P. 98. But where defendant, not admitting the plaintiff's title, allowed him to prove it without cross-examining his witnesses, or otherwise taking objection to the title proved, defendant was held not to have disclaimed plaintiff's title and allowed to shew a tenancy under the plaintiff: *Hartshorn v. Early*, 19 C. P. 139.

In case the action has been brought by some, or one of several, persons entitled as joint tenants, tenants in common, or coparceners, any joint tenant, tenant in common or coparcener in possession, may, at the time of appearance or within four days after, give notice, &c., that he or she defends as such and admits the right of the claimant to

an undivided share of the property (stating what share),
but denies actual ouster of him from the property, &c.:
Sec. 29.

Upon the trial in such case the additional question
of whether there was an actual ouster must be determined: *Ib.*

If upon the trial it be found that the defendant is joint
tenant, tenant in common or coparcener, unless actual
ouster be proved, the defendant will be entitled to judgment: Sec. 30.

These latter sections are only applicable where the action
is brought by one or more joint tenants, tenants in common
or coparceners against another or others of them, and the
title set up is consistent with that tenancy: See *Scott* v.
McLeod, 14 U. C. R. 574.

And even where this is the case, unless the defendant
avails himself of the statute by giving the notice which the
statute directs, the plaintiff must under the Act recover
without any proof of ouster: *McCallum* v. *Boswell,* 15 U.
C. R. 343; *Leech* v. *Leech,* 24 U. C. R. 321.

The only case bearing against these authorities is *Lyster*
v. *Ramage,* 26 U. C. R. 233, where I, as counsel for the
plaintiff, pressed some of the preceding authorities upon
the attention of the Court as then constituted, "with" [in
the subdued language of the Court] "quite as much urgency
as the occasion excused," but the Court, notwithstanding my
"urgency," preferred to follow some English cases decided
under the old form of procedure, and refused to give effect
to my argument.

This case does not profess to overrule any of the preceding authorities in our own Courts. So far as it is consistent with them, it may be followed. So far as it is
inconsistent with them, they should, I think, be followed
and it disregarded.

The provisions of our Act as to statements of title on
each side were intended by our Legislature to remove an
evil existing in England, and mentioned in the note to
Finlason's C. L. P. Act 258, that is, "the evil of allowing

titles to be tried without any statement of the ground of claim or defence."

These provisions in our Act direct that recovery shall only be had in accordance with the statement of title. They thereby narrow and simplify the issue for trial, and render some of the English cases, where a different procedure existed, not absolutely safe guides in the construction of our Act.

The recovery with us in ejectment, as in personal actions, is now *secundum allegata et probata.*

The writ, according to its form, is not only to eject the persons named therein, but "all *other* persons," from the possession of the land.

Therefore any other person not named in the writ may, by leave of the Court or a Judge, appear and defend on filing an affidavit, shewing that "he *is* in possession" of the land either by himself or his tenant: Sec. 9.

The Act is defective in not requiring the affidavit to shew that the person applying *was* in possession, by himself or his tenant, at the time of the issue of the writ.

Had this been so, three of the defendants, Minto, Stadtlander and Hoffman, whose title did not accrue till three days after the issue of the writ, would not have obtained leave to appear and defend.

But having been allowed to appear and defend, and there being no motion against the appearance, the appearance for all purposes relates to the issue of the writ: See *Peebles et al.* v. *Lottridge,* 19 U. C. R. 628; *Heron* v. *Elliott,* 1 C. L. J. N. S. 156. See further *Doe* v. *Challis,* 17 Q. B. 166.

No leave should be granted under the statute, either where it appears that the title of the person applying had accrued after the issue of the writ or is hostile to the title of the person or persons named in the writ: *Doe d. Horton* v. *Rhys,* 2 Y. & J. 88. See also *Driver* v. *Lawrence,* 2 W. Bl. 1259.

Where a person who ought not to have been made a defendant is improperly made a defendant, either at his own instance or that of the plaintiff, the person aggrieved may, have his name struck out of the proceedings with costs : See *Hall* v. *Yuill*, 2 P. R. 242 ; *Kerr* v. *Waldie* 4 P. R. 138. See further *Doe d. Horton* v. *Rhys*, 2 Y. & J. 88.

This is the course which ought to have been pursued in reference to the three defendants in this case, whose title, if any, accrued after the issue of the writ; but not having been adopted, we cannot, on the present application, do otherwise than treat all the defendants, by their appearance, as putting the plaintiffs to proof of their *alleged* title : See *Harper* v. *Lowndes*, 15 U. C. R. 430 ; *D'Arcy* v. *White, et al.*, 24 U. C. R. 570.

The leave, when granted, may be either to appear in lieu of the persons named in the writ or in addition to them : *Butler* v. *Meredith*, 11 Ex. 85. See further *Jones* v. *Seaton*, 26 U. C. R. 166. If the order does not say whether in lieu of or in addition to, it ought to be read as meaning in addition to the persons named in the writ : See *Haskins* v. *Cannon*, 2 P. R. 334 ; *Yeoman* v. *Steiner et al.*, 5 P. R. 466.

The mere appearance of a defendant, whether named in the writ or added by the Court or a Judge, puts the plaintiff to the proof of the title alleged in his notice. Title or no title, the defendant must succeed if plaintiff fails to prove his title. He must recover by the strength of his own title, and not by the weakness of defendants. Defendant's possession, real or presumed, is his title till a better title is proved : *Burke* v. *Battle*, 17 C. P. 478.

The plaintiff is confined to proof of the title alleged in his notice, but is at liberty, by any means in his power, to defeat the title set up by the defendants, or any of them. So the defendants, although confined to proof of the title alleged in their notice, are at liberty to defeat (and that without going into their own title) the title set up by the plaintiff: *Canada Co.* v. *Weir*, 7 C. P. 341.

Hence all defendants have in the first instance a common interest to defeat the plaintiff's title. If the title of any one of them have that effect, the others may in some cases not only use this as a shield for their own pro-

tection, but for the purpose of actually defeating the
plaintiff's title: See *Fulton* v. *Cummings*, 34 U. C. R. 331,
341; but see also *Doe Davies* v. *Creed*, 5 Bing. 327; *Doe
Wawn* v. *Horn*, 3 M. & W. 333.

On the other hand, where there is an admission of plaintiff's title by the tenant in possession, this will avail the
plaintiff not only as against him, but as against other defendants in the same interest with him: *Doe Mee* v.
Sutherland, 4 A. & E. 784; *Doe Willis* v. *Birchmore*, 9 A.
& E. 662.

It has been decided by our Court of Appeal, that if the
defendant admitted to appear by Judge's order deny the
plaintiff's right by reason of another right inconsistent
with the plaintiff's claim, and which right appears in the
evidence which the plaintiff is under the necessity of
relying upon as the foundation of his claim, that plaintiff
cannot recover against *any* of the defendants: *Fulton* v.
Cummings, 34 U. C. R. 337, 341.

The consequence is, that plaintiff may have a good title
against a person in actual possession, but after the issue of
a writ may, by the addition of another defendant who has
a better title than himself, be under certain circumstances
defeated in his action against all the defendants.

In such a case the plaintiff, after the addition of the new
defendant or defendants, if unable to strike out the added
name or names as improperly added, proceeds entirely at his
own risk, and to the same extent as if the names of the
added defendant or defendants had appeared in the writ
of ejectment when first issued.

Now to apply these decisions to the case before us.

The plaintiffs do not allege any tenancy in common with
any one of the defendants, but, on the contrary, set up a
title independent of all and hostile to all, and seek by the
strength of that title to dispossess all the defendants.

In the course of the plaintiffs' case it appears that if
they were to drop the title alleged and set up a prior title,
there would be a tenancy in common between two of the
plaintiffs and one of the defendants; but this is clearly not

the title alleged, and to which the proof must be confined at the trial in this action.

The case thus presented is certainly not one for the application of sec. 29 of the Ejectment Act.

The result is, that the plaintiffs must wholly succeed or wholly fail as to the title alleged.

The title alleged is, that there was a conveyance from Ernst Harnock to John Lage and Frederick Pries, two of the plaintiffs, and defendant Henry Herman, as trustees of the Evangelical Lutheran Church of St. Peter, and that Henry Herman was removed and discharged from the office of trustee, and the remaining plaintiff, Frederick Thedorf, appointed in his stead.

This title each and all of the defendants by their appearance, without more, deny. It is therefore for the plaintiffs to prove it, or be nonsuited as to all the defendants.

It involves proof not only of the original deed but of the *removal* of Herman, for there can be no appointment of a trustee in the place of or as successor to Herman, unless Herman be first legally removed : *Smallwood et al. v. Abbott*, 18 U. C. R. 564.

The deed which created the trust and appointed the original trustees is silent not only as to powers of removal but as to the appointment of new trustees. It is however contended that the power of removal as well as power of appointment is to be found in secs. 10, 11, and 12 of 36 Vic. ch. 135, O.

These clauses are substantially enactments of 27–28 Vic. ch. 53 of the late Province of Canada.

Neither Act was, as far as we can judge from the language used, designed to authorize the *removal* of trustees, but only to provide for the appointment of *successors* where, from some cause, there was a vacancy in the office of trustee.

The 27–28 Vic. ch. 53 is entituled "An Act to enable certain religious societies or congregations of Christians *to appoint successors* to trustees of lands held for their benefit."

It recites that land had been conveyed to trustees on behalf of certain congregations or societies of Christians in this Province *without the manner of appointing successors* to such trustees being set forth in the deeds of grant, &c., and it is expedient to provide a remedy *for such omission.*

Section 10 of 36 Vic. ch. 135, is substantially a transcript of sec. 1 of the original Act, 27–28 Vic. ch. 53, sec. 1, with the addition of the words hereafter placed in brackets.

Section 11 of 36 Vic. ch. 135 is a transcript of sec. 2 of the original Act, 27-28 Vic. ch. 53.

Section 12 of 36 Vic. ch. 136, with the exception of some added words hereafter placed in brackets, is a transcript of sec. 3 of the Act 27-28 Vic. ch. 53.

Section 10 of the Act of 1873 is as follows: " It shall be lawful for any congregation or society of Christians, of any denomination, on whose behalf lands in this Province are now, have been, or hereafter shall be held by a trustee or trustees, *without the manner of appointing successors* being set forth in the deed of grant, conveyance, will or devise of such lands, or who may be entitled to any lands without being a body corporate, at any time to assemble in a public meeting duly convened, &c., and at such meeting, by the votes of a majority of the members of such congregation then and there present, to determine in what manner the *successors* to such trustee or trustees shall be appointed, &c." [Or to appoint a trustee or trustees of any lands to which the said congregation or society is entitled, and their successors in the trust.]

Section 11 provides for the record of proceedings, the registry of the same, and the making of copies evidence.

Section 12. " *Such determination* " shall in every case have the *same effect* " *as a clause in the deed of grant,*" &c., " *setting forth the manner of appointing successors to the trustee or trustees named, would have.*" [And any lands to which any religious congregation or society, not being incorporated, is entitled, shall from time to time vest in and be held by the trustee or trustees to be appointed *as here-inbefore mentioned*, and in the successors in the trust, immediately upon the registration of the proceedings in the last preceding section mentioned; and without any or further conveyance or instrument whatsoever.]

It may be argued that the words placed at the end of section 10 and section 12 have the effect of extending the operation of the present statute beyond the design of the original Act of 1864, as recited in that Act.

But all that either Act in language provides for is the *appointment* of trustees.

The addition to section 10 ought, at furthest, to be read as providing for the case of property held in trust where the conveyance appoints no trustees ; and as this is a reading of the section beyond the operation of section 12, which declares that the determination is to have "the same effect as a clause in the deed of grant," &c., " setting forth the manner of appointing successors to the trustee or trustees named," &c., we decline at present to decide the question.

The words at the end of section 12, taken in connection with what goes before, can only be read as applying to trustees legally removed, but still living, in which case new trustees may be appointed under section 10, and, when appointed, the land is to vest in the new trustees "without any or further instrument or conveyance whatsoever," &c.

The Act does not go so far as sec. 32 of the English Trustee Act of 1850 (13 & 14 Vic. ch. 60), which provides "that whenever it shall be expedient to appoint a new trustee or new trustees, and it shall be found expedient, difficult, or impracticable so to do without the assistance of the Court of Chancery, it shall be lawful for the said Court of Chancery to make an order appointing a new trustee or new trustees, either in *substitution* for or in *addition* to any existing trustee or trustees."

The Court of Chancery, before this Act, had a general jurisdiction upon proper grounds to remove a trustee or trustees; but this jurisdiction was never exercised except where the trustee refused to act, or was so situated that he could not effectually execute the trust, misconducted himself, or became bankrupt, &c.: See *Lewin* on Trusts, 6th ed., 691.

And notwithstanding the large powers conferred on the Court by the Act of 1850, it was held that the Court had no authority, under the language used in the Act, to remove a trustee competent to act and willing to act: *Re Hodson's Settlement,* 9 Hare 118; *Re Hadley,* 5 DeG. & Sm. 67; *Re Garty's Settlement,* 3 N. R. 636; *Re Mais,* 16 Jur. 608; *Re Lincoln Primitive Methodists,* 1 Jur. N. S. 1011. And that if there was ground for removing a trustee, and it was desired to remove him, the application could not be under the Act, but by bill in the original jurisdiction of the Court: *Re Blanchard,* 7 Jur. N. S. 505, 3 DeG. F. & J. 131; *Coombes v. Brookes,* L. R. 12 Eq. 61. But see *Re Joyce's Estate,* L. R. 2 Eq. 576; *Re Stewart,* 8 W. R. 297; *Re Harrison's Trusts,* 22 L. J. Ch. 69; *Re Bignold's Settlement Trusts,* L. R. 7 Ch. 223.

The key to the meaning of our Act is to be found in the first part of section 12. Having regard to it we can only read sections 10 and 12 as providing a clause in the deed of grant, &c., "setting forth the manner of appointing successors" to trustees dead or legally removed, and not as authorizing the congregation at its caprice to remove trustees competent and willing to act.

If the Legislature intended greater effect to be given to sections 10 and 12, they have failed to express their meaning, and must we think enlarge the language used, especially in section 12 of the Act.

The title alleged by the plaintiffs, in our opinion, fails. And as all the defendants deny, and by their denial have put the plaintiffs to proof of that title, there must be a nonsuit.

MORRISON, J., concurred.

WILSON, J., was not present at the argument, and took no part in the judgment.

Rule absolute for nonsuit.

MORRISON V. SHAW.

Breach of promise—Evidence—New trial—Misdirection.

In an action for breach of promise of marriage, the only two witnesses
examined were plaintiff's brothers, who swore that the plaintiff being
pregnant, they spoke to defendant, who said he was going to marry
her, and always so intended, and that he would get the license on the
next day but one—the sister was not then present: that on the day
named, Thursday, defendant came to the house, but was kept there by
a rain storm, and promised to get the license and marry her on Monday,
to which the plaintiff, who was present, apparently assented: that on
the Monday he said he was very ill, but it would be all right when he
got better; but that this was the end of it, and they then instructed
this suit, and an action for seduction. The plaintiff was not present
and no witnesses were called for the defence. The jury having found
for defendant, the plaintiff moved for a new trial on the evidence,
filing no affidavit of her own, but the Court refused to interfere.
Held, also that a misdirection as to damages would form no ground for a
new trial, the jury having found against the cause of action.

THIS was an action for breach of promise of marriage.

The declaration contained two counts.

The first count alleged the promise to be " within a reasonable time"; and the second, " on a day now elapsed."

P ea : non-assumpsit.

Issue.

The cause was tried at the last Assizes for the county of
Wellington, before Galt, J., with a jury.

There were only two witnesses examined on the part of
the plaintiff. These were her brothers, Arthur Morrison
and James Morrison. They testified that the plaintiff was
pregnant: that in September, 1874, they spoke to defendant and asked him what he was going to do with their
sister : that he said he was going to marry her, and never
intended to do otherwise: that they asked him when he
would get the license: that he said he would do so on the
next day but one thereafter: that this conversation was on
a Tuesday : that it was not in the presence or hearing of
the sister : that on the following Thursday defendant went
to the house where their sister lived, but a rain storm came
on and they could not go out: that he stopped at the
house all night: that next day he objected to marry her as

it was so near the end of the week, but promised to go to
Mount Forest for a license on Saturday, and they were to
be married on Monday : that the sister was present and
apparently assented : that he did not go for the license on
Saturday : that his excuse was, he was very sick and
thought he would die ; but that it would be all right when
he got better : that this, however, was the end of it : that
thereupon the two 'brothers gave instructions to the plaintiff's attorney for this suit, and for an action for seduction.

This action was commenced on the 14th February, 1876.

There were no witnesses called for the defence.

The case was left by the learned Judge to the jury on
the evidence, he telling them if they believed the testimony
for the plaintiff to find a verdict in her favour for reasonable damages.   On the question of damages he told the
jury there was no evidence that the seduction took place
under a promise of marriage, and that although on the
record the question whether the plaintiff really instituted
the suit would not avail the defendant as a defence, they
might consider this matter in estimating damages.

These observations as to damages were objected to by
counsel for the plaintiff.

The jury found a verdict for the defendant.

During Michaelmas term last, *S. Richards*, Q. C., obtained a rule calling on the defendant to shew cause why
the verdict should not be set aside and a new trial had
between the parties, on the ground that the verdict was
against law and evidence, there being evidence of the
promise alleged in the declaration, and that on the evidence
the plaintiff was entitled to recover ; and also on the ground
of misdirection of the learned Judge, in stating to the jury
that there was no evidence that the seduction took place
under a promise of marriage ; and also in stating to the
jury, that although the question as to whether the plaintiff
instituted the action would not avail the defendant as a
defence, they might consider it in estimating the damages;
and on the ground that the said statements were calculated

to prejudice the plaintiff's case and were not warranted on the evidence ; and on grounds disclosed in affidavits filed.

The only affidavit filed was that of the plaintiff's attorney, in which he swore that the action was commenced by him as attorney for the plaintiff in pursuance of written instructions to that effect, signed by the plaintiff, and dated 12th February, 1876 : that these instructions were signed by the plaintiff in his office and in his presence ; and that he advised the plaintiff that her attendance would not be required at the assizes, as she could not by law be a witness for herself.

There was no affidavit of the plaintiff herself filed on the application.

M. C. Cameron, Q. C., shewed cause. The question whether there was a promise or not was for the jury, and they were not obliged to believe any particular witness or witnesses, but might give their verdict on the whole complexion of the case : *Barber* v. *Armstrong*, 6 O. S. 543 ; *Vincent* v. *Sprague*, 3 U. C. R. 283 ; *Lane* v. *Jarvis*, 5 U. C. R. 127. They having found against the cause of action, and misdirection, if any, as to the damages is no ground for a new trial : *Rogers* v. *Munns*, 25 U. C. R. 153. Besides, although there is an affidavit of the plaintiff's attorney, there is none of the plaintiff herself either as to the promise or the *bona fides* of the application.

C. Robinson, Q. C., contra. The verdict is so much against the law and evidence that it ought, in the discretion of the Court, to be set aside. The charge of the learned Judge must have prejudicially affected the plaintiff.

March 10, 1877. HARRISON, C. J.—We cannot grant a new trial on any of the grounds taken in the rule as grounds for a new trial.

Where there is a jury the jury, subject to the control of the presiding Judge as to matters of law, are the constitutional judges of the facts : *Barber* v. *Armstrong*, 6 O. S. 543. While it is true that they have not an arbitrary

discretion to reject or discredit evidence when there is
nothing in the complexion of the case to give rise to a
doubt—see *Hyde* v. *Paige*, 9 Barb. 150—it is impossible for
the Court on a motion against their verdict to lay down as
a rule that a jury must in all cases believe whatever an
unimpeached witness swears, so long as they have no direct
evidence to the contrary : Per Robinson, C. J., in *Lane* v.
Jarvis, 5 U. C. R. 127, 128.

Jurors may give credit to some parts and discredit other
parts of the evidence, or may under particular circumstances wholly discredit it : *McDermott et al.* v. *Ireson*, 38
U. C. R. 1, 11. It is not now usual for the Court in an
ordinary case to set aside the verdict of a jury on a question of fact submitted for their decision, unless it appear
that there was some misconduct on the part of the jury, or
some misdirection, conducing to the result, on the part of
the presiding judge : *Nolan* v. *Tipping*, 7 C. P. 524.

The learned Judge who presided at the trial of this
cause is not dissatisfied with the verdict. But even if this
were otherwise, it would not *per se* be any ground for
interfering with the verdict : *Hawkins* v. *Alder*, 18 C. B.
640. See further, *Brown* v. *Malpus*, 7 C. P. 185; *Regina*
v. *Chubbs*, 14 C. P. 32.

But it is urged that there was misdirection on the part of
the learned Judge which prejudicially affected the plaintiff
before the jury. It is not every remark made by a learned
Judge in the course of a jury trial that is to be deemed
misdirection : See *Greenough* v. *Parker*, 4 L. T. N. S. 473;
Henman v. *Lester*, 12 C. B. N. S. 776; *Lloyd* v. *Jones*, 7
B. & S. 475.

It is not misdirection entitling a party to a new tril
that the Judge made an inaccurate statement of the law on
some point not directly involved in the issue : *Kopitoff* v.
Wilson, 1 Q. B. D. 383.

Now there were two questions for the determination of the
jury in this case. First, the issue whether or not there was
the promise alleged ; and, secondly, the amount of damages.
The consideration of the second could only become neces-

sary in the event of the jurors having found on the first question in favour of the plaintiff. But as the jury found the first question against the plaintiff, the second did not arise. The misdirection, if any, complained of as to the want of evidence of a promise prior to the seduction, related exclusively to the first and not the second question : *Berry* v. *Da Costa*, L. R. 1 C. P. 331, 333. When this is the case, and nothing more is shewn, there is no ground for a new trial : See *Rogers* v. *Munns*, 25 U. C. R. 153.

While actions for breach of promise of marriage are generally favoured by jurors, they are not equally favoured by all jurors any more than by all Judges. There are some jurors, as well as Judges, who look upon such actions as often involving wrongs more fanciful than real. But most jurors who are asked to give large damages to a woman for loss of prospects or wounded feelings have a natural desire to see the woman who is the real or supposed sufferer, and this desire is generally gratified, although sometimes most painful to the feelings of the woman principally concerned. In this case, for some reason not explained, except in the affidavit of the plaintiff's attorney, the desire, if existing, was not gratified. When it appears, in an action for breach of promise, followed by seduction, or in an action for seduction, as is commonly the case, that the young woman is, in the language of jurors, " old enough to take care of herself," or, as is sometimes the case, " old enough to be the mother of the defendant," jurors are more or less indisposed to do much, if anything, for her. We are not informed of the age either of the plaintiff or defendant in this case. The promise said to have been made by defendant, if made, was made under very peculiar circumstances. Had it been proved by other testimony than that of her two brothers after the alleged seduction, the jury might have attached more weight to the testimony : See *Bessala* v. *Stern*, Weekly Notes, February 24, 1877, p. 46. (a) But we really do not know on what ground the jurors found against the plaintiff.

(a) Since reported L. R. 2 Q. B. D. 265.

We cannot decide that the evidence adduced on the part
of the plaintiff was such under all the circumstances that
the jury were obliged to believe it. Therefore we cannot
infer that there was misconduct on the part of the jury
because they did not believe it. A verdict cannot be said
to be against evidence, or the weight of evidence, so long
as it is in the power of the jury not capriciously, but in
the exercise of a sound discretion, and in view of all the
circumstances of the case, to disbelieve evidence. It is not
like the case where a jury has disregarded admitted facts
and their legal effect: *Holmes* v. *McKechin*, 23 U. C. R.
321 ; *Hughes* v. *Canada Permanent Loan and Savings
Society,* 39 U. C. R. 221.

This is not a case in which it can be properly said that
the jury has overlooked any admitted fact or facts. It is
not a case in which it can be said that admitted facts, if
any, pointed in a direction opposite to the finding of the
jury. It is not a case in which it can be said that the jury
in deciding the case have not given sufficient weight to any
admitted fact or facts. It is not a case of any importance
except to the parties immediately concerned.

Then as to the affidavit. The reason assigned in the
affidavit for the non-appearance of the plaintiff at the trial
was the advice of her attorney that she could not be a witness, and so need not attend. If her appearance or her
presence would have aided her action, as is sometimes the
case before jurors, we have no doubt that different advice
would have been given. Attorneys, where clients are
young or good looking generally, conceive it to be their
duty, especially in actions of this kind, to endeavour by
the presence of the young woman to strengthen the
favourable impression which the jurors are asked to take
of the evidence. But the reason given for the non-
appearance of the plaintiff at the trial, whether good or
bad, whether discreet or the reverse, is not assigned as
an excuse for non-production of her affidavit on the
present application. There was an opportunity to her
to have shewn to us by affidavit when the promise, if

any, was really made to her—that such promise without
doubt preceded her seduction ; and although such an
affidavit would not be, strictly speaking, legal evidence,
we apprehend we might have looked at it as favouring
the *bona fides* of the deponent's application for a new
trial: See *Hawker* v. *Seale,* 17 C. B. 595 ; *Smith* v. *Wood-
fine,* 1 C. B. N. S. 660. See further *Ling* v. *Croker,* 2 C. B.
N. S. 760 ; *Berry* v. *DaCosta,* L. R. 1 C. P. 31 ; *Lane* v.
Jarvis, 5 U. C. R. 129.

All that the affidavit filed discloses is the fact that two
days before the issue of the writ the attorney for the plaintiff received a written retainer from the plaintiff, which
retainer was signed by her in his presence. Had this fact
been made known to the learned Judge who presided at
the trial, he might not have made the comments which he
did as to the bringing of the action ; but as these comments, like the comments as to the absence of evidence of
a promise prior to the seduction, affected only the measure
of damages, and not the cause of action, we cannot interfere on that ground.

Where the application for a new trial is to the discretion
of the Court, that discretion must be exercised or not
according to the facts presented in each particular case.
Without saying what we might do in a different case, we
must say that in this case we see no ground for ordering a
new trial. The most we can do for the relief of the
plaintiff is, under the circumstances, to permit the present
rule to be made absolute to enter a nonsuit, the plaintiff to
pay the costs of this application : See *Thibodeau* v. *Skead*,
39 U. C. R. 387, 397.

JEMIMA HARRISON V. WILLIAM DOUGLASS.

Husband and wife—35 Vic. c. 16, s. 2, O.—Separate trade—Fraudulent contrivance.

Sec. 2 of 35 Vic. ch. 16, O., exempting from the husband's debts all proceeds or profits of any occupation or trade carried on by the wife separately from the husband, applies to all married women, whether married before or after the passing of the Act.

But this section does not apply to any occupation or trade in which the husband is held out to the world as the person conducting it, or which she cannot carry on without his active co-operation or agency. The husband need not be physically absent in order to make it her separate trade or occupation, but she cannot be properly held to carry it on separately from him, so long as he does all that is essential to its success.

Where, therefore, the husband lived on the farm with his wife, and managed it, a finding that she was carrying on the farm for herself was set aside.

As to the stock and farming utensils, which were claimed by the wife, it appeared that they had been sold under an execution against the husband, to whom they then belonged, and had been purchased by his two brothers-in-law, one of whom paid a small part of the purchase money, the other nothing, and the remainder was paid by the husband, who remained in possession as before. One of the purchasers it was said, afterwards transferred his interest to the wife, for the alleged consideration of a right to dower, which was not clearly shewn to exist, and the possession remained as before. *Held*, that the whole dealings shewed a design to protect the husband's property against his creditors, and a finding in the wife's favour was reversed.

INTERPLEADER.

The question for trial was, whether certain goods and chattels, seized and taken in execution by the sheriff of the county of Kent under a *fi. fa.*, dated 29th July, 1876, were on the day of seizure the property of the plaintiff as against the defendant, the execution creditor.

The issue was tried at the last assizes for the county of Kent before *Irving*, Q. C., acting for and at the request of Burton, J.

There was no jury.

The goods and chattels in dispute consisted in part of a buggy, a set of double harness, a bay mare, two hogs and six pigs, some oats, some beans and wheat, two stacks of hay, and two acres of corn; and for these the learned Queen's Counsel rendered a verdict for the plaintiff.

There were besides a sorrel horse, a waggon, a plough, a

harrow, and a sleigh. And as to these the learned Queen's Counsel found a verdict for the defendant.

The plaintiff was a married woman. She married Thomas Harrison, the execution debtor, about 27 years since, without any marriage contract or settlement. In 1871 he got into pecuniary difficulties. He was a farmer and living on 52 acres of the north-east part of broken front lot 93, south of the Talbot road, in the township of Howard. His brother William Harrison, and his brother-in-law, William Mooney, had been endorsing for him. A judgment was recovered in 1871 against the three of them in respect of a debt due by the husband of the plaintiff. His goods, chattels, and farming utensils were sold by the sheriff, under that judgment. William Harrison and William Mooney attended the sale, and the property was knocked down to them in separate lots. A portion of the purchase money was paid by William Harrison, and a large portion of it by Thomas Harrison, but none of it by William Mooney.

The property so purchased was allowed, notwithstanding the sale, to remain in the possession of the execution debtor on lot 93.

In 1872, lot 93, having been mortgaged, was sold by the mortgagee, and became the property of William Harrison. He thereupon leased the farm and the chattels to his brother Thomas Harrison at an annual rental of $260.

On 28th February, 1874, Thomas Harrison and his wife, the latter barring her right to dower, executed to William Harrison a quit claim of lot 93 for an expressed consideration of $150.

On the same day William Harrison executed in favour of the wife a bill of sale of the property purchased by him at the sheriff's sale for $150. but no money was paid.

The latter transfer it was said was the consideration for the execution by the wife of the quit claim as to dower.

It was not shewn whether she had joined with her husband in the mortgage under which the farm was sold.

The husband lived on the farm, and continued with the use of the stock and farming implements to manage it till

1874, when the farm was sold by William Harrison, to one Crawford.

The plaintiff and her husband then removed, taking the chattels with them, to lot 58 in the same township, in which the plaintiff had a one-third interest by inheritance, and afterwards acquired another third interest by purchase from her sister, subject to a mortgage for the whole of the purchase money,

The husband continued on that farm to manage as before, but it was said took the advice of his wife as to the crops to put in.

The learned Queen's Counsel found that the plaintiff was the occupant of the farm on which the crops in question were grown, and that she was carrying on farming there in good faith for herself.

He also apparently found in favour of the *bona fides* of the sale to William Harrison, and that at the time of the sale from William Harrison to the plaintiff there was an actual and continued change of possession of the things sold.

Most of the articles seized, except the crops, had been acquired by the plaintiff from William Harrison, under the circumstances already detailed.

The bay mare was said to have been a purchase by her after the sale of the farm implements and stock, and the two hogs and six pigs, the progeny of a pig which had been a gift to one of her children.

The plaintiff had no property at the time of her marriage, except a cow and some sheep. She sold her interest in lot 53 to one Sommerville, who paid $100 on account of the purchase money, but for some reason never completed the purchase. This was the first and only money she ever got otherwise than from her husband. She did not however apply any portion of it in the purchase of the goods in dispute.

The farm on which the property was seized was assessed in the name of the husband, but it was represented to have been so only for the purpose of giving him a vote.

·: During Michaelmas Term. last, November·30, 1876,· C. *Robinson,·* Q. C., obtained a rule. calling .on ,the·plaintiff to shew cause why the verdict obtained in this cause.by the plaintiff should. not be .set aside, and entered for the defendant, pursuant to.the ·Law Reform Amendment Act,. on the ground that the. plaintiff shewed no right to the goods, or any of them, in respect of which the, verdict was entered for the plaintiff. ·

During this term, February 8, 1877,. *Atkinson* shewed cause. The sale of ·the. husband's. goods in 1871 . was *bonâ fide.* The plaintiff afterwards legally acquired· the same. The crops belonged to her as .the farmer, and she was the owner of all the property seized. He cited *Fraser* v. *Hilliard,* 16 Grant .101.;. *Lett* v., *The Commercial Bank,* 24 U. C. R. 552; *Adams* v.· *Loomis,* 22 Grant 99 ; 35 Vic. ch. 16, sec. 2; *McCready* v. *Higgins,* 24 C. P. 233.

. *C. Robinson,·* Q. C., contra. The property, which before 1871 belonged.to the husband, never ceased to be his; and the. husband was also the owner of the crops, for. he, and not his wife, was the farmer. So .of the .horse which the wife afterwards purchased, and as to the pigs the wife shews no right whatever to them : *Lett* v. *The Commercial Bank,* 24 U. C. R. 552; *Dingman* v. ·*Austin,* 33 U. C. R. 190. The finding is clearly.against law and evidence, and should be reversed :. *Irwin* v. *Maughan,* 26 C. P. 455.·

·March 10, 1877. .HARRISON,. C. J.—The onus is by the issue on the plaintiff to establish her .right to the property in dispute.

.If .the .evidence adduced. in support of· her. claim be not clear and. satisfactory, in such a case as the present the verdict.should. be against her.

·The marriage took place long before 1872. The husband therefore was not, according to *Dingman* v. *Austin,* ·33 U. C. R. 190, deprived by the Act of that year, 35 Vic. ch. .16, .O., of his interest in his wife's land. It follows .that he.was ·rightly. in possession of the land of his wife, before and at the time of the seizure.. .

The property in the disposal of the case may be conve-
niently divided into two classes, each governed by different
considerations.

The first consists of the crops and grain, and the second
of the farming utensils and farm stock.

The argument as to the first is, that under sec. 2 of 35
Vic. ch. 16, the wife was carrying on the farm "separately
from her husband," and that in the management of it he
was no more than her servant or agent.

The first question on this is, whether sec. 2 of the Act of
1872, is applicable to a marriage which took place before
the passing of that Act.

Section 2 declares, that "all the wages and personal
earnings of a married woman, and any acquisitions therefrom, and all proceeds or profits from any occupation or
trade which she carries on separately from her husband,
&c., shall hereafter be free from the debts or dispositions of
the husband, and shall be held and enjoyed by such married
woman, and disposed of without her husband's consent, as
fully as if she were a *feme sole*."

We are of opinion that the words "a married woman"
as used in this section, mean *any* married woman, whether
married before or after the passing of the Act.

Dingman v. *Austin*, 33 U. C. R. 190, is no decision to
the contrary, for it was decided under a different section of
the Act—sec. 1.

While we agree in thinking that so much of sec. 1, as
might deprive the husband of his interest in land, where
the marriage took place before the Act, is not so to be read
as to interfere with vested rights, we concur with Blake,
V. C., in *Adams* v. *Loomis*, 22 Grant 99, in thinking that
the portions of the Act which have not that effect ought
not necessarily to be so restricted, but rather read as applicable to all married women, whether married before or
after the passing of the Act.

But we are also of opinion, that section 2 ought not to
read as applying to any occupation or trade in which the
husband is held out to the world as the person conducting it.

If the occupation or trade be such that the wife cannot carry it on without the husband's active co-operation or agency, it is not easy to discover in what sense it can honestly be called an occupation or trade, carried on by her "separately from her husband."

We do not mean to say that the husband should, in the language of Blackburn, J., in *Laporte* v. *Costick*, 31 L. T. N. S. 434, be "physically absent" in order to make the occupation or trade the separate occupation or trade of the wife, but we do not think she can be properly held to carry it on "separately from him," so long as *he* does all that is really necessary to its success.

Attempts, however ingenious, to convert the wife of a farmer into "the husbandman," and the husband into her mere servant, agent, or manager, so as to enable him to live on the farm, work the farm, derive his support from it, and do so in defiance of his creditors, are not to be encouraged.

The first part of the section in question, is substantially a transcript of sec. 1, of the English Act, 33 & 34 Vic., ch. 93, under which *Laporte* v. *Costick*, the case to which we have referred, was decided. By that case the Married Women's Act of 1870 has received the construction which we are disposed to put on the Act now before us.

The execution debtor in that case had rented a house in his own name for the purpose of his wife letting lodgings therein. She directed the repairs to be done, but the builder charged them to the husband. The furniture, which was seized upon a judgment against the husband, had been purchased by the wife with her earnings acquired from the lodgings after the passing of the Married Women's Act of 1870. The name of the husband was in the rate-book and register to enable him to vote. He lived with the wife in the house, wrote his wife's correspondence, kept her accounts, and under her directions gave orders to tradesmen for her. He was, however, unfit from ill-health to take any active part, and he did not take any active part in the general management of the house. The County Judge before whom the interpleader as to the household furniture was tried, like the learned Queen's Counsel here, found as a fact that the business was the separate business of the wife and that the husband was no more than his wife's agent for the conduct of some portions of the business. But the Court of Queen's Bench on appeal unanimouly reversed his decision, holding that there was no evidence upon which the County Court Judge could properly decide as he had done.

The case here is a weaker one for the plaintiff than the case to which we have just adverted. In that case the husband did little in the management of the business; whereas here the husband did all to make the business successful. The assertion that in doing so he consulted his wife, as to the crops to be put in, is sufficiently ludicrous to raise a smile, but not sufficiently strong to sustain a verdict.

It is a question of fact on the evidence, whether a particular occupation or trade is the separate occupation or trade of the wife : *Smallpiece* v. *Dawes*, 7 C. & P. 40 ; *Lett* v. *The Commercial Bank*, 24 U. C. R. 552 ; *Foulds* v. *Curtelett*, 21 C. P. 368. But where there is really no evidence or no sufficient evidence, even where a jury have found in favour of the separate occupation or trade, it is the duty of the Court to set aside the verdict and enter a nonsuit. See *Irwin* v. *Maughan*, 26 C.P., 455.

In this case, as there was no jury, we feel no difficulty, under the Law Reform Amendment Act, in entering a verdict for the defendant as to the crops, grain &c.

The right of the plaintiff to the stock and the farming utensils must depend on the *bona fides* of the sale by the sheriff, or rather of the purchase from the sheriff. The property then sold was unquestionably the property of the husband. If the sale was not a *bona fide* one, it is therefore still his property. The property was sold to two persons, of whom one, a brother-in-law of the plaintiff, paid a small portion of the purchase money, the other, also a brother-in-law, nothing; and the remainder was paid by the husband, who was not present at the sale as a purchaser. Notwithstanding the sale the property sold continued in possession of the husband in like manner and to the same extent as before the sale. It is true that after a time there was said to be a letting of the farm and the implements &c. by one of the purchasers at the sale to the husband. But this person afterwards, without any money consideration, and for the professed consideration of a right to dower which was not clearly shewn to exist, transferred his interest in the farm, implements &c. to the wife, and still there was no change of possession.

It appears to us that the whole of these dealings indicate a contrivance on the part of those concerned, to make the wife the owner of the husband's chattel property, without a bill of sale direct to her from the husband, without any change of possession, and without the payment of any money by her. Such a transaction cannot be supported as against the creditors of the husband: See *Graham et al.* v. *Furber*, 14 C. B. 410; *Clark* v. *Morrell*, 21 U. C. R. 596; *McKee* v. *Garcelon*, 11 Am. 200.

While most willing in a reasonably clear case to give effect to the declared intention of the Legislature, we are most anxious not to permit an Act of the Legislature to be converted either into a cloak of deceit or instrument of fraud.

If the mere assertion that a husband acted as his wife's agent was enough to protect his property from creditors, there would be a very easy means of avoiding the evident intention of the Act. Per Lush, J., in *Laporte* v. *Costick*, 31 L. T. N. S. 437.

We feel no doubt in holding here, that the general design of the parties was to protect the property of the husband from the claims of his creditors, and that the sale in 1871, as well as the subsequent management of the farm by the husband as professed agent of the wife, were fraudulent and specially intended to support the general design.

If the case were one resting entirely on the question of credibility of witnesses, we would not interfere with the finding of the learned Queen's Counsel, who saw the witnesses and heard their testimony. But as the case turns rather on general facts and circumstances, which in our opinion all point in a direction contrary to the finding, we have no hesitation in reversing the finding.

MORRISON, J., and WILSON, J., concurred.

BAILEY ET AL. V. THOMAS GRIFFITH.

Joint debtors—Relationship of principal and surety created after debt accrued—Right of surety to be treated as such.

Semble, that where *after* a right of action accrues to a creditor against two or more persons he is informed that one of them is or has become a surety only, and *after that* he gives time to the principal debtor without the consent and knowledge of the surety, he thereby discharges the surety, even though he may not have assented or been a party to the change of relationship between them.

Swire v. *Redman*, L. R. 1 Q. B. D., 536, commented upon.

In this case, however, it was *held*, upon the evidence set out below, that the plaintiffs not only knew of but assented to the change of relationship.

T., being in business, failed and made a composition with his creditors, giving his notes endorsed by W., and further secured by an assignment of certain mortgages made by T. to W.   Afterwards W. got a transfer of all T.'s business and assumed all his liabilities.

The plaintiffs were creditors of T. and received the notes for the composition.

By a written document the plaintiffs authorized the discharge of one of the mortgages made by T. to W., and assigned to secure the notes, in consideration of W. giving another mortgage in lieu thereof; and they authorized also the discharge of another of the mortgages, so far as regarded part of the property in it, in order that W. by mortgaging it again might raise money to meet the last payment on the notes. When the last note fell due, which W. by his arrangement with T. should have paid as the principal debtor, the plaintiffs by agreement with W. drew upon him for the amount at five months.   The learned Judge found that the plaintiffs knew of and assented to the arrangement between T. and W. that W. then assumed T.'s debts, and thus became the principal debtor.   In an action by the plaintiffs against T. as maker of the last of the composition notes given to them :

Held, that the plaintiffs had discharged the defendants by the time given.

And *Semble*, that the plaintiffs would also by consenting to the release of the mortgages, as above mentioned, have discharged T. to the extent to which he was thereby prejudiced.

THIS was an action brought on a promissory note, dated 1st July, 1873, for $507.24, made by the defendant, payable eighteen months after date, to William Griffith, and by the latter endorsed to the plaintiffs.

Pleas :—1. Did not make.

2. Plaintiffs not the holders.

3. Payment.

4. Acceptance by plaintiffs of a bill of exchange of William Griffith for $520.94, four months after date, and dated 4th January, 1875, in satisfaction.

5. The same plea in a different form.

The following pleas were added at the trial:—

6. On equitable grounds : that after the making and before the maturity of the said note, by a certain deed, dated the 1st day of October, 1873, and made between the defendant and the said William Griffith, the said William Griffith, for the consideration therein expressed, covenanted with the defendant that he would assume and pay certain composition promissory notes made by the defendant, among which the note sued on in this action was included, and would indemnify the defendant against all his debts, including the said note, and save him harmless from all actions in respect thereof, and at once repay him any moneys, costs, and charges he might pay through the default of the said William Griffith in observing such covenent : that the plaintiffs had notice of such deed and the said covenant therein before the maturing of said note : that after the plaintiffs had notice of such deed and covenant, and on the maturing of said note, and while the plaintiffs were the holders thereof, the plaintiffs, without the consent of the defendant, and for a good and sufficient consideration in that behalf, agreed with the said William Griffith to give him, and then accordingly gave him, time for the payment of the said note. And the defendant says that by the operation of the said deed as between him and the said William Griffith, the said William Griffith became primarily liable to pay said note, and the defendant only liable as surety in respect thereto ; and that the plaintiffs, by giving time to the said William Griffith for the payment of said note, under the circumstances above set forth, discharged the defendant from all liability in respect thereto.

7. Upon equitable grounds : that the payment of the

promissory note and certain other notes was secured colla-
terally, to the knowledge of the plaintiffs, by a certain
indenture by way of mortgage made by the said William
Griffith, in favour of one John Kerr, whereby the said
William Griffith conveyed certain lands and tenements to
the said Kerr as trustee for the plaintiffs and other
creditors of the defendant, to secure the payment of the
said note and other promissory notes : that after the
making of the said note, by deed, dated on or about the 1st
of October, 1873, and made between the defendant and the
said William Griffith, the said William Griffith, for the
consideration therein expressed, covenanted with the defendant that he would pay said note, and indemnify the
defendant against the same, and save him harmless from
all actions in respect thereof : that the plaintiffs had notice
of said last named deed and of the covenants therein, and
that after the plaintiffs had such notice, and while they
were the holders of said note, and before its maturity, the
plaintiffs, without the knowledge or consent of the defendant, along with other creditors of the defendant, procured
the said Kerr to release, and the said Kerr did at their
request release said mortgage to the said William Griffith :
that the said William Griffith from, to wit, the maturity
of said note, and at all times since, has been insolvent and
unable to pay said note and perform said covenant : that
the property so conveyed by way of mortgage to the said
Kerr, and so released from such mortgage, was of such
value that if the mortgage had not been released the plaintiffs could readily have realized thereout the full amount
of their claim in respect of said note, or the defendant, if
he had been compelled to pay said claim, could have indemnified himself thereout against all loss through having been
obliged to pay such claim.   And the defendant says that
the plaintiffs, by their said dealings with said mortgage
and the property thereby mortgaged, have prevented the
defendant from resorting to said mortgaged property to
indemnify himself against the payment of the claim sued
for herein, and that the plaintiffs ought not, having regard

-to the circumstances above set forth, to be permitted in equity to call on the defendant to pay such note.

The cause was tried at the last Toronto Assizes, before Wilson J., without a jury.

The following is his Lordship's summary of the evidence :

Thomas Griffith, the defendant, who formerly carried on business in the name of Thomas Griffith & Co., failed and went or was put into insolvency. He made a composition with his creditors for 67½ cents on the dollar, to be secured by his five promissory notes of equal amount at six, nine, twelve, fifteen, and eighteen months, and endorsed by his brother William Griffith, and to be further secured by William Griffith assigning over to the official assignee, Mr. Kerr, certain mortgages which Thomas had made to William, for endorsements which William had made to Thomas while Thomas was in business before his insolvency.

That arrangement was carried out, and the notes were given, all dated on the 1st July, 1873.

Thomas then again began business on Front street, in Toronto ; but he and his brother William not agreeing together, they referred matters to arbitration, and the result was that William got a transfer of the whole business of Thomas Griffith & Co., and assumed all the liabilities of that company, and paid to Thomas $2,000—$500 in cash and three promissory notes for $500 each.

An advertisement to that effect appeared in the *Globe*, *Mail*, and *Leader* newspapers in October, 1873, immediately after that arrangement was made ; and the advertisement required that all claims should be sent in, against Thomas Griffith & Co., to William Griffith, who would settle the same, as he had become the transferee of the estate.

Immediately after that Thomas Griffith set about to establish a business for himself ; and hearing that Whately & Co., of Toronto, were desirous of closing their business, he entered into negotiations with them for the purchase of it.

The plaintiffs were the principal if not the only creditors of Whately & Co., and Thomas Griffith was obliged to negotiate with them, or rather with Mr. Bunting, for that business. Mr. Bunting valued that stock for Whately & Co., and the Hon. Frank Smith valued it on behalf of the defendant Thomas Griffith. Their stock was valued at $6,678.97, and the defendant paid for it by giving a cheque for $2,000, and by giving in November, 1873, his three promissory notes for $1,557.99, at two, four, and six months, the cheque and notes being all endorsed over by Whately & Co. to the plaintiffs, and all of them being duly paid by the defendant.

The plaintiffs had been creditors of Thomas Griffith & Co. before their insolvency, and on the composition they received defendant's promissory notes, endorsed by William Griffith and secured by the transfer of the mortgages before mentioned to the official assignee. The note sued upon was the last of these notes, the other four having been duly paid by William Griffith as the transferee of Thomas's estate, as before mentioned, and in pursuance of the arrangement entered into between Thomas and William to that effect, and according to the advertisement of such arrangement. There was a formal deed of the arrangement entered into between Thomas and William for the purpose of the arrangement being duly carried out and observed.

Thomas then being duly started in his new business by buying out Whately & Co., carried it on, and is still carrying it on.

William carried on his business separately, and when the last composition note given by Thomas on the settlement of his insolvency, endorsed by William as before mentioned, became due on the 1st to 4th of January, 1875, to the plaintiffs, being the note sued upon, which William by his arrangement with Thomas should have paid as the principal debtor, and not only as endorser, he was not able to pay it; and he arranged with Mr. Bunting that the plaintiffs should draw upon him at four months for the amount of the note then overdue and now sued upon. The plaintiffs did so some little time after the maturity of the note, but antedated to the day of the falling due of the note. The interest of the note for $507.24, and the protest of the note, made the amount of the draft $520.94; and William Griffith accepted it. It fell due on the 4th to 7th of May, 1875, and was not paid.

William Griffith became insolvent on the 23rd July, 1875, and the plaintiffs proved upon his estate for the acceptance of $520.40, and not upon the note on or for which it was given. The note was however filed with ᴸ. r. Kerr, the same person who was the official assignee of the estate of Thomas as well as of the estate of William, among the claim papers of the plaintiffs against William Griffith, and that note was afterwards got by Mr. Meyers, attorney for the plaintiffs, from the official assignee before the commencement of this suit, and this action was commenced on it against Thomas Griffith, the maker.

The defendant contended that the plaintiffs received the acceptance of William in full satisfaction and discharge of the note. •

The learned Judge found, as proved, that an arrangement was made between William and Thomas by which William got the whole of the estate from Thomas, and was to pay all Thomas's liabilities; that the plaintiffs had notice of it at or about the time it was made, and at or about the time the advertisement of it was published, either by means of the advertisement or by means of Thomas Griffith telling Mr. Bunting of it when he (Thomas) was buying the establishment and business of Whately & Co. Thomas swore expressly that he told Mr. Bunting all about the arrangement between himself and William. And Mr. Bunting admitted in his cross-examination that he had such knowledge.

After Thomas's insolvency, and after the giving of the composition notes in settlement of his insolvency, and after William had agreed with Thomas to take all his estate and pay all his liabilities, and after the advertisement of such arrangement, and after Thomas had bought out the business of Whately & Co., and after the plaintiffs had notice and knowledge of the arrangement between William and Thomas, the creditors of Thomas, at the instance and request of William, and without notice to and consent of Thomas, entered into the following agreement with William; the plaintiffs being the third persons who signed and sealed the document.

The document, which is dated the 18th of November, 1873, begins:

"Insolvent Act of 1869. In the County Court of the County of York. In the matter of Thomas Griffith & Co., insolvents, and William Griffith, assignee of the estate of the said insolvents."

The document recites that the undersigned creditors of Thomas Griffith & Co., in consideration that William Griffith will give a mortgage on his Front-street property to John Kerr, as assignee for the creditors of the said insolvents, for the sum of $3,000, to be held by the said John Kerr in trust as collateral security for the payment of the composition notes of the said estate of the said insolvents, endorsed by said William Griffith— "do hereby consent and agree with the said William Griffith that the said John Kerr discharge, &c., the mortgage dated the 18th of January, 1873, made by Thomas Griffith to William Griffith, for $10,000 on the house and premises of Thomas Griffith in Yorkville, and which was assigned by William Griffith to John Kerr on the 30th September, 1873, as collateral security for the said composition notes. And we hereby authorize and direct the said John Kerr to take from the said William Griffith the said mortgage on the said Front-street property," &c.

By another instrument it was arranged between William Griffith and the said creditors of Thomas Griffith & Co., without notice to Thomas Griffith and without his knowledge or consent, that some further change should be made in the securities of his estate, to which instrument the plaintiffs were parties, who signed and sealed it. It was as follows :—

"Insolvent Act of 1869. In the County Court of the County of York. In the matter of Thomas Griffith & Co., insolvents, and William Griffith, assignee of their estate. We, the undersigned creditors of the estate of the above named insolvents, Thomas Griffith & Co., do hereby consent and agree that John Kerr, Esq., our trustee in this matter, shall and may be at liberty to discharge, &c., that portion of the mortgage dated 30th September, 1873, made by the said William Griffith and his wife to the said John Kerr, on his, the said William Griffith's, dwelling house and premises on the corner of College street and Spadina avenue, to secure the payment of the composition notes of the said estate endorsed by the said William Griffith, to the intent and purpose that the said William Griffith may have his dwelling house and premises unincumbered, to again mortgage the same in order to raise money to meet the last payment due to the creditors of the said insolvents on the said composition notes.

"And we, the said creditors, do hereby authorize and direct the said John Kerr to discharge the said mortgage so made to him as aforesaid by the said William Griffith, and to reconvey the estate thereby mortgaged to the said William Griffith, his heirs and assigns for ever'."

The question on these facts was, whether the defence of accord and satisfaction was proved.

The learned Judge, after stating the facts as above, rendered the following decision :—

William Griffith was unquestionably at first the endorser and surety ; and by express agreement with the creditors of and for Thomas Griffith, who was the principal debtor, they, as between themselves, certainly and expressly changed their position. William, the former surety, became the principal debtor, and Thomas, the former principal debtor, became the surety for William.

That change, although brought to the knowledge of these plaintiffs, the creditors of both William and Thomas Griffith, may be taken as not affecting the position of William and Thomas towards their creditors. The authority of *Swire* v. *Redman*, L. R. 1 Q. B. D. 536, to which Mr. Ferguson has referred, which is a very able and satisfactory judgment, determines that two principal debtors cannot by a change between themselves, constituting one the principal debtor and the other his surety, alter their original position towards the common creditor. If that is really to be considered to be the law—which it cannot properly be said to be yet, in the face of *Liquidators of Overend, Gurney & Co.* v. *Liquidators of the Oriental Financial Corporation*, L. R. 7 H. L. 348—notwithstanding the change they may make between themselves and to the knowledge of the creditor, the creditor may give, according to that case, time to one without discharging the other, or he may take the note of one or draw upon him alone for the debt without affecting the other at all, according to that case, which may be right so far. And so the mere fact of the plaintiffs drawing upon William Griffith, the endorser and surety originally—and assuming him still to be the surety—will not and could not affect the position or liability of Thomas Griffith, the principal debtor. Nor will it make any difference to the plaintiffs as creditors if at the time they gave time to William Griffith, the original surety, he had become, as between himself and Thomas, the principal debtor, and Thomas the surety—although the plaintiffs, at the time they so drew upon William, had become aware of the change of position—so long as they, the plaintiffs, were no parties to the change and did not assent to it. The case of *Swire* v. *Redman* was determined wholly upon the ground that the change of position from that of joint debtors to that of sole principal debtor of one and of surety of the other of them, as between themselves, did not change their position towards their common and original creditor; because, although he had knowledge of the change, he was no party to it, and never assented to it, nor altered his rights with respect to them in any way; and upon that ground and in that manner *Swire* v. *Redman* is distinguished from *Oakeley* v. *Pasheller*, 4 Cl. & F. 207, decided in the House of Lords, in which case the creditor assented to and was a party to the change which was made.

I am not sure that it can be said that in no case is the creditor bound to take notice of the change of position and rights of his debtors. Let me suppose that the two common debtors in *Swire* v. *Redman*, L. R. 1 Q. B. D. 536, had given a mortgage upon real estate belonging to their partnership; and upon effecting the change between themselves that one should be principal and the other surety, it was agreed between the two that the mortgage which the creditor held from them should hereafter be held by him as an indemnity for the one who had become the surety; and the creditor was notified of the change of position, and he was desired to retain that mortgage as an indemnity for the one who had become the surety, he would in my opinion, whether he approved of or assented to the change or not, be bound to deal with that mortgage so that the debtor who had become surety should receive the benefit of it. And if he after that gave it up to the one who remained debtor by the agreement of the two, or cancelled it, or made away with it in any way, he would be bound to answer for it to the one who had become the surety.

I do not think, therefore, that it can be laid down broadly that in every case the creditor can refuse to recognize the arrangements which are made by his two debtors, whether they stood originally in the place of common debtors, or one as debtor and the other as surety, if they choose to create new rights between themselves and give him notice of it. The creditor will not be bound to regard their agreements so far as they relate to their *status* towards him; but he must be bound to deal with securities he holds for his claim according to their relative rights and interest of the parties in these securities, whether he is an assenting party or not to the agreement which creates such new rights.

This case, in my opinion, may be determined on the view of the law as laid down in *Swire* v. *Redman*, L. R. 1 Q. B. D. 536; and even then, in my opinion, it should be determined against the plaintiffs on both the grounds I have just mentioned. That is because, (1) the plaintiffs were assenting parties to the change of position which was made between William and Thomas Griffith; and (2) because the plaintiffs have delivered over securities, in common with the rest of the creditors of Thomas Griffith, to William Griffith without the knowledge or consent of Thomas Griffith, who was entitled to the benefit and indemnity which these securities would have been in case of the default of William Griffith, who had become the principal debtor not only as between him and Thomas Griffith but as between them and the creditors of Thomas Griffith, including the plaintiffs.

But if it is to be determined on the construction which, before *Swire* v. *Redman*, had always been given to *Oakley* v. *Pasheller*, 4 Cl. & F. 207, and which had been given to *Liquidators of Overend, Gurney & Co.* v. *Liquidators of the Oriental Financial Corporation*, L. R. 7 H. L. 348, 360, then unquestionably the case is too clearly against the plaintiffs to admit of argument; but I shall for the present assume the law to be as it is stated in *Swire* v. *Redman*, L. R. 1 Q. B. D. 536.

Then, (1) did the plaintiffs assent to the arrangement made between Thomas Griffith and William Griffith, that William Griffith should become the principal debtor instead of Thomas Griffith, and that Thomas should be the surety of William only ? The facts shew, as already stated, that William and Thomas did make such an agreement, and that they gave public notice of it in the newspapers, and that the plaintiffs did know of such an agreement being made.

And it appears by the instrument of the 18th November, 1873, that the creditors of Thomas Griffith, including the plaintiffs, all knew of "William Griffith being assignee of the estate of Thomas Griffith & Co.," that is, that by an agreement between these two parties William Griffith had become the assignee of it all, that is, the principal debtor in respect to that estate. And upon that basis the creditors deal with William Griffith alone, by giving up to him the mortgage made by Thomas Griffith to William Griffith, and by William transferred to the official assignee, for $10,000 upon Thomas Griffith's Yorkville property, and to take in lieu of it a mortgage from William Griffith to the official assignee upon his (William's) Front-street property.

And it also appears by the instrument executed by the creditors on the 20th October, 1874, including the plaintiffs, in favour of William Griffith, that they dealt a second time with William as the assignee of the estate of Thomas Griffith & Co., and that they then released to him that part of the mortgage of September 30th, 1873, which William Griffith and wife had given upon his dwelling house and property on the corner of College street and Spadina Avenue, in Toronto, "to the intent and purpose that the said William Griffith may have his dwelling house and premises unincumbered, to again mortgage the same in order to raise money to meet the last payment due to the creditors of the said insolvents upon the said composition notes," that is, to enable William Griffith, who was the assignee of the estate from Thomas—and was the principal debtor by special bargain between these two, and to the knowledge of the creditors—to raise money upon his own property, which the creditors gave back to him, "to meet the last payment due to the creditors of the said insolvents on the said composition notes"; which had, by the agreement of which they had knowledge and which they were giving effect to, become his own debt.

It appears to me, upon these facts, that the plaintiffs and the other creditors of Thomas Griffith did, with full knowledge of the change of interest and of position made by and between William and Thomas Griffith, assent to, ratify, and give effect to the same. That being so, William then became the principal debtor and Thomas his surety ; and so, when the plaintiffs drew their bill of January 4, 1875, upon William at four months, without the knowledge of Thomas, they discharged Thomas in equity from his responsibility as such surety.

Then, as to the second question, I am of opinion that, Thomas being such surety only as just stated, the giving up and the substitution of the securities—which necessarily became his indemnity upon his becoming surety—without his consent or knowledge, indemnified him to the extent of the value of these securities, or to the loss sustained on their substitution.

And I am also of opinion that although the plaintiffs and the other creditors never assented to or became parties to the change of position agreed upon between Thomas and William Griffith, yet if the plaintiffs knew of such change, as they certainly did, that they had not the right to give up the securities which were held for the payment of these notes, to the one whom they knew to be the principal debtor, to the prejudice[of the one who was the surety, although they never expressly promised to retain the securities for Thomas Griffith ; and that they are liable to make good to Thomas Griffith the value of the securities given up, or the loss sustained upon any substitution made of these brothers. I have acted on the case cited by Mr. Ferguson, of *Swire* v. *Redman*, L. R. 1 Q. B. D. 536;

for the purpose of this suit; but the case of *The Liquidators of Overend, Gurney & Co.* v. *The Liquidators of the Oriental Financial Corporation*, L. R. 7 H. L. 348, 360, does not altogether agree with it, for in that case Lord Cairns said that "after the case of *Oakley* v. *Pasheller*, 4 Cl. & F. 207, it is impossible to contend, if, after a right of action accrues to a creditor against two or more persons, he is informed that one of them is a surety only, and after that he gives time to the principal debtor without the consent and knowledge of the surety, that under those circumstances the rule as to the discharge of the surety does not apply." The case is one deciding that a creditor having notice, after the relation of creditor to debtor is formed, that the position of the parties is different from what the creditor supposed it to be, is bound by such notice; but there in reality the position of the parties was never changed—it was only first disclosed to the creditor after his transactions with the debtor commenced. That is different from a change of position of the parties from that of two ordinary debtors to that of a debtor and surety, which is the case of *Swire* v. *Redman*. Why should parties, principal and surety at the beginning of the contract, but not known to be so by the creditor, have it in their power to alter their creditor's rights by informing him after the contract of their true position, any more than joint debtors?

In my opinion the defendant is entitled to a verdict on the pleas of accord and satisfaction. And he should be allowed to set up if necessary the giving up and substitution of securities held for his benefit as surety, of which fact of suretyship the plaintiffs had notice before the giving up and exchange of securities, by reason of which he has sustained damages to the whole amount of the note sued upon, or to a large part of it; and also the giving of time to William Griffith, the principal debtor, without the consent of Thomas, the surety.

Both of these pleas were afterwards added. See ante p. 419.

The learned Judge found a verdict for the defendant on the fourth and fifth pleas, and for the plaintiffs on the other pleas.

During this term, February 7, 1877, *Ferguson*, Q. C., obtained a rule calling on the defendant to shew cause why the verdict should not be set aside and a verdict entered for the plaintiffs for the sum of $570.18, or for such other sum as the Court might deem proper, on the ground that the verdict was contrary to law and evidence.

During the same term, February 13, 1877, *W. N. Miller*, shewed cause. The fourth and fifth pleas were proved, but if not, there was the giving up of securities, and the giving of time to the principal without the knowledge of the surety, after plaintiffs had notice that this was the relationship of the parties; and so there was a good defence under the added pleas. He cited *Swire* v. *Redman*, L. R. 1 Q. B. D. 536; *Oakeley* v. *Pasheller*, 4 Cl. & F. 207, 223, 10 Bligh, N. S. 548; *Bailey* v. *Edwards*, 4 B. & S. 773; *Liquidators of Overend, Gurney & Co.* v. *Liquidators of the Oriental Financial Corporation*, L. R. 7 H. L. 360; *Pooley* v. *Har-*

radine, 7 E. & B. 431 ; *Maingay* v. *Lewis,* L. R. 3 Ir. C. L.
495, reversed, L. R. 5 Ir. C. L. 229.

Ferguson, Q. C., contra.   The finding on the pleas of
accord and satisfaction was against evidence ; and without
assent to the change of relationship between the parties, of
which there was no evidence, the finding for defendant
can not be sustained on any of the pleas pleaded.   He
cited, in addition to the cases cited by the defendant, *Heath*
v. *Percival,* 1 Peere Wms. 682 ; *David* v. *Ellice,* 5 B. & C.
196 ; *Rees* v. *Berrington,* 2 White & Tudor, L. C., 4th ed.,
974 ; *Way* v. *Hearn,* 11 C. B. N. S. 774.

March 10, 1877.   HARRISON, C. J. — The important
question for decision in this case is, whether, after the
acceptance of the promissory note sued upon from the
defendant, he at the time being the principal debtor, and
his brother William the surety, the relationship of the
parties having been reversed, that reversal was under such
circumstances as to make it the duty of the plaintiffs to
deal with the maker of the note *only* as a surety.

The settled doctrine of a Court of equity is, that if
through any neglect on the part of the creditor a security
to the benefit of which the surety is entitled, is lost or not
properly perfected, to his prejudice, he is discharged to the
extent that he is prejudiced : *Ex parte Mure,* 2 Cox 63 ;
Williams v. *Price,* 1 Sim. & St. 581 ; *Capel* v. *Butler,* 2 Ib.
457 ; *Watts* v. *Shuttleworth,* 5 H. & N. 235, in appeal, 7
Jur. N. S. 945 ; *Pearl* v. *Deacon,* 1 DeG. & J. 461 ; *Strange*
v. *Fooks,* 4 Giff. 408 ; *Titus* v. *Durkee,* 12 C. P. 367 ; *Wulff*
et al. v. *Jay,* L. R. 7 Q. B. 756 ; *Polak* v. *Everett,* 1 Q. B.
D. 669.

It is also the settled doctrine of a Court of equity, ever
since *Rees* v. *Berrington,* 2 White & Tudor, L. C., 4th ed., 974,
that where by some binding contract time is given by a
creditor to the principal debtor, however short the time
may be, and whether the surety is benefited or prejudiced
by the giving of time, the surety is discharged.

Notwithstanding protests more or less vehement on the

part of some common law judges.—see per Williams, J.,
in *Greenough* v. *McClelland*, 2 E. & E. 434 ; per Blackburn, J., in *Petty* v. *Cook*, L. R. 6 Q. B. 794 ; per Blackburn, J., in *Polak* v. *Everett*, 1 Q. B. 672—the later
doctrine in its integrity, has been accepted by Courts of
common law when administering equity : *Darling* v,
McLean, 20 U. C. R. 372; *Mulholland* v. *Broomfield et al.*,
32 U. C. R. 369; *Titus* v. *Durkee*, 12 C. P. 367; *Grieves*
v. *Smith*, 13 C. P. 23 ; *Croydon Gas Company* v. *Dickinson*, L. R. 1 C. P. D. 707, 2 Ib., 46.

If, in the original transaction between the plaintiffs and
Thomas and William Griffith, the latter had been the principal debtor, and the former surety only, to the knowledge
of the plaintiffs when they accepted the note sued on, there
can be no room for doubt that what took place afterwards
between the plaintiffs and William Griffith, both as to
giving of time and as to giving up of securities, would be
either a discharge absolute or a discharge *pro tanto*, without reference to the alleged defence of accord and satisfaction.

The question is, whether the relationship of the parties
having afterwards been reversed with the knowledge of
the plaintiffs, the plaintiffs from the time they acquired
that knowledge were not as much bound to treat Thomas
Griffith as a surety, as if the knowledge had come to them
at the time they first received the note.

The decisions bearing on this point are not either uniform or satisfactory.

Most of the decisions relate to the law of partnership,
where on the retirement from a firm of a particular partner,
it is agreed that the remaining partner or partners shall
indemnify the retiring partner from the debts and liabilities of the firm as between themselves, in which case the
retiring partner becomes merely a surety, and the remaining partner or partners the principal debtor or debtors :
Rodgers et al. v. *Maw*, 4 D. & L. 67.

Suppose notice of this arrangement communicated to
the partnership creditors, are the latter, from the time of

such notice, bound to deal with the retiring partner only as a surety at the peril of discharging him, by giving time to the remaining partner or partners? This is the question raised and determined differently in different cases, to some of which I shall presently refer.

It is of course in the power of the partnership creditor to accept the liability of the remaining partner or partners, or of the new firm, in discharge of the liability of the old firm; but short of that the inclination of the Courts appears to be to hold that the position of the creditor under the original contract is not to be affected: see *Lindley* on Partnership, 3rd ed., vol. i., 465. See also *Swire* v. *Redman*, L. R. 1 Q. B. D. 536.

One of the earliest cases is *Heath* v. *Percival*, 1 P. Wms. 682, cited on the argument.

Sir Stephen Evans, a goldsmith, and his partner, Percival, were bound in a bond to the plaintiff for the payment of £1000 and interest. Percival retired from the firm. Sir Stephen assumed all the partnership debts. Notice was given to the creditors either to receive their money or to look to Evans only for payment. The plaintiff afterwards, instead of calling in his money, allowed it to remain in the hands of Evans at six per cent. interest. Sir Stephen became insolvent. Plaintiff then sued the residuary legatee of Percival. The question was, whether Percival was discharged by what took place between the plaintiff and Sir Stephen. And per Lord Hardwicke, p. 683: "The defendant's testator being bound in the bond, he must lie at stake until the bond be paid, and though the plaintiff continued the money on the bond, this was not material, since it was upon the credit of both the obligors. And as to the notice given by Sir Stephen to the joint creditors to bring in their securities, and that Sir Stephen alone would be hereafter liable, that being *res inter alios acta* could not bind the plaintiff; and his charging the interest did not alter the security, for still it was the bond of both," &c.

Where one of three partners, after a dissolution of partnership, undertook by deed to pay a particular partnership debt on two bills of exchange, and that was communicated to the holder, who consented to take the separate notes of the one partner for the amount, strictly reserving his right against all three, and retained possession of the original bills, it was held that notwithstanding several renewals of the separate notes he might resort to the partnership liability: *Bedford* v. *Deakin et al.*, 2 B. & Al. 210; and this even where there was a promise made to exonerate the remaining partners from all responsibility, but that promise was without consideration: *Lodge et al.* v. *Dicas et al.*, 3 B. & Al. 611.

In *David* v. *Ellice*, 5 B. & C. 196, where there was not only notice of the change in the firm, but assent to the change on the part of the plaintiff, the transfer of the plaintiff's claim from the old to the new firm with his assent, and payment by the latter of a portion of the claim, it was held that the retiring partner continued liable on the insolvency of the new firm.

The latter decision is, in *Thompson* v. *Percival*, 5 B. & Ad. 927, said by Parke, J., "not satisfactory to the profession," and by Denman, C. J., at p. 933, "not altogether satisfactory" to the Court.

A result contrary to *David* v. *Ellice* was, on some ground not clearly stated, reached by the House of Lords in the much contested case of *Oakeley* v. *Pasheller*, 4 Cl. & F. 207.

In that case the creditor continued for years to receive interest on his claim from the new firm without any knowledge or consent on the part of the retiring partner or his representatives, and it was held that by such conduct the plaintiff lost his remedy against the retiring partner, and this notwithstanding a demand by the Lord Chancellor during the argument for some authority to the effect that two original debtors could, by arrangement among themselves, convert one into a surety only for the other principal debtor.

Oakeley v. *Pasheller* is, in *Oakford* v. *The European and American Steam Shipping Co.*, 1 H. & M. 182, 9 L. T. N. S. 15, spoken of by Wood, V. C., as a strong decision and not to be stretched.

In *Swire* v. *Redman*, 1 Q. B. D. 543, 544, *Oakeley* v. *Pasheller* is justified solely on the ground that the creditor accepted the new firm as his debtors in lieu of the old firm. But in *Liquidators of Overend, Gurney & Co.* v. *Liquidators of the Oriental Financial Corporation*, L. R. 7 H. L. 348, it is supported on the broad ground that by the conduct of the creditor the surety was discharged.

In *Kirwan* v. *Kirwan*, 2 C. & M. 617, it not appearing that the creditor intended to substitute the new for the old firm, his remedy against the old firm was held to continue.

Merely taking a security for the debt from the new firm is clearly not sufficient for that purpose: *Harris* v. *Farwell*, 15 Beav. 31. See further *Brown* v. *Gordon*, 16 Beav. 302.

If the decision of this case were rested solely on the answer to the question, whether the plaintiffs had received the acceptance of William Griffith in satisfaction and discharge of the note sued on, although there is some evidence to sustain that issue—*Clarke* v. *Henty*, 3 Y. & C. 187; see *Bilborough* v. *Holmes*, Weekly Notes, Dec. 23rd, 1874, p. 301—I, as a juror, would feel compelled to find in the negative.

The fact that the plaintiffs at the time of receiving the acceptance of the draft did not give up the note is, to my mind, a strong argument against the affirmative. It would seem to me, looking at the whole of the evidence, that the draft on William was not so much intended to be satisfaction of Thomas's debt, as mere " machinery" designed for its collection: see per Blackburn in *Swire* v. *Redman*, 1 Q. B. D. 540. See further *Robinson* v. *Read*, 9 B. & C. 449; *Northamptonshire Union Banking Co.* v. *Foster*, 17 C. B. 201; *Way* v. *Hearn*, 11 C. B. N. S. 774; *The Corporation of North Gwillimbury* v. *Moore*, 15 C. P. 445.

But the question is, under the added pleas, whether the effect in law of what took place, owing to the altered situation of the parties and the knowledge of that by the plaintiffs before accepting the draft, was not to discharge the defendant, whether the plaintiffs designed to do so or not.

It is now well understood that the equity of the surety does not so much depend on contract with the creditor as on its being inequitable in him in any manner to interfere with the rights of the surety: *Hollier* v. *Eyre*, 9 Cl. & F. 1, 45; *Davies* v. *Stainbank*, 6 DeG. McN. & G. 679.

Thus in an action on a promissory note, with a plea that the defendant made the note as co-surety for a co-defendant, and that the plaintiff, at the time of the receipt of the note, having acquired that knowledge, afterwards gave time to the principal, was held to be good: *Pooley* v. *Harradine*, 7 E. & B. 431, 444; and this, where the plea is pleaded as an equitable plea, whether the plaintiff agreed or did not agree at the time to look to the defendant only as a surety : *Greenough* v. *McClelland*, 2 E. & E. 434. See further *Manley* v. *Boycot*, 2 E. & B. 46 ; *Bailey et al.* v. *Edwards*, 4 B. & S. 761.

The principle of these decisions would appear to be, that where a creditor has at the time of the contract notice of an equity existing between two persons with whom he is concerned, it is his duty so to deal with the parties as not to affect their equitable rights.

This doctrine was pushed very far in *Maingay et al.* v. *Lewis*, L. R. 3 Ir. C. L. R. 495, reversed L. R. 5 Ir. C. L. R. 229.

It was an action on the common counts. The defendant pleaded that the causes of action accrued against the defendant and one W. and S. as partners: that *after* the accrual of the cause of action there was a dissolution of the partnership by a memorandum of agreement, of which the plaintiff had due notice : that by the memorandum it was agreed that W. should take upon himself all the debts of the partnership : that after the agreement W. became the principal debtor in respect of partnership liabilities, and defendant only a surety, *of which plaintiff had notice:* that plaintiff *afterwards* took a bill of exchange at three months from W. alone for the amount of the cause of action, and thereby gave time to W., whereby defendant was discharged from liability. There was a demurrer to

the plea. The Court of Queen's Bench held the plea bad ;
but their decision was reversed on appeal, chiefly in defer-
ence to *Oakeley* v. *Pasheller*, 4 Cl. & F. 207.

The Court, in delivering judgment, looked upon the
decision of the House of Lords as settling that there may
be the relation of principal and surety between co-debtors
to which the creditor is not a party, and that; although the
relation is created *after* the co-debtors between whom it
exists have contracted the debt sued on, if the creditor,
knowing the relation, gives time to the principal debtor, he
thereby discharges the co-debtor who has become a surety,
unless the latter is proved to have assented to the giving
of time.

If this be law it supports the finding for the defendant,
whether the plaintiff did or did not assent to the change
of relationship between the brothers Griffith.

It appears to be in accordance with *Watts* v. *Robinson
et al.*, 32 U. C. R. 362; *Wilson* v. *Lloyd*, L. R. 16 Eq. 60,
and with *Oriental Financial Corporation* v. *Overend,
Gurney & Co.*, L. R. 7 Ch. 142, affirmed L. R. 7 H. L.
348.

Lord Cairns in the latter case said, at p. 360, " It appears
to me that, after the case which has been referred to at the
bar, decided by your Lordships' House, that of *Oakeley* v.
Pasheller, 4 Cl. & F. 207, it is impossible to contend if
after a right of action accrues to a creditor against two or
more persons he is informed that one of them is a surety
only, and *after that* he gives time to the principal debtor
without the consent and knowledge of the surety, that
under these circumstances the rule as to the discharge of
the surety does not apply."

The weight of authority is unquestionably in favour of
the position that, after knowledge of the creation of the
relation of principal and surety, even between joint debtors,
the creditor, without being a party to the change, and
without assenting to it, if having knowledge of it, is
bound not to act to the prejudice of the equitable rights
of the surety.

The case apparently most against this position is the case so much relied on in the argument, of *Swire* v. *Redman*, 1 Q. B. D. 536.

It is not to be overlooked that in that case the only plea was that, on the dissolution of the partnership, the creditor accepted the liability of the remaining partner and discharged the remaining partner , and for that reason apparently, *Liquidators of Oriental Financial Corporation* v. *Liquidators of Overend, Gurney & Co.*, L. R. 7 Ch. 142, L. R. 7 H. L. 348, was not cited in the argument of the case, or referred to by the Court in the delivery of judgment.

The learned judge Bramwell, B., at the trial, ruled that there was no evidence to sustain that defence, and the full Court sustained that ruling.

Although containing some severe criticisms on *Oakeley* v. *Pasheller,* 4 Cl. & F. 207, and *Maingay* v. *Lewis,* L. R. 3 Ir. C. L. R. 495, in error L. R. 5 Ir. C. L. R. 229, the decision on the ground on which it is rested, is a good one, and not in actual conflict with *Liquidators of Overend, Gurney & Co.* v. *Liquidators of the Oriental Financial Corporation*, L. R. 7 H. L. 348.

Had there been such a plea as pleaded in *Maingay* v. *Lewis*, L. R. 3 Ir, C. L. R. 495, and had the ruling been against that plea, there would have been some real conflict between the two cases.

But even if the case were in conflict with the decision of the House of Lords, and there was no evidence in this case of assent on the part of the plaintiffs, our duty would be to follow the decisions of the House of Lords in preference to that of the Queen's Bench division of the High Court of Justice.

We, however, agree with the learned Judge in thinking that in this case there was not only knowledge to the plaintiffs of the change of relationship, but assent thereto, and so the finding for the defendant should be sustained even if *Swire* v. *Redman*, 1 Q. B. D. 536, were in actual conflict with the decisions of the House of Lords, and were in other respects unexceptionable law.

The verdict should, in our opinion, be entered for the defendant on the sixth plea, and for the plaintiffs on the remaining pleas, and the rule *nisi* be discharged.

MORRISON, J., concurred.

Rule discharged.

———

BARNED'S BANKING COMPANY (LIMITED) V. REYNOLDS.

" The (Imperial) Companies Act, 1862 *"—Order making calls against past member—Right, of action thereon—Notice—Order made in defendant's absence—Finality of order—Repeal of statute—Effect of on pleas pleaded.*

Held, WILSON, J., dissenting, that an action will not lie in this country at the suit of the company on an order made under " The Companies Act, 1862," in England, in the winding up of a company, making a call upon defendant *as a part member* in respect of his shares, and directing payment thereof to one of the two official liquidators appointed.

Per WILSON, J.—The fourth plea, traversing the plaintiffs being a corporation under the Act, was good.

The articles of association of the company provided that notices required
· to be served by the company upon the members might be served either personally or left or sent by post addressed to them at their registered place of abode, and the Act provided for the keeping a register of such addresses. Per WILSON, J.—This would not apply to notices served on members, in proceedings to wind up the company, but it was not
· contrary to natural justice that the plaintiffs should recover against defendant, when the order sued upon, though made in his absence from England, and as he alleged without notice, was made after notices given in the manner thus provided for.

The sixteenth plea alleged that the order was not final, but might be varied or rescinded by the Court of Chancery in England, which Court might also order restitution to defendant of the whole or any part of the money paid under such order. The plaintiffs replied, in substance, that the payment of calls under the order is final, unless there is a surplus, which in this case there would not be; and that the order was final unless appealed against in a time fixed, which defendant had not done. Per WILSON, J., the plea was bad, for the order was final until altered; and the replication was good.

A plea that defendant was induced to take the shares by the fraud of the plaintiffs, and repudiated them as soon as he discovered the fraud, and derived no benefit from them, was clearly bad, and was not supported.

The 23 Vic. ch. 24, sec. 1, under which such defences were permitted, and had been pleaded, as could have been pleaded to the original order, was
· repealed by 39 Vic. ch. 7, O. Per WILSON, J., such repeal, under the Interpretation Act, 31 Vic. sec. 7, sub-sec. 34, O., would not affect the pleas.

DEMURRER. This case was before the Court on somewhat different pleadings, as reported in 36 U. C. R. 256.

The declaration remained as it was, and as it is therein set out, excepting that section 38 of the Imperial Statute 25 & 26 Vic. ch. 89, and subsec. 4 were then the only parts of that section which were then set out, while the present declaration set out now subsecs. 1, 2, and 3, as well. These subsections were, however, then before the Court, because the defendant had given them in full in his tenth plea, as in the report p. 261. And excepting also that in the former declaration it did not expressly appear whether the defendant was proceeded against as a past or as a present member. And it is now altered as follows—by striking out the words *and liable*, at the end of the seventh line from the bottom of p. 259—and inserting after the word "company," immediately preceding the two words struck out, "and had not ceased to be a member for a period of a year or upwards, prior to the commencement of the winding up hereinafter mentioned, and was liable in respect of the said shares."

The declaration in effect was therefore just what it was before, excepting that it was now shewn the plaintiffs were proceeding against the defendant only *as a past member* of the company.

Demurrer to the declaration :

Because it does not shew any facts or circumstances under which the laws in force in this Province give the plaintiffs any right of action against the defendant : that the declaration does not shew that under the alleged Act of Parliament, or under the laws of England, the plaintiffs have any right of action against the defendant : that it appears by the declaration that the company is being wound up by the High Court of Chancery in England and under the authority of the alleged Act of Parliament, and the plaintiffs are not shewn to have the power under the Act to sue or bring actions for any call made by the said Court : that it is not shewn that any call was made on the said shares before the order for winding up was made, or that the defendant was the holder of the said shares or of any of them at the time of making any such call or that he ever became indebted to the plaintiffs upon or in respect of the said shares or any of them : that it appears by the declaration the defendant had ceased to be the holder of any of the said shares before the commencement of the winding up of the company, and that the defendant was at most only a past member : that under the laws of this country the defendant would not be liable for any call made after he ceased to be a holder of said shares, and the declaration does not shew any provision of English law that makes him liable for any such call : that it appears the defendant, as a past member, is not subject to the same liabilities as a present member, and the declaration does not shew that any debts or liabilities of the company existed to or in respect of which the defendant was liable to contribute, or in respect of which he could be placed in the list of contributories, or that he was liable to contribute anything : that as ' the plaintiffs are suing on a law not in force in this country, and are claiming a liability which does not exist under the laws of this country, they are bound to shew that the liability they claim clearly exists under the English law, which they have not done : that it appears by the declaration that after an order has been made for winding up a company all power in regard to collecting or getting in the assets of the company is vested in the said Court of Chancery, which is specially appointed the tribunal for that purpose, and with special and extraordinary powers which cannot be enforced in this country : that it appears that any proceedings which are had are not final, and that the said Court has power to rectify the list of contributories and can at any time remove the defendant's name from such list, also, that the said Court has power to restore to the defendant all or any part of the moneys which he may pay under the said order making said calls, and that the English law, as presented by the declaration, shews that the proceedings here are not final in their character like a judgment ; and the rights of the plaintiffs, if any, can be enforced only by the said special tribunal, and not by suit at law in this country. Joinder.

The, defendant pleaded several pleas. Some of them remained just as they were at first. Some of them were modified a little, and some were now before the Court for the first time.

Pleas 1, 2, 5, 6, remained precisely as they were, and as they are set out in p. 261 of the report.

The demurrers to these pleas were just as before, and as they are set out at p. 264 of the report.

Plea 10 was just as it was, and as it is given at pp. 261, 262, excepting that the present plea alleged that long before the order was made for winding up the company, and long before the petition for winding it up, the defend-ant ceased to be the holder of any of the said shares, and, in addition to what it alleged before, that he had ceased to be a member of the said company, and excepting that the words, "but during all the times aforesaid was and still is only a past member of the said company," at the end of the said plea on p. 262, were now omitted by reason of the amendment of the declaration, and in place thereof was inserted the following : "And the defendant ceased to be a member of the said company for a period of one year and upwards prior to the commencement of the winding up of said company, in said declaration alleged."

Demurrer : that the matters therein pleaded have been adjudicated and determined by the orders mentioned in the declaration. Joinder.

Pleas 11, 12, and 13, remained as they were, excepting that each one excepted from the matters pleaded by it so much of the tenth plea as alleged the defendant ceased to be a member of the company for a period of one year and upwards prior to the commencement of the winding up of the company.

Demurrer to pleas 11, 12, and 13 : that by section 106 of the said Act set out in the declaration the order made by the Court of Chancery, and mentioned in the declaration, are conclusive as to the defendant's liability. Joinder.

The following are the pleadings which were now before the Court for the first time :—

Plea 4. That the plaintiffs were not nor are incorporated under the said Act, as alleged.

Demurrer. That the defendant having been found to be liable to contribute by the order in that behalf mentioned, is not at liberty to deny that the plaintiffs were and are duly incorporated under the said Act as alleged, and that he was a member and liable to contribute. Joinder.

Plea 8. That the said Court of Chancery did not by an order or otherwise settle the list of contributories to the assets of the company, nor declare the defendant to be or settle him on the said list as a contributory in respect of the said one hundred shares or any of them, as a member or contributory, or as included in the list of contributories as alleged.

Demurrer: that the matters therein pleaded have been adjudicated and determined by the orders mentioned in the declaration. Joinder.

Plea 14 repeats the several allegations contained in the 10th plea, except so much thereof as alleges that the defendant ceased to be a member of the said company for a period of one year and upwards prior to the commencement of the winding up of the company. And the defendant says they are respectively true in substance and in fact. And that at the time of the making of the said order for winding up of the company all calls which had at any time previously been made upon the shares in the declaration mentioned, or upon any of them, had been and were fully paid and satisfied, and there was then no indebtedness or liability whatsoever on the part of the defendant to the plaintiffs upon or in respect of the said shares or any of them, and that under the laws of England in force at the time of the making of the said order, and from thence hitherto and still in force, the right or power of making any call upon the said shares or any of them, or of enforcing any liability of the defendant as a past member of the company, was from and after the making of the said order and thenceforth has continued to be vested in the said Court of Chancery alone, and can be enforced only by that Court, and by the process thereof and within the jurisdiction of the said Court, and which Court by the said law is constituted the special and only tribunal for such purpose ; and that under the said law so in force as aforesaid, the plaintiff has not nor ever had the right or power to maintain any action or suit in England or elsewhere for the recovery of the said calls, or either of them, in the declaration mentioned, or the amounts thereof, or either of them, or any part thereof, or for the recovery of the said money, or any part thereof, so ordered to be paid, as in the declaration alleged.

Demurrer: that the plea sets up matter of law, and alleges no matters of fact which form a defence to the action. Joinder.

Plea 15 repeats the matters in the tenth plea, with the like exception as in the fourteenth plea, and then proceeds, that at the time the defendant ceased to be a member of the company all calls which at any time previously had been made upon the said shares, or any of them, had been fully paid and satisfied, and there was then no indebtedness or liability whatever on the part of the defendant to the plaintiffs, upon or in respect of the said shares or any of them ; and the defendant from a time long before he became the holder of the shares or any of them up to the time of the commencement of this suit, and from thence hitherto, was at all times resident and domiciled in either the late Province of Canada or the now Dominion of Canada, and is still resident and domiciled in said Dominion, and the defendant was not within the jurisdiction of the said Court of Chancery at any time since he ceased to be the holder of said shares as aforesaid ; and the said order by which the said Court settled the said list of contributories, and declared the defendant to be and settled him on the said list as a contributory was made, and all proceedings for obtaining or procuring said order were taken while the defendant was out of the jurisdiction of the said Court, and while the defendant was resident and domiciled as

aforesaid, and the defendant never had any notice
knowledge of any application for the said order, and never
appeared on, nor was ever heard on, any such application ;
and said order was made in his absence, and without his
knowledge; and the said alleged order, by which the said
Court made the said calls, and ordered payment as therein
mentioned, was made, and all proceedings therefor were
held and taken while the defendant was out of the jurisdiction of the said Court, and while the defendant was
resident and domiciled as aforesaid ; and the proceeding
for obtaining the said last mentioned order was commenced
by summons from the said Court, and the defendant was
not at any time before the making of the last mentioned
order served with the said summons, or with any notice
thereof, or of the application for the said order, or any of
the proceedings for obtaining the said order, and the
defendant did not appear upon nor was he heard upon any
such summons, application or proceeding, and said order
was made in his absence, and without his knowledge.

Second replication to 15th plea : that in and by the said
Companies Act,1862,sec. 25,it was and is enacted, that every
company incorporated under the Act should cause to be
kept, in one or more books, a register of its members, in
which there should be entered, among other things, the
names and addresses and the occupations of any of the
members and past members of the company, and that the
memorandum of association may, in the case of a company
limited by shares, and shall, in the case of a company
limited by guarantee or unlimited, be accompanied when
registered by articles of association, signed by the subscribers to the memorandum of association, and prescribing
such regulations for the company as the subscribers to the
memorandum of association deem expedient.   The articles
shall be expressed in separate paragraphs, numbered arith-
metically ; they may adopt all, or any, of the provisions
contained in the table marked A in the first schedule to the
said Act, when registered, they shall bind the company and
the members thereof, to the same extent as if each member

had subscribed his name and affixed his seal thereto.
And there were in such articles contained a covenant
on the part of himself, his heirs, executors, and administrators, to conform to all the regulations contained in such
articles subject to the provisions of the said Act. And that
the memorandum of association of the plaintiffs' company
was accompanied with articles of association, which were
duly registered with the said memorandum of association,
and binding on the defendant as a member of the said
company. And the said articles did adopt, among other of
the provisions contained in the table marked A, in the first
schedule to the said Act, the following provisions regarding
notices to members, that is to say :—

"Article 95 : Notices required to be served by the company
upon the members may be served either personally, or by
leaving the same, or sending them through the post in a letter
addressed to the members at their registered place of abode."

And the plaintiffs say that they did keep a register of the
members and past members of the company, in which was
entered, among other things, the name, and address, and
occupation of the defendant, in accordance with the provisions of the said Act. And that notice of the application
for the order by which the Court settled the list of contributories, and declared the defendant to be and settled
him on the said list as a contributory, and also notice to
appear and shew cause against the making of the order
making the said calls, and ordering payment by the defendant of the said calls, were duly and properly sent to the
defendant through the post, in a prepaid letter, addressed
to him at his aforesaid registered place of abode, in accordance with the provisions of the aforesaid article, and a
sufficient time previous to the making of the said orders
to enable the defendant to appear and object, or shew cause
against the making of the said orders.

Demurrer to second replication to 15th plea : Because the
replication does not allege the defendant was a subscriber
to or signed the said articles of association, or ever agreed
to be or to become bound by the said articles, or by any of

the provisions thereof.   The replication does not shew how
the articles of association became binding or obligatory on
the defendant.   The enactments of the said statute, under
the circumstances disclosed in the plea, could not give the
Court jurisdiction over the defendant, so as to make the
alleged proceedings of the said Court binding in this
country on the defendant: that even if the said provisions
as to notices were binding on the defendant, it is not
alleged that the said provisions extended or extend to services of summons, or other acts or proceedings of the Court,
or that notices of application for said orders, or either
could, under said statute, be given by the company, or was
within the operation of the said provisions : that the
language of the said provisions shews or implies, in the
absence of other allegations, that said provisions apply
only to ordinary notices to be served on or given by the
company or its members while the company was operative,
and do not apply to acts or proceedings in or before the
said Court, or to any notices thereof.

Second rejoinder to 2nd replication to 15th plea : that
the provisions regarding notices contained in the said table,
marked A, in the said first schedule to said companies Act,
1862, and which provisions the replication alleges the said
articles of association did adopt, were and are in the words
and figures following, that is to say :—

" NOTICES.

95 : A notice may be served by the company, upon any
member either personally or by sending it through the
post, in a prepaid letter, addressed to such member at his
registered place of abode."

And that the defendant was not a subscriber to, nor did
he ever sign the said memorandum of association of the
plaintiffs' company, or the said alleged articles of association ; nor did he ever agree to be or to become bound by
the said articles of association, or by any of the provisions
thereof.   And the proceeding for obtaining such order by
which the Court made the said calls, and on which the said
order was made, was commenced by summons from the said

Court, and the proceeding for obtaining said order by which the said Court settled the list of contributories, and on-which the said order was made, was commenced by act of the said Court, and all said proceedings were acts of the said Court and not of the company of the plaintiffs, and neither of the said orders, nor the application for either of them, was made or granted on any notice by or served by the plaintiffs or by the said company.

Demurrer to second rejoinder to second replication to plea 15 : because the defendant having been found liable to contribute by the order in that behalf mentioned, is not at liberty now to set up as a defence that the notices which he received, or which were sent to his registered place of abode, of the application for the said order were not properly given or sent: that the defendant admits by the rejoinder that the said orders were made by the Court, and does not allege that the said orders or either of them were or was appealed against by him, or that they were set aside, or that he attempted to have them set aside on account of the notice sent to him being improper as he alleges ; and that the rejoinder is no answer to the replication. Joinder.

Plea 16 : that under and according to the law of England in force at the time of making of the said alleged order, by which the said Court of Chancery made the said calls and ordered payment as therein mentioned, and from thence hitherto and still in force, the said order was not nor is final, but can under said law be varied, rescinded or set aside by the said Court. (*) And the payment of any money under such order was not nor is final, but said Court has power under such law to order restitution to the defendant of the whole or any part of the money so said under such order.

Demurrer to the 16th plea : because the facts pleaded do not constitute any defence, without averments that the order has been varied, rescinded, or set aside. Joinder.

(*) The words after the asterisk to the end of the paragraph were added since the former argument.

Second replication to 16th plea :that by the said Companies Act, 1862, it was and is enacted as follows :—

Section 109. The Court shall adjust the right of contributories amongst themselves, and distribute any surplus that may remain amongst the parties entitled thereto.

Section 124. Rehearings of and appeals from any order or decision made or given in the matter of the winding up of a company by any Court having jurisdiction under the Act, may be had in the same manner and subject to the same conditions in and subject to which appeals may be had from any order or decision of the same Court in cases within its ordinary jurisdiction, subject to this restriction, that no such re-hearing or appeal shall be heard unless notice of the same is given within three weeks after any order complained of has been made in manner in which notices of appeal are ordinarily given according to the practice of the Court appealed from, unless such time is extended by the Court of Appeal."

And that the payment of any money under the said order is final, except in the case of a surplus mentioned in the aforesaid section of the said Act; and that there is not nor will there be any surplus in this case; and that no notice of re-hearing or appeal from the said order in the said plea mentioned and referred to was given within three weeks after the said order had been made, nor was the time for giving such notice extended by the Court of Appeal.

Demurrer to second replication to sixteenth plea : because it does not shew that any order for payment and payment thereunder under the provision of the said Companies Act, 1862, is final.

Section 109, set out in the replication, shews that such order and payment are not final, but that payments or portions thereof may be returned to the party ordered to make payment, and that the replication is not a sufficient answer to the plea. Joinder.

Plea 17 : that the defendant was induced to become the holder of the said shares by fraud of the plaintiffs, and that he never received any benefit or advantage from or in respect of the said shares or any of them, and the defend-

ant after he had notice of the said fraud never elected to
hold or retain the said shares or any of them, but has at
all times after he had notice of said fraud repudiated and
disclaimed, and still repudiates and disclaims the said
shares and every of them, and all title thereto and all
liability in respect thereof, and within a reasonable time
after he had notice of the said fraud he gave notice of his
repudiation and disclaimer of the said shares of the
plaintiffs.

Demurrer to 17th plea: because the defendant having
been found to be liable to contribute by the order in that
behalf made, is not at liberty now to set up as a defence
that he was induced to become the holder of the shares in
the declaration mentioned by fraud. Joinder.

In Trinity Term, September 4, 1876, *Robinson*, Q. C.,
argued the case for the plaintiffs. The question is, whether
the defendant can be sued as a past member. If he can
be sued as a present member, as was decided on the former
argument, he may be proceeded against also as a past member. The defendant has pleaded many pleas which go
behind the order of the Court, and it was decided in this
case that he could do so, though by the Imperial
Companies' Act, 1862, that order is final. But the proper
view of the case, it is submitted, is, that the order operates
by way of contract under the articles of association, and
the liability is by contract rather than under a judgment
or decree. The defendant by becoming a member has
agreed to be bound by the statute governing the company,
which makes such order final and conclusive: *Copin* v.
Adamson, L. R. 9 Ex. 345, in Appeal 1 Ex. D. 000. The 14th
plea, not demurred to before, is now demurred to. It sets
up matter of law only, that an action will not lie; and that
the only remedy the plaintiffs have is by proceeding in the
Court of Chancery in England. The 15th plea also was not
before demurred to. It alleges the defendant had no notice
of the proceedings which were taken against him. The
replication is, that he had the notice which the statute

declares shall be sufficient, and which he agreed to expressly
when he became a member of the company.

S. Richards, Q. C., contra. The declaration formerly
treated the defendant as a present member. Now it is
expressly averred that he is proceeded against as a past
member. There is nothing in the way of contract with or
liability to these plaintiffs. The statute says a past member shall be liable to contribute to the assets of the company by an order of the Court of Chancery; but that does
not make him liable to the company. The statute imposes
the duty upon the past member to pay such calls, but that
does not authorize the company to sue for and collect them.
The liability of past members is not by contract, but by
statute only. The sections relating to contracts are not
on the pleadings, and cannot of course be referred to:
Re Oriental Commercial Bank, Morris's Case, L. R. 8 Ch.
800, 806, 807; *Schibsby* v. *Westenholz*, L. R. 6 Q. B. 155.
The order which was made on the defendant is not final.
The statute says only it shall be conclusive in evidence.
The facts shew the order cannot be final, for the defendant
may get the whole or part of the money back again if he
pay it. And if the plaintiffs recover a judgment at law
can the defendant ever get the money back if he is made
to pay it, and if he become entitled to have it returned to
him? That the defendant is out of the country, where
the winding up proceedings are being carried on, and
where therefore the special proceedings cannot be taken
against him, is no reason why he should be sued at law in
this country as on a general common law liability. *Story's*
Conflict of Laws, sec. 625 a. The defendant should be
proceeded against in the country where the liability
exists: *Erickson* v. *Nesmith*, 15 Gray 221; 4 Allen
233, 46 New Hamp. 371; *Stevens* v. *Evans*, 2 Burr.
1152, 1157; *Dundalk Western R. W. Co.* v. *Tap-
ster*, 1 Q. B. 667; *Steward* v. *Greaves*, 10 M. & W. 711;
Chapman v. *Milvain*, 5 Ex. 61; *Bank of Australasia*
v. *Harding*, 9 C. B. 661; *Bank of Australasia* v. *Nias*,
16 Q. B. 717; *Vestry of St. Pancras* v. *Batterbury*, 2 C.

B. N. S. 477; *Berkeley* v. *Elderkin*, 1 E. & B. 805; *Mc-Pherson* v. *Forrester*, 11 U. C. R. 362; *Donnelly* v. *Stewart*, 25 U. C. R. 398; *Smith* v. *Whalley*, 2 B. & P. 482, 484; *Emmerson* v. *Lashley*, 2 H. Bl. 248; *Patrick* v. *Shedden*, 2 E. & B. 14; *Sheehy* v. *The Professional Life Ass. Co.*, 2 C. B. N. S. 211, affirmed 3 C. B. N. S. 597. The 14th plea, setting up the true tribunal to which the plaintiff should resort, is a good matter of defence. The 15th plea is good also, because it shews a want of notice to the defendant of all the proceedings being taken against him on which it is now contended he is liable. The replication alleging a notice to the defendant of such proceedings, shews that the notice there referred to applies only to ordinary notices of the company, given by them in the management of their internal affairs, and not to such notices, or summonses, or proceedings, as are made for calls under the order of the Court on the dissolution of the company—"Companies Act, 1862," secs. 14, 25, of the Act. And they do not apply to past members. The defendant shews, in his rejoinder, the provisions of the Act as to notices, from which it is clear the notices for calls by the Court are not within its terms. And the plaintiffs demur, because they say the defendant is precluded by the adjudication in Chancery from contesting the fact of notice. The 16th plea alleges that the order made in Chancery upon the defendant to pay the calls was not and is not final. That is a good defence. The plaintiffs demur to it, because they say the order has not yet been varied or rescinded That may be, but it is no reason why the plaintiffs should seek by a recovery at law to make a matter conclusive for ever which is not intended to be so. The replication to it sets out the provisions of the statute shewing the Court will settle the rights of contributories among themselves, and will deal with any surplus that may remain according to the rights of the parties, and that a rehearing or appeal can only be had on notice, and that the defendant gave no notice of appeal, and that there is no surplus to be distributed. The defendant demurs

because the replication does not shew the proceedings to
be final, and as they are not so a suit at law cannot be
maintained. The 17th plea sets up that defendant was
induced to subscribe for the shares by the fraud of the
company. The cases are against the validity of such a
defence.

C. Robinson, Q.C., in reply. As to foreign companies he
referred to *Buckley* on Joint Stock Companies, 2nd ed., p.
186 : *Peruvian R. W. Co.* v. *Thames & Mersey Marine
Ins. Co.*, L. R. 2 Ch. 617 ; *Re Tumacacori Mining Co.*, L.
R. 17 Eq. 534 ; *Newby* v. *Von Oppen and the Colt's Patent
Fire Arms Manufacturing Co.*, L. R. 7 Q. B. 293. The
liability is under the order of the Court made under the
authority of the statute, by which every member of the
company is bound. The argument as to want of finality
of the order is self-destructive. It is that the defendant is not to pay at all because he may get some of it
back again ; but if he is to get any of it again, he must
first of all pay it. The pleadings shew, however, expressly
that there will be no surplus money, so that the defendant will never get or be entitled to get any of the
money, if he pay it, back again. The case of *Copin* v.
Adamson, L. R. 9 Ex. 345, 349, is corrected to some extent in appeal, in L. R. 1 Ex. D. 17, and shews that as
the defendant is liable by the English statute, which is
part of the charter of the company, he is liable here.
That shews that the order here as in England is conclusive in evidence.

March 10, 1877. WILSON, J.—I shall not go over any
of the ground which was reviewed in the former case
unless there is some special reason for doing so.

I shall therefore at once pass by the demurrer to the
declaration, for, although it is not now precisely as it was
before, having been since amended by describing the defendant specifically as a past member, it is in all respects substantially as it was ; for on the face of the declaration past
and present members are equally liable, and although a

past is not on precisely the like footing as a present member the declaration disclosed in my opinion, as I before stated, a full and sufficient cause of action even as against a past member. I still remain of opinion the declaration is sufficient in law, and that the company may maintain this action for the calls in their corporate name.

I am also of opinion the first and second pleas are good for the reasons before given, namely, that the calls sued for are not specialty debts.

I think, assuming the 23 Vic. ch. 24 sec. 1, to be still applicable here, although it has since the former argument been repealed by 39 Vic. ch. 7, sched. A, O, and sec. 1 No. 6, the defendant may traverse the plaintiffs being a corporate body; and that the fourth plea is good; and that the fifth, sixth, and eighth pleas are also sustainable on the same ground. The facts of the tenth, eleventh, twelfth, and thirteenth pleas founded upon sub-secs. 1, 2, 3, and 4 of section 38 of the Companies' Act, 1862, may also be pleaded under our statute giving the right to the defendant to set up any defences which he might have set up to the original suit.

The fourteenth plea alleges that all calls which were made upon the shares were paid before the winding up order, and by the law of England the calls which were made upon the defendant as a past member were made by the Court of Chancery and can be enforced in that Court only, and not in any other Court of England or elsewhere. That no doubt is so, because the order is conclusive upon the contributory, and it requires no suit to be brought in any Court to establish the liability, and when once the liability is established the Court where the proceeding is has the power to enforce payment by process of execution. But because the execution is inoperative in England by reason of the absence of the debtor is no reason why the liability he is under should not be enforced against him in the Court and by the law of the country where the debtor is found. It is just in such cases that the aid of a foreign tribunal is required. The plea in my opinion is not sufficient in law.

The fifteenth plea has not been demurred to, and no argument was had upon its sufficiency. We shall proceed to the second replication to it, which is demurred to, and to the second rejoinder to it, to which is also demurred to. The replication shews that the plaintiffs' company, under the statute, adopted a provision for giving notice to the members of matters connected with the business of the company, which, by the statute, was to be binding on each member to the same extent as if each member had subscribed his name and affixed his seal thereto, and as if he had covenanted to conform to the same. The article adopted was : That notices required to be served by the company upon the members may be served either personally or by leaving the same, or sending them through the post in a letter addressed to the members at their registered place of abode. Then the replication states that notice of the application for the order by which the Court settled the list of contributories, and put the defendant upon it, and also notice to appear and shew cause against the making of the order making the said calls and ordering payment by the defendant of the calls, were duly and properly sent to the defendant through the post, in a prepaid letter addressed to him at his registered place of abode, in accordance with the provisions of the said article, and a sufficient time before the making of the orders to enable the defendant to appear and object, or shew cause against the making of the orders. The defendant has demurred to this replication.

It is necessary to see what the declaration states, and what the fifteenth plea states or does not state, before considering the sufficiency of the replication. The declaration alleges that the defendant was a member of the company for 100 shares : that he had ceased to be a member, but not for so long as a year before the commencement of the proceedings for the winding up, and that he was liable to contribute as a past member, and that the order for calls was duly served upon him. The plea does not shew that the defendant was not resident and domiciled

in England, and within the jurisdiction of the Court of
Chancery there before he changed his residence and
domicile to Canada, nor that he was not in England and
within the jurisdiction of the Court of Chancery there at
the time he took the shares, and became a member of the
company, and also before he ceased to hold the shares,
although he was not resident and domiciled there when he
ceased to hold the shares. The plea does not shew that the
defendant was not served with a notice of the application
for the order settling the defendant on the list of contributories, although it says he had no notice or knowledge of the
application for it. Nor does it shew that the order by which
the Court made the calls, and ordered payment by the defendant, was not served upon him, or that he had not notice
of it, although he says the proceeding therefor was by
summons, and the summons was not served upon him, nor
any notice of it, nor application for the order, nor any of
the proceedings for obtaining it, nor did he appear nor
was he heard upon any such summons, proceedings, or
application, and the order was made in his absence and
without his knowledge.

The cases as to judgments obtained in the absence
of the debtor are chiefly the following : *Sheehy* v. *The
Professional Life Assurance Co.*, 13 C. B., 787, in which
it was said that a plea which alleged the defendants
were not served with any summons or process, issuing
out of the Irish Court, where the judgment was obtained,
and that the plaintiff irregularly and behind the back
of the defendants caused an appearance to be entered
for the defendants, and thereby obtained judgment, when
the defendants were not within the jurisdiction of the
said Court—although the preceding averments are presumed to mean that the judgment was signed without the
knowledge of the defendants—was insufficient, because it
was consistent with all the statements that the defendants
had full knowledge of the issuing of the summons, and it
was not to be inferred therefrom that the defendants had
not appeared in the Irish Court.

Buchanan v. *Rucker*, 1 Camp. 63, shewed the defendant was out of the jurisdiction of the Court and country in which the judgment was given, at the time the action was brought, and that he was not served with any process in the action, and that a judgment in such a case could not be binding, when, for anything that appeared, the defendant never was within the jurisdiction of the Court.

Douglas v. *Forrest*, 4 Bing. 686, was a recovery had in Scotland, without notice or service of process, against a native born Scotchman who had gone abroad, leaving property there, and it was sustained.

Becquet v. *MacCarthy*, 2 B. & Ad. 951, was a case where a judgment in the Mauritius was obtained against one who was absent from the Island, and was founded on process served upon the Attorney-General there, according to the law there; and it was held that such recovery was not so contrary to natural justice as to render the judgment void when the party had resided in the Island at the time the cause of action accrued, although he had withdrawn himself from it before the proceedings were commenced.

In *Shibsby* v. *Westenholz*, L. R. 6 Q. B. 155, Blackburn, J., said, at p. 161: "If at the time when the obligation was contracted the defendants were within the foreign country, but left it before the suit was instituted, we should be inclined to think the laws of that country bound them: though before finally deciding this we should like to hear the question argued."

In *Copin* v. *Adamson*, L. R. 9 Ex. 345, the action was on a French judgment. The defendant pleaded he was not at any time before resident or domiciled in France, or within the jurisdiction of the Court, or subject to French law: that he was never served with any process, nor had he any notice or opportunity of defending himself. The plaintiff replied that the defendant was a holder of shares in a French company, having its legal domicile at Paris, and that he thereby became subject, by the law of France, to all the liabilities belonging to the holders of shares, and in particular to the conditions contained in the statutes or

articles of association. By these statutes it was provided
that all disputes arising during liquidation between shareholders should be submitted to the French Court: that
every shareholder provoking a contest must elect a domicile, and in default election might be made for him at the
office of, &c.: that all summonses, &c., should be validly
served at the domicile formally or impliedly chosen: that the
company became bankrupt, and defendant's unpaid calls
became payable to the plaintiff as assignee : that he made
default and provoked a contest : that he never elected a
domicile, and thereupon the plaintiff caused summonses,
&c., to be served at the office aforesaid: that by the law
of France that was the defendant's implied domicile of
election for the purpose of service, and the same was regular,
and that the defendant was bound to appear but did not,
whereupon judgment by default was recovered against him.
There was a like replication to the preceding one, stating
the law of France to be the same as the matters which are
contained in the above statutory articles of association, but
omitting all reference to the statutes or articles of association.   On demurrer the first replication was held good, and
the second replication [Kelly, C. B. dissenting to the judgment on the second replication] was held bad.   The first
replication was held sufficient by the whole Court, because
the defendant had by his own contract by becoming a
member of the company bound himself to be governed by
the French law, while the second replication was held bad
by the majority of the Court, because the French law did
not bind the defendant without his express assent, (which
was not stated,) to submit himself to French law.

The Court relied on the case of *The Bank of Australasia*
v. *Harding*, 9 C. B. 661, where a company was incorporated
in Australia under a local Act, and the Judges in that case
were of opinion that the defendant was bound by the provisions of that local Act because he was a member of the
company which was incorporated by it; that it must be
assumed he was an assenting party to it and that it was
passed at his request.   The Chief Baron, in the case in

L. R. 9 Ex. 345, was in favour of carrying the law further than his two brother Judges.

The case in appeal is reported in L. R. 1 Ex. D. 17 where the judgment was affirmed. The appeal was on the judgment on the first replication only.

Lord Cairns, L. C., said, at p. 19, "The question might arise, whether, without any express averment, by the law of France or by that of every civilized country, the shareholder would not be bound by all the statutes and provisions of the company in which he was a shareholder. * * * It appears to me that, to all intents and purposes, it is as if there had been an actual and absolute agreement by the defendant; and that, if it were necessary to bring an action against him on the part of the company, the service of the proceedings at the office of the Imperial procurator, if no other place were pointed out, would be good service."

This replication shews there were articles of association which were registered and were binding on the defendant as a member of the company as if he had signed and sealed the same, and had covenanted to conform to all the regulations of the articles subject to the provisions of the Act.

There can be no question then that the notices sent by letter through the post prepaid to the defendant's registered address are a full and perfect notice by his own voluntary consent and agreement of such notices as are within the terms of the article in question. That article according to the replication is, "That notices required to be served by the company upon the members may be served either personally or by leaving the same," &c. Are the notices by which the Court settled the defendant on the list of contributories, and by which he was called upon to appear and shew cause why the order for payment of the calls should not be made, notices to be served by the company upon the members? I do not think they are. The company is not properly the party proceeding in such a winding up. The company does not apply for or obtain the order. It is the liquidator who acts for and represents in

these matters the creditors of the company, and who uses
the company's name for all necessary purposes and upon all
proper occasions to enforce the creditors' rights by and in
the name of the company. The company is being proceed against, as it were adversely in these cases.

The plaintiffs cannot conclude the defendant, therefore,
on the ground of contract by him to be bound by such a
notice according to the terms of the articles of association.
But that is not the whole question. It is, upon such a
notice, which the replication shews was given, is it contrary to natural justice that the plaintiffs should recover
against the defendant for these calls, when he had notice
of the application to put him upon the list of contributories, and notice also to appear and shew cause against
the making of the order declaring the calls he was required
to pay? And when such notices were communicated to
him in the very manner he had stipulated that the general
notices of the company should be communicated to him?

I think there is not one of the cases which says that it
is; but on the contrary they shew, in my opinion, that it
is not. It may not have been quite regular to proceed
with the summons by merely notifying the party of it
in place of serving it, but an irregularity may be cured:
Sheehy v. *Professional Life Ass. Co.*, 13 C. B. 787, per
Maule, J., 794.

The plea itself, as before mentioned, does not exclude
the presumption of several facts as to service and notice
of some of the proceedings upon and to the defendant, and
it may be it admits sufficient by not denying them to
shew the recovery was not against natural justice.

It is sufficient to say the replication states such facts,
although not with the intent or in the manner pleaded, to displace the plea, which sets up in effect a recovery against
natural justice: *Sheehy* v. *Professional Life Ass. Co.*, 2 C.
B. N. S. 211' in Ex. Ch. 3 C. B. N. S: 597.

The defendant knew the company was established under
The Companies' Act, 1862, and that it was registered and had
its domicile in England. He knew also it was liable to

be wound up, and if it were, that the proceedings for that purpose would be taken in England in the Court of Chancery there, against all persons liable to be placed upon the list of contributories, and he knew, too, that he was one of those who were liable to be settled upon such list, and who might be made answerable for calls.

The presumption, too, is, that the defendant subscribed for and took his shares, and thus became a member of the company while he was in England.

He contracted engagements by that act, which it became his duty to fulfil. And he knew that the preliminary steps to give effect to that responsibility must first be taken in England. Under these circumstances it cannot justly be said, with the notices which the defendant has had, which are admitted by the replication and by the rejoinder, and in part by the plea, that the recovery for these calls, which was had against him in England, was contrary to natural justice and void. I am of opinion the second replication to the fifteenth plea is sufficient in substance.

Then as to the second rejoinder to the second replication to the fifteenth plea. It sets out the article as to notices to be given by the company in its terms. Then it alleges that the defendant was not a subscriber to nor did he sign the memorandum of association, nor the articles of association, nor did he ever agree to become bound by the articles of association, or by any of the provisions thereof.

It does not appear to be necessary that the defendant should sign the memorandum of association, nor the articles of association. But it is plain if he became a member of the company, which his fifteenth plea expressly shews he did do, that by the wording of the statute he did become bound as if he had signed and sealed the same, and as if he had covenanted to observe the same.

While the membership is admitted and the enactment referred to is not denied, the defendant cannot dispute the plain terms of the liability, which the fact of his being a member has thrown upon him. The rest of the rejoinder has been already disposed of. It is agreed the proceedings in question were not such as were taken by the company, and therefore the defendant cannot have it said to him that he agreed to receive notice and service of such proceedings in the manner in the replication and rejoinder; but I am of opinion, if the defendant were notified in that manner, as he admits he was, that the recovery against him in England, based upon such notice and service, is not contrary to natural justice. I therefore, as a consequence, hold the rejoinder to be insufficient in law.

The sixteenth plea alleges that the order making the call and directing payment, is not final, but can be varied or rescinded by the Court, and the payment of money under it is not final, because the Court may order restitution of the whole or any part of the money to the defendant which he may. And the plaintiffs have demurred to it because it is no defence.

I considered this point before on the former argument and I am of the same opinion as I was then, that the plea is not a defence in law. If it is a defence in this action, it is a defence to the enforcement of the calls in England by means of an execution which issues from the Court when payment is refused by the member. But if that were a defence, then it would be an idle proceeding to carry on a winding up suit.

So long as the Court has the power to direct payment to be made, it has the power to enforce it by the necessary mandatory process.

The judgment sought by the plaintiffs in this case is auxiliary to the proceedings in England. The judgment if recovered here will practically be under the direction of the Court there, which has full power over the persons of the parties who will control the judgment if obtained.

The defendant's idea of want of finality is, that as he has a chance of getting back something, he should, therefore, not pay anything. It is not good reasoning, for he can never get back anything until he first pay something. And there is no want of finality, as the defendant says there is, if he is not to pay at all, for that is the most final of all proceedings.

There is some confusion on this point where there should not be any.   A decree or order may not be final when it is collateral or when it is conditional in some way to the performance of some other act, or when there is an option to the party to do one thing or the other.   But when the sum to be paid is settled, it cannot be said then not to be final for the purpose of that payment made or to be made, because there is something afterwards to be done or which may be done with respect to that money : *Sadler* v. *Robins,* 1 Camp. 253; *Henderson* v. *Henderson*, 6 Q. B. 288.

In *Vanquelin* v. *Bouard,* 15 C. B. N. S. 341, p. 367, Erle, C.J., said : " The twelfth plea, to the first count, alleges that the judgment in the first count mentioned was a judgment by default for want of an appearance by the defendant in the Court of the Tribunal of Commerce, and by the law of France would become void as of course on an appearance being entered. I apprehend that every judgment of a foreign Court of competent jurisdiction is valid, and may be the foundation of an action in our Courts, though subject to the contingency, that by adopting a certain course the party against whom the judgment is obtained might cause it to be vacated or set aside.   But until that course has been pursued, the judgment remains in full force and capable of being sued upon.   The plaintiff, therefore, must have judgment on the demurrer to this plea."

So in *Scott* v. *Pilkington*, 2 B. & S. 11, where an action is brought on a judgment of a foreign Court the pendency of an appeal in the foreign Court against that judgment is no bar to the action, although it may afford ground for the equitable interposition of the English Court in which the action is brought to prevent, the possible abuse of its process and in proper time to stay execution.

All those cases against suing on judgments in the Division Courts in the Superior Courts of this country, and on County Court judgments in England in the Superior Courts there, are founded on different considerations altogether than the consideration arising from the want of

finality, or from the refusal of one Court to aid another.
They are based upon the ground that these smaller Courts
have different powers and a larger equitable jurisdition
than the higher Courts have in such cases, and the policy
of the law was to preserve the suitors of these Courts where
the costs were not so high as in the other Courts, from being
harassed in the higher and more expensive Courts, and they
have no reference whatever to the rule, which guide the
Courts of one country in giving aid and effect to the
judgments of another country.

In *Patrick* v. *Shedden*, 2 E. & B. 14, the order sued
upon was plainly an interim or interlocutory proceeding,
entitling the party to levy his costs, while the appeal was
pending in the House of Lords, the costs to be accounted
for afterwards, and so it was held an action would not lie
for them as the proceeding was not final.

In *Berkeley* v. *Elderkin*, 1 E. & B. 805, it was held that
an action would not lie in the Superior Court upon a judgment of the County Court, because the Legislature had provided a cheap remedy for suitors in County Court cases,
and that object of the Act would be defeated if an action
could be maintained in the Superior Courts upon such
judgments. Again, there were goods which were exempt
from seizure under the County Court process, which would
not be protected from seizure under the Superior Court
execution. And besides, there was no imprisonment in the
County Court but for contempt, none by way of punishment.
And the Judge had the power to order the payment of the
debt by instalments, and to rescind and alter that order by
any other he might make, as to debt and costs, as he might
think just. And the Court held, therefore, the judgment
was not a final proceeding upon which an action would lie.

The like decision was pronounced in several cases in our
own Courts in actions upon judgments in the Division
Court. I shall only refer to *Donnelly* v. *Stewart*, 25 U.
C. R. 398.

But can it be said if the debtor left the jurisdiction of that
inferior Court and went abroad, that he could not be sued
in the foreign Court upon such a judgment ? I think not.

And in this case more particularly must the payment be enforced, because the very purpose and object of the winding up suit must be frustrated if the payments are not made as they must necessarily abide the result of a further and later disposition of them.

In re East India Cotton Agency, Furdoonjee's case, L. R. 3 Ch. D., 264: it was held that a shareholder resident in Bombay, of a joint stock company registered in England, could not put upon his list of debts and liabilities the shares which he had in the company before the winding up of the company had commenced, because the extent of that liability, or whether there would be a liability or not, was incapable of proof; and the debtor, although he got his discharge in Bombay, was put on the contributory list of shareholders in England.

The Financial Corporation v. *Lawrence*, L. R. 4 C. P. 731, was a case in which the like rule was applied to an inspectorship deed executed by the debtor in England.

In *Ex parte Pickering, Re Pickering*, L. R. 4 Ch. 58, 61, Wood, L. J., said :—"While the concern is a going concern, the amount of liability to future calls is incapable of being estimated ; but when the company is being wound up this state of things is altered, and the contributory is a debtor for an amount which the Legislature assumes to be capable of being estimated."

If in a foreign country the unpaid shares of a company being wound up can be placed upon the list of creditors as a debt due or contingently due to the company, and is then a provable debt, and for which the subsequent discharge to the debtor would release him, then it is quite plain it is a debt taken notice of and capable of being dealt with by the foreign Court, just as any other debt is noticed and dealt with. It appears to be a case in point, and to be a complete answer of itself as a matter of authority, to the objection upon which the whole defence rests, that this is not a debt which can be proceeded for in a foreign country.

The sixteenth plea, therefore, is, in my opinion, not sufficient in law.

The plaintiff has then replied to the sixteenth plea, to the effect that the payment of calls is final, unless there is a surplus fund, and that there will be no surplus; and that all proceedings are final, unless they are appealed against within a given time, which the defendant has not done. And the defendant has demurred to it.

That replication, although not necessary, is not bad in law. It shews facts which are intended to convince the defendant that if he once pay the money he has not the slightest chance of ever getting any part of it back again. The demurrer to it cannot be maintained from what I have said as to the fifteenth plea.

The seventeenth plea, as to the defendant having been induced to take the shares by fraud of the plaintiffs, and that he repudiated the shares as soon as he discovered the fraud, and that he derived no benefit from the shares, was not argued. We suppose because the authorities are so strongly against the validity of such a plea, so long as the party has not had his name removed in fact from the company's list of members.

Our attention has been called to the fact that since judgment was given in the case on the former argument the 23 Vic. ch. 24 sec. 1, under which the pleas have been pleaded impeaching every matter in like manner as it could have been done to the original proceeding itself, has been repealed by the 39 Vic. ch. 7, sec. 1 and sched. A., O. The question is, does that affect the pleas which were pleaded under and by the authority of that Act, and preclude the defendant from any longer contesting the merits of the orders which were made by the Court of Chancery in England imposing upon him the liability which is the subject of the action

"The Interpretation Act," 1868, sec. 7 sub-sec. 34, enacts that, "The repeal of an Act at any time shall not affect any act done or any right or right of action existing, accruing, accrued, or established, or any proceedings commenced in a civil cause, before the time when such repeal shall take effect; but the proceedings in such case shall be conformable when necessary to the repealing Act."

And sub-sec. 35 enacts that "No offence committed, and no penalty or forfeiture incurred, and no proceeding pending under any Act at any time repealed, shall be affected by the repeal, except that the proceedings shall be conformable, when necessary, to the repealing Act."

In this case there was by the exercise by the defendant to plead as he had done under the Act since repealed, "an act done, or a right existing, accrued, or established," and perhaps also it may be said there were by the pleas pleaded "proceedings commenced in a civil cause before the time when such repeal shall take effect."

It may also be said that under the words "No proceeding pending under any Act at any time repealed shall be affected by the repeal,' also entitle the defendant to maintain his pleas under the repealed Act. The object of the Legislature was plainly not to divest or disturb any thing done, or any right acquired under a statute, because that statute was afterwards repealed.

The effect of a repeal of a statute at common law is as was stated by Tindal, C. J., in *Kay* v. *Sherwin*, 6 Bing. 576, 582, "I take the effect of repealing a statute to be, to obliterate it as completely from the records of the Parliament as if it had never passed; and it must be considered as a law that never existed, except for the purpose of those actions which were commenced, prosecuted, and concluded while it was an existing law."

In *Morgan* v. *Thorne*, 7 M. & W. 400, where the Judge who tried the cause postponed granting the certificate to deprive the plaintiff of costs until the motion for a nonsuit was disposed of, and before that time a new statute came into force which repealed the earlier statute under which the Judge would have given the certificate, it was held that the certificate he then gave was void.

In *Charrington* v. *Meatheringham*, 2 M. & W. 228, the defendant was entitled by statute to treble costs on the plaintiff being nonsuited, which statute was in force at the time of the trial, but before judgment was entered the statute was repealed, and it was held the defendant was not entitled to tax treble costs.

In *Miller's Case*, 1 W. Bl. 451, it was held that an insolvent who had done everything under the statute to entitle him to his discharge was deprived of the discharge by the repeal of the statute. See also *Butcher* v. *Henderson*, L. R. 3 Q. B. 335.

The effect of the common law rule would have been to remove the provision of the statute which permitted the defendant to plead to the merits of the original proceeding in this action upon it in like manner as he could have done to the original proceeding itself, as if it had never existed. But our own special legislation has, I think, preserved and maintained his rights as he had them under the law which was in force when he exercised them.

It seems, without regard to the facts of this case, a just and correct principle of law, and it is certain that injustice was done under the contrary rule according to some of the cases which have been cited.

The result of my opinion is, that the declaration is good in law against the demurrer to it.

That the first, second, fourth, fifth, sixth, eighth, tenth, eleventh, twelfth, and thirteenth pleas are good.

The fourteenth plea is bad.

The second replication to the fifteenth plea is good.

The second rejoinder to the second replication to the fifteenth plea is bad.

The sixteenth plea is not good.

The second replication to it, so far as it is of any consequence to say so, is sufficient in law.

The seventeenth plea is not good.

HARRISON, C. J.—I am sorry to say I am compelled to dissent from the result at which my learned brother Wilson has arrived as to the sufficiency of the declaration.

I shall, as shortly as possible, state the grounds of my dissent.

The declaration before amendment was against the defendant as a member of the company for a debt due by him as a contributory, and the Court as then constituted, for reasons then expressed by my brother Wilson, held the declaration good.

It is not necessary for me to say whether or not I concur in that decision, pronounced as it was before I became a member of the Court, for although not bound by all the reasons assigned by any particular Judge or Judges for reaching a particular conclusion, I am, as a member of this Court, bound by a former decision of the Court. the result of judicial deliberation, till that decision be reversed by a majority of the Court or by some higher authority. See *McGee* v. *McLaughlin,* 23 U. C. R. 90.

But the declaration as now amended is against the defendant as a past member, whose only liability, it is argued, is under the statute, and under a statute which gives no express power to the company in liquidation by action to enforce that liability.

I am not, therefore, I think, in any manner concluded by the former decision of this Court from stating and I deem it my duty unreservedly to state my opinion as to the cause of action, if any, disclosed in the present declaration.

To sustain this declaration it is not, in my opinion, enough for the company to shew a liability of some kind on the part of the defendant, but the company must shew a liability to themselves as plaintiffs, or in respect to which they, as plaintiffs, are expressly authorized to sue.

So long as a person remains a member of an incorporated joint stock company, and there is a portion of his subscribed stock unpaid, there is a liability to the company after calls duly made by the company, and it may be that this liability continues after the company is placed in liquidation, for in that case the company, although not beneficially entitled to the money, is "suing in its own name for its own debt." See *United Ports and General Insurance Company* v. *Hill et al,* L. R. 5 Q. B. 395.

But this cannot be where the person is sued as a past member—in other words, has before suit ceased to be a member of the company, and thereby all privity of contract between him and the company has also ceased. The liability, if any, which then ensues, appears to me not to be a liability to the company, but a liability solely to the creditors of the company—a liability created by statute, and which can only be enforced in the special manner which the statute directs. See *Macbeth* v. *Smart*, 14 Grant, 298; *Ryland* v. *DeLisle*, L. R. 3 P. C. 17; *Re Paraguassu Steam Tramroad Company, Black & Co.'s case*, L. R. 8 Ch. 254; *Benner* v. *Currie*, 36 U. C. R. 411; *McGregor* v. *Currie*, 26 C. P. 55.

In my opinion, therefore, the declaration discloses no cause of action against the defendant, and for that reason I decline to express any opinion as to the sufficiency of any of the many subsequent pleadings.

I think the defendant is entitled to judgment on demurrer.

MORRISON, J., concurred with Harrison, C. J.

Judgment for defendant.

THE ROYAL CANADIAN BANK v. ROSS.

Banks—Transfer to of Warehouse Receipts—34 Vic., c. 5, D.

The 34 Vic. c. 5, secs. 46 and 47, D., permits the transfer to a bank of a bill of lading, or warehouse receipt, to secure an antecedent debt, where the understanding at the time of contracting such debt was, that the bill of lading should be transferred as collateral security.

In this case it appeared that the bank agreed to make advances to S. & Co. to purchase coal and stone, to be secured by bills of lading and warehouse receipts for such coal and stone when received. The transfer of such receipts to the bank, after the arrival of the goods, was held to be authorized; and it was held no objection that the agreement was to give a receipt for goods of which, at the time, the person was not possessed.

Six months had elapsed after the giving of the receipt before the seizure of the goods by the creditors of S. & Co., but the bank had taken possession of these goods with the consent of S & Co., and were selling them in order to repay their advances. *Held*, under 34 Vic., ch. 5, sec. 50, D., that they were entitled to hold the goods, notwithstanding the lapse of time.

THIS was an interpleader issue, directed to try the ownership of a quantity of plaster seized at Belleville on

14th March 1876, by the sheriff of the county of Hastings, as being the property of Messrs. George Simpson & Co., at the instance of the defendant, a judgment creditor of that firm.

The firm of George Simpson & Co. was formed in 1868, and consisted of Messrs. George and James H. Simpson.

Their business was importing stone for plaster, grinding it and selling it, as well as storing grain, coal, &c., and acting as general warehousemen and wharfingers.

It was in 1870 that the firm first began to import the stone plaster and grind it. They imported about 600 tons a year. The importations were made in the summer and ground in the fall and winter. Sales usually commenced about the month of February in the year following the importation. There were generally about 300 tons of plaster on hand.

In 1872 James H. Simpson retired from the firm, but, as he afterwards continued to act for the firm, the fact of his retirement was not known to the bank.

The firm in 1873 made an agreement with the Royal Canadian Bank at Belleville for advances to be made by the bank for the purpose of purchasing coal and stone plaster, the same to be secured by bills of lading and warehouse receipts on the coal and stone when received, the stone to be then ground into plaster by George Simpson & Co. at their mill in Belleville and sold ; they accounting from time to time to the bank for the proceeds, in reduction of the amount of advances from time to time made by the bank.

Advances were made by the bank to the firm in 1873, and on 5th December 1873 a warehouse receipt covering 500 tons of plaster was made by George Simpson & Co. in their own favour, and was by them endorsed to the bank for the purpose of securing the advances in accordance with the original understanding.

On 10th April 1874 Mr. John Young succeeded the former agent of the bank at Belleville. He, in July of that year, agreed with the firm of George Simpson & Co. to make advances to the firm to the extent of $6,000 for the same purposes as in the preceding year, such advances to be secured as before.

In August, 1874, Mr. Young, under the agreement, discounted a note for the firm of $1,750.

During the following month of September a bill of lading for 250 tons of stone plaster, dated Oswego 24th September, 1874, was transferred to the bank under the agreement. It was accompanied by a draft for $575, United States currency, which the bank retired.

This cargo on its arrival was found to be 16 tons short making only 234 tons.

The bank shortly afterwards discounted paper for the firm to the amount of about $5,800.

In October, 1874, a warehouse receipt for 234 tons of plaster stone, the cargo covered by the bill of lading, was given to the bank.

About the same time a further warehouse receipt for 300 tons more of plaster stone was given to the bank under the agreement to secure advances.

On 28th January, 1875, the firm gave the bank a warehouse receipt for 534 tons of plaster and stone.

This was intended to cover and to consolidate the previous receipts for 234 and 300 tons of stone plaster, respectively.

Renewal notes were from time to time discounted by the bank for the firm.

Some moneys were paid to the bank in reduction of the indebtedness of the firm to the bank, which in June, 1875, reduced the claim of the bank to $6,100,

About this time a note on demand was drawn for the amount of $6,100, and a warehouse receipt given to the bank for 300 tons of plaster then actually being in the possession of the firm.

This was sworn to have been the plaster made from the stone covered by the bill of lading and previous warehouse receipts.

No stone plaster was afterwards received by the firm at Belleville.

The note for $6,100 was discounted by the bank, and the proceeds applied in payment of the then existing indebtedness of the firm to the bank.

In July, 1875, George Simpson left for British Columbia, and the bank took possession of the plaster covered by the last warehouse receipt.

Before and at the time of the seizure the bank had possession of the plaster, and was making sales of it for the purpose of repaying the advances which had been made on it.

The cause was tried at the last Chancery Sittings for the county of Hastings, before Proudfoot, V. C.

Several objections were raised as grounds of nonsuit, but the learned Vice Chancellor overruled them, reserving leave to the defendant to move to enter a nonsuit, and a verdict was entered for the plaintiffs.

During Easter Term, May 29, 1876. *Hodgins*, Q. C. obtained a rule calling on the plaintiffs to shew cause why the verdict should not be set aside, and a nonsuit entered, on the following grounds :—

1. The statute only allows the bank to acquire and hold warehouse receipts on property stored or deposited with the warehouseman at the time of the advance of the money by the bank, and on the understanding being had that warehouse receipts are to be given, and does not authorize the bank to acquire warehouse receipts on property not owned by the warehouseman or stored or deposited with him at the time of the advance being made by the bank, but to be acquired by him subsequently.

2. The agreement to give warehouse receipts at the time of an advance being made by the bank must be an agreement to give some specific receipt or receipts upon some specified property, and upon some specified quantity, and not an agreement to give warehouse receipts in general terms.

3. There could not be a valid agreement under the statute to pledge property not then in existence.

4. The warehouse receipt dated 3rd June, 1875, was not dated on the day it bears date, but was antedated for a fraudulent purpose by George A. Simpson & Co. or J. H. Simpson, and therefore was not a valid receipt.

5. That more than six months had elapsed from the date of receipt or possession thereof by the bank before seizure under defendant's execution, and the receipt, therefore, was of no force or effect.

6. If the manual possession of the receipt by the bank was only about four months before the examination of James Young, the manager of the bank, as sworn to by him, it must have been received by him after defendant's execution and after seizure thereunder.

7. The warehouse receipt was never handed over to the possession of the manager of the bank, and pledged as collateral security for the due payment of any bill or note discounted by said bank, in the regular course of its banking business.

8. There never was any legal transfer of said warehouse receipt covering said ground plaster under the Act entitled "An Act relating to Banks and Banking," the bill, note, or debt not having been negociated or contracted at the time of the acquisition of such warehouse receipt by the bank, or upon the understanding and agreement that such warehouse receipt should be transferred to the bank.

9. That there was no such firm in existence as George A. Simpson & Co. at the date of the warehouse receipt or when the receipt was given.

10. If that firm was in existence when the receipt was given, George A. Simpson & Co. were not warehousemen within the meaning of the Act.

11. The bank never had possession of the plaster covered by said receipt.

12. At the time of the receipt being given, George A. Sinpson & Co. were in insolvent circumstances and were not able to meet their engagements, of which the plaintiffs had full notice, and the giving of the receipt to the Bank was a fraudulent preference within the meaning of the statutes, and therefore void as against creditors.

Or why the verdict should not be set aside upon the like grounds, and a new trial ordered, or a verdict entered for the defendant.

During Hilary Term last, *Geo. D. Dickson*, shewed cause. The bank claims the plaster both under the bill of lading and under the warehouse receipts, and is, under the general understanding upon which the money was advanced, entitled to hold it.: Consol. Stat. C. ch. 54; 24 Vic. ch. 23; 31 Vic. ch. 11, D.; 34 Vic. ch. 5, D.; *Todd* v. *Liverpool & London & Globe Ins. Co.* 18 C. P. 192, in appeal, 20 C. P. 523; *McBride* v. *The Gore District Mutual Ins. Co.*, 30 U. C. R. 451; *Ontario Bank* v. *Newton*, 19 C. P. 258; *Bank of British North America* v. *Clarkson*, 19 C. P. 182; *Royal Canadian Bank* v. *Miller*, 29 U. C. R. 266; *Llado et al.* v. *Morgan*, 23 C. P. 517; *Coffey* v. *The Quebec Bank*, 20 C. P. 110, 555.

Hodgins, Q. C., contra. There was no new advance at the time of the transfer of any of the warehouse receipts. The change from stone to ground plaster so changed the property as to free it from the operation of the receipt. The plaster was so mixed that it was impossible to say how much, if any, of what was seized was covered either by the bill of lading or the warehouse receipt. The agreement was for a future advance on property not in *esse*, and the receipts given under that agreement were inoperative.

March 10, 1877. HARRISON, C. J.—The first eleven objections taken to the recovery of the bank may be substantially reduced to the number of three:

1. The right of George Simpson & Co. to make warehouse receipts, and whether warehouse receipts were made by that firm.

2. The right of the bank to receive warehouse receipts under a preceding agreement to make advances on the security of warehouse receipts to be afterwards given.

3. The right of the bank to hold the property under the warehouse receipts after the expiration of six months from the giving of the same.

The legal sufficiency of these objections must be decided on the proper reading of the Act relating to Banks and Banking, 34 Vic. ch. 5, D.

No bank coming under the operation of that Act is allowed, directly or indirectly, to lend money or make advances upon the security, mortgage, or hypothecation of any goods, wares, or merchandise except as authorized by the Act : sec. 40.

The bank may take, hold, and dispose of mortgages and hypotheques upon real and personal property by way of additional security for debts contracted to the bank in the course of its business : sec. 41.

The bank may acquire and hold, among other things, any receipt given for cereal grains, goods, wares, or merchandise stored or deposited in any cove, wharf, yard, harbour, warehouse, mill, or other place in Canada, or shipped in any vessel, or delivered to any carrier for carriage from any place whatever to any part of this Dominion, as collateral security for the due payment of any bill of exchange or note discounted by such bank in the regular course of its banking business : sec. 46.

The bank may also receive warehouse receipts for any debt which may become due to the bank under any credit opened or liability incurred by the bank for or on behalf of the holder or owner of the bill of lading, receipt, &c., or for any other debt to become due to the bank. Ib.

No transfer of the bill, warehouse receipt, &c., is to be made under the Act, unless the bill, note, or debt be negotiated or contracted at the time of the acquisition thereof by the bank, or upon the understanding that such bill or receipt would be transferred to the bank : sec. 47.

The bill, note, or debt may be renewed, or the time for payment thereof extended by the bank, without affecting the security. Ib.

The warehouseman giving the receipt, &c., and the person transferring it to the bank, may be one and the same person : sec. 48.

No cereal grains or goods, wares or merchandise (other than timber, &c., for which special provision is made,) shall, except with the consent of the person pledging the same, be held for a period exceeding six months: sec. 50.

Without the aid of this statute the transfer of warehouse receipts to the bank would not pass the interest of the owner of goods embraced therein to the bank : *Deady* v. *Goodenough*, 5 C. P. 163, 176 ; *Glass* v. *Whitney*, 22 U. C. R. 290, 294.

The Legislature having provided for the transfer under certain conditions, it is necessary for the bank, in order to hold the property as against the creditors of the transferor, to shew that the transfer was made under the conditions prescribed : *Bank of British North America* v. *Clarkson*, 19 C. P. 182 ; *Royal Canadian Bank* v. *Miller*, 29 U. C. R. 266 ; *Royal Canadian Bank* v. *Carruthers*, Ib. 283.

Much of the business of the country now done with banks is done by means of the transfer of warehouse receipts, and the Legislature has from time to time, according to the exigencies of commerce, amended and extended the law so as to facilitate the doing of business in that manner.

While the Legislature at first may have intended only to provide for the storing of goods with some public warehouseman, the taking of a receipt from him, and the transfer of such receipt as a security for advances, it is manifest that by the power given to a warehouseman to store his own property, give a receipt to himself and transfer that receipt to the bank, the law is greatly extended.

This particular extension, in the absence of some system of Government registration or Government inspection, may be much abused, and has in some instances been so abused as to be productive of rank frauds : *Todd* v. *The Liverpool & London & Globe Ins. Co.*, 18 C. P. 192; in appeal, 20 C. P. 528 ; *Box* v. *The Provincial Ins. Co.*, 15 Grant 337, reversed on appeal, 18 Grant 280.

But considering the magnitude and multiplicity of the transactions, the wonder is, in the present loose state of the law, that the frauds are not more numerous.

Unless it appears that the person or persons giving the warehouse receipt was, at the time of giving it, a warehouseman of some kind, the receipt will be of no value as a transfer of property: *Ontario Bank* v. *Newton*, 19 C. P. 258.

This is the foundation of the right, and if this be wanting, the entire superstructure must of course fall to the ground.

When the warehouse receipts in question here were given, George Simpson was carrying on the business of warehouseman under the name, style, and firm of George Simpson & Co.

It would seem that, so far as the bank is concerned, his brother James H. Simpson held himself out as a partner; but this is of no consequence, for whether the firm was composed of the two or the one, that firm did make and transfer the warehouse receipts to the bank.

Then were these receipts, or any of them, transferred to the bank under such circumstances as to make the property therein described the property of the bank ? The Consol. Stat. C. ch. 54 sec. 8, only permitted the receipts to be transferred to a bank, "as collateral security for the due payment of any bill of exchange or note discounted by such bank in the regular course of its business." But the present Act goes further. It permits the warehouse receipt, &c., "for any debt which may become due to the bank *under any credit opened or liability incurred by the bank* for or on behalf of the owner of such receipts, or for any *other* debt to become due to the bank," and provides for advances on a previous "understanding that such receipts would be transferred to the bank :" 34 Vic., ch. 5, secs. 46, 47, D.

The title of the plaintiffs is rested principally on the warehouse receipt of June or July, 1875. The original was lost. The contents were satisfactorily proved. The copy produced was not of the same date as the original. This leads to some confusion in the testimony about it. But upon the whole evidence it would appear to have been given to the bank at the end of June or beginning of July, 1875, and for an honest purpose. It covered 200 or 300 tons of plaster then in store. But no actual advance of money was made at the time of its transfer to the bank. Unless we can look behind it to see what took place between the parties before it was given, the argument that it was for a past due debt would be entitled to some weight.

Now the statute not only enables the bank to accept the transfer of a warehouse receipt as collateral security for the due payment of a bill or note at the time discounted, but for any debt which may become due to the bank upon any credit opened—that is, *previously* opened; or for any debt or liability incurred—that is, *previously* incurred —by the bank for or on behalf of the owner of the receipt. If this meaning were doubtful upon the reading of sec. 46 standing by itself, the doubt is removed upon reading it in connection with sec. 47. While the latter declares that no transfer of the receipt shall be made to secure the payment of any bill, note or debt, unless negotiated or contracted at the time of the acquisition thereof by the bank, this is only one of the alternatives of the section. The other alternative is thus expressed, "or upon the understanding that such bill of lading or * * * receipt, *would* be transferred to the bank," &c.

The effect of reading the sections in conjunction is to permit the transfer of a bill of lading, &c., to secure an antecedent debt, where the understanding was, at the time of the contracting of the debt, that such bill of lading, &c., should be transferred as collateral security for the payment of the debt.

It is argued that an agreement to give a warehouse receipt on goods of which the person at the time is not possessed, is no valid transfer of the property. In one sense this is true; but this is only in a limited sense. In equity while it is held, as at law, that a contract to transfer property which is not in existence cannot operate as a conveyance simply because there is nothing to convey, still if a person agree to sell or mortgage property, real or personal, of which at the time he is not possessed, and

receive the consideration for the contract, if he afterwards
acquire the property equity stamps it as the property of
the person who paid the consideration for its transfer, and
will compel the vendor or mortgagor to convey it according
to contract : *Holroyd* v. *Marshall*, 9 Jur. N. S. 213 ; *Re
Thirkell*, 21 Grant 492. See further *Mason* v. *McDonald*,
25 C. P. 435, 439.

It is on this principle that a transfer of a debtor's
property to secure a past advance may be upheld against
creditors in bankruptcy, on proof that the debt was
contracted upon the understanding or agreement that the
property should be transferred : *Hutton et al.* v. *Cruttwell*,
1 E. & B. 15 ; *Harris* v. *Rickett*, 4 H. & N. 1 ; *Allan* v.
Clarkson, 17 Grant 570.

The transfer when made, as it were, relates to the antecedent agreement on the faith of which the debt was
contracted, and so the transfer when made, although in
one sense made to secure an antecedent debt, is a valid
transfer because springing from and sustained by the
original agreement.

To this extent it appears to us that the Legislature, by
the Act of 1871, intended to allow banks to take warehouse receipts, although no bill or note is actually discounted
at the time of the transfer—that is, although the proceeds
of the bill or note, if any, at the time said to be discounted,
are not then paid to the owner of the warehouse receipt,
he having previously obtained the advance.

It is not for us to question the wisdom of legislation,
It is our duty to give effect to legislation as best we can,
in accordance with the language which the Legislature has
used.

It appears to us that the understanding which took place
between the bank and Simpson & Co. in 1873 and 1874,
was such as the Legislature has authorized, and that the
subsequent warehouse receipts, given as they were on
property at the time of giving *in esse*, must be sustained.

It is sworn not only that there were the 300 tons of
plaster to answer the receipt of June or July 1875, but

that the same was the produce of the stone of which the bank received the bill of lading in September, 1874.

No question was raised at the trial as to the effect of the conversion of the stone into plaster, and could not well be raised by the warehouseman or his creditors in the face of the fact that in the receipt of June, 1875, the merchandise is described as plaster, and was then plaster.

But it is further argued that before the seizure six months had expired after the giving of the receipt, so as to make the holding of the bank against the creditors of the pledgors unlawful.

In this particular, also, the law now is not what it was in 1859. The Consol. Stat. C. ch. 54, sec. 9, did not permit the holding of the goods, under any circumstances, for a longer period than six months. The effect of the expiration of the six months without a sale by the bank was to revest the property in the original owner. The present Act not only provides for the extension of the time for the payment of the debt without affecting the security:— sec. 47—but permits the holding of the goods for a longer period than six months, where held with the consent of the person who pledged the same: sec. 50.

Where the bank. within the six months, with the consent of the pledgor, obtains possession of the property pledged, the bank then in good faith proceeds to sell and is selling at the expiration of the six months and at the time of the seizure, it must, in our opinion, under the statute, if necessary, be held that the bank is in possession with the consent of the person pledging, so as to enable the bank, as against his creditors, to hold notwithstanding the expiration of the six months.

This, in effect, disposes of all the objections taken in the rule except the twelfth, and that is, that at the time the last receipts were given George Simpson & Co. were in insolvent circumstances and were not able to meet their engagements, of which the plaintiffs had full notice, and the giving of the receipt was a fraudulent preference. The evidence fails to sustain this objection and nothing was said—probably because nothing could be said—in its support at the argument. The rule *nisi* must be discharged.

MORRISON, J., concurred.

Rule discharged.

LEPROHON v. THE CORPORATION OF THE CITY OF OTTAWA.

Government officers of the Dominion—Income tax.

Held, (Harrison, C. J., *dissentiente*) that the corporation of the city of Ottawa could legally impose a tax upon the official income of officers of the Dominion Government, the Legislature having given, and having the right under the B. N. A. Act to give, the power to impose such tax.

Held, also that an officer of the House of Commons of the Dominion at Ottawa, paid out of moneys voted by the Parliament of Canada, is an officer of the Dominion Government.

THE declaration contained a count in trespass to goods and trover.

The only plea necessary to be mentioned is the third which alleged that the plaintiff, being a resident inhabitant of the city of Ottawa, was assessed for $18.07 for taxes on certain personal property and income in the city : that the defendants, by their collector of taxes, demanded payment thereof from the plaintiff at his place of residence, but that he did not pay the same, and after fourteen days had elapsed from the time of demand, the taxes remaining unpaid, the defendants authorized their collector to levy and collect the same, which he did by distress and sale of the plaintiff's goods, &c.

The plaintiff replied that he was not at any time liable to be assessed by the defendants for the income tax in the plea mentioned.

The defendants took issue on the replication.

The cause was tried before Moss, J., at the last Assizes for the county of Carleton.

The following admissions were made at the trial :—

1. The plaintiff is a resident of the city of Ottawa and a householder therein, and liable to the municipal assessments of the city generally.

2. The plaintiff is an officer of the House of Commons of the Dominion of Canada, whose salary is paid out of moneys voted by the Parliament of Canada in the annual supply bill under the head of " House of Commons salaries and contingencies, per clerks estimate, as prepared under the Internal Economy Act, 31 Vic. ch. 7, " such salary being paid to the plaintiff at the city of Ottawa, the seat of Government of the Dominion of Canada, out of the moneys there deposited and being, and belonging to the said Dominion; and the plaintiff's office is in the city of Ottawa.

3. In respect of his income derived from such salary, being a salary of $1,500 per annum, he was assessed and taxed for the year 1875 for the amount of $18.07, under the authority of the Assessment Act of the Province of Ontario ; and his name being on the revised assessment roll of the city for the year 1875 for said amount, the collector of the defendants, after protest by the plaintiff, proceeded to sell, and did sell, the plaintiff's goods in order to realize and did realize the amount of the tax, with costs and charges.

The plaintiff claimed to be exempt from any tax or assessment on his income by reason of such income being derived from his salary payable to him under an annual vote of the Parliament of Canada, and therefore not assessable under any existing law or laws.

The sole question raised at the trial was, whether the corporation of the city of Ottawa could legally assess and collect from an officer of the House of Commons a tax or assessment upon his income, deri ved as aforesaid.

The learned Judge was of opinion that the plaintiff was exempt, and entered a verdict in his favour for $25.

The opinion was as follows:—

Moss, J.—As the learned counsel candidly informed me at the outset, this is a test case, and it is intended to ultimately obtain an expression of opinion from the Supreme Court of the Dominion upon the question involved. My own individual opinion, therefore, is a matter of little importance, and I might, without any impropriety, have contented myself with entering a verdict *pro formâ*. But as I am desired to express an opinion I shall endeavour to do so before entering a verdict.

This case is one of considerable difficulty ; the time and opportunities I have had to investigate the subject, have been wholly inadequate to that full consideration which it must ultimately receive ; and I have made no attempt to reduce my views to writing. I have endeavoured, however, to form an opinion upon the various points submitted to me by the learned counsel in the course of their able argument.

The question which it seems convenient first to consider is, whether, upon the proper construction of the Assessment Acts of Ontario, the income of an officer of the House of Commons is liable to taxation. On behalf of the plaintiff in this case, who is an officer of the House of Commons and whose salary is payable in the manner stated in the admissions, it was argued that upon the true construction of the Assessment Acts, the Legislature of Ontario, so far from imposing any charge upon the income of such an official, had declared it to be exempt With this contention I am not able to agree. By the Act of 1866, which was in force at the time the British North America Act was passed and Confederation established, the salaries of officials in the position of the plaintiff were exempt ; and in the Ontario statute of 1869, relating to the assessment of property, that exemption was continued, the language of the statute being only varied from that of 1866 so far as the changed circumstances of our political condition rendered necessary. By the Act of 1869 it was clear that these official salaries were not subject to taxation. Sub-section 25 of section 9 expressly includes, among the exemptions from liability to taxation, the annual official salaries of the officers and servants of the House of Commons resident at the seat of Government at Ottawa. The plaintiff is a servant of the House of Commons resident at the seat of Government at Ottawa, and therefore if that clause had continued in force he would have been exempt by the express enactment of the Legislature. But, sub-section 25 of section 9 of that Act was repealed by the Act of 1871, and therefore, in the existing statute law of the Province, there is no express exemption of the salary of a person occupying the position of the plaintiff.

But it was argued that an exemption was constructively contained in sub-section 12 of the same section, which exempts any pension, salary, or gratuity or stipend, derived from Her Majesty's Imperial Treasury, or elsewhere out of this Province. The contention of the plaintiff was, that this was a salary derived out of this Province. I do not think that exemption extends to the present case. The course of legislation seems to me to be quite opposed to this construction being placed upon sub-section 12. That sub-section is to be found in the Acts of 1866 and 1869, and contains precisely the same words " or elsewhere out of this Province." Notwithstanding the use of these words, the Legislature, when it desired to manifest its intention of exempting such salaries, deemed it necessary to use express language. This appears equivalent to a legislative declaration that the words in the 12th sub-section did not cover the case. If they did, the express exemption in the 25th sub-section was wholly unnecessary. It may be said that this was done for greater precaution. But, even if that explanation was otherwise unsatisfactory, what is to be said of the repeal of sub-section 25 by the Act of 1871 ? It cannot admit of serious doubt. I think that the intention of the Legislature in repealing the Act was, to remove these official salaries from the list of exemptions. On the whole, I think that upon the construction of the Ontario Assessment Acts the Legislature of Ontario have not exempted the incomes of officers of the House of Commons from liability to assessment.

The grave question then arises, whether the Provincial Legislature had power to impose a tax upon the salaries of such officers. I need not say that I approach the solution of this question with very grave doubt and very great hesitation. It is a constitutional question, involving delicate considerations and affecting very considerable interests. The best conclusion which I have been able to form is, that upon the construction of the powers which are vested in the Legislature of Ontario, the officers in the position of the plaintiff are not liable to be assessed upon their incomes. I look first, as I am bound to look, at the language of the British North America Act. Upon the terms of this statute the defendants relied for finding the power to impose a tax upon these incomes. The 2nd, 8th, and 13th sub-sections of the 92nd section are the clauses upon which the defendants mainly rely. The object of the 92nd section was, to define the matters with which the Provincial Legislature should alone have the power to deal, and to describe the subjects which should be withdrawn from the legislative control of the Dominion Parliament. The second sub-section gives the Legislature of each Province power to legislate in relation to direct taxation in the Province, in order to the raising of a revenue for Provincial purposes. I am of opinion that the assessment in question cannot be said to be a matter of direct taxation in order to the raising of a revenue for

Provincial purposes.   It is an assessment levied for raising
moneys for municipal purposes.   Then the Legislature of each
Province has also power, by the 8th sub-section, to make laws
relating exclusively to matters coming within the class of municipal institions in the Province.   Now, no doubt under this
sub-section it belongs to the Provincial Legislature to determine
generally the mode of assessment for municipal purposes and on
what property taxation should be levied.   The power to authorize the mode of assessment and levy of taxes for municipal
purposes, it may be conceded, is impliedly contained in the power
to legislate generally with respect to municipal institutions.   But
the extent and limits of this power are not expressly stated.   It
arises by implication and necessary intendment, not by express
enactment.   I do not think that that section of itself contains
any express authority to levy such a tax as that in question.   The
13th sub-section, which gives the exclusive legislative jurisdiction
over property and civil rights, does not appear to me to be
applicable.

On the whole, I do not find in the British North America
Act that there is an express provision either authorizing or prohibiting any tax on such incomes.   That being the case, there
being no express provision. and the instrument which forms the
great charter of our constitution being silent on the subject, it
appears to me that the Court will have to consider the question
in relation to the Federal character of the Dominion.

The question has been frequently considered in that aspect in
the United States.   Numerous decisions of the Supreme Court
and of the State Courts were referred to by the learned counsel
during the argument.   Now it is quite true, as suggested in the
argument, that these decisions are not binding upon the humblest
Judge of this Province, but they are the opinions of eminent
jurists, distinguished for learning, and deeply versed in the solution
of questions of constitutional law.   I think, therefore, that their
reasoning will probably be found to furnish us with a safe guide in
the determination of these questions.   This reasoning seems to me
cogent and conclusive.   It is so entirely applicable to the case in
hand that I could not come to any other conclusion than that I
have indicated without being prepared to impugn its correctness.
I have said that I find no express provision in the British North
America Act either authorizing or prohibiting this assessment.
Now the Courts of the United States have proceeded directly
upon the assumption that there is no express provision which
regulates this subject.   They do not proceed upon the construction
of any particular language in the constitution, but they place
their decisions upon the foundation of broad and general principles.
They rest them upon the character of the essential relations
existing between the Federal Government and the State Governments, and upon the estimate of the powers which must be vested
in or removed from each respectively.   Now in the great case of

McCulloch v. *Maryland*, 4 Wheat. 316, in which that eminent jurist Chief Justice Marshall pronounced judgment, he laid down the principle that the States have no power of taxation or otherwise to retard, impede, burden, or restrain in any way the powers vested in the general government. That was the general doctrine upon which the judgment of the Court proceeded in that important case. The learned Chief Justice very fully considered the nature of the relations which subsisted between the Central and State Governments, and held that it would be contrary to the character of the Federal Union to permit State legislation of a character that would impair in any way the effective execution of the general powers which had been entrusted to the central authority. In that case it was unnecessary to consider pointedly the power to tax officers of the United States upon their income, but the principles laid down were quite enough, in my opinion, to extend to such a case. In subsequent cases they were held so to extend. In the case of *Dobbins* v. *Commissioners of Erie County*, 16 Peters 435, to which I was also referred by Mr. Cockburn, the question was raised expressly. There the Supreme Court of Pennsylvania held that a law was constitutional by which the State had assumed to tax an officer of the United States. The question, therefore, was raised directly and pointedly before the Supreme Court. It was held that upon the reasoning of the case in 4 Wheaton, and upon the legitimate extension of its principles, such a law was unconstitutional. I cannot do better than refer to the language which was used by the learned Judge who pronounced the unanimous opinion of the Court in that case. After pointing out the inanimate objects, the use of which the constitution contemplated, and the management of which had been entrusted to the central authority, such as ships-of-war, which were the means of carrying out the object of the Central Government and could not be taxed by the State, he proceeded, at page 448 : ' Is not the officer more so who gives use and efficacy to the whole ? Is not compensation the means by which his services are procured and retained ? It is true it becomes his when he has earned it. If it can be taxed by a State as compensation, will not Congress have to graduate its amount with reference to its reduction by the tax ? Could Congress use an uncontrollable discretion, in fixing the amount of compensation, as it would do without the interference of such a tax ? The execution of a national power by way of compensation to officers can in no way be subordinate to the action of the State Legislatures on the same subject. It would destroy also all uniformity of compensation for the same service, as the taxes of the States would be different.'

Now, the reasoning employed in that case is precisely applicable to that on which I am giving my opinion. Without expressing dissent from these views, and without, so to speak, overruling the case, I could not come to any other conclusion. Our circumstances, it appears to me, sufficiently resemble the circumstances that existed in these cases to render the principles entirely applicable. There is but one other case to which I shall refer, *Buffington* v. *Day*, 4 Law Times, U. S. Supreme Court Reports (a). In that case Mr. Justice Nelson said : ' It is conceded in the case of *McCulloch* v. *Maryland*, that the power of taxation by the State was not abridged by the grant of a similar power to the Government of the Union ; that it was retained by the States, and that the power is to be concurrently exercised by the two Governments, and also that there is no express constitutional prohibition upon the States against taxing the means or instrumentalities of the General Government ; but it was held, and we agree properly held, to be prohibited by necessary implication, otherwise States might impose taxation to an extent that would impair, if not wholly defeat the operations of the Federal authorities when acting in their appropriate sphere. These views, we think, abundantly establish the soundness of the decision of the case of *Dobbins* v. *Commissioners of Erie*, which determined that the States were prohibited, upon a proper construction of the constitution, from taxing the salary or emoluments of an officer of the Government of the United States, and we shall now proceed to shew that upon the same construction of 'that instrument, and for other reasons, the Government is prohibited from taxing the salary of the judicial officers of the State.   It is a familiar rule of construction of the Constitution of the Union, that the sovereign power vested in the State Governments by their respective Constitutions remain unaltered and unimpaired, except so far as they were granted to the Government of the United States.

In this case the Central authority, in the exercise of its appropriate functions, appointed the plaintiff to a position of emolument. In the exercise of its proper powers it assigned to him a certain emolument.   This emolument the plaintiff is entitled to receive for the discharge of duties for which the Central Government is bound to' provide.   I do not find in the British North America Act that there is any express constitutional prohibition against the Local Legislatures taxing such a salary, but I think that upon the principles thus summarized in the case which I have just cited there is necessarily an implication that such power is not vested in the Local Legislature.   I therefore, in accordance with these views which I have just imperfectly expressed, have thought it right to enter a verdict for the plaintiff, and I think he should have a certificate to entitle him to full costs."

During Michaelmas term last, November 20, 1876, *Bethune*, Q. C., obtained a rule *nisi* calling on the plaintiff

---

(a) Reported *sub nom. The Collector* v. *Day*, 11 Wall. 113, 132.

to shew cause why the verdict should not be set aside, and a verdict entered for the defendants, pursuant to the Law Reform Act, on the ground that the plaintiff was not entitled to recover, and on the ground that the defendants were legally entitled to impose the taxes in respect of which the plaintiff's goods were seized.

During the same term, December 2, 1876, *Robinson*, Q.C., shewed cause. It may be that the Legislature of Ontario did not mean to exempt from taxation the salaries of the officers of the Dominion Government living at Ottawa or elsewhere : see 29–30 Vic. ch. 53, sec. 9, sub-sec. 23 ; 32 Vic. ch. 36, sec. 9, sub-secs. 12, 25 ; 34 Vic. ch. 28, sec. 1 ; *Nickle* v. *Douglas*, 35 U. C. R. 126 ; 37 U. C. R. 51. But we deny the power of that Legislature to tax them. It rests, under sub-sec. 8 of sec. 91 of the British North America Act, with the Legislature of the Dominion to pass laws for " the fixing of and providing for the salaries and allowances of civil and other officers of the Government of Canada," and this power cannot constitutionally be interfered with by the Provincial Legislature under sub-secs. 28 or 13 of sec. 92 of the same statute : *Shaw* v. *Shaw*, 12 C. P. 456 ; *Secretary of War* v. *The City of Toronto*, 22 U. C. R. 551 ; *Secretary of War* v. *City of London*, 23 U. C. R. 476. This Act forms our constitution, and on this question it should receive the same construction as the constitution of the United States. There are, no doubt, distinctions between the two constitutions, but no difference can be shewn which should make the American decisions or the reasoning on which they are founded inapplicable. It applies perhaps with greater force to us, where the reserved powers are with the Central or Dominion Government, and not with the Provinces : *Regina* v. *Taylor*, 36 U. C. R. 183, 191 ; *Re Slavin and The Corporation of the Village of Orillia, Ib.* 159, 174 ; *Regina* v. *Taylor*, 36 U. C. R. 183, 224 ; *McCulloch* v. *State of Maryland*, 4 Wheat. 316, 325, 391, 425, 428, 436 ; *Dobbins* v. *The Commissioners of Erie County*, 16 Peters 435, 448 ; *Cooley* on Constitutional Limitations, 2nd ed., 484.

Power to tax involves the power to destroy, and this, if permitted to any extent, would be an encroachment on the powers of the Dominion Legislature: *The Collector v. Day*, 11 Wall. 113; *Melcher v. The City of Boston*, 9 Met. 73; *Cooley* on Constitutional Limitations, 2nd ed., 482; *Sedgwick* on Constitutional Law, 2nd ed., 507, 508, notes. The plaintiff, although in the employment of the House of Commons, is an officer of the Dominion for the purposes of the exemption: 31 Vic. ch. 27, D.; *Taylor v. Campbell*, 33 U. C. R. 264.

M. C. Cameron, Q. C., and *Bethune*, Q. C., contra. Taxation is the rule, exemption the exception. Under our constitution express language is required to create the exemption. And in this respect our constitution differs from that of the United States. Ours, in sec. 125, declares that "No lands or property belonging to Canada or to any Province, shall be liable to taxation." This is the only exemption from taxation. The maxim, *expressio unius est exclusio alterius*, applies. Taxation here is not on the office, but on personal property, income being the measure of value: 32 Vic. ch. 36, sec. 36, O. This comes under municipal institutions and matters of a local nature: Sec. 92, sub-secs. 8, 16, British North America Act. The tax is not on the officer, *qua* officer, but on all persons deriving income, from whatever source: 32 Vic. ch. 36, sec. 21, O. Besides, an officer of the House of Commons is not an officer of the Dominion, if there be any such exemption. Here there is no question of reserved power: *Dow v. Black*, L. R. 6 P. C. 272. The decisions of the United States Supreme Court are inapplicable. If the salaries of Dominion officers are exempt from taxation, so would be the franchise of every corporation created under Dominion authority.

March 10, 1877. HARRISON, C. J.—The only question argued before us was, whether the official salary of the plaintiff an officer of the House of Commons of the Dominion of Canada, is exempt from municipal taxation, and that question must be decided on the proper interpretation to be placed on the British North America Act, 1867.

When that Act became the supreme law of the Provinces, then for the first time united, the annual official salaries of the officers and servants of the several departments of the Executive Government and of the two Houses of Parliament, resident at the seat of Government, were, in the Province of Ontario, by express legislation, exempt from municipal taxation: 29 & 30 Vic. ch. 53, sec. 9, sub-sec. 23.

A similar exemption was declared in the Ontario Assessment Act subsequently passed: 32 Vic. ch. 36, sec. 9, sub-sec. 25; but in 1871 the Legislature of Ontario assumed to repeal the exemption: 34 Vic. ch. 28, sec. 1, O.

When the question is as to the interpretation of a statute which extends equally to several Provinces, unless it be made to appear that the law on the point under investigation was the same in each Province before and at the time of the passing of the statute, no reliable argument is furnished for its interpretation.

We are not informed as to the law of exemptions in the several Provinces of Nova Scotia and New Brunswick at the time of the passing of the Act, and so must adjudicate on the question now before us without light, if any, in that respect from either of these Provinces.

The British North America Act, which is now our written constitution, has, like the constitution of the United States, federally united several communities, before the union having separate governments and separate parliaments, ruling and legislating independently of each other, and without reference to each other's interests.

In each constitution (that of the United States and ours) we see traced in strong characters the separate functions of the executive, the legislature, and the judiciary departments of government; and provision is made in our constitution for the independent exercise of the executive and legislative functions, not only by the central authority, but by the authorities of each Province.

Neither constitution attempts to make provision for

all exigencies that may arise in the exercise of these functions.

In considering the constitution of the United States the eminent Jurist Chief Justice Marshall felicitously said : " A constitution to contain an accurate detail of all the subdivisions of which its great powers will admit, and of all the means by which they may be carried into execution, would partake of the prolixity of a legal code, and could scarcely be embraced by the human mind. It would probably never be understood by the public. Its nature, therefore, requires, that only its great outlines should be marked, its important objects designated, and the minor ingredients which compose those objects be deduced from the nature of the objects themselves" : *McCulloch* v. *The State of Maryland,* 4 Wheat. 317, 407.

In our present enquiry we are alone concerned with the legislative powers conferred on the Parliament of the Dominion of Canada, and the Parliaments of the several Provinces.

These are to be found so far as expressed in sections 91 and 92 of the British North America Act.

The former section, 91, confers on the Parliament of Canada power to make laws for the peace, order, and good Government of Canada, in relation to all matters not coming within the classes of subjects by the Act assigned exclusively to the Legislatures of the Provinces.

The latter section, 92, assigns certain classes of subjects described exclusively to the Legislatures of the Provinces.

The inference which I draw from the reading of these two sections is, that unless a particular legislative power be found clearly to have been conferred on the Provincial Legislatures by sec. 92, it remains as an unenumerated power with the Legislature of the Dominion, but that where it can be said without doubt to have been conferred on the Provincial Legislatures the action of those bodies within the sphere of their jurisdiction, and subject only to the power of disallowance to which I shall presently refer, is supreme. See *Re Goodhue,* 19 Grant 366 ; *L'Union*

St. Jacques DeMontreal v. *Belisle*, L. R. 6 P. C. 31; *Dow et al.* v. *Black, Ib.* 272.

In this respect there is a difference between our constitution and that of the United States, for by the Tenth amendment of the constitution of the United States it is provided that " The powers not delegated to the United States by the constitution, nor prohibited by it to the States, are reserved to the States respectively, or to the people."

Where under our constitution a bill passed by the Houses of Parliament is presented to the Governor-General for the Queen's assent, he shall declare, according to his discretion, but subject to the provisions of the Act and to her Majesty's instructions, either that he assents thereto in the Queen's name, or that he withholds the assent, or that he reserves the bill for the signification of her Majesty's pleasure : sec. 55.

Where the Governor-General assents to a bill in the Queen's name, he shall, by the first convenient opportunity, send an authentic copy of the Act to one of her Majesty's principal Secretaries of State ; and if the Queen in Council, within two years after the receipt thereof by the Secretary of State, thinks fit to disallow the Act, such disallowance (with a certificate of the Secretary of State of the day on which the Act was received by him) being signified by the Governor-General by speech or message to each of the Houses of Parliament, or by proclamation, shall annul the Act from and after the day of such signification : sec. 56.

The provisions of the Act as to the assent to bills, the disallowance of Acts, and the signification of pleasure on bills reserved, are made to extend and apply to the Legislatures of the several Provinces, as if those provisions were re-enacted and made applicable in terms to the respective Provinces and the Legislatures thereof, with the substitution of the Lieutenant-Governor of the Province for the Governor-General, of the Governor-General for the Queen and for a Secretary of State, of one year for two years, and of the Province for the Dominion of Canada : sec. 90.

The effect as regards bills passed by the Provincial Legislatures, I take to be as follows :—

1. The Lieutenant-Governor of the Province, on presentation of a bill for his assent, shall declare according to his discretion, but subject to the provisions of the Act, either that he assents thereto in the Queen's name, or that he withholds the Queen's assent, or that he reserves the bill for the signification of the Governor-General's pleasure.

2. Where he assents to a bill, he must, by the first convenient opportunity, send an authentic copy of the Act to the Governor-General, and if the Governor-General in Council, within one year after receipt thereof, thinks fit to disallow the Act, such disallowance being signified by the Lieutenant-Governor by speech or message to the Provincial Parliament, shall annul the Act from and after the day of such signification.

The power of the Governor-General in Council to disallow a Provincial Act is as absolute as the power of the Queen to disallow a Dominion Act, and is in each case to be the result of the exercise of a sound discretion, for which exercise of discretion the Executive Council for the time being is in either case to be responsible as for other Acts of executive administration.

It is not to be expected that the Governor-General in Council will be so far able to examine all Acts passed by the Provincial Legislature as to foresee all possible constitutional difficulties that may arise on their construction, and therefore an omission to disallow is not to be deemed in any manner as making valid an Act, or a part of an Act, which is essentially void as being against the constitution : See *Regina* v. *Wood*, 5 E. & B. 49, 55.

While the Act confers on the Parliament of Canada power to make laws as to the fixing and providing for the salaries and allowances of civil and other officers of the Government of Canada (sub-sec. 8 of sec. 91), it confers on the Parliaments of the Provinces the power to make laws as to municipal institutions, as to property and civil rights, and generally, as to all matters of a merely local or private nature in the Provinces: Sub-secs. 8, 13, and 16 of sec. 92.

The latter powers are subject to the declaration in sec. 125, that "no lands or property belonging to Canada or to any Province shall be liable to taxation."

Power is, by sec. 131, given to the Governor-General in Council, until the Parliament of Canada otherwise provides, from time to time to appoint such officers as deemed necessary or proper for the effectual execution of the Act; and by sec. 130 it is provided that until the Parliament of Canada otherwise provides, all officers of the several Provinces having duties to discharge in relation to matters other than those coming within the classes of subjects by the Act assigned exclusively to the Legislatures of the Provinces, shall be " officers of Canada," and shall continue to discharge the duties of their respective offices under the same liabilities, responsibilities and penalties as if the union had not been made.

An office, says Marshall, C. J., is a public charge or employment, and he who performs the duties of the office, is an officer. If employed on the part of the United States, he is an officer of the United States: *United States* v. *Maurice*, 2 Brock. 96, 102.

Although the plaintiff was not appointed by the Governor-General of Canada, but by the House of Commons of Canada, of which it is admitted he is an officer, he is, I think, for the purpose of the question before us, to be deemed as much an officer of Canada and of the Government of Canada as if appointed by the Governor-General in Council.

The same word, owing to the poverty of our language, is often used in different places to express different ideas. The word Government may in a general sense be taken to express the ruling powers of a country, including legislative and executive, or in a more limited sense only the chief executive officers to whose administration the executive duties of Government are especially delegated.

In the former sense Parliament or the Legislature is as much a department of Government as the Executive, and it is in this sense I think the plaintiff should be held an officer of the Government of Canada, although not appointed by the Executive Government of Canada.

Every argument which can be urged in favour of the exemption from taxation of the salaries of officers appointed by the Executive Government is as applicable to an officer appointed by either branch of the Legislature of the Dominion of Canada as to officers appointed by the Governor in Council.

The great question therefore is, whether there is such an exemption as claimed on the part of the officers of Canada, whether appointed by the legislative or executive departments of the General Government.

In the determination of this question I propose, so far as necessary, to refer only to the decisions of the Supreme Court of the United States, and not to any of the decisions of State Courts in conflict with the decisions of the Supreme Court.

It is not pretended that on the face of the British North America Act there is in words any exemption from "municipal taxation" of the salaries of such officers, but the argument is, that the exemption is as necessarily intended and as effectual as if expressed in words. The principal argument against the exemption is, that the Imperial Legislature having, in sec. 125, provided for certain exemptions, none others should be inferred, according to the maxim, "*expressio unius est exclusio alterius.*" But this maxim, although general, is by no means of universal application. See per Lord Campbell, in *Saunders* v. *Evans et al.,* 8 H. L. C. 721, 729.

The sages of the law (according to Plowden) have ever been guided in the construction of statutes by the intention of the Legislature, which they have always taken according to the necessity of the matter, and according to that which is consonant to reason and good discretion : *Plowden,* 205 b.

By sub-secs. 2 of sec. 10 of the constitution of the United States, it is provided, that "No State shall, without the consent of Congress, lay any imposts or duties on imports or exports, except what may be absolutely necessary for executing its inspection laws," &c., and from this it was argued that with the exception stated any State had power to lay on taxes not being imposts or duties on imports or exports on any person or property within its territorial jurisdiction; but in no case has the Supreme Court of the United States ever given effect to this argument.

The leading case on the point is *McCulloch* v. *The State of Maryland*, 4 Wheat. 317, mentioned in the judgment of Mr. Justice Moss. In that case it was held that a law of the State of Maryland imposing a tax on the operations of the bank of the United States was unconstitutional.

In delivering judgment Chief Justice Marshall said, at p. 425 : " That the power of taxation is one of vital importance : that it is not abridged by the grant of a similar power to the government of the union : that it is to be concurrently exercised by the two governments, are truths which have never been denied. But, such is the paramount character of the constitution, that its capacity to withdraw any subject from the action of even this power, is admitted. The States are expressly forbidden to lay any duties on imports or exports, except what may be absolutely, necessary for executing their inspection laws. If the obligation of this prohibition must be conceded—if it may restrain a state from the exercise of its taxing power on imports and exports—the same paramount character would seem to restrain, as it certainly may restrain, a state from such *other* exercise of its power as is in its nature incompatible with, and repugnant to, the constitutional laws of the union."

In a subsequent part of the same judgment (at p. 432), the same learned and distinguished Judge said: " If the States may tax one instrument, employed by the Government in the execution of its powers, they may tax any and every other instrument. They may tax the mail; they may tax the mint; they may tax patent rights; they may tax the papers of the custom house; they may tax judicial process; they may tax all the means employed by the Government, to an excess which would defeat all the ends.

of Government. This was not intended by the American
people. They did not intend to make their Government
dependent on the States."

The result, as expressed at p. 436, was, that " The States
have no power by taxation or otherwise, to retard, impede,
or burden, or in any manner control the operation of the
constitutional laws, enacted by Congress, to carry into execution the powers vested in the General Government." But
it was said that this ".does not extend to a tax paid by the
real property of the bank in common with the other real
property in the State, nor to a tax imposed on the interest
which the citizens of Maryland may hold in this institution (the United States Bank) in common with other property of the same description throughout the State."

The tax was held to be unconstitutional, because on the
franchise of the bank, and so on *an instrument employed
by the Government of the union* to carry its powers into
execution.

It is reported that William Pinckney said of this cele-
brated decision, that in it he saw a pledge of the immor-
tality of the union : *Pomeroy's* Constitutional Law, 189.

The Supreme Court a few years afterwards, although a
revision of the case was requested, deliberately affirmed it :
Osborn v. *The Bank of the United States*, 9 Wheat. 738,
859, 860.

The views expressed in the later case were afterwards
affirmed in *Brown* v. *The State of Maryland*, 12 Wheat.
435, 446.

It was for some time a question whether a tax on stock
of the United States Bank came within the rule laid down
in *McCulloch* v. *The State of Maryland*, or within the
exceptions noted at the end of that decision. And notwithstanding the argument that great injustice was done
to others by exempting men who were living on the
interest of their money from the payment of taxes, thereby
establishing a privileged class of public creditors; who,
although living under the protection of the Government,
are exempted from bearing any of its burdens, the

majority of the Judges of the Supreme Court, including Chief Justice Marshall, in *Weston* v. *The City of Charleston*, 2 Peters 449, decided that a tax on stock of the United States Bank, held by an individual citizen of a state, is a tax on the power "to borrow money on the credit of the United States," and cannot be levied by or under the authority of a State consistently with the constitution.

Chief Justice Marshall in delivering judgment in the last case said, at p. 467 : "The right to tax the contract to any extent, when made, must operate on the power to borrow before it is exercised, and have a sensible influence on the contract. The extent of this influence depends on the will of a distinct government. To any extent, however inconsiderable, it is a burden on the operations of government. It may be carried to an extent which shall arrest them entirely."

A State tax imposed on the State bonds or other securities of the United States was for similar reasons held unconstitutional : *Bank of Commerce* v. *New York City*, 2 Black 620. But the stock of State banks are under certain limitations liable to taxation. See *The Providence Bank* v. *Billings*, 4 Peters 514 ; *Van Allen* v. *The Assessors*, 3 Wall. 573, 596 ; *The People* v. *The Commissioners*, 4 Wall. 244 ; *Society for Savings* v. *Coite*, 6 Wall. 594; *Provident Institution* v. *Massachusetts*, *Ib.* 611.

The case, however, which on the facts most resembles the case before us is, *Dobbins* v. *The Commissioners of Erie County*, 16 Peters 435, 443. In that case the Supreme Court of the United States held that a State had no power to tax an officer of the United States for his office or its emoluments. It was said to be the only instance of a tax being rated in the State of Pennsylvania upon the salary of an officer of the United States. The officer was in command of the revenue cutter Erie, on the Erie station. He had been for several years resident and domiciled in Erie city, and voted there. He was rated for the years 1835, 1836, and 1837, for $500, the salary of his office. The State law was, that an account should be taken

" of all offices and posts of profit," and that it was the duty of assessors " to rate all offices and posts of profit, professions, trades, and occupations, at their discretion, having a due regard to the profits arising therefrom." It was plain, therefore, that the tax was on the *emoluments* of the office, and not simply on the office. But whether it was the one or the other, it was pointed out by Mr. Justice Wayne, who delivered the judgment of the Court, the tax could not be sustained.

The learned Judge said, at p. 445 : " The emoluments of the office, then, are taxable, and not the office. But whether it be one or the other, we cannot perceive how a tax upon either conduces to comprehend within the terms of the Act the office or the compensation of an officer of the United States. It will not do to say, as it was said in argument, that though the language of the Act may import that offices and posts of profit were taxable, that it was the citizen who holds the office whom the law intended to tax, and that it was a burden he was bound to bear in return for the privileges enjoyed and the protection received from the Government : and, then, that the liability to pay the tax was a personal charge, because the person on whom it was assessed was a taxable person."

In answer to such suggestions, the learned Judge proceeded to say, at p. 448 : "The obligation upon persons to pay taxes is mistaken, and the sense in which a tax is a personal charge is misunderstood. The foundation of the obligation to pay taxes, is not the privileges enjoyed or the protection given to a citizen by government, though the payment of taxes gives a right to protection. Both are enjoyed as well by those members of a State who do not, because they are not able to, pay taxes, as by those who are able and do pay them. Married women and children have privileges and protection, but they are not assessed unless they have goods or property separate from the heads of the families. The necessity for money for the support of the States in time of peace or war, fixes the obligation upon their citizens to pay such taxes as may be imposed by lawful authority. And the only sense in which a tax is a personal charge, is, that it is assessed upon personal estate and the profits of labour and industry," &c.

In a subsequent part of the same judgment, the same learned Judge, at p. 448, said: "The execution of a national power by way of compensation to officers, can in no way be subordinate to the action of the State Legislatures upon the same subject. It would destroy also all uniformity of compensation for the same service, as the taxes by the States would be different. * * * The powers of the National Government can only be executed by officers whose services must be compensated by Congress. The allowance is in its discretion. The presumption is, that the compensation given by law is no more than the services are worth, and only such in amount as will secure from the officer the diligent performance of duties. The officers execute their offices for the public good. This implies their right in reaping from thence the recompense the services they may render may deserve, without that recompense being in any way lessened, except by the sovereign power from whom the officer derives his appointment, or by another sovereign power to whom the first has delegated the right of taxation over all the objects of taxation, in common with itself, for the benefit of both. And no diminution, in the recompense of an officer is just and lawful, unless it be prospective, or by way of taxation by the sovereignty who has the power to impose it; and which is intended to bear equally upon all according to their estate. The compensation of an · officer of the United States is fixed by a law made by Congress. It is in its exclusive discretion to determine what shall be given. It exercises the discretion and fixes the amount, and confers upon the officer the right to receive it when it has been earned. Does not, then, a tax by the State upon the office, diminishing the recompense, conflict with the law of the United States which secures it to the officer in its entireness? It certainly has such an effect; and any law of a State imposing such a tax cannot be constitutional, because it conflicts with a law of Congress made in pursuance of the constitution, and which makes it the supreme law of the land."

It would appear to be the result not only of this but of other cases, that the State, having no power directly to tax the income, *eo nomine,* has no power indirectly to do so by calling the income personal property and then taxing it under a new name. If such a course were permitted it would be a plain evasion of the law: *Bank of Commerce* v. *The City of New York,* 2 Black 620; *Bank Tax Case,* 2 Wall. 200.

The conclusion, according to *Pomeroy's* Constitutional Law, sec. 305, to be drawn from all the cases may be summarily stated as follows: " States may exert their power of taxation generally upon persons and property within their boundaries; but they cannot thereby interfere with any of the functions of the nation. They cannot tax national property; or the evidences of the national debt owned by individuals; or banks incorporated by the nation as a part of its general scheme of finance; or salaries of national officers. *In a word, all the means which are employed by the nation to carry on its legitimate functions are entirely beyond the reach of the several States.*" See further, *Cooley's* Constitutional Limitations, 2nd ed. 482; *Cooley* on Taxation, 56; *Hilliard* on Taxation, 148; *Sedgwick* on Constitutional Law, 2nd ed., 507 and note.

If this be a sound conclusion under the constitution of the United States, where the reserved powers are with the States or the people—and there it is now beyond question the law of the land—it cannot be less sound as applied to our constitution, where the reserved powers, I think, appear to be with the General Government.

The converse of *Dobbins* v. *Commissioners of Erie County,* 16 Peters 435, 443, arose in *The Collector* v. *Day,* 1 Wall. 113, where an attempt was made by the National Government to tax the salary of a Judge appointed by a State, and was for similar reasons held to be unconstitutional.

The principles to be deduced from the cases appear to be, that the National Government and the State Governments are, as it were, distinct sovereignties, that the means and instrumentalities necessary for the carrying on of either Government are not to be impaired by the other: that as the power to tax involves the power to impair, the exercise of such a power by the one Government on the income of the officers of the other is inconsistent with independent sovereignty of the other; and that in such cases exemption from taxation, although not expressed in the National Constitution, exists by necessary implication.

These principles appear to me to be, if possible, more applicable to our constitution than to that of the United States of America.

It does not, however, follow from them that railway corporations and other corporations, created by or under the authority of the Dominion Legislature for *other* than Government purposes, would be more free from municipal taxation than companies incorporated by the Provincial Legislatures.

For these reasons I concur in the decision of the learned Judge who tried the cause.

In my opinion the rule *nisi* should be discharged.

MORRISON, J.—After the best consideration I have been able to give to this case, I have arrived at the conclusion that our judgment should be in favour of the defendants.

The British North America Act defines by secs. 91 and 92 the exclusive objects of legislation which are respectively within the jurisdictions of the Parliament of Canada and the Provincial Legislatures. The terms used designating such respective objects, classes, and powers of the local Legislatures are necessarily general, and in some instances difficult of an accurate or certain interpretation when it becomes necessary to define in detail what matters are or are not within the particular class, or are limited or excluded by some other power or class assigned to the Parliament of Canada. Among these terms are sub-sec. 8

of sec. 92, "Municipal Institutions in the Province;" sub-
sec. 13, "Property and civil rights in the Province;" sub-
sec. 16, "Generally all matters of a merely local or private
nature in the Province."

In neither secs. 91 or 92 is there to be found any expressions indicating the exemption of any person, or the property or income of any person from taxation, whether
Dominion, Provincial, or Municipal. We have therefore
to consider whether there is anything to be found in any of
the respective powers implying any exemption, or whether
there is any principle authorizing us to imply that the
officers or employees of the Dominion Government are not
liable to be assessed or taxed for municipal purposes as
other residents within a municipality.

That the subject of exemption from taxation was considered by the framers of the British North America Act
is apparent from section 125, which declares that "No
lands or property belonging to Canada or any Province
shall be liable to taxation."

It appears to me that this express exemption of public
property determines the limit of exemption, and by implication all other property is liable under the respective
powers conferred by the 91st and 92nd sections.

Under the class "municipal institutions within the Province," the making of a law for the assessment of personal
property for municipal purposes is certainly a law in relation to a matter within that class, and is consequently
within the exclusive power of the Provincial Legislature;
but it is argued that upon some general principle, which we
are to imply, the officers and employees of the Dominion
Government are not liable to the same extent of taxation
for municipal purposes as other residents.

There is no such principle or usage that I am aware of
recognized in England; but it is said that our system of
government and constitution is like that of the United
States, and we have been referred to cases decided in the
United States Courts as indicating the principle I have
referred to; and it has been argued that our system of

confederation is so similar to that of the United States that the grounds upon which those decisions have been decided are applicable to the state of things existing in this country and the respective powers of the Dominion Parliament and the Provincial Legislatures. But it seems to me those cases are quite distinguishable, and were decided upon grounds and for reasons that do not apply here.

The several States of the Union are sovereign independent States. Their constitutions and powers are not expressly designated or limited, but the constitution of the United States is limited ; as said by Chancellor Kent, it "is an instrument containing the grant of *specific powers*, and the Government of the Union cannot claim any powers but what are contained in the grant, and given either expressly or by necessary implication": *Kent's* Com. vol. i., 12th ed., p. 313.

The distinguishing character of our system is, that the British North America Act is an Act of the Imperial Parliament conferring certain specific powers upon the Parliament of Canada, and certain specific powers upon the Provincial Legislatures, with this other important difference from the federal constitution of the United States, that the Dominion Government have in their hands a check upon the Legislatures of the Provinces in the power of disallowing any statute passed by them, and so may prevent any legislation which tends to obstruct, defeat, or impede the constitutional acts of the Dominion Parliament or Government. The Provincial Legislature is in that respect not like a sovereign State of the Union, but subordinate to that of the Dominion Government, and there are consequently not those grave difficulties and dangers to be apprehended here, as suggested in the cases in the American Courts, from the Legislatures of the States of the Union, and which no doubt pressed upon the learned Judges of the Supreme Court who had to consider the cases we have been referred to.

I may here remark that this is not the case of the Local Legislature enacting that the officers of the Dominion

Government shall pay any particular tax, or that the office itself shall be taxed; but the Act complained of is, the exercise of an alleged municipal right to assess personal property of residents within the municipality.

The Assessment Act, 32 Vic. ch. 36, O., and the amending statute 34 Vic. ch. 28, O., are unquestionably constitutional. They contain no clause or provision in violation of the British North America Act. All that can be said is, that the officers of the municipality of Ottawa, under the authority of the assessment laws, assessed the plaintiff for his personal property in the manner pointed out in the 35th section of the 32 Vic., which provides that the ratepayers last year's income in excess of $400 shall be held to be his net personal property for the current year, unless he has other property liable to assessment, in which case such other property and such excess shall be added together and constitute his personal property liable to assessment.

The cases we have been referred to in the United States Courts, more particularly the leading case of *McCulloch* v. *The State of Maryland*, 4 Wheat. 316, are, I think, quite distinguishable, and do not apply. The general principle laid down is, that the several States have no power of taxation or otherwise to retard, impede, burden, or restrain in any manner the powers vested in the General Government; but the principle so laid down in that case has been limited by a subsequent judgment of the Supreme Court in the case of *The National Bank* v. *Commonwealth*, 9 Wall. 353.

Mr. Justice Miller, who delivered the judgment of the Court, after stating that the principle laid down in *McCulloch's Case* had been repeatedly affirmed, said, at p. 361: "The doctrine has its foundation in the proposition, that the right of taxation may be so used in such cases as to destroy the instrumentalities by which the Government propose to effect its lawful purposes in the States, and it certainly cannot be maintained that banks or other corporations or instrumentalities of the Government are to be wholly withdrawn from the operation of state legislation. The most important agents of the Federal Govern-

ment are its officers, but no one will contend that when a
man becomes an officer of the Government he ceases to
be subject to the laws of the state.   The principle we are
discussing has its limitation, a limitation growing out of
the necessity on which the principle itself is founded.
The limitation is, that the agencies of the Federal Government are only exempt from State legislation so far
as that legislation may interfere with or impair their
efficiency in performing the functions by which they are
designed to serve that Government.   Any other rule would
convert a principle founded alone on the necessity of
securing to the government of the United .States the
means of exercising its legitimate powers into an unauthorized and unjustifiable invasion of the rights of the States.
The salary of a federal officer may not be taxed ; he may be
exempted from any personal service which interferes with
the discharge of his official duties, because those exemptions
are essential to enable him to perform these duties.   But
he is subject to all the laws of the state which affect his
family or social relations, or his property, and he is liable
to punishment for crime."

And, again, in *Thomson* v. *Pacific R. W. Co.*, same vol.
at p. 590, Chief Justice Chase, in delivering judgment,
says, commenting on *McCulloch* v. *Mayland*, 4 Wheat.
316 : " It is true that some of the reasoning in the case of
McCulloch v. *Maryland* seems to favour the broader doctrine.   But the decision itself is limited to the case of the
bank, as a corporation created by the law of the United
States, and responsible in the uses of its franchises to the
Government of the United States.   *   *   We do not
think ourselves warranted in extending the exemption
established by the case of *McCulloch* v. *Maryland* beyond
its terms.   *   *   *   We do not doubt the propriety or the
necessity, *   *   * of maintaining the supremacy of the
General Government within its constitutional sphere.   We
fully recognize the soundness of the doctrine, that no State
has a 'right to tax the means employed by the Government
of the Union for the execution of its powers,' but we think

there is a clear distinction between the means employed
by the Government and the property of agents employed
by the Government. Taxation of the agency is taxation
of the means; taxation of the property of the agent is
not always or generally taxation of the means. No one
questions that the power to tax all property, business, and
persons, within their respective limits, is original in the
States and has never been surrendered. It cannot be so
used, indeed, as to defeat or hinder the operations of the
National Government; but it will be safe to conclude, in
general, in reference to persons and State corporations
employed in Government service, that when Congress has
not interposed to protect their property from State taxation, such taxation is not obnoxious to that objection.
We perceive no limits to the principle of exemption which
the complainants seek to establish. It would remove from
the reach of State taxation all the property of any agent
of the Government. Every corporation engaged in the
transportation of mails, or of Government property of any
description, by land or water, or in supplying materials for
the use of the Government, or in performing any service of
whatever kind, might claim the benefit of the exemption."

The case of *Dobbins* v. *Commissioners of Erie*, 16 Peters
435, upon which the plaintiff chiefly relies, is, I think, also
distinguishable. That case was rested upon the provisions
of an Act of Congress authorizing the collection of duties,
and for that purpose the use of revenue cutters and officers to command them, and the Act of Pennsylvania
providing that an account should be taken of all offices
and posts of profits, and making it the duty of assessors to
rate all offices and posts of profit at their discretion, &c.
The Court held that the officer who was in command of a
revenue cutter, was equally, with the vessel, her guns, &c.,
means to enforce the law, and that a tax upon such an
officer, was an interference with the constitutional means
of the United States, within the principle laid down in
McCulloch's case. I am not at all disposed to admit that
that decision was a sound one. I may also refer to the case

of *The Collector* v. *Day*, 11 Wall. 113, to shew that the decision in *Dobbins's Case* was rested mainly upon the ground that he was captain of a revenue cutter.

Nelson, J., in delivering judgment, said, at p. 127, the rule and principle of the case (*Dobbin's Case*)was, that "the exemption rests upon necessary implication, and is upheld by the great law of self-preservation; as any government, whose means employed in conducting its operations, if subject to the control of another and distinct government, can exist only at the mercy of that government. Of what avail are those means if another power may tax them at discretion?"

I cannot see that such reasoning can apply to the relations existing between the Government of the Dominion and the Provinces, or to the case of this plaintiff, or any clerk or person employed in any office of the Dominion Government.

I also refer to the case of *Melcher* v. *City of Boston*, 9 Metc. 73, a case somewhat like the one before us, as shewing the view entertained by the learned Judges of the Supreme Judicial Court of Massachusetts, of the decision in the case of Dobbins.

The learned Judge who delivered the judgment of the Court, said, p. 75: "The plaintiff relies upon the case of *Dobbins* v. *Commissioners of Erie*, 16 Peters 435, as an authoritative decision governing the present case. Giving to that decision all the force and effect of a judgment of the highest tribunal upon the question there raised, yet there arise, in the case at bar, two important questions for our consideration: 1st. Was the plaintiff an officer of the United States, in any such sense as would entitle him to the immunities from taxation which were adjudged to attach to Dobbins, as a captain of the United States revenue cutter? 2nd. May not a tax upon "income" be assessed upon all citizens of Massachusetts residing therein, as well where such income is derived from the National Government, by way of compensation for services rendered to it, as from any other source"? And after referring to the Act of Congress

regulating the post office department, and the position of
the plaintiff as a clerk, &c., he said :—" The case in
16 Peters, 435, already referred to, was essentially different.
Dobbins was a captain of the United States revenue cutter.
He was an officer of the United States, appointed by the
President, under the provisions of a statute creating the
office.   It was a clear case of one holding an office under
the United States Government.   The statute of Pennsylvania, under which the question arose, authorized the
assessment of a tax ' upon all offices and posts of profit.
The tax was upon the office.   The taxing power assumed
to deal with him as one holding an office.   In the case at
bar, no such recognition of the party as a public officer
exists, and no tax was assessed upon the office.   *   *
As it seems to us, the plaintiff has failed to bring himself
within the case of *Dobbins* v. *The Commissioners of Erie ;*
not being an officer of the United States in any such sense
as will exempt him from taxation in common and in like
manner with all other citizens and residents of Massachusetts.   He is therefore liable to taxation ' for income,' and
that as well for income derived from compensation for
services rendered to the National Government, as from any
other source."

The learned Judge then says, that it is not necessary to
express any opinion upon the second question, whether a
tax upon " income" may not be well assessed upon one holding a public office under the General Government, and
proceeds, at p. 77: " But we deem it proper to say, that
such form of taxation may present a different question, and
authorize a different decision from that in *Dobbins's Case,*
16 Peters 435.   The tax upon income is not a tax upon the
office directly, it would seem to be only carrying out the
great principle of assessing taxes proportionally and equally,
according to the ability of the persons taxed.   Its form is
unobjectionable, pointed at no particular class, whether
office-holders or otherwise, but embracing, as proper subjects of taxation, all who place themselves under the protection of our Local Government, and participate in common

with others in the free enjoyment of our schools, our humane institutions, the protection of our laws and the benefits resulting from their due administration, our public ways, and all those beneficent objects for which these taxes are assessed. We are not disposed to assume in advance that the Supreme Court of the United States will decide that a tax ' upon income' will be illegal, if assessed upon a resident of Massachusetts, deriving his income from the compensation allowed him for services as an officer of the United States."

The Court held that the tax was properly demanded of the plaintiff. The judgment in this case seems to have been acquiesced in, as it does not appear to have been carried further. It seems to me to be a decision quite applicable to the case now under judgment.

If the principle or rather suggestion of impairing the efficiency of the officer, by reason of his pecuniary means being affected by such taxation, can be invoked to entitle the plaintiff to exemption, upon the like principle every employee of the Dominion Government ought to be exempt from any law which might be passed compelling payment of debts by the application or attachment of any moneys, the proceeds of an officer's income or emolument received by him. And it would be pushing the principle of implication to an unreasonable length to assume that the Dominion Government, when fixing salaries, &c., did so contemplating such immunity from taxation. If they entertained such a view, we may assume that the Government would have so indicated by some legislative enactment. If the Dominion Parliament under power 8, sec. 91, had enacted that all the salaries and allowances of its officers should be exempt from Provincial or municipal taxation, I should have had difficulty in saying whether such an Act would be constitutional, or not an encroachment upon the powers conferred on the Provincial Legislature.

The Dominion Parliament has not so declared. As said by Chase, C. J., in *Thomson* v. *Pacific R. W. Co.*, 9 Wall.

579, 591, when Congress has not interposed to protect and exempt their officers or employees, the taxation in question is not obnoxious to the principle contended for by the plaintiff."

The general rule in construing statutes is, that where a general power is conferred any particular power is also conferred; and so in the case of *L'Union St. Jacques de Montreal* v. *Belisle*, L. R. 6 P. C. 31, the Privy Council observe that the scheme of enumeration in the British North America Act was to mention various categories of general subjects which may be dealt with by legislation. "Such legislation," they said, p. 36, "is well expressed by Mr. Justice Caron when he spoke of * * *faillite*, bankruptcy and insolvency, all which are well known legal terms, expressing systems of legislation with which the subjects of this country, and probably of most other civilized countries, are perfectly familiar. The words describe in their known legal sense provisions made by law for the administration of the estates of persons who may become bankrupt or insolvent, according to rules and definitions prescribed by law, including, of course, the conditions in which that law is to be brought into operation, and the manner and effect of its operation."

And so in like manner the terms "Municipal Institutions in the Province" necessarily include the whole government of municipalities, and the subject of taxation upon all persons and property within the municipality. And, as an example of the wide interpretation put on the classes of subjects enumerated in sec. 92, I may refer to *Dow* v. *Black*, L. R. 6 P. C. 272. It was there argued that the second class, "Direct taxation within the Province in order to the raising of a revenue for Provincial purposes," only meant a revenue for general purposes, that is, taxation incident to the whole Province. But their Lordships of the Privy Council saw no ground for giving so limited a construction to the class; but they held that it enabled the Provincial Legislature, whenever it saw fit, to impose direct taxation for a local purpose upon a particular locality within the Province.

I may also refer to section 129 of the British North America Act, which declares that all the laws in force in the Province shall continue as if the union had not been made, subject to be repealed, abolished, or altered by the Parliament of Canada, or the Legislature of the Province, according to the authority of the Parliament or the Provincial Legislature.

Now, in Ontario the right to tax the personal estate and income of officers of the Government in common with all others, existed at the time of the passing of the British North America Act. It is true that for some special reason the officers of the then Government residing at Ottawa, were exempt, not, I take it, as a matter of right, but for some special reason at the time. In 1859, the Ontario assessment law was repealed, but virtually re-enacted, exempting the like officers of the Dominion Government, and by the 34 Vic. ch. 28, O., this exemption was repealed. Can it be said that the Ontario Legislature acted unconstitutionally in doing so ? I think not, and if the authority to assess officers of the Government existed at the time and after Confederation, the Parliament of Canada, if the right of so exempting its officers is within any of its powers, has not in any way repealed or abolished the right of the Province to do so.

If the plaintiff is right in his contention, and the principle is pressed to its consequences, any officer or employee in the service of the Dominion, such as the customs, excise, the post-office department, in the Public Works and Government Railways, and various other officers, would be equally exempt.

On the whole I see no ground, either by implication or otherwise, for holding that this plaintiff is exempt from the operation of our Assessment Laws or the mode of assessing and arriving at the amount of his personal estate which he complains of. I cannot apply the reasoning upon which the American authorities are based, and say that this assessment is a tax on the operations of the Dominion Government, or, to use the words of the learned Judge of the Supreme Court of the United States, on one of its instrumentalities, in the sense used by them.

I think the defendants are entitled to our judgment, and that the rule should be absolute to enter a verdict for them.

WILSON, J.—It is plain that the Assessment Act, 32 Vic. ch. 36, sec. 9, O., amended as it has been by 34 Vic. ch. 28, sec. 1, O., does not exempt the income of officers of the Dominion residing in Ontario.

The general enactment of that statute is, that all land and personal property in the Province of Ontario shall be liable to taxation, subject to certain exemptions —:

And *personal property* is, by section 4, declared to include all goods * *· income, and all other property, except land and real estate as defined by section 3.

And by section 5: *Property* includes *both* real and personal property, as above defined.

Some of the exemptions are those in the following sub-secs. of sec. 9 :—

11. The personal property and official income of the Governor-General of the Dominion of Canada, and the official income of the Lieutenant-Governor of the Province.

13. All pensions of $200 a year and under, payable out of the public moneys of the Dominion of Canada, or of the Province.

14. The income of a farmer, derived from his farm, and the income of merchants, mechanics, or other persons, derived from capital liable to assessment: 33 Vic. ch. 27, sec. 2.

21. The annual income of any person, provided the same does not exceed $400.

22. The stipend or salary of any minister of religion, and the parsonage or dwelling house occupied by him, with the lands thereto attached.

The repeal of the 25th sub-section, which in express terms applied to this case, is a very significant fact against the allowance of such an exemption.

But it is said, if this claim cannot be supported on the

ground of an exemption, that it is still maintainable, because it is an unconstitutional tax which the Local Legislature cannot impose. That, of course, can only arise under the Confederation Act.

Section 91 confers upon the Dominion Legislature exclusive authority over a variety of matters, and among others over :—

Sub-section 3: The raising of money by any mode or system of taxation.

Sub-section 8: The fixing of and providing for the salaries and allowances of civil and other officers of the Government of Canada.

Section 92 confers upon the Provincial Legislature exclusive authority over the following, among other matters :

Sub-section 2: Direct taxation within the Province in order to the raising of a revenue for Provincial purposes.

Sub-section 8: Municipal institutions in the Province.

Sub-section 13: Property and civil rights in the Province.

Sub-section 16: Generally all matters of a merely local or private nature in the Province.

Section 125 enacts that no lands or property belonging to Canada or any Province shall be liable to taxation.

I am quite sure that section 91, sub-section 3, does not apply, because that refers to the raising of money by the Dominion Legislature by any mode or system of taxation, and this is not a case of that kind.

Nor does sub-section 8, because the power, which seems an essentially needful one that the Dominion Parliament should fix and provide for the salaries of the civil and other officers of the Dominion, cannot by any interpretation be held to exclude the right of assessment of that salary by the Provincial Legislature.

Section 92, sub-section 2, does not apply here, because that is confined to taxes imposed by the Legislature for Provincial purposes.

Sub-sections. 8, 13, and 16, do, however, apply, and by them the Local Legislature has the power to tax or to exempt from taxation, or to confer upon Municipalities the power to tax the salaries of Dominion officers.

The assessment in question is one imposed by municipal
authority.   It is also an assessment made in respect of *property* as defined by the Assessment Act; and it is really
in respect of matters of a merely local or private nature in
the Province, because the amount so raised or to be raised
is to be applied to merely local or private matters in the
municipality of the city of Ottawa.

The only ground upon which an exemption can be claimed
by the plaintiff is, that the Dominion Government having
employed him and having given him a remuneration for
his services, that it would be or might be detrimental to
the public interest if that remuneration should be lessened
by any municipal burden put upon him, taxing that
income, inasmuch as the payment made to him must be
presumed to be necessary for the due performance of his
duties and the maintenance of that proper social position
and dignity required of a public officer.

It is upon that ground, and for that cause partly, but
not altogether, that the half-pay of an officer cannot be
attached or assigned.   Such allowance is partly in respect
of services thereafter to be rendered, but it is not a permanent grant—it is voluntary, and may be withdrawn at
any time : *Flarty* v. *Odlum*, 3 T. R. 681.

In *Ex parte Hawker, Re Keely,* L. R. 7 Ch. 214, it was
held the retiring pension of an officer could not be taken
by the assignee in bankruptcy.

In *Dent* v. *Dent*, L. R. 1 P. & D. 366, it was held that
the pension of a retired officer received wholly in respect
of past services, was liable to sequestration—but that half-
pay could not be taken, as it was partly in respect of future
services.   The sequestration would relate only to pay actually due : *Knight* v. *Bulkeley*, 4 Jur. N. S. 527.

A superannuation allowance is not a debt which can be
attached: *Innes* v. *The East India Co.,* 17 C. B. 351.

It is clear that the assignment of a salary of a public
officer would not be supported.

The assignment of the whole of a pension for past services, or of half-pay, or of an annuity granted by Parliament to maintain the dignity of a title—as in *Davis* v. *Duke*

of Marlborough, 1 Swan. 74—or of the pay of an officer, or the attaching them for debt or taking them in insolvency, so far as it can be done or cannot be done, are entirely different from this case, which is the claim to exemption for payment of an ordinary municipal tax upon a salary or income, which every one else with a few exceptions is subjected to.

The doctrine of public policy, which is treated of very freely in the different cases on the subject of pay and pensions before referred to, and in the others which are therein cited, is in no way violated by a tax of this kind. The plaintiff, as a public officer, is not a person over whom the Dominion Legislature has exclusive jurisdiction, and it cannot be said that the imposition of the tax upon his income is an unwarranted interference with him by the municipality under the authority of the Local Legislature.

He might with more reason claim to be exempt from statute labor, or from the requirement to remove snow, ice, &c., from the sidewalk opposite his house, because that might take him away from his public duty.

He would, but for the special exemption granted to him and to many others by the jury law, be liable to serve as a juror.

He has no privileges but such as are specially given to him. His office or duties give him none. He is subject to arrest like any other person.

The case of *McCulloch* v. *The State of Maryland*, 4 Wheat. 316, determined that a bank established by the National Government of the United States could not have a tax upon its issues imposed upon it by a State in which it had established a branch bank, nor could it be restricted by such State to the issue of notes of such denominations as it prescribed.

The charter also provided that the collectors and receivers of the national revenue should receive payment in the notes of that bank, while the State of Maryland declared that it should be penal to pay in such notes unless they were first duly stamped by the authority of that State.

The Court held that the tax was upon the franchise which Congress had created, and that the tax was unconstitutional.

But it is expressly declared that the real property of the bank in the State was liable to taxation, and also the proprietary interest which the citizens of the State held in the bank in common with others.

So also *Weston* v. *The City of Charleston*, 2 Peters 449, determined that a tax imposed by any State or under the authority of any law of the State, upon stocks issued for loans made to the National Government was unconstitutional, because it was a tax upon the contract which the Government had made with the holders of the stocks that they should receive upon it a certain interest or benefit, and any such tax would operate prejudicially to the credit of the Government.

Two of the dissenting Judges intimate that if the tax had been on the income of the holder of the stock in common with his other sources of income, in place of the stock *eo nomine*, it might not have been objectionable.

The plaintiff contends that if the franchise of a bank corporation, or the stocks of the United States, each of them created by the National Government, cannot be taxed, neither can he be taxed, because he in his own person as a public officer, receiving a public salary, stands on quite as good a vantage ground as such a corporation, or as such stock : and that he is as much the principal with respect to the tax in question as the franchise or the stock was in the two cases just mentioned.

I do not think he can maintain that, because there is no tax put upon him as a public officer, nor is there a capitation tax put upon him in any form. His income is taxed. That of course reduces his salary, and the fear on the ground of policy is, that it may diminish his zeal for and his usefulness in the public service.

That is the danger to be averted, and the difficulty we are called upon to meet.

The case of *Dobbins* v. *The Commissioners of Erie*

County, 16 Peters 435, is one which does, it was contended, apply in favour of the plaintiff. In that case the State, under the words "all offices and posts of profit," imposed a county rate upon the captain of a revenue cutter, an officer of the National Government, and it was held that such a tax could not be supported.

The Court, at page 449, said : " The officers execute their offices for the public good. This implies their right of reaping from thence the recompense the services they may render may deserve, without the recompense being in any way lessened, except by the sovereign power from which the officer derives his appointment."

The Collector v. *Day,* 11 Wall. 113, decided the converse case to the last,—that a State judicial officer could not be taxed by the National Government.

These cases do not in the least apply to the claim of the plaintiff.

I am not much impressed with the force or reasoning of the case of *Dobbins* v. *The Commissioners of Erie County,* 16 Peters 435, just mentioned. In that case the National Government had a certain jurisdiction over the officer, and so also had the State Government. He was accountable to the National Government for nothing but his official conduct. He was amenable to the State Government, while a citizen of it, for everything else and in every other respect. And why his *income,* as distinct from his office or post, should not be subject to local taxation in like manner as that of every other citizen of the State, I do not quite understand.

If the tax had been on the income of all officers of the National Government, or had been in way restrictive or exceptional, I could understand the objection that was made to it. But when it subjected him to the like and to no other or greater liability than was imposed on every citizen over whom in common with himself the State had jurisdiction, the conclusion that was come to seems to me inconsequential, and the grounds of it very imaginary.

The case of *Melcher* v. *The City of Boston,* 9 Met. 73, is very much opposed to the one before referred to.

But granting it full authority in cases under the like circumstances, it does not follow that it is entitled to prevail here. .

The Local Legislature had at the time of confederation full power over such a tax, and that power is expressly granted to it, or rather has been preserved to and reserved for it, under the head of "municipal institutions."

That these salaries were at that time by a special clause of exemption not then taxed does not alter the case, because the *power* over all such matters remained with, or was granted to the Local Legislature and to these municipal bodies to deal with as theretofore, and that which had before been an exemption could not have been under-stood as intended always to be an exemption, or to be an irrevocable declaration that such salaries never would be taxed.

I cannot conceive that such a *power* to deal with exemptions as we pleased which unquestionably existed before, and at the time of confederation, and which has not been interfered with, directly or indirectly, by that Act, can now be questioned on the fanciful ground that the like tax put on the plaintiff's income or salary which is put upon all other incomes of every kind, but a few which have been excepted, can be considered illegal and unconsti-tutional because it is an assumption of power, or because it is opposed to public policy, or that its tendency is to diminish the plaintiff's usefulness in the public service by reducing his salary below the amount which the Dominion Government has thought fit to estimate his services and usefulness at. That a grant or seizure of the salary for debt should not be allowed, is comprehensible, but that an income tax should be illegal is not to me reasonable. These two matters are different in their nature, consequence, and purpose, and are not to be confounded by any gener-alities that a right to tax is a right to destroy. The municipality was also dealing, as it has the right to do, with a matter affecting property and civil rights, for income is expressly property by the Assessment Act. The

question must always be, and only be, is there the power
to tax ?

If there is, there is nothing more to be said.   If there is
not, that also puts an end to enquiry.

The opinion whether there is such power or not may
and will depend upon many considerations of more or less
importance, and the consequences of either view must also
be considered as aids to the judgment to be formed, but
only as aids, for the question must still come back to this
point : is there, or is there not, such a power ?

In my opinion there was, and there is, such a power to
tax ; and the rule should be made absolute for the defendants, treating the plaintiff, as I have throughout, as an
officer of the Dominion Government.

Rule absolute.

———

BACON v. CAMPBELL, HAYES, DODDS, AND BOOKLESS.

Lease—Covenant not to assign—Breach—Forfeiture—Waiver.

The plaintiff leased land for ten years from 1st December, 1871, to oné
    D., who covenanted that neither he nor his assigns would assign,
    transfer, or sub-let the premises without the plaintiff's consent in
    writing first obtained, with a proviso for re-entry.   D. mortgaged his
    interest to one H. to secure him against his endorsement of a note for
    D., the proceeds of which D. expended in converting the premises into
    a race-course and pleasure grounds and erecting buildings thereon.
    This note being dishonoured, H. informed the plaintiff of the mortgage,
    and that owing to the plaintiff's absence it had been taken without his
    consent, whereupon the plaintiff waived all objections on this ground,
    and declared that he would take no advantage of the omission,. and H.
    then paid the note, and afterwards expended a large sum in foreclosing
    the mortgage and improving the premises.
H. having foreclosed, advertised the land for lease.   One W. took posses-
    sion in May, 1874, on the understanding that he was to have the place
    for five years, with the privilege of remaining the whole of the original
    term, at a rent of $530 a year, and there was to be a written agreement,
    to be drawn up if possible so as not to affect H.'s lease.   He remained
    ten months, and made improvements, and while in possession sub-let
    part of the land to one C. for $300 a year.   W. gave up possession to
    H. in April, 1875, not being able to obtain the written agreement which

had been promised to him; and on arbitration with H. the arbitrators awarded to W. $524 in full for improvements, "less $224 due for rent," on which basis they settled. H. notified C. in October, 1874, not to pay any money for rent unless authorized by H.

Held, MORRISON, J., dissenting, that what took place between H. and W. was a breach of the covenant; and *Semble*, that the lease was forfeited also by the dealing between H. and C.

Per MORRISON, J.—The parties intended only that there should be an assignment if the plaintiff would consent to it, and there was no forfeiture.

Held, also, that the plaintiff had waived the forfeiture caused by the mortgage to H.

EJECTMENT for part of park lot 27, formerly in the township of York but now in the city of Toronto, containing by admeasurement 23 acres and 30 perches.

The writ was issued 5th June, 1875.

The plaintiff claimed title by virtue of breaches of covenant contained in a lease from the plaintiff to one Patrick Davy, dated 1st December, 1871, whereby the plaintiff demised the land in question to Davy for ten years from 1st December, 1871, and which lease contained a covenant on the part of the lessee that he should not nor would at any time during said term, assign transfer or sub-let the premises without the license or consent of the plaintiff in writing.

The notice of title alleged that Patrick Davy, on or about 16th July, 1872, assigned the lease to the defendant Hayes, without such license or consent : that the defendant Hayes, on or about 1st June, 1874, sub-let the land to one Wardell : that Hayes or Wardell sub-let the premises, or some part thereof, to the defendant Campbell; and that Hayes, on or about 20th May, 1875, sub-let the premises, or some part thereof, to the defendants Bookless and Dodds, or one of them.

The notice claimed that in consequence of the said breaches of covenant, or some of them, the plaintiff was entitled to possession.

The defendant Hayes, besides denying the plaintiff's title, pleaded a defence on equitable grounds.

The equitable plea alleged the lease from the plaintiff to Davy: that Davy, by deed dated July 16th, 1872, mort–

gaged his interest to defendant Hayes, to secure him from loss in the event of his having to pay a promissory note for $1000, made by Davy, and endorsed by Hayes: that the proceeds of the note were expended by Davy in converting the premises into a race-course and general pleasure ground, and erecting the necessary buildings thereon: that Davy failed, at the maturity of the note, to pay it: that payment thereof was demanded of the defendant Hayes: that Hayes thereupon, in October, 1872, called on the plaintiff and made known to him that the note had been endorsed by the defendant Hayes: that the mortgage was given by way of security, but that in consequence of the absence of the plaintiff from the country the mortgage was taken without the consent of the plaintiff: that the plaintiff did thereupon waive all objections to the mortgage on the ground or by reason of the same having been made without his consent in writing, and declared that he would take no advantage of the omission to obtain his consent: that defendant Hayes, relying upon the waiver and declaration, paid the amount of the promissory note, and afterwards with the knowledge, consent, and approval of the plaintiff, expended a large sum of money in foreclosing the mortgage, and in making improvements upon the said lands, and in carrying out the covenants contained in the lease   The plea concluded with the averment that the premises were demised to Davy for the express purpose of being constructed into a race-course and general pleasure ground, and that the defendant had not at any time sub-let or assigned the premises, or any part thereof.

There was judgment by default against the defendants other than Hayes.

The cause was tried at the Toronto Winter Assizes for 1876, before Morrison, J., without a jury.

. The lease from the plaintiff to Davy was proved. It was dated 1st December, 1871, to hold for ten years from 1st December, 1871, at the annual rental of $232, payable quarterly, on the 1st of March, June, September, and December in each year.

The mortgage from Davy to the defendant Hayes, dated July, 1872, was also proved. Proof was also given of the waiver and declaration alleged in the equitable plea, and that the same took place under the circumstances stated in the plea.

The learned Judge held that part of the plea proved, but the question was, as to the remaining part of the plea, which alleged that defendant Hayes had not assigned or sub-let the premises without leave, and which was not expressly determined by the learned Judge.

The lessee covenanted for himself. his executors, administrators, and assigns, that neither he nor they would at any time during the term " assign, transfer, or sub-let the said premises hereby demised," without the license or consent of the lessor, his heirs or assigns in writing, for that purpose first had and obtained.

The proviso was for re-entry for nonpayment of rent, or " if the lessee, his executors, administrators, and assigns shall assign or sub-let the said premises without such license as aforesaid," or in case of breach of any of the covenants therein contained.

In March, 1874, Hayes having foreclosed his mortgage from Davy, through his solicitors, Messrs. G. & H. B. Morphy, advertised the land to be leased.

In May, 1874, Wardell took possession of the lands, on the understanding that there was to be an agreement to be drawn up by Hayes's solicitor. The agreement was, if possible, to be drawn up in such a manner as not to affect Hayes's lease. No such written agreement, however was drawn up. The understanding was, that Wardell was to have the premises for five years, with the privilege of continuing oh for the whole of the remainder of the term, under the original lease. The rent to be paid was $530 per annum. Wardell, on this understanding, took possession, and remained in possession for about ten months. During this time he made improvements on the premises. While in possession Wardell sub-let a portion of the lands to defendant Campbell. He sub-let to him the house and garden.

Campbell was to have the portion sub-let for three years with the privilege of five years. Campbell was to pay $300 a year and taxes. Wardell gave up possession to Hayes in April, 1875. He gave up possession because he was never able to get the written agreement which had been promised to him. The amount to which he was entitled for improvements was settled by arbitration, The arbitrators awarded to Wardell "the sum of $524 in full for improvements, less $224 due for rent" to Hayes. Hayes availed himself of the deduction and settled with Wardell on the basis of the award.

Campbell, in October, 1874, was notified in writing by Hayes "not to pay any money for *rent*" to any one unless authorized by Hayes to do so. When Wardell gave up possession Campbell owed him over $200 for rent. Hayes was to accept as part of what was due him by Wardell the money which Campbell owed Wardell. After Wardell gave up possession Campbell took the whole of the premises from Hayes; $70 were paid by Campbell to a niece of Hayes as rent. Campbell made improvements, as he swore to the value of $400.

Campbell, with the assent of Hayes, rented the racecourse to Dodds and Bookless on the 22nd and 24th May, 1875. Campbell had the exclusive privilege of selling refreshments during the two days, and Dodds and Bookless had the receipts at the gates. For the two days the course was in the possession of and under the control of Dodds and Bookless.

The learned Judge, on the whole, although not free from doubt, entered a verdict for the defendant Hayes. Leave was reserved to enter a verdict for the plaintiff.

During this term, February 26, 1876, *Crombie*, obtained a rule calling upon all the defendants to shew cause why the verdict rendered for the defendant Hayes should not be set aside, and a verdict entered for the plaintiff, pursuant to leave reserved at the trial.

During Michaelmas term last, November, 28, 1876,
66—VOL. XL U.C.R.

McMichael, Q.C., *Monkman* with him, shewed cause. As to the transfer to the defendant Hayes, the equitable plea of waiver was proved, and there was no assignment or sub-letting by Hayes. They cited Consol. Stat. U. C. ch. 90 sec. 4; *Addison* on Contracts, 7th ed., 580, 581 ; *Ward* v. *Day,* 4 B. & S. 337, 5 B. & S. 359 ; *Doe* v. *Laming,* 4 Camp. 73.

Richards, Q. C., *Crombie* with him, contra. The equitable plea as regards Hayes was not proved, and even if it were, there were sub-lettings subsequent to that which operated as a breach of the covenant. They cited *McCord* v. *Harper,* 26 C. P. 96 ; *Doe d.* v. *Eykins,* 1 C. & P. 154 ; *Fawcett* on Landlord and Tenant, 286, 287 ; *Smith's* Landlord and Tenant, 2nd ed. 144.

February 6, 1877. — HARRISON, C. J. — The plaintiff in his notice of title claims title not only because of the assignment from the lessee to the defendant Hayes, but because of the alleged sub-letting of the premises by Hayes to Wardell, and afterwards to Campbell, and the sub-letting to Dodds and Bookless.

If the defendant's equitable plea had only averred a waiver of the right to enter because of the transfer from the lessee to defendant Hayes, it would have been no answer to the claim. But as the plea concludes with the averment that the defendant " did not at any time sub-let or assign the premises, or any part thereof, in any manner contrary to the true intent and meaning of the covenant," it is, if true, a sufficient defence.

I agree with the finding of the learned Judge who tried the cause, so far as the transfer to the defendant Hayes is concerned. The evidence shews that the plaintiff did elect not to take advantage of that transfer as a cause of forfeiture, and declared his intention to that effect to the defendant. The ordinary mode of waiving a right of forfeiture of the kind is by receipt of rent. But this is not the only mode. Other acts besides the acceptance of rent have been held to be a waiver of a right of entry, when they shew an intention on the part of the landlord that the lease shall continue.   See *Doe* v. *Meux,* 4 B. & C. 606 ; *Doe Nash* v. *Birch,* 1 M. & W. 402 ; *Doe* v. *Lewis,* 5 A. & E. 277 ; *Dendy* v. *Nicholl,* 4 C. B. N. S. 376 ; *Toleman* v. *Postbury,* L. R. 6 Q. B. 245 ; *Collins* v. *Hasbrouck,* 15 Am. 407.

When a landlord, in express language, having had his attention drawn to the cause of forfeiture and with full knowledge of all the circumstances, elects not to take advantage of the forfeiture, and so expresses himself to the person against whom he might otherwise enforce it, I think he is bound both at law and in equity by the election.

In *Ward* v. *Day,* 4 B. & S. 337, Crompton, J., at page 352, said, " If a man, having an option, by some solemn act, declares his determination and election, he cannot afterwards recede from it."

In the same case, 5 B. & S. 362, Sir William Erle said, " When a landlord elects not to take advantage of a forfeiture, and declares to the party against whom he could enforce it that he will not do so, he is bound by the election."

These and other like observations are cited and approved by Hagarty, C. J., in *McCord* v. *Harper,* 26 C. P. 101, 102. See also *Pellatt* v. *Boosey,* 31 L. J. C. P. 281.

The uncontradicted testimony of the defendant Hayes, and of his solicitor, Mr. Morphy, established that there was such an election, and such a declaration on the part of the plaintiff.

But this does not prevent the plaintiff relying upon any subsequent assignment or sub-letting on the part of Hayes if any such appear to have been proved.

If the rule in *Dumpor's Case,* 1 Smith L. C., 7th ed., 41, had not been interfered with by the Legislature we might be obliged to hold that the plaintiff having in effect licensed the first assignment, the condition was at an end, but sections 1, 2, and 3, of 29 Vic. ch. 28, taken from the English Statutes 22 & 23 Vic. ch. 35, sec. 2, and 23 & 24 Vic. ch. 38, sec. 6, prevent us so holding.

The first of these enactments, 29 Vic. ch. 28, sec. 1,.

provides that "Where any license to do any act which, without such license, would create a forfeiture, or give a right to re-enter, under a condition or power reserved in any lease heretofore granted, or to be hereafter granted, shall at any time after the passing of this Act, be given to any lessee or his assigns, every such license shall, unless otherwise expressed, extend only to the permssion actually given, or to any specific breach of any proviso or covenant made or to be made, or to the actual assignment, under-lease, or other matter thereby specifically authorized to be done, but not so as to prevent any proceeding for any subsequent breach, unless otherwise specified in such license," &c.

The second, 29 Vic. ch. 28 sec. 3, in order to prevent the supposed operation of *Dumpor's Case*, where what is relied upon is a waiver and not a license, enacts that where any actual waiver of the benefit of any covenant or condition in any lease, on the part of any lessor or his heirs, executors, administrators, or assigns, shall be proved to have taken place after the passing of this Act, in any one particular instance, such actual waiver shall not be assumed or deemed to extend to any instance or any breach of covenant or condition, other than that to which such waiver shall specially relate, nor to be the general waiver of the benefit of any such covenant or condition, unless an intention to that effect shall appear.

We have therefore to deal with the subsequent, if any, breaches of the covenant, not to assign or sub-let, and without reference to anything that had transpired before they happened.

The covenant is a reasonable one. Its purpose is to prevent any person other than the tenant or the person of whom the landlord approves having possession as a tenant or sub-tenant of the land demised.

While a landlord may have confidence in the tenant or some other person to whom the tenant proposes to assign, it does not follow that he will have equal confidence in any or every person who may, without his knowledge or consent, be let into possession of the land, either as a tenant or sub-tenant.

The landlord, at all events, has reserved to himself the option of withholding his consent to transfers or sublettings, by the express covenant that any transfer or subletting made without his consent in writing shall be void, and this is followed by a right of re-entry if the covenant be broken.

In *Holland* v. *Cole*, 1 H. & C. 67, it was held that an assignment under the Bankruptcy Act of 1861, to trustees for the benefit of creditors, was a breach of the covenant.

In *Varley* v. *Coppard*, L. R. 7 C. P. 505, it was held that an assignment by one partner to another of his undivided interest in the demised premises, was a breach of the covenant.

In *Doe Dingley* v. *Sales*, 1 M. & S. 297, where the tenant agreed with a person to enter into partnership with him, and that such person should have the exclusive use of the back chamber and some other parts of the demised premises and of the rest jointly with the defendant, and that person entered into possession under the agreement, it was held that the covenant was broken.

Letting rooms to mere lodgers would not be a breach of the covenant *Doe d. Pitt* v. *Laming*, 4 Camp. 73. But letting a portion of a room in a factory with steam power for working lace machines at a certain sum per annum, payable quarterly, where the person to whom the letting is made takes exclusive possession of the portion let, would, it is presumed, be a breach of the covenant. See *Selby* v. *Greaves*, L. R. 3 C. P. 594.

It will not be necessary to decide as to the effect of the letting to Dodds and Bookless, if we should be of opinion that what took place between Hayes and Wardell, or between Hayes and Campbell, did amount to a sub-letting.

It may be laid down for a rule that whatever words are sufficient to explain the intent of the parties, that the one shall divest himself of the possession and the other come into it for such a determinate time, whether they run in

the form of a license, covenant, or agreement, are of themselves sufficient, and will in construction of law amount to
a lease for years as effectually as if the most proper and
pertinent words had been used for that purpose   *   *

  * for a lease for years, being no other than a contract
for the possession and profit of the land on the one side
and a recompense of rent or other income on the other; if
the words made use of are sufficient to prove such a contract in what form soever they are introduced, or however
variously applicable the law calls in the intent of the
parties, and models and governs the words accordingly :
Bac. Ab. "Leases," K.

A license from one person to another to inhabit a house
for the purpose of a joint business free of all rent except
taxes, is to be deemed a demise of it to the person who is
to inhabit it : *Right dem. Green* v. *Proctor,* 4 Burr. 2209.

The general rule in the case of a writing is, that if there
are words shewing a present intention that the one is to
give and the other is to have possession, a tenancy is
created : Per Parke, B., in *Bicknell* v. *Hood,* 5 M. & W.
104, 108.

Although the writing provide for the future execution
of a lease, yet if the writing and the circumstances shew
an intention for the immediate transfer of possession from
the one person to the other, and occupation thereafter, the
relation of landlord and tenant will be held to have existed
without any lease ever having been executed : *Poole* v.
Bentley, 12 East 168 ; *Doe Jackson* v. *Ashburner,* 5 T. R.
163 ; *Doe Walker* v. *Groves,* 15 East 244 ; *Baxter d. Abra-
hall* v. *Browne,* 2 W. Bl. 973. See further *Warman* v.
Faithful, 5 B. & Ad. 1042 ; *Chapman* v. *Bluck,* 4 Bing. N.
C. 187, 193.

In the latter case Tindal, C. J., said, after speaking of
the writing in question : " But we may look at the acts of
the parties also, for there is no better way of seeing what
they intended than seeing what they did under the instrument in dispute." See further *Gore et ux.* v. *Lloyd,* 12 M.
& W. 463.

Without deciding that when the question is, as to the meaning of a writing, we can in every case look at the acts of the parties otherwise than as strengthening the opinion formed as to the meaning of the writing—see per Lord Abinger in *Alderman* v. *Neate*, 4 M. & W. 704, 716—in a case like the present, where there is no writing to construe, and where the question of sub-letting entirely depends on the words and acts of the parties, there is no difficulty in the way of the fullest consideration of the conduct of the parties.

Wardell obtained the exclusive possession of the land. This was from Hayes and under an agreement for the execution of a lease of some kind by Hayes. Wardell occupied for ten months. Before leaving there was a settlement between the parties on the basis of an award. A certain sum was found to be due to Wardell for improvements during his occupation. From this sum was deducted $224 for what is called "rent" in the award. One of the arbitrators afterwards endeavoured to qualify the use of the word rent, by saying that when that word was used rent was not intended. What else was intended? Nothing else is suggested. Now can it be said that a man who allows another to go into possession of land under an agreement for a lease, and who afterwards accepts rent for ten months' occupation by that person, never let the premises to that person? I think that it is not too much to hold in such a case that there was a letting. Both parties intended an immediate transfer of possession. Neither party intended that until the execution of the lease there should be no rent paid. Their subsequent conduct shews the reverse. See *Chapman* v. *Towner*, 6 M. & W. 100.

Besides, I incline to think that what took place between Hayes and Campbell also amounted to a breach of the covenant. Campbell was the sub-tenant of Wardell for a term certain at a certain money rent. Hayes so far recognized his tenancy that he forbid Campbell to pay rent otherwise than to himself, Hayes.

To decide that what took place between Hayes and Wardell was not in the creation of the relation of landlord and tenant, and so a breach of the covenant against sub-letting without license in writing would be to enable tenants to set their landlords at defiance, while without license of the landlord placing others in exclusive possession of the premises, and afterwards receiving rent for the occupation.

While acknowledging that forfeitures are not to be favoured, and that this is a particularly hard case of forfeiture, we must see that contracts are fairly performed by the parties contracting.

The covenant not to assign or sub-let was as binding on defendant Hayes as on the original lessee, and by the terms of that covenant the landlord, because of the breach by Hayes of the covenant, is entitled to recover possession of the land demised.

We cannot permit ourselves to be influenced by any argument or consideration of hardship. Where the controversy is as to the performance or non performance of a contract the question of hardship must in the determination of the controversy by a Court of law be cast aside. But even if admitted, there might be something said in favour of the hardship to landlords of permitting persons in whom they have no confidence exclusively to occupy their lands, and that contrary to the express language of the contract of demise.

Courts of equity do not usually relieve parties against a forfeiture occasioned by the breach of a covenant not to assign or sub-let. And one reason is, that the forfeiture almost always arises from the wilful default of the lessee : See *Davies* v. *Mortin*, 2 Chan. C. 127; *Lovat* v. *Lord Ranelagh*, 3 V. & B. 31 ; *Hill* v. *Barclay*, 18 Ves. 63; *Bamford* v. *Creasy*, 7 L. T. N. S. 187.

The rule must, in my opinion, be made absolute to enter a verdict for the plaintiff.

WILSON, J., concurred with the Chief Justice.

MORRISON, J.—In this case I was not satisfied at the trial that there was any tenancy created or any intention to create a tenancy that in law would work a forfeiture. All that the parties intended was, that there should be an assignment if the plaintiff would consent to it. I still retain that opinion, but as the learned Chief Justice and Mr. Justice Wilson are of a different opinion, I do not think it necessary to postpone the giving of judgment to enable me to write a formal one, and I therefore merely say that I dissent.

Rule absolute.

MOLSON'S BANK V. DONALD MCDONALD.

Promissory note—Discharge of endorser by giving time—Mortgage—Collateral security.

One M., the maker of certain promissory notes payable to and endorsed by the defendant, gave to the plaintiffs, the endorsees, a mortgage on land, with a proviso to be void on payment of $4,300, with interest in one year, " the said sum of $4,300 being represented by certain promissory notes now under discount, and held by the said mortgagees, and any renewals or substitutions therefor that may hereafter be given for the same. All to be paid within one year from this date."

After the execution of this mortgage, the notes sued upon were handed to the plaintiffs by M. to renew notes then held by them and referred to in the mortgage, the defendant having endorsed them in blank and entrusted them to M. for that purpose.

Held, that no agreement to give time for the payment of the notes could be implied from the mortgage ; and the parol evidence, set out in the case, shewed that the mortgage was intended only as collateral security.

The mortgage was a second one, and the defendant alleged that by the neglect of the plaintiffs in permitting a foreclosure of the first mortgage instead of obtaining a sale, he had suffered loss, which he claimed to deduct from plaintiffs' balance. Upon the evidence stated in the report, it was held that no such negligence was shewn, and the Court refused a reference to the Master, or leave to amend the pleadings.

ACTION against defendant as endorser of three promissory notes as follows :

1. Made by D. M. McDonald on the 28th June, 1875, payable to plaintiff or order, for $525, three months after date, and endorsed by plaintiffs.

2. Of the same date, made and endorsed by the same parties, payable three months after date, for $1,500.

3. Dated 29th June, 1875, and endorsed as before for three months for $1,500.

Pleas. 5 : That after the endorsement and delivery of the notes to the plaintiffs, and before they became due, &c., without the consent of the defendant, and for a good consideration in that behalf, the plaintiffs agreed with the maker to give him, and gave him, time for the payment of the said notes for one year after they should respectively become due.

6. That the notes were notes made by the maker in renewal of certain other notes made by him and endorsed by the defendant for the accommodation of the maker, and as his surety only, &c.; and that the plaintiffs, before the notes became due, without the consent or knowledge of the defendant, agreed with the maker that in consideration that the maker would execute and deliver to the plaintiffs a deed by way of mortgage of freehold premises in the city of Toronto, to secure the amount of the said notes and other notes made by the maker to the plaintiffs, the plaintiffs would give to the maker time, for the term of one year from the 26th of April, 1875, for the payment of the said notes and any renewals, &c.: that the maker executed the mortgage, &c., and the plaintiffs accepted the same and gave the maker the said time for payment of the notes; and the defendant afterwards, and after the said notes became due, but without having any knowledge or notice of the agreement or the making of the mortgage or that time had been given, did, at the request of the plaintiffs, endorse the notes in the declaration, the same being renewals respectively of the promissory notes so held by the plaintiffs at the time of the making of the said agreement.

7. On equitable grounds : that the notes in the declaration were renewals of other notes made by the maker and endorsed by the defendant, as in the last plea mentioned that while the plaintiffs were the holders of the said notes, and before the same were renewed, the plaintiffs required

the maker to give them, and he accordingly gave them, security therefor by way of mortgage upon certain freehold premises belonging to him, &c., which mortgage was the second mortgage, &c.: that afterwards, and after the said notes had been renewed, &c., the first mortgagee filed his bill in the Court of Chancery to foreclose the equity of redemption in the said premises, in which suit the plaintiffs and the maker were made parties defendants : that such proceedings were had, &c., that the plaintiff therein was about to obtain a final order of foreclosure, &c., of the premises, and the said maker being desirous that the said premises should be sold under the decree of the Court in the said suit, instead of being foreclosed, was about to take the procedings necessary for that purpose, whereupon the plaintiffs informed the said maker of the notes that they the plaintiffs, had already taken such proceedings; and the said maker, believing that the plaintiffs had taken such proceedings, did not himself take the same, whereas in fact the plaintiffs had not and wholly omitted, &c., to take any such proceedings, whereby, and by reason of the mere negligence of the plaintiffs in that behalf, the equity of redemption in the said premises, which were of great value and more than sufficient, if the same had been sold, &c., to pay both of the said mortgages, was foreclosed : that the defendant never had any notice or knowledge of the suit until after the equity of redemption had been foreclosed, and the defendant has by the mere default, &c., of the plaintiffs, as aforesaid, been deprived of the benefit of the said security so given by the said maker, and is discharged and released from his liability on the said notes.

Issue.

The case was tried at the Toronto Summer Assizes of 1876, before Patterson, J.A., without a jury.

The promissory notes being admitted, the following evidence was taken at the trial :—

The mortgage in question was dated 26th April, 1875, and made between D. Mitchell McDonald *et ux.*, to the defendants, the Molson's Bank, covering certain property in the city of Toronto.

"Proviso, mortgage to be void on payment of $4,300, with interest, as follows : the said sum of $4,300, with interest, in one year from the date hereof. The said sum of $4,300, being represented by certain promissory notes now under discount, and held by the said mortgagees, and any renewals or substiutions therefor that may hereafter be given for the same, all to be paid within one year from this date."

At the end of the mortgage was a further proviso :

" It is hereby agreed that during the currency of these presents the said mortgagor shall be entitled to a release of any one or more of the before mentioned parcels of land, on payment by him to the said mortgagees of the sum of $1,000 for each parcel so discharged, to be applied in his indebtedness, or as an assignment to the said mortgagees of the first mortgage, on such parcel or parcels so released, for whatever sum the said mortgagor shall receive from any purchaser of such parcel or parcels, provided such mortgage not to be less than $1,000, and that the mortgagor's indebtedness amounts to that sum."

The following is the memorandum of instructions referred to in the evidence of Mr. Morris, defendants' solicitor, and in the judgment, where the facts are sufficiently stated : " Instructions from McDonald 14/4/75. Mortgage for $3,000 from Donald Mitchell McDonald, and Jane, his wife, to Molson's Bank as collateral security for the undermentioned notes in the hands of the bank, and any renewals thereof, and also for any indebtedness to the bank, to be settled by Mr. Robertson in case of default of payment of notes."

Then follows the properties and the encumbrances thereon ; also a memorandum of the proviso for releasing part, last above mentioned in the mortgage.

At the close of the case the learned Judge found as follows : " I hold that there is no agreement to be implied from the mortgage to give time for the payment of the notes ; but that even if there was such an agreement the notes now in question were given by the defendant with the full knowledge of the facts on the part of the agent to whom he entrusted the endorsements to be given to the bank. The last plea was not proved, and I do not think any

laches or negligence shewn on the part of the bank in not
asking for a sale, which would make it proper in the interests of justice that I should amend the pleas. The evidence
on the plaintiffs' part is, that they obtained an estimate of
the value of the mortgaged property, which exceeded only
by a very small sum $4,000. The prior encumbrance was
only about $400 short of that. On consultation they de-
cided that it was not prudent to redeem. The mortgagor
and principal debtor did not suggest that they should apply
for a sale, and did not, on his own behalf or on behalf of
the defendant, his surety, take any steps to obtain a sale,
which they could have had, although he now puts a much
higher value on the property than was obtained by the
plaintiffs at the time. The plaintiffs could not have had
a sale without advancing at any rate $80, and the mort-
gage to the defendants being not only for securing the
notes in question, but also for another note of $800 and
upwards, there does not seem to be any such a margin
of value shewn as to make it reasonable to hold that
the plaintiffs committed any default with regard to the
defendant."

The learned Judge therefore entered a verdict for the
plaintiffs, and $3,664.06 damages.

In Easter term, May 31, 1876, *Bethune*, Q. C., obtained
a rule *nisi* to set aside the verdict, on the ground that the
defendant was discharged by the giving of time to the principal debtor; or why it should not be referred to the Master
in Chancery to enquire what amount, if any, the defendant
lost by the neglect of the plaintiffs in reference to the
mortgage in permitting the foreclosing of the mortgage
by a prior mortgagee; and why the amount of the verdict
should not be reduced by the amount the Master should so
find; and why the defendant should not have liberty to add
a plea on equitable grounds, setting up that the plaintiffs
took from the principal debtor, D. Mitchell McDonald, a
mortgage or security for the amount of the cause of action
sued for in the cause, and afterwards neglected to ask for

a sale in a suit by a prior mortgagee of the lands embraced
in the plaintiffs' mortgage, and neglected to communicate
with the defendant upon the subject, whereby the plaintiffs' mortgage was foreclosed, and the defendant lost the
benefit thereof; and averring that the property embraced in
that mortgage was worth more than the prior mortgagee's
debt, and praying that the plaintiffs might be compelled to
make good the loss, and that the amount of it might be
deducted from the plaintiffs' claim.

During Michaelmas term, November 25, 1876, *C. Robinson,* Q. C., shewed cause. The evidence shews that the
mortgage was intended to be, and was executed and
accepted as collateral security only for the notes, and there
was no time given for the payment of the notes as alleged
in defendant's plea, either upon the face of the mortgage
or otherwise. The acts on which the defendant relies for
his discharge from liability were done with the knowledge
of his agent, duly authorized to act for him and trusted
with his endorsements. No laches or negligence on the
plaintiffs'. part, in dealing with the mortgage or property
covered by it, was shewn in evidence.

He cited *McInnes* v. *Milton,* 30 U. C. R. 489; *Shaw et
al.* v. *Crawford,* 16 U. C. R. 101; *Gore Bank* v. *McWhirter,*
18 C. P. 293; *Chitty* on Contracts, 10th ed., 717 : *Twopenny*
v. *Young,* 3 B. & C. 208; *Polak* v. *Everett,* L. R. 1. Q. B. D.
669; *DeColyar* on Guarantees, 280; *Proctor* v. *Robinson,*
35 Beav. 329.

Bethune, Q. C., with him *Spencer,* contra. The evidence
shews a binding contract to extend the time to pay the
debt for a year from 26th April, 1875, made between the
plaintiffs and the principal debtor, of which the defendant had no knowledge, and by which he was discharged:
Rees v. *Berrington,* 2 White & Tudor, 974, 990, 2 Ves. 540;
Samuel v. *Howarth,* 3 Mer. 272, 278; *Calvert* v. *London
Dock Co.,* 2 Keen 638; *The General Steam Navigation Co.*
v. *Rolt,* 6 C. B. N. S. 550; *Moss* v. *Hall,* 5 Ex. 46; *Pooley*
v. *Harradine,* 7 E. & B. 431; *Howell* v. *Jones,* 1 C. M. &

R. 97 ; *Combe* v. *Woolf*, 8 Bing. 156 ; *Bailey* v. *Edwards*, 4 B. & S. 761. The notes sued on were given as renewals of the notes first endorsed by defendant, and were so given in ignorance of the extension of time, and cannot affect his discharge : *Bell* v. *Gardiner*, 4 M. & G. 11 ; *Mills* v. *Guardians, &c., Alderbury Union*, 3 Ex. 590. The mortgage given to the bank by D. M. McDonald contains proof of the extension of the time, and parol evidence should not have been received in denial of that agreement : *Ex parte Glendining*, Buck 517 ; *Boultbee* v. *Stubbs*, 18 Ves. 20 ; *Mathews* v. *Holmes*, 5 Grant 1, 35 ; *Young* v. *Austen*, L. R. 4 C. P. 553 ; *Abrey* v. *Crux*, L. R. 5 C. P. 37 ; *Wallis* v. *Littell*, 11 C. B. N. S. 369 ; *Lindley* v. *Lacey*, 17 C. B. N. S. 578. At all events, if admissible the weight of the parol evidence is in defendant's favour and goes to establish the agreement to give time : *Bamfred* v. *Iles*, 3 Ex. 380 ; *Strange* v. *Fooks*, 4 Giff. 418, 412 ; *Bonser* v. *Cox*, 4 Beav. 379, 6 Beav. 110 ; *Bonar* v *McDonald*, 3 H. L. 226 ; *Pybus* v. *Gibb*, 6 E. & B. 902; *Blest* v. *Brown*, 8 Jur. N. S. 603. The plaintiffs' neglect to inform the defendant of the foreclosure proceedings on the prior mortgage, by which the defendant was prevented from securing the property, would discharge the defendant to some extent : *Mutual Loan Ass.* v. *Sadlow*, 5 C. B. N. S. 449 ; *Pearl* v. *Deacon*, 24 Beav. 186 ; *Pledge* v. *Buss*, Johns. 663, 666 ; *Watts* v. *Shuttleworth*, 5 H. & N. 235 ; *Mayhew* v. *Crickett*, 2 Swanst. 185, 191. There should be a reference to ascertain the value the mortgage would have had but for plaintiffs' neglect. The action is brought too soon and should have been delayed for a year from the 26th April, 1875. D. M. McDonald was not defendant's agent.

They also cited *Wulff* v. *Jay*, L. R. 7 Q. B. 756 ; *Clarke* v. *Henty*, 3 Y. & C. Ex. 187 ; *Lake* v. *Brutton*, 8 DeG. McN. & G. 452 ; *Leader* v. *Homewood*, 5 C. B. N. S. 546 ; *Bell* v. *Gardiner*, 4 M. & G. 11 ; *Mills* v. *The Guardians, &c., of Alderbury Union*, 3 Ex. 590 ; *Haynes* v. *Hare*, 1 H. Bl. 659.

February 6, 1877. MORRISON, J.—The defendant is sued in this action as endorser of three promissory notes made by his son, Mr. Mitchell McDonald, and he contends that he has been released from his liability thereon, as he was only an accommodation endorser and surety for his son, by reason of the plaintiffs having, without his consent, given time to the maker for the payment of the notes in question, by the taking of a mortgage from the maker on certain property as a security for the payment of the notes.

The evidence at the trial, as to the object of taking the mortgage and the giving of time, was very contradictory, the defendant's witness, his son, swearing to a state of facts which is denied and positively contradicted by the plaintiffs' witnesses in many important particulars; and as to that part of the case, I think the evidence preponderates very strongly in favour of the plaintiffs' contention, that the mortgage was given and taken as collateral security only, and that there was no giving of time to the maker in the sense contended for by the defendant.

The evidence shews that Mr. Mitchell McDonald was indebted to the bank upon a note for over $800, with which this defendant was not connected: that the former being pressed by the bank for the payment of that note, proposed to give the bank a mortgage on certain properties as a security for its payment: that during the negotiations, Mitchell McDonald, being the maker of three other notes held by the bank and endorsed by this defendant, and then maturing, he was informed by the bank manager that he required those notes paid; he then proposed to the bank manager that these notes might also be secured in the same mortgage—I take it to induce the bank manager to consent to their being renewed when they fell due, so as to enable him, the maker, to meet the notes at the close of the navigation of the year 1875, when he expected to be prepared to pay the notes—and that the mortgage should be a collateral security for the payment of the notes and renewals. Under these circumstances the bank manager assented, saying that if it was any inducement to him, he would allow them to be renewed to the close of the navigation. Mr. Mitchell McDonald, who is himself a barrister and attorney, put himself in communication with the bank's solicitor to have the mortgage prepared.

These three notes amounted in all to $3,525, and the proposal to give the security was made about the 14th of April, 1875. On that day the maker gave the instructions to the bank solicitor for the preparation of the mortgage, stating the properties, &c. The instructions were reduced to writing by Mr. Morris, the bank's solicitor, and by those instructions it appeared and was stated that the mortgage was to be a collateral security for the notes then held by the bank and any renewals of them. The mortgage was executed on the 26th of April, 1875, and made in the usual form, the proviso in the mortgage stating that the mortgage was to be void on payment of $4,300 in one year from the date thereof, the said sum of $4,300 being represented by certain promissory notes then under discount and held by the plaintiffs, and any renewal or substitution thereof that might thereafter be given for the same, all to be paid within one year from the date of the mortgage.

At the time the mortgage was executed there were prior mortgages on the lands to a very considerable amount.

After the making of the mortgage, on the 2nd of June, 1875, two of the notes in question in this suit, one for $1,500, and one for $525, were made by Mitchell McDonald payable three months after date, to the defendant and specially endorsed by him, and were given to the bank as renewals ; and they expressed in the bodies of the notes to be " in renewal of paper endorsed by him " ; and on the 29th of July the other note in question, for $1,500, also at three months, was also made and endorsed by the defendant. These three notes were handed to the bank by Mitchell McDonald, the mortgagee, to retire and renew the notes then held by the bank, the blank, or partially blank, notes endorsed by the defendant being entrusted to the maker for that purpose. The mortgage itself does not specifically refer to notes endorsed by defendant—only to notes of the mortgagor generally.

It appeared, however, at the trial that the notes referred to in the mortgage included the notes endorsed by the defendant, and that the notes now in question were renewals

of these notes. The language of the proviso being so-
general, it was necessary to shew by parol evidence what.
was meant and intended by the parties.

I quite concur with the learned Judge who tried the
cause, that the mortgage contains no implied contract
that time should be extended for the payment of the notes.
If there is an implied agreement, it is to renew the notes
when they fall due, and that necessarily required the consent of the defendant, and that is what is fairly to be
inferred, and I would say was the intention of the parties,
viz., to renew the paper with the same names to the end
of the season, at which time the mortgagor said he could
pay the notes; and in pursuance of that arrangement these
notes were produced to the bank endorsed by the defendant,
the defendant having left these notes with the maker,
as his agent, to deliver them to the bank for the purpose
of renewing the notes previously held by the bank.

There is nothing in the mortgage restraining the plaintiffs from pursuing any remedy they thought proper on the
notes themselves, or any stipulation not to sue the notes
after they were due. As said by Sir John Robinson, C. J.,
in *The Bank of Upper Canada* v. *Sherwood*, 8 U. C. R. 118
—a case very similar to this—" The mortgage may or may
not have extinguished the first notes, depending on the
language of it. That, however, would only be on the
technical ground of merger; but that principle could not-
be applied to the notes now sued on, which were given
long after the mortgage was made. As to these notes, the
only question can be, whether they were binding when
given and endorsed; for in respect to them nothing that
could affect their validity was done afterwards. Why
should they not be binding?—As between Bethune and
the plaintiff there was a good consideration. There was
no reason why Mr. Bethune could not legally give them
his notes for the debt due, though secured by mortgage.
The assignment, as set out, does not postpone the time
for paying the notes. All that can be said is, that it gives
the plaintiff the additional security of certain steamboats,

subject to a defeasance if the money should be paid on the 1st of August, 1849. That did not restrain the remedy on the notes themselves if not paid according to their tenor."

The parol evidence here shews that the mortgage was intended merely to be a further and collateral security, and the subsequent acts of the parties shew such to be the case.

The proviso contemplated a renewal of the notes, and that the mortgage was a security for the ultimate payment of the notes.

As held in the *Gore Bank* v. *Eaton*, 27 U. C. R. 335, a case in one respect somewhat like this, the proviso applied only to the remedy against the land.

Assuming that the mortgage was given as collateral security, which I think is clear from the evidence, as said by Sir John Robinson, C. J., in giving judgment in *Shaw et al.* v. *Crawford*, 16 U. C. R. 101, "the intent evidently was, that the mortgagor was not to be disturbed under the mortgage until the time that was mentioned in it; but that is, the holders of the note, the plaintiffs, might be at liberty to deal with that independent of the mortgage."

In *Strong* v. *Foster*, 17 C. B. 201, Jervis, C. J., in giving judgment, at p. 215, says: "Then, assuming that this is a case of suretyship, I take the rule in equity to be the same as the rule at law, viz., that mere forbearance on the part of the creditor to sue the principal debtor will not release the surety. This is distinctly laid down by Lord Eldon in *Samuel* v. *Howarth*, 3 Meriv. 272. The mere fact of the creditor remaining inactive is not enough to enable the surety to say that time has been given to the principal debtor, and that therefore he is discharged. What has been done here to alter the situation of the parties? Foster was bound to pay the note when at maturity. It was his duty to enquire whether Smeator had paid it, if he had reason to believe that he would do so. Nothing has been done by the bank that I can see, to change the rights or liabilities of the parties. The defendant has not been prejudiced by any act of theirs, or prevented from enforcing any remedy he was entitled to."

Williams, J., at p. 219 said : " What I understand by
a giving of time in such a case is this—the surety has a
right at any moment to go to the creditor and say, 'I
have reason to suspect the principal debtor to be insolvent
therefore, I call upon you to sue him, or to permit me to
sue him.' If the creditor has voluntarily placed himself in
such a position as to be compelled to say he cannot
sue him, he thereby discharges the surety. The case
would then fall within the general doctrine as to principal
and surety, which equally obtains in law and in equity,
that, if the creditor does any act to alter the position of the
surety, he thereby discharges him. There is no pretence
for saying that time has been given in that sense in the
present case."

And Crowder, J., at p. 221 said, " I have always
understood that the giving of time which discharges a ·
surety, supposes a state of things where the creditor has
by some binding contract precluded himself from enforcing his remedy against the principal debtor as but for
such contract he might have done."

And Willes, J., in his judgment referred at p. 223 to
the case of *Fentum* v. *Pocock*, 5 Taunt. 192, as expressly
deciding that where the holder of a bill of exchange, accepted for the accommodation of the drawer, took a
cognovit from the drawer for payment by instalments, he
did not thereby discharge the acceptor, whether the holder
at the time of the taking the bill knew that it was an
accommodation bill or not, and that learned Judge further
said, with regard to that case : " It is supposed that Lord
Eldon, in the *Bank of Ireland* v. *Beresford*, 6 Dowl. 233,
expressed a doubt upon that ; but I think it will be found
that he adopts the view taken by Sir James Mansfield and
the rest of the Court of Common Pleas in that case."

In *Bell* v. *Banks*, 3 M. & G. 265, Coltman, J., says, " It is
not a sufficient ground for discharging the surety that the
principal has taken a further security from the principal
debtor without the privity of the surety, although he may
be thereby induced to forbear from enforcing his demand

against the principal. Here the creditor has not fettered himself in any way."

And Maule, J., at p. 267 said, "With reference to the discharging of sureties it is well known in law, that giving time means the putting it out of the power of the creditor to sue during the extended time."

On the whole case I am of opinion there was no giving of time for the payment of the original notes, or any binding stipulation in respect to them, or to the renewals, nor anything done on the part of the plaintiffs to discharge the defendant from liability, nor anything done injurious to the defendant as surety or inconsistent with his rights; and that the plaintiffs are entitled in this respect to hold their verdict.

The defendant's rule also seeks a reference to the Master in Chancery to enquire what amount, if any, the defendant has lost by the neglect of the plaintiffs in permitting the foreclosure of the mortgage by the prior mortgagees, and that the amount of the verdict be reduced by such amount. And also to add a plea on equitable grounds, setting up that the plaintiffs took from Mitchell Mc-Donald a mortgage for the amount of the cause of action sued for, and afterwards neglected to pray a sale by the prior mortgagees, and neglected to communicate with the defendant on the subject, whereby the mortgage was foreclosed and the defendant lost the benefit thereof, and averring that the property embraced in the mortgage was worth more than the prior mortgage debt, and praying that the plaintiffs may be compelled to make good the loss and the amount be deducted from the plaintiffs' claim.

It is quite clear from the evidence given at the trial that after the prior mortgagees took steps to foreclose their mortgage, the amount due thereon being about $3,700, the bank manager made enquiry as to the value of the property, and the question of value was fully considered by the officers of the bank: that they also employed a competent person of twenty years' experience in dealing in real estate in this city, where the lands in question were situate. This valuator gave evidence on the trial, and he stated the value at $3,700. Under these circumstances the plaintiffs did not think it advisable to go to the expense of praying a sale.

The defendant's son, the mortgagor, at the trial valued the property at a much higher value; but although so deeply interested in his own right, as well as his father's, the defendant, he did not think it necessary or advisable to ask for a sale, nor did he ask or advise the plaintiffs to do so, but he permitted the final order of foreclosure to go.

I must say that the whole of the testimony of the defendant's son is most unsatisfactory, and the defendant cannot complain if the most unfavourable view is taken of it. If the defendant relied on the value of the mortgaged property being much beyond the amount of the prior mortgagee's debt and the alleged negligence of the plaintiffs in not asking for a sale, as a ground for reducing his liability on the notes, he ought to have been prepared with and produced other and reliable evidence shewing such greater value. The defendant himself on the trial, when asked, could not say what the value of the property was.

The learned Judge who tried the case was of opinion that there was not any laches or negligence shewn on the part of the bank in not asking for a sale: that the value of the property did not appear to be such as to make it reasonable to hold that the plaintiffs committed any default in that respect with regard to the defendant; and he also, at the trial, refused to amend the last plea, as he saw nothing in the interests of justice that would make it proper he should allow an amendment of the plea.

I perfectly concur in the view taken by the learned Judge. In a case like this, after a verdict for the plaintiffs we ought not to grant a new trial, or order a reference to Chancery, or grant leave to add the new plea which is here asked, without some foundation being laid by the evidence at the trial, or upon affidavits shewing facts to justify us in doing so, if the plea had been on the record.

The evidence given at the trial warranted a finding in favour of the plaintiffs on such a plea.

On the whole I am of opinion that the rule should be discharged.

HARRISON, C.J., and WILSON, J., concurred.

Rule discharged (a).

JOHANNA COOLEY, EXECUTRIX, AND THE REV. HENRY
BRETTARGH, AND MATTHEW BURNS, EXECUTORS OF THE
LAST WILL OF SAMUEL COOLEY, DECEASED, V. ANN
SMITH, ALLEN WEBSTER SMITH, AMBROSE SMITH,
ALONZO SMITH, AND HARRIET SMITH.

*Registry Law—Equitable interest—Possession—Notice—Offer to purchase—
36 Vic. ch. 10, O.—Corroborative evidence—Pleadings in Chancery—
Admissibility of evidence.*

In ejectment it appeared that M., owning the land in question, conveyed it in 1852 to W. J. M., who in the same year mortgaged to the Trust & Loan Company. They in 1858 conveyed to W., who in 1859 mortgaged it again to them, and in 1860 they conveyed to C., who devised it to the plaintiffs. All these conveyances were duly registered. Both W. J. M. and W. were acting as trustees or agents for M.

For the defence it was shewn that M. in 1852 verbally agreed to sell the land to one P. S., who paid the purchase money and took possession as a purchaser. In 1859 he received a bond from M. to convey to him in two months, but he never obtained a conveyance, and the bond was never registered, nor could it be under the Registry law when it was given. He died in 1859, and his wife and children, the defendants, had continued to hold possession ever since. C. when he purchased in 1860 had notice of such possession.

Held, following *Grey* v. *Ball*, 23 Grant 390, the last decision in Chancery, though opposed to earlier cases, that knowledge of the possession held by the plaintiffs having an equitable interest was not sufficient to affect the registered title, and that the plaintiffs therefore were entitled to recover; but a new trial was granted, with costs to abide the event, to enable defendants to shew, if possible, that C. in fact bought subject to M.'s equity of redemption.

Held, also, that offers to purchase made by defendants, not having been accepted, and an alleged lease signed by them, without proper advice, under which they had paid no rent, should not, under the circumstances, preclude defendants from relying upon their equitable title.

Held, also, that the bond, which was produced, for the conveyance of the land, without any payment to be made, was sufficient corroborative evidence of defendants' statement of the verbal bargain by plaintiffs and payment of the purchase money, under 36 Vic. ch. 10, sec. 6, O.

(*a*) This case has since been affirmed on Appeal.

C., in the answer in a suit in Chancery, having stated the sum paid by him, and the facts : *Semble*, that the pleadings in this suit, having been put in by defendants, were some evidence as against them of such payment: but as a new trial would not have been granted for the reception of such evidence, even if inadmissible, the point was not determined.

THIS was an action of ejectment brought on the 11th of November, 1875, for the recovery of possession of part of block A. in the broken front of the township of Sidney, composed of lots 138, 139, and 140, on the north side of King street, and lot 142, adjoining and immediately in the rear of lot 138 ; lot 141, immediately in the rear of lot 139, and broken lot immediately in rear of 140, the last mentioned lot being on the south-west side of Heber street, formerly in the village of Annwood, now in the village of Trenton.

The plaintiffs claimed title under and by virtue of a deed from the Trust and Loan Company of Upper Canada, to Samuel Cooley, their testator, dated 19th February, 1860.

The defendants, besides denying the title of the plaintiffs, pleaded an equitable defence.

The equitable plea alleged that the defendant Ann Smith was the widow, and the other defendants the children of Philo Smith, deceased : that some time in 1852 Philo Smith agreed to purchase the lands in question from Adam Henry Meyers, who was then the owner thereof: that he paid the whole of the purchase money, and entered into possession, but received no conveyance : that Meyers afterwards, in fraud of Smith, conveyed the lands to one W. J. Macaulay in trust for himself, Meyers, for the purpose of enabling Macaulay to mortgage the same to the Trust and Loan Company for the loan of a sum of money to him, Meyers : that the equity of redemption was afterwards conveyed by Macaulay to Meyers : that the mortgage became in default : that the mortgagees, under power of sale contained in the mortgage, offered the lands for sale: that one R. M. Wilkinson, at the request of Meyers and his agent, became the purchaser of the lands : that neither Meyers nor Wilkinson having the money to pay for the lands, the money was raised by the execution of a mortgage on the said and other lands to the Trust and Loan Company : that the last mentioned mortgage also contained a power of sale : that default was made in the second mortgage : that the lands were thereupon sold by the mortgagees to Samuel Cooley for $3,500, of which sum Cooley paid $2,000, being the money of Meyers, and Meyers himself paid the remainder to the mortgagees : that Cooley in making the purchase was the agent of Meyers : that Meyers and Cooley colluded for the purpose of defrauding Philo Smith : that Cooley when he purchased the land well knew that Philo Smith had previously purchased and paid for the said lands. The plea concluded by submitting that in equity the plaintiff was not entitled to maintain the action, and should be ordered to execute a conveyance to the defendants.

The plaintiffs replied that Samuel Cooley was a purchaser for value, without notice : that the title is a registered title : that the plaintiffs are entitled to the benefit of the Registry Acts : that Cooley, on or about 20th February, 1866, in the Court of Common Pleas, ejected two of the defendants, who afterwards, on 24th July, 1868, accepted a lease of the lands from Cooley : that these defendants are Ann Smith and Allen Webster Smith, who have since remained in possession. The replication concluded by claiming the benefit of the Statute of Frauds against the defendants, and that owing to laches the defendants could not succeed.

The case was tried at the last Assizes, at Belleville, before Wilson, J., without a jury.

The following admissions were made by the defendants :

1. Patent of the lands in question to the Rev. John Strachan, dated 29th February, 1804.

2. Bargain and sale. 18th June, 1845. John Strachan, described as the Lord Bishop of Toronto, to Adam Henry Meyers, consideration £60, of the lands in question, registered 28th June, 1845.

3. Bargain and sale. 3rd January, 1852. Adam Henry Meyers to William James Macaulay, consideration £1,000

registered 23rd July, 1852; of the lands in question and
other lands.

4. Mortgage, 24th June, 1852, William J. Macaulay to
the Trust and Loan Company, of the lands mentioned in
the last deed, to secure £400; registered 24th July, 1852.

5. Bargain & Sale, 11th December, 1858, from the Trust
and Loan Company to R. M. Wilkinson, consideration £400,
registered 17th February, 1860, of the lands in question.

6. Mortgage, 10th August, 1859, from R. M. Wilkinson
to the Trust and Loan Company, to secure repayment of
$2,950, on the lands in question and other lands.

7. Bargain & Sale, 15th February, 1860, from the Trust
and Loan Company to Samuel Cooley, consideration $2,950,
of the lands in question and other lands; registered on 16th
February, 1864.

8. Will of Samuel Cooley, dated 15th February, 1875,
devising the lands in question to the plaintiffs on certain
trusts therein contained.

This closed the case for the plaintiffs.

The following admissions were thereupon made by the
plaintiffs :—

1. Bond dated 12th July, 1859, in the penal sum of £500,
from Adam Henry Meyers to Philo Smith, conditioned for
the conveyance by Meyers to Smith, his heirs and assigns
within two months from date, of "that certain dwelling
house, tract of land and premises situate in the village of
Trenton, now occupied by the said Philo Smith, being
composed of the several lots or pieces of land heretofore
conveyed by the Lord Bishop of Toronto to said Adam
Henry Meyers," &c., being the lands in question.

2. Copy of bill in Chancery filed 28th October, 1869, by
Perlee Chard, against Adam Henry Meyers and Samuel
Cooley, in reference to south half lot 22, in the 3rd concession of Rawdon—which was one of the lots contained
in the deed from Meyers to Macaulay, by him mortgaged
to the Trust and Loan Company, and by the company
sold and conveyed to Wilkinson, who again mortgaged
the land to the company, who afterwards sold the same to

Cooley, alleged to be an agent for Meyers—and praying, among other things, the restraint of an action of ejectment brought by Cooley against the plaintiff.

3. The answers of Cooley and Meyers, in which it was alleged that the sale to Cooley was for value, stating the facts and denying fraud and collusion.

4. Decree dated 22nd September, 1859, referring it to the Master to take an account, and ordering a conveyance from Cooley to the plaintiff on payment of the amount, and in default bill to be dismissed.

5. Order dated 23rd February, 1873, dismissing the bill with costs as against defendant Cooley, for non-payment of the money found due by the Master's report.

Objection was made to the admission of the bill and answer as evidence between the parties in this suit.

An exemplification of a judgment in ejectment recovered by Cooley on 17th July, 1866, against Mary Ann Smith and Allan W. Smith, was also put in evidence, and a *hab. fac. poss.* therein issued.

Also a lease dated 24th July, 1868, from Cooley to the defendants in the ejectment suit, of the premises in question, for one year from 24th July, 1868, at the yearly rent of $48.

Mary Ann Smith, one of the defendants, and widow of Philo Smith, was the first witness called for the defence. She proved that her husband died 31st July, 1859 : that he was in possession of the land as a purchaser for seven or eight years before his death, and up to the time of his death : that he bought the land from Meyers, paying him $1000 for it : that their possession was well known to Cooley : that Cooley lived in the same village : that Meyers told Smith that this land and Chard's land were reserved and deeds to be made to them : that Cooley afterwards brought ejectment against defendant : that the action was not tried : that Cooley told her to go home and he would give her a deed : that she signed some paper which Cooley insisted she should sign or be pnt out of possession : that there was no agreement to pay rent, and that she always refused to pay and never did pay any rent to Cooley.

Allen W. Smith, her son and one of the defendants, was also called as a witness for the defence. He proved that at the time he signed the lease he was under age; that he did it rather than have his mother thrown on the street by the sheriff's officers, and through fear of the officer who said if he did not sign it he (the officer) would handcuff him; he did not know anything about a trial or any agreement to pay rent, but on the contrary, told Cooley that the land was theirs under the bond from Meyers.

The action of ejectment appeared to have been defended by Adam Henry Meyers, who it would seem did as he pleased, without communication with or instructions from the defendants.

Objection was made to the testimony of Mrs. Smith as being uncorroborated, within the meaning of 36 Vic. ch. 10, sec. 6, O., but the learned Judge held that the bond was confirmatory of her evidence, as it provided for a conveyance by Meyers in two months without in any manner referring to payments to be made.

It also appeared from independent testimony that Smith and his family had been in possession of the land for more than twenty years before action, and that it was known to all the villagers, of whom Cooley was one.

Offers to purchase from Cooley, made by Mrs. Smith, were also given in evidence.

The learned Judge found that the offers to purchase made by Mrs. Smith were merely made for the sake of peace, and as there was no acceptance of them should not be allowed to prejudice the title of any of the defendants.

He also held that the recovery in ejectment in 1868, by Cooley against Mrs. Smith and her son, and the subsequent execution of the lease by them, was not binding on the defendants, so as to prevent them from setting up their real defence.

He found as facts that in 1852 Philo Smith purchased the land from Meyers for $1,000, and paid the purchase money: that immediately thereupon Philo Smith took possession as a *bond fide* purchaser: that in 1859 he received from Meyers the bond for a deed: that no deed was executed, but that Smith and his family had ever since remained in possession: that Cooley before he acquired title to the land had notice of such possession.

The learned Judge thereupon entered a verdict for the defendants, and ordered the plaintiffs to convey the real estate to the defendants in such manner as the children and the widow of Philo Smith, who died intestate, were respectively entitled to hold the land.

During Michaelmas term last, November 23, 1877, *Cameron*, Q. C., obtained a rule to shew cause why the verdict should not be set aside and a verdict entered for the plaintiffs, pursuant to the Law Reform Amendment Act, on the ground that the plaintiffs proved their title to the land in question, and that the defendants failed to prove the defence set up by them on the law and evidence; and for the improper admission of the evidence of two of the defendants as to matters occurring before the death of the plaintiffs' testator without the same being corroborated by other material evidence, and that the defendants should not have obtained a verdict on such evidence; and that the plaintiffs' testator was a purchaser for value without notice of the alleged equity of the defendants, and that there was no evidence of any such notice, and that the plaintiffs are entitled to the benefit of the Registry Acts as pleaded by them, and the defendants are barred by their acquiescence and laches; and for the improper reception of copies of the pleadings in a Chancery suit of *Chard* against *Meyers*, the decree in the said suit only being admissible.

During the same term, December 1, 1877, *Bethune*, Q.C., shewed cause. The possession of Smith was notorious to all the villagers, of whom Cooley was one, and so he must have had notice of it: *Jones* v. *Smith*, 1 Hare 60; *Kerr* on Frauds, 175, 183. Notice of the possession was, under the circumstances, notice of the defendants' title: *Gray* v. *Coucher*, 15 Grant 419. And the case is not affected by the Registry Acts: *McMaster* v. *Phipps*, 5 Grant 15, 253; *Moore*

v. *The Bank of British North America*, 308 ; *McLennan* v. *McDonald*, 18 Grant 502. The plaintiffs' testator therefore was in equity a trustee for the defendants, and the defendants are entitled to a conveyance. There was no evidence of the payment of purchase money by their testator independently of the deed, and this is not sufficient : *Ferrass* v. *McDonald*, 5 Grant 310, 313 ; *Jones* v. *Beck*, 18 Grant 671. The lease which two of the defendants signed was obtained by oppression, and so is not binding on them : *Kerr* on *Frauds* 137, 138; *McLaurin* v. *McDonald*, 12 Grant 82. The testimony of the defendants was corroborated not only by the bond executed by their testator, but by the fact of the long continued possession in his lifetime and afterwards : *Stoddart* v. *Stoddart*, 39 U. C. R. 203.

Hector Cameron, Q. C., contra. Mere possession is not notice of the defendants' title : *Grey* v. *Ball*, 23 Grant 390 ; *Bell* v. *Walker*, 20 Grant 558; *Sherboneau* v. *Jeffs*, 15 Grant 574 ; *Barnhart* v. *Greenshields*, 9 Moore P. C. 18. The possession was not even corroborative evidence of the testimony of the defendants, and there was no other corroborating evidence: *Stoddart* v. *Stoddart*, 39 U. C. R. 203. Defendants put in the answer of Cooley in the Chancery suit of *Chard* v. *Meyers*, where it was distinctly sworn that Cooley paid the whole of the purchase money to the Trust and Loan Company, and this is independent of the deed to Cooley. Besides, the equitable title relied on by the defendants was not proved, and even if proved, no order can in this suit be made for the execution of a conveyance : *Kennedy* v. *Bown*, 21 Grant 97 ; *French* v. *Taylor*, 23 Grant 436 ; *Best* v. *Hill*, L. R. 8 C. P. 10 ; English Judicature Act, 36 & 37 Vic. ch. 66, sec. 24, sub-secs. 2 and 3; and at all events can not be made without bringing in all the owners of the other lands affected, for the purpose of marshalling : *Miller* v. *Smith*, 23 C. P. 47; *Bondy* v. *Fox*, 29 U. C. R. 64; *Haynes* v. *Gillen*, 21 Grant 17 ; *McLellan* v. *McDonald*, 18 Grant 502; *Severn* v. *McLellan*, 19 Grant 220.

March 10, 1877. HARRISON, C. J.—This is an action of ejectment for the recovery of the possession of land.

Until recently there could be no equitable defence pleaded in such an action: *Neave* v. *Avery et al.*, 16 C. B. 328.

But it is now by sections 4, 5, and 6, of the Administration of Justice Act, 1873, provided that in addition to denying the plaintiff's title, the defendant may state by way of defence any facts which entitle him on equitable grounds to retain possession: that such a defence may be set up to the whole or part of the property mentioned in the writ; and that the plaintiff may reply such facts as avoid the defence on equitable grounds. See *Carrick* v. *Smith*, 34 U. C. R. 389.

It is by sections 1, 3, 8, and 9, of the same Act provided, that Courts of law and equity shall be as far as possible auxiliary to one another: that any party to an action at law may, by plea or subsequent pleading, set up facts which entitle him to relief upon equitable grounds, although such facts may not entitle such party to an absolute, perpetual, and unconditional injunction in a Court of equity: that for the purpose of carrying into effect the objects of the Act, and for causing complete and final justice to be done in any action at law, the Court, or a Judge thereof, may, at the trial or at any other stage of the action or proceeding, pronounce such judgment or make such order or decree as the equitable rights of the parties respectively require; and that in case any equitable question cannot be dealt with by a Court of law so as to do complete justice between the parties, there may be a transfer of the action or proceeding made to the Court of Chancery.

The power being to a Court of law to do *complete* justice between the parties, either by itself making all necessary orders or by a transfer of the cause, when expedient, to the Court of Chancery, the latter Court will not now, according to its reported decisions, entertain bills for *any portion* of the justice which, under the amended law, might, directly or indirectly, have been obtained in the common law action: *Kennedy* v. *Bown*, 21 Grant 95; *McCabe* v. *Wragg*, *Ib.* 97;

Demorest v. *Helme,* 22 Grant 433, 433 ; *French* v. *Taylor,* 23 Grant 436 ; *Victoria Mutual Fire Ins. Co.* v. *Bethune, Ib.* 568·

If we should, on the law and evidence, uphold the finding of the learned Judge in this case, and agree with him in thinking that a conveyance ought to be executed by the plaintiffs to the defendants, in order to do complete justice between the parties, it would be, according to these decisions, our duty, if necessary, to add parties to the suit, direct enquiries to be made, accounts to be taken, and in all respects act like a Court of equity, so as to fully dispose of the rights of the parties : *Boulton* v. *Hugel,* 35 U. C. R. 402. See also *Scott* v. *Dent,* 38 U. C. R. 30, 37.

Unless satisfied that the equitable defence set up by the defendants is proved in point of fact and good in point of law, it is our duty, as the plaintiffs' title is *primâ facie* admitted, to decide in favour of the plaintiffs.

We agree with the learned Judge in thinking that the defendants should not, by reason of the offers to purchase said to have been made by one of the defendants and the execution of the lease by two of the defendants, be precluded from setting up their defence as pleaded.

While the offers to purchase may as against the defendants making them be held some slight evidence of title in the person to whom the offers were made—See *Penlington* v. *Brownlee,* 28 U. C. R. 189—not having been accepted, and there being no change whatever in the position of the parties in consequence of the offers, we ought not to preclude defendants from shewing that at the time the offers were made they really had a good equitable title, and for the sake of peace were only negotiating for the legal title. See *Dixon* v. *Baty,* L. R. 1 Ex. 259.

Then as to the lease. The defendants had no legal adviser. They did not understand the effect of what they were doing. What they did was apparently done under circumstances of oppression. An undue advantage was taken of their helpless condition. They ought not, under these circumstances, by the mere execution of the paper called a lease, and never having paid rent thereunder, to be precluded from asserting the title, if any, which before and at the time of the execution of the lease they enjoyed, and of which it is not pretended they have since in any manner divested themselves.

Nor can we say that the defendants, who all the time were in actual possession of the land, claiming it as owners, paying no rent to any body, were so far guilty of laches as to disentitle them to the relief now asked, if in other respects entitled to it.

We agree with the learned Judge in thinking that the testimony of Mrs. Smith was corroborated by other material evidence, so as to entitle the defendants to the verdict, if in point of law the facts shew they have a right to it.

The bond executed by the plaintiffs' testator, conditioned for the conveyance of the land in two months, without any provision for payment of purchase money, is not only evidence of a previous contract of purchase, but of the payment of the purchase money, and so materially corroborates the evidence of Mrs. Smith, who says that there was a bargain for the purchase of the land, followed by payment of the purchase money.

When to this is added the fact of actual possession from the time when the bargain is said to have been made in 1851 or 1852, and that in the lifetime of the alleged bargainor, and no payment of rent to him, or claim of rent by him, although he knew of the possession, the corroboratory evidence is strengthened.

It is not necessary for us to decide that the latter is of itself sufficient, but taking the two together we feel no doubt as to the correctness of the ruling of the learned Judge under the statute 36 Vic. ch. 10, sec. 6, O.: *Stoddard* v. *Stoddard*, 39 U. C. R. 203.

The only remaining matter, before determining the principal points in the case, is the question of the alleged improper reception of the pleadings in the Chancery suit of *Chard* v. *Meyers*. If this evidence be rejected there will be no evidence, independently of the deed, that Cooley

was a purchaser for value. In the answer to the Chancery
suit he swears he was, states the amount he paid, and gives
all the circumstances. This was put in by the defendants,
and without more was, we think, some evidence of the
payment of the money as against the defendants: *Bondy*
v. *Fox*, 29 U. C. R. 64. If we were to give effect to the
plaintiffs' present contention we should undoubtedly weaken
the plaintiffs' position as a purchaser for value.

So far as the defence is concerned, we are of opinion that
it is quite as strong without as with the contested testimony, and are unable to hold that any substantial wrong
was done to the plaintiffs by the admission of the evidence.

We would not, under the circumstances, grant a new
trial, even if this evidence were inadmissible, and so need
not now determine whether or not it was strictly admissible: *Smith* v. *Murphy*, 35 U. C. R. 571 ; *McDermott* v.
Ireson, 38 U. C. R. 1.

Having stripped the case of collateral matters, we shall
now proceed to consider the main grounds of the equitable
defence and reply. These are, as regards the defence, that
before the plaintiffs' testator acquired title the intestate of
the defendants had acquired a good equitable title, of which
the plaintiffs' testator had notice when he purchased; and
as regards the reply, that under any circumstances the
plaintiffs are entitled to priority under the operation of
the Registry Acts.

The reply also puts the defendants to proof of the allegations contained in the plea. See 36 Vic. ch. 8, sec. 6.

In equity a purchaser of property, with notice of an
equity binding the person from whom he takes, is himself
bound by the equity to the same extent and in the same
manner as his vendor: *Taylor* v. *Stibbert*, 2 Ves. Jr. 437.
See also *Dunbar* v. *Tredennick*, 2 B. & B. 304, 310.

Notice is either actual or constructive, but there is in
general no difference between them in consequences: *Pros-
ser* v. *Rice*, 28 Beav. 68 ; *Wormald* v. *Maitland*, 35 L. J.
N. S. Ch. 69.

Actual notice, as the words import, consists of express

information of the fact, and embraces all grades of evidence, from the most direct and positive proof to the slightest evidence from which a jury would be justified in finding notice. See *Boursot* v. *Savage*, L. R. 2 Eq. 134.

Constructive notice is where there is notice enough to excite the attention of a man of ordinary prudence to call for further enquiry, and in such case the person is bound by a knowledge of all the facts which would have been the result of the enquiry if made. *Ib.*

Hence, if the purchaser has actual knowledge of an equity affecting the property in the hands of his vendor, or of facts which raise the presumption of knowledge, he is as much bound by the equity as the vendor himself: *Carter* v. *Carter*, 3 K. & J. 617 ; *Cory* v. *Eyre*, 1 DeG. J. & S. 149 ; *Leigh* v. *Lloyd*, 2 DeG. J. & S. 301; *Newton* v. *Newton*, L. R. 6 Eq. 135 ; *Hunter* v. *Walters*, L. R. 11 Eq. 292 ; *Directors, &c.*, v. *Robson*, L. R. 7 H. L. 496.

Possession is *primâ facie* evidence of seisin : *Doe Keogh* v. *Calhoun*, 1 U. C. R. 157 ; *Eccles* v. *Paterson*, 22 U. C. R. 167 ; *Hunter* v. *Farr*, 23 U. C. R. 324 ; *Asher et al.* v. *Whitlock*, L. R. 1 Q. B. 1 ; *Board* v. *Board*, L. R. 9 Q. E. 48.

Where a man is in actual possession of real property, the fact of his possession is to be imputed as knowledge of his title to a purchaser who acquires the property without making enquiry as to the title : *Taylor* v. *Sibbert*, 2 Ves. Jr. 437 ; *Crofton* v. *Ormsby*, 2 Sch. & Lef. 583 ; *Allen* v. *Anthony*, 1 Mer. 282, 284; *Jones* v. *Smith*, 1 Hare 60 ; *Bailey* v. *Richardson*, 9 Hare 734; *Holmes* v. *Powell*, 8 DeG. M. & G. 572 ; *Attorney General* v. *Stephens*, 2 K. & J. 724 ; *Barnhart* v. *Greenshields*, 9 Moore P. C. 18, 32 ; *Gray* v. *Coucher*, 15 Grant 419.

It appears to us that the plaintiffs' testator before and at the time he purchased the land in question had, on the authority of these cases, at least constructive notice of the equitable title of the defendants.

So far as the plea is concerned, we agree with the learned Judge in thinking that the defendants, on the law and evidence, are entitled to judgment.

But it is insisted that under the operation of the registry laws the plaintiffs are notwithstanding entitled to judgment.

The Act which was in force at the time of the oral agreement of purchase in 1852, and at the time of the subsequent giving of the bond in 1859, was 9 Vic. ch. 34 of the late Province of Canada.

It provided, in the case of a registered title, that every deed and conveyance not registered should be adjudged fraudulent and void against any subsequent purchaser or mortgagee for valuable consideration, unless registered before the registry of the deed or mortgage of the subsequent purchaser,—sec. 6; but did not provide for the registry of a mere bond for conveyance of land or other contract of purchase.

The latter was not done by the Legislature till 1865, when the 29 Vic. ch. 24 was passed. Section 34 of that Act provides for the registry of bonds and agreements for the sale and purchase of land.

While mere priority of registration determines the right to the property as between parties claiming under different instruments capable of registration—*Doe Robinson* v. *Allsop*, 5 B. & Al. 142; *Drew* v. *Lord Norbury*, 3 Jones & L. 267; *Moore* v. *Cuthbertson*, 27 Beav. 639; *Robson* v. *Carpenter*, 11 Grant 293; *Holland* v. *Moore*, 12 Grant 296; *Stephens* v. *Simpson*, 12 Grant 493, 15 Grant 594—it has never been held, at all events in equity, independently of the statutes to which we shall hereafter advert, that registration is any protection against an unregistered title incapable of registration of which the subsequent purchaser for value had notice: *Sumpter* v. *Cooper*, 2 B. & Ad. 223; *Wright* v. *Stanfield*, 23 Beav. 639. See further *Eyre* v. *McDowell*, 9 H. L. 619; *The Agra Bank* v. *Barry et al.*, L. R. 7 H. L. 135.

The late Chancellor Blake, in *McMaster* v. *Phipps*, 5 Grant 258, expressed the opinion that the statute 9 Vic. ch. 34, did not in any manner affect equitable rights not created by deeds, conveyances, or written instruments of any sort, but which arose upon parol agreements or grew out of the conduct of the parties.

Such was also the opinion of the present Chancellor in *Harrison* v. *Armour*, 11 Grant 303, on a review of the English authorities bearing on the point.

Courts of equity have held that it never could have been the intention of the Legislature to give to a party a priority of right to commit a fraud, and that notice of a prior equity is for the purposes of the Act, if applicable, equivalent to registration: *Bank of Montreal* v. *Baker*, 9 Grant 298.

In the latter case the late Chancellor VanKoughnet, at p. 301, said : " While the Act declares that registration shall be notice, it does not provide that notice of an unregistered conveyance shall not affect a registered conveyance."

The cases in our Court of Chancery, as to whether the notice should as against a registered title be actual, are not uniform.

In *Sodon* v. *Stevens*, 1 Grant 346, where the unregistered title was by deed capable of registry, the late Vice-Chancellor Esten expressed a doubt as to the sufficiency of constructive notice to defeat the registered deed of a subsequent purchaser for value.

In *Waters* v. *Shade*, 2 Grant 457, where at the time of the second sale and conveyance the prior equitable title of the plaintiff was not in such a shape as to be capable of registry, it was held by Esten, V. C., that the possession of the property by the first but unregistered purchaser was not of itself notice of the title of the first purchaser, so as to defeat the subsequent registered title.

Such also was the ruling of the same learned Judge, concurred in by the present Chancellor, in *Ferrass* v. *McDonald*, 5 Grant 310. See further *McCrumm* v. *Crawford*, 9 Grant 337.

But in *Moore* v. *Bank of British North America*, 15 Grant 308, 310, there was a discussion as to the necessity for actual notice where the title was incapable of registration.

The suit was first heard before the late Chancellor VanKoughnet, who made the following note : " Whatever

opinion I may have individually entertained on this ques-·
tion, I learned from both my brother Judges—Esten and
Spragge, V.CC.—that it was considered as settled law in this
Court, that constructive notice, such as that by possession,
&c., did not avail against a registered title.   My brother
Spragge still considers that to be the view on which the
Court has acted in such a case.   This being so, I think I
should dismiss the bill, with costs, leaving it to the plaintiff
to seek for a different declaration of the law either on
rehearing or appeal."

On the rehearing, in the absence of the Chancellor in
England, Mowat, V. C., combatted, at p. 310, any such view
as follows : "It appears that the impression his Lordship
thus had at the moment of what had been theretofore held
was not quite correct. It had theretofore been supposed that
constructive notice of an unregistered deed, which was
capable of registration, did not avail against a registered
deed ; but no such doctrine had been laid down where the
unregistered claim was not founded on an instrument
capable of registration.   On the contrary, in that class of
cases, it had been distinctly held in this country, as well as
in England, that the Registry Act did not apply, and that
constructive notice was as effectual as in other cases ; and
this appears to have been his Lordship's own view of what
was the correct principle."

The decision of the majority of the Court, consisting of
the present Chancellor and Mowat, V. C., was that in the
case of an unregistered deed of a date antecedent to the
Act of 1865, and not founded upon a deed or conveyance
capable of registration, constructive notice, such as possession of the property, is sufficient notice against a subsequent
registered conveyance.

In *Gregg* v. *Coucher*, 15 Grant 419, where the equity
arose before the Act of 1865, possession was held, by the
present Chancellor, sufficient notice of the equitable title
as against the subsequent registered deed, although there
was no pretence of actual notice.

The Act of 1865, 29 Vic. ch. 24, enacted as follows :—

Sec. 65, "Priority of registration shall, *in all cases*, prevail, unless before such prior registration there shall have been *actual* notice of the prior instrument by the party claiming under the prior title."

Sec. 66, " No equitable lien, charge, or interest affecting land, shall be deemed valid *in any Court* in this Province after this Act shall come into operation, as against a registered instrument executed by the same party, his heirs or assigns," &c.

These sections were re-enacted as sections 67 and 68 of 31 Vic. ch. 20, O.

The question is, whether these sections should be read as affecting equitable interests which arose before, and which are sought to be enforced after the passing of the Act of 1865.

If the sections be read as in any manner interfering with vested rights, they ought not to be read retrospectively: *Moon* v. *Durden*, 2 Ex. 22 ; *Pettamberdass* v. *Thackoorseydass*, 7 Moore P. C. 239 ; but if read as merely affecting procedure, they may and ought to be read retrospectively: *Wright* v. *Hale*, 6 H. & N. 227 ; *Kimbray* v. *Draper*, L. R. 3 Q. B. 160.

In *McDonald* v. *McDonald*, 14 Grant 133, and *Moore* v. *The Bank of British North America*, 15 Grant 308, the Court of Chancery refused to read the sections as applying to equities which arose before the passing of the first Act. But in *Sherboneau* v. *Jeffs*, 15 Grant 574 ; *Bell* v. *Walker*, 20 Grant 558, and *Grey* v. *Ball*, 23 Grant 390, the same Court, without referring to the previous decisions, appear to have held the reverse.

In *Sherboneau* v. *Jeffs*, the equitable title arose in 1860, but the late Chancellor Vankoughnet held the case to be governed by sec. 67 of the Act of 1865, and to require proof of actual notice as against the subsequent registered title.

In *Bell* v. *Walker*, 20 Grant 558, where the equity arose before the passing of the Act of 1865, Strong, V.C., expressed no opinion on the point, but Blake, V.C., expressed

a strong opinion in favour of reading the Act as applicable
to equities which arose before its passing, and Chancellor
(Spragge) said he was inclined to agree with the latter
opinion.

In *Grey* v. *Ball*, 23 Grant 390, the Chancellor took a
more decided view in favour of the construction of the
Act expressed by Blake, V.C., in the previous case, and at p.
394, said : "It would be an anomaly, looking at the way in
which equitable interests are dealt with by these Acts, to
hold possession by the person having such interest *per se*
notice against a registered title, when possession by a person having a 'prior instrument' would not be notice."

The last case is undistinguishable from the one now
before us. It is the most recent exposition of the law on
the point in the Court of Chancery. The equitable interest
there arose before the Act of 1865. There was possession
by the person having the equitable interest. And it was
held, under the operation of the recent Act, that knowledge of such possession was not sufficient to affect the
registered title.

It only remains for us, when deciding a question of
equity, regardless of our own opinion, to follow the last
equity case in point, although in conflict with prior cases
in the same Court, leaving the parties dissatisfied to take
the opinion of the Court of Appeal as to which set of the
conflicting decisions is the one which truly expresses
the law.

The sections are in other respects so expressed as to have
caused differences of opinion between the late Chief Justice
of this Court, in *Bondy* v. *Fox*, 29 U. C. R. 64, 72, and the
present Chief Justice of the Common Pleas, and Mr. Justice
Gwynne, in *Millar* v. *Smith*, 23 C. P. 47, 56.

The latter conflict, so far as the decision of the case
now before us is concerned, is of no consequence, but we
mention it in the hope that if there be further legislation
it will be such as to remove all existing points of conflict.

In *Forrester* v. *Campbell*, 17 Grant 379, it was argued
that the effect of the Acts of 1865 and 1868 is to make

equitable titles void as against subsequent registered instruments, whether the parties entitled under these instruments had or had not notice of the equity, but the Court
refused to give effect to the contention.

The decision of *Forrester* v. *Campbell*, 17 Grant 379,
was afterwards followed in *Wigle* v. *Setterington*, 19 Grant
512.

In *Severn* v. *McLellan*, 19 Grant 220, the learned Judge
found actual notice. It does not therefore decide anything
as the point now before us.

No title was set up by the defendants through length
of possession. The defence was entirely rested on the
equitable title alleged. That defence cannot avail as
against the replication, according to the most recent
decisions of the Court of Chancery.

We are therefore obliged, in the present state of the
authorities, to make the rule absolute to enter the verdict
for the plaintiffs.

But if defendants desire a new trial, either for the purpose of proving that Cooley at the time of his purchase
colluded with Meyers, or purchased under such circumstances that Cooley was only a mortgagee—see *Chard* v.
Meyers, 19 Grant 358—or for the purpose of raising any
other defence which they think can, in the event of another
trial, be established, the rule may, under the circumstances
of this case, be made absolute for a new trial, costs to abide
the event; the defendants to have till the first day of next
term to make the election.

WILSON, J.—The land was owned by Adam Henry
Meyers. On the 3rd of January, 1852, Meyers conveyed
to Wm. James Macaulay, and he on the 24th of June, 1852,
mortgaged to the Trust and Loan Company. The Trust and
Loan Company, on the 11th of December, 1858, conveyed
to R. M. Wilkinson, and he on the 10th of August, 1859,
mortgaged to the Trust and Loan Company, and the company on the 15th of February, 1860, conveyed to Samuel
Cooley.

71—VOL. XL U.C.R.

Cooley's will was made on the 15th of February, 1875, devising the land to the plaintiffs.

These conveyances were all duly registered.

Meyers gave a bond on the 12th of July, 1859, to Philo Smith (the two defendants being his wife and son) to convey the land in question, a small part of the farm which Meyers conveyed, and which was mortgaged to the Trust and Loan Company.

It appeared that Philo Smith bought the land by verbal agreement only from Meyers, and went into possession of it seven or eight years before his death, and that he remained in possession of it until his death on the 31st of July, 1859, only a few days after he had got the land, and that his widow and the family have been in possession of it ever since.

Whether Philo Smith had bought and taken possession before Macaulay mortgaged to the Trust and Loan Company on the 24th of June, 1852, is of no consequence, because that mortgage was afterwards put an end to by the conveyance from the company to Wilkinson on the 11th of December, 1858, and because Wilkinson was acting as agent or trustee for Meyers, lending his name for Meyers's benefit, as Macaulay had done before him, to facilitate probably the transactions with the company, which could be better transacted through others than through Meyers.

The conveyance to Wilkinson in December, 1858, and the mortgage by him on the 10th of August, 1859, to the company, must be considered as matters done and transacted by Meyers.

Then the facts are : Meyers had sold to Philo Smith the land in question in this suit seven or eight years before the 12th of July, 1859, who went into possession of it, and who, or those claiming under him, have had possession of it ever since.

On the 12th of July, 1859, Philo Smith, having before that paid for the land, got a bond from Meyers to convey the land to him, which was the first document of any kind he received from Meyers. That bond was not registered.

On the 10th of August, 1859, Wilkinson, for Meyers, mortgaged the whole farm and other lands to the Trust and Loan Company for $2,950; and the company, on the 15th of February, 1860, conveyed the mortgaged property to Samuel Cooley, who duly registered.

The plaintiffs rely on a registered title, and the defendants do not, but upon notice, which they say secures to them the benefit of a registered title.

The bond to Philo Smith of the 12th of July, 1859, might have been registered before Wilkinson for Meyers made the mortgage to the Trust and Loan Company on the 10th of August, 1859.

If it had been, it would still have been necessary to shew that the Trust and Loan Company, in order to gain precedence of them, knew in dealing with Wilkinson they were dealing with him for Meyers. It is not probable they did know it; although that fact might, from the long transactions prior to that time about this property, have been established, as it is very probable that Meyers may have been brought into connection with them frequently during the time from the giving of the first mortgage in June, 1852, till the giving of the second mortgage in August, 1859.

But assuming the company knew that in August, 1859, they were dealing in effect with Meyers, there is no reason to believe that the company had notice in fact of the claim of any one under Philo Smith to the land in question.

The defendants were in fact however there as vendees, as Philo Smith as vendee had been for years in possession of the land before the company's mortgage of August, 1859.

Was that possession notice to the company that the defendants had a claim to the land? Or are the company bound by the fact of that possession to have had notice of it? The statute which was in force at these dates was the 9 Vic. ch. 24.

By that Act it is declared that after any memorial has been registered, every deed, &c., made and executed, of the lands, or any part thereof, contained in the memorial shall be adjudged fraudulent and void against any subsequent purchaser or mortgagee for valuable consideration unless it is registered.

I am of opinion the Trust and Loan Company had constructive notice of Philo Smith's interest by reason of his long and actual possession of the land, of which fact they must be deemed to have had notice: *Holmes* v. *Powell*, 8 DeG. M. & G. 572; *Barnhart* v. *Greenshields*, 9 Moore's P. C. 18. And as to Cooley, he had actual notice of such possession when he bought in 1860, and for long before it, and that should have put him upon further enquiry. The course of decisions here has been, even under the old Registry Acts, that actual notice of a prior unregistered claim was required to be proved to cut out a prior registered one; and that constructive notice, by the fact of possession, was not sufficient of itself to do so, unless the equitable claim was one which could not be registered.

The bond of the 12th of July, 1859, could have been registered before the company acquired the title which is now set up of the 10th of August, 1859; and of that bond there is no reason to suppose the company had any notice or knowledge, any more than they had of the possession.

Whether Cooley knew of it or not is of no moment, so long as he claims from one who did not know of it. In order to defeat Cooley, the defendants must shew not only that he knew of the possession or bond, but that the company also knew of the possession or bond. For his knowledge is of no avail, unless his vendor knew of such matters also. It is useless to say whether *actual* notice is or should be the proper rule under the early Registry Acts; or whether constructive notice, by means of possession, is sufficient to defeat a prior registration, because if that is to be contested it must be in appeal.

It is said that secs. 66 and 68 of the Registry Act of 1868 are retrospective in their operation, and that the defendants will be required to meet that view of the case too.

As to sec. 66, that registration shall constitute notice of such instrument to all persons claiming subsequently to it, that clause has no effect here, because Philo Smith did not claim subsequently but prior to the company and to Cooley. And probably it may be retrospective, because it relates rather to that which is or is declared to be evidence, and so is a matter of procedure.

But sec. 68,—which declares that no equitable lien, &c., shall be deemed valid in any Court after the Act comes into operation as against a registered instrument executed by the same party, his heirs or assigns, and tacking shall not be allowed to prevail in any case against the provisions of the Act—relates not to matters of procedure but to matters of estate and interest in lands; and such rights are not to be defeated, or avoided, or made null, but by the plainest language, and such language is not used here. There are two cases in favour of the retrospective operation, but there are two cases also against it. If Cooley was protected by the notice or knowledge only which the company had, that may apply only to the extent of the mortgage interest, and not to his purchase of the equity from the company, if he did purchase it.

I think the defendants should be allowed a further opportunity to discover and ascertain if possible whether Cooley, when he bought in 1860, did not in fact buy subject to the rights of Meyers's equity of redemption, and if so, then such proceedings may be taken by the defendants to require the plaintiffs to account from the time of the purchase, and if there be a balance owing to them to resort to the other lands before having recourse to the defendants' property.

There is great reason to believe that the equity suit, which established in Meyers's lifetime the fact that Cooley was merely the assignee of the mortgage, and not the absolute purchaser of the land, was and is true in fact: *Chard* v. *Meyers*, 19 Grant 358. And when all the evidence is given upon that point which can be given, the Court can then determine whether the defendants are entitled

.to maintain their claim against the legal rights of the plaintiffs.

The case will be, of course, open to the defendants to strengthen their case in any other respect as they may be advised.

The rule will be absolute for a new trial, with costs to abide the event.

MORRISON, J., concurred.

Rule absolute for new trial.

HALL v. MERRICK.

Prvmissory note—Signature in blank by married woman—Alteration— Guarantee.

The plaintiff had signed notes for the accommodation of M., and declined to continue doing so, or to renew such paper, unless M. would give him a guarantee. Defendant, M.'s wife, had been in the habit of signing blank notes for M. when asked, and M. having a blank form of note signed by her, filled it up as follows, for the amount of the plaintiff's paper then falling due :—

April 3. 1871. Four months after date I promise to pay to William Hall, or order $1264, at the Bank of Toronto here. *This note to be held as collateral security.* Value received.

The words in italics were inserted at the plaintiff's request.
The defendant had no communication with the plaintiff.
Held, that the defendant was not liable, for the instrument was not a promissory note, not being for the payment of money absolutely ; and if a guarantee, there was nothing to shew that she ever signed or intended to sign such a contract, or authorized the conversion of the note into it.

THIS was an action tried before Hagarty, C.J.C.P, at the Toronto Fall Assizes, 1876.

The declaration contained a count on a promissory note for $1,264, made by the defendant, at four months' date, and the common money counts ; also, a count setting out that in consideration that the plaintiff would make and deliver to one J. D. Merrick certain promissory notes for the accommodation of the said Merrick, &c., the defendant promised the plaintiff to be responsible to him for the payment of the amount thereof: that the plaintiff delivered

to said Merrick the said notes, and Merrick afterwards
made default in the payment thereof, and the plaintiff was
obliged to pay the same, and all conditions were fulfilled,
&c., yet the defendant did not pay the plaintiff the amount
of said promissory notes, &c.

Fourth count : that in consideration that the plaintiff
would make and deliver to J. D. Merrick certain promissory notes for the accommodation of the said Merrick, and
for the purpose of enabling him to raise certain moneys, the
defendant, by her certain agreement in writing in the words
and figures following, that is to say :—

"$1264.   April 3, 1871.

"Four months after date I promise to pay to William
Hall, or order, twelve hundred and sixty-four dollars, at
the Bank of Toronto, here. This note to be held as collateral security ; value received.

"SARAH J. MERRICK."

—agreed to pay the plaintiff the sum of $1264; and the
plaintiff delivered to the said J. D. Merrick the said
promissory notes, and Merrick afterwards made default in
the payment thereof, and the plaintiff was obliged to pay
the same, &c., and all conditions were fulfilled, &c., yet the
plaintiff did not pay the said $1264.

Pleas : 1. To the whole declaration : that the time of
making the alleged note, promises, &c., was before the
passing of the Married Women's Property Act of 1872, and
at said time the defendant was and still is the wife of J.
D. Merrick.

2. To first count, did not make the note as alleged.

3. To first count, that the note was made by the
defendant at the request and for the accommodation of her
husband J. D. Merrick as collateral, security for the payment by him of certain notes before then made, &c., and
endorsed by the plaintiff for the said Merrick, and upon the
terms that the said note should be held as such security,
and except as aforesaid there never was any value or consideration for the making or payment of the note of the
defendant, and that the notes so made and endorsed by the

plaintiff were, before the commencement of this suit, paid and satisfied, &c.

4. To first count: note not stamped as required by law.

5. To first count, on equitable grounds: that the note was made for the accommodation of her husband, J. D. Merrick, and as his surety, &c., to secure the payment of certain notes made, &c., by the the plaintiff for the accommodation of J. D. Merrick, &c., and that plaintiff agreed to give J. D. Merrick time for the payment of the said notes, beyond the time when the said notes were due and payable.

6. To second count: never indebted.

7. To third and fourth counts: did not promise, &c.

8. To third and fourth counts: no default by J. D. Merrick in payment of the said notes.

9. To third and fourth counts: payment by J. D. Merrick.

10. To third and fourth counts, on equitable grounds: that the defendant made the promise and agreement, &c., as surety, &c., and without the consent of defendant the plaintiff gave time to J. D. Merrick for the payment of the debt.

Replication to the first plea: that the promises and debts in the plea mentioned were made, &c., for the defendant upon her express promise to pay the same out of her separate estate, and upon the faith and credit thereof.

To fourth plea: that the plaintiff, as soon as he acquired knowledge that the note was insufficiently stamped, double stamped the note.

Issues on all the other pleas.

The plaintiff was examined at the trial, and it appeared from his evidence that in the year 1871 the plaintiff was liable on accommodation paper which he had given to J. D. Merrick for a considerable amount: that the plaintiff declined signing any more unless he got a guarantee: that J. D. Merrick asked the plaintiff if he would take the defendant's (his wife's) guarantee: that the plaintiff assented: that J. D. Merrick afterwards produced the note or instrument now in question; the plaintiff stating that the guarantee was to cover any loss that might arise through his obliging

J. D. Merrick. He further stated that he never saw the
defendant in reference to the matter, and had no communication whatever with her.

The defendant was also called by the plaintiff. She
testified that she never saw the plaintiff in reference to the
note, and that she never heard of him until after this suit
commenced; and that she never agreed to become guarantee for her husband's (J. D. M.) debts: that she signed a
piece of blank paper with nothing on it but the printing:
that she had been in the habit of signing blank notes at
her husband's request, because he asked her to do so, and
that it was never explained to her what the notes she
signed in blank were for, or how they were to be used:
that she did not know what the note now in question was
for: that such blank notes were to be used in J. D. Merrick's business, and he was to protect them.

J. D. Merrick was also examined, and he stated that he
received from the plaintiff accommodation and other paper:
that in April, 1871, he had a considerable amount of the
plaintiff's accommodation paper, and that the plaintiff insisted on his getting his brother's or his wife's (defendant)
name: that the witness had a blank note signed by his
wife lying in his drawer, and he filled it up for the amount
of plaintiff's paper then falling due, the plaintiff asking
him to insert on its face the words "collateral security,"
the witness stating that it was given to the plaintiff as
security, and that the intention of the guarantee was, to
secure the notes he had signed for the witness up to that
time, and he was to give him renewals: that nothing was
said about the then present or future obligations: that he
inferred it was to cover the future as well as the past: that
it was the only blank note of the defendant's he had, and
he could not say that it was a blank intended for the plaintiff: that he never spoke to defendant about the plaintiff.

The instrument produced at the trial was as follows :—

$1264.   April 3, 1871.

Four months *after date I promise to pay to* William
Hall, *or order*, twelve hundred and sixty-four dollars, *at*

the Bank of Toronto here. This note to be held as collateral
security. *Value received.*

Due.   (Signed)   SARAH J. MERRICK.

The words in italics as above were printed.

At the close of the case several objections were taken to
the plaintiff's recovery, and which are stated in the rule
nisi.

The learned Chief Justice entered a verdict for the
plaintiff for $1,071.50, being the amount of moneys alleged
to have been paid by the plaintiff on account of J. D. Merrick, and reserved leave to the defendant to move to enter
a verdict for her, &c., and leave to the plaintiff to increase
the verdict.

In Michaelmas term, November 23, 1876, *E. Crombie*, for
defendant, obtained a rule to enter a verdict or nonsuit, or
to reduce the verdict, or for a new trial, on the following
grounds: that the paper writing signed by the defendant was
not a promissory note : that if a promissory note, it was not
and is not duly stamped : that whether the same was a promissory note or not, the defendant, being a married woman at
the time she signed it, was not liable under the circumstances
under which it was signed by her and received by the plaintiff: that being a married woman, she could not contract in
the manner shewn by the evidence to guarantee the debt of
her husband: that the said writing is not a sufficient promise
under the Statute of Frauds to charge the defendant for
the debt, &c., of her husband, as claimed in the two last
counts of the declaration : that the evidence shewed that
the alleged note was given to secure renewals of notes
made by the plaintiff for the accommodation of defendant's
husband, and there was no evidence of such renewals, &c. :
that subsequent to the time of said defendant having become surety to the plaintiff, the plaintiff altered the mode
of dealing with J. D. Merrick.

On the same day, *J. K. Kerr*, Q. C., obtained a rule to
increase the verdict to the amount of $1,264, the amount
of the guarantee, or to such other amount as the Court
might think the plaintiff entitled to.

During this term, February 15, 1877, both rules were argued. *J. K. Kerr*, Q.C., for the plaintiff. The document in question is a good promissory note, or if not it is a sufficient guarantee. He cited *Fahnestock* v. *Palmer*, 20 U. C. R. 307; *La Banque Nationale* v. *Sparks*, 27 C. P. 320 (a); *Greenham* v. *Watt*, 25 U. C. R. 365; *Palmer* v. *Baker*, 23 C. P. 302; *Williams* v. *Lake*, 2 E. & E. 349; *Barkerville* v. *Corbett*, 3 C. & P. 162; *Walson* v. *McLaren*, 19 Wend. 557; *McKane* v. *Joynson*, 5 C. B. N. S. 218; *Manning* v. *Mills*, 12 U. C. R. 515; *Van Wart* v. *Carpenter*, 21 U. C. R. 320; *Bateman* v. *Phillips*, 15 East 272; *Jenkins* v. *Ruttan*, 8 U. C. R. 625; *Byles* on Bills, 9th ed., 90; *Westhead* v. *Sproson*, 6 H. & N. 728; *Wood* v. *Priestner*, L. R. 2 Ex. 66, 282; *Ellis* v. *Emmanuel*, L. R. 1 Ex. D. 157; *Gray* v. *Seckham*, L. R. 7 Ch. 680.

E. Crombie for defendant. The document sued on is not a note by reason of the words in it, "this note to be held as collateral security." It is not even now sufficiently stamped. The evidence shews that it never was intended by Mrs. Merrick as a guarantee, even if she could be a guarantor for her husband. He cited *Cholmeley* v. *Darley*, 14 M. & W. 344; *Robins* v. *May*, 11 A. & E. 213; *The Corporation of the County of Perth* v. *McGregor*, 21 U. C. R. 459; *Waterous* v. *Montgomery*, 36 U. C. R. 1; *Shand* v. *Du Buisson*, L. R. 18 Eq. 283.

March 10, 1877. MORRISON, J.—The principal questions raised in this case are, first, whether the plaintiff is entitled to recover upon the instrument in question as a promissory note, and if not, whether he can do so as a guarantee. As to the first point, one of the main requisites of a promissory note is, that it contains a promise to pay unconditionally a sum certain, and if the note at the time of its making, whether on its face or by an endorsement, is made or rendered payable on certain conditions, that will deprive it of its character as a note.

(a) Affirmed on appeal; not yet reported.

One of the earliest cases is that of *Carlos* v. *Fancourt*, 5 T. R. 482, which decided that a note payable on a contingency, or not payable at all events, was not a note within the statute of 3 & 4 Anne.

In *Hartley* v *Wilkinson*, 4 M. & S. 25, where the note was subject to a stipulation endorsed on it, Lord Ellenborough, C. J., said, p. 26: "How can it be said that this note is a negotiable instrument for the payment of money absolutely, when it is apparent that the party taking it must inquire into an extrinsic fact, in order to ascertain if it be payable?" Bayley, J., said at page 26: "This note cannot be said to be payable at all events."

And in *Ayrey* v. *Fearnsides*, 4 M. & W. 168, where the note had on its face after the words *for value received*, "and all fines according to rule," it was argued that these words might be rejected as surplusage, or as being insensible. The Court held that they could not do so, as it was quite possible they had a meaning, and if so, it was certainly not a promissory note.

And so in *Chlolmeley* v. *Darley*, 14 M. & W. 344, where the note was unobjectionable on its face, but it had a memorandum, which was endorsed at the time of making, that it was given to secure floating advances made by the banking company to one of the makers.

In *Robins* v. *May*, 11 A. & E. 213, where a note for £500, payable twelve months after date, stated on its face to be held as collateral security for moneys owing to the payees, Lord Denman, C. J., at page 216, said: "The instrument is no promissory note, and cannot be declared on as such. It gives notice on the face of it, to all the world, that the promise is only a conditional one." Patteson, J., said, p. 216, "The note is, in substance, a promise to pay if another person named in it does not pay. If it had been indorsed before it was due, it would have been worthless in the hands of the indorsee."

I may also refer to the cases in our own Courts of *Palmer et al.* v. *Fahnestock*, 9 C. P. 172, and *Fahnestock et al.* v. *Palmer* 20 U. C. R. 307.

These authorities all go to shew that the plaintiff cannot recover on this instrument as a promissory note.

Then as to the second question raised. Is there any evidence to support either of the last two counts: viz., that in consideration of the plaintiff delivering to J. D. Merrick accommodation notes, the defendant promised to be responsible to the plaintiff for the amount thereof, or agreed to pay to the plaintiff $1,264; or, to put it briefly, can the plaintiff recover upon this instrument or writing as a guarantee? I think not. The evidence shews that the defendant had entrusted her husband with a printed form of a promissory note, to which she put her name, the spaces for the payee's name, amount, &c., blank, to enable her husband to make use of it as a negotiable promissory note. The printed form itself excludes any other idea or intention, and there is not the slightest evidence that it was contemplated that this blank note or her name should be used for any other purpose. The defendant never had at any time any communication with the plaintiff, nor did her husband communicate to her that the plaintiff required her to guarantee his debt, or to become responsible to the plaintiff for any accommodation paper he had given or might give to her husband.

What appears to have taken place is simply this: The plaintiff had accommodated J. D. Merrick by giving him his name on notes. He demurred continuing to do so, or to renew such paper, unless Merrick would give him a guarantee. Merrick having this blank note, signed by the defendant, in his drawer, produced it and filled it up with an amount agreed on between him and the plaintiff; and at the instance of the plaintiff, he, Merrick, inserted the words stating that the note was held as collateral security.

Under these circumstances the plaintiff received the alleged guarantee, the defendant having no knowledge of the transaction or the use made of the blank note. On the other hand, the plaintiff had knowledge that the instrument was a blank note without any promise or stipulation.

on the part of the defendant guaranteeing any debt of the plaintiff. There is no evidence that the defendant ever intended to sign any guarantee, or that this note she so signed should be converted into one.

It is no doubt a rule of law that if a person puts his name to or indorses a form for a note, with blanks for the amount, &c., and gives it to another person, that such person has a general unlimited authority to fill up the blanks, and to any amount, and issue it as a promissory note: *McInnes* v. *Miller*, 30 U. C. R. 489.

I may here refer to the case of *Foster* v. *McKinnon*, L. R. 4 C. P. 704, a case the reverse of this. There the defendant signed his name to what he thought and considered to be a guarantee to enable the party to obtain an advance of money from his banker. It turned out to be a bill of exchange.

Byles, J., in giving judgment, at page 712, referred to the rule I have mentioned, where a person puts his name to or endorses a blank note or bill, and said : " In these cases, however, the party signing knows what he is doing ; the indorser intended to indorse, and the acceptor intended to accept, a bill of exchange to be thereafter filled up, leaving the amount, the date, the maturity, and the other parties to the bill undetermined. But in the case now under consideration the defendant, according to the evidence, if believed, and the finding of the jury, never intended to endorse a bill of exchange at all, but intended to sign a contract of an entirely different nature. It was not his design, and, if he were guilty of no negligence, it was not even his fault that the instrument he signed turned out to be a bill of exchange."

So here the defendant did not sign a blank guarantee or intend to do so, for the evidence clearly shews that she contemplated signing and did sign a blank negotiable promissory note, which she entrusted to her husband to be filled up and used as such ; and that such blank note was, at the instance of the plaintiff, without the knowledge of the defendant, converted into what the plaintiff now alleges is a guarantee on the part of the defendant to repay any moneys the plaintiff might have to pay on account of her husband.

There is no evidence that she intended to be or was a party to any such contract. The implied authority given to her husband by signing the blank printed form of a negotiable note cannot, I think, be extended to the conversion of the blank form into quite a different contract.

In *Hanbury* v. *Lovett*, 16 W. R. 795, where the defendant gave B. an acceptance in blank to renew a bill, and authorized B. to fill up the amount, B. added, before the defendant's signature, "payable at 145 Euston Road." The jury found that no express authority had been given to B. to make the bill payable at any particular place. It was there contended that for the convenience of commerce a person to whom a blank acceptance is given was not bound to treat it as a general acceptance.

Martin, B., in giving judgment, said, p. 796: "We are all of opinion that this acceptance does not bind the defendant. The allegation is, that the giving this blank acceptance to B. is giving him the power to fill it up so as to make it payable at whatever place he might choose. It is clear to me that he has no such authority to do so, and his having done it vitiates the acceptance."

Bramwell, B., said, p. 796: "The short way to dispose of it is, to say that no evidence was given of any authority to fill up this bill except with a general acceptance. What is the difference between a bill drawn as this bill was and a bill drawn and accepted in the ordinary way, and then altered so as to make it payable at a particular place?"

So here there is no evidence of any authority to alter the blank promissory note into a guarantee. On the whole I think the defendant is entitled to our judgment on these points, and it becomes unnecessary to consider the other points raised.

The defendant's rule to enter a nonsuit will be made absolute, and the plaintiff's rule discharged.

HARRISON, C. J., concurred.

WILSON, J., was not present during the argument, and took no part in the judgment.

Rules accordingly.

MCARTHUR V ALISON.

Landlord and tenant—Breach of covenant—Entry by landlord—Wrongful distress—Trespass—Trover.

Defendant leased land to one M. for five years from the 1st December, 1874, by a lease in the statutory short form, containing covenants not to sublet or assign without leave, &c.   On 26th February, 1876, defendant finding the premises vacant, and going to ruin, the door of the house broken and open, fences down, &c., reentered and nailed up the door, and on the 29th leased it by deed to one G. for five years. On the 9th March the plaintiff, who had been hired to work for M., receiving the use of the house and part of the crops for his pay, broke into the place, and remained there until 17th April, when defendant seized under a distress for rent, there being none due, and removed the plaintiff's stove, &c.   The plaintiff then promised to leave on the 19th, and gave up the key to defendant as a symbol of possession, and G.'s stove was put up in place of the plaintiff's.   On the 19th, when G. and defendant went there, M. resisted their entrance, and they came to blows. M. and defendant had an arbitration, which resulted in an award that defendant should pay $18 costs to M., and that M. should give up possession, as he had broken his covenants in the lease.   The plaintiff sued defendant for trespass to the land, and in trover, and the jury found a verdict for $100.

Held, that the plaintiff could not recover for the trespass, having no title to the land, for if he went in under a lease from M., and not as his servant only, that of itself constituted a forfeiture, and entitled defendant and G. to enter.

A verdict was thereforee ntered on the trover count for 1s. damages for the injury done to plaintiff's stove, and for defendant on the other counts.

DECLARATION : 1st and 2nd counts in trespass, *quare clausum fregit*; a count in trover for a stove ; and a count for assault.

Pleas: not guilty ; lands not plaintiff's, &c. ; goods not plaintiff's ; a plea to the trover count, that plaintiff's goods were encumbering the close of the plaintiff, and that the defendant removed the same doing no unnecessary damage.

The cause was tried before Harrison, C. J., and a jury, at the Owen Sound Fall Assizes, 1876.

From the evidence given at the trial it appeared that the defendant demised the premises in question, the south half of lot 11, in the 12th concession of Collingwood, County of Grey, by indenture of lease to one Miller for five years from the 1st December, 1874, at a rental of $120 for the first year, &c., first payment payable on 1st December, 1875. The lease was made according to the statutory short form, and contained covenants to pay the rent, to repair, and not to sublet or assign without leave, and that the lessee should summer fallow at least five acres each year and clear the portion of all stones, &c., with a proviso for re-entry on non-performance of any of the covenants. On the 26th February, 1876, the defendant finding the premises vacant, the door of the house broken and open with two panels out, floor broken down, &c , and appearances indicating that cattle had been in the house the summer previous, the fences down, and, as said by a witness, everything wrecked, so that the house was unfit for use or for any person to live in it, re-entered the premises, and nailed up the door of the house, &c. It appeared also that no summer fallowing had been done : that on the 29th February the defendant leased the premises by deed to one Goldsmith for five years : that the defendant saw Miller and told him he had taken possession of the place : that on the 17th April, 1876, defendant was informed by Gold-smith that McArthur, plaintiff, had broken open the house. It appeared also that defendant, with a view of getting plaintiff off the premises and removing his goods, gave a landlord's warrant to one Longhead to seize for rent : that they entered the house and stated that they were seizing for rent, and after some words began to put out of doors the things in the house : that after removing the stove the plaintiff then agreed to leave the place on the 19th April, the plaintiff delivering the key as a symbol of giving up possession to the defendant, and the plaintiff's goods and his family were allowed to remain until the 19th. On the

19th, when defendant and Goldsmith went to the premises, Miller appeared and was there in the house, and threatened to attack defendant if he entered. He did do so. A row took place, and blows were struck. Eventually the defendant and those with him were arrested and brought before a magistrate, when Miller and defendant entered into arbitration bonds to settle their differences.

On the 28th April the arbitrators made their award, awarding that defendant should pay $18 costs to Miller, and that Miller should forthwith quietly and peaceably give up possession of the premises, as he, Miller, had, as they found, broken his covenants in his lease by subletting and non-performance of other covenants. At this arbitration the plaintiff was examined as witness for Miller. According to the plaintiff's testimony he was hired to work for Miller in March, 1876, after the re-entry of defendant, and he was to have the house on the premises, some pasturage and a part of the crops for his pay: he went into posession on the 9th March, and was there until the 17th April, when defendant and the others came to the house to seize: they began removing his stove and put it out, he threatening to assault the parties: his wife persuaded him to submit, and he then promised, as stated, the defendant to leave on the 19th April: Goldsmith's stove was put up in place of plaintiff's: next morning he went to look for a place, and on his return he found defendant in possession. On the 19th he left for a team. He returned and found Miller and defendant there. Fighting followed and plaintiff's things were placed on the next lot. He went as a witness before the magistrate, and on his return he found Goldsmith in possession and plaintiff's family had left the place. He appeared as a witness before the arbitrators, and did not pretend to have any claim on his own behalf, and assenting to what was done. It appeared also that Miller had sublet the premises to one McCallum in 1875.

At the cloes of the case it was objected, on the part of the defendant, that plaintiff could not recover: that the defendant had entered for non-repair of the premises, &c.,

and that the plaintiff was only the hired servant of Miller,
and that he had given up possession to defendant. For
the plaintiff it was contended that defendant should not
be allowed to take advantage of the forfeiture, as he afterwards received rent and distrained. The charge for the
assault was not pressed.

The learned Chief Justice overruled the objections,
leaving the following questions to the jury: 1st. Were the
premises out of repair on 26th February, 1876? Answer,
Yes. 2nd. Did the defendant enter for non-performance of
covenants? Answer, No. 3rd. Did the plaintiff on the
17th April give the key to defendant as a symbol of
possession, promising to remove his goods on 19th April?
Answer, Yes. 4th. Did the plaintiff, in the arbitration
proceedings, know that Miller was himself claiming to hold
the premises and assent to the proceedings? Answer, No.
The jury assessed the damages at $100, and the learned
Chief Justice entered a verdict for that amount, reserving
leave to move.

In Michaelmas term, November 22, 1876, *Fleming*
obtained a rule *nisi* for a nonsuit, on the ground that
Miller having been adjudged not entitled by the award to
possession, the plaintiff had no right to the land in question: that the evidence shewed that there was a breach of
covenant in the lease, for which the defendant was entitled
to enter and did enter: that if plaintiff was a sub-tenant
of Miller, then defendant was entitled to enter by reason
of the forfeiture: that defendant had received possession
of the premises on 17th April, and plaintiff's refusal
afterwards to go out of possession justified the entry; or
why a verdict should not be entered on the finding of the
jury on the questions submitted to them; or for a new trial.

During the same term, December 2, *Kerr*, Q. C., shewed
cause, and cited *Manning* v. *Dever*, 35 U. C. R. 294; *Addison* on Torts, 273; *Platt* on Leases, Vol. ii., 260; *Lees* v.
Fisher, 12 U. C. R. 604; *West* v. *Dodd*, L. R. 4 Q. B. 634;
Fawcett, L. & T. 241; *Chase* v. *Scripture*, 24 U. C. R. 598.

Fleming, contra, supported the grounds taken by his rule and contended that the entry of the 26th February entitled defendant to succeed, and that the plaintiff should not recover even nominal damages.

March 10, 1877. MORRISON, J.—The principal question which arises is, whether this plaintiff is, entitled to recover damages for a trespass to the land in question. First. I think it is quite clear that the plaintiff while in possession of the land was merely there as the hired servant of Miller, who had leased the premises from the defendant, and that he went on the premises on the 9th March; and it is equally clear that the defendant, who had rented the place to Miller, on visiting the premises on the 26th February, 1876, found them vacant, the door and windows broken; the fences down, the place in fact in a state of ruin, cattle having been allowed to be in the house during the previous summer : that, under these circumstances, he re-entered for a breach of covenant, and took possession, nailing up the house so as to keep animals out, and putting up the fences, &c. ; that on the 28th February he re-let the premises by deed for five years to one Goldsmith : that, learning in April from the latter that the plaintiff had taken possession of the house, the defendant, in order to get the plaintiff out of the house, made a landlord's warrant and under that authority entered the house to remove the plaintiff's goods and put him out of possession : that the bailiff having commenced to remove the things, among them a stove which was taken out, the plaintiff then agreed if defendant refrained from removing the things he would leave the place on the Wednesday following, and as a giving up of possession handed the defendant the key, and Goldsmith's stove and some other things were put into the house, defendant and Goldsmith being there the following day and on Wednesday.

On the latter day Miller appeared, and probably at his instance plaintiff refused to carry out his agreement to leave, and the parties came to blows, and eventually, defendant and those with him were arrested at the instance of Miller, and brought before a magistrate. They then forthwith left their differences to arbitration.

The arbitrators adjudicated and, among other things, awarded that Miller had forfeited his lease, and that he was quietly and peaceably to give up possession of the premises. In the meantime plaintiff's family had left the premises and the plaintiff's goods were removed to the next lot, and returned to the plaintiff.

According to the plaintiff's testimony the injury done to his things did not exceed three or four dollars, including the breaking of a stove. I cannot see upon what ground the plaintiff is entitled to recover for a trespass to the land. The premises he had no title to. He went into possesion after the entry of the defendant on the 26th February, and then only as the servant of Miller; but assuming that he went in under a letting from Miller, as he contended, that of itself constituted a forfeiture, and entitled the defendant and Goldsmith to enter on the 17th or 19th April.

It is quite clear that there was a breach of covenant to repair, and that the defendant entered on the 26th February. The jury found that the premises were then out of repair. They found also, I think erroneously, that the defendant did not enter for such breach, although I think it is clear he did, and he followed it up by re-letting the premises for five years to another tenant ; and the jury found also that the plaintiff on the 17th April delivered to the defendant the key as the symbol of giving him the possession and promising to leave the premises and remove his goods on the 19th.

The only difficulty the case presents, is, whether the plaintiff is not entitled to a verdict for at least nominal damages for the injury done to the plaintiff's stove when the defendant removed it on the 17th April. I do not think the defendant was justified, without notifying the plaintiff of his object and intention, to remove his property in the way he did.

If, instead of doing so under pretence of a landlord's warrant, which he had no right to make, he had told the plaintiff that he required him to leave the premises as he was entitled to the possession of them, and to remove his property, giving him a reasonable opportunity to do so, he might have acceded to the request; but, instead of doing so, the defendant claimed to remove the property under a distress for rent when none was due, and which plaintiff contended was the fact as he knew it was paid. The defendant, without any notice, forcibly removed the plaintiff's stove and injured it to some extent. Both parties are very much to blame.

If a verdict had been entered for the defendant I would not have disturbed it; but as the verdict is for the plaintiff, and the damages assessed were principally for the supposed trespass to the land, and as I think the plaintiff is entitled to a verdict on the third count, he should retain a verdict on that count and 1s. damages, and the verdict should be entered on the other counts for the defendant.

HARRISON, C. J., and WILSON, J., concurred.

Rule accordingly.

NICHOL v. THE CANADA SOUTHERN RAILWAY COMPANY.

R. W. Co.—Surface Water—Obstruction of—Liability—Limitation clause,
C. S. U. C. ch. 66, sec. 83,—Neglect to fence.

The plaintiff sued defendants for not constructing and maintaining a sufficient culvert under their railway where it crossed the plaintiff's land,
so as to prevent as little as possible the flow of a natural water-course
there; and in another count, for neglect to fence off their railway from
plaintiff's land adjoining when requested. A count in trespass was
added. The jury found $390 damages on the second and third counts,
and 1s. damages on the first. There being no evidence of any natural
stream: *Held*, that the plaintiff could not recover on the first count, for
the interference with the flow of surface water formed no ground of
action, and there was no charge of negligence in constructing the railway.

McGillivray v. *Great Western R. W. Co.*, 25 U. C. R. 69, commented upon and distinguished.

As to the neglect to fence, defendants pleaded not guilty by statute, C. S.
U. C. ch. 66, specifying sec. 83, among others, but at the trial they
raised no question under that clause as to the plaintiff's damages being
confined to six months, and it was not shewn clearly how much of the
damage accrued beyond that time. It seemed probable, however, that
only eight or ten weeks would be excluded if the clause applied, and
the Court refused to interfere on this ground. *Quære*, whether the
clause would apply, this being an act of omission.

Quære, also, as to the liability of defendants for acts of their contractors,
but this point was not determined, as they were bound by the statute
C. S. U. C. ch. 66, sec. 19, to fence on request, and a request was
proved.

DECLARATION. The first count stated that the plaintiff,
was possessed of lot 26, in the 3rd concession of the
township of Oneida, in the county of Haldimand, through
which runs a natural creek, drain, stream of water, or water-
course, and that the defendants' line of railway, crosses
above the level part of the plaintiff's land, and the creek
&c., and it became their duty to construct, keep, and maintain a proper and sufficient culvert underneath the line of
railway where it crosses the creek, &c., on the plaintiff's
land, or sufficient ditches along the side of the railway so
as to prevent as little as possible the natural flow of the
water in the creek, &c., through the plaintiff's lands underneath the line of railway, or along the side thereof.
Breach. Whereby the water of the creek, &c., has been
from time to time penned back upon and overflowed the
plaintiff's land to a much greater extent than it would have
done, so that the soil, &c., have been greatly injured.

Second count : that the defendants' line of railway, which
is constructed on the plaintiff's land, divides the plaintiff's
land into two portions adjoining the railway on either side
thereof, and it became the duty of the defendants within
six months after they had taken possession of that portion
of the plaintiff's land required for the use of the railway,
and when thereto required by the plaintiff, within a reasonable time after such request, at their own cost and charges
to set and make on the land of the plaintiff so taken for
the use of the railway, and from time to time to maintain
and keep in repair a sufficient post, rail, hedge, ditch, bank,
or other sufficient fence or support to keep off hogs, sheep,
and cattle from the lands of the plaintiff adjoining the railway, and thereby divide and separate, and keep constantly
divided and separated the lands of the plaintiff so taken
for the use of the railway. Breach. Whereby the plaintiff
has lost the use of his land, &c., and divers hogs, sheep, and
other cattle for want of such fences, &c., broke and entered
the plaintiff's land and destroyed the grass, &c.

3. Trespass : the count being in the general form.

4. Money counts.

Pleas.—1. To first, second, and third counts : not guilty,
by statutes 33 Vic. ch. 32, secs. 1 and 4 ; Consol. Stat. C.
ch. 66, secs. 2, 8, 9, 10, 11, 19, 83, and 123.

2. To same counts : that plaintiff was not possessed of
the lands.

3. To first count : that a natural creek, drain, stream of
water, or water-course, over which the defendants' line of
railway crosses, does not run through the said land as
alleged.

4. To fourth count : never indebted.

Issue.

The cause was tried at Goderich, at the Spring Assizes of
1873, before Wilson, J. The evidence material to the case
was as follows :—

Edmund Decew, Provincial Land Surveyor, said : The
railway crosses the lot about the centre. A water-course
is on the north side of the railroad on the plaintiff's land.

It has been obstructed by the earth thrown out on making the railroad, and now forming the railway embankment, about eight feet high there. Before the embankment the water escaped across the land now occupied by the railway. The defendants, on the north side of the railway, cut a culvert across the plaintiff's land to let the water off, but the ditch they dug westerly was made only for a few yards and it should have been made for about 26 rods, which would have carried the water off; and the ditch they have dug is filled up as if by the earth which has been washed through the culvert, so that about two-thirds of an acre have been damaged by the lying water. Farms there are selling for $50 an acre. That is the lowest price.

Cross-examination.—The plaintiff's lane up through his farm crosses by a bridge over the railway. There is a cutting there for the railway. The bridge is about 15 feet above the bank. The rise to the bridge on each side commences about 50 or 60 feet from the bridge. The approaches to the bridge are by an earthen embankment. There is a culvert across the north embankment in the lane. The flow through the culvert is from east to west. The ditch on the west of the culvert has been made only one or two rods. It should have been carried as far as the westerly termination of the railway cutting, where the water would have fallen into the side drains of the railway. The water coming from the plaintiff's bush west of the culvert flows to the railroad side drains. The defendants could have extended the ditch westerly far enough to remove the water at very little expense. It is good arable land on the east side of the culvert. It was under crop when I saw it lately. The water-course is made from the rain-fall only. I thought only about two-thirds of an acre damaged by the overflow. That piece was low and wet.

John Decew, Provincial Land Surveyor, a son of the first witness, said: Two acres of the plaintiff's land were covered by the earth thrown out by the defendants from their cutting and thrown outside of their own land. On the east of the lane the plaintiff's land slopes from north to south and from east to west. It is a kind of basin. About two acres of that high land drain into this water-course. The defendants should provide a culvert and ditch to carry off a waterfall or watershed on two acres of land to the east of the lane and culvert. To the west of the lane a part of the north land slopes to the west and part to the east. The lane is the point of depression of these slopes, The culvert in the lane has been put in at the lowest level. The lowest part of the plaintiff's land is at the west of his lot, and that is the highest part of the rail track, for the track ascends from east to west. If the ditch had been cut westerly from the culvert, it would have prevented any mischief happening at the point on the lane and about there. The natural flow of water from the plaintiff's west limit is still to the west.

Walter Nichol, the plaintiff, said : The defendants took possession about the beginning of September, 1871. They threw the fences down on my land, one side a rail fence, and the other a stump fence. I told the men to put the fence up. They referred me to the engineer. I spoke to him. He said he had nothing to do with the work, and if I stopped the work I would do it at my own responsibility. They never put up the fences, They are not up yet. They have 90 feet across my lot. At first the men threw down only about 90 feet of my fences for their track, but as they began to throw the stuff back on my land they removed the fences along the sides of the lane still more, so that they moved my fences south of their ground about 80 feet, and north of their ground 70 or 80 feet. They also threw my east fence down between Mr. Hamilton, who owns lot 27, and myself. I put it up for a while, so did Mr. Hamilton, but they were always thrown down, and at last we let the fences alone. I had a fence along the north of my lot, and so had Hamilton along the concession line There was a fence also between my lot and Hamilton's. The men threw Hamilton's fence at the north on the con-

cession line open, then they crossed his land on to mine at
their railway track. The cattle came often in from the
concession through that road on to my land, and also hogs,
sheep, and horses. I lost my hay crop in the north-east
and south-east fields, and also in the north-west and south-
west fields, 12¾ acres east, and 11 acres west, less railway
track, 3¾ acres, leaving 20 acres, and at 1¼ tons of hay per
acre would be 25 tons of hay, worth from $15 to $16 a ton
this last winter. I intended to have taken off a crop of
clover seed after the first crop of hay, which would have
been 2 bushels to the acre, or 40 bushels. I paid $5.75 a
bushel yesterday at Caledonia, and got 1½ bushels of clover
seed at that rate. There were cattle over my fields all last
summer. My five cows ran over it, too, with the strange
cattle. Could take no crops off that land. I had plenty
of pasture for my cattle without their being in that field.
Cattle came in also on the west side, but not so often. In
the latter end of June last I ploughed up the fields to the
east, when I found my crops spoiled. I intended to sow it
with wheat. I notified Mr. Kingsmill, of Toronto, the
secretary of the company, that I intended to sow the fields,
and that I required them to be fenced. I put in my fall
wheat. The field is not fenced yet. It has received great
damage from cattle, sheep, and hogs. Last Saturday a lot
of hogs and cattle came along the railway from the west on
to my land. Martin owns the land west of me. The cattle
come on now along the track, both from east and west. I
sowed about 10 acres of wheat. There is more than one
acre of the fields to the east covered by the earth thrown
out by the defendants on my land beyond their own line.
My 10 acres of sowed wheat are damaged to the full half of
the value of the crop. I estimated the field at $20 an acre
before it was damaged. The natural course of the water
before the railway was made was from the low point to the
north of the track to the low point south of it, then westerly
to a bit of low ground near the west line of the lot, and then
westerly on to lot 25. Defendants have made a culvert north
of the track across the lane, and they have dug a ditch west-

erly a little way. The culvert is always full of water, because there is not escape enough for it. A drain I had along my lane has been stopped by the defendants' embankment made on my lane as my approach to the over-crossing or bridge made for me. The water kills and injures over one acre to the north of the track. The defendants' men drew the timber for my over-crossing on to my south-west field, and did all the framing there. I wanted them to put it on the high ground. They left all the waste of the framing on the land. I lost about half an acre of clover killed by it, and I was two days with one of my boys picking up the waste and hauling it away.

Cross-examination : I have a lane from south to north along my whole lot. There is a side line to the west of Martin's lot 25, and another to the east of me between lots 29 and 30. Docherty, a contractor with the defendants, threw my fences down at the west, and at my lane, and Callaghan, another contracter, threw my fences down at the east. I notified Mr. Kingsmill about the fencing. The company settled with me so far as the arbitration was concerned, but not for the land they covered with their cutting. I agreed to sell to the company at $100 an acre for any other land they might want. It was in May, 1872, I complained to Mr. Kingsmill of the want of fences. Before that time Hamilton's cattle came on along the line on my land, my own cattle also came in on my own fields. Hamilton turned them off sometimes, so did I. At last I gave it up, for the fences were always thrown down. The company have covered with waste earth about two and a-half acres of my land. Cattle, &c., have come in on west from Martin's side. The company, on the east line between Hamilton and myself, have taken the fences down as far as they have carried the waste earth back, and that is beyond their 90 feet. I have got a very good over-crossing. If I did not get it I was to get $1,200.

There was a good deal of evidence on the same matters given by other witnesses for the plaintiff.

For the defence. *Junius A. Fagg* said : I was an engi-

neer on the eastern division of this railway. The work
was let in sections to contractors. Two sections met on
the plaintiff's land. Docherty had the contract to the west
of the plaintiff's land, and east so far as the east side of
plaintiff's centre lane, and Callaghan to the east of that.
It is the business of the contractor, under the directions he
has from the company, to keep the fences up. None of my
men or staff took down the fences. The company gave no
directions to the men. They would instruct the contractor
or his foreman. The railway is in a deep cutting going
through the plaintiff's land. There was a fill for about
200 feet at the west side of the plaintiff's lot. From there
we began to cut easterly all across the lot. The west part
of the lot was the lowest. There the water spread to the
north into a bush, as well as towards the centre, where the
embankment and track are. Some of the water off the
high land at the east would find its way to the bank. A
culvert was put in north of the embankment.

Cross-examination: It is only a small part of the plaintiff's land would drain to the east, the rest would drain to
the west. I was at the plaintiff's land last week after a
heavy rain, and I saw no water left at the culvert nor about
it. I saw more water on the high land in pockets than on
the low land. No water backed up there. The culvert
may be 125 feet north of the centre line of the track. The
plaintiff's approach to the bridge is the only obstruction to
the former flow of the water, and to obviate that the culvert
was made. From the west end of the culvert there is a
fall westerly of 2 feet in a 100 feet, and no obstruction
west of the culvert has been placed, excepting a little waste
earth at the west end of the cut, and that might hold a
little pool of water not three feet wide, and I think that
would not back it on the plaintiff's land. The piece of
wet land I saw was six hundredths of an acre. The land
about is very high, and more might run down to the culvert
than the culvert would for half an hour be able to carry
off.

There was other evidence not material to be stated.

The plaintiff claimed—

For 25 tons of hay at $15	$375
Forty bushels of clover seed, at the rate of 2 bushels for 20 acres, at $5.75	230
Half of wheat crop of 10 acres spoiled, $20 per acre	100
Damage to half an acre of clover on south-west field by laying lumber on it, and labour in clearing it off from waste stuff left on it........	25
Total....................	$730

There was a good deal of discussion on the legal rights of the parties at the trial, which it is not material to state, as there was no objection taken for any alleged misdirection.

The jury found as follows :

For 20 acres meadow................	$260
Loss of crop of clover seed	100
Damage to wheat	25
Damage to the half acre of clover land	5
Total.....................	$390

Verdict for plaintiff and damages just stated, $390, on the second and third counts.

The jury found the plaintiff did sustain a little damage by the water as in the first count stated, and they assessed the damages on it at one shilling, and gave a verdict for defendants on the fourth count.

In Easter term, May 22, 1873, *Crooks*, Q. C., obtained a rule calling on the plaintiff to shew cause why the verdict for the plaintiff should not be set aside and a verdict entered for the defendants on the first and third counts, pursuant to leave reserved, and also why the verdict for the plaintiff on the second and third counts should not be set aside, and a new trial granted, upon the law and evidence, on the following grounds : 1. As to the second count, no legal liability attached to the defendants thereunder, as the company was not required to fence off their line of railway from the plaintiff's land, and any damage proved did not arise from any default of the company in that respect.   2. As to the third count, any damage which was occasioned to the plaintiff arose from the default of the contractors for the construction of the railway under the company, and from the contractors' omission during construction to keep up the line fences ; and the company is not liable in law for such default.   3. Upon the ground that the damages were excessive, and if otherwise allowable, that only a moderate amount thereof can, under the law and evidence, be attributable to the defendants.   4. Upon the ground that the injury complained of occurred more than six months before the commencement of this action.

In Michaelmas term, November 25, 1873, *MacKelcan* shewed cause. The defendants are liable for stopping the natural drainage of the land by their embankment : *McGillivray* v. *Great Western R. W. Co.*, 25· U. C. R. 69 ; *Crewson* v. *Grand Trunk R. W. Co.*, 27 U. C. R. 68 ; *Vanhorn* v. *Grand Trunk R. W. Co.*, 18 U. C. R. 356 ; *Vanhorn* v. *Grand Trunk R. W. Co.*, 9 C. P. 264 ; *Lawrence* v. *Great Northern R. W. Co.*, 16 Q. B. 643. The defendants are themselves liable, although the work and injury were done by their contractors : *Hole* v. *Sittingbourne and Sheerness R. W. Co.*, 6 H. & N. 488 ; *Ellis* v. *Sheffield Gas Consumers' Co.*, 2 E. & B. 767. As to the limitation of the six months, that point was not taken at the trial—it is now raised for the first time. If effect is given to it, the provision does not apply to acts of non-feasance, and the second count is for not fencing. Consol. Stat. C., ch. 66, sec. 83, is the limitation clause, and secs. 13 and 19 relate to the fencing. The authorities as to the application of the clause are *Reist* v. *Grand Trunk R. W. Co.*, 15 U. C. R. 355, 364 ; *Snure* v. *Great Western R. W. Co.*, 13 U. C. R. 376, 381 ; *Soule* v. *Grand Trunk R. W. Co.*, 21 C. P. 308, 315.

Crooks, Q. C., supported the rule. The first count the plaintiff failed upon. No natural stream existed to be obstructed, and of course none could be proved : *McGillivray* v. *Millin,* 27 U. C. R. 62 ; *Lawrence* v. *Great Northern*

R. W. Co., 16 Q. B. 643. The second count was not proved,. because no requisition was made by the plaintiff upon the defendants to fence. The obligation is to fence against adjoining proprietors. The cattle that did the injury were strange cattle trespassing on the adjoining lands, and against which the defendants were not bound to fence : *Ricketts* v. *East and West India Docks and Birmingham R. W. Co.,* 12 C. B. 160 ; *Fawcett* v. *York and North Midland R. W. Co.,* 16 Q. B. 610. As to the third count, the defendants. are not liable for what was proved under it, nor for what was done under any of the counts, because the acts were done by the contractors of the defendants, who were independent of the defendants, and for whom therefore the defendants were not liable : *Steele* v. *South Eastern R. W. Co.,* 16 C. B. 550 ; *Daniel* v. *The Directors of the Metropolitan R. W. Co.,* L. R. 5 H. L. 45. As to the Statute of Limitations, it is not an answer for not fencing, for that is a continuing duty ; but it is an answer to the damage occasioned by not fencing : *McCallum* v. *Grand Trunk R. W. Co.,* 31 U. C. R. 527. The plaintiff claims to hold the whole $390 damages on the second and third counts. As to the $5 on the third count, for damage done to the clover land, the defendants do not object ; but they object to the plaintiff recovering any greater sum upon that count, and they dispute his right to recover on the second count at all.

March 10, 1877. WILSON, J.—It is unquestionable law that water collecting in bogs and marshes, or mere surface water caused by the falling of rains or the melting of snow, and not constituting a stream flowing in a defined channel, are not governed by the like law which relates to what are commonly called and known as running streams.. That has been definitely settled by the highest tribunal.

Chasemore v. *Richards,* 5 Jur. N. S. 873, *Rawstron* v. *Taylor,* 11 Ex. 369, *Broadbent* v. *Ramsbothom,* 11 Ex. 602, shew that the owner of land on which such water is may do with it as he pleases, and the adjoining proprietor has. no right to have it flow to his land.

We have in several cases followed these decisions, and we have also expressed our opinion that there is the corresponding right of the adjoining proprietor to do as he pleases with his land, and to exclude the flow of such surface water on to his land from the higher level.   I refer to *McGillivray* v. *Millin*, 27 U. C. R. 62.

If the plaintiff had sold the land to a private person in place of to this railway company, he could not have complained if the private purchaser had constructed such an embankment as the defendants have done, or a solid stone wall, making no allowance for the escape of the drainage or surface water from one part of his land to the other so separated by the intervening piece which had been sold, nor would he have had any right of way or communication across the land so sold which severed his farm.

If the plaintiff have any other or different rights against this company, it cannot be by reason of his being a vendor and their being vendees, nor by reason of the mere fact that the parcel of land he had sold had prejudiced his rights, and had therefore created of necessity an easement or burden upon the land of the purchaser to the extent of such alleged injury.   That should have been guarded against at the time of conveyance by such proper reservations and covenants which he desired for the purpose, and which would have had the assent of the purchaser to his taking the land so burdened and holding it for ever as a servient tenement.

McGillivray v. *Great Western R. W. Co.*, 25 U. C. R. 69, is a decision that an action will lie for building an embankment unskilfully and negligently as part of the line of railway across the land which was the owner's, and which interferes with his drainage, because that is evidence of building it in a negligent and unskilful manner, when a proper culvert made in the embankment would have given a free passage to the surface water; and many authorities are cited there in support of such an action.

Whether it is maintainable or not need not be decided now, even as it is there laid.   If so, it can only be by the statute, but there is nothing in the statute conferring upon the plaintiff any new rights of action which he did not possess before.

No doubt in giving up his land he can claim for any injury done or which may be done to his course of drainage, and it would properly be admissible as an item of damages.

Here there was an arbitration between the plaintiff and defendants, and he got $100 an acre for his land, and he gave a receipt in full for the " right of way and damage over " his land.

That would not exclude a recovery for a cause not known at the time, and therefore not contemplated by either party —*Lawrence* v. *Great Northern R. W. Co.*, 16 Q. B. 643—if the plaintiff would, but for such damages as were settled for, have had a cause of action.

It is sufficient to say that the first count is not for negligence and unskilfulness in making their embankment, but for a default of duty in not providing for the escape of the water, and in the case of mere surface water there is no such duty; as *Wallace* v. *Grand Trunk R. W. Co.*, 16 U. C. R. 551 ; *Vanhorn* v. *Grand Trunk R. W. Co.*, 18 U. C. R. 356, and *McGillivray* v. *Great Western R. W. Co.*, 25 U. C. R. 69, shew.

There was no *natural* stream in this case as alleged in the count, and the case entirely fails.

If there had been a natural stream the averment of duty would have been well laid in the count.

There was no pretence for saying there was ever more than mere surface water.

The verdict must therefore be entered for the defendants on the first count.

As to the question upon the second and third counts, it is whether the acts were of that nature that the defendants are not responsible for them ?

That the work was done by the contractors of the company, and by the workmen of the contractors, there is no reasonable doubt.

It was not very plainly proved at the trial how the work

in question was in fact done by the contractors, whether they got their plans, &c., and proceeded as independent contractors, or whether the company did not all the time by their engineers and other officials constantly superintend, direct, and control the work while it was in progress.

There is very little doubt that the latter was the mode and style of operations, as it is in all works of an important nature, and in such a case the defendants would be directly responsible for all that the men did in the course of that work, although they were not the workmen of the company : *Burgess* v. *Gray*, 1 C. B. 578; *Sérandat* v. *Saïsse*, L. R. 1 P. C. 152; *Pendlebury* v. *Greenhalgh*, L. R. 1 Q. B. D. 36 ; and upon which authorities we acted in the case of *Grassick* v. *The City of Toronto*, lately before us.

As a fact, therefore, I should be disposed to say that the defendants continued to have such a control and direction of the work as to be answerable for the mode in which it was carried on.

It is not material here to consider whether the defendants are liable for the fences being thrown down and kept down, or whether the contractors who actually threw them down and kept them down should be resorted to. The law is not always quite plainly expressed in such a case.

It is settled that when work is let by contract, and the contractor does something collateral and beyond his contract, that the employer is not responsible, but the contractor only : *Knight* v. *Fox*, 5 Ex. 721; *Hole* v. *Sittingbourne and Sheerness R. W. Co.*, 6 H. & N. 488.

And when the contractor does the very thing he was engaged to do, and it is an injury, the employer may be made liable : *Ellis* v. *Sheffield Gas Consumers' Co.*, 2 E. & B. 767.

And also that the employer would not be responsible where a contractor was doing the work, dangerous if not carefully done, and he had no reason to believe the contractor would not be duly careful : *Daniel* v. *The Directors &c., of the Metropolitan R. W. Co.*, L. R. 5 H. L. 45.

It is also said when a person is doing work under an

Act of Parliament he cannot relieve himself from responsibility by employing a contractor : *Gray* v. *Pullen*, 5 B. & S. 970 ; and there is a good deal also said of the same kind in *Hole* v. *Sittingbourne and Sheerness R. W. Co.*, 6 H. & N. 488.

If the plaintiff were complaining of the neglect to keep up his fences by the defendants, as at the common law, we would be obliged to decide whether the defendants or their contractors should be held liable. But here the plaintiff complains that the defendants were requested under the statute to fence off their line from his land, and they neglected and refused to do it. The defendants denied that request, but in my opinion it was proved at the trial from the documents which were then produced, but which are not now forthcoming. There then arose a statutory duty upon them to perform it, and that they certainly failed to perform : Consol. Stat. C. ch. 66, sec. 19.

The plaintiff is then entitled to recover for the injury he sustained in consequence of the want of fencing, unless his damages are restricted to a period within six months before the beginning of the action.

The plaintiff cannot be prevented from recovering some damage, because his right, as was admitted by Mr. Crooks, is a continuing right. And the plaintiff further contends that he is not to be confined to the period of six months before the bringing of the action, because section 83 applies to acts of commission and not to mere omissions by the defendants.

The plaintiff further argued that the defendants were not entitled to raise the question as to the six months, because they took no proper objection at the trial, and they raised it by their rule for the first time. The defendants gave notice of that section as one of those they relied upon as a defence under the general issue, but they certainly made it no part of their case at the trial. The action was brought on the 9th of January, 1873, so that the six months open to the plaintiff would extend back to the 9th of July, 1872.

Now how much damage accrued, if any, before that day I cannot say. The defendants began their work about the beginning of September, 1871. It is probable that all the injury complained of was that which was sustained in the year 1872, and of course after the spring opened. So that there would be only eight or ten weeks before the beginning of the six months—if the limitation does apply —which would be beyond that day. And it cannot be worth while in a case of this kind, when the damages are not large, although they are perhaps somewhat larger than they should have been, to grant another trial, which could only be upon the payment of costs, in order to relieve the defendants from some supposed amount of damages which the plaintiff has got by reason of their own remissness in not raising that defence specifically at the trial, as they should have done.

The case of *Reist* v. *Grand Trunk R. W. Co.*, 15 U. C. R. 355, decides that the 83rd section does not apply to acts of nonfeasance. However it may be, it is not necessary we should re-open this long pending litigation to settle with precise accuracy how much, if any, of the sum given for damages was before the 9th of July, 1872, when the fault is wholly that of the defendants that it was not done at the time, and when, in my opinion, it would result in leaving the parties as to damages in all probability exactly where they are.

The rule will be to enter the verdict for the defendants on the issues to the first count, and that the residue of the rule be discharged.

MORRISON, J., concurred.

HARRISON, C.J., was not present at the argument, and took no part in the judgment.

Rule accordingly.

DAVIS v. McWHIRTER, ASSIGNEE.

Sale of goods—Fraudulent design not to pay—Rescission—Stoppage in transitu.

P., carrying on business at Woodstock, on the 28th August, ordered eight half chests of tea from the plaintiff, who lived at Bowmanville, at five months' credit, through H., the plaintiff's traveller, who called upon him to solicit orders. The order was given on the 28th August, 1876, and the tea arrived at Woodstock by rail, on the 4th September. The railway company addressed the usual notice of arrival to P. as consignee, which notice came on the 5th into the hands of defendant, an attachment in insolvency against P. having on that day been received by defendant as official assignee. Defendant on the same day demanded the goods from the freight agent of the company, tendering the freight, but the agent refused to deliver them. The plaintiff's agent telegraphed to him on the 6th to hold the tea; and on the company's application, an interpleader was granted.

Semble, that the *transitus* was at an end, on the authority of *Bird* v. *Brown*, 4 Ex. 797.

P. had previously purchased tea from the plaintiff, giving his note at five months, which matured on the 4th September, though the usual credit was five months. H. said that he remarked to P., when making the sale in question, that there were extra hands behind the counter, for which P. accounted by the alleged increase of his business; and he added that he was not in immediate need of these teas, but wanted to get them. H. said he thought P. was doing well and intended to pay, but he made no enquiries as to his standing, or as to probable payment of the note then maturing. On or shortly before the 5th September, P. absconded, owing over $3'000, and leaving assets to pay only about five cents in the dollar. None of his employees were examined at the trial.

Held, that the fair inference from all the circumstances, (which are more fully set out in the case) was that P. ordered the goods fraudulently, with a preconceived design of not paying for them; and that on this ground the plaintiff was entitled to recover.

THIS was an interpleader issue, tried before Sinclair, Co. J., of Wentworth, sitting for the Chief Justice of this Court, at the last Winter Assizes for Hamilton, without a jury, to try whether eight half chests of tea in the warehouse of the Great Western R. W. Co., at Woodstock, were the property of the plaintiff as against the defendant, the assignee in insolvency of one Palmer.

From the evidence given at the trial it appeared that Palmer, who was carrying on business at Woodstock, ordered the teas from the plaintiff, who carried on business at Bowmanville, through one Hands, a commercial traveller, who was soliciting orders for the plaintiff, and who called on Palmer for that purpose, Palmer stipulating for five months' credit.

The order was given on the 28th August, 1876. Hands sent forward the order on that day to the plaintiff. Palmer had previously purchased tea from the plaintiff for which he gave his note at five months, and which note would mature on the 4th September. The plaintiff received the order for the tea on the 30th August, and he sent off the goods from Bowmanville to Woodstock, at which place they arrived on the 4th September. The railway company addressed the usual notice to Palmer, as consignee, of the arrival of the goods. The notice came to the hands of the defendant on the 5th September. On the same day a writ of attachment issued against Palmer, and during the afternoon of the same day, 5th September, the defendant being official assignee, on receipt of the writ of attachment, served a copy of the writ on the freight agent of the railway company, and demanded the goods, tendering the freight charges. The agent refused to deliver the goods.

On the 6th September the plaintiff telegraphed the railway agent to hold the teas, and that he had written him instructions, which telegram he received at 11.15 a.m. on the 6th. The plaintiff also wrote the same day to the company's agent, directing him to hold the teas subject to his order. He replied on the 7th, that he had the tea in the warehouse. Both parties thus having demanded the tea, on the company's application this interpleader was ordered.

It appeared that Palmer had absconded, how long before the issuing of the writ of attachment did not appear. The defendant thought not more than forty-eight hours. The liabilities of Palmer were found to be $3,279, excluding the teas in question. His stock was valued at $800, and realised $520; his book debts were worthless; there were no other assets, while $240 was due for rent and taxes, leaving about $270, less the amount of the insolvency expenses, to be divided among his creditors, about five cents on the dollar.

A good deal of evidence was given for the purpose of shewing that Palmer had been selling his goods at much lower prices than other dealers, and that he was disposing of them rapidly, and in doing so created suspicion : that on the 28th August, when the plaintiff's travelling agent called on Palmer soliciting orders, he remarked to Palmer that there were extra hands behind the counter : that Palmer said he was compelled to have them, as his business was increasing, especially since he gave up the liquor traffic : that he said he was not in immediate need of the teas, but that he wanted to get them : that while he said nothing to the plaintiff's agent about his pecuniary affairs, he created an impression that his business was increasing and prospering, and that the agent believed that to be the case.

The defendant called no witnesses.

At the close of the case the learned Judge gave judgment as follows, for the defendant :—

SINCLAIR, Co. J.—On the issue of the writ in insolvency against Allen Palmer, and on the delivery thereof to the defendant on the 5th day of September, 1876, all right and title which Palmer had in the teas in question vested in the defendant under the 16th section of the Insolvency Act of 1875.

Of course the plaintiff, the vendor of the goods, would have the same right to stop them *in transitu* after the property in them became vested in the defendant as official assignee, and before the *transitus* ended, as he would have had if these goods had remained the property of Palmer. Before any notice by the vendor to the carriers—the Great Western R. W. Co.—of Palmer's insolvency, and forbidding their delivery of the goods, the defendant had tendered to the carriers their freight on the teas. They had been sold on five months' credit, so that there remained nothing but payment of freight to give Palmer or those claiming under him the right of possession as well as property in the teas.

On tender by the defendant to the station agent of the Great Western R. W. Co. at Woodstock of their freight, and on his demanding the teas, which it appears he did, the company became simply wrongdoers. Until some claim that they were bound to recognize was made, they should have recognized the right of the consignee, or those claiming under him. The *transitus*, in my opinion, was at an end on tender by the defendant, as Palmer's assignee, of the freight, and his demanding possession of the goods : *Bird* v. *Brown*, 4 Ex. 797, per Rolfe, B.

I may say that Mr. MacKelcan did not strenuously argue this view of the case, but maintained that if the plaintiff could not, under the circumstances, rescind the sale as being fraudulent, that at least he had the right to stop *in transitu*. For the reasons already given, and on the authority of the case just cited, I am quite clear that that right was gone on the 6th September, when the plaintiff first notified the railway company : *Ex parte Gibbes*, L. R. 1 Ch. D. 101.

The main contention on the part of the plaintiff's counsel was, that the teas had been fraudulently purchased of the plaintiff, through his travelling agent, by Palmer, without his having any intention of paying for them. If this were so, a long series of cases, commencing with *Martin* v. *Pewtriss*, 4 Burr. 2478, and ending with the latest cases at common law of *Clough* v. *London and North-Western R. W. Co.*, L. R. 7 Ex. 26, and *Morrison* v. *The Universal Marine Ins. Co.*, L. R. 8 Ex. 40, decide that the plaintiff had a right to rescind the sale.

The difficulty I have is, in deciding whether or not the facts here bring this case within the principle of these authorities. It appears that plaintiff's traveller was in Woodstock on the 28th August last. The insolvent, Palmer, had carried on business there as a general grocer for a few years before that time. He appears to have been doing a thriving business, and selling large quantities of goods. It was remarked that he had been selling lower than other dealers in the same kind of goods, for which he gave the reason I shall presently mention. He did not go to the plaintiff or his agent to buy these goods ; but, on the contrary, the plaintiff's agent went to him. Palmer at first did not want to buy ; but, with the anxiety to sell which is proverbial with that class, the plaintiff's agent induced Palmer to buy the teas in question, the latter not wishing to buy them unless he got five months' instead of four months' credit for them. There had been a previous transaction between the same parties ; the same agent had previously sold Palmer, on plaintiff's account, a bill of goods amounting to $212, and for which his note for that amount was then outstanding. It, too, had been sold at five months' credit, although the usual credit in this branch of trade is four months. This note matured on the 4th day of September, 1876. It was a subsisting liability of Palmer's when this second bill of goods was sold to him ; yet, before making sale, plaintiff's traveller did not inquire of Palmer or anybody else the probability or possibility of his paying this outstanding debt. No questions were asked of him about that, nor was inquiry made in any way of this man's circumstances or mode of doing business. The plaintiff's travelling agent said, from all he saw, that Palmer fully intended to pay for the goods at the time he purchased them. This man at this time saw Palmer's stock, as he had done in the March or April previous, and did not remark that it had been depleted, or that

the goods were disappearing mysteriously or otherwise, or that
Palmer was letting his stock run down.   The only remark which
the seller's agent ventured to make, according to his own story,
was that Palmer appeared to have too many hands in the store.
Palmer appeared to satisfy his mind on this subject by saying
that his increasing business required it.   From the evidence of
this witness I am satisfied that he was exceedingly anxious to sell
Palmer the goods : that he went out of his usual course to give
him better terms than he did the plaintiff's customers generally :
that he considered Palmer good, and did not take the slightest
precaution to ascertain his commercial standing.

It is urged that it is hard that the plaintiff should lose his teas,
if it be that defendant is entitled to hold them.   I do not think
so.   If he has any one to blame it is himself in giving such unlimited discretion to the traveller for his house ; and that person
also, for the over anxiety to sell goods, regardless of the prospect
of their being paid for.   So long as merchants will pursue the
reckless policy which has driven many of them to ruin, of doing
as this plaintiff's agent did, just so long should they fail to receive
the slightest sympathy for their losses.

But it is urged that because Palmer bought these goods on
the 28th of August, and absconded on or shortly before the 5th
of September, that I must find, as a necessary consequence, that
he did not intend to pay for them at the time of the purchase.
To use the words of Lord Tenderden in *Ferguson* v. *Carrington*, 9
B. & C. 59, "It is submitted that I should find that Palmer bought
the goods with the preconceived design of not paying for them,
from the facts appearing in evidence."   In order to determine
this, it is necessary to take a glance at the evidence.   The principal witness was the station agent of the Great Western R. W.
Co., at Woodstock, who spoke of a conversation with Palmer, in
which that person told him how it was he could sell lower than
others in the same trade.   Palmer told witness that his mode of
dealing was in this way : "He purchased such goods as these at
say five months' credit, and sold them off as soon as possible for
cash.   With the cash he would again purchase goods, getting a
good reduction on the trade prices.   He would again sell these
goods off as soon as possible at trade prices for cash, and as he
said, would turn over the money two or three times before his
original bill of goods would become due."   Now, there is a danger
of doing this kind of business ; but it will be found that the
grains and material part of our farm produce are bought and sold
on as small a margin as was the insolvent's discount for cash, on
goods purchased in that way.   So long as he could turn his money
quickly he might succeed, but otherwise disaster would be inevi-
table.   The attempt to shew that Palmer undersold the others in
the same line of business completely failed.   But if he did do so,
which might be inferred from his own account of his system of

doing business, I do not see that it alters the case. His success or failure depended upon the contingencies I have mentioned.

In all the cases I have met, the purchaser, or some one in his interest, or in collusion with him, either got possession of the goods or tried to obtain them. This was relied on, and very properly so, to shew the fraudulent mind the purchaser had in purchasing the goods. He did not want them for the purpose of honest trade, but for immediate sale or disposal, and to possess himself of their proceeds. If the insolvent had here contemplated fraud, his great object would have been to get possession not only of these goods, but other goods which he had bought of Simpson, Stewart & Co., of Hamilton, and which were in the railway company's freight shed at the time these teas were. He could have waited until these came into his possession, sold them at a sacrifice,. and put the money into his pocket, or re-shipped the goods to Detroit or some where else, that he might there have them. From the circumstance that Palmer did not wait to get possession of the goods he ordered from plaintiff and others, and left hurriedly, I think his absconding suddenly must be looked for to other causes. Something must have occurred after he purchased these goods to have induced him to abscond. He may have taken stock and ascertained that his mode of business had proved disastrous. He might then have realized on all available assets, or fraudulently disposed of them. If at the time the goods were sold the plaintiff's. agent saw no indications of anything wrong, he might have done many things between the 28th August and the 5th day of September, to indicate an intention to abscond, yet not have it in his mind at that time. It appears to me a strange circumstance that none of those in the absconder's employ were called by the plaintiff. It was not suggested they were out of the country. If it had been proved by one of the many clerks which were seen in the store on the 28th August that Palmer had been preparing for flight—that he had been doing that which was irreconcilable with any other opinion—then I would have some fact on which to found an opinion ; but as the case now stands, I would simply have to presume fraud by guess, which I am not disposed to do. Indeed, I think, on the authority I am just about to refer to, it is my duty not to do so. *Ex parte Whittaker, Re Shackleton,* L. R. 10 Ch. App. 446, was not mentioned to me by counsel in this case. It was a case in which the facts were found stronger than in this, yet the Chief Judge in bankruptcy refused to presume fraud, and his decision was upheld by the Lords Justices in Appeal.

As a matter of fact, I find that it is not proved that Allen Palmer at the time he purchased the goods in question, did not intend to pay for them. It is a question, as suggested by Lord Justice Mellish, at page 441, whether the vendor can rescind the sale after bankruptcy.

Mr. MacKelcan suggested that this sale was a fraud under the Insolvent Act. It is a sufficient answer that this plaintiff does not claim under that statute : *Squire* v. *Watt*, 29 U. C. R. 328.

During this term, February 8, 1877, *R. R. Loscombe* obtained a rule *nisi* to set aside the verdict, and to enter a verdict for the plaintiff, or for a new trial, on the ground that there was a right of stoppage *in transitu*, and that the purchase made by Palmer was a fraudulent one.

During the same term, February 14, 1877. *Robertson,* Q. C., shewed cause. The grounds taken by the learned County Court Judge support his finding. There was no right of stoppage *in transitu*, under the circumstances. The whole transaction was an honest one, as far as Palmer was concerned. He referred to *Bird* v. *Brown*, 4 Ex. 786 ; *Heinekey* v. *Earle*, 8 E. & B. 410, 423 ; *Graham* v. *Smith*, 27 C. P. 1 ; *Ex parte Whittaker, Re Shackleton*, L. R. 10 Ch. 446 ; *Squire* v. *Watt*, 29 U. C. R. 328.

Loscombe, contra. The stoppage *in transitu* was valid, being made by the agent of the Grand Trunk for whoever was concerned, and it was afterwards ratified by the plaintiff. The facts are wholly against the learned Judge's finding as to the *bona fides* of Palmer. He cited *Heinekey,* v. *Earle*, 8 E. & B. 410 ; *Whitehead* v. *Anderson*, 9 M. & W. 518 ; *Graham* v. *Smith*, 27 C. P. 1 ; *Howell* v. *Alport*, 12 C. P. 375 ; *Lewis* v. *Mason*, 36 U. C. R. 590 ; *Ascher* v. *Grand Trunk R. W. Co.*, 36 U. C. R. 609 ; *Pollock* on Contracts, 481.

March 10, 1877. MORRISON, J.—As to the right of the plaintiff to stop the goods *in transitu*, the case of *Bird* v. *Brown*, 4 Ex. 786, is a strong authority in favour of the defendant's contention. There it was held that where an unauthorized agent stopped goods *in transitu*, his act could not be rendered effectual to defeat the consignee's title by the consignor's ratification of the act after the *transitus* was ended.

Rolfe, B., in giving judgment, said, at p. 797 : "As to the first point, we are of opinion that there could be no stoppage *in transitu*, after the formal demand of the goods by Bird on the 11th May, and the subsequent delivery of them to the defendant, (who assumed to act for the plaintiff). The goods had then arrived at Liverpool, and were ready to be delivered to the parties entitled. Bird, on behalf of the assignees, demanded the goods and tendered the amount due for the freight. Assuming there had been no previous stoppage *in transitu*, the masters of the several ships were thereupon bound to deliver up the goods to Bird as representing Carle & Telo, and they could not, by their wrongful detainer of them, and delivering them over to other parties, prolong the *transitus*, and so extend the period during which stoppage might be made. The *transitus* was at an end when the goods had reached the port of destination, and when the consignees, having demanded the goods and tendered the amount of the freight, would have taken them into their possession but for a wrongful delivery to other parties."

I have some difficulty in reconciling the decided language in *Bird* v. *Brown*, 4 Ex. 786, with other authorities, but as our judgment is in favour of the plaintiff upon another ground, it is not necesssary to consider the matter in that respect.

Then as to the second question, whether the purchase by Palmer was fraudulent. After a careful perusal of the evidence, I cannot concur in the conclusion arrived at by the learned Judge, viz., that it was not proved that Palmer at the time he ordered or purchased the teas did not intend to pay for them.

In my judgment the evidence sufficiently establishes, and is strong to shew that Palmer at the time he gave the order was either in a state of hopeless insolvency and intended absconding, having no intention of paying for the teas, or if not insolvent he was disposing of his goods with a dishonest intent, putting the proceeds in his pocket, with a view at a fitting opportunity of absconding, and ordered

these goods with a preconceived design of not paying for
them or even receiving them, for I think it is a fair inference to be drawn from his conduct that he ordered the teas
to lull suspicion.

Palmer had purchased previously teas from the plaintiff,
and his note for that purchase was falling due within a
few days after the travelling agent called at his place.   The
latter had no reason to suspect that the new order was not
given *bonâ fide,* or that Palmer was insolvent.

It is also noticeable that in reply to a remark of the
agent that Palmer said he was compelled to have extra
hands behind his counter as his business was increasing,
and further saying that although he had no immediate use
for the teas that he wanted to get them.   To my mind these
remarks were strong circumstances to induce the agent to
solicit and take the order, and to lead him to believe that
Palmer was doing a prosperous and increasing business.
His absconding within a few days after, and the small
amount of assets he left behind him, makes it evident those
statements were entirely false.

In many cases from the very nature of the fraud it is
difficult to prove it by direct evidence, and a person in
many cases has to depend upon various circumstances
calculated to shew the concealed purposes of the party who
commits a fraud.

Kent, in his Commentaries, vol. ii., p. 484, says: "A
deduction of fraud may be made, not only from deceptive
assertions and false representations, but from facts, incidents,
and circumstances, which may be trivial in themselves, but
decisive evidence in the given case of a fraudulent design."

It is a settled rule that if a purchaser obtains goods upon
credit with a preconceived design of not paying for them,
the act is fraudulent, and the seller on discovering the
fraud may reclaim his property, or if he obtains goods,
knowing that they never would be paid for, and intending
to abscond, or to throw them into an immediate bankruptcy,
&c., he is guilty of a fraud: *Earl of Bristol* v. *Wilsmore,*
1 B. & C. 514; *Noble* v. *Adam,* 7 Taunt. 59 ; *Load* v. *Green,*

15M. & W. 216; *Ferguson* v. *Carrington,* 9 B. & C. 59.
Mere insolvency would not be enough to avoid the sale.
If Palmer gave the order with the honest intention of continuing his business, and paying for the goods if he was
able to do so, the plaintiff could not rescind the contract
on the ground of fraud.

The facts given in evidence negative and are quite inconsistent with any such conclusion, while they furnish
sufficient grounds for inferring that he ordered the goods
with a preconceived design of never receiving or paying
for them, or by absconding subjecting them to the effect
of an insolvency.

I cannot think with the learned Judge, that, because
Palmer did not wait to receive the teas, but absconded
before their arrival, that his doing so rebutted a fraudulent
intention or any preconceived design of not paying for
them. It is more likely that his motive in ordering the teas
was, as I have said, to lull suspicion, to create confidence,
to enable him to carry out his dishonest intentions.

It is to be feared that fraudulent traders in many cases
make such fraudulent purchases when entirely insolvent,
with a view of increasing the assets of their estates.

The learned Judge seemed to think that the case of *Ex
parte Whittaker, Re Shackelton,* L. R. 10 Ch. 446, justified
him in arriving at the conclusion he did. In my opinion
it is quite distinguishable. There Shackelton had purchased wool at an auction, which, by the conditions of
sale, was to be paid for on delivery. Whittaker knowing
Shackelton, and believing him to be well off, Shackelton
making no representations, he allowed him to take the
goods away on Saturday. On the Monday following
Shackelton was adjudicated a bankrupt, in his absence,
having been previously served with a debtor's summons
for a small debt, which he failed to comply with, and so
committed an act of bankruptcy.

The wool remained in Shackelton's possession, and no
attempt to raise money on it. The Chief Judge in the
Court below said : " Here, without a particle of evidence,

without a shadow of reason, I am asked to convict this
man of fraud. How can I guess what sort of defence he
might have had to the proceedings in bankruptcy ? Concealment there was none in this case—misrepresentation
there was none."

Mellish, L. J., at p. 449, said : " It is true, indeed, that a
party must not make any misrepresentation, express or
implied, and as at present advised, I think that Shackelton
when he went for the goods, must be taken to have made
an implied representation that he intended to pay for them,
and if it were clearly made out that at that time he did not
intend to pay for them, I should consider that a case of
fraudulent misrepresentation was shewn, but I do not think
this sufficiently made out. The debt for which he was
proceeded against was a small one, and he did not attempt
to raise money on these goods. I cannot say that he may
not have thought that he could come to some terms with
the petitioning creditor, and stop the bankruptcy proceedings." James, L. J., saying : " He might suppose that he had
a chance of paying Ragg's small debt, and stopping the
bankruptcy proceedings."

There the only evidence was, that proceedings in bankruptcy were commenced, and that before any adjudication
Shackelton, in the ordinary course of his business, bought
the goods at an auction without telling the vendor that a
petition had been presented against him. The Chief Judge,
no doubt, believing that the bankrupt had supposed he
would arrange with the petitioning creditor, and had
omitted to appear.

Here the evidence is quite different, Palmer leading their
agent to believe that he was doing a prosperous and increasing business, disposing of his goods as mentioned at
the trial, absconding a few days after he gave the order,
and just a day before a five months' note he gave for the
former purchase fell due, leaving behind him a mere trifle
of assets, and no explanation offered or given to rebut the
strong presumption that he, Palmer, was acting dishonestly.
As noticed by the learned Judge, the persons employed

by him might have been called if any explanation could
have been given for his conduct.

With every respect for the opinion of the learned Judge
who tried the case, I think it was sufficiently made out
that Palmer ordered the teas with a preconceived design
of not paying for them, and that upon that ground the
plaintiff is entitled to our judgment.

This is just one of those cases where justice requires
that we ought if we find there is evidence to authorize
us consistent with law to give judgment in favour of a
person who sold goods for which he was not to be paid,
and so prevent them being applied in payment of the debts
of others.

I think the rule should be made absolute to enter a
verdict for the plaintiff.

HARRISON, C. J.—I have read the able judgment of the
learned Judge of the County Court in this case.

If the only question were, the right of the plaintiff to
the property on the ground of stoppage *in transitu* I should,
following *Bird* v. *Brown*, 4 Ex. 786, have agreed with him
in holding that the *transitus* was at an end when the goods
reached their destination on the line of railway, and when
the defendant, as assignee in insolvency of the consignee,
had tendered the freight to the railway company: See
Wiley et al. v. *Smith*, in Appeal. 1 App. 179.

But I am unable to agree with the learned Judge in
thinking that the consignee at the time of the purchase
did intend to pay for the goods. His absconding a few
days afterwards, taking with him all his then available
assets, I think raises the presumption that he was not
acting honestly when purchasing the goods. Had it
appeared in evidence that there was some such cause as
supposed by the learned Judge for his sudden flight, the
presumption would have been rebutted. But in the absence
of some rebutting circumstances, other than the non-arrival
of the goods before his flight, the presumption of fraud
must, I think, prevail. There is no doubt much anxiety

77—VOL. XL U.C.R.

on the part of travellers to sell goods for houses whom they represent, and in consequence some very imprudent sales are made. But in this case it seems to me the learned Judge attached too much importance to the supposed anxiety of the traveller to sell. From all that he could see, or all he could learn at the time of sale, he had every reason to believe that Palmer was doing an increasing and profitable business. But the fact was not so. This must have been known to Palmer at the time of the purchase. Looking at his subsequent flight without other explanatory cause, it is not too much to infer that the cause was the unhealthy condition of his business, and that at the time of the purchase he contemplated what a few days afterwards he did.

One cannot fail to see that justice is entirely with the demand of the plaintiff. If the facts proved will warrant an inference in accordance with the demands of justice. that inference ought to be drawn. I think they do warrant the conclusion of fraud at the time of the purchase, and so agree in making absolute the rule.

WILSON, J., was not present at the argument, and took no part in the judgment.

Rule absolute.

DONNELLY V. BAWDEN.

Malicious arrest—Reasonable and probable cause—Objection taken too late.

Where in an action for malicious arrest the facts are uncontradicted the question of reasonable and probable cause must be decided exclusively by the Judge.

The action at the trial was treated as one for malicious arrest, and in that view a nonsuit was entered. In term it was argued that the action was really one of trespass, and that the whole case should have been left to the jury as such, but the Court held that it was too late to urge this.

DECLARATION: that the defendant on the 1st day of March, 1876, at the village of Lucan, &c., then being one of the constables and peace officers in and for, &c., did unlawfully, maliciously, and without reasonable and probable cause, and without any authority in that behalf, assault, beat, arrest, take into custody and imprison and place the plaintiff in irons, and conveyed him through divers public streets and highways to a certain building in the said village, and there detained, confined, and kept the plaintiff prisoner for a long space of time, to wit, for the space of four days, whereby the plaintiff suffered, &c.

Plea: not guilty, by statute, Consol. Stat. U. C. ch. 126, sec. 11, Public Act.

The case was tried before Burton, J., at the last Fall Assizes at London.

At the close of the plaintiff's case, the plaintiff himself being the principal witness, a nonsuit was moved for by the defendant's counsel, and the note made by the learned Judge upon entering the nonsuit was as follows:—

The plaintiff has not proved that the defendant acted maliciously and without reasonable and probable cause. I think the conviction of the plaintiff with his brothers and others who were convicted of several offences, under the peculiar circumstances of the village at that time, when a general terrorism prevailed, and the military had to be called out, and other offences were daily occurring, is sufficiently shewn in the plaintiff's own evidence to warrant me in holding that there was reasonable and probable cause for the course taken by the defendant, and that there is no evidence of his having acted maliciously.

During Michaelmas term, November 21, 1876, *Glass*, Q. C., obtained a rule to set aside the nonsuit and for a new trial, on the ground that the nonsuit was contrary to law and evidence, and that from the evidence adduced at the trial on behalf of the plaintiff the question of absence of reasonable and probable cause should have been left to the jury.

During this term, February 8, 9, *Meredith* shewed cause. There is no count in trespass. The objection in the rule was not taken at the trial and cannot be taken now, and it is at all events untenable.

Glass, Q. C., contra. The point that this is really an action of trespass was not distinctly taken at the trial, but it is an action of trespass and should have been so treated, and the whole case left to the jury. The case should be considered on its merits. He cited *Neil* v. *McMillan*, 25 U. C R. 485, 491; *Bout* v. *Cradock*, 27 L. J. Ex. 314; *Cotterell* v. *Hughson*, 7 C. P. 277; *Taylor* on Evidence, 6th ed., sec. 1390.

March 10, 1877.—MORRISON, J.—The only question raised by the rule is, that specifically referred to in the rule itself, viz.: that the learned Judge should have left to the jury the question of absence of reasonable and probable cause.

As said in *Taylor* on Evidence, 6th ed., p. 39 : "It is now clearly established, albeit the wisdom of the rule has recently been stoutly disputed," referring to the case of *Lister* v. *Perryman*, L. R. 4 H. L. 521, "that the question of probable cause must be decided exclusively by the Judge, and that the jury can only be permitted to find whether the facts alleged in support of the presence of absence of probability, and the inferences to be drawn therefrom, really exist."

In this case the only evidence adduced at the trial was on the part of the plaintiff, and the case rested principally on the plaintiff's own testimony; and where the facts in evidence are uncontradicted, it is the duty of the Judge to decide whether there is reasonable or probable cause, and the Judge has a right to act upon all the uncontradicted facts of the case. In the learned Judge's notes I find no such objection taken at the trial as mentioned in the rule. But assuming that it was so taken, I do not think the learned Judge could have left the question to the jury.

During the argument Mr. Glass contended that the action was one of trespass, and not an action on the case; and that the whole case should have gone to the jury as in an action of trespass; and as the defendant had not shewn any justification for the arrest by shewing a warrant the plaintiff was entitled to a verdict.

The learned Judge reports that the case was not so launched or presented at the trial, nor was that view taken of it; but that it proceeded, as an action on the case for having maliciously and without reasonable or probable cause arrested the plaintiff. The counsel for the defendant during the argument stated that if any such view had been presented or contended for he should have pleaded a justification, and would have been prepared to prove it.

The ground of nonsuit noted by the learned Judge is quite inconsistent with any such contention.

After reading the evidence at the trial, we do not think this is a case in which we ought to relax any rule in favour of the plaintiff. We therefore discharge the rule, as the ground taken in it is unsustainable.

HARRISON, C. J., concurred.

WILSON, J., was not present at the argument, and took no part in the judgment.

Rule discharged.

THOMPSON V. BASKERVILLE.

Lease—Forfeiture—Waiver.

Declaration for trespass to land. Plea, *liberum tenementum.* Replication, a demise by defendant to plaintiff for a term unexpired. Rejoinder, averring a breach of covenant to repair, and defendant's entry thereupon. Surrejoinder, that upon the alleged breach and forfeiture defendant accepted rent accrued due after the forfeiture, which was thereby waived. *Held,* surrejoinder bad, for there could be no waiver after entry.

DEMURRER.   Declaration : trespass to real estate.

Plea : *liberum tenementum.*

Replication : a demise to plaintiff by the defendant for a term which is not yet expired.

Fifth rejoinder : that the lease was subject to a condition for making void the same, and allowing the defendant to reenter if the plaintiff did not during the lease keep the fences, &c., in repair, and averring that the plaintiff had broken that covenant, whereupon the defendant entered.

Sixth rejoinder : similar to the fifth, but as to the premises other than the fences.

Surrejoinder ; that after the happening of the said several alleged breaches, and the incurring by reason thereof of the said alleged several forfeitures, the defendant accepted payment of rent which accrued due after the said alleged forfeitures for the said demised premises, by operation and reason wheref the said several alleged forfeitures were waived.

To this surrejoinder the defendant demurred, on the ground that it did not answer the fifth or sixth rejoinders, or any of them, by reason that the breaches alleged in each of the said rejoinders are continuing breaches, and the forfeitures alleged therein are not shewn by anything contained in said surrejoinder to have been waived ; also, that the said surrejoinder confesses, but does not avoid the forfeiture alleged in the said fifth and sixth rejoinders, or any of them.

The demurrer was argued by *Osler,* Q. C., for plaintiff. The surrejoinder does not state to what time the breach continued, whether to that of entry or action brought.

The surrejoinder is demurred to because it is alleged that the breaches in the rejoinder are continuing breaches, and on these pleadings, we contend, that the question of whether there can be a waiver after entry cannot arise. The acceptance of rent was a waiver, at all events, whether before or after entry. The defendant ought to have pleaded that the forfeiture continued. He cited *Goodright d. Walter* v. *Davids,* Cowp. 803 ; *Arnsby* v. *Woodward,* 6 B. & C. 519 ; *Dendy* v. *Nicholl,* 4 C. B. N. S. 376 ; *Pellatt* v. *Boozy,* 31 L. J. C. P. 281 ; *Cole* on Ejectment, 409 ; *Doe d. Nash* v. *Birch,* 1 M. & W. 402.

Browning, for defendant. The breaches alleged in the defendant's rejoinder are continuing breaches with entry thereupon, and are so pleaded: *Chit.* Prac., 2nd ed., 755. Acceptance of rent waives past breaches only : *Munston* v. *Gladwin,* 6 Q. B. 953. The doctrine of the leading cases of *Goodright* v. *Davids,* Cowp. 803, and *Arnsby* v. *Woodward,* 6 B. & C. 519, that acceptance by a landlord of rent accrued due subsequent to a forfeiture is a waiver of the forfeiture, does not apply to the case of a continuing breach : *Ambler* v. *Woodbridge,* 9 B. & C. 376 ; *Doe d. Baker* v. *Jones,* 5 Ex. 498. The surrejoinder of the plaintiff confesses the breach and defendant's entry thereupon. The surrejoinder to be good should allege, first, that the breach had ceased, and, second, that rent was accepted before entry : *Baker* v. *Jones,* 5 Ex. 498. The surrejoinder here does not shew this. The entry of defendant completed the forfeiture and avoided the lease : *Somers* v. *Buller,* 5 U. C. Q. 369. A deed once void cannot be set up again. Acceptance of rent under such circumstances may at best create a tenancy from year to year ; but it would be a departure for plaintiff to allege a yearly tenancy now : *Ib.* The defendant cannot new-assign : the premises the breach, the entry, and time of entry are each rendered certain by the pleadings.

September 22, 1876. GALT, J.—There is no doubt, as was contended by Mr. Browning, that the breach of a condition to repair is a continuing breach, and therefore, that although all prior breaches are waived by acceptance of rent after the landlord has knowledge of the breaches complained of, yet the right of re-entry continues after such receipt, and consequently such waiver will not re-establish the term if the breach of the condition still continues. In the surrejoinder demurred to, it is alleged that after the happening of the said several alleged breaches, &c., the defendant accepted rent, &c. This evidently points to the time when the action was brought, and therefore if the premises remained in such a state of repair as to constitute a breach, the proper way to raise the question is, by new-assigning, when it would be incumbent on the defendant to prove that after the waiver, by acceptance of rent, there had been a further or continuing breach of covenant. To give effect to the demurrer would be to say that the plaintiff cannot, in case of a covenant to repair, reply a waiver.

The question as to the right of the defendant to re-enter will come up on the trial of the traverse, and if it shall appear on the trial that the plaintiff had been guilty of a breach of covenant after the acceptance of rent by the defendant, the defendant will be entitled to a verdict.

Judgment for plaintiff.

From this judgment the defendant appealed to the full Court, and the case was re-heard during this term.

Osler, Q. C., for the plaintiff. The argument was similar to that before Mr. Justice Galt.

Browning, for the defendant.

At the close of the argument judgment was given for defendant, on the ground that there could not be a waiver by acceptance of rent after entry.

A DIGEST

OF

ALL THE REPORTED CASES

DECIDED IN

THE COURT OF QUEEN'S BENCH;

FROM TRINITY TERM 40 VICTORIA TO HILARY TERM 40 VICTORIA.

ACTION.

Notice of.]—*See* COUNTY ATTORNEY—SALE OF GOODS,1—REGISTRAR. *See* MORTGAGE—PUBLIC COMPANY.

AFFIDAVITS.

To hold to bail—Sufficiency of.]—*See* BAIL.

AGENT.

See INSURANCE, 2.

ALTERATION.

Of cheque.] — *See* BANKS AND BANKING, 1.
Of note.]—*See* BILLS AND NOTES, 3.

AMENDMENT.

Of pleadings refused.—*See* BILLS AND NOTES 2.

APPEAL.

See BILLS AND NOTES, 1.—CONVICTION, 1, 2.

ARBITRATION AND AWARD.

Motion to set aside — Practice.]—A rule *nisi* to set aside an award must be drawn up on reading the award or a copy of it. The objections taken to the award were, that having been made *ex parte*, and without hearing witnesses, it was void and it was urged that it might therefore be set aside without producing it; but, *Held* otherwise. *Re Hinton* v. *Meade,* 24 L. J. Ex. 140, not followed. *Re Johnson and Montreal and City of Ottawa Junction R. W. Co.,* 359.

ARCHITECT'S CERTIFICATE.

See BUILDING CONTRACT.

ARREST.

See MALICIOUS ARREST.

ASSESSMENT OF DAMAGES.

See BOND.

ASSESSMENT ROLL.

Mode of ascertaining who, on the roll, are entitled to vote under the Temperance Act of 1864.] — *See* LIQUOR, SALE OF, 2.

ASSESSMENT AND TAXES.

1. *Tax sale—Delay in obtaining deed—Registry—29 Vic. ch. 24, sec. 57.*]—The sheriff, on the 9th October, 1860, sold the land in question for taxes to the plaintiff, gave a certificate of the sale, but for some reason not explained plaintiff did not obtain his deed until the 17th September, 1866, and he registered it on the same day, within one year from the passing of 29 Vic. ch. 24. There was no proof of any neglect or misconduct on his part in not procuring the deed sooner.

Held, that the delay in registering did not, under 29 Vic. ch. 24, sec. 57, avoid the deed as against the purchaser of the land who had first registered : that the deed not having been questioned within the time limited by the protecting statutes, was within their operation ; and that the plaintiff, bringing ejectment in 1870, was entitled to recover. *Carroll* v. *Burgess*, 381.

2. *Government officers of the Dominion—Income tax.*]—*Held*, (HARRISON, C. J., *dissentiente*) that the corporation of the city of Ottawa could legally impose a tax upon the official income of officers of the Dominion Government, the Legislature having given, and having the right under the B. N. A. Act to give, the power to impose such tax.

Held, also, that an officer of the House of Commons of the Dominion at Ottawa, paid out of moneys voted by the Parliament of Canada, is an officer of the Dominion Government. *Leprohon* v. *The Corporation of the City of Ottawa*, 478.

See COVENANTS FOR TITLE.

ATTORNEY AND SOLICITOR.

See TRESPASS.

BAIL.

Order to hold to bail—Sufficiency of affidavits – Rule nisi.]—In order to support an order to hold defendant to bail, the plaintiff need not disclose in his affidavit the names of the persons on whose information he founds his belief that defendant is about to leave the province, where he files also other affidavits, stating facts which would justify such belief ; in that case, it is the same as if the plaintiff had stated that these deponents had informed him of the facts stated in their affidavits.

A rule *nisi* to set aside the order for such alleged insufficiency in the plaintiff's affidavit must point out the objections specifically. *Watson* v. *Charlton*, 142.

BAILIFF.

Division Court.] *—See* TRESPASS— SALE OF GOODS.

BANKS AND BANKING.

1. *Cheque—Alteration in date— Payment by bank—Negligence.*]—The plaintiff, a merchant and customer of defendants' bank, having a note payable there on the 28th January, 1873, made a cheque payable to himself or bearer, and left it with defendants to meet the note. The cheque however was not used for that purpose nor returned to the plaintiff, but the note was paid by defendants and charged to the plaintiff's account. The cheque was afterwards, on the 31st January, 1874, presented to the defendants by some one unknown, the year having been changed from 1873 to 1874, and it was paid by defendants without noticing the alteration, and

charged to the plaintiff's account. How it got out of defendants' bank was not ascertained.

Held, that the alteration avoided the cheque : that defendants therefore were not warranted in paying it; and that the plaintiff was entitled to recover back the money.

Quære, whether, if the cheque had not been void, the defendants, on the ground of negligence, would, on the facts more fully stated in the case, have been liable to the plaintiff for paying it.

Per WILSON, J., the cheque must be considered to have been paid when the note for which it was given was handed over by defendants to plaintiff, and on that ground defendants could not have been made liable upon it. *Beltz* v. *Molson's Bank*, 253.

2. *Banks—Transfer to, of warehouse receipts—34 Vic. c. 5, D.*]—The 34 Vic. ch. 5, secs. 46 and 47, D., permits the transfer to a bank of a bill of lading, or warehouse receipt, to secure an antecedent debt, where the understanding at the time of contracting such debt was that the bill of lading should be transferred as collateral security.

In this case it appeared that the bank agreed to make advances to S. & Co. to purchase coal and stone to be secured by bills of lading and warehouse receipts for such coal and stone when received. The transfer of such receipts to the bank, after the arrival of the goods, was held to be authorized; and it was held no objection that the agreement was to give a receipt for goods of which, at the time, the person was not possessed.

Six months had elapsed after the giving of the receipt before the seizure of the goods by the creditors of S. & Co., but the bank had taken possession of these goods with the consent of S. & Co., and were selling them in order to repay their advances. *Held*, under 34 Vic., ch. 5, sec. 50, D., that they were entitled to hold the goods, notwithstanding the lapse of time. *The Royal Canadian Bank* v. *Ross*.

See BILLS AND NOTES, 1—PUBLIC COMPANY.

_____

BARRISTERS CALLED.

32.

_____

BILLS AND NOTES.

1. *Accommodation maker and indorser—Relation of suretyship—Consideration.*]—Action on a note for $1,500, dated 25th July, 1872, made by defendant payable to the order of S., and alleged to have been endorsed by S. to the plaintiffs.

It appeared that one M., on the 17th January, 1872, had given his bond to the assignee in insolvency of S. conditioned if S. should fail to pay forty-three cents in the $ by the 10th July, to pay to the assignee $500, or so much as should be required to make up the deficiency. S. got the defendant to make this note for his accommodation, and got F. to endorse it afterwards, in order to give it to M. as security against his bond, which he did. M. having been sued on this bond, compelled F. to pay him the amount of the note, and F. and his partner then sued defendant as maker.

The learned Chief Justice of the Common Pleas, who tried the case without a jury, found that defendant, when he signed the note, understood from S. that F., one of the plaintiffs, would endorse as co-surety, and that defendant would be liable only for half the amount; but that F. knew nothing of this, but endorsed in the ordinary way, considering that defendant would be liable to him for the whole.

Held, WILSON, J., dissenting, that the relationship of co-sureties between F. and defendant was not established, so as to prevent the plaintiffs from recovering from defendant more than half the amount of the note.

Per WILSON, J.—F. and defendant each knew that the other was a surety for S., and that being so, there was the relation of suretyship between them for the common debtor.

Ianson v. *Paxton*, 23 C. P. 439, and its effect as a judgment of our Court of Appeal, commented upon.

Held, also, that M. held the note on a good consideration as between himself and the other parties thereto. *Fisken* v. *Meehan*, 146.

2. *Discharge of endorser by giving time—Mortgage—Collateral security.*]—One M., the maker of certain promissory notes payable to and endorsed by the defendant, gave to the plaintiffs, the endorsees, a mortgage on land, with a proviso to be void on payment of $4,300, with interest in one year, "the said sum of $4,300 being represented by certain promissory notes now under discount, and held by the said mortgagees, and any renewals or substitutions therefor that may hereafter be given for the same. All to be paid within one year from this date."

After the execution of this mortgage, the notes sued upon were handed to the plaintiffs by M. to renew notes then held by them and referred to in the mortgage, the defendant having endorsed them in

blank and entrusted them to M. for that purpose.

Held, that no agreement to give time for the payment of the notes could be implied from the mortgage; and the parol evidence, set out in the case, shewed that the mortgage was intended only as collateral security.

The mortgage was a second one, and the defendant alleged that by the neglect of the plaintiffs in permitting a foreclosure of the first mortgage instead of obtaining a sale, he had suffered loss, which he claimed to deduct from plaintiffs' balance. Upon the evidence stated in the report, it was held that no such negligence was shewn, and the Court refused a reference to the Master, or leave to amend the pleadings. *Molson's Bank* v. *McDonald*, 529.

3. *Signature in blank by married woman—Alteration.—Guarantee.*]—The plaintiff had signed notes for the accommodation of M., and declined to continue doing so, or to renew such paper, unless M. would give him a guarantee. Defendant, M.'s wife, had been in the habit of signing blank notes for M. when asked, and M. having a blank form of note signed by her, filled it up as follows, for the amount of the plaintiff's paper then falling due :—

April 3, 1871. Four months after date I promise to pay to William Hall, or order, $1264, at the Bank of Toronto here. *This note to be held as collateral security.* Value received.

The words in italics were inserted at the plaintiff's request.

The defendant had no communication with the plaintiff.

Held, that the defendant was not liable, for the instrument was not a promissory note, not being for the payment of money absolutely; and if a guarantee, there was nothing to shew that she ever signed or intended to sign such a contract, or authorized the conversion of the note into it. *Hall* v. *Merrick*, 566.

See BANKS AND BANKING, 1—DONATIO MORTIS CAUSA—HUSBAND AND WIFE, 1.

BOND.

Bond—8 & 9 Wm. III. c. 11—Assessment of damages—Execution for penalty.]—The plaintiffs sued on a bond in $1,000 penalty, conditioned to convey land, alleging non-performance. A verdict was rendered at the trial for $1,000, and 20 cents for detention, no damages being assessed on the breach; and execution was afterwards issued endorsed to levy the $1,000 and costs taxed. *Held*, the bond being within the statute of 8 & 9 Wm. III. ch. 11, and the plaintiff having paid the 20 cents and costs, that execution must be stayed, for that the penalty could not be levied. *Greer et ux.* v. *Johnston*, 116.

BRAKES.

Duty of railways as to use of.—*See* RAILWAYS AND R. W. Cos., 2.

BREACH OF PROMISE.

Evidence—New trial—Misdirection.]—In an action for breach of promise of marriage, the only two witnesses examined were plaintiff's brothers, who swore that the plaintiff being pregnant, they spoke to defendant, who said he was going to marry her, and always so intended, and that he would get the license on the next day but one—the sister was not then present: that on the day named, Thursday, defendant came to the house, but was kept there by a rain storm, and promised to get the license and marry her on Monday, to which the plaintiff, who was present, apparently assented: that on the Monday he said he was very ill, but it would be all right when he got better; but this was the end of it, and they then instructed this suit, and an action for seduction. The plaintiff was not present and no witnesses were called for the defence. The jury having found for defendant, the plaintiff moved for a new trial on the evidence, filing no affidavit of her own, but the Court refused to interfere.

Held, also, that a misdirection as to damages would form no ground for a new trial, the jury having found against the cause of action. *Morrison* v. *Shaw*, 403.

BUILDING CONTRACT.

Omission to sign specifications—Right to sue on quantum meruit.]—The plaintiff agreed in writing, on the 19th February, to build a house for the defendant according to the plans and specifications of one R., with alterations made by I., for $25,000. Afterwards some alterations were agreed upon, and on the 30th April a contract was executed by plaintiff and defendant by which the plaintiff was to build the house for $26,596, and this contract recited that the plaintiff had agreed to do all the work required according to certain plans and specifications prepared by R., with certain suggestions and amendments made by I., and signed by the plaintiff, subject to the various stipulations and conditions mentioned in the contract. The plans were signed by the plaintiff, but not the specifications; but he finished the building according to the specifications prepared, and from time to time obtained certificates for payment from the architect for the work executed as under the contract, in accordance with its provisions, by which the money was to be paid on such certificates, no extra work was to be paid for without a written order, and in the event of any dispute the architect was to be the sole and final judge.

Held, that the plaintiff's omission to sign the specifications could not entitle him to set aside the contract as not complete, and to claim for the work done as upon a *quantum meruit,* without the architect's certificates. *Gearing* v. *Nordheimer,* 21.

BY-LAW.

Conviction under.]—*See* CONVICTION.

See LIQUOR, SALE OF, 2.

CERTIFICATE OF ARCHITECT.

See BUILDING CONTRACT.

CERTIFICATE FOR COSTS.

See COSTS.

CERTIORARI.

Where a conviction for an offence, not a crime, is affirmed on appeal by the Sessions, the writ is not taken away by 38 Vic. ch. 4, O. *Re Bates,* 284.

CHATTEL MORTGAGE.

See TRESPASS.

CHEQUE.

Alteration of.]—*See* BANKS AND BANKING, 1.

CHURCHES.

See RELIGIOUS INSTITUTIONS.

COLLECTOR.

Of inland revenue — Delivery of Temperance By-law to.]—*See* LIQUOR, SALE OF, 1.

"COMPANIES' ACT, 1862,"
(IMPERIAL.)

See PUBLIC COMPANY.

COMPENSATION.

For injury to houses by train passing on street.]—*See* RAILWAYS AND R. W. Cos., 1.

COMPOSITION AND DISCHARGE.

Setting aside deed of.]—*See* INSOLVENCY, 1.

CONSIDERATION.

See BILLS AND NOTES, 1.

CONSTITUTIONAL LAW.

See ASSESSMENT AND TAXES, 2.

CONTRACT.

See BUILDING CONTRACT — STATUTES, CONSTRUCTION OF.

CONVICTION.

1. *Summary conviction — Notice of appeal—33 Vic. ch. 27, D.*]—It is not essential that the notice of appeal under 33 Vic. ch. 27, D., from a summary conviction, should be signed by the party appealing. A notice, therefore, "that we, the undersigned D. N. and C. N." of, &c., following the form given by the Act in other respects, but not signed, was held sufficient. *Regina* v. *Nichol et al.,* 76.

2. *Certiorari*—38 *Vic. ch. 4, O.—By-law.*]—In the case of a conviction for an offence not being a crime, affirmed on appeal to the Sessions, the writ of *certiorari* is not taken away by the 38 Vic. ch. 4, O.

Where the conviction purported to be for an offence against a by-law, but shewed no such offence, it was quashed; and it was held, that it could not be supported as warranted by the general law. *Re Bates*, 284.

Variance between conviction and warrant.]—*See* LIQUOR, SALE OF, 3.

CORPORATION.

See PUBLIC COMPANY.

CORROBORATIVE EVIDENCE

See REGISTRY LAW.

COSTS.

Trespass to land after notice—Right to costs—Suggestion—C. L. P. Act, sec. 225.]—The plaintiff, in an action for trespass to land, in which the pleas were only not guilty and leave and license, recovered one shilling damages, and the Judge refused to certify for costs. The plaintiff then applied for leave to enter a suggestion on the record that the trespasses were committed after notice, and for an order, on such entry, that the master should tax full costs.

Held, that sec. 325 of the C. L. P. Act not being repealed by the 31 Vic. ch. 24, O., the plaintiff was entitled under it to enter the suggestion; but that the proviso to that section—not to be found in the corresponding Imperial enactment, 3 & 4 Vic. ch. 24, sec. 3—would prevent him from recovering more than Division Court costs, without a certificate. *Howden v. Donnelly*, 119.

On indictment for obstructing highway.]—*See* WAYS, 1, 2.

COUNTY ATTORNEY.

Notice of action.]—The defendant, being county crown attorney and clerk of the peace, received certain promissory notes belonging to the plaintiffs with the depositions from a magistrate on the committal of certain persons for obtaining such notes by false pretences. At the trial before the County Judge the prisoners were acquitted, the learned Judge saying that the prosecutors' remedy, if any, was in Chancery. The defendant refused to give the notes up to the plaintiffs on demand, saying that he would return them to the committing magistrate, and the plaintiffs thereupon brought trover and detinue.

The learned Judge, who tried the case without a jury, having found that defendant acted *bonâ fide* in such refusal: *Held*, that he was entitled to notice of action under C. S. U. C. ch. 126: that he was an officer fulfilling a public duty within that statute; and that the refusal, though erroneous, was an act done by him in the supposed discharge of such duty. *McDougall et al. v. Peterson*, 95.

COVENANTS FOR TITLE.

Pleading.]—A declaration on a covenant against encumbrances by defendant, or his wife, or any one claiming under them, alleged as a breach that at the time of making said covenant a large sum was in arrear for taxes duly imposed, without shewing that they accrued while defendants owned the land or were caused by his acts. *Held*, bad. *Silverthorne v. Lowe*, 73.

COVENANT.

Not to assign lease—Waiver of breach.]—*See* LANDLORD AND TENANT, 1.

To repair—Breach of—Waiver.]—*See* LANDLORD AND TENANT, 3.

CRIMINAL LAW.

1. *Forgery—Evidence.*] — On an indictment for feloniously offering, &c., a forged note commonly called a Provincial note, issued under the authority of 29-30 Vic. ch. 10, D., for the payment of $5, it appeared that the prisoners had passed off a note purporting to be a Provincial note under the statute, knowing that the figure 5 had been pasted over the figure 1, and the word five over the word one. No evidence was given that the note so altered was a note issued by the Government of Canada; but it was shewn further, that when the attention of the prisoners was called to the alteration, they said, " give it back if it is not good," and that on its being placed on the counter one of them took it up and refused to return it, or substitute good money for it. *Held*, that looking at the particular character of the forgery—*i. e.*, an alteration—and the conduct of the prisoners, the onus was on them to dispute the validity of the writing, if a defence; and a conviction was sustained. *Regina* v. *Portis et al.*, 214.

2. *Larceny—Recent possession—Evidence.*]—On an indictment for stealing cooper's tools on the 5th of November, 1874, it appeared that the prisoner was not arrested for nearly two years afterwards. During that time—it was not shewn precisely when—he was proved to have sold several of the tools at much less than their value, representing that he was a cooper by trade, and was going to quit it, which was proved to be untrue. It was proved also that he was in the shop from which the tools were stolen the night before they were taken, and frequently; and that when arrested he offered the prosecutor $35 to settle and buy new tools, and offered the constable $100 if he could get clear.

Held, that though the mere fact of the possession by the prisoner, after such a lapse of time, might not alone suffice, yet that all the facts taken together were enough to support a conviction for larceny. *Regina* v. *Starr*, 218.

See WAYS.

CROWN LANDS.

See FREE GRANT LANDS.

DAMAGES.

1. Recovery of three cents and no costs against magistrates, under C. S. U. C. ch. 126. *Stoness* v. *Lake et al.*, 320.

2. Recovery in trespass of costs of quashing conviction, as damages for sale under distress warrant, issued under such conviction. *Hallet* v. *Wilmot et al.*, 263.

Assessment of.]—*See* BOND.

See MISDIRECTION.

DEED.

Registration of Sheriff's.]—*See* ASSESSMENT AND TAXES, 1.

DELAY.

See ASSESSMENT AND TAXES, 1.

DELIVERY.

Of bill or note.]—*See* DONATIO MORTIS CÁUSA.

DISTRESS.

Wrongful distress.] — *See* LAND-
LORD AND TENANT, 2.

DIVISION COURT BAILIFF.

*Notice of action against—Suffi-
ciency of.*]—*See* SALE OF GOODS, 1.

See TRESPASS.

DONATIO MORTIS CAUSA.

Gift inter vivos—Delivery.]—B.,
who died in 1874, had made a will
in which there was a devise to the
plaintiff, his illegitimate daughter;
but this having given offence to his
family he destroyed it and made
another, and at the same time signed
a promissory note, payable to the
plaintiff, for $2,000. He placed
this note in a pocket book, where it
remained till after his death, but
shortly before his death he shewed
it to a witness, and said it was to be
paid after his death, and then handed
it with the pocket book to the witness, but afterwards took them back.
He told this witness that he would
talk more about it to her another
time, and asked her to tell P., his
legitimate daughter and his executrix, that he had shewn the witness
the note, which the witness did, and
told the testator that she had done
so. It was proved also that he said
he had made provision for the plaintiff.

Held, that the plaintiff could not
recover, for the note could not be
claimed by her either as a *donatio
mortis causa* or as a gift *inter vivos,*
there having been no delivery of it
by the testator.

Quære, whether such a note may,
by manual delivery, be the subject
of a gift. *Rupert* v. *Johnston,* 11.

DOUBLE INSURANCE.

See INSURANCE, 2.

DUNKIN ACT.

See LIQUOR, SALE OF, 1, 2.

EASEMENT.

*Right of way—Severance of tene-
ments—When the right will pass—
"Appurtenances"—Pleading.*]—Declaration for breaking and entering
the plaintiff's close, being a yard in
the rear of a certain shop and premises, and throwing down a brick
wall there.

Plea : that before the alleged trespass one J. D. was seized in fee of
the said shop and premises, and of
the said close : that the occupiers of
the shop enjoyed as of right and
without interruption a certain way
on foot and with cattle from a public
lane over said close to said shop and
premises, and therefrom over said
close to the lane : that afterwards J.
D., by deed, dated 12th July, 1849,
demised the shop and premises, *with
all the appurtenances,* to L. & W. as
trustees for a term of years, which
it was agreed by the deed should be
renewed, and which was afterwards
renewed ; and that the defendants
became and are assignees of the term,
and took possession of the shop and
premises under the assignment : that
after the demise to L. and W., the
executors of J. D. dem sed to S. the
said close, subject to said way, and
the same afterwards became vested
for a term in the plaintiff : that afterwards the defendants during their
term, and in their own right, entered
the close to use said way, and in
using the same broke down part of

said wall, which obstructed said way. On demurrer to this plea:

Held, by HARRISON, C. J., that the plea might be read as alleging a defined way, necessary and convenient for the enjoyment of defendants' property before the lease from J. D., constructed across the plaintiff's close, for the use and enjoyment of defendants' shop, and visible to all persons when the plaintiff acquired title: that so reading the plea, the way may be said to be an "appurtenance" to defendants' premises, which passed from J. D. by the deed under which defendants claimed, and that the plea therefore was good.

On appeal this judgment was reversed, on the ground that the plea could not be read as alleging an apparent and continuous easement necessary for the proper enjoyment of defendants' premises, without which it would not pass under the deed.

Per BURTON, J.—Upon a severance of tenements, easements used as of necessity, or in their nature continuous, will pass by implication of law; easements not continuous or apparent, but used from time to time only, will not.

Per PATTERSON, J.—A right of way is not such a continuous easement as to pass by implication of law with a grant of the land; only a way of necessity will so pass. A way used by the owner of two tenements over one for access to the other, is not in law appurtenant to the dominant tenement, so as to pass with a grant of it, under the word "appurtenances," unless the deed shews an intention to extend the meaning of that word, and to embrace the way, or the grant is of all ways "used and enjoyed," or words are used shewing an intention to include existing ways, in which case a defined existing way will pass. *Harris* v. *Smith et al.,* 33.

EJECTMENT.

By wife without joining her husband. *Johnstone* v. *White,* 309.

Proof of title in.]—*See* RELIGIOUS INSTITUTIONS.

ELECTIONS.

Under Temperance Act of 1864—*Closing poll too soon.*]—*See* LIQUOR, SALE OF, 2.

ESTOPPEL.

See INSURANCE, 2—WAYS, 1.

EVIDENCE.

Admissibility of.]—In an action of ejectment the plaintiff claimed under one C., who it was alleged had bought the land and paid for it, and C., in the answer in a suit in Chancery, having stated the sum paid by him, and the facts: *Semble.* that the pleadings in this suit, having been put in by defendants, were some evidence as against them of such payment; but as a new trial would not have been granted for the reception of such evidence, even if inadmissible, the point was not determined. *Cooley et al.* v. *Smith et al.,* 560.

See BREACH OF PROMISE—CRIMINAL LAW, 1, 2—EJECTMENT—REGISTRY LAW — SALE OF GOODS — WAYS.

EXECUTION.

Priority of.]—*See* TRESPASS,

EXECUTORS AND ADMIN-
ISTRATORS.

Will and probate set aside—Rights of executor.]—The plaintiff, as executor of one W., having paid money to defendant, as a legatee under the will, and the will with the probate having been afterwards set aside by a decree of the Court of Chancery, the plaintiff was held entitled to recover back the money. *Haldan* v. *Beatty*, 110.

FENCE.

Neglect of R. W. Co. to put up.]—*See* RAILWAYS AND R. W. COS., 3.

FINE.

Where defendant convicted of obstructing a highway.]—*See* WAYS, 1, 2.

FIRE INSURANCE.

See INSURANCE.

FORFEITURE.

See LANDLORD AND TENANT, 1, 3.

FORGERY.

See CRIMINAL LAW, 1.

FRAUD.

Sale of goods, fraudulent design not to pay for.]—P., at Woodstock, bought 8 half-chests of tea from plaintiff at Bowmanville, on 25th August, and the tea arrived on the 4th September. On 5th September, P.

absconded. *Held*, from these and other circumstances stated in the report, that P. ordered these goods fraudulently with the design of not paying for them. *Davis* v. *McWhirter*, 598.

See HUSBAND AND WIFE, 3—INSURANCE, 3.

FREE GRANT LANDS.

Sale of timber by locatee—31 Vic. ch. 8, 37 Vic. ch. 23, O.]—Land within the free grant territory was located on the 12th of August, 1870. On the 2nd of April, 1872, the locatee sold to the defendant all the pine and other timber thereon, stipulating that ten years should be allowed for taking it off, and the defendant paid the purchase money in full. The patents for the lands issued in 1876, and the defendant afterwards cut timber, for which the patentees brought trespass.

Held, that under 31 Vic. ch. 8, and the order in council of 4th October, 1871, confirmed by 37 Vic. ch. 23, O., the locatee had a right to make the sale : that no limitation as to the time within which the timber should be removed could be implied from these statutes ; and that the plaintiff therefore could not recover. *Hutchinson et al.* v. *Beatty*, 135.

GENERAL AVERAGE.

Vessel—Unseaworthiness — General average.] — The defendant's schooner was engaged to carry a cargo of timber from Spanish River to Chippewa. She left Spanish River with the timber on the 15th October, and anchored on that day at Bayfield Sound, leaking badly, where she remained till the 10th of November, and was then towed by a tug to

Sarnia. There she got a steam pump, and with it on board was towed to the Welland canal, where she arrived on the 25th November, and being frozen up the cargo had to be unloaded. The defendant refused to give up the lumber unless, in addition to the freight, the plaintiff would pay his share for general average of (1) the expenses incurred for charges of the tug, $1,200; (2) use of hawser, $50; (3) use of steam pump, $315; (4) telegrams, protest, adjustment, $25; (5) extra help discharging, $120.

Held, that if the vessel had been seaworthy the first, second and fifth items would not have been chargeable; and that the third might be; but,

Held, also, that the evidence, set out below, shewed the vessel to have been unseaworthy at the commencement of and during the whole voyage, and that the expense was occasioned thereby; and that defendant therefore had no claim. *Chaffey* v. *Schooley*, 165.

GIFT.

Inter vivos.]—*See* DONATIO MORTIS CAUSA.

GUARANTEE.

Construction of.] — Defendant's son, living at St. Catharines, applied to the plaintiffs, merchants in Hamilton, to supply him with goods, and on the 12th April they wrote to him that they would execute his order if he could get the endorsation of his father. On the 13th the son wrote to them to send the goods, and that he would get his father's endorsation if required. On the 17th the plaintiffs wrote proposing, in view of future business, and to save the trouble of getting an endorsement with each transaction, that the father should give a continuous guarantee. The son on the 19th wrote that he would get this, and urged them to send the goods at once, which they did on the same day, with a form of guarantee for the father to sign. On the 21st the son wrote to his father, who lived at Woodstock, "I am buying some goods" from the plaintiffs, and enclosing the guarantee for his signature. The father, not liking this form, wrote another, as follows: "Woodstock, 20th April, 1875. Gentlemen—In consideration of your supplying my son with what goods he may from time to time require of you this season, on your usual terms of credit, I do hereby guarantee the payment of the same." The defendant, as the Court inferred from the evidence, was not aware when he signed this that his son had already obtained any goods from the plaintiffs. After the guarantee, in May and June, further goods were purchased by the son.

Held, that the guarantee applied only to the goods purchased after it, not to those previously furnished. *Wood et al.* v. *Chambers*, 1.

See BILLS AND NOTES, 3.

HIGH SCHOOLS.

By-law to raise money for.]—*See* SCHOOLS.

HIGHWAY.

Obstruction of.]—*See* WAYS, 1, 2.

HUSBAND AND WIFE.

.1. *Married woman—Liability of* —35 *Vic. c.* 16, *O.*]—A married woman in August, 1874, gave a promissory note with her husband, to the plaintiffs, for money due by him, which they accepted on the representation, which was true, that she had separate estate, the only consideration being their forbearance of the husband's debt.

Held, that she was liable, under 35 Vic. ch. 16, O. *Kerr et al.* v. *Stripp,* 125.

2. *Separate estate—C. S. U. C. ch.* 73, 35 *Vic. ch.* 16—*Ejectment— Outstanding term.*] — The plaintiff was married to her present husband in 1859, without any marriage settlement, and he, before that year, had reduced into possession the land in question.

Held, that she was not entitled to sue for it without joining her husband in ejectment, either under C. S. U. C. ch. 73, or 35 Vic. ch. 16, O., such land not being her separate property, and the husband not being divested by the last mentioned Act; and that she would not have been entitled even if her husband had not reduced it into possession.

The patent issued in 1836 to C., who apparently had made some agreement for sale to D., who transferred it to the plaintiff. The plaintiff in 1846 conveyed the land to her sons, and in 1862 a deed, for a nominal consideration, was executed by C. to the plaintiff. The learned Judge, who tried the case without a jury, having found that this last deed was made to the plaintiff as a trustee to enable the title of her sons to be perfected: *Held,* that on this ground also the land could not be her separate estate.

The evidence shewed that the plaintiff's son had for some time been in possession as a tenant under lease, at a yearly rent. *Semble, per* HARRISON, C. J., that this also would have been a bar to plaintiff's action. *Johnstone* v. *White,* 309.

3. 35 *Vic. c.* 16, *s.* 2, *O.—Separate trade—Fraudulent contrivance.*]— Sec. 2 of 35 Vic. ch. 16, O., exempting from the husband's debts all proceeds or profits of any occupation or trade carried on by the wife separately from the husband, applies to all married women, whether married before or after the passing of the Act.

But this section does not apply to any occupation or trade in which the husband is held out to the world as the person conducting it, or which she cannot carry on without his active co-operation or agency. The husband need not be physically absent in order to make it her separate trade or occupation, but she cannot be properly held to carry it on separately from him, so long as he does all that is essential to its success.

Where, therefore, the husband lived on the farm with his wife, and managed it, a finding that she was carrying on the farm for herself was set aside.

As to the stock and farming utensils, which were claimed by the wife, it appeared that they had been sold under an execution against the husband, to whom they belonged, and had been purchased by his two brothers-in-law, one of whom paid a small part of the purchase money, the other nothing, and the remainder was paid by the husband, who remained in possession as before. One of the purchasers it was said, afterwards transferred his interest to the wife, for the alleged consideration of a right to dower, which was not clearly shewn to exist, and the possession remained as before. *Held,* that the whole dealings shewed a design to protect the husband's property against his creditors, and a finding in the wife's favour was reversed. *Harrison* v. *Douglass,* 410.

[Signature in blank, by wife, of a note to be used by husband for his own business.] — See BILLS AND NOTES, 3.

See BREACH OF PROMISE.

INCUMBRANCE.

Concealment of—When insuring.] —*See* INSURANCE, 3.

INDICTMENT.

See WAYS, 1, 2.

INFORMATION.

For sale of liquor—Insufficiency of waiver.]—*See* LIQUOR, SALE OF, 3.

INLAND REVENUE.

See LIQUOR, SALE OF, 1.

INSOLVENCY.

Insolvent Act of 1875—Composition and discharge—Withdrawal of claim.]—At a meeting of the creditors of an insolvent one L., as receiver in Chancery of the estate of W., claimed on two notes annexed to his affidavit, stating that according to his information and belief he held no security. The amount was then entered among the proved claims. During the meeting, however, the solicitor for the endorsers on these notes came in, and shewed that security was held for them, of which L. was not aware ; and L. then stated that owing to this he would withdraw his proof and notes ; and he took no further part in the proceedings. The affidavit had not been marked as received and filed, and three days afterwards the notes were given up to L. by the assignee. The claim, nevertheless, had been entered on the list of debts proved, certified by the official assignee under section 52 of the Insolvent Act of 1875, and remained there ; but in the estimate and calculations made at the meeting it was not taken into account, being understood as withdrawn. Afterwards a deed of composition and discharge was procured, the creditors who signed it representing less than the amount required if this claim were included, but more if it were excluded.

Held, that the claim should not be considered as proved, having been erroneously retained and included in the certificate ; and that the deed therefore was valid. *Rooney et al.* v. *Lyon,* 366.

INSURANCE.

1. *Fire policy—Non-occupation of premises.*]—A fire policy, granted to the plaintiff on a dwelling house in a town, contained the following condition : "Unoccupied dwelling houses, with the exceptions undermentioned, are not insured by this association, nor shall it be answerable for any loss by fire which may happen to, in, or from any dwelling house while left without an occupant or person actually residing therein. The temporary absence of a member or his family, however, none of the house-

hold effects being removed, is not to be construed into non-occupancy. And this condition is not construed to apply to the temporary non-occupation of small dwellings for the accommodation of hired help on a farm, the main dwelling on the same continuing to be occupied. But the main dwelling house must not be unoccupied for longer than forty-eight hours at any one time."

The plaintiff lived several miles from the house, which was leased to a monthly tenant, who had removed his goods within forty-eight hours before the fire, and no one had resided in the house for ten days before. The fire took place on the 10th September, and the tenant's month was up on the 24th. He was in arrear for rent, for which his goods had been distrained, but the plaintiff, who had a person ready to take possession, did not suppose that the tenant would leave until his month was up.

Held, that the exception as to forty-eight hours applied only to dwellings on a farm : that the condition, which required an actual residence of the occupant, was broken ;. and that the plaintiff could not recover.

Held, also, that a demand of the claim papers and proof of loss, without reference to this condition, could not be construed as a waiver of it: *The Canada Landed Credit Co.* v. *Canada Agricultural Ins. Co.,* 17 Grant 418, dissented from on this point.

No such waiver having been set up at the trial, which took place without a jury, *quære*, as to the propriety of allowing it to be urged in term. *Abrahams* v. *The Agricultural Mutual Assurance Association,* 175.

80—VOL. XL U.C.R.

2. *Double insurance—Same agent for both companies—Estoppel.*]—The plaintiff and one Morris, who was local agent at Barrie for defendants and for the Hastings Mutual Insurance Company as well, went together to one M., who filled up two applications for insurance, which were signed by the plaintiff, one for insurance with defendants on his grist mill, and the other for insurance with the Hastings Company on fixed and movable machinery in the mill. The agent, thinking the former insurance was on the building only, and the latter on the machinery only, ·did not inform defendants of the other insurance, and the application to defendants stated that there was no other insurance on the property.

Held, that there was a further insurance on part of the property insured by defendants ; but

Held, also. WILSON, J., dissenting, that the defendants, under the circumstances, could not set it up to defeat the plaintiff's claim, defendants' agent having prepared the application with a full knowledge of the facts. *Shannon* v. *The Gore District Mutual Fire Ins. Co.,* 188.

3. *Mutual Ins. Co.—False statement as to title—Concealment of encumbrance—36 Vic. ch. 44, sec. 36, O.*]—The plaintiff, in his application for insurance with defendants, a mutual insurance company, answered " Yes " to the question, " Does the property to be insured belong exclusively to you ?" and to the question, " If encumbered, state to what amount," he made no answer. The defendants' agent, who took the application, said the plaintiff told him there was a mortgage for $100 on the building, which he was about to have discharged, and that he, the agent,

therefore thought it unnecessary to insert it in the application, and gave no notice of it to the company. The plaintiff said the agent filled up the application, which he signed without reading it, and that he told the agent of the mortgage, but did not say that he was going to remove it.

Held, that there was no false statement as to title; and that there was no concealment as to the encumbrance, for the omission to mention it was sufficiently explained; and that the defendants, after the issue of the policy on the application, and after the fire, could not take advantage of the omission as avoiding the policy under 36 Vic. ch. 44, sec. 36, O.

Quære, whether the "false statement" or "concealment" mentioned in that section must not be fraudulent, in order to avoid the policy. *Sinclair* v. *The Canadian Mutual Fire Ins. Co.*, 206.

4. *Mutual insurance policy — Assignment to mortgagee — Subsequent insurance by mortgagor—Effect of on rights of mortgagee—Pleading.*]—A mortgagee, becoming assignee of a policy under the Mutual Insurance Act, 36 Vic. ch. 44, O., by an assignment duly ratified by the company, becomes—whether he has given his own note, or the directors have assented to retain the premium note of the mortgagor—a person insured to the extent of his own interest, and is, in the event of loss, entitled to recover in his own name to the extent of his claim. By such assignment he acquires a separate independent interest under the policy, and the policy as against him is not avoided by a contract for further insurance made by the mortgagor without his knowledge, and which he could not prevent, nor by any acts of a similar kind beyond his control.

Held, that although the assignment might by agreement so bind him, the terms of the assignment in this case, hereinafter mentioned, were not sufficiently clear to have that effect.

The declaration alleged that defendants by their policy insured one B. for $3,000 on a manufactory and stock : that afterwards, with defendants' knowledge and consent, he assigned all his interest in the policy to the plaintiffs, as collateral security for a mortgage by B. to them for $3,000, on the property insured : that defendants ratified and confirmed said policy to and in favour of the plaintiffs : that the premises were burned ; and that by force of the statute the plaintiffs became under the said assignment interested in the said policy as the insured, and entitled to all rights as if they had been the original parties insured.

Defendants pleaded that the assignment was accepted by plaintiffs, and the consent given by defendants, subject to the condition that the plaintiffs should be bound by all the terms and conditions of the policy, as B. was bound by the same, and that the policy should continue voidable as though such assignment had not been executed, and the said policy was not otherwise ratified or confirmed to the plaintiffs : that it was a condition of the policy that any insurance on the premises by the act or with the knowledge of the insured in any other company, without the consent of defendants, should avoid the policy; and that B. effected other insurances, specified, without defendants' consent.

The plaintiffs replied, 2. That the said assignment was not accepted by plaintiff, nor was defendants' consent thereto and the ratification by them to the plaintiffs, as in the declaration and plea mentioned, on the terms or subject to the condition that the plaintiffs should be bound by any terms which would render the policy voidable by any act or omission of B. ; but by virtue of said assignment, consent, and ratification, the plaintiffs became entitled to all the rights and subject to all the conditions to which B. had been subject, before the assignment, &c., and not otherwise ; and that the said insurances effected by B. were without the plaintiffs' consent or knowledge ; 3. That the alleged insurances effected by B. were not of the same interest as that insured by the plaintiffs under said policy in the declaration mentioned, and said insurances were not effected by plaintiffs or with their knowledge or consent

Held, that the second replication was bad, as being in effect a demurrer to the plea, and neither traversing nor confessing and avoiding it ; and that the plea was bad, and the third replication good. *The Mechanics' Building and Savings Society* v. *Gore District Mutual Fire Ins. Co.*, 220.

See MORTGAGE.

JOINT DEBTORS.
See PRINCIPAL AND SURETY.

JOINT STOCK COMPANY.
See PUBLIC COMPANY.

JUSTICE OF THE PEACE.

Action against magistrates—Pleading—Damages.]—A count alleging that defendants were justices of the peace, &c., and assuming to act as such justices, but without any jurisdiction or authority in that behalf, caused a distress warrant to be issued against the plaintiff's goods for $56, which they had adjudged the plaintiff to pay under and by virtue of a certain conviction made by them without any jurisdiction, and caused the plaintiff's goods to be sold thereunder, which conviction was afterwards duly quashed on application of the plaintiff to this Court, whereby the plaintiff lost the use and value of his goods, and was put to costs in getting the conviction quashed.

Held, a count in trespass ; and *held*, also, that the plaintiff was properly nonsuited, the cause of action being the seizure of the plaintiff's goods under warrants, issued upon three convictions of the plaintiff, for alleged offences under the Act relating to the sale of spirituous liquors, two only of which had been quashed, and a conviction for assault ; and therefore an act done by defendants in the execution of their duty, as justices, with respect to matters within their jurisdiction.

Quære, if the plaintiff had been entitled to succeed in trespass, whether he could have recovered the costs of quashing the convictions as damages. *Hallett* v. *Wilmot et al.*, 263.

LANDLORD AND TENANT.

1. *Lease—Covenant not to assign—Breach—Forfeiture—Waiver.*]— The plaintiff leased land for ten years from 1st December, 1871, to one D., who covenanted that neither he nor his assigns would assign, transfer, or sub-let the premises without the plaintiff's consent in writing first obtained, with a proviso for re-entry. D. mortgaged his interest to one H. to secure him against his endorsement of a note for D., the proceeds of which D. expended in converting the premises into a race-course and pleasure grounds and erecting buildings thereon. This

note being dishonoured, H. informed the plaintiff of the mortgage, and that owing to the plaintiff's absence it had been taken without his consent, whereupon the plaintiff waived all objections on this ground, and declared that he would take no advantage of the omission, and H. then paid the note, and afterwards expended a large sum in foreclosing the mortgage and improving the premises.

H., having foreclosed, advertised the land for lease. One W. took possession in May, 1874, on the understanding that he was to have the place for five years, with the privilege of remaining the whole of the original term, at a rent of $530 a year, and there was to be a written agreement, to be drawn up if possible so as not to affect H.'s lease. He remained ten months, and made improvements, and while in possession sub-let part of the land to one C. for $300 a year. W. gave up possession to H. in April, 1875, not being able to obtain the written agreement which had been promised to him; and on arbitration with H. the arbitrators awarded to W. $524 in full for improvements, "less $224 due for rent," on which basis they settled. H. notified C. in October, 1874, not to pay any money for rent unless authorized by H.

Held, MORRISON, J., dissenting, that what took place between H. and W. was a breach of the covenant; and *Semble*, that the lease was forfeited also by the dealing between H. and C.

Per MORRISON, J.—The parties intended only that there should be an assignment if the plaintiff would consent to it, and there was no forfeiture.

Held, also, that the plaintiff had waived the forfeiture caused by the mortgage to H. *Bacon* v. *Campbell et al.*, 517.

2. *Breach of covenant—Entry by landlord—Wrongful distress—Trespass—Trover.*]—Defendant leased land to one M. for five years from the 1st December, 1874, by a lease in the statutory short form, containing covenants not to sub-let or assign without leave, &c. On 26th February, 1876, defendant finding the premises vacant, and going to ruin, the door of the house broken and open, fences down, &c., re-entered and nailed up the door, and on the 29th leased it by deed to one G. for five years. On the 9th March the plaintiff, who had been hired to work for M., receiving the use of the house and part of the crops for his pay, broke into the place, and remained there until 17th April, when defendant seized under a distress for rent, there being none due, and removed the plaintiff's stove, &c. The plaintiff then promised to leave on the 19th, and gave up the key to defendant as a symbol of possession, and G.'s stove was put up in place of the plaintiff's. On the 19th, when G. and defendant went there, M. resisted their entrance, and they came to blows. M. and defendant had an arbitration, which resulted in an award that defendant should pay $18 costs to M., and that M. should give up possession, as he had broken his covenants in the lease. The plaintiff sued defendant for trespass to the land, and in trover, and the jury found a verdict for $100.

Held, that the plaintiff could not recover for the trespass, having no title to the land, for if he went in under a lease from M., and not as his servant only, that of itself constituted a forfeiture, and entitled defendant and G. to enter.

A verdict was therefore entered on the trover count for 1s. damages for the injury done to plaintiff's stove, and for defendant on the other counts. *McArthur* v. *Alison*, 576.

3. *Lease—Forfeiture—Waiver.*]— Declaration for trespass · to land. Plea, *liberum tenementum.* Replication, a demise by defendant to plaintiff for a term unexpired. Rejoinder, averring a breach of covenant to repair, and defendant's entry thereupon. Surrejoinder, that upon the alleged breach and forfeiture defendant accepted rent accrued due after the forfeiture, which was thereby waived. *Held,* surrejoinder bad, for there could be no waiver after entry. *Thompson* v. *Baskerville*, 614.

LAND, SALE OF.

See REGISTRY LAWS.

LARCENY.

See CRIMINAL LAW, 2.

LEASE.

See LANDLORD AND TENANT.

LICENSE INSPECTOR.

See LIQUOR, SALE OF, 1.

LIMITATIONS, STATUTE OF.

R. W. Co.'s neglect to fence.]— *Quære*, whether C. S. U. C. ch. 66, sec 83, would apply to neglect to fence, this being an act of omission. *Nichol* v. *Canada Southern R. W. Co.*, 583.

LIQUOR, SALE OF.

1. *Temperance Act of* 1864—*Delivery of by-law to collector.*]—The issuers of licenses appointed under 37 Vic. ch. 32, O., supersede the collector of inland revenue under the Temperance Act of 1864 ; and under that Act and the 39 Vic. ch. 26, O., it was held unnecessary to deliver a copy of a by-law passed on the 29th June, 1875, under the Temperance Act, to the collector of inland revenue.

Semble, that if it had been, the person to whom it was delivered in this case was, under the facts stated, sufficiently shewn to be such collector.

It was objected that the applicant for a mandamus to the inspector of licenses to inspect and report on his premises, so as to enable him to apply for a license, did not shew that he was a natural born or naturalized subject, as required by the by-law ; but *Held,* that such objection could not have prevailed, for he was shewn to have been duly licensed up to 1st May, 1876, and no exception had been made to him. *Re Lake and Blakeley*, 102.

2. *Temperance Act of* 1864 — *Voting for by-law—Poll closed too soon.*]—Where a by-law under the Temperance Act of 1864 had been carried in a county by 193 majority, but it appeared that in one township, where the names of the qualified municipal electors on the assessment roll were more than 800, the poll was left open only two days, leaving 250 votes unpolled there, the by-law was set aside.

The names of owners appearing in the 6th column of the roll, under the heading "Owners and address," should be counted, in order to ascertain the number of electors, although not appearing in the second column headed, "Name of occupant or other taxable party," and not bracketed or numbered in the first column. *Re Johnson and the Corporation of the County of Lambton.* 297.

3. *Conviction — Insufficiency of information—Waiver of—Variance between conviction and warrant— C. S. U. C. c. 126, s. 17.*]—The plaintiff, on an information against him under 37 Vic. ch. 32, O., for selling liquor without a license, was brought before the defendants, magistrates. It was proved that this was his second offence, though the information did not charge it as such. The plaintiff disputed the evidence as to the first conviction, but did not object to the information, and the magistrates convicted and adjudged him to be imprisoned for ten days which they had power to do only for a second offence, *Held,* that the plaintiff had waived the objection to the information, and that defendants were not liable in trespass.

Held, also, that the variance between the conviction and the warrant for plaintiff's arrest, the former saying nothing as to hard labour and the latter providing for it, could not deprive the defendants of protection under the statute, Consol. Stat. U. C. ch. 126.

Held, also, that in any event defendants could not have been liable for plaintiff's suffering caused by the harsh regulations of the prison during his confinement; and that having been proved to have been guilty of the offence for which he was convicted, he could have recovered only three cents and no costs, under Consol. Stat. U. C. ch. 126, s. 17. *Stoness* v. *Lake et al.,* 320.

MALICIOUS ARREST.

Reasonable and probable cause— Objection taken too late.]—Where in an action for malicious arrest the facts are uncontradicted the question of reasonable and probable cause must be decided exclusively by the Judge.

The action at the trial was treated as one for malicious arrest, and in that view a nonsuit was entered. In term it was argued that the action was really one of trespass, and that the whole case should have been left to the jury as such, but the Court held that it was too late to urge this. *Donnelly* v. *Bawden,* 611.

MANDAMUS.

To issue license.]—*See* LIQUOR, SALE OF, 1.

MARRIAGE.

Breach of promise of.] — *See* BREACH OF PROMISE.

MARRIED WOMAN.

See HUSBAND AND WIFE.

MEMORANDA.

32.

MISDIRECTION.

As to damages, forms no ground for a new trial. *Morrison* v. *Shaw,* 403.

MONEY PAID.

See WILL, 1.

MORTGAGE.

Of vessel—Purchase by mortgagee —Loss of vessel—Right to sue for mortgage money.]—Declaration on defendant's covenant by deed to pay money. Plea: that the deed mentioned was a mortgage and re-conveyance of a vessel sold by plaintiff to defendant, to secure the purchase money therefor; and that while the plaintiff was mortgagee the said vessel and all defendant's interest therein was sold, and the plaintiff became the absolute owner of said vessel, whereby the mortgage became merged and satisfied. Replication, on equitable grounds, that the vessel, being a British ship, was seized for wages due to the crew, and sold at Detroit, in the United States, solely through defendant's default: that by the law of the United States the wages formed a lien prior to the mortgage, and the plaintiff, wholly to protect himself, and not to gain any advantage over defendant, became the purchaser: that he offered and was always willing to re-convey and deliver her to defendants on being paid the mortgage money and the sum paid by him at such sale, which defendants refused to pay: that the plaintiff, having possession of the vessel, insured her, and on her loss by the perils of the sea received the insurance money, which the plaintiff is and always has been ready to apply to the purchase money.

Held, on demurrer, affirming the judgment of Gwynne, J., a good replication, and that the plaintiff, under the circumstances stated, was not precluded from recovering on the covenant. *Parkinson v. Higgins et al.*, 274.

Negligence in enforcing payment of collateral second mortgage.]—See Bills and Notes, 1.

MORTGAGOR & MORTGAGEE.

See Insurance, 4.

MUNICIPAL CORPORATIONS.

See Schools.

MUTUAL INSURANCE.

See Insurance, 3, 4.

NEGLIGENCE.

See Banks and Banking—Railways and R. W. Co's., 2.

NEW TRIAL.

See Misdirection—Railway and Railway Co's., 3—Sale of Goods, 1.

NONSUIT.

Where plaintiff sued for seizure of his goods under warrants issued on three convictions, two of which only had been quashed. *Held*, that he was properly nonsuited. *Hallett v. Wilmot et al.*, 263.

NOTICE.

See Registry Law.

NOTICE OF ACTION.

See County Attorney, 1—Registrar, 1, 2—Sale of Goods. 1—Trespass.

NOTICE OF APPEAL.

See Conviction, 1.

OFFER TO PURCHASE.

See Registry Law.

OFFICERS.

Of Dominion Government—Taxation of income of.]—See Assessment and Taxes, 2.

OTTAWA.

Water commissioners of.] — *See* WATER COMMISSIONERS.

PAYMENT.

Of cheque.]—*See* BILLS AND NOTES, 1.

Proof of.]—*See* EVIDENCE.

PENALTY.

Execution for.]—*See* BOND.

PLEADING.

A replication was held bad, as being in effect a demurrer to the plea, and neither traversing nor confessing and avoiding it. *The Mechanics' Building and Savings Society v. The Gore District Mutual Fire Ins. Co.*, 220.

Special count held to be a count in trespass.] — *See* JUSTICE OF THE PEACE.

See COVENANTS FOR TITLE—EASEMENT.

PLEADINGS IN CHANCERY.

Admissibility of in evidence.]—*See* EVIDENCE, 1.

PRINCIPAL AND AGENT.

See SALE OF GOODS, 2·

PRINCIPAL AND SURETY.

Joint debtors — Relationship of principal and surety created after debt accrued—Right of surety to be treated as such]—*Semble*, that where *after* a right of action accrues to a creditor against two or more persons he is informed that one of them is or has become a surety only, and *after that* he gives time to the principal debtor without the consent and knowledge of the surety, he thereby discharges the surety, even though he may not have assented or been a party to the change of relationship between them.

Swire v. *Redman*, L. R. 1 Q. B. D. 536, commented upon.

In this case, however, it was *held*, upon the evidence set out in the report that the plaintiffs not only knew of but assented to the change of relationship.

T., being in business, failed and` made a composition with his creditors, giving his notes endorsed to W., and further secured by an assignment of certain mortgages made by T. to W. Afterwards W. got a transfer of all T.'s business and assumed all his liabilities.

The plaintiffs were creditors of T. and received the notes for the composition.

By a written document the plaintiffs authorized the discharge of one of the mortgages made by T. to W., and assigned to secure the notes, in consideration of W. giving another mortgage in lieu thereof ; and they authorized also the discharge of another of the mortgages, so far as regarded part of the property in it, in order that W. by mortgaging it again might raise money to meet the last payment on the notes. When the last note fell due, which W. by his arrangement with T. should have paid as the principal debtor, the plaintiffs by agreement with W. drew upon .him for the amount at five months. The learned Judge found that the plaintiffs knew of and assented to the arrangement between T. and W. : that W. then assumed T.'s debts, and thus became the principal debtor. In an action by the plaintiffs against T. as maker of the last of the composition notes given to them :

Held, that the plaintiffs had discharged the defendants by the time given.

And *Semble,* that the plaintiffs would also, by consenting to the release of the mortgages, as above mentioned, have discharged T. to the extent to which he was thereby prejudiced. *Bailey et al.* v. *Griffith,* 418.

Release of surety by giving time.] —See BILLS AND NOTES, 2.

See BILLS AND NOTES, 1, 2.

PUBLIC COMPANY.

" The (Imperial) Companies' Act, 1862 "—Order making calls against past member—Right of action thereon —Notice—Order made in defendants' absence—Finality of order—Repeal of statute—Effect of on pleas pleaded.] —*Held,* WILSON, J., dissenting, that an action will not lie in this country at the suit of the company on an order made under " The Companies' Act, 1862," in England, in the winding up of a company, making a call upon defendant *as a past member* in respect of his shares, and directing payment thereof to one of the two official liquidators appointed.

Per WILSON, J.—The fourth plea, traversing the plaintiffs being a corporation under the Act, was good.

The articles of association of the company provided that notices required to be served by the company upon the members might be served either personally or left or sent by post addressed to them at their registered place of abode, and the Act provided for the keeping of a register of such addresses. *Per* WILSON, J. —This would not apply to notices served on members, in proceedings to wind up the company, but it was not contrary to natural justice that the plaintiffs should recover against defendant, when the order sued upon, though made in his absence from England, and as he alleged without

notice, was made after notices given in the manner thus provided for.

The sixteenth plea alleged that the order was not final, but might be varied or rescinded by the Court of Chancery in England, which Court might also order restitution to defendant of the whole or any part of the money paid under such order. The plaintiffs replied, in substance, that the payment of calls under the order is final, unless there is a surplus, which in this case there would not be ; and that the order was final unless appealed against in a time fixed, which defendant had not done. *Per* WILSON, J., the plea was bad, for the order was final until altered ; and the replication was good.

A plea that defendant was induced to take the shares by the fraud of the plaintiffs, and repudiated them as soon as he discovered the fraud, and derived no benefit from them, was clearly bad, and was not supported,

The 23 Vic. ch. 24, sec. 1, under which such defences were permitted and had been pleaded, as could have been pleaded to the original order, was repealed by 39 Vic. ch. 7, O. *Per* WILSON, J , such repeal, under the Interpretation Act, 31 Vic. sec. 7, sub-sec 34, O., would not affect. the pleas. *Barned's Banking Co.* v. *Reynolds,* 435.

PUBLIC SCHOOLS.

See SCHOOLS.

QUANTUM MERUIT.

See BUILDING CONTRACT.

RAILWAYS AND R. W. CO'S.

1. *Train passing along a street— Houses injuriously affected—Right to compensation.*]—A railway company was permitted by the corpo-

ration to run their track along Cherry street in the city of Hamilton, which was only thirty feet wide. The plaintiff, owning a brick cottage and frame house on the street, complained that the trains passing caused the houses to vibrate, and the plaster to fall off the walls, and alleged loss of tenants thereby; but the evidence as to any structural injury caused by the railway was contradictory, and the Court held that it was not sufficiently made out.

Held, affirming the judgment of HAGARTY, C. J. C. P., that the plaintiff was not entitled to compensation under the Railway Act. *Re Devlin and the Hamilton and Lake Erie R. W. Co.*, 160.

2. *Two lines crossing—Collision —Use of brakes—Negligence.*]—The defendants' railway crossed the Grand Trunk Railway on a level. The train on the defendants' line was approaching the crossing, and the air brakes for some reason did not act. It was too late after discovering this to stop the train with the hand brakes, or by reversing the engine, though every effort was made, and a collision occurred with a train on the other line, of which the plaintiff was a conductor, by which he was seriously injured. It was shewn that these brakes were in common use on railways, and that the brakes in question had been twice examined and frequently used on that day, and found all right and effective. The learned Judge, who tried the case without a jury, held that defendants were liable, for that the air brakes should have been applied at a sufficient distance to enable the train to be stopped by other means in case of these brakes giving way.

Per HARRISON, C. J.—The finding was right.

Per MORRISON, J.—There was no evidence of negligence, for the defendants were not bound to have any other than air brakes, and were justified in depending upon them.

WILSON, J., being absent, and the Court thus equally divided, MORRISON, J., withdrew his judgment, so as to avoid the expense of a re-argument, and enable the defendants to appeal. *Brown v. The Great Western R. W. Co.*, 333.

3. *Surface water—Obstruction of —Liability — Limitation clause, C. S. U. C. ch. 66, sec. 83—Neglect to fence.*]—The plaintiff sued defendants for not constructing and maintaining a sufficient culvert under their railway where it crossed the plaintiff's land, so as to prevent as little as possible the flow of a natural water-course there; and in another count, for neglect to fence off their railway from plaintiff's land adjoining when requested. A count in trespass was added. The jury found $390 damages on the second and third counts, and 1s. damages on the first. There being no evidence of any natural stream : *Held*, that the plaintiff could not recover on the first count, for the interference with the flow of surface water formed no ground of action, and there was no charge of negligence in constructing the railway.

McGillivray v. *Great Western R. W. Co.*, 25 U. C. R. 69, commented upon and distinguished.

As to the neglect to fence, defendants pleaded not guilty by statute, C. S. U. C. ch. 66, specifying sec. 83, among others, but at the trial they raised no question under that clause as to the plaintiff's damages being confined to six months, and it was not shewn clearly how much of the damage accrued beyond that time.

It seemed probable, however, that only eight or ten weeks would be excluded if the clause applied, and the Court refused to interfere on this ground. *Quære*, whether the clause would apply, this being an act of omission.

Quære, also, as to the liability of defendants for acts of their contractors, but this point was not determined, as they were bound by the statute C. S. U. C. ch. 66, sec. 19; to fence on request, and a request was proved. *Nichol* v. *The Canada Southern R. W. Co.*, 583.

See ARBITRATION AND AWARD.

REASONABLE AND PROBABLE CAUSE.

See MALICIOUS ARREST, 1.

REGISTRAR.

1. *Notice of action.*]—*Held*, that a Registrar was not entitled to notice of an action against him for neglecting and refusing to furnish a statement in detail of fees charged by him, as required by 38 Vic. ch. 17, sec. 7, O., and claiming a mandamus; such neglect and refusal being an act of omission. *Ross* v. *McLay*, 83.

2. *Notice of action.*]—A registrar is entitled to notice of an action brought against him to recover back fees charged by him in excess of those allowed by the statute 31 Vic. ch. 20, O. *Ross* v. *McLay*, 87.

REGISTRATION.

Of Sheriff's Deed.]—*See* ASSESSMENT AND TAXES, 1.

REGISTRY LAW.

Equitable interest — Possession — Notice—Offer to purchase—36 Vic. ch. 10, O.—Corroborative evidence.]—In ejectment it appeared that M., owning the land in question, conveyed it in 1852 to W. J. M., who in the same year mortgaged to the Trust and Loan Company. They in 1858 conveyed to W., who, in 1859, mortgaged it again to them, and, in 1860, they conveyed to C., who devised it to the plaintiffs. All these conveyances were duly registered. Both W. J. M. and W. were acting as trustees or agents for M.

For the defence it was shewn that M. in 1852 verbally agreed to sell the land to one P. S., who paid the purchase money and took possession as a purchaser. In 1859 he received a bond from M. to convey to him in two months, but he never obtained a conveyance, and the bond was never registered, nor could it be under the Registry law when it was given. He died in 1859, and his wife and children, the defendants, had continued to hold possession ever since. C. when he purchased in 1860 had notice of such possession.

Held, following *Grey* v. *Ball*, 23 Grant 390, the last decision in Chancery, though opposed to earlier cases, that knowledge of the possession held by the plaintiffs having an equitable interest was not sufficient to affect the registered title, and that the plaintiffs therefore were entitled to recover; but a new trial was granted, with costs to abide the event, to enable defendants to shew, if possible, that C. in fact bought subject to M.'s equity of redemption.

Held, also, that offers to purchase made by defendants, not having been accepted, and an alleged lease signed by them, without proper advice, under which they had paid no rent, should not, under the circumstances, preclude defendants from relying upon their equitable title.

Held, also, that the bond, which was produced, for the conveyance of the land, without any payment to be made, was sufficient corroborative evidence of defendants' statement of the verbal bargain by plaintiffs and payment of the purchase money, under 36 Vic. ch. 10, sec. 6, O. *Cooley et al.* v. *Smith et al.*

RELIGIOUS INSTITUTIONS.

36 *Vic. ch.* 135, *O.*—*Removal and appointment of trustees—Ejectment—Proof of title.*]—The 36 Vic. ch. 135, secs. 10, 12, respecting the property of religious institutions, authorizes only the appointment of successors to trustees dead or legally removed, and does not empower the congregation to remove trustees competent and willing to act.

The three plaintiffs in this case claimed title under a conveyance to two of them, and to H., one of the defendants, a trustee of the congregation named, alleging that H. had been since removed from the office of trustee, and the plaintiff T. appointed in his stead. Defendants denied the plaintiffs' title. The conveyance contained no clause for the removal of trustees or the appointment of new ones, and the congregation under the statute above mentioned, had assumed to appoint the plaintiff T. in place of H. *Held,* that the plaintiffs must wholly succeed or wholly fail as to the title alleged, and that the appointment of T. being invalid, a nonsuit must be entered. *Lage et al.* v. *Mackenson et al.,* 388.

REPEAL OF STATUTE.

Effect of.]—*See* PUBLIC COMPANY.

RIGHT OF WAY.

See EASEMENT.

RULES AND ORDERS.

1. A rule *nisi* to set aside an order to hold a defendant to bail for insufficiency in the plaintiff's affidavit must point out the objections specifically. *Watson* v. *Charlton,* 142.

2. A rule *nisi* to set aside an award must be drawn up on reading the award or a copy. *Re Johnson and Montreal and City of Ottawa Junction R. W. Co.,* 359.

Calls made under (English) Companies' Act 1862—Finality of orders for.]—*See* PUBLIC COMPANY.

SALE OF GOODS.

1. *Division Court bailiff—Notice of action—Sale of business — Evidence of bona fides.*]—The Consol. Stat. U. C. ch. 126, sec. 10, requiring notice of action, does not apply to the case of a Division Court bailiff acting under an execution, which is specially provided for by ch. 19, sec. 193; and a notice, therefore, to such bailiff, not having endorsed upon it the name and place of abode of the plaintiff, as required by the former, but not by the latter Act, was held sufficient.

Upon the evidence set out in the case, the jury having found that the business carried on by the execution debtor was that of his brother, and carried on by the execution debtor as his agent, a new trial was granted, with costs to abide the event. *Stephens* v. *Stapleton,* 353.

2. *Sale of goods by agent—Power of agent to bind principal.*]—The defendants, merchants in Toronto, arranged with L. & H. in London, England, for a consideration specified, that all goods bought by defendants in England should be charged to L. & H. by the various sellers, with whom L. & H. were to settle. The plaintiffs' agent K. sold goods to defendants on credit, and the plaintiffs' draft on L. & H. having been protested, they sued defendants. The evidence was contradictory as to K.'s knowledge of defendants' arrangement with L. & H., and as to whose credit the sale was made upon.

The jury were directed that the plaintiff was bound by K.'s arrangement for payment, if any, made with defendants; and were asked to say whether the goods were sold on the credit of L. & H., looking only to them for payment, or to defendants, on their own credit, in the ordinary way, and they found for defendants. *Held*, that the direction was right; but upon the evidence, more fully stated in the case, a new trial was granted on payment of costs. *Creighton et al.* v. *Janes et al.*, 372.

3. *Fraudulent design not to pay—Rescission—Stoppage in transitu.*]—P., carrying on business at Woodstock, on the 28th August, ordered eight half chests of tea from the plaintiff, who lived at Bowmanville, at five months' credit, through H., the plaintiff's traveller, who called upon him to solicit orders. The order was given on the 28th August, 1876, and the tea arrived at Woodstock by rail, on the 4th September. The railway company addressed the usual notice of arrival to P., as consignee which notice came on the 5th into the hands of defendant, an attachment in insolvency against P., having on that day been received by defendant as official assignee. Defendant on the same day demanded the goods from the freight agent of the company, tendering the freight, but the agent refused to deliver them. The plaintiff's agent telegraphed to him on the 6th to hold the tea; and, on the company's application, an interpleader was granted.

Semble, that the *transitus* was at an end, on the authority of *Bird* v. *Brown*, 4 Ex. 797.

P. had previously purchased tea from the plaintiff, giving his note at five months, which matured on the 4th September, though the usual credit was four months. H. said that he remarked to P., when making the sale in question, that there were extra hands behind the counter, for which P. accounted by the alleged increase of his business; and he added that he was not in immediate need of these teas, but wanted to get them. H. said he thought P. was doing well and intended to pay, but he made no enquiries as to his standing, or as to probable payment of the note then maturing. On or shortly before the 5th September P. absconded, owing over $3,000, and leaving assets to pay only about five cents in the dollar. None of his employees were examined at the trial.

Held, that the fair inference from all the circumstances, which are more fully set out in the case, was that P. ordered the goods fraudulently, with a preconceived design of not paying for them; and that on this ground the plaintiff was entitled to recover. *Davis* v. *McWhirter*, 598.

See GUARANTEE—TRESPASS.

SALE OF LAND.

See REGISTRY LAW.

SCHOOLS.

High Schools.]—A County Council is not authorized. under 37 Vic , ch. 27, sec. 47, O., to raise money by by-law for a High School not in existence, but in contemplation only. *Re Sharp and the Corporation of the County of Peel,* 71.

SEPARATE ESTATE.

See HUSBAND AND WIFE.

SEPARATE TRADE.

Of wife..] — *See* HUSBAND AND WIFE, 3.

SHERIFF'S DEED.

Delay in registering.]—*See* ASSESSMENT AND TAXES, 1.

SHIPS AND SHIPPING.

See GENERAL AVERAGE—MORTGAGE.

SPECIFICATIONS.

To building contract—Omission to sign—Effect of.]—*See* BUILDING CONTRACT.

STATUTE.

Repeal of after action commenced —Effect on pleas pleaded.] — *See* PUBLIC COMPANY.

STATUTES.

C. S. U. C. ch. 73.]—*See* HUSBAND AND WIFE, 2.

C. S. U. C. ch. 126.]—*See* COUNTY ATTORNEY—LIQUOR, SALE OF, 3.

C. L. P. Act, sec. 325.]—*See* COSTS.

Temperance Act, 1864.]—*See* LIQUOR, SALE OF, 1.

Companies' Act, 1862 (Imperial).]—*See* PUBLIC COMPANY.

5 & 6 Wm. & M. ch. 11, sec. 3.]—*See* WAYS, 2.

8 & 9 Wm. III. ch. 11.]—*See* BOND.

3 & 4 Vic. ch. 24, sec. 3 (Imperial).]—*See* COSTS.

23 Vic. ch. 24, sec. 1.]—*See* PUBLIC COMPANY.

29 Vic. ch. 24, sec. 57.]—*See* ASSESSMENT AND TAXES, 1.

31 Vic. ch. 1, sec. 7, sub-sec. 34, O.]—*See* PUBLIC COMPANY.

31 Vic. ch. 8, O.]—*See* FREE GRANT LANDS.

31 Vic. ch. 20, O.]—*See* REGISTRAR, 2.

31 Vic. ch. 24, O.]—*See* COSTS.

33 Vic. ch. 27, D.]—*See* CONVICTION, 1.

34 Vic. ch. 5, secs. 46, 47, D.]—*See* WAREHOUSE RECEIPTS.

35 Vic. ch. 16, O.]—*See* HUSBAND AND WIFE,

35 Vic. ch. 80, sec. 41, O.] — *See* STATUTES, CONSTRUCTION OF.

36 Vic. ch. 10, O.]—*See* REGISTRY LAW.

36 Vic. ch. 44, sec. 36, O.]—*See* INSURANCE, 3.

36 Vic. ch. 104, sec. 17, O.] — *See* STATUTES, CONSTRUCTION OF.

36 Vic. ch. 135, O.]—*See* RELIGIOUS INSTITUTIONS.

37 Vic. ch. 23, O.]—*See* FREE GRANT LANDS.

37 Vic. ch. 27, sec. 47, O.] — *See* SCHOOLS, 1.

37 Vic. ch. 32, O.]—*See* LIQUOR, SALE OF.

38 Vic. ch. 4, O.]—*See* CONVICTION, 2.

38 Vic. ch. 17, sec. 7, O.—*See* REGISTRAR, 1.

39 Vic. ch. 7, O.]—*See* PUBLIC COMPANY.

39 Vic. ch. 26, O.]—*See* LIQUOR, SALE OF, 1.

STOPPAGE IN TRANSITU.

See SALE OF GOODS, 3.

SUBSEQUENT INSURANCE.

See INSURANCE, 4.

SUMMARY CONVICTION.

See CONVICTION, 1.

SURETY.

See BILLS AND NOTES, 1, 3.

TAXES.

See ASSESSMENT AND TAXES.

TAX SALE.

See ASSESSMENT AND TAXES.

TEMPERANCE ACT OF 1864.

See LIQUOR, SALE OF.

TIMBER, SALE OF.

On Free Grant Unpatented lands.]
—*Hutchinson* v. *Beatty*, 135.

TITLE.

False statement as to, when insuring.]—*See* INSURANCE, 3.

TRESPASS.

Division Court bailiff — Interpleader issue — Detention of goods after judgment for plaintiff—Notice of action—Liability of attorney.]— Defendant C., a Division Court bailiff, was employed by the plaintiff to sell certain goods under a chattel mortgage given to the plaintiff by one L. Defendant C. advertised and took possession of them, and afterwards executions came into his hands against L., under which the attorney for the execution creditors told him to seize these goods. The plaintiff claimed them, and obtained judgment in his favour upon an interpleader issue. Defendant C. refused on demand to give up the goods to the plaintiff until he should consult the attorney, who told him to use his own judgment. The plaintiff having brought trespass and trover.

Held, that C. was liable : that he was not entitled to a demand of perusal and copy of the warrants under which he acted, for the action was not brought by reason of any defect in the process : that the jury were warranted in finding, as they did, that he did not believe that he was discharging his duty as bailiff in refusing to give up the goods after the decision of the interpleader, which finding disentitled him to notice of action : that the execution creditors were also liable ; but that the attorney was not, for he had told C. only to use his own judgment. *Stewart* v. *Cowan et al.*, 346.

See COSTS. — JUSTICE OF THE PEACE.—LANDLORD AND TENANT.

TROVER.

See LANDLORD AND TENANT, 2.— TRESPASS.

TRUSTEES.

Removal and appointment of under 36 *Vic. ch.* 135, *secs.* 10, 12, *O.*]— *See* RELIGIOUS INSTITUTIONS.

UNSEAWORTHINESS.

See GENERAL AVERAGE.

VARIANCE.

Between conviction and warrant.]
—See LIQUOR, SALE OF.

WAIVER.

Of conditions of insurance policy.]
—See INSURANCE, 1.

Of forfeiture.]*—See* LANDLORD AND
TENANT, 1, 3.

WAREHOUSE RECEIPTS.

*Banks—Transfer to, of warehouse
receipts—34 Vic. c. 5, D.*]—The 34
Vic. ch. 5, secs. 46 and 47, D., permits the transfer to a bank of a bill
of lading, or warehouse receipt, to
secure an antecedent debt, where the
understanding at the time of contracting such debt was, that the bill
of lading should be transferred as
collateral security.

In this case the bank so agreed to
made advances to S. & Co. to purchase coal and stone, to be secured
by bills of lading and warehouse
receipts for such coal and stone when
received. The transfer of such receipts to the bank, after the arrival
of the goods, was held to be authorized ; and it was held no objection
that the agreement was to give a
receipt for goods of which, at the
time, the person was not possessed.

Six months had elapsed after the
giving of the receipt before the
seizure of the goods by the creditors
of S. & Co., but the bank had taken
possession of these goods with the
consent of S. & Co., and were selling them in order to repay their
advances.

Held, under 34 Vic. ch. 5, sec. 50,
D., that they were entitled to hold

the goods, notwithstanding the lapse
of time. *The Royal Canadian Bank
v. Ross*, 466.

WARRANT.

*To Division Court bailiff, demand
of perusal and copy.*]*—See* TRESPASS.

WATER COMMISSIONERS OF OTTAWA.

*35 Vic. ch. 80, s. 41, O.—Construction
of.*]—The 35 Vic. c. 80, s. 41, O., incorporating the defendants, as amended
by 36 Vic. c. 104, s. 17, O., provides
that " all work under the said commissioners shall be performed by contract, excepting the laying of the
water pipes, and such other works as
in the opinion of the engineer of the
said commissioners can be more
profitably performed by day work " :
Held, that the words " by contract "
did not necessarily mean by contract
under seal, so as to relieve the defendants from liability for work done
upon an executed parol contract.
*McBrian et al. v. The Water Com-
missioners for the City of Ottawa*,
80.

WATERS AND WATER COURSES.

*Obstruction of by railway embank-
ment.*]*—See* RAILWAYS AND R. W.
Co's., 3.

WAYS.

*Indictment for obstructing high-
way—Previous conviction—Estoppel
—Costs—Fine.*]—Where the defen-

dant had been convicted of nuisance in obstructing a certain highway, by a fence, and after removal of such a fence by the sheriff under process replaced it on the same highway, though not in precisely the same line as before : *Held*, that the former conviction was conclusive against the defendant as to the existence of the alleged highway, and that he could not again raise the question on this indictment for obstructing the same highway.

Where the indictment was removed into this Court by the prosecutors : *Held*, that the defendant was not liable to costs ; but the Court ordered that one-third of the fine imposed should go to the prosecutors, and suggested that the Government might on application order the remaining two-thirds to be paid to them, the whole fine being less than their costs incurred. *Regina v. Jackson*, 290.

2. *Indictment for obstructing highway—Costs—5 & 6 W. & M. ch. 11 —Fine.*]—A township municipality prosecuting an indictment for obstructing a highway in the township, which indictment had been removed on defendant's application into this Court, and the defendant convicted thereon : *Held*, to be "the party aggrieved" within the 5 & 6 W. & M. ch. 11, sec. 3 ; and the defendant, having to pay their costs and his own, amounting to over $400, was fined only $1.

Right of way.]—*See* EASEMENT.

———

WILL.

Legacy paid in mistake.]—Where plaintiff, as executor of W., paid money to defendant, as legatee, under the will, and the Court of Chancery set aside the will and probate, the plaintiff was held entitled to recover the money back. *Haldan v. Beatty*. 110,

———

WORDS.

"*Appurtenances.*"]—*See* EASEMENT.

"*By contract.*"] — *See* WATER COMMISSIONERS OF OTTAWA.

"*Party aggrieved.*"]—*See* WAYS, 2.

———

WORK AND LABOUR.

See BUILDING CONTRACT.

Lightning Source UK Ltd.
Milton Keynes UK
UKHW020621120219
337137UK00005B/566/P